THE FEUDAL KINGDOM OF ENGLAND

1042-1216

A HISTORY OF ENGLAND
IN ELEVEN VOLUMES

General Editor: W. N. Medlicott

THE PREHISTORIC AGE IN BRITAIN
BY STANLEY THOMAS

ROMAN BRITAIN
BY C. E. STEVENS

THE ANGLO-SAXON AGE
BY D. J. V. FISHER

THE FEUDAL KINGDOM OF ENGLAND*
BY FRANK BARLOW

THE LATER MIDDLE AGES IN ENGLAND*
BY B. WILKINSON

THE TUDOR AGE*
BY JAMES A. WILLIAMSON

THE STUART AGE
BY IVAN ROOTS

EIGHTEENTH CENTURY ENGLAND*
BY DOROTHY MARSHALL

THE AGE OF IMPROVEMENT*
BY ASA BRIGGS

LATE NINETEENTH CENTURY ENGLAND
BY MAURICE SHOCK

CONTEMPORARY ENGLAND*
BY W. N. MEDLICOTT

* *Already published*
Some of the titles listed are provisional

THE FEUDAL KINGDOM OF ENGLAND

1042–1216

by

FRANK BARLOW

LONGMAN
London and New York

LONGMAN GROUP LIMITED
London

*Associated companies, branches and representatives
throughout the world*
*Published in the United States of America by Longman
Inc., New York*
Second edition © Frank Barlow 1961
Third edition © Longman Group Limited 1972

First published 1955
Second edition 1961
Third (and first paperback) edition 1972
Sixth impression in paperback 1980

Library of Congress Cataloging in Publication Data

Barlow, Frank.
The feudal kingdom of England, 1042–1216.
(A History of England in eleven volumes)
Bibliography: p.
Includes index.
1. Great Britain—History—Medieval period,
1066–1485. 2. Great Britain—History—Edward,
the Confessor, 1042–1066. I. Title. II. Series.
DA175.B26   1976   942.02   75–34449
ISBN 0–582–48237–2

*Printed in Great Britain by
Richard Clay (The Chaucer Press), Ltd.,
Bungay, Suffolk*

INTRODUCTORY NOTE

ONE of the effects of two world wars and of fifty years of ever-accelerating industrial and social revolution has been the growing interest of the citizen in the story of his land. From this story he seeks to learn the secret of his country's greatness and a way to better living in the future.

There seems, therefore, to be room for a rewriting of the history of England which will hold the interest of the general reader while it appeals at the same time to the student. This new presentation will take account of the recent discoveries of the archæologist and the historian, and will not lose sight of the claims of history to take its place among the mental recreations of intelligent people for whom it has no professional concern.

The history will be completed in a series of nine volumes. The volumes will be of medium length, and it is hoped that they will provide a readable narrative of the whole course of the history of England and give proper weight to the different strands which form the pattern of the story. No attempt has been made to secure general uniformity of style or treatment. Each period has its special problems, each author his individual technique and mental approach; each volume will be able to stand by itself not only as an expression of the author's methods, tastes, and experience, but as a coherent picture of a phase in the history of the country.

There is, nevertheless, a unity of purpose in the series; the authors have been asked, while avoiding excessive detail, to give particular attention to the interaction of the various aspects of national life and achievement, so that each volume may present a convincing integration of those developments—political, constitutional, economic, social, religious, military, foreign, or cultural—which happen to be dominant at each period. Although considerations of space will prevent minute investigation it should still be possible in a series of this length to deal fully with the essential themes.

A short bibliographical note is attached to each volume. This is not intended to supersede existing lists, but rather to call attention to recent works and to the standard bibliographies.

W. N. MEDLICOTT

PREFACE

THE theme of this book is the feudal kingdom of England and the men who made it. I have tried to tell a story—for to my mind history without a story is meaningless—and to tell it in as much detail and depth as I can. The only continuous thread which the sources give to the historian of this period is the fortunes of the great men—the bishops, the barons, and, above all, the kings—and it is not stupid to accept in the main this contemporary scale of values, for, although history is in a sense made by every living creature, only a few men have the power, material or intellectual, to exert an appreciable influence on events.

Yet the history of a distant period becomes little more than a fairy tale unless the background, which the contemporary writer takes for granted, can be re-created. And it is this evocation of a past age which is so difficult. If the historian uses a technical vocabulary his world is closed except to the few, and the use of specialized terms divorces the story from the towns, churches, and fields which we know. But to avoid technicalities is no less dangerous, for modern equivalents are often cumbersome and usually misleading. My plan has been to interrupt the narrative occasionally with digressions of an analytical and explanatory character; and I am aware that this sort of compromise has its disadvantages too.

Medieval sums of money require, perhaps, a prefatory explanation. During the period covered by this volume the only coin in general circulation in western Europe was the silver penny of various and fluctuating standards (see below, pp. 24, 187). The shilling (12 pence), mark (160 pence), and pound (240 pence) were units of account, the value of which depended on the type of penny required, e.g. sterling or angevin, and also on the method of payment, by tale or by weight. Hence the amount of silver represented by any financial expression can usually be determined. But to convert that into a modern value is beyond the wit of man. Those interested in the problem may consult E. Victor Morgan, *The Study of Prices and the Value of Money* (Historical Association, Helps for Students of History, No. 53), 1950.

The historian takes a risk when he dispenses with footnotes. He cannot qualify generalizations or support his individual views. Nor can he—and this must be his liveliest regret, for any attempt to give references to original authorities in a book of large scope and modest size is a pretence—thank by acknowledgement the authors of those monographs and learned articles which make the writing of general histories possible. It is hoped that the index, which I have tried to make as complete as possible, will serve in the place of cross-references.

In conclusion, I should like to thank my colleagues, Mr. G. W. Greenaway and Mr. L. J. Lloyd, who have done their best to save me from blunders and infelicities, and all those other friends who have helped me with advice and encouragement.

FRANK BARLOW

UNIVERSITY COLLEGE, EXETER
10 *June*, 1954

PREFACE TO SECOND EDITION

For this edition I have made a few corrections - and I thank those who have pointed out errors - and also have revised passages where the latest research of others or my own studies have caused me to change my view. The most extensive re-writing is in Chapter 1.

F.B.

UNIVERSITY OF EXETER
2 *July*, 1961

PREFACE TO THIRD EDITION

I have again corrected a few errors and revised those parts where my own or the research of others has made me wish to express myself differently. I have to thank my colleague Dr J. S. Critchley for re-reading the book and making useful suggestions.

F.B.

UNIVERSITY OF EXETER

22 September 1971

CONTENTS

CHAPTER 9

THE ANGEVIN EMPIRE

CHAPTER 10

THE ANGEVIN DESPOTISM

MAPS AND CHARTS

I

ENGLAND IN THE REIGN OF EDWARD
THE CONFESSOR

I

B Y 1042 western Europe, helped by an improvement in the
climate, was beginning to recover from the last of those
disasters which had kept it in poverty and ignorance since the
collapse of the Roman Empire. The assimilation of the Vikings was
in progress; and never again were marauders to terrify the Atlantic
coast, threaten a precarious civilization, obliterate political boundaries, and disturb capriciously the development of the existing
kingdoms. But the political map had been left untidy. Spain was
largely in the hands of the Moslems; the Middle Kingdom had
bequeathed a legacy of political ambiguity to a corridor running
from the North Sea to the Mediterranean; the Viking migration had
confused the allegiance of the northern maritime territories; and
political authority, shattered by invasion or enfeebled through the
disappearance of institutions and the loss of agents, was dispersed
among a numerous military aristocracy.

The traditional cultural and political affiliations of England had
been profoundly affected by the Scandinavian colonization of
eastern England, eastern Ireland, and the Neustrian seaboard at the
end of the ninth century. Hitherto the Anglo-Saxon kingdoms had
been in closest touch with those Germanic peoples which had
created barbaric simulacra of imperial rule within the confines of
the Roman empire, and with that Celtic fringe which had retained
some memory of its Roman inheritance; and England herself had
played no trivial part in the transmission of such classical culture
as had been acquired from those sources. But the conquests and
settlements of the Vikings, that ringed the northern waters, brought

England fitfully within a Scandinavian orbit; and it was not until England was subjugated by the Normans, themselves of Viking origin, yet gallicized in part, that she swung once more, and finally, to face her southern neighbours.

Scandinavian influence was at its height in England during the rule of the Danish dynasty. But the empire of Cnut disintegrated after his death in 1035; and when Edward, the son of Aethelred II and Emma of Normandy, was accepted as king of the English in 1042, ties with the north were loosened. Edward, who united the lines of Cerdic and Rollo, although by upbringing and taste more Norman than West-Saxon, was neither 'English' nor 'French'. He was representative of that coarse synthesis of the dominant European traditions which the Normans had achieved.

The recognition of Edward as king in England after Harthacnut had fallen dead at the marriage feast of Tofig the Proud and Osgot Clapa's daughter was little more than the acceptance of the one immediately available candidate from the large field of claimants that the political upheavals of the last fifty years had produced. The Danish Cnut had supplanted the West-Saxon Aethelred and had married his widow, Emma of Normandy; and since each king had also had children by another wife there were four distinct lines of royal descent in 1035. By 1042, however, the two direct lines from Cnut had failed; and the sons of his sister, Estrith—Svein, Beorn, and Osbern—were the kin nearest to the main Danish stem. But the rights of these children of Estrith had been barred by a treaty made by Harthacnut, the son of Cnut and Emma. In 1038-9 Harthacnut, while ruling in Denmark, had sought to extricate himself from his war with Magnus of Norway so that he should be free to enforce his claim to England against Harold Harefoot, Cnut's son by Aelfgifu of Northampton. He had accordingly made a treaty with his northern rival by which, if either died childless, the other was to inherit his dominions. And so, when Harthacnut died without issue in 1042, Magnus entered into possession of most of Denmark, despite Svein's resistance, and prepared to invade England, although it probably lay outside the scope of the treaty.

The English royal family was in a condition no less confused. The children of both of Aethelred's marriages had taken refuge abroad during the Danish domination of England. The elder line was represented by Edmund Ironside's son and grandson, who lived in Hungary, entirely isolated from English affairs until 1054. The sons of

Aethelred and Emma, however, Edward and Alfred, had been brought up at the neighbouring Norman court by their uncle, Duke Richard II, and after his death had remained with their cousin, Duke Robert I the Magnificent. They had been completely abandoned by their mother, who devoted herself to the children and kinsmen of her second marriage with Cnut, and who only turned to Edward as a last resort. When her youngest son, Harthacnut, succeeded to the English throne on the death of Harold Harefoot in 1040, so weak was his position that it was decided to bring over from Normandy his middle-aged half-brother. Edward arrived in 1041 and was recognized as joint ruler. This belated family reunion secured the crown for Edward when Harthacnut died unexpectedly in 1042. Although there was no general enthusiasm for his cause and it was rumoured that Emma now favoured Magnus of Norway, Edward's descent from Cerdic attracted the English and his lineage from Rollo satisfied the Danes. He also showed considerable political skill in rallying support, and was eventually crowned king at Easter 1043.

II

The kingdom which Edward had been called to rule after an exile of some twenty-eight years was bounded in the west and north by the limits of the Mercian and Northumbrian earldoms. The frontier with Wales had the greater stability, for Offa's Dyke had mostly followed the highland contour, and marked the chosen limit of Anglo-Saxon penetration. The northern boundary had no such natural support, and was liable to great fluctuation. The Viking settlements had cut greater Northumbria in two, and the further part had fallen under the influence of the Celtic Highland powers. King Edgar had recognized this situation by granting Lothian to the king of Scots; and in 1042 'English' Northumbria was still confined to south of the Tweed; but west of the Pennines Earl Siward had pushed his earldom north at the expense of Strathclyde and was ruling up to the Solway Firth. The Welsh principalities and the Scottish kingdoms were not, however, completely independent of the English king. The king of Scots was the man, or vassal, of the English king for Lothian and the other English estates that he held. In addition, although Scottish kings were always ready to confuse the issue, the rulers in Scotland, like those in Wales, had for centuries acknowledged the general overlordship of English kings. The wider relationship was still personal, and the king of Scots submitted only when he thought it useful or when constrained. But repeated acts of commendation had forged a bond that could be given a more feudal stamp when Scottish claimants swore fealty to the English king before they attempted with southern help to obtain the northern crown. Edward and his lieutenants were temporarily to master Wales; but more indirect means had to be employed to secure political influence in Scotland. The two countries were, indeed, too remote for immediate control from Wessex.

England herself, however, was relatively small and, like all western Europe, thinly populated. Although her people were fruitful, the primitive means of exploiting natural resources prevented the population from rising much above a million. But in consequence society was youthful and resilient. Men and women came slowly to maturity, married late, and died too soon. The stock of inherited knowledge, therefore, was kept small and the standard of acquired skill remained low. But the predominance of young people in society enabled gaps caused by pestilence or war to be quickly filled. The desperate pressure of a redundant population on a limited and inelastic supply of food and the cruel, inevitable elimination of the weaklings gave rise to the cardinal sins of gluttony, avarice, and envy and to some which were too ordinary to be numbered, such as brutality and callousness. But from them sprang also the adventurousness that is so characteristic of the age, the reckless disregard of the odds, the heroism of those for whom there could be no turning back. England, therefore, was not of such a size as to be beyond the capabilities of a vigorous king; and the kingdom had a political unity which could not be matched elsewhere in Europe. Yet behind the façade of an organized state were provincial distinctions of culture and fissile tendencies which were no less remarkable.

The rich diversity of the English landscape, with its great forests, wooded plains and valleys, mountain ridge, downs, wide moorland, and frequent marsh and fen, fostered a variety in ways of life. The density of the population decreased from east to west and from south to north owing to the greater fertility of the plains; but there were no natural lines of cleavage and few homogeneous tracts of sharply contrasting features. Upon this geographical variety had been laid the different social patterns of the several races of settlers; and these had been moulded by the administrative peculiarities of the various early kingdoms.

It is difficult when surveying England in the eleventh century to point with confidence to any distinct characteristics arising from racial differences among the original Germanic settlers, except, perhaps, to the customs of Kent and its mysterious Jutes; but where Angle and Saxon had mixed extensively with the Celt, as in Bernicia and western Wessex, an ethnic individuality is apparent; and where in the mountains and on the moors pockets of even older races had been left undisturbed men of small stature existed, pagan and aloof, to provide a tradition of fairies and witches which outlasted their physical survival. Even more noticeable in the time of Edward were the yet undefaced boundaries of the earlier Anglo-Saxon kingdoms. Greater Wessex and Mercia were distinct from the rest of the country in their system of land-holding; Bernicia, Deira, East Anglia and Essex, and Kent with in part Surrey, Sussex, and Hampshire, had each its individual peculiarities. The different field systems of the agricultural economy together with the social individualities, which in part create, in part arise from the economic pattern, seem to correspond to the areas of those kingdoms; and these separate cultures persisted until medieval methods of farming were swept away.

The Scandinavian migration and conquests of the ninth century had introduced another complicating factor. The settlement of four Viking armies on the land in northern and eastern England affected the racial stock, the social habits, the language (including personal and place-names), and the law of a large part of the kingdom. The density of the colonization in the several areas is not easily determined. But there was some Scandinavian intrusion into Northumbria, especially Yorkshire; eastern Mercia, massed round the 'five boroughs' of Derby, Nottingham, Leicester, Stamford, and Lincoln —Lincolnshire probably having the greatest density in the whole kingdom; and East Anglia. In these areas Danes predominated among the colonists; but fresh waves of Norwegian settlers, mostly from Ireland, had broken over the north-west coastal area, from Cumberland to the Wirral, and given Lancashire the most mixed population in England. Danish law, moreover, ran far beyond the districts of heavy settlement. It dominated almost the whole area which had been subject to the control of the invaders, the division north of the Thames and east and north of Watling Street. And during the rule of Cnut and his sons a Scandinavian aristocracy had been planted throughout the country. The cultural distinction between Anglo-Saxon and Danish England was the most profound in eleventh-century England, and it was still real two centuries later. Yet the Danelaw had enjoyed total political independence for only a short period, and preserved few political ambitions. It may have preferred a king of its own race, but it rarely exerted itself to that end. It may be that Scandinavian colonization had reinforced existing provincial distinctions, as in the case of Northumbria; yet, on the whole, the population accepted the rule of English kings who made no attempt to interfere with its customary mode of life.

Eleventh-century England was an agricultural and pastoral country, with most of the population deriving its livelihood directly from the soil. Its economic and social life turned on a large number of provincial centres, each the focus of the local roads and tracks: a system more characteristic of its culture than the great trunk roads which the Romans had left behind. It was a decentralized kingdom, in which, to the inhabitants, the village was more important than the shire, the shire than the province, the province than the state. The retinues of the nobility, the occasional armies, the merchants and pedlars moved through a country people that stood and watched them pass, and then turned back to its own business.

III

Anglo-Saxon society was strongly aristocratic, and the agricultural population was organized to support the monarchy and a nobility both lay and clerical.

A caste nobility, the *eorlcund*, had been present in the Germanic hordes that occupied Britain in the fifth century, and appeared again in the Scandinavian armies of the ninth century. But a warlike aristocracy suffers heavy casualties, and the important territorial families of the eleventh century were not in general of great antiquity. They were largely descendants or members of the ministerial class which served the kings and the greatest men. Thegns were in origin servants, who owed personal and especially military service to their masters; and the official character of their position was still clear in the eleventh century. But the practice of rewarding them with land had gone far by this time to convert them into a local aristocracy with an almost hereditary rank. They were not a homogeneous class. The standing of a servant depends on the importance of his master and on the length and value of his service. Among the thegns, at one end of the scale, were men who possessed estates in many shires acquired through generations of royal service, and, at the other,

were men indistinguishable from land-holding freemen except by
their rank. Nor did they form an exclusive circle. Ordinary freemen
could still rise to the thegnage in royal service, and even a merchant
who had ventured thrice across the North Sea using his own capital
could acquire the rank with its privileges.

Above the thegns were the earls. Their number was small in the
eleventh century, their estates vast, and their position almost hereditary. But as rulers of a province under the king they were the
king's servants, and he made them and broke them if he could. The
higher clergy had an official character similar to that of the lay aristocracy. Bishops and abbots were the ministers of their churches, they
were appointed to their offices by the king, and their endowments
were due to royal generosity.

The power of the nobility had been, and was still being, formed by
accretions from both above and below. From the king came grants
of almost everything that was in his power to give: land, privileges,
financial and judicial customs, and services. From inferiors came men
seeking a lord. The double process was common to all western
Europe, and in general produced what is known as feudalism. The
essential feature of feudal society as it developed within the Carolingian empire, especially between the Loire and the Rhine, was the fief
(*feudum*), from which the descriptive word was coined at the beginning of the seventeenth century. In this basic institution two independent strands were joined: a personal bond between two free men—
a superior (the lord) and an inferior (the vassal)—and a method of
land tenure, whereby the vassal held a benefice of his lord. The
personal relationship, deriving from an act of commendation, the
putting oneself under the protection, the 'mund' of a lord, appears
in all Germanic societies and was fully present in England. The
English words *thegn* and *cniht* were similar in meaning (youth,
servant) to the Celtic *gwas*, from which the low-Latin *vassus* (vassal)
was formed (in the middle of the eleventh century Gospatric lord
of Allerdale and Dalston addressed a writ to his *wassenas* in Cumbria);
and the Englishman when acknowledging a lord performed some
symbolic gesture of submission similar to the Frankish homage, a
ceremony in which the vassal, on his knees, placed his hands between
those of his lord's and swore an oath of fealty. This solemn contract
obliged the man to serve and obey his lord, and obliged the lord to
protect and maintain the man. In Gaul the lord usually acquitted
part of his obligation by giving his vassal the right to enjoy for life

the fruits of a property which still belonged to the lord. This usufruct was called a benefice, and a benefice given to a vassal became known as a fief.

The benefice was in origin a Roman institution which the Franks had adopted. The Anglo-Saxons, however, had felt Roman influence mainly through the church, and their land laws had shown quite a different development. The main desire of those who had a claim on the king's gratitude—his servants and the church—was to receive land under a tenure which was not precarious; and the church had introduced the charter or diploma (*boc,* book) which conveyed land, or rights over land, in the terms of the vulgar law of the late Roman Empire. A royal grant by book created a *ius perpetuum,* an estate which could be passed to heirs and could not lawfully be resumed by the king. In the eleventh century the church and most of the lay aristocracy held some book-land.

For the church book-land meant land which could not be lost. For the aristocracy the power to alienate, and especially to bequeath, was the most attractive aspect of the tenure. Yet although the grant by charter appears absolute, without consideration, unburdened with future conditions, the charter was not the grant. It was only the evidence for a grant which had been made verbally and symbolically according to Germanic custom. And it may be that the real terms of the grant were often obscured. For by Germanic law every gift required a counter-gift, some return to the benefactor. Hence there is reason to think that the formulae of Roman conveyancers as used by the clerks of the royal household at the behest of illiterate kings can be misleading; that when land was booked to a church the counter-gift was at least prayers for the soul of the benefactor; and that when the king booked land to his lay servants, or the owner of book-land granted it to another, the counter-gift could include a purchase price or the performance of services.

Also, since the eighth century, kings, when granting land by book, had reserved their right to the common burdens which lay on land, that is to say, the maintenance of fortifications and bridges and the performance of military service (sometimes called *trimoda necessitas*). And so, although the duty was not created by the grant, it becomes easy to understand how the author of that eleventh-century private collection of customs, the *Rectitudines singularum personarum,* could come to write that a thegn holds his land in return for military service. King Edgar and his successors had granted, or

restored, wide powers of local government to the reformed monasteries, for with the grant of land and hundreds by book went the
duties of administering justice and producing soldiers and ships.
For example, the triple hundred of Oswaldslow, created for Worcester, was a 'ship-soke', and the bishop of Worcester became responsible for the provision and command of sixty warriors, the comple-
ment of a warship. It is no accident that several abbots were at the
battle of Hastings. And some precarious aspects clung even to
book-land. On the evidence of wills as well as of the laws we know
that secular holders of such land were obliged at death to return to
their lord a substantial heriot in land, money, horses, and arms.
Moreover, book-land was forfeited to the king if his thegn neglected
his duties, including fyrd service.

The true benefice, and approximations to it, can also be found in
England. Most peasants had lost the absolute ownership of their
lands and were considered to be the tenants of their lord, rendering
service and rents in return for the use of his property. Moreover,
leases were common enough in the last century of the Old-English
kingdom. The church rejoiced to receive in perpetuity and as
absolutely as possible, but hated to give in the same way. Yet it had
its own servants to reward and needed the service of thegns. It could
not properly, above all in form, permanently alienate possessions for
which it was merely the trustee. Therefore it either used or introduced the 'loan' (*lǽn*) of land, which was in effect a benefice.

These leases were extremely useful. All landowners paid servants
by lending land to them. We find land leased to stewards and reeves,
to a woman in return for lessons in gold embroidery, and to a
monastic scribe. Land could also be leased for rent in money or
produce. Heads of families created life-interests in land for their
widows, younger children, and other dependants. Most ecclesiastical
communities appear to have granted leases to some of their household retainers (*cnihtas*) and thegns in return for the performance of
two kinds of service. First, personal service to the grantor, their
immediate lord, and secondly, those common burdens owed to the
king of which, in a feudal context, military service is the most
significant. In the language of the Anglo-Norman feudal lawyers the
fief was burdened with *intrinsec* and *forinsec* service. It is possible that
the lay nobility did likewise. But evidence is lacking. There seems to
have been no social stigma attached to holding land on lease. In 1012
Edmund Ironside, the king's son and heir, accepted an estate from

the monastery of Sherborne on loan. In 1015 the Aetheling Aethelstan was leasing an estate, apparently of eight hides, from his father, King Aethelred. Archbishops, bishops, and abbeys, earls and thegns, men and women, all were willing to take land on loan.

Loans of land conveyed no more than the usufruct. Ecclesiastical leases (and it is unfortunate that only church archives have survived) seem usually to have been for three lives; but leases for shorter periods can also be found. Every lease contained a strict reversionary clause. But it was hard to enforce. Some grantors accepted the difficulty and made provision in the lease for its renewal after the term had expired. The hereditary tendency was strong. Bishop Oswald of Worcester described loans as benefices. And it is clear that leases made by English churches to thegns and cnihts (and we cannot ignore the possibility that secular landowners were imitating) were not unlike contemporary feudal grants in Gaul. In this connexion it should not be overlooked that *lǽn* is cognate with *Lehen*, the German word for a fief, from which *Lehnswesen* (feudalism) has been formed.

Leases were usually granted by lords to inferiors. There was also a contrary movement. Men were commending themselves to lords, sometimes together with their lands. The type of bargain made must have varied with the circumstances. In the higher branches of society the tie was essentially personal—the traditional relationship of the Heroic Age. And in a less heroic period it had lost some of its sacredness. In the Midlands and north of England there were old landed families who could still command the deep loyalty of their men. But it is significant that when Godwine, earl of Wessex, threatened rebellion in 1051, his following melted away. Beneath this level, however, commendation normally involved the man's land as well as his allegiance. There is ample evidence from the East-Anglian church lands that many small freeholders had by commendation, for the sake of piety, gain, or security, made themselves into tenants of the church, unable to withdraw their commended lands from the estate even if they themselves were free to depart. And such a bargain made them not unlike vassals with fiefs. Moreover, all those men throughout the country who had accepted land on loan from a lord, or were supposed to have done so, were in a dependent position. In western and central England most of the peasants were held to be cultivating their lord's land; and they owed automatic allegiance to him and could not withdraw it. It seems, indeed, that

among the lower orders commendation was more widely and deeply
territorialized than in Gaul.

Feudal elements and inchoate feudal arrangements were certainly
present in Edwardian England. In Gaul the dukes and counts had
become the vassals of the king, their honours, offices, and estates
had been assimilated to benefices, and the fief had become the normal
holding of even the greatest men. England had not advanced so far.
The thegn owned some book-land, which could usually be granted
away with the permission of the king or some other lord, and held
other estates by unknown tenures. But superimposed on this
largely freehold structure were the leases which gave it flexibility.
The question of crucial importance is whether the network of
leases had become of greater significance than the underlying freehold organization. It seems, on the available evidence, that the more
substantial English landowners did not hold much property on loan.
England, therefore, was not so feudal as Gaul. But she was probably
developing in the same direction; and most of the features associated
with true feudalism can be found in the Old-English kingdom.

Agricultural wealth and the possession of commended men in
themselves gave political power to lords; and some aspects of lordship must be considered as arising from the economic situation and
as independent of royal surrender. But these were reinforced in
Anglo-Saxon England by the privileges granted by the king. When
the king granted an estate to a thegn or a church he usually alienated
most of his economic rights over the inhabitants of that estate—the
right to take money and food rents and to exact miscellaneous
services, such as keeping the king's house and estate in repair,
building shelters on his hunting expeditions, and carting his produce
and stores. The transfer of these customs to a private lord did not
immediately affect the position of those who owed them. Royal
customs became seignorial customs; and the king's reeves were
simply replaced by seignorial reeves.

The king also granted judicial rights to the nobility. Law was still
in the eleventh century mostly folk-law, popular and immemorial
custom; but there seem to have been no folk-moots. The shire and
hundred courts were controlled by the king's servants; and the
countless immunities which disrupted the system were in the hands
of the aristocracy. Jurisdiction was profitable; therefore judicial
customs could be alienated by the king, and treated as negotiable
assets by the recipient, in the same way as any other profitable right.

It is unlikely that the beneficiary automatically organized his private courts. The profits of justice rather than its administration were the prize. But in the long run the principle held good that the reward must be earned; and hence most types of case and most types of court, as well as the penalties and issues of justice, passed into the hands of the lay and clerical aristocracy. In the franchisal courts private instead of royal reeves supervised the procedure and collected the revenue; but in all other respects franchisal and public courts should have been indistinguishable. The immunist was, in a sense, a royal official.

Another force, too, helped to mould the pattern of private juris-diction. Commendation did not of itself make the man officially subject to his lord's jurisdiction; and few lords possessed even limited judicial rights over all their men. But the feeling was strong that a lord was responsible for those men under his *mund*—his family and his dependants; some landowners, like the abbot of Ely, had by royal grant soke over all their commended men wherever they might live or work; and it is believed that on the eve of the Norman conquest all substantial landowners in England had 'sake and soke', usually with 'toll and team', within at least their demesne. This jurisdiction, largely 'civil' in character, and mostly at the expense of the shire courts, covered many of the forms of action under folk-law, including cases of stolen chattels and disputes over land. The 'criminal' element was small, and was not greatly increased when 'infangentheof' and some minor offences normally reserved to the king were added to it. Apart from the right to hang a thief caught in the act (infangentheof), the jurisdiction extended no farther than medleys, assaults, and woundings, and stopped well short of capital offences. By continental standards sake and soke was 'low' justice; and, although larger franchises existed, it is clear that the English kings had not by this type of grant squandered their jurisdictional rights. Many grants of sake and soke were made to private indivi-duals and churches by the king. But by the eleventh century the right had become almost an appurtenance to an estate. It would be rash to conclude that it had in every case been created by a formal act of alienation; and it is clear that it had come to be regarded as a traditional right of lordship. When sake and soke was exercised over dependent villages it was, to use a later expression, manorial jurisdic-tion; where it lay over free men it can be called seignorial. The halimote (hall-moot) remained throughout the Middle Ages a court of customary and ancient law; but the profits went to the lord; the lord's representative presided; and it was the means by which both the immemorial custom of the manor and the economic subjection of the tenants were perpetuated and enforced.

Where jurisdictional rights greater than those covered by the formula 'with sake and with soke, with toll and with team, and with infangentheof' were concerned, the express agency of the king is more discernible. Grants of exemption from the hundred courts, or grants of whole hundreds, were relatively common in the late Old-English period; and the monastic franchises in East Anglia provide an extreme example of this practice. In King Edward's day Peterborough had eight hundreds, Ramsey two, Ely groups of two, five-and-a-half, and one-and-a-half, and Bury St. Edmunds the eight-and-a-half hundreds annexed to the manor of 'Bedricsworth', which had been part of Edward's mother's dower. Kings Cnut and Edward even occasionally bestowed on favoured immunists cases which touched the king alone. Bury St. Edmunds, for example, had sake and soke and six royal forfeitures in its group of hundreds. With the alienation of hundredal jurisdiction and 'reserved' cases there is no doubt that the grantees became private royal officials. They were rarely allowed to assimilate this jurisdiction to other judicial powers which they may have enjoyed, and a strong monarchy always required and sometimes inspected their title to these courts. Nevertheless, such rights in private hands strengthened other aspects of lordship; and they were especially valuable where territorial lordship was weak. The combination of seignorial rights, commendation, and hundredal jurisdiction gave a lord considerable control over a man and his land.

The alienation of royal rights to the nobility is often regarded as a fragmentation of the state. For Gaul this is true enough. But in Britain there had been no Romano-Germanic kingdom to disintegrate, and the power of the kings and of the nobles had grown in step. The more the petty kingdoms coalesced, the more the kings were forced to alienate that portion of their original rights which they could no longer exercise in person. Yet the power of Edward was certainly as great as Edgar's, and was much greater than that which the predecessors of Alfred had enjoyed; so it is clear that the monarchy had on balance acquired more authority than it had dispersed. The dukes in Gaul had stolen the prerogatives of the kings; but the earls in England were in the place of once independent rulers. Throughout the English kingdom were landowners, large and small, living on their family estates or on book-land, who owned no lord except the king, and many more whose tie to any other lord was frail. The king of the English had in no way been squeezed out of all territory except his own demesne. Moreover, the idea of public authority had not disappeared. Each lordship was a fragment of, and on the same pattern as, the royal authority; and each lord was in a sense a royal official, rewarded for his services by permission to collect the appropriate royal revenue.

Landownership, commendation, and alienated or usurped *regalia* were the tangled threads in Anglo-Saxon lordship. Different bundles of these threads were held in different hands; and different results were achieved as they were spread over individual cultures. Land-ownership was probably still the dominant ingredient. By charter or will owners alienated land with its stock and men as though they were disposing of slave estates; and the contrast between landowner-ship and simpler lordship produced the distinction between 'inland' and 'outland'. Inland was land in which no one but the lord had proprietary rights. Whether this land was organized as home farms round his halls, let to agricultural tenants in return for rent and services, or loaned to thegns and cnihts, it was, in descending degrees of emphasis, the lord's inland or, in Norman terminology, his demesne. The characteristic feature of outland was that the lord possessed over the landholders, whose scattered tenements formed it, merely seignorial rights, and enjoyed only those customs which had once been rendered to the king.

All important landowners exploited their estates indirectly. Units were formed out of the individual properties, or manors, to produce a *feorm* or 'farm'—a fixed render—and these were often organized into provisioning and revenue groups, the former supplying the lord and his household with a fixed amount of food for consumption (the 'food farm'), the others, usually the more inconveniently situated parts, providing a fixed render of money or produce for sale through the hands of a manager (a 'farmer'). The royal demesne was still organized in this way in 1066: estates in Old Wessex (Dorset, Somerset, Wiltshire, and Hampshire) were providing 'farms of one night', and the rest of the demesne mostly fixed money payments. Likewise, the abbey of Ely, a house refounded in 970, had by 1066 out of its demesne lands scattered in 116 villages in six shires, valued at about £900 a year, organized 33 'manors' to provide 56 food farms,

each a week's food for the abbey, and left about as many in reserve
to breed stock and grow crops for the market. Such a simple organization was applicable to the most heterogeneous collection of
estates, and hides from us the diversity of the societies which lay
under the wide grasp of the lords.

IV

If we are to believe the evidence of the Anglo-Saxon laws, the
fundamental cleavage in free society below the king lay between the
thegn and the ceorl, the gentle and the simple of Victorian writers.
The barrier was not impassable. A ceorl could thrive, and achieve
the higher status. But the stratification appears sharp and significant.
It certainly determined a man's position before the law, fixing the
value of his life, of his peace, and of his oath. Nevertheless, such a
simple classification throws little light on a society rich in the diversity of its economic and social groupings. It suggests the existence of
an enormous substratum of peasants, equal and free, below a modest
and level aristocracy. The picture, however, is false. Within the ranks
of the thegnage were wealthy and poor, important and insignificant
men; and there was little uniformity in the social and economic
condition of the ceorls.

The sharpest division among the ceorls was probably that between
those who ran a farm and those who did not. In areas where inheritance was impartible there was for every head of a household holding
a share of the village fields a group of landless kinsmen and farm
labourers. These dependants were often of the same legal status as
the landholder; but their economic and social position was far
inferior. There was also the distinction between those who farmed
their own land and those whose land belonged to their lord. The
tenant-farmers were slipping into the half-free class which lay
between the full ceorls and the slaves.

The slaves, the freedmen, and the half-free were in part relics of
subject peoples, in part Englishmen who had lost their freedom either
through misfortune or the operation of the law. The number of
slaves in the Old-English kingdom has probably always been underestimated. Most surviving Anglo-Saxon wills order the enfranchise-
ment of some or all of the slaves on the estates; and slaves were still
numerous in 1086 despite the movement towards freedom which the
Norman conquest probably accelerated. Hence an intermediate
class, which the Normans would call 'villein', was being created both

by the descent of impoverished or oppressed ceorls and by the ascent of enfranchised slaves. The one set had lost its economic independence; the other was gaining a place in the rural economy; and both made a substantial render to their lord in return for their use of his land and, sometimes, of his stock. It seems possible, therefore, that the largest social class in Anglo-Saxon England was composed of men who can best be described as half-free, and that the largest economic class was made up of men who had either no agricultural holding or, at most, a cottage and a garden. The 'peasant-proprietor' was very rare in eleventh-century England.

The landed ceorls, and, perhaps, some of the poorer thegns, were farmers—usually 'mixed-farmers', for, owing to the difficulty of transport, corn was grown wherever possible. The farmers and their labourers lived in villages, except where the lie of the land made that difficult or where social custom encouraged settlement in hamlets; and these, usually small, villages and tinier hamlets are those we know to-day. But in some parts of the country the aspect has been greatly changed. The countryside has become emptier of men—a single farm having often replaced a village—and more closely covered with fields and hedges.

In Mercia and central Wessex (even, perhaps, in Devon) the agrarian unit was usually the whole township, and not the individual farm. The arable land round the village lay open, with no permanent hedges and few trees. For the purpose of cultivation it was divided into two fields, which were put under corn in alternate years, a rotation which allowed ample time for the recovery of the land between one crop and the next. Each of the great fields was subdivided into ploughing units, called *culturae* or furlongs; and a farmer's holding consisted of a number of quarter-acre strips, scattered throughout the furlongs in the two fields. These dispersed farms were roughly equal, and the system of agriculture required, and presupposed, much communal activity. Although the practical details of farming methods in the eleventh century are by no means clear, it is reasonable to think that the scarcity of draught animals and the intermingling of the strips must usually have led to co-operative ploughing; and the field rotation, the defence of the growing crops, the common use of the lands when fallow, and the intercommoning on the waste around and within the arable bound the cultivators into a tight community and allowed no deviation from the village scheme.

This equality of stake, interlocking of holdings, and regularity of pattern betoken both a rigid social custom and, probably, the presence of an external power interested in its maintenance. The whole system depended on the custom whereby each farm descended intact to a single son—whether the eldest, the youngest, or the father's favourite—a custom which produced the 'stem-family'. The practice involved little hardship at a time when the population could increase but slowly. Yet outside this area holdings could usually be broken up, and even in the Midlands the natural predisposition of mankind towards division among heirs sometimes asserted itself. Hence it cannot be without significance that the Midland villages had been subject to the power of lords from a very early time; and it may well be that equality was the result rather of economic servitude than of the preservation of a primitive idyllic polity.

The typical family holding in the open fields of these Midland villages was a 'yardland' (latinized as 'virgate'), nominally of 30 acres, named after the unit of measurement used for the width of the strips, the land-yard or rod (latin, *virga*) of from 15 to 21 feet. In the rest of the kingdom, however, area was estimated in quite different ways. The commonest unit was the amount of land that could be cultivated by the standard plough and its team. In Deira the measure was the ploughland of eight oxgangs, the carucate and bovate of Latin documents; in East Anglia the eruing, and also terms which point to a family share, as man-lot or the full-holding, in Latin *plena terra;* in Kent the sulung and yoke; and in Sussex there had once been wystas, another plough unit. Such terms have no association with the strip, and suggest a more individual type of husbandry. Villages surrounded by open fields are found outside Mercia and central Wessex; but rarely outside that area existed its characteristic feature: the complex of equal holdings, divided between two fields, scattered among furlongs, and cultivated according to a common scheme.

The most striking contrast to the economy of the Midlands is provided by Kent. This culture, at one time common to all the 'Jutish' territory in the south-east of England, had by the eleventh century yielded in part to the West-Saxon conquerors, and some of its characteristics had disappeared from Hampshire, Surrey, and Sussex. The fundamental peculiarity of the whole area was its hamlet settlements, each with a single field held by a group of kinsmen. This is the antithesis of the open-field system of the Midlands:

scattered hamlets instead of a nucleated village, compact holdings assessed in yokes in the place of the dispersed virgates, and joint family inheritance—a custom known as gavelkind—instead of a single stem of descent. Each hamlet was a distinct agrarian unit; but it can be seen in its entirety only when set within the lathe, as the ancient sub-divisions of Kent were called. Between Surrey and Sussex and into Kent ran the great forest of Andred. Round the coast and by the rivers were salt pastures. To each lathe was attached part of the forest and part of the saltings; and these rights were sub-divided between the hamlets within the lathe. Thus each family tenement consisted not only of a plot of land but also of grazing and other rights in wood and pasture often at some distance from the arable. And in this feature another contrast is seen with the Midland village with its circumscribed and usually unbroken boundaries. There is no reason to think that in the eleventh century the inhabitants of Kent did not grow subsistence crops in their fields like the farmers elsewhere; but there was no hindrance to a specialized economy when market conditions allowed.

The type of husbandry followed at this time in East Anglia, Lincolnshire, and the East Riding of Yorkshire is obscure, and evidence for the northern parts has been destroyed by the devastations of William the Conqueror. The East-Anglian culture appears to have lain midway between those of Kent and of the Midlands, for although there were nucleated villages with open fields, the farming seems to have been individual. It is possible that an unknown system of Anglian origin had broken down during the Danish wars and Scandinavian settlement. Certainly it appears that there was no regular rotation of crops between two village fields and no equal division of the farms between the fields and the furlongs; but whether racial habits, Anglian or Danish, or the plentiful supply of wattles for fencing and the interest in the breeding of sheep were responsible is still an unsolved problem. For individual farming leads to an unstable social organization, which makes it more difficult for the historian to approach the unknown through the known.

The parts of England already reviewed were under permanent cultivation by the plough. The principal produce was corn, winter wheat and rye and spring barley and oats, with peas and beans as the subsidiary crop, and hay the valuable gift of nature. Wheat and, especially, rye were grown for bread, oats and barley for animal fodder, porridge, and beer. The type of grain that was grown depended to some extent on climate and soil; and the type of stock varied according to the amount and quality of the pasturage. The usual domestic animals were sheep, goats, and cows—all milch animals—pigs for eating, and draught beasts—oxen and horses—as well as poultry. It was the dung of these animals that made such a relatively intensive farming possible.

In Bernicia and Cornwall, owing to the nature of the country, agriculture was subordinate to pastoral pursuits. And this contrast was intensified by difference of race. Cornwall was purely Celtic, and Northumbria had a large Celtic infusion. Yet the economic organization was similar to Kent's. The true economic unit in those parts was the small 'shire' (as Coldinghamshire, Berwickshire, and Howdenshire in the north and Triggshire and Powdershire in Cornwall) —corresponding to the lathe—to which belonged the hills, moors, and waste on which family groups of inhabitants, scattered in hamlets and small villages, intercommoned. The main occupation of the hill country was the keeping of cattle, sheep, and bees, and the rhythm of life was not the rotation of the fields but the movement between the summer pasture on the moors and the winter grazing in the valleys and farm closes. Where land was cultivated, a part of the small hamlet fields was improved in turn, mulched with the winter manure, and cropped with a succession of spring-sown grains until exhausted; at which time another portion, restored to fertility by long fallow, was brought into cultivation. In more favoured places there was an 'infield', which was in permanent cultivation, supplemented by 'outfields' reclaimed occasionally from the moor. The way of life was quite distinct from that of the true cornlands.

The variety in method of cultivation of the soil found in eleventh-century England is only one expression, perhaps the fundamental expression, of different provincial cultures. The same lack of uniformity is seen in the social condition of the class of working farmers.

Lordship was most effective in western Mercia and central Wessex, where there was the oldest tradition of settled government, the immediate presence of the king, compact village communities, and sometimes a servile Welsh population. In this area all the threads of lordship tended to be gathered into the same hands; and the integration of the village life was conducive to the level subjection of the whole township, although, even here, it was unusual for a whole village to be under the same lord for all purposes. The lord's inland (in the narrowest sense of the word) was divided between the fields like the strips of the yardlands, but often in blocks of whole furlongs; and it was cultivated for him by the household slaves and the villagers —the *geburs* who had a share in the fields and the *cotsetlan* who had merely a plot. None of these men was completely free. Their descendants were the servile manorial villeins.

Outside this area lordship over the agricultural classes was less firmly rooted in the soil. The Danish provinces can be considered together, for they present some similarities; yet it is by no means certain that they shared a uniform culture, or that all the common peculiarities were of Danish origin. It cannot be doubted that the settlement of some Scandinavian armies on the land at the end of the ninth century created new social groupings and gave rise to distinct cultures; yet the traditional view that Scandinavian colonization re-established a more primitive freedom has to meet the difficulty that society was freer in East Anglia than in the area which has been called the essential Danelaw, the district between the rivers Welland and Tees, and that society was freest of all in Kent where the Danes had not settled. Nor can it be without significance that the characteristic unit of lordship in the Danelaw, the soke, was peculiar to England and that the sokes bore English names. The idiosyncrasies of East Anglia and Northumbria lie deeper, perhaps, than is sometimes allowed. It is also possible that part of the individuality arose after the time of settlement. For instance, the long immunity of these almost autonomous provinces from the taxation and burdens of the Old-English monarchy and, especially, from the greed of the church freed them from some of the main economic pressures on the ceorl.

Fundamentally soke implied jurisdiction, and a soke comprised those men under the jurisdiction of another. The relationship may sometimes have been based originally on the military ties between the common soldiers and their captains; but it found formal recognition in the alienation of public courts by the king. Some sokes were formed by the grant of whole hundreds to a lord, some by granting jurisdiction over all a lord's commended men; others, perhaps, by the grant of all unattached men within a hundred or group of hundreds. A soke could, therefore, extend over a wide area. The Lincolnshire soke of Waltham involved the inhabitants of 16 villages; the Yorkshire soke of Gilling the men of 21; while in East Anglia Necton soke lay in 9 different hundreds. The soke had also acquired an economic significance by the eleventh century. A lord always had jurisdiction over his 'villeins'; and even in the freest areas he usually had soke over his commended men. Hence soke and estate were largely synonymous. Between the Welland and the Tees the soke appeared as a complex of demesne (the inland, together with its scattered berewicks) within an area of jurisdiction and tribute organized round it (the sokeland, or outland). Similar conditions will be found in Kent. Soke and lathe were not unlike. In East Anglia the texture of society was rather looser, and the sokes were more scattered and possibly less stable than in the northern Danelaw. Villages were divided between several lords; the men themselves could be divided between different lords, one lord having his soke, another his commendation. But even here aggressive lords, like the abbot of Ely, were consolidating soke and estate.

The agricultural population of this society cannot be classified according to the Wessex categories. In 1066 the abbot of Ely exercised rights over some 1,200 freemen and sokemen living in 200 villages, 1,100 villeins, almost as many cottagers, and nearly 300 slaves. The villeins, cottagers, and slaves, the cultivators of the abbot's inland, descendants of native Anglian peasants, Danish freedmen, and depressed sokemen, were doubtless similar in status to the corresponding classes in the Midlands. The numerous body of sokemen was, however, a unique feature of this area. These men had smaller arable tenements than the Midland farmers—their holding in the northern Danelaw was from one to two oxgangs, with one oxgang as perhaps the standard, and the normal holding of the sokeman and freeman of East Anglia seems to have been even less—but it is likely that many of them were engaged in sheep farming, and that their rights of pasture were more important than their cornfields. And in the social sphere their comparative economic independence of their lord's demesne, the diversity of their personal relationships, and their indisputable freedom distinguish them sharply from the villeins. Yet the commendation and service which they owed to their lords had become attached to their holdings, so that the tenements of some freeman and of most sokemen could not be separated from the lord's estate by the action of the tenant; and the economic freedom of even these men was in jeopardy.

The Danelaw was a country of large villages surrounded by the township fields; Kent and the south-east was a land of hamlets; yet there were similarities in their social and governmental organizations. The hamlets of Kent had anciently been grouped in lathes, and the dues and services that had been assessed on the hamlets in sulungs and yokes were rendered at the royal town within the lathe. The grant of an estate from the king to a lord could lead to few economic changes. If a home farm were acquired it consisted of scattered fields; and it was hard to organize the inhabitants of the lathe as the labour force for that demesne. Lordship, therefore, was predominantly seignorial. There was the familiar distinction between the lord's demesne and the outland, those hamlet fields which remained in the ownership of their peasant families. Grants of jurisdiction, too, were of no great help in creating a territorial lordship. Individual farming had supported no moot which could be used to further the economic policy of the lord. The local court was that of the lathe; and a whole lathe or a fragment of a lathe in private hands resisted amalgamation with seignorial jurisdiction.

In pastoral areas lordship was more archaic. It resembled that relationship between chieftain and clan which lasted for centuries more in Celtic areas, except that Anglo-Saxon kinship was never quite so solid. The tribute due to the lord was divided between the hamlets within the 'shire', without further repartition—each hamlet owing food rents in cattle and corn, payments, possibly in kind, for the right to pasture beasts in the shire forests and moors, and miscellaneous personal duties, such as giving hospitality to the lord, accompanying his progresses, and rearing his dogs. There was little, if any, seignorial demesne. The lord was a chieftain, not a landlord. And this difference is seen also in jurisdiction. The lords of the Northumbrian 'shires' usually controlled a hundred court; and such franchisal jurisdiction together with the inherent right which a lord had over his followers was all that he possessed. The northern peasants were called bonders, husbandmen, and their holding the 'full husbandland'. Set within a pastoral economy foreign to the greater part of England, the status of the bonders remained equivocal and difficult to bring into line with the tenures known elsewhere. In Cornwall, however, alien assessments had been in part superimposed. There was the 'Cornish acre', a plough unit sometimes as great as 64 Midland acres; and from the domination of Wessex had followed even the introduction of the Saxon hide and yardland.

The complexity and variety of the social and economic structure in eleventh-century England has often been stressed. Basically it was due to the persistence of different provincial cultures, and to the long and largely uninterrupted development of Germanic institutions. The benefice or fief, which in northern Gaul had almost standardized the system of land tenure, was gaining ground; but it had not yet transformed the estates of the official nobility. In some ways eleventh-century England was not unlike Gaul in the Carolingian period. The exceptional power of the Crown had prevented offices from changing into fiefs and royal servants from becoming simply vassals. English society was, therefore, in a sense archaic. It had not become feudal as society was feudal between the Loire and the Rhine. But this really feudal area was but a small part of western Europe; and the surrounding countries—Germany, Italy, Aquitaine, and Christian Spain, together with England—each had indigenous peculiarities yet had much in common. The main English aberrations consisted in the existence of a noble class of thegns, recognized by the law, and still owing services in virtue of its position; in the Nordic prejudice of that class against a military organization based on the private castle and cavalry troops; and in the dominance of the personal tie, the relative integrity of property rights, and the rarity of the fief among the aristocracy, so that many characteristic feudal features, such as knight-service and serjeanty, could be approached only through fictions. Yet English society should not be regarded as an oddity and studied out of context. In its aristocratic organization and the dominance of the warrior class, in its dispersal of public authority, and in its association of almost all duties with the possession of land it takes its place securely within a family of countries, of which none was identical in structure with another, none even internally homogeneous, but of which all were formed out of the amalgam of Roman and Germanic institutions and have always felt themselves akin.

V

At no time in the Dark Ages had the movement of trade been entirely halted in Europe; and by the eleventh century, in the relative peace after the settlement of the Viking marauders, and stimulated by the sea traffic of those adventurers, it was once more gathering momentum. England lay athwart the end of two great European trade routes from the Orient—that through Russia to the Baltic, where the island of Gotland was the distributive market, and that from the Adriatic to the Low Countries by way of the Rhineland. Its south-eastern harbours faced northern Gaul; and Ireland stood across from Bristol and Chester. Much cross-Channel traffic went to Wissant, a harbour formed by a breach in the sand dunes between Cap Gris-Nez and Cap Blanc-Nez, and then linked up with the system of

Roman roads radiating from the old Roman port of Boulogne. Already, however, there were signs of regular trade connexions. The men of Rouen had a settlement at Dowgate in London; the men of the emperor (probably the citizens of Cologne) and of Flanders (perhaps the hanse of Bruges, which comprised the gilds of the northern Flemish towns) also resorted there; and King Edward himself bestowed a group of Sussex ports on the Norman abbey of Fécamp.

The English ports seem to have been quite active in the eleventh century; but we have only scraps of information about the nature of the trade. Chester imported marten skins from Ireland, and Bristol sent back slaves. London in King Aethelred II's reign received lumber, fish, blubber, cloth, gloves, pepper, wine, and vinegar from the Rhineland, the Low Countries, Normandy, and northern Gaul. Scandinavia modelled its coinage on the English pattern. In general England imported the luxuries required by the church and the aristocracy, and, although it sent out some articles of fine quality, such as illuminated manuscripts and gold embroidery, for which it was famous, it exported mainly animal and dairy produce.

Internal trade was facilitated by the abundance of silver pennies. England almost had a money economy. In Edward's reign the number of coins cut from the pound, mark, or *öre* (weights and units of account) varied according to the economic situation. Pennies of 18 gr. (300 to the lb.) were usual until 1051 when they were raised for a time to 27 gr. More reforms were made in 1065. King Edward granted to Dover freedom from toll throughout England in order to facilitate the distribution of imported articles; but the bulk of internal trade was concerned with goods of domestic origin—cattle, salt, and iron implements. Salt was obtained from sea-water and brine springs at many places in England, and metals were extracted on a small scale wherever alluvial deposits could be found or veins easily worked.

Such conditions were unfavourable to the growth of a large merchant class in England, and few towns display true urban characteristics. The English boroughs of the eleventh century were those fortified towns which had been constructed for the defence of the countryside by both sides during the Danish wars. Sometimes repaired Roman cities, sometimes fortresses newly laid out on a grid pattern, most became governmental centres as well. The borough was usually the seat of a mint, of a market, and, sometimes, of the shire and hundred courts. But it was in no way sharply detached from the countryside. As with other royal estates a royal reeve—here a port-reeve—administered it for the king; it was assessed in the normal way in hides or carucates to the national burdens; except in the case of London it had no special urban court; and the system of land tenure within the walls was not radically different from that out-side. Tenements were usually held by payment of rent (landgable) and by performance of various personal services—a tenure similar to that of several agricultural classes, but especially suited to merchants, and capable of modification according to their needs. Most boroughs were on royal demesne; but the king had not infrequently alienated tenements, customs, and jurisdiction here as elsewhere. Hence there was often the same variety of lordship within a borough as in the rural village. Nobles and churches owned tenements, the customs due from them, commendation over inhabitants, and rights of sake and soke.

This unspecialized condition of the Edwardian boroughs does not, however, mean that they were all purely agrarian units; nor does the lack of self-government exclude the existence of a rudimentary com-munal organization. It seems that the *burhwaru*, or burgesses, properly called, were not all those who lived within a borough, but those inhabitants responsible for the borough customs. Such men were not necessarily traders; yet the large population of some towns and the dwindling of the borough fields make it certain that agricultural pursuits were sometimes subsidiary to activities characteristically urban. Estimates of the population of the English towns, although all based on Domesday statistics, vary considerably. It is, however, generally agreed that at least twenty towns had populations of over a thousand, and, according to one modern authority, Ipswich had over 3,000 burgesses, Thetford almost 5,000, Lincoln and Norwich between 6,000 and 7,000, and York about 9,000. No figures can be given for Winchester, the seat of the treasury, or London, certainly the largest town, because they were omitted from Domesday Book. On the population evidence alone it is clear that not a few of the larger English boroughs were real towns and not merely fortified administrative stations. Then London is known to have possessed three local and specialized courts, the folkmoot, husting, and ward-moot; and it is possible that in those other boroughs which formed the centre of a hundred or wapentake the court had developed a character of its own. There is also evidence that gilds had been formed in a few of the larger towns. Some of these may have had purely social functions; but the London gild of cnihts may already have become an association of wealthy merchants, and the chapmen gild of Canterbury can probably be traced back to Edward's reign. Moreover, when King Edward made an arrangement with the ports of Dover, Sandwich, Romney, Hythe, and Fordwich, by which they were to furnish him with ships and men in return for the profits of jurisdiction, he recognized that each had a community with which he could deal, and which could assume responsibility for a financial and administrative transaction.

The revenue which boroughs produced for their owners included the landgable and its associated services, tolls on sales, and the profits of the mint and of jurisdiction. The revenue was usually farmed by the sheriff from the king, and, as in the case of the shire courts, the king shared the profits with the earl in the proportion of two to one. This earl's 'third penny' was probably a reward for his duties in connexion with the defence and maintenance of these important institutions.

The English towns of the eleventh century were rudimentary and formless compared with the self-governing, privileged urban republics of the high Middle Ages. But the towns of most importance under Edward the Confessor were still pre-eminent under Edward I; and the reasons which had made them great in the eleventh century were those which made them even greater as time went by. We cannot doubt that the beginnings of a brisk foreign traffic and of a lively internal market had already, before the Norman conquest, started to transform the more favourably situated Anglo-Danish boroughs into urban trading and industrial communities.

VI

Christianity was the official religion in England. Heathen cults and magical practices were condemned by law, and an organized church and priesthood were maintained by the people. The popular religion, however, was informed by pagan festivals and deeply coloured by superstitions with which the church had compromised. It is likely, indeed, that many men were not even nominal Christians; but the church was not strong enough to compel, and the pagans felt no active hostility towards it.

The organization planned for the church in Britain by Pope Gregory I, as expressed in his letter of 22 June 601 to Augustine of

Canterbury, had been found impracticable, and the Edwardian church had peculiarities of form due not only to its unbroken and natural development during four-and-a-half centuries but also to the initial compromises which the complete disappearance of Roman institutions from the country forced on its founders. Appreciations of the Anglo-Saxon church are often vitiated either through failure to recognize insular peculiarities which had been sanctioned by the very creators of this outpost church, or through the making of an unsympathetic comparison with continental churches, such as the Norman, which had been organized anew after collapse.

The Roman plan for Britain had been followed as far as possible. Two independent provinces had been created, with metropolitan sees at Canterbury (instead of London) and at York; and subordinate territorial dioceses had been formed, although not to the number originally intended nor on the classical pattern. Instead of the projected twelve dioceses in each province, there were in 1042 thirteen south of the Humber and but one to the north, a disparity due to the inequality in wealth and to the difference in the political history of the two divisions. Of more importance was the inability of the founders of the English church to model the dioceses on a Roman administrative framework, with the episcopal sees placed in great urban centres. In Britain the dioceses had perforce to coincide with the areas ruled by the local kings, and the sees to be situated in any convenient settlement. This expedient caused the area of the bishop-rics to fluctuate as the boundaries of the petty kingdoms changed; and while this flexibility gave them a power of survival superior to that possessed by the more rigidly organized continental churches, it appeared disorderly once the hierarchical system had elsewhere in Europe been established anew after the catastrophic disruption of the ninth century.

The theocratic nature of the Old-English kingdom—characteristic of all western Europe at this time—meant that church and state shared many characteristic features; and the church appeared more as a loose confederation of bishoprics under the king than as an independent hierarchical organization. Pope Gregory I had not intended the archbishop of Canterbury permanently to have primacy over York, and there is no evidence that, save under exceptional circumstances, the southern metropolitan had ever enjoyed the legal rights of a primate, although a superiority arising from his rule of the politically and economically more important province and of the oldest and most revered church was usually recognized in practice. The absence of recorded conflict in the Anglo-Saxon period, in contrast to the endemic strife which followed, implies that Canterbury did not meddle with York and, moreover, that neither archbishop exercised much control over his subordinate bishops. National and provincial synods were on occasion held in England; but the metropolitans enjoyed precedence and honour in their provinces rather than real governmental powers.

The absence of an active hierarchical principle had led to a blurring in the territorial organization of the church by the eleventh century. The custom whereby the archbishop of York held also the bishopric of Worcester obscured the division between the two provinces; and the inability of Stigand, archbishop of Canterbury, to perform archiepiscopal functions between 1059 and 1066, owing to papal displeasure, led to such confusion that after the Norman conquest the northern metropolitan claimed for his province not only Worcester, but Lichfield and Dorchester as well. The dioceses, too, were losing the character of distinct units; and a development is noticeable similar to that which had taken place in their secular counterparts, the earldoms. Just as, since the reign of Cnut, shires were grouped arbitrarily to form great provincial earldoms, so it had become not unusual to combine two, and occasionally three, dioceses under one bishop. In Edward's reign Lyfing held Cornwall, Crediton, and Worcester; Leofric Cornwall and Crediton; Ealdred Worcester with Hereford and Ramsbury, and then Worcester and York; Heremann Sherborne and Ramsbury; and Stigand Winchester and Canterbury. This practice was due partly to the poverty of York and the south-western dioceses, partly to administrative convenience. It was advantageous, for instance, in view of the Welsh menace, for Ealdred to combine Worcester and Hereford between 1056 and 1060; and he administered Ramsbury in addition because Bishop Heremann abandoned his see from 1055 to 1058.

Just as in the state the most effective governmental unit was the earldom, so it was the bishopric in the church; and the state sometimes interfered to strengthen the power of the bishop. The royal laws required the holding of diocesan synods for the rule and edification of the lower clergy, and these were occasionally held. Canon law, the special law of the church, was studied in England; and several compilations, useful to a bishop, have survived. The English manuals were derived in the main from penitentials of native origin, from the eighth-century Irish collection of canons, and from the Carolingian revision of the fifth-century collection of Dionysius Exiguus, known as the *Dionysio-Hadriana*. Hence, although most of the important texts are represented, the law was generally old-fashioned: it reflected more the Carolingian than the contemporary position. Certainly there was no great interest in canon law in England, and this can be attributed to the limited scope of the bishop's jurisdiction in ecclesiastical cases and over ecclesiastical persons. Where penance was the appropriate punishment, it was imposed by the church; but most moral offences were covered by the folk-law and royal legislation, and to this law the clergy as well as the laity were subject. The church had, therefore, little independent jurisdiction, and the bishops had beyond the synod no machinery of government. A good and efficient bishop perambulated his diocese, preaching to the people, confirming boys and girls, consecrating churches, and generally overseeing the condition of his flock. He could do much in person by virtue of his office; but if he himself was slack, there was anarchy.

Originally, there had been no parish other than the bishop's diocese; and this had gradually been subdivided as other churches were founded within the bishopric. By the eleventh century the medieval parish system, which has survived little changed to the present day, was already present in its rudiments; and almost every village had a church of some sort. Boroughs often had many. The gradual growth of a parish organization had left its mark on the status of the churches. The earliest foundations were called in the eleventh century the 'old minsters', a name which reveals that they had once been, if not monasteries, at least colleges of clerks on the same pattern as the cathedral minsters; and usually they were still served by a body of clergy. Such churches had mostly been founded by the bishops themselves or by the king; and their endowments were large and their parochial rights paramount. In process of time lesser churches had been built, often by the lay nobility on their estates within the parishes of the old minsters; indeed, by the eleventh century a thegn was expected to own a church. These lesser churches were the predecessors of the typical medieval parish church. Their endowment of land, in Wessex and English Mercia often of one or two yardlands, was sufficient to support only a single priest; and their parochial rights were less comprehensive than those of the old minsters. The eleventh-century laws also mention a class of 'field churches'—chapels without a cemetery, which had not yet acquired even a limited parochial status.

The church had been growing independently of the bishops; and as they had not sought to make their government more effective by subdividing their dioceses into archdeaconries—the usual expedient in the western church—they had never gained much control over those local churches which were privately owned. Wherever the Germanic people had been converted to Christianity men regarded the churches they founded as private property, and classed them with mills and sheep-folds as a productive appurtenance to their estates. Hence a bishop found it difficult to administer his diocese as a unity. He had unlimited control only over his own proprietary churches; and when churches within his diocese were owned by another bishop it was often hard for him to prevent their attachment to the other see. The churches, for instance, which stood on the estates which the archbishops of Canterbury possessed in Sussex became isolated and outlying parts of the diocese of Canterbury; and such peculiars often lasted until the nineteenth century.

It was, however, the institutional formlessness rather than any special laxity of government which set the English church apart in the eleventh century, for all provinces were anarchic, and the independence of the proprietary church was usual throughout Europe. The authority of the owner of a church, who appointed his priest, invested him with suitable lands or endowments, and treated him as a servant, was greater in practice than that of the bishop, who must sanction the appointment by institution and who had the right of spiritual discipline. Such a priest, similar in land-holding and status to the other village cultivators, came very close to servitude in strongly manorialized areas. And had clerical celibacy, which was the aim of reformers in England as on the continent at this time, been achieved, it appears that the position of the lower clergy would have suffered, for a married and often hereditary priesthood acquired a customary position and revenue which protected it to some degree against the arbitrary will of the owners of the churches.

As the village priest was so bound up in the life of the agricultural community, a high moral standard or exceptional zeal is not to be expected. But there is no reason to doubt that normally he did his duty according to the requirements of the age. A large body of edifying literature both in Latin and in English was written in the tenth and eleventh centuries—the vernacular literature without parallel elsewhere in Europe—and most of this was intended for the instruction of the lower clergy and to provide material suitable for sermons. Aelfric had produced at the end of the tenth century his *Catholic homilies*, two sets of forty sermons in the native tongue. Byrhtferth of Ramsey had composed in 1011 his *Manual*, a practical handbook for the clergy, written in Latin and explained in English. The church required the lower clergy to minister to and instruct the people, and it provided the necessary education. It was not only in England that priests were married, and it was not only abroad that the custom was recognized as an abuse. But to estimate or to compare moral tones is a thankless task. St. Wulfstan was for a time a parish priest, and there must have been others like him to leaven the lump.

The revenue of all churches came basically from their endowment of land; but free-will payments and taxation under the authority of the state became increasingly important. Thanksgiving offerings had by the eleventh century usually hardened into a tariff for spiritual services. The cathedrals 'sold' chrism to their daughter churches; the parish priests charged for baptism, and required the gift of part of a dead man's chattels, a due known as soul-scot, and in later times as the mortuary. Tithe had originally been a Christian duty; but by the eleventh century payment was enforced by the secular law. In its form of a tenth of the gross increase of all crops and animals it pressed heavily on the cultivators. The destination of tithe was various in the Edwardian period. The old minsters had retained a substantial portion; but the proprietors of land and churches claimed and exercised some control over its employment, and part of the tithe went to the lesser churches and even occasionally into secular hands. The use of tithe for the endowment of monasteries, which became widespread later, does not, however, seem to have been common in the Anglo-Saxon period. The state had also imposed national taxes for the support of the church, such as plough-alms and church-scot.

Benedictine monasticism had been revived in England after the Danish invasions and settlements of the ninth century, and a wave of pious enthusiasm, which reached its climax in the reign of Edgar (959-75), had caused the establishment of more than forty houses, all south of the Humber, and planted thickest in Wessex, western Mercia, and the Fenlands. The movement had native roots, but was greatly influenced by the reformed monasteries of Lotharingia,

especially through Ghent, and of Cluny through Fleury-sur-Loire.
A uniform rule for the new monasteries, the *Regularis concordia,* an
eclectic code based on the observances in the best continental houses,
was drawn up by an English synod in Edgar's reign; yet the monasteries remained independent units, and it seems that individual
variety in ritual was never completely suppressed. The special
feature of the monastic revival in England was that its inspirers were
the bishops supported by the kings; and this close connexion
between the episcopacy and monasticism strongly affected the texture
of the English church. The bishops of Winchester, Worcester, and
Sherborne and the archbishop of Canterbury reformed their cathedral chapters by substituting monasteries for colleges of canons—a
practice which remained peculiar to England; and monks were
chosen as bishops far more frequently than was the general custom
in western Europe at this time. Hence the whole English church was
permeated with the ideals of the monastic renaissance; and if this led
to some dilution of its strength, it at least avoided that strife between
the bishops and the monasteries which was common outside
England. In the middle of the eleventh century the archbishop of
York, and the bishops of London, Exeter and Wells, re-established
the traditional canonical life of their cathedral clergy by imposing a
quasi-monastic rule. Elsewhere the cathedral minsters were still
served by colleges of secular clerks with little corporate sense.
When Edward came to the throne the first reformed monastery,
Glastonbury, was about a century old; and it is possible that the
passage of time and the political unrest before and after the reign of
Cnut had led to some slackening of zeal in English monasteries.
Edward himself, claimed as a lover of monks, seems to have considered that English observance was not up to the best continental
standard—attributable, he thought, to the novelty of monasticism in
England, and hence the need for a laxer rule; but his apparent
indifference to practical measures of reform suggests that the position
was at least satisfactory.

Such was the internal structure of the English church in Edward's
reign. But in no way was it an isolated or self-sufficient organization.
It was part of the church universal, of which in the west the successor to St. Peter was recognized as head; and it was also closely
enmeshed with lay society in England. Although the two English
provinces were directly subordinate to the papacy, the control was
extremely light. This state of affairs was not due to a conscious policy

of independence pursued by the English church. Rome had founded the church in Britain, and the *ecclesia Anglorum* remembered its founder with pious gratitude. Indeed, in the intercourse between the mother and the daughter churches the overtures came usually from the English side. It was the distance, and, until the middle of the eleventh century, the degradation of the papacy which created a practical barrier. Official relations were confined principally to two matters. The right of the pope alone to confer metropolitan authority on a bishop had never been questioned; and each new English archbishop on promotion either petitioned by legation or in person for the symbol of his authority, the circlet of white wool worn round the neck with a pendant before and behind, such as appears on the arms of the see of Canterbury, known as the *pallium*, or pall. In the eleventh century the personal visit of both archbishops to Rome had become usual. It was not always a popular custom: the journey was dangerous and the papal court rapacious; but no archbishop could function without the *pallium*. The case of Stigand proves this undisputedly. Stigand, an Englishman, who had served Cnut as chaplain and was seemingly at the head of Edward's *scriptorium* in the early years of his reign, after holding the bishoprics of Elmham and Winchester, was appointed archbishop of Canterbury by the king in 1052 after his Norman predecessor, Robert of Jumièges, had been expelled by the party of Godwine, earl of Wessex. The view in England was that Robert had fled and resigned his see; actually he obtained papal letters of restitution which he could not use. However that may be, the pope accepted a similar revolution at Dorchester; and Stigand did in fact obtain the *pallium* in 1058-9 from Pope Benedict X. Benedict was an intruder, and later the church regarded him as a usurper. Stigand was, therefore, merely unlucky in the moment chosen for his application. But as soon as the English church learned that Benedict was no true pope, it refused to recognize Stigand as archbishop; and the only periods during which Stigand consecrated bishops were during the pontificate of Benedict and after the Norman conquest. The second regular connexion between England and the papacy was that ancient custom, the annual payment of tribute from England, called Romescot or Peter's Pence, which was still maintained under Edward.

Other official business was unusual and sporadic. Leofric's removal of his see from Crediton to Exeter received the approbation of Pope Leo IX; a dispute between bishops over the boundaries of their sees was settled by Pope Nicholas II; the same pope insisted at the time of Ealdred's visit for the *pallium* that the new archbishop should surrender the diocese of Worcester, and sent cardinal legates to England both to see that this was done and to review the position of the church in England; occasional malefactors were required to obtain a papal penance: and with the pontificate of Leo IX (1048-54) began again the regular trickle of papal privileges in favour of monasteries into England.

The position was, then, that the papacy had not yet given its full attention to England, and that England still sought on occasion and when considered appropriate the help of the pope. English prelates were present at Leo IX's councils in 1049 at Rheims and in 1050 at Rome and Vercelli. English bishops went to Rome for consecration in 1061. English nobles still kept up the custom of visiting the city of the apostles. Both Tostig, earl of Northumbria, and his brother, Harold, earl of Wessex, made the journey with their retinues; and if King Edward himself was prevented from following the example of Cnut, he made amends by rebuilding a monastery in honour of St. Peter.

The connexion between England and Rome was slight, but devoted; the relations between church and state in England were most intimate. The Anglo-Saxon kings had been exceptionally pious, and their rule was theocratic. Indeed, Edwardian England reproduces many of the characteristic features of the Carolingian renaissance, when Frankish king and his bishops, and Frankish emperor and the pope worked harmoniously together in the government of western Europe. In England the bishops and the heads of certainly the more important monasteries were appointed by the king with the advice of the witan; prelates were always among the counsellors of the king; and it was naturally in the witenagemot that major matters of church policy, such as the creation or suppression of dioceses and the moving of sees, were decided. The legislative codes issued by the king dealt with spiritual as well as secular offences; but sometimes a specialization can be observed, and sections of the codes appear to be deliberations of church synods promulgated under royal authority—a Carolingian custom, which was still followed in churches other than the English. Edward himself was no legislator, and he made no known additions to the codification of Cnut; but the rights of the church were under his care. As he declared in a charter he granted in 1050 to the new cathedral church at Exeter, 'It is right and proper for us, whom God has appointed to rule over men, . . . to take in hand . . . the affairs of the church and correct those things which in our eyes do not appear to be just, . . . directing them to the advancement of both this life and the life hereafter.'

If the king assumed responsibility for the good government of the church, he expected in turn that the bishops should share in the task of administering the kingdom. Indeed, he regarded the bishops as the spiritual counterpart to the earls. The bishop presided over the shire court with the earl or, in his absence, the shire-reeve; and they provided justice according to the appropriate law for both laymen and clerk. The king's orders were addressed to the bishop, earl, and thegns of the shire. Bishop and earl were the twin pillars on which the public government of the king was based. Yet the confusion in function did not in England lead to some of the grosser abuses of the age. Bishops were not invested by ring and staff but by a writ sent to the shire court. Prelates were rarely scions of the highest nobility, as in Normandy in the first half of the eleventh century, but were selected mainly either from the monasteries or from the king's writing office (*scriptorium*), later known as the chancery. This had been the policy of Cnut; and it was maintained by Edward, and also by William I. Six monks from houses that had been reformed in the tenth century were promoted by Edward, including Ealdred, monk of Winchester and abbot of Tavistock, who held several sees before becoming archbishop of York, and Wulfstan, who in 1062 was promoted from the headship of the cathedral priory to the bishopric of Worcester. One foreign monk, Robert from St. Ouen and abbot of Jumièges, was made bishop of London and then archbishop of Canterbury. The number of clerks from Edward's *scriptorium* who gained promotion was rather larger, and in this class there was a marked foreign element. Three were Lotharingians, two were Normans, and of the five Englishmen, one, Leofric, had been educated in Lorraine. Among these royal clerks was Stigand, the unsatisfactory archbishop of Canterbury. But he should not be regarded as typical. Curial bishops were as a rule excellent administrators, respectable in character, and devoted to the king.

It is, however, within the class of monastic bishops that men can best be found for comparison with the more distinguished 'Norman' prelates, such as Lanfranc or Anselm. Ealdred, who rose to be archbishop of York, was probably the most illustrious of Edward's bishops, Wulfstan of Worcester the best. Ealdred, despite his monastic origin, was a man of affairs. While bishop on the Welsh border he was involved in the problem of the march, negotiating treaties, and even, on one occasion, defending his territory by arms. His reputation for administrative skill led to the accumulation of bishoprics in his hands; and, although we know little about his pastoral work, he stands out as a builder and as a reformer. He rebuilt the monastic church at Gloucester, and in his archdiocese he completed the building programme of his two predecessors at the great collegiate churches of York, Southwell, and Beverley, increased their endowments at his own expense, and insisted on a regular communal life for the canons who served them. Like Stigand he was immersed in the secular affairs of the kingdom, but unlike his fellow archbishop he managed to keep clear of faction, and he served Kings Edward, Harold, and William with equal disinterestedness. It was as a diplomatist that Edward found Ealdred most useful. The bishop was active in all internal crises, and was employed by Edward on foreign legations. He became a great traveller, journeying to Cologne, visiting Rome twice, and in 1058 making a pilgrimage to Jerusalem by way of Hungary, undismayed by Earl Svein's death on a similar venture six years before. The cardinal legates, who returned with Ealdred from Rome in 1061, found the archbishop congenial company. He was the type of cosmopolitan Anglo-Saxon, the administrative bishop, the practical reformer. He was conscious of no inferiority when the Normans came; he knew how to put a Norman sheriff in his place; and William's wide changes in the English church did not begin until after Ealdred's death.

If we know Ealdred largely from the record of his public acts, we know Wulfstan through a biography, written by his chaplain, which concentrates on the bishop's private life. Both pictures are, therefore, distorted; but each is complementary to the other. The portrait we have of Wulfstan is that of a stern moralist, of an indefatigable devotee to a personal ministry, of a saint to whom tardy justice was done by the papal canonization in 1203. Despite Wulfstan's education as a boy in the abbeys of Evesham and Peterborough, his office of schoolmaster in Worcester priory, his love of books, and the encouragement he gave to the writing of history, which led to the composition of the chronicle called 'Florence of Worcester's', he is given no special reputation for learning; and despite his intimacy with King Harold, the favour of King William and Archbishop

Lanfranc, and his commission to the sub-prior, Hemming, to sort and record the monastic archives—to which we owe the production of the second and third Worcester cartularies of the eleventh century, inferior, indeed, to the first compilation, but proof of his business sense—he is made to appear simple and innocent of all worldly wisdom. Certainly as a public figure Wulfstan was overshadowed by Ealdred, who never surrendered the ultimate control of Worcester affairs after he had been deprived of that bishopric in 1062, nor, it must be confessed, all the episcopal estates; and in local affairs Wulfstan was eclipsed by Aethelwig, abbot of Evesham. But what caught the imagination of his contemporaries and gave him the power of healing and of working miracles—which assured his lasting reputation—was the extreme asceticism of his life and his punctilious observance of spiritual duty. Characteristic of Wulfstan was the personal mission that he conducted in his small diocese. Always on the move, he visited regularly in turn all parts of his bishopric, preaching peace and repentance, baptizing, confirming, hearing confessions, and urging the building of churches which he consecrated when built. There is nothing local in the characters of Ealdred and Wulfstan. Each represents an episcopal type which has appeared in all periods of ecclesiastical history. It is, therefore, significant that such good examples of both types should have existed in the English church on the eve of the Norman conquest.

Until papal centralization had broken down local custom there was no uniform pattern of church government in western Christendom; and the individual and archaic English church was only one of many diverse provinces. The English church had advanced precociously up to the time of the Carolingian renaissance; but after the eighth century, apart from the revival in monasticism, it had made little progress. The same limited virtue gave rise to both phases. English strength lay in its conservative tradition. Its scholars had rescued what they could of patristic and classical learning, and had handed it on. But they took no interest or part in the original developments which followed. The new law, the new theology, the new striving after independence aroused no stir in English circles. The church was, therefore, in a sense, backward and in need of reformation. But its general moral and cultural tone was in no way inferior to the average European standard.

VII

In the eleventh century the nobility lived in barn-like halls and the peasants in hovels; and conscious creative activity was centred in the church, which alone provided the physical setting for many types of artistic production. The laity were not barbarous; but, since few men could afford much luxury, their life was dominated by traditional and utilitarian crafts. Buildings in stone, sculpture and metal work, embroidery, the copying of manuscripts, and literature itself, were essentially *opera Dei*, works to the glory of God, for the encouragement of the Christian life, and for the delight and wonderment of the people.

Christian art had been in origin the art of the Roman empire; and, as imperial Rome still lived gloriously in Byzantium, most western artistic styles were derived directly or indirectly from the Christian east. England in the eleventh century was in immediate contact with Constantinople; but it had felt Byzantine influence mainly through the Carolingian empire and, latterly, through its surviving portion, the Ottonian empire in Germany. North-eastern England was also affected by Scandinavian culture, and western England by Irish. Art styles could travel swiftly, by means of manuscripts and textiles, even in this period of restricted communication; and many models were available to English craftsmen. The English were an artistic people. The first flowering of their art had been in Northumbria; in the eighth century Mercia had taken the lead; and with Alfred Wessex had come to the fore. English craftsmen had, therefore, a great tradition, which was powerful enough to assimilate the foreign themes. We find, then, in England many quite different styles in currency, but for the most part expressed in a characteristic native idiom. And the craftsmanship was superb. One of the first actions of Duke William after the conquest of England was to rob the churches of their artistic treasures in order to distribute magnificent largesse throughout Normandy and at Rome.

Many English churches were built of wood, and all but one of these have perished. Even the stone buildings have suffered badly. It is impossible to-day to compare the more important buildings of that age with the fine examples of the Norman period which are still standing, for no great Saxon church remains. North Elmham is in ruins; Canterbury was burned; others were pulled down to be replaced by larger churches in later styles. Only among the parish churches are fragmentary examples yet to be seen of a distinguished native school of architecture. And so thoroughly have Anglo-Norman romanesque and Norman-French gothic stamped themselves on the country, that these few specimens of the insular style now appear exotic intrusions into the accepted form.

The general style which prevailed in tenth- and eleventh-century England was Carolingian romanesque, and England shared with the Rhineland the purest tradition. The churches were remarkable for the equal importance given to the east and west ends, which led sometimes to a double transept or double apse, for their towers, and for the presence of an atrium or forecourt at the west end. Arches, doorways, and windows were usually round, although in England a taste for straight lines gave rise sometimes to triangular piercings. Carved decoration was sparse and the moulding on piers and arches poor. A common type of capital was the modified cube, the cushion form, introduced in the eleventh century from Germany, and later adopted and developed by the Normans. But the churches were probably plastered and painted inside, and the external walls were sometimes lavishly adorned by pilaster strips and blind arcading—a style likewise imitated from the Rhineland. These barbarized antique churches, polychromatic within, and adorned with porticos, apses, and pillars, and with clusters of turrets and cupolas, still had something in common with the Christian East. The gulf between them and Lincoln cathedral or Westminster abbey is profound.

It is believed that English churches were generally smaller than those which had recently been built in Normandy in a new romanesque style which was moving northwards across France; and it is probable that by 1066 many had ceased to satisfy the more ambitious standards of the age, for there had been a tradition in the English church that it was sacrilege to pull down and rebuild the works of saintly founders. Edward the Confessor, however, rebuilt Westminster abbey in the Norman style; and it is likely, even had the Norman conquest not taken place, that the English tradition would have been modified by the architectural fashions of northern France. Yet old habits were still strong. Ealdred, archbishop of York, who had visited Cologne, disregarded the style favoured by the English royal court, and into the new presbytery he had built at Beverley introduced a screen 'skilfully fashioned of Teutonic work'. Thus a living tradition of some distinction, basically classical in form, with the inspiration renewed from the Carolingian empire and especially from the cities of the Rhine, changed its direction sharply when the Normans began to rebuild the greater churches of England.

Sculpture in stone—and examples in other *media* have not survived —had a more localized tradition, and shows a greater diversity of style. The great Anglian school of sculpture, itself of diverse inspiration, was in decay in the north, where Scandinavian and Celtic themes had become popular. Ornamental slabs and standing crosses were decorated with all sorts of interlace and plaiting and sometimes with the elongated animals and leaves which the Norsemen had transmitted from Scythia. The best figure sculpture, the Roods and the Madonnas, was produced in the south, mostly on Byzantine models, although the iconographical tradition was various and the themes seem to have reached England by various routes and from different places of origin in the Christian East. The technical skill and the artistic merit vary considerably; but some of the pieces which are assigned to the eleventh century, such as the Romsey rood and the York Virgin, are sophisticated work of astonishing quality.

Most of the monasteries which had been refounded in the south of England in the tenth century had organized workshops. Book production—the writing, decorating, and binding of manuscripts— was the basic task; but all sorts of church furniture, carved ivories, metal, enamel, jewel work, and embroidery, were produced. In these arts, too, the dominant influence was Byzantine, although, again, the influence had reached England through various channels. England was most famed on the continent for its metal work, embroidery, and manuscripts. The making of books had greatly expanded during the revival of monasticism, and the quality of the decoration had become so high that it had influenced continental *scriptoria*. The models used in England were for the most part of Carolingian origin; but one of the most characteristic styles which developed—rather incorrectly known as the 'Winchester style'—was a local achievement. The initial letters scrolled with acanthus leaves and the outline drawings of this school represent English calligraphy at its best. The artists treated the antique designs so freshly that the delicate and animated patterns formed by the fluttering drapery, the craned necks, and the large expressive hands of the figures have an independent and high artistic merit. In the art of calligraphy itself an even older style was still holding its own. The 'insular script' or 'national hand', an Irish modification of the Roman half-uncial hand of Gaul brought to England by the Scottish missionaries of the seventh century, had made temporary headway even on the continent of Europe in the eighth century. But with the tenth-century renaissance of English monasticism 'Carolingian minuscule', a late-eighth-century Frankish development, had begun to find favour in the English writing-offices. In the eleventh century these two styles stood side by side.

The main impression created by Anglo-Saxon works of art, apart from their beauty, is their antique form. Except for the Scandinavian themes, which had pushed their way into areas where the artistic tradition was in collapse, and for the Celtic idiom of the west, the style of English products belonged to that ancient Mediterranean world from which the kingdom had received its religion. Even the silver pennies showed Byzantine influence. Yet there was an English style. The architects built their churches high and narrow; the sculptors had a love for nature; and the decorators used a characteristic sinuous line. English art was at one with the church it served: Roman to the core, yet insular in expression.

There was no standard vernacular speech in the eleventh century. Provincial tongues were more than dialects. But an almost uniform literary prose and an 'official' English had been created from the West-Saxon, which were remarkable aberrations from the general pattern of European cultural development. The official English of the king's writs was brought into being by the precocious growth of a central government and the need of the court to communicate in the vernacular with its lay servants. The literary language arose from the creative talent and the educational zeal of a people who had been stimulated by classical learning but had not adopted a romance tongue. From the European point of view, shared by many who wrote in English, the vernacular literature was a sign of failure. Latin was the proper vehicle for scholarship; and English style was affected by the Latin studies of its exponents. This attitude of shame explains how it was that literary English disappeared soon after the Norman conquest. The new generation of scholars wrote only in Latin. Vernacular history and homilies, even vernacular poetry, were not deeply bound up with, nor did they become symbols of, patriotism and incipient nationality. Nevertheless, while the nobility and the clergy were dominated by the native tradition, England possessed a corpus of literature which could be enjoyed by layman and clerk alike. There was an integration of culture in the Old-English kingdom which was not to come again until Chaucer's time,

VIII

The king, his servants, and the government of the kingdom are considered last in this survey of Edwardian England not because they were of little importance, but because many aspects of the royal administration were comparatively recent, and obscure organizations more expressive of the fundamental nature of English society. The territorial kingdom, as opposed to the rule of peoples, was a new concept; the administrative framework of shire and hundred was an innovation of the tenth century; the earldoms had been transformed by Cnut; and the monarchy itself had steadily increased in power since Alfred.

In the division of the territorial kingdom into smaller administrative units can be seen that characteristic feature of the late Old-English period—a specious uniformity half-concealing an ancient diversity of form. Uniformity appeared in the partition of the greater part of the kingdom into shires, much as we know them to-day, and the repartition of the shires into hundreds or wapentakes; diversity is seen in the way in which these often exotic units followed no invariable pattern and sometimes fitted uneasily over earlier native institutions. The shires had no common origin, and as entities differed greatly in age. The more ancient, which represented subdivisions within a kingdom, as the Wessex shires, or a kingdom itself, as the counties of the south-east, possessed an organic unity which was not to be expected in central England, where the shire was an artificial creation of the tenth century. Different, too, were the shires in the areas colonized by the Vikings, which kept for long their character of armies settled on the land. Nevertheless, they had all been given a common function in the tenth century: each was an area of local government under a royal official (originally the ealdorman and later the sheriff), a subdivision in the national assessment to geld, and the seat of a folk-court.

Except in the northern Danelaw the shires were divided into hundreds. The Wessex hundred, itself not discernible before the tenth century, was probably a division of the older *regio*; and the new institution was introduced into the other provinces as the kings of Wessex extended their rule. Where the shires were artificial the hundreds were equally neat; but elsewhere the hundred superseded or absorbed Cornish 'shires', the rapes of Sussex and, perhaps, of Surrey, the lathes of Kent, and East-Anglian ferdings and leets. In the northern Danelaw, however, the trithing and wapentake perdured. The hundreds and wapentakes, despite their natural diversity, had in the eleventh century some common governmental functions. Each possessed a court; each was responsible for certain police and military duties; and most of them were sub-units in the repartition of the geld. Over the hundred was a royal servant, the reeve; but the smaller hundreds often kept their ancient grouping as fragments of a *regio*, and were attached for administrative purposes to a nuclear royal town. By Edward's time the whole organization was riddled with immunities and complicated by anomalies, and as a system existed no more.

The power of the king within his kingdom may appear insignificant when analysed according to function; but in dissection the intangible authority is lost. Primitive kingship was the focus of racial emotions far stronger than those that subsist to-day. An Anglo-Saxon king had a potency independent of his capacity as a ruler; he had a representative and symbolical character, which at the time could be expressed only in terms of ancient lineage and in his relationship to the gods, or to the Christian God. He was descended from Cerdic, Gewis, Woden, and from Adam. He had been anointed king with holy oil and shared some of the characteristics of the sacred priesthood. Edward's biographer calls him *Christus Dei*, God's anointed; and as the vicar of God he ruled by divine grace. The king played the leading part in the propitiatory ritual of his people, holding courts on days of festival that were older than Christianity; and a well-favoured king meant a prosperous people. Yet the cult of kingship placed no trammels on the person who wore the crown. Strength of personality, skill in war, wisdom in council, could make the individual king the arbitrary ruler of his kingdom. Succession to such a crown was naturally limited to members of the royal family, and only a Cnut or a Harold could disregard that fundamental assumption. Yet the old Germanic tradition that each new ruler required the assent and approbation of his people was still alive; and the church, which favoured the elective principle, could give it sharp expression. In normal times and in ordinary circumstances the eldest son of the dead king was accepted without question. He had been brought up to govern and had often been his father's support in his declining years. The idea of an indivisible kingdom descending automatically according to the rules of primogeniture was not fully formed in England before the close of the thirteenth century; but it arose out of earlier habits. Even though the will of the late king, the violence of faction, or the wise deliberation of the magnates some-times disturbed the normal descent of the Anglo-Saxon crown, the succession is more easily described as hereditary than as elective, provided it is remembered that the candidate had to be accepted by the nobles and anointed and crowned by the church.

It is often difficult to distinguish between the acts of the king and those of his wise men (*witan*). It was impossible, and probably considered improper, for the king to rule without help and advice. Aethelred II, Edward's unfortunate father, was called in derision 'Unraed', the king without counsel. But the king took counsel when and where he chose. There was no constitutional theory. He was always accompanied by his family and his household servants. Bishops, abbots, and earls were often in attendance. The local nobility and churchmen came into court as the king travelled round and then went out again. At the great church festivals, especially at Christmas and Easter, the king held more solemn courts with richer banquets for larger assemblies. But Edward once held an important council in mid-Lent. So the king was never without advisers, and even if he reserved the more serious business, such as hearing notable cases, issuing laws, making treaties, granting estates by book, imposing geld, and appointing earls, bishops, and abbots, for the more ceremonial occasions, he was constrained by no constitutional theory. A king could be accused of wrongful action and of taking foolish advice, but not of incorrect procedure.

Moreover even the larger councils were domestic. The king's guests at court were all his men, and had usually been given their office by him or his predecessor. They were his servants and 'familiars', and, although they were not usually servile, they were in the presence of their master, their lord and king. Even Edward the Confessor, who suffered overmuch from the advice of his family, earls, and bishops, often took his own line and could sometimes dominate his divided counsellors. The part of the court closest to the king, his household, was characteristic of the simple economy of a territorial magnate, with servants who still kept their domestic names. The nomenclature was insular, but the system was European. Thegns serving as butlers, table-waiters (stewards), and chamber-lains—'stallers' as they all could be called in and after the Danish period—were the main secular servants; priests and clerks served the king's oratory. The king's administrative servants in the country at large were also characteristic of the private estate rather than of the kingdom. The king's thegns formed an aristocracy in the shire; the king's reeves governed his estates and the hundreds, and specialized members, the port reeves and the shire reeves (sheriffs), supervised the royal interests in the boroughs and the shires. But although the royal administration was simple and domestic it was efficient.

A group of clerks, whose main duties in the travelling court were primarily religious, also acted as scribes. There was no chancellor, although Regenbald, one of Edward's clerks, is given that style in Domesday Book, and hardly a formal *scriptorium*. Earlier the main work had been the writing of the land-books, also known as diplomas or charters, by which the ceremonial granting of land was recorded for posterity; but by Edward's reign the diploma had yielded to the writ in the king's court, because it suffered from two great disadvantages: it was composed in the florid and bombastic style which betrays the deep influence of Celtic Latin on the English, and it was unauthentic, that is to say it incorporated no device by means of which the genuine original could be distinguished from a later copy or fabrication. Hence by the eleventh century the diploma was becoming again more a private than an official document; and it passed out of general use after the Norman conquest. Not so the writ. This form, a terse grant of land or privileges written in English with a hanging wax seal, created perhaps under Aethelred, was adopted by the Normans, and became the prototype of most of the diplomatic forms used in England in the Middle Ages: the writ-charter, the letters patent, and the letters close. And Edward's seal, three inches across, bearing a portrait of the king enthroned in majesty on both sides—derived apparently from the imperial seal of the successors of Otto III (983–1002) through Cnut, who used a double image to signify his two kingdoms and to allow the writ to be sealed open—was the first of its kind in Europe and the prototype of most 'great' seals.

No extensive archives were kept by the secretariat. Copies of writs were not taken, and documents which had to be preserved were stored with the king's relics in the chapel. But it should be remembered that the Norman court had no chancery and no seal at this time. The easy routine of the English *scriptorium* and the distinction of its products were signs of a long history; and the diplomatic forms current in Edward's day—diploma, chirograph, and writ—were not only splendid achievements but (except for the diploma) of permanent influence in England.

The financial machinery of the Anglo-Saxon kings is characterized by a similar rudimentary precocity. Some of the king's money was kept with him in a box in his bedchamber under the care of bower-thegns (chamberlains) and hrægel thegns (servants of the wardrobe); but for the collection and auditing of the royal revenues there was required also a treasury at Winchester, the capital of Wessex, and subordinate storehouses, staffed, perhaps, by *horderes*, keepers of the gold-hoard. The routine items of royal revenue—the profits of jurisdiction, the customs of boroughs, and the *feorms* of the royal estates—were farmed for each shire by the sheriff; and these stereotyped amounts together with special items were paid by him at Winchester. The treasury also supervised the collection of geld when imposed—*heregeld*, the one national tax in Europe at this time. The arithmetic was comparatively simple; but the treasury not only accounted, it also checked the money either by weighing the coins or by assaying their silver content. No other fisc in Europe had developed so far; and it was accepted and developed by the Normans. Its archives, like those of the *scriptorium*, have disappeared. Its records were superseded by, and started anew with, Domesday Book.

The kingdom was too large for the king to exercise even his limited royal powers always in person; and beneath him were the earls. The organization of the earldoms had been greatly changed during the rule of the Danish dynasty. The Old-English ealdorman, or *dux* (duke), had often ruled no more than a single shire, and sometimes could trace descent from the ancient kings or nobility of its independent past. But the mortality among the aristocracy had been heavy during the Danish wars; and the Englishmen whom Cnut appointed earls were rarely from the old families. Moreover, the unification of the kingdom had made another change overdue. Provincial governors were required; and Cnut reduced the earldoms in number, so that they corresponded roughly to the greater kingdoms of the ninth century, Northumbria, Mercia, East Anglia, and Wessex, although it is likely that other men with the title of earl had subordinate rule within the major circumscriptions. While these changes greatly affected the political importance of the office, the office itself remained essentially the same. It was a royal appointment, held during the king's pleasure, and created no hereditary rank. The duties of an earl were vice-regal. He exercised in his earldom those rights which the king had in the kingdom at large. He kept the peace and maintained good justice. He commanded the military forces of his province and was answerable for its defence. He received orders from the king and was responsible for their execution. He was a necessary subordinate officer in the government of the enlarged territory that the tenth- and eleventh-century kings had to rule. But, although the office did not harden into an hereditary rank before the twelfth century, the drift towards hereditary succession was always strong, and only the vigilance of a strong monarchy could withstand it. Cnut and Edward were, indeed, really successful only in one direction. They prevented the earldoms from assuming a fixed territorial area, and were always able to create new earldoms and vary the combination of shires that each contained. But the same process which had occurred in the ministerial office of thegnhood was at work in the office of the earls, and could not completely be gainsaid. The sons or, at least, the eldest sons of earls expected to be earls also; and appointments were often found for them, culminating usually in succession to their father's earldom on his death.

One of the results of the transformation of the earl into a provincial governor was the increased importance of the shire-reeve, for the shire was still the basic administrative, financial, and judicial unit in the kingdom. The shire-reeve had come into existence with the shires and hundreds in the early tenth century, and he drew his duties from two directions. He kept most of the functions of a king's reeve and he acquired new responsibilities as the ealdorman's deputy in the shire. In the former capacity he was responsible for the administration of the royal demesnes, for the collection and enforcement of all the royal customs—the *feorm*, labour and carrying services, rents, geld, and judicial profits—for the general supervision of the king's interests, and for the maintenance of the police system. He was appointed by the king, and held office at the king's pleasure, and, as a royal agent, knew no superiors save the earl and the bishop. As the deputy of the earl, the sheriff presided in the shire court with the bishop, exercised judicial duties in the hundred courts, commanded the shire contingents in the fyrd, and performed all those duties which were beneath the enhanced dignity of the earl. By Edward's reign the sheriff had become a very important man. He usually possessed, or acquired, estates within the shire, and he travelled with a mounted escort. And in the sheriff the king had an instrument which could be used to break down variety in custom and to unify the administration of the country. The decrease in the number of the great comital families between 1042 and 1066 was so rapid that had

King Harold overthrown the single rival native dynasty—Earl Aelfgar's sons—an administrative despotism might have arisen without the aid of a Norman conquest.

With the advice of the witan, with the help of his earls, and through his personal servants the king ruled the country. The oldest function of the king was to make war; but by the eleventh century this operation had widened into a more general responsibility for the peace of the kingdom. Edward the Confessor took command of the fleet when invasion was threatened; but he never led the army into battle. Although Edward's campaigns were fought by his earls, the army was the king's army; no other person had the right to employ troops except in the king's service or in the country's interest.

The composition of the armed forces at the disposal of the king and of his lieutenants varied according to the purpose. At times of invasion and of local disturbance all men capable of bearing arms could be expected to play their part; and the shire levies, especially in the coastal areas and in the Danelaw, where the fighting tradition of the ordinary freeman was still strong, possessed even in the eleventh century a military importance. But for more regular expeditions, and for campaigns outside the boundaries of the shires, the impressment of such a host was neither practical nor desirable. The king required a select quota of trained and well-equipped warriors—men, if possible, with a helmet, byrnie, and horse—and the provision of this type of army was in the main secured by assessing the land to service. Many varieties of bargain were struck by the king with different localities and with different lords for military service; and among these was the finding of a soldier for each five hides of land in the estate. Even this scheme led to divergent practices. In the west Midlands compact five-hide tenements, or units made up of scattered lands, were often created in order to meet the military obligations of the estate; in eastern England, where 'inland' was rare, the military service was not always territorialized, but ran upon the undivided lordship. In all cases the warrior received money for his expenses from those who stayed at home, according to some customs at the rate of four shillings the hide, his wages for two months. Hence in practice within the southern part of England the thegn had become the ordinary soldier of the late Old-English period. The churches, in particular, are found granting land on loan to thegns for the express purpose of fulfilling the churches' military obligations; and when large estates were granted by the king to thegns, the owner had to answer the king's summons to the army together with a number of companions computed according to the hidage. In the north of England, where more primitive conditions persisted, military service was less territorialized; and it is possible that a rota among those liable to fight rather than a landed assessment was generally in use. The army, whether mobilized from the mass of the free inhabitants to defend the shire, or from select representatives to join a royal expedition, was called the *fyrd* when the main composition was English, or the *here* when Danes predominated. The system was not entirely disregarded by the Norman kings, and it was reformed by the Angevins after the short hey-day of the feudal knight.

The English navy was equipped and manned in a similar way. Traces of a territorial organization, whereby groups of three hundreds were responsible for providing a long ship with sixty oarsmen —that is to say, one man for each five hides—are discernible in Warwickshire; and Edward the Confessor contrived an even more specialized arrangement when the Kentish ports agreed to provide a fleet in return for the profits of their courts.

The armies and the navies were produced by expedients which modified the primitive obligation of all free men to fight, but which did not transform its national and territorial character. The internal structure, however, of an army so gathered was moulded by other ideas. Men followed and fought round their lords; and it was lordship and not territorial grouping—although these attachments were not necessarily in opposition—which gave discipline and coherence to the fyrd. The earl was supported by his thegns, those thegns by their thegns and men, and so down to the rank and file. On the eve of the Norman conquest, a thegn, Eadric, the holder of five hides on loan, had the office of steersman of the bishop of Worcester's ship and commander of the bishop's troops; and those soldiers would fight under the banner of St. Mary of Worcester. Territorial in recruitment, aristocratic in organization, the fyrd was in these features characteristic of the age.

Even though fyrd service was largely specialized in Edward's day, it was still insufficiently professional to meet all the needs of the king and of his military officers. To secure a bodyguard and to provide an immediately available striking force the kings had since the beginning of the eleventh century maintained foreign, mostly Scandinavian, mercenaries. In 1012 Aethelred II had taken the Jómsviking,

Thorkell Hávi (the Tall), with forty-five ship's crews into his service; and this custom was abandoned only in 1051, when Edward dismissed the last five ships. The English thegnage had lost much of its original character by the eleventh century, and King Cnut employed housecarles—domestic warriors—as a bodyguard. His successors, and the earls and the great nobles, imitated the practice. The royal housecarles guarded the king's person, they formed his garrison in important towns, and they could be employed on important administrative missions. Their alien extraction, their special military code of honour, and their professional training made them the *corps d'élite* of any army put into the field. Few of them survived the murderous battles of 1066. Thus the king had a professional cadre of troops under his hand, his thegns and the forces of his earls at call, and a varying proportion of all the free men of the nation at his service when custom required or necessity impelled. As a military system it was cumbrous and weighted by too long a tradition. It usually failed in face of a professional invader; but for local defence against pirates, for general peace duties, and for occasional expeditions against the Welsh or Scots it served its purpose.

To pay the wages of the foreign seamen and housecarles English kings imposed a tax, *heregeld*, on the whole country. It had its precedent in the large sums collected to buy off the Danes, and so the tax was called in natural error Danegeld when reimposed by the Normans. The king who introduced the tax, probably Aethelred II, did not impose a new and uniform rating system on the kingdom, but utilized existing provincial assessments to tribute. In Mercia and Wessex, for instance, the land was already assessed in hides, and the tax was imposed at so many shillings the hide. The principle which underlay the hidage was that provincial quotas were sub-divided between the shires, and then repartitioned among lesser administrative units, sometimes the hundreds, sometimes older and obsolescent units, such as the rapes of Sussex. The smallest rateable unit was the township, often assessed at 5 or 10 hides. Similar systems obtained in Deira and in Kent, where the carucate and sulung respectively replaced the hide; but in East Anglia a different, less territorialized, method of rating was employed, under which the township paid a proportion of the amount of tax laid on the leet, an ancient subdivision of the shire.

The hides, sulungs, and carucates of the assessments had never borne a close relation to the actual acreage of a province; and in the eleventh century they were merely artificial fiscal entities, corresponding little to the yardlands, ploughlands, and holdings of the farmers over which they lay. Hence the rateable value to the geld of the shires and of the localities was archaic from the beginning, and by Edward's day, as a result of block reductions in assessment and beneficial diminutions or total exemptions in favour of individual estates, the system had become unequal in incidence and bewildering in complexity. It is significant that King William I, when he reimposed the tax, felt unequal to the task of rationalizing this valuable but incomprehensible inheritance from his cousin. The Domesday survey took no heed of the underlying systems, and recorded merely the assessment to geld of each estate; and it has been left to modern scholars to regroup the Domesday assessments and to reconstruct the principles on which the tax was originally imposed.

The fundamental weaknesses of the assessment are obvious; the failure of the kings to improve upon it, even to control it in their interest is manifest. By 1066 the tax had become a custom lying on land, hardly different from many other customs. Yet the very imposition of the tax was a great achievement of the Old-English monarchy. It was without parallel in contemporary Europe, and was not bettered anywhere for centuries to come.

The judicial powers of the Anglo-Saxon kings were small, but large for the time. The king was not yet the fountain of justice: he was more the ultimate temporal avenger of violations of a customary code of behaviour. Law was the birthright of the individual man. It was the immemorial custom which bound men of his class and of his locality. The law protected, and put a price on, a man's life, the integrity of his body, limb by limb, the peace of his dwelling, and his goods. A man looked to the popular courts to enforce his rights under the law. For every infraction of his rights due compensation (*bot*) had to be paid by the offender to the injured man if retaliation was to be avoided, and should a man be killed the value of his life (his *wer*) must be offered to his relations to buy off their feud. Judgment in the court depended largely on correct pleading; and the basis of proof was the oath of the lawful man, supported, if necessary, by the oaths of helpers, and supplemented, in cases of deficiency, by the ordeal. Thus crime was considered a tort, an occasion for the payment of appropriate damages to the victim or his kin; and the judicial system was ritualistic, highly technical, and irrational, in that it presupposed divine intervention throughout the course of the pleading. This great mesh of law was almost entirely independent of the king. It was personal and local. Custom differed from estate to estate, from shire to shire, and especially from province to province. The distinction between West Saxon, Mercian, and Danish law was erased only when a new common law spread from the royal court long after the end of the Saxon royal dynasty.

Yet the Old-English monarchy had never capitulated to the threatening stranglehold of law. Many of the great kings between Aethelberht and Cnut had issued legislative codes, timid in their innovations, it is true, but formative of a tradition that the dooms pronounced by the king were the most authentic expression of the law. Moreover, in the century-and-a-half before the Norman conquest the kings had become more confident in the judicial sphere. They had reorganized the popular courts, and put them under the control of their servants; and they had extended the operation of the royal peace, and introduced a conception of crime.

The shire court, which met at least twice a year in the eleventh century, was concerned mainly with the traditional cases under folk-law, of which theft and violence were probably the most important. The procedure was archaic; but the constitution of the court was new. Official presidents—bishop and earl, or the sheriff in the absence of the earl—were in charge; and attendance of suitors had become conventionalized. The townships and the hundreds sent representatives, and, apart from the litigants, usually only the thegns attended in person. It is clear that by Edward's day the king's thegns formed the leading suitors in most shires, and that the function of declaring the law of the shire and of giving judgment had passed to them. In the Danish shires an hereditary class of lawmen had a similar position. In this way the shire court had become an organ of local government in close touch with the king. Royal writs under seal went down to the bishop, earl, and thegns of the shire; and that assembly, which was at the same time both a meeting of the local aristocracy and a body of royal servants, executed the king's commands. By the middle of the eleventh century the administrative drive emanating from the royal household, operating through the writ, and directed to the shire court, was beginning to weld the country together. Norman tyranny had useful instruments to hand.

The hundred courts were even more closely connected with the crown, for their main judicial purpose was the administration of police schemes which the king had devised. The hundred, under the presidency of the king's reeve, or, in the case of exemptions, under a private reeve, met every month. By a law of Cnut every free man over the age of twelve had to be a member of a hundred and of a tithing—in theory a tenth part of a hundred—and the tithing and hundred were responsible for the good behaviour of its members. In the twelfth century twice a year at the 'law days' the view of frank-pledge—an inquisition into the state of the tithings—was held by the sheriff in the hundred court; and this procedure may be as old as Edward's reign. But, except possibly on the law days, not all free men attended the meetings even of the hundred court in the eleventh century. As with the shire court suit had been conventionalized and often territorialized. Attendance at court was burdensome to the small man; and he escaped from it if he could. It is possible that the commonest form of suit to the hundred court was from the priest, the reeve, and four men from each township. The suitors were known as hundredors, and the duty was often attached to certain pieces of land.

Besides remodelling the courts, English kings had jealously preserved their right to the penalties for the more serious offences. The 'reserved' cases—which in the Norman period became known as the pleas of the crown—included murder (concealed homicide), treason, arson, attacks on houses, open theft, persistent robbery, coining, homicide, wounding, mayhem, and rape—the first seven being unemendable, capital offences since Cnut's reign—and also those disobediences and derelictions of duty which closely touched the crown, such as neglect of a royal order, the giving of unrighteous judgment, and the failure of a king's thegn to perform fyrd service. Naturally, too, the king took the penalties for breaches of his peace.

The peace which an eleventh-century malefactor might disturb was no seamless mantle spread over the whole country. Each lawful man was entitled to the peace of his person and of his home; and at this time every breach of the peace was the infraction of some local, perhaps temporary, individual peace. The peace of the king was more potent than the peace of an earl, or of a thegn, or of a ceorl; and breaches of it incurred a heavier penalty; yet even the king's peace was limited to areas—essentially to his presence—to seasons, and to persons whose safety he had guaranteed; and even when extended by means of writ, messenger, or subordinate officer it remained both manifold and particular. Yet a start had been made which in time was to revolutionize the administration of the law. The peace given under the king's hand became later a legal fiction and covered the whole country. And offences against the king's peace came to be regarded as offences against the community, as crimes. The church, too, had played a part in this new attitude towards violation of the law. To the church many of the breaches were sins, infractions of the moral code, offences to God, evils for which damages could not by themselves atone. Even so, the old view which inspired the folk-law was not dead in Edward's day. When Bishop Wulfstan once preached at Gloucester on his usual text of peace, one of his auditors complained that although he had killed a man by accident he could not buy peace and pardon at any price from the five brothers of the dead man. And Wulfstan had to work a miracle before the avenging kinsmen would call off their blood feud.

This analysis of some aspects of Anglo-Saxon monarchy and of the king's position within his kingdom reveals both the limitations on the scope of royal initiative and the increasing potentialities of his effective power. As the Old-English monarchy came to an end in 1066 the concern with potentialities is natural, for only in the light of some view of the direction in which the state was moving can an appreciation be made of the changes which the Norman conquest effected. Yet few historians have ventured to predict the course on which the Anglo-Danish kingdom was set. There have been historians who believed that the English state was basically wholesome and lacked only strong direction; there are others who hold that society was decadent and drifting into anarchy. Neither view is wholly satisfactory. England was closest in structure and development to that other Carolingian fossil, Germany. Yet its society was too vigorous and lively to merit the charge of decadence. Nor should the kingdom's looseness in texture and fissile tendencies be overstressed through a false comparison with modern political groupings. By contemporary standards the Old-English state was remarkable for its compactness, its administrative machinery, and its organic unity. Even so weak a king as Edward the Confessor could control the kingdom through perilous times. Cnut had been the master of his people. Harold, or Harold's son, might easily have been the same. The powers of the crown were great for the man who could use them. But the riddle of the future cannot be read because so much depended on the character of the individual king.

2

THE REIGN OF EDWARD THE CONFESSOR

I

THE reputation of Edward as man and as king has steadily deteriorated since the Middle Ages. His piety has lost its savour; his passion for hunting is found incongruous; and his political policy finds few modern defenders. To his contemporaries he appeared benign, honest, pious, and sporadically rash. There was much of his father, Aethelred, in him, and also, perhaps, a vein of patient endurance from his mother. No appraisal of Edward is likely to value him above mediocrity; yet no view can be fair which does not take into account the great difficulties he had to meet. And when his problems are considered, the twenty-two-and-a-half years of peace that England enjoyed under his rule will, perhaps, be considered no small achievement.

The strength of all native kings since Alfred, and of the bretwaldas before him, had lain fundamentally in the possession of an ancestral kingdom and in the personal devotion of servants whether household or landed thegns. The Danish rulers of England, having no special attachment to any one of the submerged kingdoms, had widened the conception of English kingship by divorcing it from its local and particular associations; but Cnut's plan of reserving no English province for his direct rule, and his grant of Wessex as an earldom to his upstart favourite Godwine, had weakened the position of any successor who had not his quasi-imperial power. And when the Scandinavian empire collapsed, it was evident that the main support of the English monarchy had been removed. When Edward became king the royal demesnes were still at his disposal,

and were sufficient for his estate; but he found a stranger ruling as
earl in his ancestral kingdom of Wessex, and was deprived of the
personal service of those thegns whom his forebears had rewarded
with land. His power as king was to depend on the extent to which
he could utilize the authority of earls who mostly had no tradition of
loyalty either to him or to his family.

The succession of earls in this period, even to the greater appointments, is not firmly established. In 1042, however, Siward was earl
of Northumbria, Leofric of Mercia, and Godwine of Wessex.
Leofric, alone, came of an old ruling family. He was the son of
Leofwine, ealdorman of the Hwicce under Aethelred, and husband of
Godgifu (Godiva), who has imperishable association with Coventry.
Leofric seems to have possessed the old-fashioned virtues of integrity
and loyalty, and to have given disinterested service to his royal
masters. Siward was a Dane who had married the grand-daughter of
the native line of earls. He had firmly identified himself with Northumbrian ambitions, and the direction of his interest lay north. He
probably wanted nothing more than to be left alone. Yet it should be
remembered that the cession of Lothian to the king of Scots had
permanently altered the balance of power in the north, and that
truncated Northumbria had to rely increasingly on southern support
in order to escape from the ambition of the Scottish kings. The rise
of the house of Godwine, from thegn to king in three generations,
was so meteoric that it naturally became the subject of saga. By the
early twelfth century it was widely believed that Godwine was the
son of a swineherd. In fact, his father, Wulfnoth, was probably a
Sussex thegn. In saga Godwine is portrayed as a cunning, eloquent,
greedy, sacrilegious, and ambitious man—a caricature which stresses
the qualities necessary for such a quick rise to power. Yet one who
knew his sons and his daughter Eadgyth thought caution and
patience characteristic of the family. Early adherence to King Cnut
set Godwine on his way. He was made earl before 1018, and married
Gytha, the sister of Cnut's brother-in-law, Earl Ulf, who came of a
Danish family renowned for its descent from a bear. The earl of the
West Saxons was strong enough and sufficiently adroit to hold his
position intact through the reigns of Harold Harefoot and Harthacnut. The deed which left the darkest stain on his character was his
being accessory to the murder of Edward's brother, Alfred, on a visit
to England in 1036. Alfred was fatally blinded after his arrest by
Godwine; and, although the earl lawfully purged himself of wrong-

ful action, his moral guilt was generally supposed.

Godwine's support greatly helped Edward in 1042–3. The new king was not a weakling. He was still in the prime of life, an active man and a keen soldier, experienced in the ways of the world, with the skill to survive and the determination to keep the throne at any cost. What he lacked was loyal support. In any case he had to work with Godwine. If at times he resented his dependence on the earl, political realism prevailed. When after nine years they quarrelled it proved to be a misfortune for them both.

In these circumstances it is not surprising that Edward should have developed a household that was to give offence, especially to Godwine. A stranger in England, Edward welcomed servants from Normandy and its environs, and made modest attempts to endow some of his foreign friends with office and land. An earldom in the west was given before 1050 to his nephew Ralf, the son of his sister Godgifu and Drogo, count of the Vexin; large, but not extravagant estates were bestowed on two Bretons, Robert fitzWimarc (a relative of the king) and Ralf 'the staller'; and smaller grants were made in the usual way to others of his servants. The promotion of Normans within the English church, which followed naturally from the composition of Edward's chapel, was on a similar small scale, but provoked more criticism, because some of the most important positions were involved. It is clear that Edward at no time commanded a personal following equal in power to that at the disposal of any one of the three great earls. His only chance of freedom lay in the rival aspirations of his provincial governors.

It is, indeed, easy to exaggerate the Norman element in Edward's court. It was confined almost entirely to the royal household and chapel, and has left little trace in the attestation to royal charters. The early courts of Edward were very like the later courts of Cnut. Scandinavian blood and culture remained strong among the aristocracy, and provided the dominant influence in the first years of the reign. It is significant that when Godwine's eldest son, the half-Danish Svein, murdered his cousin, the Danish Earl Beorn, Estrith's son, in 1049, Edward and the army (and the word used in the Chronicle is *here*, normally employed for the Danish army) pronounced a Viking sentence of dishonour upon him, declaring him *nithing*. And even more remarkable is the story in the longer saga of Olaf Tryggvason, possibly an addition of the thirteenth century, that 'King Edward made it a custom to relate the saga of King Olaf

Tryggvason to his great men and his bodyguard on the first day of Easter; and he chose that day rather than any other for the telling of the saga, saying that Olaf Tryggvason was superior to other kings as much as Easter day is superior to the other days of the whole year'. Olaf had returned to Norway from raiding England in 994, had won a kingdom, and converted it to Christianity at the point of the sword; so he may well have been Edward's hero. But, even if the story is false, it shows at least that in the north Edward was remembered as a Scandinavian king among his warriors, a character which acts as a corrective to the colourless saint he became in English tradition.

While the internal problems which faced Edward were difficult, the external position was menacing. Edward cannot have been unaware from the beginning that Magnus of Norway or Svein of Denmark, or even some other pretender, would invade if conditions allowed. There had been a Scandinavian party in England in 1042, which included the Queen-mother Emma; and the landing of a Viking force on the eastern coast would have been the signal for grave defections. Edward was spared an immediate invasion first through the civil war in Denmark, which immobilized Svein, and then by the attempt of Magnus to make good his claim to Denmark, which Svein withstood with small success, but with unconquerable determination. The danger was even more acute because Edward's relations with Flanders were unfriendly, and Magnus's fleet could have used Bruges as its advanced base. As it was, Count Baldwin V gave the shelter of his ports to Viking pirates who raided the English south-east coast in 1048. Edward's mother, Emma, when exiled by Harold Harefoot, had taken refuge in Flanders in 1037; and Emma and Harthacnut's invasion forces had been collected at Bruges during the winter of 1039–40. No doubt these two had poisoned Count Baldwin's mind against Edward. Certainly Baldwin offered a welcome to all exiles from England in the first decade following Edward's accession; and his hostility to the English king is an important thread in the political history of these years. He received Godwine's son Svein after both his banishments, and Godwine himself in 1051.

Edward's friends lay farther south and east. The count of Boulogne, Eustace II, a Flemish vassal, had married Edward's sister Godgifu, after she had been widowed in 1035 by the death of Drogo, count of the Vexin; and Eustace was to appear in English history at two of the most critical points in the next quarter of a century, in 1051 and 1066. From Normandy Edward could expect no immediate help. Robert the Magnificent was dead, and William II (the Bastard), Edward's cousin once removed, was in his unquiet minority, protected only by the care of his overlord, Henry I, king of the Franks. Edward was on good terms with Henry and may have remembered William with anxious affection. The German king, Henry III, was also in the family circle. He had married in 1036, while his father, the Emperor Conrad II, was alive, Edward's half-sister, Gunnhild (Kunigunda), the daughter of Emma and Cnut. But she had died on the Adriatic two years later, and her only child, Beatrix, was made abbess of the royal abbey of Quedlinburg near Goslar in 1046. Henry's second marriage in 1043 to Agnes of Poitou did not disturb his friendly relations with England. Both he and Henry, king of the Franks, sent embassies to Edward's coronation in 1043; and in 1049 Edward gathered his fleet at Sandwich, and Svein of Denmark brought his ships down the coast to provide a naval blockade, while Henry, now Roman emperor, stamped out the rebellion in Lorraine which had lasted four years and which involved Edward's enemies Baldwin V count of Flanders and his son, Baldwin margrave of Antwerp.

With friends and enemies thus disposed, the danger from the ambition of Magnus of Norway was taken seriously in England. Svein, as the weaker party and as Godwine's nephew, received English help against his rival, but never as much as he asked or as Godwine wished to send. His brothers, too, were favoured. Beorn was given an earldom and Osbern an honourable position in England. In the course of the year 1046 Magnus expelled Svein from Denmark, and in 1045 and 1046 the English fleet was called out to meet the threat of a Norwegian invasion. But Svein, exiled in Sweden, joined forces with one of the most romantic characters in that heroic northern world, Harold Hardrada, the man who in 1030 had survived the stricken field of Stiklestad where St. Olaf died; who had found his way to Byzantium and served in the Varangian regiment of the imperial bodyguard; whose eastern journeys were soon to become legendary; and who was now back with a Russian wife and the desire for a kingdom. The renewed hostilities which sprang from this alliance prevented Magnus from sailing for England, and his death in 1047 entirely changed the position in the north. With the generosity of an old warrior, Magnus bequeathed Norway to his uncle, Harold Hardrada, and Denmark to Svein Estrithson. Each got his kingdom, but inherited also the legacy of war. Svein, too, was menaced by the power of the German empire and distracted by the ravages of Wendish pirates. Hence it was Harold Hardrada who first asserted his shadowy claims to the English throne only to find in 1066 an end to his wanderings in an English grave.

The death of Magnus in 1047 was considered by Edward to mark the end of the period of external danger, and he carried out an important military reform. In Lent 1050 he reduced the foreign mercenary fleet from fourteen ships to five, and in the next year paid off the rest. He was thus able to remit for a time the tax, *geld*, by which the force had been maintained, and improve the coinage. Edward may have been buying support for his appointment of William of Normandy as his heir. To compensate for this loss of naval strength Edward made an arrangement with the men of certain south-eastern ports by which, in return for the profits of jurisdiction in their courts, they were bound to provide ships and seamen for the king; and in this bargain is to be seen a factor which contributed to the growth of the Confederation of the five boroughs, the Cinque Ports. Moreover, there still remained the duty of the shires to provide ships when necessary. Yet, although the foreign position justified this surrender of an immediate striking force in favour of an arrangement less costly, and in fact no foreign invasion in strength took place before 1066, and then after ample warning, the action was ill-conceived. However useful the professional fleet could have been against an invasion in force, it was even more useful against unexpected and piratical raids by foreign and domestic enemies. Against returning outlaws, in particular, the native fleet was bound to be uncertain, and the national levy impossibly slow.

II

In foreign policy Edward had largely waited on events. His domestic policy was equally opportunist. The distribution of the royal estates and the Wessex lineage of the Old-English kings made it inevitable that Edward should reside like his ancestors in the south of England, that is to say within the earldom of Godwine; and the earl of the West Saxons aimed from the beginning at controlling the king. Edward had not a strong character; but he had the long rancour and the sporadic rashness of the weak. At the next court after his coronation in 1043 he took the three great earls with him to

Winchester to punish his mother Emma for her neglect and opposition; and he left her powerless by confiscating most of her lands and wealth. But he soon restored her to favour. In these years it was the king who was being plundered. Godwine was extortionate. His eldest son, Svein, was soon made earl, and in 1050 his earldom is known to have comprised the Mercian shires of Hereford, Gloucester, and Oxford, and the Wessex shires of Berkshire and Somerset. Godwine's second son, Harold, was appointed earl of East Anglia about 1045; and about the same time Godwine's nephew, Beorn Estrithson, was given an earldom in the eastern Midlands. Moreover, early in 1045 Edward married Godwine's daughter Eadgyth, thereby giving public recognition to the close relations between king and earl. This political marriage caused no surprise at the time, and the suggestion that it was not consummated is connected either with the later belief in Edward's chastity and holiness or with the view that he constantly hated Godwine and his family. For neither supposition is there good historical evidence. Edward had not married in exile probably because he had not held a suitable estate, and even if at forty he was a confirmed bachelor he knew where his duty lay. He needed an heir of his body to stabilize the position both of himself and of his adherents, and he married at almost the earliest opportunity. It may be that he proved to be impotent, although Eadgyth could have been barren. There is no way of knowing. Edward and his wife were healthy and seem to have been a normal, although childless, couple.

Godwine was probably at the height of his power and influence in 1045. The decline which followed is in part attributable to the behaviour of his son Svein. This ruffian outraged religious sentiment in 1046 by seducing the abbess of Leominster, and military honour in 1049 by murdering his cousin, Earl Beorn. He suffered exile for both offences, in 1046 passing through Flanders to the Scandinavian war, in 1049 returning to Flanders; yet Godwine condoned the crimes, and used his influence to secure Svein's recall in 1050 and his restitution to an earldom. Such evil lawlessness must have weakened Godwine's position with the king and his reputation in the country. What is more, Edward had used Svein's disgrace to strengthen the royal influence in the west. It seems that rule over part at least of Svein's earldom was entrusted to Ralf, Edward's nephew, during the exiles, and it was decided to establish some French garrisons in Herefordshire, where certainly one castle, and possibly three, had been built and garrisoned by 1051. This was an innovation in England, and a foretaste of William's reign. Beorn's death, too, was a loss to the house of Godwine; and Harold's power in East Anglia had probably been weakened by the estates given to the Bretons, Robert fitzWimarc and Ralf the Staller.

The growing estrangement between Edward and Godwine is seen in the clash of interest over the appointment to bishoprics. Between 1042 and 1051 ten vacancies occurred in the thirteen dioceses within the province of Canterbury. Half were filled by Englishmen, of whom only two call for special mention. Stigand, an opportunist clerk, was promoted to Elmham in 1043 and transferred to Winchester in 1047. His irregular translation to Canterbury in 1052 and his flagrant pluralism were to cause embarrassment to Edward and Harold. Ealdred became bishop of Worcester in 1047, and as archbishop of York crowned William. Two sees were given to clerks with Lotharingian connexions. The alien Heremann received Ramsbury in 1045, and Leofric, native born but educated abroad, was appointed to Devon and Cornwall in 1046. It is likely that traditional English relations with the reformed Lotharingian church rather than political reasons were responsible for these appointments, although the friendship of the house of Godwine with Flanders may have played a part. The promotion of Normans, however, within the English episcopate, although rare, was bitterly opposed by Godwine and his friends, probably because it symbolized the independent action of the king. In 1044 Edward gave London to Robert Champart, abbot of Jumièges, an old friend who obtained considerable personal influence over his benefactor, and in 1050 the king appointed one of his Norman chaplains, Ulf, to the see of Dorchester. On 29 October 1050 Archbishop Eadsige died ; and the struggle between earl and king for control of the southern episcopate came to a head. The monks of Christ Church elected one of themselves, Aelfric, probably a kinsman of Godwine, as archbishop; but Edward refused to accept him; and in 1051 king and witan gave Canterbury to Robert of Jumièges. To soften the blow Spearhafoc, abbot of Abingdon, was appointed bishop of London. The new archbishop, however, was more intransigent than the king. It seems that he wished another Norman to succeed him at London (possibly William, a royal chaplain, who later got the see), and he returned from his visit to Rome for the pallium with papal authority to refuse consecration to Spearhafoc. But Edward let Spearhafoc, who was his goldsmith, remain in London. Robert then turned against Godwine and accused him of having despoiled Canterbury of lands in Kent, and tempers rose fast. It is probable that Godwine realized by now that he was not to be the grandfather of a king. His influence was on the wane, and the archbishop had resurrected the old charge that the earl had contrived the murder of Alfred.

There are signs that Godwine was preparing for action. He had negotiated a marriage between his third son, Tostig, and Judith, daughter of Baldwin IV of Flanders, and half-sister of the reigning count, whose relations with Edward had always been strained; and it was while Godwine was at the marriage feast of his son in the autumn of 1051 that a fortuitous event occurred which snapped his patience, and brought England very close to war. Eustace of Boulogne arrived on a visit to his brother-in-law, and his retinue was involved in a murderous brawl at Dover within Godwine's earldom. This was more than the earl could stand. He and his sons, earls Svein and Harold, mobilized the forces of their earldoms, and on 1 September concentrated at Beverstone in the Cotswolds, twenty miles south of Gloucester, where Edward held his court. They demanded the surrender of Eustace of Boulogne and of the garrison of the castle which the Frenchman, Osbern Pentecost, had built at Ewias Harold in the Golden Valley near Hereford.

Edward, too, saw that the crisis had arrived; and he accepted the challenge. He summoned Earls Siward and Leofric to him, and they came with their armies, prepared to defend the king against a rebellious earl. Earl Ralf, too, supported his uncle. In face of this unexpected firmness Godwine had either to fight or submit. To his credit he was not prepared to wage civil war. He temporized, and finally gave way. Initiative passed to the king. It was settled that a witenagemot should be summoned to London for Michaelmas at which Godwine should stand his trial, and the charges he was to face seem to have comprised not only those arising out of his recent behaviour but also the old accusation of complicity in Alfred's death. This was the moment of Edward's triumph. In London his Norman friends, especially the archbishop, encouraged his vindictive attack. The northern earls still stood fast; and Godwine's military force had dwindled since his inaction at Gloucester. Foreseeing his inevitable condemnation, Godwine lost heart, and did not stand his trial. He fled from Southwark to Bosham, and, with his wife, his sons Svein, Tostig, and Gyrth, and Tostig's wife Judith, crossed to sons Svein, Tostig, and Gyrth, and Tostig's wife Judith, crossed to Bruges. His sons Harold and Leofwine rode to Bristol and sailed for Ireland. The king had ample revenge. Godwine and his sons were outlawed, and the queen was banished to a West-Saxon nunnery. Earl Leofric was rewarded by the grant to his son, Aelfgar, of Harold's earldom; Svein's earldom was divided between Edward's nephew, Ralf, and the royal kinsman, Odda of Deerhurst; but at least the greater part of Wessex was kept in the king's hands. Spearhafoc was expelled from the see of London, and the king's Norman chaplain, William, put in his place. But Edward went too far. The northern earls had rallied to the king against the threat of rebellion, and were prepared to see Godwine stand trial for his misdeeds; but their interest cooled as Edward and his foreign advisers passed from judicial action to the satisfaction of personal revenge; and when Edward used his new freedom to increase his connexions with Normandy, the earls reverted to neutrality, and did nothing to prevent the counter-revolution.

Not only had Edward's re-establishment of royal power in the kingdom unsettled the earls, his foreign schemes probably affronted Godwine. Norman apologists for the Conquest writing shortly after it had taken place claimed that it was at this time, through the agency of Robert of Jumièges that Edward made William his heir. It is indeed likely that Edward made a treaty with William in 1051 in order to restrain the Norman-Flemish alliance and dissuade those maritime powers from harbouring Scandinavian adventurers. That he also promised him the succession is possible. One English annalist believed that the duke visited Edward in the winter of 1051–2 and it may have been then that Edward gave William as hostages two members of Godwine's family whom he had in his hands, probably since September 1051, when he was forcing the earl to stand trial. Norman friendship was the key to England's security, and it is likely that this view was accepted by all Edward's counsellors. The king's childlessness was a diplomatic asset. No doubt he was courted by his kinsmen and doubtless he made promises to some. In a sense there was a succession problem throughout the reign. But Edward seems to have cared more for his own security than for the cause of any of the pretenders. If a promise was made to William it cannot have been intended seriously. Edward was not yet fifty and could remarry. William was only twenty-three. All the same, Godwine, as the father of the queen and interested in his wife's nephew, Svein

Estrithson, king of Denmark, and possibly also in Flanders, may have been angered by Edward's nomination of William. The feelings of Earls Leofric and Siward are unknown. But it seems likely that even if Edward had died immediately, search would have been made, as three years later, for another descendant of Aethelred while the earls maintained a regency government. There was only a small Norman party in the country. The archbishop of Canterbury and two bishops would have been for William, perhaps Earl Ralf and his vassals, and the handful of Edward's foreign servants. The duke had possible means of entry into England. Edward had given some estates on the coast of Sussex to the abbey of Fécamp in Normandy and Bosham was held by Osbern, Edward's Norman chaplain, a kinsman of both Edward and William. But it is unlikely that Edward deliberately created a bridge-head for William. Maritime estates were the obvious reward for a Norman monastery.

William was the bastard offspring of Duke Robert and Herleva (Arlette), daughter of a tanner of Falaise; and he succeeded to the duchy as a boy of seven when Robert died in 1035 at Bithynian Nicaea (Isnik) on his return from a pilgrimage. His mother married after Robert's death Herluin vicomte of Conteville; and the children of this marriage, Robert, count of Mortain, and Odo, later bishop of Bayeux, were ever close to the new duke. The minority of William had been disturbed by the conspiracies of the many nobles irregularly related to the ducal house; but his position had been finally secured by the victory of his overlord, King Henry of the Franks, over the Norman rebels at Val-ès-dunes in 1047. In 1052 William was a young prince of note, yet had not achieved such distinction as to disquiet the Anglo-Danish nobility. King Edward was, however, to live for fourteen more years; and with the return of Earl Godwine any promise of the throne to William seems to have been studiously forgotten, except by the Norman duke. Within a short time of the negotiations William married Matilda, daughter of Baldwin V of Flanders. This union had been prohibited by Pope Leo IX in 1049 on the ground of consanguinity, and the displeasure of the church embarrassed the duke until 1059, when Pope Nicholas II dispensed with the impediment. But the political advantages from the marriage were considerable. An alliance with the imperial fief of Flanders improved William's strategic position; and in his wife ran the blood of the kings of Wessex as well as other distinguished strains.

In the autumn of 1051 the family of Godwine had fled to bases

from which they could return by force if need be. The old man and
three of his sons were at Bruges, where Harthacnut and Emma had
gathered their invasion forces twelve years before. Harold and
Leofwine were at the Norwegian port of Dublin under the protection
of Dermot, king of Leinster and 'of the foreigners of Dublin'. In
both places ships and desperate crews could be recruited; and sea
communications were so good that a concerted expedition could be
planned for the summer of the next year. Godwine sailed from the
river Yser in June, too early for Harold; but he probed Edward's
defences, and rallied his supporters in Kent. On his second sortie in
September he sailed direct to Wight, and joined forces with Harold
and Leofwine west of Portland. The younger adventurers had sailed
from Dublin with nine ships to the Bristol Channel, provisioned by
force near Porlock, and rounded Land's End. The combined fleets
cruised eastwards up the English Channel, receiving reinforcements
from the very ports which recently had been bound to provide the
king with ships, and sailed up the Thames to Southwark. Edward
was with an army on the north bank; but this time it was Godwine
and not he who was in a position to fight. Wessex was for its earl;
Earls Leofric and Siward stood neutral and aloof; London itself
declared for the returning outlaws. It was the turn of the Normans
to flee before judgment. The archbishop of Canterbury and the
bishop of Dorchester broke out of London and escaped abroad.
Lesser men hurried for refuge to friends in the country. Edward had
to accept terms. Godwine swore that he and his sons were innocent
of the crimes imputed to them, and the family was restored to its
former position. The Lady Eadgyth was recalled to court. Only
Svein was not there to enjoy a third return from exile. Accepting
penance, he had left Bruges on a pilgrimage to Jerusalem, and died
in Lycia on the return journey. So Ralf kept an earldom in the west;
and Odda, too, was compensated on the Welsh border; but the hated
castle in the Golden Valley was dismantled. There was no general
proscription of foreigners. Sentence of outlawry was passed on those
who had perverted the law or tampered with its good administration;
but many who had caused no offence were untouched. The ecclesiastical position was settled in a similar way. Robert of Jumièges and
Ulf were allowed to remain in exile; and Robert's Benedictional
and fine English Missal are still at Rouen. Stigand, a political opportunist, was given Canterbury, and held it together with Winchester.
Another Englishman, Wulfwig, was appointed to Dorchester. But

Spearhafoc was not restored to London; the Norman William was allowed to return.

The moderation of the settlement of 1052 justified the neutrality of the northern earls. Doubtless they would have interfered again had Godwine's terms been extortionate; but they were prepared to allow Edward to take some punishment for his vindictive revenge and his reckless surrender to a foreign party. Their attitude is shown in the quiet way in which Aelfgar, Leofric's son, surrendered the East Anglian earldom to Harold. The whole episode, indeed, reveals the strength and weakness of the Anglo-Saxon kingdom. Provincial jealousy and rival ambition seem powerful enough to tear the state asunder; yet a strong sense of community, that could exist independent of the king, is manifest at moments of crisis. To call this feeling 'nationality' is to go too far; but to ignore the common sentiment is to disregard the facts. Norway, Denmark, and Sweden were at this time crystallizing into separate states. In England, with its growing diversity of stock, a counter-movement might be expected; yet Danish Siward, English Leofric and Godwine, Anglo-Danish Svein and Harold, Anglo-Norman Edward, were all caught up in a web which they found hard to break. There was in England a respect for traditional rights and for the due observance of law which twice in these two years operated to curb naked violence and to protect the integrity of the state. On the first occasion this respect overthrew a rebellious earl; on the second it supported an exile seeking his inheritance. On balance it is the strength of the state rather than its incoherence which is the more remarkable.

III

The restoration of the house of Godwine through military operations in 1052 did more than put the earl of Wessex back in his dominant position; it destroyed the king's confidence in his personal schemes of independent action. But the death of Godwine on 15 April 1053 changed the balance of the provincial powers once more. Its immediate result was to strengthen the standing of the Mercian house. When Harold succeeded to his father's West Saxon earldom, Aelfgar, Leofric's son, replaced Harold again in East Anglia. These moves put the Mercian family completely athwart the Midlands, and left Godwine's family with a single earldom in the hands of a man who as yet lacked his father's personal influence and reputation.

Nevertheless, the closeness of the Wessex family to the king, the succession of able brothers growing up with claims to rule, and probably the increasing influence of Eadgyth over her husband, worked in its favour. Ralf's earldom, which included the shires of Hereford and Oxford, is perhaps the most interesting in this period, for it anticipates the Welsh marcher earldoms that William was to establish. Castle building, which had been checked in 1052, was resumed, and Ralf began to train the men of his earldom to fight on horseback. This military reorganization was an answer to the threatening power of Gruffydd ap Llywelyn; but it seems to have been too novel, or too timidly handled, to have been much of a success at the time.

In 1055 the mighty Earl Siward died, far from battle, but harnessed for war, like a true Viking. In the previous year he had lost his eldest son, Osbeorn Bulax (timber-axe), killed during the opening and decisive phase of a northern campaign which led to the expulsion of Macbeth from the Scottish throne, and the setting up in his place of Malcolm, son of the Duncan, king of Scots, whom Macbeth had in 1040 slain in open war. Siward's other son, Waltheof, was considered in 1055 too young for this dangerous earldom; and Edward granted it to Harold's younger brother, Tostig. The wisdom of this act cannot be gainsaid. It brought a separatist province under the closer control of the king, for Tostig was a favourite of both Edward and Eadgyth, and yet did not unduly enhance the power of the sons of Godwine, for the two earldoms they held were separated by the wide and compact Mercian dominions. It is true that the concentration of the great earldoms in the hands of only two families must have sharpened their rivalry; but it is difficult to see what other course the king could have followed. And Tostig was a good choice for the office. As the son of Gytha he was no alien by blood, and as the brother-in-law of the Count of Flanders he had the standing for his task. Both Tostig and Judith were benefactors to the church, while Tostig, even if secretive and sometimes harsh, was to prove himself a strong ruler and a bold adventurer. In 1065 the Northumbrians were to drive him out. But others after Tostig were to find the government of Northumbria beyond their powers; and his failure is, perhaps, better explained by regarding it as a premature attempt by king and earl to subjugate a refractory province, than as the inevitable conclusion of an ill-conceived project. Tostig ruled for ten years. At first Malcolm III (Canmore) was weak, and looked to his

English connexions for help. Even in 1059, two years after Macbeth's death, Malcolm came south with Tostig and the two northern prelates to meet his old benefactor, King Edward, at Gloucester. So close, indeed, were Malcolm and Tostig that they are referred to as 'sworn brothers'. But in substituting the anglicized Malcolm for Macbeth the earls of Northumbria had raised a danger to their province. With Malcolm begins the transformation of the Scottish monarchy from a Celtic chieftaincy to a government on the English pattern. The basis of Malcolm's power lay in the lost English territories south of the Forth. His ambition became to add the country south of the Tweed, to recreate the old Northumbria. Tostig held him in check by friendship; after Tostig's fall Northumbria was to quail before an ambition pent-up too long.

From 1053 until 1057, when Earls Ralf and Leofric died, the two great provincial houses in England were roughly in equilibrium; but the king's policy had been changed. He had to look outside Normandy for an heir. In the circumstances Edward 'the exile', the surviving son of Edmund Ironside, became the obvious choice; and so it was that in 1054 Ealdred, bishop of Worcester, was sent to the court of the Emperor Henry III to enquire about the Aetheling and to negotiate for his return. The bishop waited at Cologne for a year, and then came back alone. The Aetheling had lived in Hungary for most of his forty years, and hesitated, no doubt, before exchanging a secure position at the Magyar court for a tempting but uncertain future. Towards the end of 1056 negotiations were renewed. Harold, earl of Wessex, crossed to Flanders, and may have journeyed even farther afield, in an attempt to make contact with Edward, or again to press him to come. Next year the exile stood once more on English soil, only to die before he met the king. The succession question was again thrown completely open. Edward Aetheling left by a foreign wife an infant son, Edgar, and a daughter, Margaret. The boy never found much favour among the English nobility, and his wanderings and misfortunes were to surpass even those of his father. The girl was to become the saintly wife of Malcolm III, king of Scots, and to be the mother of three northern kings.

The other deaths in 1057 were almost as momentous as that of the Aetheling. In August or September Leofric, earl of the Mercians, died, and in December the king's nephew, Ralf. The redistribution of the provincial governorships was entirely in the interest of the sons of Godwine. Aelfgar surrendered East Anglia for the paternal earldom of Mercia, and was replaced by Harold's brother, Gyrth. The shires of south-eastern England were grouped in a new earldom for yet another brother of Harold, Leofwine; and Harold received in compensation Herefordshire, which Ralf had held. The death of Leofric was far more disastrous to his family than the death of Godwine had been to his. In 1058 Mercia was completely ringed by the earldoms of Harold and his brothers.

It is easy, however, to exaggerate the rivalry between the houses of Leofric and Godwine. Each had its 'ancestral' earldom, and expected others to be found for sons reaching military age. Each, no doubt, was eager for power, without necessarily denying a place to the other. Yet as Mercia became isolated by the earldoms held by Harold's brothers, it seems to have looked to Wales for a counterpoise.

Wales, which contained a mixture of some of the most ancient colonists of Britain, remnants of peoples who had been pushed back into the mountain fastnesses by successive waves of conquerors, had never since the migratory period been a danger to the English. Its isolation and the poorness of its grazing grounds, broken with but few fertile valleys, had helped to preserve a primitive and simple but attractive way of life. The social organization was tribal, the economic life almost entirely pastoral. Physical barriers hindered the attainment of political unity, and only rarely could a native chieftain achieve even a brief hegemony over the scattered and proudly independent cantrefs. Although Christian since Roman days, Wales had been little disturbed by alien influences. The Vikings were familiar with its coastline—there are fiords in Wales: Milford and Haverford—but had never settled down there. And the Saxon march knew the Welsh only as cattle raiders, as uneasy and turbulent neighbours.

Yet some English influence was inescapable. Any Welsh chieftain who rose to more than tribal power was bound to come into political contact with English officials and to feel the cultural pull of the English royal court. And it is significant that the greatest Welsh king in the Dark Ages, Hywel Dda, Hywel the Good, who became ruler of all Wales in the first half of the tenth century, was much attracted by Wessex and even codified Welsh custom in imitation of Alfred's work. In the eleventh century another prince of courage and ambition, Gruffydd ap Llywelyn, king of Gwynedd and Powys in the north, began to climb to supreme power. In 1039 he had secured his flank by defeating a Mercian army near Welshpool, and by 1055 had subdued the southern princes and made himself ruler of Deheubarth and Morgannwg and king of all Wales. But Gruffydd's entanglement in English affairs was to have results less happy than Hywel's, for the apprehension he aroused provoked a new phase in Anglo-Welsh relations, a phase which was to end only with the political subjection of his country to the English crown in the thirteenth century.

In the spring of 1055 Aelfgar, earl of East Anglia, was banished for 'treason'. He soon returned from Ireland to Wales with a Viking fleet, allied with Gruffydd, and invaded Herefordshire. In October Earl Ralf, defending his earldom in the French military style which he had introduced, was defeated, and could not prevent the sack of his shire town. Harold, earl of Wessex, led an army against the invaders, refortified Hereford, and accepted the allies' plea for peace. Aelfgar was restored to his earldom, and Gruffydd kept his conquests. In June 1056 Leofgar, the new bishop of Hereford, one of Harold's clerks, attempted to punish the Welsh king, and lost his life in a battle near Glasbury on Wye, in which the sheriff of Hereford and many others fell. Again Harold took the field, and once more he came to terms with Gruffydd. The Welsh prince swore that he would be a faithful under-king to Edward, and in return was confirmed in possession of those English lands which he had occupied along the border. The most important of these was that strip between the rivers Dee and Clywd in the north; but in the Maelor district, round Oswestry, about Chirbury, and north and south of the Wye were areas which had been cleared by the Welsh of their ancient colonies of Englishmen. In this sparring contest the honours had lain with Gruffydd, and Harold had acquired little military glory.

In 1058, one year after he had moved from East Anglia to Mercia, Aelfgar was outlawed again, and once more for reasons which remain obscure. His subsequent actions followed the familiar pattern, except that this time his return had the fortuitous support of a Viking fleet not only drawn from Norway, the Hebrides, Orkney and Dublin, but also under the command of no less than Magnus, son of Harold Hardrada, king of Norway. Gruffydd, too, was involved. This formidable invasion secured the restoration of Aelfgar to his earldom; but of the military operations we know nothing. Some time later Gruffydd married Ealdgyth, a daughter of Aelfgar, which cemented the Mercian-Welsh alliance. But Aelfgar disappears from genuine record after the summer of 1062, and subsequent events suggest that either he was incapacitated about that time or it was then that he died and was succeeded by his young son, Edwine.

The succession of this boy proves that there were restraints (perhaps both moral and external) on the ambition of the house of Godwine. And Mercia's weakness was turned to the advantage of the kingdom and not to the enrichment of a rival family. In 1062 Gruffydd, mistaking the position, ravaged Worcestershire. In the winter Harold made a lightning raid with mounted troops into North Wales—a move which foreshadows his rapid marches in 1066—and only just failed to capture Gruffydd at Rhuddlan. He then withdrew and planned a campaign with his brother Tostig, earl of Northumbria. At the end of May 1063 Harold sailed from Bristol and harried the Welsh coast; Tostig penetrated North Wales by the coastal plain. In a savage war without pitched battles Gruffydd was worn down and encircled by the invaders, and then murdered by his crestfallen companions. His head was sent to Edward; Gwynedd and Powys were divided between two kinsmen, and the land surrendered in 1056 withdrawn; while the Celtic portions of South Wales were allowed to revert to their old princely families. Harold's reputation became great and in time legendary; and it was long before the Welsh menace was to be feared again.

IV

Between 1063 and 1065 the English kingdom was at peace. The overwhelming power in the hands of the sons of Godwine, and their harmonious relations with the court, gave the English state unity, stability, and strength. Yet, if it is the actions of the king's servants which call for most attention in the years after 1052, the growing reputation of the king should not be overlooked. To those who glanced back across the Norman Conquest this was the rule of Solomon, a golden age. According to Edward's first biographer, perhaps Folcard, a monk of St Bertin's at St Omer, or Goscelin, another monk of that house who joined Heremann bishop of Ramsbury in England, the king lived a simple, rustic life. After mass the hunt, and after the hunt the conversation of holy men. Although he could still flash with anger like a lion, he was reaching the sweetness and tranquility of old age. The snowy hair and beard, thé rosy countenance were the conventional outer-trappings of a wise old king; the long translucent fingers, the good works, the lack of children, revealed a man aspiring to sanctity, one 'who lived like an angel in the squalor of the world'. It was in these last years that some men at court began to suggest that Edward, like Robert the Pious,

king of France, before him, had the power to cure the sick. Aethelred
II, his father, was sung by the Icelandic poet Gunnlaug as the
warrior king and lord whom his men obeyed as a god. Edward to his
biographer was God's anointed, *Christus dei.*

Edward left a memorial to his taste in the abbey he built outside
London, a church which, rebuilt by King Henry III, was to find a
permanent place in the hearts of Englishmen and to become a
national mausoleum. His wife, Eadgyth, and his brother-in-law, Earl
Harold, were builders, too. Harold reconstructed the church that
Tofig the Proud had erected at Waltham to house the Holy Rood,
the thaumaturgic crucifix that had been found in Somerset. The new
collegiate church for a dean and twelve canons was consecrated on
3 May 1060. Eadgyth rebuilt the church of the nuns at Wilton,
consecrated anew in 1065. But the greatest project was the king's.
Outside the west gate of London, on Thorney, an island in the
Thames, formed by the delta of the Tyburn Brook, stood a Benedictine monastery dedicated to St. Peter, and called, in relation to the
cathedral church of St. Paul's, the West Minster. This Edward
rebuilt in the new Norman romanesque style at the cost of a tithe of
his revenue over many years. It was completed on the eve of his
death, and he was buried in the church. This magnificent building
was a marvel to contemporaries, and its picture can still be seen on
the Bayeux tapestry.

In 1064 Edward was approaching sixty, and, although still vigorous, could not be expected to last much longer; but we know little
of the hopes of the foreign claimants or of the secret ambitions which
Harold, or even Tostig, may have had. William of Poitiers, the Conqueror's panegyrist, tells us a story about the chief characters which is,
a little later, also told in pictures, but for a rather different purpose, on
the Bayeux tapestry, that splendid embroidery stitched for William's
half-brother, Odo. In 1064 or 1065 (the date is conjectural) Edward
sent Earl Harold as his ambassador to Normandy in order to confirm
his nomination of William as his heir. Harold sailed from Bosham,
made an unexpected landing in Ponthieu, the county of Guy I, a
vassal of the duke of Normandy, was arrested and held for ransom,
and in the end was released through the intervention of the duke.
At Bonneville-sur-Touques or at Bayeux he confirmed his business
on oath and made various associated promises which fully committed
him personally to the scheme. He accompanied William on a campaign into Brittany, acquiring a reputation for great physical strength,

and received many honours from his host. Earl and duke had made a solemn compact. As the story is blatant Norman propaganda it is unlikely to be true in all detail and may even be wrong in substance. There seems no reason to doubt that Harold went as Edward's ambassador to Normandy. But the Norman apologists may have changed the purpose of the mission. Edward seems still to have been hale and hearty. It may be that Harold went to confirm the old treaty of alliance between the two courts, or merely to exchange gifts and assurances of friendship, a common practice of the time. In addition Harold could have been sounding out William's intentions or even looking for supporters for his private schemes. The true story cannot now be told. But the oath that Harold took, whatever the terms may have been, was a fateful act. In 1066 he could be denounced as a faithless vassal and perjurer. And we do not know his reply.

If the mission of Harold to Normandy reveals a disturbance in foreign affairs the events in Northumbria show how deceptive was the peace at home. In the autumn of 1065, while Earl Tostig was hunting with the king near Salisbury, apparently unaware of his danger, a revolt broke out in Northumbria, which rapidly assumed the character of a provincial uprising against Tostig's rule. His severity was the general cause; a heavy tax he imposed and the murder of some thegns at his instigation were probably the immediate occasions. In October, Tostig was deposed by a rebel moot at York; Morkere, the younger brother of Earl Edwine of Mercia, was elected in his place; and, after Tostig's treasure had been secured and his housecarles killed, the Northumbrian army under its new leader marched south, and was joined by the Mercian forces under Edwine, for the insurgents knew that force alone could persuade the king to accept this revolution. Earl Harold met the rebels at Northampton, and attempted to mediate, while Edward demanded war. Tostig apparently accused Harold of having incited the rebellion against him and Harold would not fight the Northumbrians and Mercians to restore his brother. At the end of October the king submitted. Tostig was outlawed, and Morkere appointed earl in his place. In 1065 as in 1052 Edward had to yield to force; but again the legalities were observed. It was the sorrowful king and not a rebellious province which formally substituted Morkere for Tostig. The political results of this cloaked rebellion were important. It caused the king's death, for Edward's grief and mortification were such that he never fully recovered from the shock. Its influence on Harold's fortunes are, however, less easy to discern. Tostig never forgave his brother's neglect, and his invasion next year in company with Harold Hardrada contributed in no small measure to Harold's defeat by Duke William. But if Tostig, as the favourite of the old king, had himself hopes of the crown, and if, had this ambition been disappointed, his loyalty to his brother would have been insecure, then Harold gained by the substitution. Edward lived long enough to see his buildings finished at Westminster. In 1065 the midwinter witenagemot was summoned to London instead of the usual Gloucester, and on 28 December the new church was consecrated. The king was too ill to attend the ceremony. He died on 5 January 1066, and was buried in the minster.

The reign of Edward the Confessor lacks the ruthless grandeur that informs the rule of his predecessor Cnut and of his successor William. Compared with those kings his direction appears uncertain, his policy wilful, his achievement small. But if Edward had left an able son, or Harold had advanced to glory, then the Confessor might well have been judged the wise and pacific king, who, by husbanding his country's strength after troubled years, made possible the great deeds of his successors. Be that as it may, Edward's reign has a character of its own; and if it is rarely appreciated it is because, although Edward's failings are common to all times, his virtues were purely medieval. A weak man, riding—uneasily and petulantly— political storms which he could not control, he nevertheless left the royal powers unimpaired; and from a mistaken view of his character and piety was built a picture of a Christian king that served as an ideal until the ideal itself lost favour. The interest of the Normans in the reign was at first utilitarian. Edward and his nobles were the legal 'ancestors' of William and his barons; and the titles of the last English landowners and their foreign successors were carefully recorded in that great land register—Domesday Book. But gradually the upstart Normans appropriated the English past. The first generation of Anglo-Norman historians wrote with pride of English saints and heroes; lawyers collected 'the laws of King Edward'; and in time the memory of the last 'legitimate' English king was cherished by the conquered and the conquering race alike. Pope Innocent II rejected the first attempt to get Edward recognized as a saint in 1139 owing to the political disorder in England; but on 7 February 1161 Pope Alexander III rewarded Henry II's espousal of his cause by issuing a bull of canonization. Angevin interest in St. Edward the Confessor reached its zenith with Henry III, who rebuilt Westminster Abbey and named his eldest son after the saint. Nevertheless, Henry's great-grandson, Edward, the victor of Crécy, styled himself 'the third after the Conquest'. The cult of the saint could not blur the tradition that a revolution in English history had taken place in 1066.

3

THE NORMAN CONQUEST OF ENGLAND

I

I<small>T</small> is recorded in the earliest life of Edward the Confessor that in a vision which Bishop Beorhtwald of Ramsbury had of St. Peter granting the crown to Edward and at the same time imposing a celibate life upon him, Edward exclaimed, 'What then of the stock which will reign after me?' To which St. Peter replied, 'The kingdom of the English is the kingdom of God, and it has pleased God to make provision for its future.' But when Edward had his fatal stroke, no man knew with certainty what God's pleasure was, or even, it seems, what Edward himself desired. The dying man had apocalyptic visions, and prophesied woe to his country. Archbishop Stigand whispered that the king raved; and still the watchers waited. At the close Edward commended his wife, his retainers, and his kingdom to Harold, earl of Wessex. On 5 January 1066 Edward died; and on the next day he was buried and Harold chosen and crowned in his place.

The indecorous haste of the coronation betrays the anxieties of the time, but in no way means that Harold's succession was ill-considered or supported by but few. Edward's fatal sickness had coincided with the Christmas witenagemot, at which, in view of the Westminster ceremonies, attendance must have been large. If there were nobles who favoured Edgar Aetheling or Duke William as king, Edward's dying bequest served to stifle their desires. It is possible that the widow Eadgyth was not Harold's warmest supporter, for Tostig had been her favourite brother; and she retired to Winchester, where later she received honourable and friendly treatment from King William. But there is no evidence that Edwine, earl of Mercia, or Morkere, earl of Northumbria, was hostile to the choice of Harold. Morkere, indeed, may well have been grateful to the West Saxon earl. The magnates must have been in rough agreement before

Edward died; and the immediate coronation reveals that they were fully aware of the dangers they were incurring. A challenge from the duke of the Normans was to be expected; an incursion by Harold Hardrada, king of Norway, was likely; and the events of the last year had added the peril of raids from the outlawed Tostig and his sworn ally, Malcolm, king of Scots. The free acceptance of a man outside the English royal house was a striking breach in tradition; yet it should be remembered that Harold had noble blood through his Danish mother, Gytha, and that his sister had been Edward's consort. Edgar Aetheling was clearly unable to raise much of a party, and obtained only half-hearted support after Harold's death. It may be argued that a stronger position would have been created had Edgar been crowned and had Harold remained as the power behind the throne. But Edgar was incapable of inspiring such loyalty, and Harold was unwilling to efface himself.

Harold's reign of nine months was taken up almost entirely with political and military preparations for the inevitable conflict, and it is easier to judge him as a general than as a king. The man himself seems without greatness, but in no way negligible. To a contemporary Harold appeared of fine physique, a good captain and a brave soldier, magnanimous and affable, patient like all his family, steadier and less brilliant than Tostig, a strong ruler of his earldom, and a stern lover of justice. He had had long and varied military experience. In 1052 he had sailed with pirates from Dublin; between 1055 and 1063 he had fought the Welsh; and in 1064 he had been in William's cavalry against the Bretons. If he normally fought like his ancestors on foot with battle-axe and shield-wall, he also knew the feudal horseman and his tactics. His political education, too, was extensive. He had visited Rome, and studied the countries through which he passed; he had been on embassies to north Gaul, and was familiar with the Flemish and Norman as well as with the English court. It is easy to picture him as an old soldier and, perhaps, Harold was happiest on campaign; but he had ruled successfully as earl for twenty years, and there is no reason to think he would have been less capable or more inspiring as king.

One of Harold's first acts was to secure the loyalty of Northumbria, which not unnaturally showed reluctance to accept the southern magnates' choice of king, especially as the new ruler was Tostig's brother. But the opposition seems to have been passive, and unsupported by the new earl, for a peaceful progress through the province by Harold in company with a bishop well-known at York, Wulfstan of Worcester, won the fealty of the nobles. Even so, Harold thought it wise to bind Edwine and Morkere more closely to him. He put away his concubine, Eadgyth 'Swan-neck', and married their sister, Ealdgyth, the widow of Gruffydd. She bore him a posthumous child, whom she named after her slain husband. Yet not Venus but Mars ruled that fateful year. At Easter, while the contestants for the English throne gathered their forces together, 'Halley's' comet blazed across the sky, a portent of disaster to a credulous people.

Tostig, who had taken refuge in Flanders, his wife's country, moved first. In May 1066 he raided the south coast of England, passed safely up the Channel, and, penetrating the Humber, ravaged Lindsey. Earls Edwine and Morkere drove him off, and the outlaw sailed north to Scotland. Tostig was out for his earldom rather than for the kingdom, and when he was repulsed he waited to see what the greater enemies of his brother could do. It is possible that he was in touch with Harold Hardrada, and encouraged him to invade. The king of Norway had made peace with Svein of Denmark in 1064, and was ready with his veteran troops for his last adventure.

As soon as William II, duke of the Normans, heard that his cousin had died and Harold had been chosen in his place, he began to prepare to upset his successful rival. Military and diplomatic schemes went hand in hand. The political events of the last few years in Europe had favoured William well. In 1060 his overlord, King Henry I, had died, and Baldwin V of Flanders, William's father-in-law, became guardian and regent for the youthful Philip I, Baldwin's nephew. As the count was also related to the outlawed Tostig he neither prevented his vassals from joining William's forces nor put any hindrance in the way of the Norman duke. Among the Flemish vassals was Eustace II, count of Boulogne, the brother-in-law of the deceased English king, and a friend of William. Also in 1060 had died Geoffrey Martel of Anjou, and his county, the hereditary enemy of Normandy, was later disputed between his two nephews, Geoffrey the Bearded and Fulk 'le Réchin'. Consequently in 1063 William was able to conquer the border county of Maine. In 1064, with Harold in his company, William had chastised Brittany. To the north, Guy of Ponthieu was his vassal, so that the whole coastline from Ushant to the Scheldt was under the control of William, his dependants, or his friends. Harold, indeed, had no allies abroad, save only, perhaps, Svein of Denmark; for the Emperor

Henry III had died in 1056 leaving a boy as heir, and Pope Alexander II had no cause to favour the family which supported Stigand
as archbishop of Canterbury.

The general situation was propitious to William's cause; but the
almost miraculous success of the expedition and the utter collapse of
a rival party in England could not have been expected by even the
most optimistic in the spring and summer of 1066. The invasion
itself must have appeared hazardous; and it is unlikely that any
detailed plans for the conduct of a campaign on English soil were
ever made. It would be a mistake to credit William with a strategic
skill much greater than that which Svein Forkbeard, Cnut, Harold
Hardrada, or any of his Viking precursors had possessed. When
William laid his project before the Norman barons in the great
council of his duchy the most he could have offered with sincerity
was an expedition which might produce plunder, might wrest
provinces from the rule of Harold, and might ultimately, perhaps,
lead to the conquest of the whole kingdom. The fortunes of the
Normans in Sicily must have been the precedent which dominated all
men's minds. Yet although the uncertainties which masked the out-
come of this enterprise should not be overlooked, the fearless determination of the duke and his military and diplomatic skill must be
recognized as the instruments of his victory. The provision of troops
and ships for such an undertaking was not within the Norman
barons' feudal obligation. In any case a force sufficient for the invasion could not be raised from Normandy itself. Hence allies and
mercenaries had to be enrolled. The army which William eventually
led was not so much the ducal forces of Normandy as a miscellaneous
contingent under Norman leadership brought together by promise
of gain and by hope of adventure. William's relatives, friends, and
feudal vassals made the largest contributions. Most of the great
Norman families were represented in the army. Bretons, possibly
under their count, formed the second largest national contingent.
Count Eustace of Boulogne brought his men, and Flemish volunteers
were numerous. Other units were attracted from all French-speaking
lands.

The recruitment of soldiers, the building of a fleet of transports on
the pattern of Viking ships, and the assembly of military supplies
formed but a part of William's preparations. By diplomacy he sought
to protect his duchy during his absence and also to enlist for his
cause the sympathy of Europe. The regency which ruled for

Henry IV in Germany and even King Svein of Denmark promised neutrality. Negotiations with the pope were more momentous. Alexander II was approached as an influential power, as the mouthpiece of the only law with international pretensions, and, especially, as the supreme judge in ecclesiastical cases, for they were spiritual charges that William brought against Harold. William's ambassador to the curia, Gilbert, archdeacon of Lisieux, had a good cause to plead. He could point to William's relationship to Edward, to the bequest of the throne in 1051–2, and to Harold's oath of 1064. He could create prejudice against Harold, and strengthen William's case, by repeating the current story, true or false, that Harold had been consecrated by the excommunicate Stigand. It was easy in fact to represent Harold as a perjured usurper fraudulently crowned. To these legal charges Harold could make no reply since he had neglected to be represented at Rome. William could in addition make attractive promises. He could undertake to reform the English church and to resume payment of Peter's Pence, which appears either to have fallen into arrears or to have been interrupted by the political disturbance. It seems that Gilbert also held out hopes that the duke, if successful, would hold England as a papal fief. Again the precedent of the Normans in Sicily was apposite, and must have influenced the moves of the negotiators. It is certain, however, that William gave no specific undertaking through Gilbert; it is even possible that in dangling this glittering reward before the pope the ambassador was exceeding his instructions; but both William and the papal party appear to have accepted ambiguities during, and for some time after, the negotiations in the hope of turning them to future advantage. William's chief supporter at the court of Alexander II, the Cardinal Hildebrand, later Pope Gregory VII, found the College of Cardinals unenthusiastic for an enterprise which would bring the horrors of war to a peaceful and friendly Christian country, errant, perhaps, but traditionally loyal; and it needed all Gilbert's skill and all Hildebrand's fanatical vision to carry the day even against an unrepresented opponent. In the end William probably received the papal blessing, and he enlisted the Norman and neighbouring churches to pray for the success of his expedition. But William of Poitiers, who describes the sympathy of the European powers for the duke's cause, no doubt makes too much of words that cost nothing. Nor could William have been deceived. Although superstitious, he knew that he must rely on the skill and courage of his army.

II

By August William's preparations were complete. The transports were assembled in the mouth of the Dives; the army was encamped nearby; and William intended presumably to sail due north to the Isle of Wight and Southampton water. All waited on a south wind. In England Harold had regarded Tostig's raid in May as the warning signal, and mobilized his forces. The plan of defence was local and simple. Earls Edwine and Morkere were primarily responsible for the defence of their earldoms against Tostig and, if it so chanced, Harold Hardrada; the king and his brothers were to defend their earldoms against William of Normandy. Harold himself commanded a fleet which he based on the Isle of Wight in order to intercept the invaders. As it turned out Harold had mobilized too soon. An anti-cyclone centred to the west of the British Isles remained stationary in August bringing a northerly air stream down the North Sea and the Channel. Harold Hardrada took advantage of it to leave Norway; but William could not sail. Early in September Harold's forces disintegrated. Four months' inactivity had been disheartening to a defensive army, and the harvest tasks had become urgent. The fleet, too, had run out of supplies, and on 8 September, when the anti-cyclone began to break up, Harold transferred his headquarters to London, and lost many of his ships in the operation. A few days later William's fleet also suffered losses when it moved, or was driven, up Channel before it found a haven off Saint-Valery at the mouth of the Somme within the territory of Guy of Ponthieu.

Harold Hardrada, with one of his wives, several of his children, and, perhaps, with two to three hundred ships, touched at Shetland and Orkney, gathering reinforcements on the way, and in September reached the Tyne, where he was joined by Tostig. The invaders, after ravaging for supplies, sailed up the Humber and the Ouse, disembarked at Riccall, and marched on York. Earls Edwine and Morkere put themselves in front of the city, and were heavily routed on 20 September at Gate Fulford. York seems to have surrendered to the victors a few days later; but the army encamped at Stamford Bridge on the river Derwent, seven miles east of the city. King Harold had moved to the help of the earls on hearing of the Viking landing. He hastened with his troops up the Roman road, passed through York on 25 September, and pushed straight on to engage the enemy. In a savage and conclusive battle Harold Hardrada, Tostig, and an Irish king were slain; and when Harold allowed the remnants of the Scandinavian forces to re-embark, they needed, it is said, but twenty-four of their ships. Harold's house-carles and thegns must have suffered losses, too, in so bloody an encounter; and these two northern battles sapped the English military strength on the eve of the Norman invasion. The battle of Stamford Bridge is overshadowed by the battle of Hastings; but it also has a claim to be considered one of the decisive battles of English history. The crushing defeat of the Norwegian adventurer by the Anglo-Danish Harold was almost the final episode in the Scandinavian history of England. Hope of seizing the English throne withered slowly in Trondheim, in Roskilde, and in Odense, where the winter nights were long and the sagas without end; but never again did northern ambition severely shake the power of an English king.

On 27 September, two days after Harold's victory, the south wind blew at last. Duke William embarked his forces, and crossed during the night to Pevensey Bay, where he made an unopposed landing in the morning. He then took advantage of the strange peacefulness of the coast to transfer his base to the more easily defensible Hastings; a motte and bailey castle was thrown up to protect the lodgement; and for a fortnight the Normans reconnoitred and pillaged the hinterland, as though they were uncertain of how best to exploit their good fortune. The forces which William had brought with him have been variously estimated. Modern historians are of the opinion that the armies which faced each other at Hastings were of not more than 7,000 men. The names of few of those who fought in the battle are known—no more than 32 members of the Norman host have been identified with certainty; but the equipment of the troops is familiar through the meticulous detail of the Bayeux tapestry. The invading army was a mixed force of cavalry and foot. All the knights and some of the infantry wore a light metal helmet, conical in shape with a nose-piece attached, a byrnie (a coat of chain mail with short sleeves and legs, lined with leather or fabric, worn next to the skin in battle), and, usually, puttees on the legs, and carried a kite-shaped shield made of leather stretched on a wooden frame. The war horses, bay, roan, or black Percheron stallions, were unprotected. The stir-rups were long, and the riders wore spurs at their ankles. The arms of the knights were the spear or lance and the sword. The infantry mostly had short bows and a capacious quiver. The bri-gading of cavalry and archers gave William a force more useful in attack than in defence. But, unless horses could be procured in number, the battle had to be fought near his base.

When Harold heard at York of William's landing he left the sheriff Merleswein in command in the north, ordered the earls Edwine and Morkere to rally their men and follow him south, and retraced his steps down the Great North Road. At London he waited for less than a week, and then led his army towards Hastings. Harold's intentions will never be clear. His troops, weary with marching and fighting, needed rest; in time reinforcements from the north and the west would come in. A prudent general would have waited before launching an unprovoked attack on a new enemy. Yet Harold had a victorious army; and the permanent problem of defence in the Anglo-Saxon period was that of intercepting a mobile raider and of bringing him to battle. To catch William at his base and destroy him before he had time to build up an impregnable position and receive reinforcements was a course which must have had its attraction for the headlong victor of Stamford Bridge. It must be remembered, too, that the invader was ravaging Harold's earldom, and that both duty and self-interest pressed Harold to go to the immediate assistance of his people. An advance towards Hastings, however, did not commit Harold irrevocably to battle. The threat of an attack would force the duke to call in his forces, and Harold could contain the enemy while gaining that precious delay; at the same time by getting closer to the Normans he could obtain the initiative and choose his moment. In the event Harold was out-manœuvred, and accepted a battle on the enemy's terms. The skill of a general is relative to the ability of his opponent; and the charge of rashness levelled against Harold by contemporaries as well as by some modern historians seems unfounded. Harold was noted for his caution. His failure lay in getting too close to the enemy without having the opportunity for a surprise attack; and his misfortune consisted in being faced by a rival who desired a decisive encounter near his ships, who believed that God would vindicate the just in the ordeal of battle, and who had the genius to exploit his opportunity to the full.

Harold marched from London down the only road which penetrated Andredsweald; and on the evening of 13 October he came out of the forest about nine miles from Hastings, too late for an immediate surprise assault on William's camp. He halted his men at Sandlake ('Senlac' to the Normans), where the road followed a ridge flanked by steep escarpments. The place was a natural fortress. In front the ground fell gently away and then rose to the higher Telham Hill. On both flanks were marshy streams. The position could not be turned, and it blocked William's way. Disengagement was possible back along the ridge, and the Weald offered its refuge in the rear. William snatched the chance to fight. At daybreak his army moved out of Hastings, and when the road topped Telham Hill the English host came into sight beneath them. Harold had accepted the challenge. His men were massing on the ridge. In front were the best armed thegns to form the shield-wall; behind were those with less armour, supporting the line by weight, and ready to throw spears, axes, and even stones. Archers seem to have been few. In the rear, to the left of the centre, was the highest point, marked later by the high altar of Battle Abbey; and there stood Harold and his brothers Gyrth and Leofwine, under the writhing red and golden dragon standard, surrounded by their housecarles. To the Normans the English army seemed a solid phalanx of warriors.

The Normans armed on Telham Hill and deployed on the forward slope in view of the English. The invaders advanced in three divisions. On the left were the Bretons, possibly under Alan the Red or his brother Brian; on the right were the French and Flemings under Eustace of Boulogne; and in the centre were the Normans under their duke. Each cavalry division was preceded by two lines of infantry: light skirmishers armed with bows in the van, and in support crossbowmen, archers, and swordsmen. Early accounts of the battle are not as clear or reliable as is sometimes supposed, and the action cannot be described in detail. It is certain that in the early stages the invaders suffered a near-disaster. The infantry could not get through the barrage of missiles, and the cavalry, cut down by the swung axes, could not break the shield-wall. Some of the attackers gave way and fled, drawing English troops down in pursuit. In the confusion the whole French army wavered and recoiled. A cry went up that the duke was dead, and panic seized the attackers. But William wheeled his knights and cut down the pursuing footmen in the open; and once the Norman leaders had rallied their men it was found that no irreparable loss had been suffered. Indeed, it was probably in this phase of the battle that Harold's two brothers were killed; and although the English were still able to close their ranks, they had let their best chance of a quick victory slip away.

After the failure of the main assaults the fighting became less organized. Under the hail of arrows and spears English soldiers dropped, but there were others to take their place; and the shield-wall was still too strong to be broken by a general cavalry charge. But whenever the Norman archers caused disarray, knights thrust into the breaches, hacking and spearing. In the lulls squadrons of cavalry galloped up, and swerved away or turned tail in real or simulated flight. Groups of English, maddened by the hours of standing and waiting, and harassed by archers out of range, dashed forward to strike a few last blows in the open, and were cut to pieces by knights who came in from flank and rear. The English army was gradually worn down. The dead were heaped on the ridge; the crescent of the standing pressed more closely round the king. Long before the end the position had become hopeless, unless the on-coming night would give respite or reinforcements should arrive. But there was no retreat until Norman knights burst into the last groups fighting under the standard, and Harold fell, perhaps un-recognized. Then the English broke, and the few survivors streamed back along the road, pursued by horsemen, many of whom crashed down the escarped sides of the ridge in the failing light.

The Normans suffered heavy casualties in the battle; but the English forces were annihilated. The battle of Hastings is remarkable not only for the clash of fighting styles, and for the demonstration that archers with cavalry could destroy an immobile defensive infantry mass, but also for the classical display of the older art by the vanquished and for their heroic discipline. It is no wonder that Harold, the perjured usurper, is styled on the Bayeux tapestry Harold the king. In William, Harold had met his master as a general; but the Anglo-Danish housecarles and thegns and the king who fought under the dragon standard were magnificent in defeat.

By dawn on 15 October Duke William knew that he had killed his rival together with his brothers, and that he had won such a victory that others would hesitate before taking up arms against him. He was content to wait and to refresh his mauled army. After five days' rest at Hastings, during which time reinforcements arrived from Normandy, William marched east and secured the Kentish ports. By the end of October he had reached Canterbury, and then fell sick. According to one authority William was immobilized for a month; other evidence points to a quick move on London. The attack was, however, repulsed; and the duke, after burning the transpontine suburbs, pushed upstream and then westward through Hampshire into Wiltshire, while his fleet lay conveniently at Chichester. Winchester, the seat of the treasury and the residence of Eadgyth, Edward's widow, submitted during this progress; but the respite allowed the English leaders full time to consider their next moves. Earls Edwine and Morkere had reached London shortly after the day of the battle, and among the notabilities who gathered there were the two archbishops and Edgar Aetheling. At a witenagemot held early in November, possibly influenced by news of William's serious illness, Edgar Aetheling was elected king by the magnates, the citizens of London, and the seamen; but the indecision of Edgar's supporters is revealed by their failure to proceed to a coronation. It is clear that those few who still could have raised an army to fight against the invader had no clear-cut opposition to William's cause and had no will to continue the struggle. William had a respectable claim to the throne, and he had shown that he wielded mighty power. The emergence of no effective opposition in the two months which followed the battle of Hastings meant that William had won the throne by means of a personal contest with his rival. He had no need to conquer England.

It was, perhaps, because William appreciated the political situation that he ventured to cross the Thames at Wallingford in Berkshire and march up the Icknield Way towards the Wash, far from a secure base. At Wallingford Archbishop Stigand made his submission. The foray to the north of London brought in the other leaders. At Little Berkhamstead appeared Edgar Aetheling, Earls Edwine of Mercia and Morkere of Northumbria, Ealdred archbishop of York, Wulfstan bishop of Worcester, Walter bishop of Hereford, and representatives of the city of London. They offered William the crown, and he accepted it after consultation with his advisers. William entered London; and on Christmas Day, 1066 he was crowned in Westminster Abbey by Ealdred, archbishop of York, in the traditional way.

Three months after his landing at Pevensey William was king of England. His rivals, Harold Godwinesson and Harold Hardrada, were dead; Edgar Aetheling was a pensioner at his court; the earls of Mercia and Northumbria were honoured guests in his train; the leaders of the church had given him their support; London, Winchester, and the south-eastern ports were under his control; his writ ran in shires which had not seen his troops. William claimed to

rule by hereditary right, as Edward's lawful successor; and by the
end of 1066, certainly by February 1067, when he left England for
an eight months' visit to Normandy, William's political authority
was as effective as had been Harold's in the year before. If the period
of conquest is considered as ending only in 1071, when the last of the
native insurrections had been suppressed, it must be remembered
that in those first five years William was acting as an English king,
dealing with problems similar to those which might have occupied
Harold had he survived. But William's struggle to keep his throne
and his successful breaking of all resistance transformed the power
of the English monarchy, and led to changes in the composition of
the nobility and of the higher clergy, in governmental method, and in
the arrangement of society. After William had reigned for twenty
years the result of the battle of Hastings had become not simply the
substitution of William for Harold as king, but the intrusion of the
Norman way of life into many spheres of activity. It is convenient,
therefore, to close the story of the Norman conquest of England in
1086, for in that year William surveyed his kingdom; and the
description of the land and of its inhabitants which was then made,
and which has survived in the form of Domesday Book and some
associated documents, witnesses both to the confident power which
the king had established and to the changes in the social order
which he and his barons and prelates had made.

III

William was both the lawful successor of King Edward and a
foreign conqueror ruling, at first precariously, by military power.
Many of his acts express a sense of lawful continuity. The immediate
disturbance in the kingdom was small. The spoils of those who had
been killed in the battle of Hastings and the proceeds of a geld were
for a time sufficient reward for the king and his followers. At the
coronation William had taken the traditional oath to hold just law;
soon he confirmed to London the laws it had enjoyed under King
Edward; and later he ordained for the whole kingdom, according to
an early-twelfth-century compilation, that all men should have and
hold the law of King Edward as to lands and all other things
together with those additions which he, William, had established for
the good of the English people. The use William made for some
years of the services of influential Englishmen also helped towards
a smooth transition from the old order to the new. The great nobles,

it is true, obtained only an ornamental position in the state. They were kept at court, and deprived of administrative power; and the king's suspicion is shown by his widespread demand for hostages. This policy was, perhaps, justified, for none of the magnates remained steadfastly true; but it is possible that the king's distrust likewise contributed to the result. The virtual suspension of the earls of Mercia and Northumbria made it necessary for the king to rely on their ecclesiastical counterparts; and in this trust William was not betrayed. Ealdred, archbishop of York, remained as viceroy in Northumbria; Aethelwig, abbot of Evesham, was appointed to a similar position in Mercia. In both provinces, however, William appointed earls for the marches. Englishmen had perforce to be employed in Northumberland; but Cheshire, which was excluded from Aethelwig's competence, Hereford, and Shrewsbury received Norman earls. In Mercia, William had also the support of Wulfstan, bishop of Worcester. Northumbria and even Mercia were later to give great trouble to the king; but the immediate trust William gave to their spiritual leaders delayed revolt and restrained it when it came. The use of these three prelates was dictated by governmental needs. The favour shown to the suspended archbishop of Canterbury either demonstrates how desperate the king was for native support or reveals William's gratitude for his early adherence to his cause, for the irregularity of Stigand's position had been denounced by William. Yet William not only kept Stigand as one of his advisers at court, he even allowed him to consecrate Remigius as bishop of Dorchester in 1067—a quite inexplicable vagary—and his fall did not take place until the country had been completely settled and a comprehensive reform of the English church undertaken.

The active support of these ecclesiastics for the new king and the outward loyalty of the leading nobles secured the adherence of the mass of the people. William called out English troops for his march on Exeter in 1068, and the fyrd co-operated in the suppression of many local uprisings. There can be no doubt that William's reign opened far more auspiciously than had the reign of Cnut. Yet the person of the conqueror could not be entirely disguised, although the building of castles was the only overt sign of military occupation during the early years.

Castle building was a deliberate policy of the king and of his lieutenants; but it should not be thought that it was controlled by a strategic master-plan. With few exceptions the royal castles were

erected in towns, with the purpose of dominating their dense populations and of providing secure administrative centres. The king's
castles were entrusted to castellans, often the sheriffs of the counties.
The foreign barons were encouraged to build private strongholds;
and by 1100 some five or six thousand castles had risen in England,
planted thickest in Herefordshire and Shropshire, and sited usually
in fertile valleys. This activity probably led to the evolution of the
motte and bailey castle out of the simple ring-work which was the
usual Norman type. A stockade and a tower (keep), both of wood,
surmounted the earthen mound (motte), which was formed by dig-
ging a surrounding ditch; and a base-court, or bailey, lay adjacent,
protected by ditch and rampart. The bailey could serve as quarters
for a garrison and as a shelter for other troops, and the keep as a
watch-tower and, perhaps, as the last defensive position. Such
castles, easily built, and as easily rendered useless before retreat,
provided a system of defence in depth for the whole country which
was to prove the salvation of the Normans in the years of turmoil.

Disorders and insurrections were frequent in England until 1071
but only in one phase did they even approach the dimensions and
unity of a national uprising. The south-east of England remained
quiet except for a revolt in Kent in 1067, when the rebels, although
aided by an invasion by Count Eustace of Boulogne, who had
quarrelled with the king, failed to capture Dover. Disturbance was
greater in the more remote parts of the kingdom, traditionally
anarchic, open to foreign intervention, and as yet unsettled by the
Normans. In Northumbria disorder was endemic and almost purely
domestic; but it was especially dangerous to William because it could
be incited or exploited by the Scottish and Danish kings as well as
by disaffected native leaders. The Welsh March was turbulent, and
the interference of Welsh princes allowed an English thegn, Eadric
the Wild, to wage private war on his enemies. Devon and Cornwall,
the extremity of Wessex, had given refuge to Harold's mother,
Gytha, and to his children by Eadgyth 'Swan-neck', Godwine,
Edmund, and Magnus; and, even when the sons had been expelled
and had lost their popularity, the danger of their invasions from
Scandinavian Ireland remained. Elsewhere revolt was local and
particular, provoked by specific oppression and by the dislike of the
population for individual barons and officials. Geld was collected
extortionately; but in the nature of things the king had no general
policy of such unpopularity as to cause a mass uprising against his

rule. There was no race hatred and no shameful exploitation of a conquered country. Some of the risings and rebellions seem to have been concerted—doubtless there were wide conspiracies and invitations to any possible ally—but the plans and even the aims of the leaders are impenetrably obscure. The main characters, Edgar Aetheling, earls Edwine, Morkere, Gospatric, and Waltheof, Svein Estrithson, Malcolm Canmore, Eadric the Wild, Hereward, and Harold's sons all seem aimless malcontents, selfish adventurers, or freebooters, such as were produced whenever the traditional bonds of medieval society were weakened for a moment. William and his barons were occasionally in grave danger; but the opposition can rarely be considered patriotic, was never organized, and was always devoid of a leader with a noble cause to plead.

William's regents, his half-brother, Odo of Bayeux, earl of Kent, and his cousin and steward, William fitzOsbern, earl of Hereford, had kept order during the king's absence in Normandy in 1067; but the situation was uneasy. On William's return in December he called for the submission of Exeter, which was still outside his immediate control. Exeter replied as York may have answered King Harold two years earlier: it would pay its accustomed tribute and perform its due services, but it would not swear fealty or receive the king within its walls. This was the voice of a semi-autonomous province, not the defiance of a rebel city; but, whereas Harold had used persuasion in Northumbria, William tried force in Devon. His wrath, however, found no victim. A march in winter to the west and an eighteen-day siege of Exeter led only to the city's surrender on favourable terms. A royal castle was built, but the customs were not increased. Harold's family escaped, his mother in the end to an honourable exile in Flanders, his sons to a life of piracy from the Irish ports. William subdued Cornwall by his presence, and then returned in order to welcome his wife Matilda on her first visit to England and to have her crowned as queen.

William's personal authority in Mercia and Northumbria had not yet been effectively asserted, and the independence of the Scottish March, the old Bernicia, from which the county and earldom of Northumberland were formed, caused him constant disquiet. In 1067 the king dispatched Copsi, one of Tostig's old associates, to dispossess Oswulf, a local magnate who was then in power; but both claimants were killed in 1068. The earldom was then bought from the king by Gospatric, another sometime companion of Tostig, who like Waltheof, Siward's son, earl of Huntingdon and of other shires, could trace descent from Earl Uhtred of King Aethelred's day, and who, therefore, inherited one of the longest and most famous blood feuds in the north. But in 1068 a series of conspiracies among the native English, in which Gospatric was involved, came to a head; and the north broke into general revolt. Edgar Aetheling was probably at the nominal head of the insurgents; earls Edwine, Morkere, and Gospatric, and the sheriff Merleswein were leading members; Malcolm, king of Scots, and Welsh princes were involved; and Harold's sons, probably quite independently, raided south-west England. The revolt seemed of formidable dimensions; but the archbishop of York discountenanced it; a royal campaign into Mercia secured the speedy surrender of Edwine and Morkere, who were restored to favour; and when William had reached York by way of Warwick and Nottingham, which he fortified in order to secure his return, even Malcolm was willing to swear fealty through ambassadors. Edgar Aetheling, however, together with his sisters and Gospatric and Merleswein, took refuge in Scotland.

The events of 1068 formed merely a prologue to the main action. Towards the end of the year the king appointed a Flemish adventurer, Robert of Comines, to replace Gospatric as earl, and in January 1069, Robert and his army were massacred in the city of Durham. The exiles at the court of King Malcolm came south and joined the citizens of York in an attack on the castle; and, although the king relieved the garrison, and threw up another fortress, the tide of insurrection was rising fast, and Viking marauders were approaching on both sides of the island in the hope of profiting from the expected chaos. In midsummer 1069 two of the sons of Harold once more ravaged Devon, but were eventually driven off. In autumn the fleet of a more dangerous invader appeared off the south-east coast. King Svein of Denmark had dispatched a force of some 240 ships under his brother Osbern, Estrith's son, who had lived in England during the early years of Edward the Confessor's reign; and with Osbern were at least two of Svein's sons, Harold and Cnut. The Danes followed the usual coastal route, and entered the Humber on 8 September after unsuccessful attacks on Dover, Sandwich, Ipswich, and Norwich. They were joined by the forces of Edgar Aetheling, Gospatric, and Waltheof; the local population was not hostile; and on 21 September the combined armies sacked York and took the castles while the old archbishop, Ealdred, died. Sympathetic risings in Staffordshire and Shropshire emboldened the outlaw Eadric the Wild with his Welsh allies and also men from Chester to attack Shrewsbury. Rebellion flared up also in Devon and Cornwall and in Dorset and Somerset. The Norman hold on the kingdom was tested as never before or again. The pressure was severe. But the desperate purpose of the Normans and their superior military organization gave them a clear advantage over an incoherent and aimless opposition. And this was fortunate for the country. The ravaging, to which William was driven in order to check his enemies, spared England the general anarchy which would have followed the destruction of the Norman power.

William undertook the repression of the northern rebellion. Elsewhere order was restored chiefly by the local garrisons and barons aided by the loyal elements of the fyrd. As the king rode north the Danes withdrew down the Humber and eventually encamped on the farther bank. After detaching some of his forces in order to contain them William turned against the Staffordshire rebels, and defeated them. On his way back to meet the Danes he learned that they had re-entered York, so he advanced from Nottingham on the northern capital, and by laying waste the surrounding areas drove the invader out. Devastation and depopulation were the traditional methods chosen by the king to deny the countryside to the Danes and to punish a rebellious people. After Christmas William extended his ravaging up to Durham and as far as the Tees. There Gospatric and Waltheof submitted. Both were restored to their earldoms, and Waltheof was promised William's niece, Judith, for wife. The king could still show mercy as well as terror to his enemies. In January 1070 William struggled back to York; and then, pushing his troops almost beyond the limits of endurance, crossed the Peakland to Chester, and ravaged Cheshire and Shropshire in their turn. From Chester, where he built a castle, he came again to Stafford; and either now or earlier on his northward progress Staffordshire and Derbyshire were harried by the stern commander. When William finally left Mercia in order to review his troops at Salisbury the revolt had been extinguished and the invasion had been checked. The devastation of Northumbria and Mercia made it certain that the Danes would confine their activities to the coast. William had won a terrible and costly victory.

The king paraded his army at Salisbury in the spring of 1070 and paid off most of his mercenaries. In May, King Svein himself took

over command of his fleet; but he, too, came to realise that his forces
were inadequate alike to make permanent conquests and to dispute
the throne with William. The collection of booty had become the
one profitable aim. The Vikings left the Humber for Ely, and,
joining up with an English outlaw, the thegn Hereward, plundered
the abbey of Peterborough. In June the Danish fleet entered the
Thames, and then finally set sail for home. Its spoils were great, but
its political achievement had been small. Order was fast returning to
the English kingdom. Eadric the Wild submitted to the king and
was pardoned. Only in the Fens, where Hereward and his companions remained in possession of Ely Abbey, was the country
unsubdued, and a refuge still open for English malcontents. In
April 1071 earls Edwine and Morkere, who had taken no active part
in the great uprising, fled once more from court. Edwine made for
Scotland, and was killed on the way, apparently by his men. Morkere
joined Hereward on the island of Ely. The king decided to suppress
this last centre of disaffection. A short campaign based on Cambridge
cleaned up the Fens. Morkere surrendered, and was kept prisoner in
Normandy. Hereward escaped; and his future actions belong to
folklore rather than to history.

IV

The unsuccessful revolts of 1067–71 completed the ruin of the
English thegnhood. At the battle of Gate Fulford Northumbrian and
Mercian thegns had been slaughtered; at Hastings it was the turn of
the thegns of Wessex and of the east. No doubt many of the dead left
heirs or heiresses, and, although the lands of those who fell in the
battle of Hastings were forfeited, unimportant 'traitors' could usually
redeem their lands by making suitable gifts to the avaricious king.
The uprisings, however, led to forfeitures on a wide scale and to new
grants to Norman lords. By 1086 only two Englishmen, Thurkill of
Arden and Colswein of Lincoln, still held large estates directly of the
king. Smaller native tenants, especially north of the Humber, where
the Norman colonization was always thin, remained quite common;
but the southern thegnage had as a body been submerged or displaced by the foreigner. Reduction in status and curtailment of
holding must have been the fate of most of the thegnly class. Many,
however, were entirely dispossessed. Some became outlaws, like the
famous Eadric the Wild and Hereward; some settled in Lothian;
some scattered widely over Europe—one group possibly finding

asylum in Denmark, another joining the Varangian regiment of the Eastern Empire. The Anglo-Scandinavian nobility had disappeared. The fate of the native earls illustrates this well. By 1070 only two English earls still held office, Waltheof and Gospatric, and of these only the former was an Edwardian creation. The earl of East Anglia, Ralf de Gael, can also, perhaps, be added to this group, for there was English blood in the family. His Breton father had served Edward the Confessor as 'staller', and had been made earl by William in the first years of his reign. None of the three, however, was to last much longer. Gospatric was deprived of the earldom of Northumberland in 1072 and replaced by Waltheof; and in 1075 Waltheof and Ralf were involved in the rebellion of Roger, earl of Hereford, Ralf escaping to Brittany and suffering disinheritance, Waltheof being executed as a traitor. William allowed the great Anglo-Scandinavian earldoms to expire with the families that had held them. His new creations were strategically placed for the defence of the kingdom. In 1066–7 Odo of Bayeux was given Kent and William fitzOsbern Hereford. In 1070–1, after the suppression of the great rebellion, Chester was granted to Hugh d'Avranches and Shrewsbury to Roger of Montgomery. Earl William also held the Isle of Wight and Earl Roger Sussex. Foreigners were appointed to the earldom of Northumberland after 1075. Hence all the south-eastern ports were in trusted hands and the Welsh and Scottish marches were guarded.

The ruin of the Anglo-Scandinavian nobility was followed by the purging of the Edwardian episcopate. William had secured papal support for his claim to the throne by promising to reform the English church; and in the spring of 1070 three legates of Pope Alexander II arrived in England to start the work. The moment was well chosen. The country had been brought under control, and Ealdred, archbishop of York, was dead. The legates had orders to depose Stigand and all bishops consecrated by him; but this simple principle hardly met the king's requirements, for a Norman monk, Remigius, had been consecrated bishop of Dorchester by Stigand, and most of the English bishops had satisfactory orders. The legates were complaisant; and at the councils of Winchester (Easter 1070) and Windsor (Whitsun) Stigand of Canterbury, Aethelric II of Selsey, Leofwine of Lichfield, Aethelmaer of Elmham, and Aethelwine of Durham were deposed on various grounds, not all of which are clear. To the vacancies in the two archbishoprics and five bishoprics the king appointed four clerks from the royal chapel, one

Norman and one Lotharingian clerk, and one monk, Lanfranc, abbot
of Caen. As a result of these changes only three English-born bishops
remained—Leofric of Exeter, a clerk of foreign education, Wulfstan
of Worcester, and Siweard of Rochester, an old man who died in
1075; and no Englishman was raised to the episcopate for several
generations thereafter. The monasteries were treated less severely.
Few English abbots were deposed; but as they died they were
replaced by Norman monks. By the end of William's reign only
unimportant houses still had English rulers.

The widespread substitution of foreigners, especially of Normans,
for natives in important church positions was doubtless inspired
largely by political ends, although coloured by reforming zeal. Some
of the new appointments were excellent, and none was scandalous,
except, perhaps, that of Turold to Peterborough Abbey; but the
large proportion of chancery clerks who obtained the mitre proves
that possession of the right loyalties and of the accepted culture was
William's first requirement of a bishop. The king cannot be blamed
for this. Whatever may have been his original intentions or his early
expedients, he had been driven by the events of 1066–71 to fashion a
Norman state in his English kingdom.

By 1070 the building of a new order in church and state had
begun; and the progress was not interrupted during William's lifetime by any serious misfortune. Some external dangers to his rule in
England remained, principally from Scotland and Denmark. Wales
held no threat. The Welsh March attracted the boldest Norman
settlers, and these consolidated and extended Harold's territorial
gains, especially in the north. As the earldom of Hereford lapsed in
1075, William intervened in South Wales in 1081, when he penetrated to St. Davids and built Cardiff castle; but generally he was
content to leave Welsh affairs to his earls and barons. Scotland,
however, required continual care. In 1070 King Malcolm III
(Canmore) ravaged as far south as Cleveland, while Gospatric, earl
of Northumberland, instead of meeting the foe, retaliated by laying
Cumbria waste. When Malcolm withdrew from England with his
booty and his slaves he took with him also Edgar Aetheling and his
sister Margaret, whom he married about this time. William could not
deal with Malcolm until the campaigning season of 1072. He then,
supported by a fleet on his eastern flank, penetrated the northern
kingdom up to Abernethy on the River Tay; and Malcolm submitted, did homage to William, gave as hostage his son, Duncan, by

an earlier marriage, and apparently agreed to expel his brother-in-law, for Edgar soon after left for Flanders. The Yorkshire knights still bragged about this victory in 1138; but the north had not been tamed. In 1079 Walcher, the Lotharingian bishop of Durham, whom the king had made earl of Northumberland three years before, could not prevent a foray by Malcolm down to the Tyne; and in the next year the episcopal earl, caught up in a local feud, was murdered at Gateshead. The king had to intervene once more. He sent his half-brother, Bishop Odo of Bayeux, to chastise the disturbed province, and later in the year his eldest son, Robert, to punish the king of Scots. Robert built Newcastle as a defensive fortress on the way back. Cumbria had been lost; Northumberland had become a march; and the frontier had in effect receded to the Tyne.

The danger of a Scandinavian invasion was William's greatest fear; and the hostility of Flanders since 1071 added to the peril. Svein Estrithson, king of Denmark, died in 1074. He had been much concerned with English affairs since he received his difficult inherit-ance in 1042; yet he had achieved little outside his own country. He was succeeded by five sons in turn; and it was the second of these, Cnut II, king in 1080, who inherited his father's ambition to reunite Denmark and England. Cnut, who had sailed with the Viking fleet in 1069–70, intervened again in an English rebellion, this time when Roger, earl of Hereford, the son of the first Norman earl, and Ralf de Gael, earl of East Anglia, with the complicity of earl Waltheof, revolted against King William in 1075–6. But his fleet of some 200 ships arrived in the Humber too late to save the earls; and he with-drew to Flanders after pillaging York minster. When Cnut succeeded his brother Harold III as king he began to build up a great naval coalition against England. King Olaf III of Norway, Harold Hardrada's son, and Robert 'le Frison', count of Flanders, Cnut's father-in-law, promised aid. The Danish ships were gathered in Lim Fiord for the invasion; but domestic disputes and mutinies held Cnut back; and in July 1086 Cnut was assassinated in the church of Odense on Fyen Island. The expedition never sailed. Scandinavian anarchy had saved England yet again; and the northern calendar had gained another dubious saint.

William, however, had been much alarmed by the threatened invasion. In 1085 he recruited a very large force of cavalry and foot in Brittany, Maine, and France, which he quartered on his English barons; and, as in 1070–1, he devastated the eastern coastal areas of

England. At the Christmas court he ordered a survey of his kingdom to be made, the results of which were recorded in the two volumes of Domesday Book. On 1 August 1086 he held a court at Salisbury and received homage and fealty from all his barons and from their most important followers. Cnut was dead before this extraordinary security measure was taken; and later in the year William left again for Normandy, never to return.

Domesday Book—and the name proves it—has always been regarded with awe. Its minute description of the country and of its inhabitants received only grudging admiration at the time, but has fascinated all generations since. It was, of course, the bible of the treasury; and a bible that has been searched unceasingly both in the way of business and for general historical information. As an historical document it is of unique importance, since careful and imaginative analysis of its data allows us to acquire an exacter knowledge of society in the late Old-English and early Norman periods than can be formed of any preceding era and of many succeeding ages.

The immediate occasion of the survey was probably the confusion which attended the quartering of mercenaries on the baronial demesne in 1085, and the king's sudden realization at this moment of peril that he did not know the full resources of his kingdom and the exact economic and territorial position of his barons. Domesday Book records for England the possessions of all the major landowners within each shire, and, taking the manor as the basic economic unit, lists for each its name, its holder in King Edward's day and at the present time, its assessment to geld, its extent, resources, capital equipment, men and, sometimes, stock, its value before 1066, at the time of grant, and at the present day, and, finally, some opinion on its true exploitable capacity or value. From these statistics the king could obtain a clear view of the value of the royal estates and of the holdings of the individual barons. He had also a book of hides, a list of rateable values—useless, indeed, owing to the form in which the information was presented, for reassessing the incidence of geld, but convenient in its definitive record of the liability of each estate. It will be seen that the inquest was not altogether a measure taken in panic, and that it was planned on lines more comprehensive than the needs of the moment required.

The judicial aspect of the inquiry shows very well how both long and short term policies converged to produce an authoritative written record of the many facts which interested the government. The replacement of the native aristocracy by foreigners—although the legal fiction had in every case been maintained that the newcomer was the heir to his predecessor, and so inherited exactly the same position—together with the high-handed and surreptitious encroachments inevitable at a time of dispossession and disorder, had naturally caused instability of title. Disputed claims to land and to superiorities over land, some older than the Conquest, some created by it, were many; and the churches, always the victims of spoliation in anarchic times, especially were involved in a maze of puzzling litigation. In 1085 William decided to settle the results of the revolution in landownership once and for all. Hence the Domesday inquest can also be regarded as a judicial eyre. The royal commissioners settled many cases, and recorded others for future decision.

The machinery used for making this description in 1086 was of mixed parentage. The inquest itself with its use of the sworn testimony of local inhabitants—the jury—is generally considered a Norman device; but the information was returned for the shires—although many individual estates were scattered widely over the country—and the hundred courts were used to verify the statistics. The general form of the returns to the inquiry is, however, feudal. We have chosen to close the history of the Norman conquest with the compilation of Domesday Book because it is the best record of the success of that conquest. Its conception and its execution reveal the immense power and drive of the king. Shire by shire the survey records the estates of the king and of his tenants-in-chief; and we see that the Normans have inherited the land. And in their inheritance they have silently transformed the law. Domesday Book is a book of fees, a feodary. All land is within or appurtenant to a manor; from the manors are formed fiefs, baronies, and honours; and the greatest honour of all is the honour of England, the kingdom conquered and owned by William the Bastard.

4

THE ANGLO-NORMAN KINGDOM

I

THE Anglo-Norman state which was formed gradually after 1066 was unlike both the Anglo-Danish kingdom of Edward the Confessor and the Norman duchy of William II. Nor can it be regarded as merely an amalgam of English, Danish, and Norman elements. The mixture suffered a chemical change; and the result was new and unique. It is not, therefore, always easy to determine the precise filiation of the post-Conquest institutions in England. Norman, Breton, Flemish, 'French', English, and Danish forms, often similar in purpose and little different in appearance, were brought together; and, even when one of them can be seen in the end to have dominated the others, it had often by that time itself been modified by the silent pressure of another custom. The problem of isolating the individual contributions is, moreover, made more difficult by the obscurity of Norman in comparison with English history. It is all too easy when an administrative practice seems to have had no exact Anglo-Danish antecedent to conclude that there must have been a Norman prototype.

The superficial disparities between England and Normandy in 1066 disguise a basic similarity of condition. Normandy was, of course, smaller and only a duchy, and a state with a relatively short history. It had, moreover, been assimilated into the political framework of Gaul, and into the cultural life of Latin Christendom, so that the Normans called themselves 'French' in England. These were important differences. But Normandy and England were geographically alike. The landscape of Normandy and Brittany repeats that of England and its Celtic west; and similar economic conditions generally produce similar social structures. The same Scandinavian conquests formed both the English Danelaw and Normandy, and both sets of colonists intermingled with natives of a common racial mixture. Although attempts have been made to contrast the peaceful peasant conservatism of the English Danelaw with the restless aristocratic adaptability of Normandy, the antithesis seems forced. The pattern of settlement appears to have been similar on both sides of the water; both colonies were equally accommodating in some directions and stubborn in others; but whereas in England the cultural and linguistic differences between Anglo-Saxon and Dane were slight, and modification consequently less noticeable, in Normandy it was necessary to adopt a Romance tongue.

The latinization of Normandy was to have important effects in England; yet the linguistic assimilation had been completed only by 1028; and the preponderant Scandinavian character of Normandy must always be borne in mind. The colonization itself was spread over several generations; and even under Duke William II a contrast can be seen between the more anciently occupied territory, that in east Normandy, secured by the treaty of St. Clair-sur-Epte in 911, and the western portions conquered and ceded before the pact of Gisors negotiated by Duke Richard I and King Lothair in 965. Thus the migratory period came to an end only a century before the Norman conquest of England, and the newer, and probably thicker, settlements in the west were more resistant to Latin culture than was the area surrounding Rouen. But even after the county, or duchy, had been stabilized within its historic boundaries and accepted as an integral part of Gaul the attitude of the Norman dukes remained equivocal. In 996 Richer of Rheims referred to the Norman duke as 'king of the pirates', and in 1013–14, while King Aethelred and his family were taking refuge from Svein and Cnut at Richard II's court, the duke harboured the pagan forces of Olaf Haroldsson, the future saint, which had been ravaging between the Baltic and Spain for the last ten years. Yet this tenacious holding to a traditional and individual way of life was matched by the same lack of political ambition that has been observed in England. In 911 Rollo accepted the overlordship of Charles the Simple, king of the Franks; and it is now agreed that he did homage as a vassal and took back his conquests as a fief. The suzerainty was transferred from the Carolingian to the Capetian dynasty without trouble—indeed, Norman support contributed greatly to the success of Hugh Capet; Dukes Robert I and Richard II accepted their subordinate position without ambiguity;

and it was only through the efforts of his Capetian overlord that William the Bastard was able to maintain his hold on the rebellious duchy. Nevertheless, the Norman dukes exercised all the royal rights in the fief—coining deniers with the ducal name thereon, enjoying an unlimited jurisdiction, and controlling the bishoprics—and the willingness of the dukes to perform services to their overlords varied according to their relative strengths. For the relations between a lord and a vassal depended ultimately on the power that each disposed; and the authority which Duke William II acquired in the years after Val-ès-Dunes and during the minority of King Philip I gave him a practical independence which none of his ancestors had enjoyed.

The gradual adoption of the French language and of Christianity by the Normans was due in part to convenience, in part to the respect paid to a superior civilization. Rollo accepted baptism in 911, just as Guthrum had in 878; but Rollo probably renounced his new faith before he died, and a heathen reaction followed the assassination of Duke William I in 942. Organized religion had collapsed in Normandy under the impact of the Scandinavian invasions in the same way as it had in eastern England. The diocesan system had disintegrated; there was a gap in the succession of bishops; monasticism had disappeared; and the sacred edifices had been destroyed. The re-establishment of the church in Normandy was, however, encouraged by Duke Richard I (942–96) after he had asserted his authority. As in England the foundation of monasteries was the precursor of more general reform, and the impetus came from the same areas, Flanders and Cluny, although in Normandy Cluniac influence was the later and the more important. In 1000 there were but four abbeys in Normandy. By the middle of the century the nobles had begun to imitate the duke; and in 1066 the number of foundations had risen to at least twenty great abbeys and six nunneries. Duke Richard I's refoundation of the monastery of St. Wandrille in 961 with monks from Ghent is as early as the beginning of the monastic renaissance in England. But the movement was slower to gather momentum in Normandy, and the entry of William of Dijon with Cluniac monks into Fécamp in 1001 marks more truly the opening of the decisive period. Thus Norman monasticism was at least a generation newer than its English counterpart, and to this factor is due in some degree its greater piety and zeal at the time of the Conquest. Besides a difference in tone between the two churches there was also a difference in culture. However cosmopolitan the

English church may appear under Edward the Confessor the traditional mode of life was strong enough to modify all foreign influence. But the Norman church was in culture part of the Neustrian church and parcel of Latin Christendom. In 1066 seven great Norman monasteries were ruled by foreigners—three Germans, one from Gaul, and three Italians.

Two of the ultramontanes were not only important in the ecclesiastical life of Normandy but were to play great parts in English history, Lanfranc of Pavia and Anselm of Aosta. Lanfranc, the son of a 'lawman' at Pavia, rejected as a young man the family career of expounding Lombardic custom, and travelled to Gaul in search of humaner learning. A second renunciation, this time after he had become a successful teacher at Avranches, led to his entering the new monastery of le Bec Hellouin, on a tributary of the River Risle; yet, because of the poverty of the house, the monk soon began to teach again. The renown of Lanfranc's pupils proclaims the distinction of his teaching, and his reputation as the father of monks testifies to the sincerity of his conversion. The traditional medieval curriculum, the *trivium* and *quadrivium*, had been quickened through the rediscovery of that corpus of the works of Boethius—later known as the *Logica vetus*—which made available for the eleventh century the ideas of Greek philosophers, including Aristotle. Novel logical categories, such as substance and accidents and genera and species, served to stimulate many branches of learning; and when the old theology was expressed in the new terms orthodoxy had to be defined afresh. Lanfranc excelled as a dialectician, that is to say as a teacher of the art of argument. His protracted and eventually successful controversy over the doctrine of the Eucharist with that even more distinguished teacher, Berengar of Tours, stimulated a theological interest in Normandy and prepared the way for a general European advance on Carolingian standards. But Lanfranc was essentially of the old world—the theocratic order, the undivided universe ruled by the God-king and the king-god, the divinely appointed nobles, and the princely bishops and abbots. It is typical that Duke William II should have employed him sometimes as an adviser and confidential agent in Normandy. And when Lanfranc, as an old man, left his abbacy of Caen to become archbishop of Canterbury he stamped his own and his master's pattern on the English church.

Anselm, born at Aosta, and related through his mother to the counts of Maurienne, had as a young man travelled even more widely than Lanfranc in search of learning. In 1060 he too became a monk at le Bec; and he succeeded Lanfranc as prior of that house in 1063, and became abbot in 1078. Anselm's cheerful piety, his perspicuous goodness, and his lovable nature impressed all who encountered him; and his fame as a teacher confirmed le Bec's position as the leading school of orthodoxy in the West. A deep study of the Christian fathers, a suspicion that the old cosmic theories were being questioned, and the inheritance of a dialectic sharpened by his master Lanfranc and of a grammar refined by Berengar of Tours enabled Anselm to expound the traditional theology persuasively to an audience composed mainly of simple monks. His work was a great memorial to a world that was almost dead. For at this time the improvement in technique among scholars was so rapid that within two generations the great achievements of the mid-eleventh-century masters were already derided as fumbling efforts. Anselm was in a way the last of the Fathers. The gulf between him and the twelfth-century masters of the Paris schools, of whom Abailard was the great precursor, is profound.

The importance of Lanfranc and the brilliance of Anselm are unquestionable. But the achievements of a Lombard and of a Burgundian have, perhaps, thrown an undeserved lustre over the intellectual life of Normandy in 1066. The Normans themselves were not a particularly artistic or speculative race; and the Norman bishops and abbots of England were in general no more distinguished for theological interest than were their Anglo-Saxon predecessors. They had merely been educated in a different school.

Whereas in England king and bishops had been the instigators of monastic reform, in Normandy the secular church had been indifferent or hostile to the ducal policy, and so came more slowly under reformative influence. The Norman bishops had usually been scions of the ducal and baronial houses, and even in 1066 three of the seven Norman bishops were related to the duke. But William had gradually broken with tradition and appointed foreigners, monks, and clerks of his chapel. Yet this reform of the Norman episcopacy was very new in 1066: it was, for instance, only eleven years since Rouen had received its first archbishop of the new type, the monk Maurilius of Fécamp, later reputed a saint.

The Norman church had been created under the inspiration of the dukes, and was firmly under their control. The bishops and the abbots of ducal houses and of those under ducal protection were appointed and invested in the court of the duke. There was a separate law for the church; but the duke was the judge of its competence. Church councils occasionally legislated; but the duke sanctioned and approved. The church had wide estates; but the duke treated them almost as ducal demesne. And by putting himself between the Norman church and the papacy and insisting that all traffic should pass through him, the duke kept the leadership in his own hands. There was no opposition in Normandy to this state of affairs. The strife between church and state which was developing in the Empire aroused no echo in the duchy. An aristocratic episcopacy and a monastic organization under ducal patronage and informed by Cluniac ideals were slow to be moved by the new stridency in papal circles.

The territorial aristocracy of Normandy was no more ancient than the Norman church. Few of the families notable in 1066, and even more famous after they had acquired English lands, could trace their pedigree beyond the times of Duke Richard II, and many were the creations of William II. Often related to the dukes or their consorts, they had been endowed from the ducal estates or from old church lands. The highest title employed in Normandy—that of count, equivalent to the English earl—had not been assumed by any noble except the ruler before the eleventh century; and even on the eve of the conquest of England its use was confined to members of the ducal family, and had not become strictly hereditary. A class of ministerial nobility, such as the English thegnhood, had not yet emerged. Normandy was thoroughly feudal. Land tenure was securely based on the fief, and all secular and many ecclesiastical offices were tending to become fiefs. The barons enjoyed extensive jurisdictional rights—although, as in England, most of them were franchisal—and they had enfeoffed many knights on their estates. Norman feudalism was mature by eleventh-century continental standards, but it was primitive compared with twelfth-century English conditions. Only rudimentary traces of all those obligations, such as relief, wardship, marriage, and suit of court, which later became so important a feature of Anglo-Norman feudalism, have as yet been discovered in Normandy before 1066.

The power of the duke over his nobles depended largely on force. There had developed in Normandy little of that tradition of an organic state ruled by law under a divinely appointed king which was so pervasive in England. The dukes had for the most part been strong; and William II, after he had survived twelve years of anarchy and crushed four revolts between 1047 and 1053, had exceptional power. He had been able, therefore, to carry further his father's policy of giving more precision to the military aspect of feudalism and of organizing it in the ducal interest. The older territorial families had not been conscious that their endowments were conditional grants, or that they were held in return for specific service to the duke. The greater men had maintained warriors and enfeoffed knights merely in order to use them in their private wars. But Dukes Robert I and William II, taking advantage of successions and forfeitures, had gradually clamped on the fiefs of their vassals the duty of providing a fixed quota of knights for the ducal army—a larger unit when the duke fought for himself and a lesser when he aided his overlord—and claimed the right in an emergency to call out all men who could bear arms, a custom which was known later as *retrobannus* or *arrière-ban*. The bishop of Bayeux, for example, is believed to have had the service of some 120 knights for his own purposes; and he owed the duke 20 knights for the ducal and 10 for the royal army. The later dukes had also put restrictions on private war and controlled the freedom of the barons to build castles. Yet it was not until the Norman dukes had become English kings that real order was sporadically enforced in the duchy.

The governmental machinery in such a state was naturally simple. Duke William II made much progress in organizing his duchy as a centralized entity distinct from the rest of Gaul, especially through his position as head of the Norman church; but the dukes had developed few organs of institutional rule. The ducal court (*curia ducis*), composed mainly of kinsmen and personal friends—for there was no class of thegns, and few bishops habitually attended—was even more domestic than the private household of an English king. The most important officials were the duke's seneschal or steward (*dapifer*), his butler, and his chamberlain. The constables and marshals were as yet very minor servants. On occasion the duke appointed delegates—often bishops—to hear judicial cases; but the duke had no proper chancery and no seal, and consequently could issue neither writs nor charters: his diplomas were usually drawn up by the beneficiary and were authenticated by holograph crosses. The duke's financial administration was in advance of that of his Frankish contemporaries, but was simple compared with the English. He employed *vicomtes*—deputies, it must be remembered, of the count of Rouen, the duke of Normandy—and *prévôts* (reeves) to collect his revenue; and these servants paid their farm into the duke's chamber (*camera*), where the chamberlain guarded the coffers. The English sheriffs were renamed *vicomtes* by the Normans, for the two offices were basically similar in function; but it should be noticed that the Norman *vicomtes* were often members of the great baronial families and that the office had in many cases been turned into a fief. No body like the larger meetings of the *witan* existed in Normandy. Occasionally, as before the invasion of England, the Norman duke deliberated with his barons in a *magnum concilium*, a great council; but this expedient was rare and devoid of English ceremonial and tradition. The duke was unaccustomed to legislate, except in church councils; and Norman law, French in origin, but developing as a provincial custom, had not been committed to writing even in the shape of ducal dooms. And, although the Norman dukes had inherited from the Frankish kings a tradition of the use of the Carolingian *missi dominici* and of the sworn investigation, which, as English kings, they were to refashion as the eyres and jury, it cannot be gainsaid that, compared institutionally with England in 1066, Normandy was a very primitive state. Its only excellencies consisted in a partly reformed church with its Latin culture, in a hard-headed, ruthless, talented, and usually adaptable aristocracy, and in its form of society, which, being organized for war, made the duchy especially well fitted to conquer and to hold, and which, as it contained within itself seeds of a discipline that germinated during the period of the military occupation of England, proved capable of engendering a new and fruitful system of government.

II

The main effects in England of the Norman conquest were such as might almost be deduced from a study of the earlier history of each country. The general economic and social organization of England and the massive governmental imprint imposed on it by generations of kings and their bishops and earls passed through the conquest little changed. The Normans introduced no new method of agriculture and probably no new system of estate management. The laws of the people were not much altered, and for many purposes the foreign settler became subject to the indigenous customs. The framework of shire and hundred or wapentake and the ancient ecclesiastical dioceses endured. William as king was the successor of

Edward and remitted none of the traditional powers of the English monarchy; but if he could add to them, either from Norman practice or from the advantage which a military conquest and a new beginning gave, he did so. The English chancery with its writ and seal, the English treasury and the Danegeld, and, possibly for a time, the English witenagemot, were accepted by the Normans; and they were driven harder than ever before. Wider changes and novelties sprang from the creation of a foreign aristocracy both lay and clerical. The new baronage organized itself in a pattern which owed more to Normandy than to England but which was peculiar to the Anglo-Norman state; and the new bishops and abbots, under the spur of the king and the guidance of the primate, transformed the English church. But even more important than the changes effected in the first generation of Norman rule were the unrealized potentialities of the situation. King, baronage, and church had each increased its strength; and, provided that anarchy could be avoided, such a conjuncture was bound to lead to a rapid growth in institutions and to the evolution of a new polity. And perhaps most important of all was the opening of England to recurrent and accumulative streams of Frankish influence. Had the Norman dynasty lasted, the earliest wave of French settlers might have been assimilated in time, in the same way as the Scandinavian aristocracy introduced by Cnut had been absorbed, without its radically affecting the broad lines of indigenous development. But after William's grandson, William the Aetheling, Henry I's son, had lost his life in the wreck of the *White Ship*, the English crown passed to a count of Boulogne, a member of the house of Blois, and then to a count of Anjou; and with the sons and descendants of Henry II the influence of Aquitaine on England became profound. Hence much of the importance of the Norman conquest of England is germinal. And the land which nourished the alien seed, the new strains which were later introduced, and the cross-fertilization from many sources which followed, must all be taken into account when the development of England in the years after 1066 is brought under review.

William I was more than a Norman duke and more than an Old-English king. He took the prerogatives of each, and made himself more powerful than either. His two sons, who reigned in turn after him, were not a whit less strong. William inherited the royal demesne swollen by the estates of the earldoms he destroyed, increased the area of forest, and hunted as indefatigably as his saintly predecessor.

He wore his crown in court on the great festivals; he issued under the great seal writs in English and, occasionally, in Latin—for French did not become an official language in the Norman period; he collected the old tax, the Danegeld, often and extortionately, except from the manorial demesne (in its narrowest sense) of himself and of his tenants-in-chief, and he provided for the treasury in Domesday Book a new and detailed record of its incidence; he made few changes in the law, and his sons less, but enough to show that the will of the king was superior to custom. Norman priests gradually took their place in the chapel and chancery; but Edward's *scriptorium* had been staffed largely by foreigners, and the essential character of that institution was not changed by an alteration in title. Nor was the treasury as an office of receipt and storage affected by the Conquest. The Anglo-Saxon methods of counting, weighing, and assaying the silver pennies remained; and the money was still kept at Winchester. Most of the English sheriffs had been replaced by Normans before 1071, and, as the office of *vicomte* was not unlike that of the shire-reeve, the foreign title gained ground. But, although the dignity of the office was enhanced through its grant to substantial tenants-in-chief, who often were also royal castellans, the shrievalty remained unaltered in essentials; and, although the dangers of independence and feudalization arose, few shrievalties did in fact become hereditary, and generally a more powerful monarchy was able to control its more powerful servants.

Not all the foreigners who settled in England after 1066 owed their land to the express grant of the king. Some married English widows or heiresses; some bought or inherited estates. Nor does there seem to have been for the natives a general surrender and regrant of land. But the principle was soon asserted, and affected native and foreigner alike, that all land belonged to the king, and that every other tenant held a benefice immediately or mediately of him. This thorough feudalization of England increased the actual and the potential power of the monarchy. All absolute freeholds, even ecclesiastical alods, disappeared. Every holder of land was a link in a chain which led ultimately to the king; and the links were forged as firmly as medieval man could contrive. William also made sure that the groupings under the great vassals should not develop into the most vital units in the state. At Salisbury in 1086 he made all the important rear-vassals do homage to him. The Anglo-Saxon chronicler, the authority for the event, describes the participants as

...ne landowners of any account all over England, whosesoever
...n (vassals) they might be'; and, even if these words are interpreted in the narrowest sense possible, the ceremony is still of great
importance for English history. The kings of the Franks had long
since lost the power to take a general oath of allegiance from their
subjects. In their truly feudal kingdom a rear-vassal owed no duty
except to his immediate lord or lords. No vassal of the duke of
Normandy when doing homage to the duke reserved his fealty to
the king of the Franks. And so it was all down the feudal ladder.
Nor are there any clear English precedents for William's action since
Edmund's reign (939–946). It is possible, therefore, that William
innovated; and by so doing he started the divergence of English
from Frankish feudalism. For the practice of taking general oaths of
allegiance was repeated by William's sons, and it was reinforced and
made a principle of law by King Henry II. The *leges Henrici*, an
unofficial law-book dating from 1114–8, states that each vassal owes
his lord fealty, saving that which he owes to God and to the prince
of the land. And 'Glanville' in Henry II's reign and Bracton in
Henry III's repeat the principle. In this way the king, and his
lawyers, maintained the thesis that every man in the kingdom owed
his main loyalty to the king and not to his immediate lord. Such an
idea, of course, ran counter to normal feelings, and was more an
expression of royal policy than of the common attitude. It cannot,
indeed, be proved to have had any independent influence on the
behaviour of English feudal tenants before the thirteenth century. But
the assertion of the principle and its reiteration until it began to have
effect was one of the forces which moulded the kingdom of England.

The complete feudalization of England also unified and simplified
the land law. All free holdings were assimilated to the fief; and so
ubiquitous were fiefs in England that they soon ceased to be differen-
tiated by name. The great fiefs that William I created for his more
important vassals out of the confiscated estates of the 'traitor' thegns
were all held by military service; and all the bishops and most of the
abbots were likewise given military duties. But not even gifts to God
himself—grants in free, pure, and perpetual alms—were alodial in
England. When the grantor acquitted the ecclesiastical recipient
from all rent and service due to him (intrinsec service)—and this was
rare—and when the land was also made free of service due to the
superior lords of the grantor (forinsec service)—which was rarer—
and when even a symbolical render, such as a rose, was not required,

/

there remained the characteristic duty of prayer and intercession for the soul of the benefactor, which brought the tenure of free-alms, or frankalmoin, into line with the fief. The tenure of all those domestic servants, such as cooks, bakers, ushers, and porters, of those hunting servants, and of many of those non-chivalrous dependants who had been granted fiefs as a reward for their professional services was termed serjeanty; and all the Norman kings continued to grant new serjeanties despite the growing disadvantages of the method. Knight-service, frankalmoin, and serjeanty were the three distinct tenures introduced by the Normans; but so pervasive were feudal ideas that all the free native tenures which survived the disaster were brought within the new system; and, since they had in common the render of money and non-servile labour dues in return for the tenement, they were classified as 'free-socage' by the twelfth-century lawyers. The universality of the fief helped to unify the kingdom. In the twelfth century the distinction between the free man and the servile peasant, between the free holding and the precarious holding in villeinage, began to become sharper than elsewhere in Europe; but above that line no deep barrier arose between different types of free tenure.

The logic and symmetry of Anglo-Norman feudalism were due to its imposition on a conquered country by a strong king. William I made sure that the power of the monarchy was unassailable. From each of his more important vassals he required the service of a number of knights for duty in the royal castles and army. This *servitium debitum* may possibly have been defined by William when he first granted a fief; but it is more likely that the various feudal services due from the honours were settled gradually and, indeed, were often modified; and always there was the tendency for the liability to decrease. The military assessment seems to have been heavier in England than in Normandy, but it was probably from the beginning lighter than the Old-English requirement of one man from each five hides of land. As the pre-Conquest military obligation is several times described in Domesday Book it also probably remained in force. It is not easy, however, to relate the Old-English and Anglo-Norman liabilities to the field armies described by the chroniclers. These were made up of cavalry and infantry, and included barons, thegns, knights, mercenaries, and auxiliaries. Always there were several nationalities, and wherever William fought after 1066 he seems to have had some English troops with him. He and his barons exploited every right and called up the type and number of troops that were suitable for the occasion. In times of danger, William and his sons called out a general levy of troops. To English writers this was the fyrd; and that William II should threaten defaulters with the Scandinavian penalty of *nithing* shows how many threads came together in this enduring custom. More novel was the employment of knights on castle-guard. Fiefs were grouped in 'castleries' round the more important fortresses so as to facilitate the rendering of guard service by rota; and it seems that castle-guard was the heaviest burden which lay on military vassals, for it had to be performed in peace as well as in war. William I encouraged his barons to build private castles; yet he insisted on his ducal right to garrison them with his own troops in case of need; and from the beginning he prohibited private war. This restriction on a traditional right of continental barons may well have been a security measure aimed at husbanding the king's barely adequate military strength; but it was perpetuated as a stringent rule except on the turbulent marches.

Feudal tenure provided the king with a garrison for his castles and a cavalry force when required, it supplied him with the service of menials, and it yielded revenue. But it is not so certain that it provided him with counsel. The great councils which William held were far more like the witenagemot than the *curia ducis*, and were still called by native writers by the English name. Indeed, it cannot be doubted that in the transitional period, while English bishops, earls, and thegns thronged the court, the witenagemot still lived. Nevertheless, the feudal idea that suit of court was an incident of tenure had an increasing effect when the great men of the kingdom became predominantly Norman. It was the duty of a lord's vassals to give him advice, and the lord's duty to seek their counsel; and honorial courts, based on this principle, were being organized throughout England. Yet it may be doubted whether the composition of the king's council can at any time be fully explained by tenure. Although the king's barons attended his councils, the right of anyone to be present irrespective of the wish of the king was never seriously asserted in the Norman period. Nor is it likely that bishops and abbots attended the councils solely by reason of their holding baronies of the king: they attended, as before, primarily because they were the witan of the country. The archbishop of Canterbury, indeed, claimed, and usually obtained, the position of principal adviser to the king. Others—officials, menials, and visitors—were present because it was the king's will. The king was something more than a lord of vassals; and, although feudal theories became progressively clearer, the logical expression of them in the field of counsel—chapter 14 of Magna Carta—was only put forward when feudalism as a method of government was already in decay.

The changes in the king's household were more immediate but, perhaps, no more fundamental. William brought his own servants with him; and the Anglo-Danish officials—the thegns, the house-carles, and the stallers—gave way to men holding offices of Roman and Frankish origin. But the seneschals or stewards, the constables, the marshal, the chamberlain, and the butler still performed the same type of personal service to the king in his hall and chamber as the Anglo-Danish officials had done in hall and bower. They, together with the chancellor in the chapel, formed the permanent core of the king's court; and, as the scope of royal government grew, so they developed into officers of state. Some acquired only an increased dignity; but some, in company with new officials, became ministers of constitutional importance.

It will be clear, then, that in the development of the post-Conquest monarchy two influences worked side by side. The Anglo-Norman kings were the lords of feudal vassals; and the elaboration of a code of relations based on the feudal tie had the effect of producing a monarchy with contractual duties towards the barons and, more widely, a society knit together by a mesh of mutual obligations. But a king was always more than *primus inter pares*. He was an anointed ruler, different in kind from his subjects. The Anglo-Norman kings managed to retain most of the rights and with them much of the symbolic grandeur of their English predecessors, and added to them some governmental procedures that came from the Roman empire by way of the Franks. The bare command of the king, especially when expressed in his writ under seal, had an absolute authority. Hence the practical effect of the increased power of the king was to prepare the way for an institutional despotism operating through 'prerogative' rights that could be checked only by desperate rebellion and, theoretically, by the application of feudal ideas of mutual duties, which themselves knew no sanction except the renunciation of fealty (*diffidatio*) and, in the last resort, war on the autocratic king.

III

The men to whom William granted large fiefs in his new kingdom
were not necessarily those who had fought in the battle of Hastings.
Most of his soldiers were mercenaries, and received from the king
merely their hire. The main beneficiaries were members of those
leading Norman families, often related to the ducal house, which had
supported William's project. A few neighbouring princes, among
whom may be named Counts Eustace of Boulogne and Alan of
Brittany, obtained substantial fiefs; but the new aristocracy of
England was predominantly of Norman extraction and normally of
honourable descent. Their followers, however, especially their
knights, were of more motley origin; and it should be noticed that,
whereas to the king all his foreign vassals were 'French', baronial
documents often recognized subsidiary nationalities such as Breton
and Flemish. The new barons were enfeoffed with the scattered
estates of the English 'traitors', and no man was allowed to conquer
for himself, except at the expense of the Welsh and Scots on the
borders. William deliberately created a few compact lordships on the
marches, such as the earldoms of Chester and Shrewsbury and the
honour of Cornwall, and organized some fiefs round important
castles; but in general the new baronies conformed to the usual
Frankish type and consisted of dispersed members. There is, indeed,
no evidence that the baronage particularly desired concentrated fiefs.
A string of castles across the country gave at least as much military
power as a circumscribed group; scattered manors facilitated travel
and social intercourse; and administrative efficiency was dearly
bought at the cost of isolation and boredom.

The land was granted by the king to be held under all the old
conditions. With the estates went sake and soke, the traditional
customs, and the commendation which the former owner had
enjoyed. The only changes lay in the revision of the military service
required by the king and in the closer tie of feudal vassalage in
which the foreigners were already caught and which in time
entangled all free classes. The substantial tenants-in-chief of the
king—especially those assessed at a quota of knights—were known
as barons, and their estates as baronies or honours. About 170
baronies were created by William I. They varied in size from the
great lordship of his half-brother, the count of Mortain, which
contained about 800 manors—the bulk of Cornwall together with

substantial holdings in Devon, Somerset, Dorset, Berkshire, Sussex, Northamptonshire, and Yorkshire—to modest estates such as the barony of Gilbert de Bretville, which consisted of 19 manors divided between Wiltshire, Berkshire, and Hampshire.

Even if William I immediately and arbitrarily fixed the military service of his barons (and this is unlikely), the other mutual rights and duties of lord and vassal was defined much more slowly. William's new English barons came from several lands and were used to no uniform law. The customs of relief (the payment to a lord for investiture with a fief, especially by the heir after the death of a vassal), wardship (the arrangements made when the heir to a fief was under age), marriage (the right of the lord to control the marital alliances of his vassals, especially those of heiresses), and aid (the right of the lord to obtain financial help from his vassals on proper occasions) were familiar to all, but often in different forms. Hence the law governing the relations between the king and his tenants-in-chief was in frequent dispute; and some points remained unsettled even after the Great Charter of 1215. But each definition of the law created new law. English precedents can be found for most of the 'incidents' of feudal tenure; but it is unlikely that the mutual duties of a foreign king and his foreign vassals owed much to Old-English custom. Magna Carta settled the vexed question of the sum to be paid as relief by the heir to a barony at £100. It can hardly be thought that the amount of heriot payable by an Old-English thegn closest to the king had any influence on this.

As soon as the great fiefs had been created by the king the process of sub-infeudation began. The barons in their turn usually granted part of their land to kinsmen and to men who held lands of them in Normandy. So Montgomery shared his acquisition with Pantulf and Tosny with Clères. Such mesne vassals, who often were responsible for producing a fraction of the *servitium debitum* assessed on the honour, and who had sake and soke within their fiefs and often their own castles, were their lord's barons, and are usually termed 'honorial' barons in order to distinguish them from the barons of the king. By 1086 many of the great barons had granted away at least half their honours, as a rule the poorer and remoter members. Walter Giffard, whose barony centred on Buckinghamshire, had, for instance, granted out 51 of his 71 manors to vassals. It was easy for a generous or ostentatious baron to dissipate quickly his economic capital, especially as the king did not ordinarily interfere. But the

Domesday Inquest of 1086 not only betrays William's ignorance of the internal structure of the baronies he had created two decades before: it also reveals his curiosity.

To answer the king's military requirements and to protect the new order against internal insurrection and foreign invasion the barons at first kept knights in their household ready to snatch their byrnies from the walls and to leap on their tethered horses. These foreign warriors were more like housecarles than thegns; but it was the English word *cniht*—meaning the household retainer of a lord—which soon mastered the French *chevaler* as the vernacular for *miles*. As the danger to the Norman settlement receded barons began to enfeof knights with land. Policy varied from barony to barony. Knights were enfeoffed more quickly in the west than in the more vulnerable east. The abbot of Evesham had already settled his quota on the land by 1072 and the bishop of Hereford by 1085, while the bishop of Worcester was not far behind. But more important for the future welfare of the barony than the time of enfeofment was the number of knights enfeoffed. A baron could grant fees to the exact number of knights required of him by the king, to more, or to less. If to more, then he had a safe margin to cover accident and had also a following to satisfy his pride or to further his private schemes. If to less, then he kept the balance in his household or, later, relied on hiring knights from the pool of landless younger sons or on commuting his service. By the middle of the twelfth century about 6,500 knights had been enfeoffed on the baronies, although the *servitium debitum* owed to the king was only about 5,000. The churches had for the most part enfeoffed more than their quotas, for each new bishop or abbot had a different set of relatives and dependants to reward; some baronial excesses were considerable—the Bigods, for example, owed 60 and had enfeoffed 125; but a surprisingly large proportion of the lay baronage never created fiefs for all the knights for which they were answerable. Those barons who kept the largest part of their honours in their own hands—in demesne—did the best for their descendants. The possession of many vassals and knights conferred prestige and was useful for a time; but it crippled the economic position of the barony when there was a greater demand for corn and animals in the markets and demesne farming became profitable. Individual barons followed their private inclinations in the early years, and, although the king sometimes meddled with the arrangement of ecclesiastical fiefs, in general he respected the privacy of the honours.

In the early Norman period the knights had little social standing and, like the thegns, they were expected to be at their lord's bid and call. Indeed, some English thegns learned the new technique of fighting and became knights; when knights were enfeoffed it was often with old thegn land; and on some ecclesiastical baronies, where the sense of continuity was strong, thegns were not replaced by knights until the loans fell in. The regular work of the knight was to accompany his lord on his progresses and expeditions and perform miscellaneous riding duties. In time of war he was required to campaign for at least two months at his own expense; and every year he had to give 40 days to training and castle guard. Knights were not rich. Often their harness was their lord's, and they rarely at first obtained a fully heritable fief. For the most part they were still common soldiers without the glamour of chivalry.

The kingdom was made up of honours and baronies, and each was a kingdom in microcosm. The baron inherited all the rights which his English predecessors had possessed in the estates; and if he acquired greater rights in the years after the Conquest he obtained them through royal grant. Some of the new earls controlled their shire courts and had their own sheriffs, and so became possessed in their honours of almost all the rights which the king had in the kingdom at large. But franchises never ceased to be alienated regalities and their owners private royal officials. Thus the Norman conquest had no radical effect on the public side of private lordship. Greatest change came from the reorganization of the estates as fiefs. Just as the king, so the baron had his barons, his knights, his body of administrative servants, his court for his vassals, his castles, and his monasteries and churches. The honorial court had the same importance in the honour as the king's court had in the whole kingdom. Its domestic staff—varying in elaboration according to the importance of the honour, but repeating in essentials the pattern of the king's household—was responsible for the routine administration of the estate. But it was normally reinforced by the presence of some honorial barons; and on some occasions all the vassals were required to attend, for only the duty of suit of court could hold a straggling honour together. The jurisdiction of the honorial court was probably something new in England, and it was the creator of a novel body of law, the law of the honour. The honorial vassals had come together in a foreign land, each half-remembering a different set of customs; and through disputes over service, relief, wardship, marriage, dower, and all the other mutual duties of lord and vassal, and vassal and vassal, a uniform code was gradually created for each honour. These feudal laws were not written down. Tradition and the memory of men gathered together in a court, not legal records, are characteristic of the feudal age. And, although William I's sons had little respect for the integrity of the honour, and so modified the pattern which their father had made that the century-and-a-half after Domesday Book remains a nightmare to the scrupulous genealogist, it seems true to say that the Anglo-Norman honour developed a tighter, more organic, and more coherent structure than the Old-English estate had ever possessed and than the continental Norman lordship had as yet acquired. Thus Anglo-Norman feudalism was made in England, and, although custom varied from honour to honour, insular peculiarities both in structure and in terminology soon became apparent.

The life of the new aristocracy was not greatly different from that of the old. There was the same lack of privacy in hall or castle, the press of servants and retainers, the stifling promiscuity that drove the rare individual into a hermitage or on to a solitary path. There was, perhaps, an even greater disdain of agriculture and a greater love of war or its substitutes—the chase, hawking, and military training and sport. The physical ideal was still the coarse athletic figure; courage and fidelity remained the spiritual ideals. The haunting spectre continued to be the tedium which assails isolated communities of limited intellectual interest, and for which there is no remedy but fresh outbursts of physical distraction. It was a restless, drunken, and emotional society, gorged after 1066 with unaccustomed wealth.

The Normans brought with them, of course, new traditions. The Anglo-Danish thegnage was remarkable for its comprehensiveness and for its enjoying a legal status partly divorced from wealth and tenure. In essence thegnage was closest to serjeanty—thegns were servants, *ministeriales*—but it comprised also those whom the Normans would call barons and knights. It was, moreover, a sharply defined class possessing special privileges under the law. Both these attributes were alien to the Norman aristocracy. In a truly feudal society position depends on wealth and tenure and is always relative. A noble caste does not exist. Yet the Normans, in common with the 'French', were developing a new conception of nobility based on knighthood.

The Germanic initiation ceremony of girding a young man with arms and striking him with the fist had disappeared in England, and it was reintroduced by the Normans at a time when the old simplicity was being elaborated into something far different. Already in 1066 a code of chivalrous behaviour was taking form, fundamentally secular in inspiration, as the name *courtoisie* (the manners of courts) betrays, but tinged with ecclesiastical influence. The basic standards were still the qualities of a martial and sport-loving society; and the earliest encrustations were the eccentricities, the prodigalities, and the ostentation which proclaim freedom from want and shameless contempt for the economies of the peasantry and bourgeoisie. William Rufus, the third son of William the Conqueror, is typical of this phase. But contemporary with Rufus and his brother-in-arms for a season, was William IX, duke of Aquitaine, one of the earliest known troubadours, the Provençal poets who sang of a new type of love. The origins of 'courtly love' are perplexingly obscure and have been hotly debated. But the sexual code which dominated the lyric poets of the Languedoc was new and original: it was a sophistication of a rich and enfranchised secular society, and was in reaction alike from the gross animality of contemporary behaviour and the puritan ethics of the church. Instead of a brutal and fleeting conquest of the hapless maid by the powerful knight, the themes of the troubadour are the long and arduous courtship of the superior lady by the inferior male, the disappointments and tribulations of an unrequited yearning for an object of beauty and grace. The suitor is the vassal, serving his lady in a noble adventure. Instead of the Christian ideal of marital fidelity and the practical utility of the union, in courtly love the passion must be illicit and the ends a refined sensuality. It may be that courtly love was always a phantom sophistication; it is possible that the 'Platonic' strains, which ruled at William Rufus's court, have always been underestimated; but through its influence on literature it helped to raise the status of women and to vulgarize a romantic conception of love which has never been without effect on European society, especially in wealthy circles.

Courtly love was but one aspect of the more polished manners, appropriate to a courtier, which were spreading through aristocratic society in the twelfth century. At the same time the church was taking a larger part in the ceremonies of knighthood and introduced thereby the more humane ideals of a Christian warrior. Already by the middle of the twelfth century courtly love had been codified into an artificial system; and in the end chivalry became a punctilious code of social etiquette, meaningless except as a class distinction. The inspiration was always French, and in England the sway of chivalry varied according to the strength of French influence. For better or for worse English habits were seldom as refined as French; and in England the chivalrous code never become the hallmark of a distinct and exclusive noble caste.

IV

The erection of a feudal superstructure in England in the years after 1066 could not fail to affect all classes in time. Although the Norman conquest was not, and was not followed by, a mass migration, and the Norman lords showed no great interest in demesne farming—indeed, the trend which persisted until the thirteenth century was the indirect exploitation of demesne and the commutation for money of labour services—the intrusion of foreign lords caused everywhere some disturbance and probably in most places led to an increase in the old 'farms'. Moreover, in the eastern parts of England estates were consolidated and manors created by finishing the process of making commended men into tenants, by turning all personal into tenurial bonds. Even so, it is not believed that there was a wholesale depression of the peasantry, despite the apparent evidence to the contrary which can be read into Domesday Book. That survey disregards most of the finer Old-English distinction in social standing and puts the bulk of the cultivators, except in some eastern counties, into one of two groups: *villani*—villagers, those with a landed stake in the village fields—and *bordarii* or *cotarii*—cottagers, the village labourers and craftsmen. If the later significance of *villanus*—the servile villein—is disregarded as anachronistic, then the classification is fair enough in an economic context. It need not even surprise us that a number of groups of petty thegns holding a small estate as joint heirs or that an even larger number of sokemen —or the descendants of these—are described as *villani* in 1086. The terminology is new, and serves its purpose; it will, in the case of the word *villanus*, possibly have a harmful effect on the future history of some of the families thus described; but there is no need to suppose that its use signifies that by 1086 the individual rights of all the cultivators had been disregarded, or that a levelling policy had been systematically followed by the Normans. Some simplification was probably inevitable in the circumstances, and those whose political freedom or social standing accorded ill with their economic position were the natural victims. But against this should be set the rapid disappearance of the large class of slaves. The 'villein' class had for long been forming both from above and below. It is likely that the Norman conquest merely accelerated the process, but, on balance, had a liberating effect.

English towns suffered badly during the period of Norman conquest. Some were involved in the fighting; many were partly cleared for the building of castles; and from most the king required a larger financial return. Trade was disturbed. The Scandinavian connexion was broken. After 1071 Flanders was hostile, and by 1074 France was unfriendly. No increase in the old commerce with Rouen nor the small influx of foreign merchants and artizans could compensate for these disasters; and there is nothing to show that 1066 was a turning point in the mercantile or industrial history of England. Normandy had only one city which could compare with the greater English boroughs; and it is unlikely that Norman institutions had much immediate effect on insular urban development. The king confirmed to London its old laws; the old customs of many towns were carefully recorded in Domesday Book; and it seems that the Norman kings granted no new privileges to the boroughs and made few changes in the administration. In general, the old boroughs passed through the Norman conquest scarred but little altered; and developed slowly on conservative lines until the middle of the twelfth century, when a period of rapid expansion began. But while the old boroughs were restoring their fortunes, new towns were being built by the Normans. In some parts of the country, especially on the Welsh march, a Norman borough became an almost usual adjunct to a Norman castle, for the new lords saw in trading communities both a source of revenue and a contribution to peaceful settlement. To these artificial creations the founders granted the free customs of the little Norman *bourgs* they had fostered at home; and since the earl of Hereford, William fitzOsbern, was castellan of Breteuil, built about 1060, it was the customs of Breteuil which were conferred on Hereford, and from there were diffused more widely. Thus English and Norman customs stood side by side, sometimes in the same town; and it was not until later kings began to sell privileges to the boroughs that a common development towards a free, self-governing, and more uniform urban status can be descried in England.

In none of the languages spoken in western Europe was it possible to distinguish between a 'town' and a 'village'. The urban unit was something new and alien in an agricultural and feudal economy. Merchants were oddities, who needed special royal protection. They had to struggle against every traditional authority—against unsuitable jurisdiction, against hampering tolls and restrictions on movement, and against plundering barons and extortionate princes. They lived by exchange, and the profits of exchange—except in so far as they represented the wages of labour and transportation—were considered usurious by the church and illicit by conventional morality. The bourgeoisie, therefore, developed its own ethics, different alike from those of the peasantry and from those of the aristocracy. The merchant was only less suspect than the Jew, who began to find a footing in the English towns after the Conquest; and the ghetto was merely a cell within another ghetto—the town itself.

The area of natural woodland and waste was still large in eleventh-century England, and it provided sport and food probably for most classes. Colonization had already dotted the relics of primeval forest with dens, leys, and fields; but the heath and scrubland were of little use to agriculture. The Old-English kings had owned their private chases, and the royal hunting preserves were greatly extended under the first three Norman kings. William I widened the boundaries of his forest in Hampshire to form the 'New Forest'—a notorious action because some villages and hamlets were destroyed on the outskirts. But the depopulation was exceptional: forests were not completely closed to farming. The king drew revenue from pannage, a rent for the pasturing of swine and other beasts, and from fines for purprestures—penalties for encroachment, but virtually agricultural rents. And the real importance of the growth of the royal forest lay in another direction. William introduced into England from Normandy a special forest law of Frankish origin in order to protect his hunting. This law, additional to, and in no way supplanting, all other laws, was thrown arbitrarily across vast areas of England. By the reign of Henry I the whole of Essex was 'forest', and there were few counties which had not extensive preserves within them. The law protected the venison—the red deer (which William I loved as though he were their father), the fallow deer, the roe, and the wild boar—and the vert—the vegetation which nourished and harboured the animals—by penalties which became progressively severer under the Normans; and a special forest administration was gradually created to enforce the law.

The royal forest was disliked by the nobles because it limited their own chases. It was hated by the church for its inhumanity and for its disregard of clerical privilege. It was detested by the people because it hampered their agriculture, harassed them in their ordinary life, restricted their right to take wild beasts and wood, and introduced but another legal hazard of which they had to beware. But the forest produced food and revenue for the king; and the strength of a medieval king can be gauged by his success in defending his forests against the general opposition.

V

The changes made in the English church after the replacement of English by foreign bishops in 1070 were designed both to give it greater structural coherence and to reform its culture on the Norman pattern. The number and size of the English dioceses were not altered until King Henry I founded Ely and Carlisle, but several episcopal sees were resited in 'cities' in accordance with the precepts of canon law. Lichfield was moved to Chester and later to the monastery of Coventry: Sherborne to Old Salisbury: Selsey to Chichester: Elmham to Thetford and then, after an attempt to enter Bury St. Edmunds had failed, to the monastery of Norwich: Dorchester to Lincoln: and Wells to the monastery at Bath. Dioceses were gradually divided into territorial archdeaconries, the number varying according to the size of the bishopric, and the archdeaconries into rural deaneries. As the dioceses often perpetuated the boundaries of the ancient sub-kingdoms, and the archdeaconries and rural deaneries not seldom corresponded to the shire and hundred, the territorial framework of the church remained thoroughly English. What, however, had been a loose confederacy of bishoprics was reorganized on a strictly hierarchical principle, and it must be recognized that feudal ideas quite as much as ecclesiastical discipline contributed to the result. The southern bishops were firmly subordinated to their Canterbury metropolitan, and oaths of canonical obedience were required which resembled the fealty of a vassal. Moreover, both political and ecclesiastical purposes worked for the unity of at least the English church under one primate. For William such a plan meant the ecclesiastical subordination of the separatist province of York; for Lanfranc it promised greater authority and a united reform movement. The scheme was naturally opposed by the Norman archbishop of York; but William and Lanfranc carried the day; and in 1072 a compromise was achieved. York lost its claim to the dioceses of Worcester, Lichfield, and Dorchester, but received in compensation metropolitan rights over all Scotland; and the archbishop of York was forced to acknowledge the primacy of Canterbury and to agree to attend the synods of Canterbury with his suffragans. Thus Lanfranc became, as the English Eadmer describes him, 'primate of all Britain and patriarch of all islands on this side of the Channel'. The settlement, however, was basically unstable. Primacies were everywhere being weakened by the increased power of the papacy and by the tendency, supported by the False Decretals, for the pope to deal directly with bishops and to disregard the mesne authorities; hence Canterbury was to find it difficult to maintain an effective primacy over the reconstituted northern province. Nor could York, even with the steady backing of the papacy, subdue the Scottish bishops. For the moment the arrangement served William and Lanfranc well; but the totality of the innovation could not be retained.

The Old-English church had been closely enmeshed with the temporal life of the kingdom; and at least one aspect of this confusion appeared disorderly to William and Lanfranc. About the year 1072 the king empowered the church to hold its own spiritual pleas separate from the hundred courts, and forbade lay judges to interfere in spiritual causes. The terms of the royal writ on which we depend for this information leave many questions unanswerable. There is no definition of the ecclesiastical cases and crimes which are to be heard by the bishop or archdeacon according to the canons and the episcopal laws, and there is no special mention of clerical offenders. We know that in the twelfth century a hierarchy of spiritual courts (courts Christian), from the archdeacon's to the primate's—with, of course, the inevitable number of franchises, liberties, and 'peculiars'—developed in England; and we can learn from ecclesiastical lawyers the extent of the jurisdiction claimed for those courts; but the early history of ecclesiastical jurisdiction in England is as yet extremely obscure. We know, however, a little more about Norman conditions—especially from the decrees of the council of Lillebonne held in 1080—and it may safely be considered that these practices were in the main transferred to England.

In Normandy the bishop's jurisdiction was exercised under the duke's ultimate control; it appears hardly different in operation from other types of franchisal authority; and it seems rather to be composed of diverse threads than to have arisen from the application of a single principle. The bishop had forfeitures arising out of breaches of the special peace which lay over churches, their inhabitants, and their visitors. He received fines from all those acting *contra Christianitatem*, that is to say from adulterers, sorcerers, and all offenders against the moral code; and he had jurisdiction in matrimonial affairs. He also had fines from his criminous or delinquent subordinates—from members of his household, from clerks and their servants. But his jurisdiction over clerical persons was not exclusive. Clerks had to answer in lay tribunals for some matters, such as disputes over secular fiefs, and they were subject to the forest law. Finally, the bishop supervised the ordeal—a competence expressly recognized by the English writ—and he enforced the Truce of God, a peace expedient which was not introduced into England.

Even with the help of this Norman evidence the English picture remains obscure. The Norman information is more concerned with the financial rights of a bishop than with the measure of his jurisdiction. Receipt of a penalty, or of part of a penalty, does not always mean that the penalty was imposed in the recipient's court; and, although in the English writ bishops are ordered to hear spiritual causes in a special place, bishops continued for a while to sit in the shire court, and this tribunal is not mentioned in the writ. Later, the church claimed jurisdiction over all spiritual persons and in all spiritual cases, that is to say, exclusive competence to judge the offences of clerks whatever the crime might be, and exclusive cognizance of all breaches of the moral code, whether committed by a clerk or by a layman. The fullness of this jurisdiction was certainly not achieved, and probably not claimed, in the Norman period. But in ecclesiastical courts ran the special law of the church —canon law—and the more that branch of jurisprudence was studied, the more active the clergy became in striving for an unfettered competence. Archbishop Lanfranc introduced into England his private collection of the canons, made at le Bec out of an abridgement, possibly his own, of the pseudo-Isidorian papal decretals (the 'False Decretals'), joined to a complete text of the councils. This collection obtained a wide circulation, and seems to have held the field for some time; but it was replaced in the twelfth century by better compilations—the fuller *Decretum* of Burchard, the more orderly collection of Anselm of Lucca, the popular *Pannormia* of Ivo of Chartres, and, finally, in the second half of the twelfth century, Gratian's *Concordia discordantium canonum*, which was to remain the standard textbook for the western church. In 1072 the full panoply of the *forum ecclesiasticum* was a thing of the future, and William introduced a practice which the church was never to disdain even in its days of pride. The sheriff was to compel men to accept the bishop's jurisdiction; and thereafter the custom arose whereby the sheriff arrested obdurate excommunicates on receipt of a royal writ sued out by the ordinary, and surrendered the offender to the ordinary's court. And this custom helps to remind us that however great the differences between church and state became, the state still offered its physical aid to the church and the church was willing to terrorize the king's enemies with its spiritual ban.

The deliberative and legislative powers of the Norman church were transferred to England, and differed little from those which had been enjoyed by the Old-English church. Ecclesiastical synods, especially primatial synods, were held more frequently during the period of active reform, 1072–86, than of late; but they were summoned by the king, graced by his presence, usually met at court in conjunction with the *magnum concilium*, and required royal approval for their decrees. The control of the king may be considered greater, the participation of the lay nobles less than before. The aim of the canons issued by these synods was to bring the English church up to the best standards of the time, and little was decreed that had not been attempted in the past by the better English bishops. The duties of a bishop were redefined: he was to hold synods, visit his diocese, and maintain ecclesiastical discipline. The unchastity of clerks was condemned, and great efforts were made to secure an unmarried clergy. The first synod of Winchester (1070) threatened all unchaste clergymen with the loss of their office; but the third synod of Winchester (1076) softened the blow. Only canons were immediately to abandon their wives; deacons and priests were not to take wives in the future. No doubt this reforming zeal, springing from the king and primate and activating most of the bishops, reached all branches of the church. But, like all reforming movements, it ran down in time; and in the reign of William II, who had no interest in the church's ideals, it came quickly to an end.

William I had originally intended to reform the English church through the help of Cluniac monks, and, although this scheme fell through, his chief instrument, Lanfranc, was a monk. Nevertheless, the impact of the conquest on English monasticism, although great, was not of radical importance. The foreign monks, who gradually replaced the native abbots, had no common rule to impose, for the Norman houses had been as independent as the English, and their practices were not in general different from those prescribed by the *Regularis Concordia*. The English calendar, full of uncouth but cherished saints, came in for criticism; and force was required at Glastonbury to persuade the monks of the superiority of the use of Dijon over Gregorian plainsong. Lanfranc composed original *consuetudines* for his own monastery, Christ Church, which were adopted by Durham; and individual revisions of the monastic customs were made elsewhere. Discipline was, no doubt, tightened up at first; and an ambitious rebuilding programme swept away the English fabrics by then often a century old. It is significant, perhaps, that few new houses of monks were founded by the first settlers. They endowed their Norman monasteries with some of the spoils of England; but the great monastic movement on the morrow of the Conquest was of purely English inspiration. From Evesham and Winchcombe a band of monks went north in search of simplicity and, it may be thought, an English way of life; and they or their adherents refounded or created Jarrow and Monkwearmouth —these monks later migrating to Durham—Tynemouth, Whitby, St. Mary's at York, and Melrose. There seemed at first even a danger that the monastic cathedral, an English peculiarity, might be abolished by some of the new bishops; but Lanfranc intervened, and the effect of the Conquest was in the end to increase the number. By about 1100, nine of the seventeen English episcopal sees were in monasteries; and the custom was to last, not always with happy results. Far more consequential, however, than modifications in the constitution of individual monasteries was the gradual replacement of English by Norman monks. The great Benedictine houses of England never entirely lost their royal and 'national' tone; but, as they ceased to be strongholds of a vernacular culture, some of the intimate ties which had bound them into the community were broken for ever. New waves of monastic fervour were to sweep over England in the twelfth and thirteenth centuries; but worldly circles had lost their enthusiasm for the ideal long before the sixteenth century, and monks were already considered unsuitable candidates for bishoprics within a generation of the Norman conquest.

The village priest was only slightly affected by the Conquest. Owing to his low social position he was not disturbed by an influx of foreign clerks; and as a rule he remained married despite the reform drive. His economic position probably showed the same development as that of the 'villein': at first little altered, but later depressed. The pensions paid by the clerks serving proprietary churches seem to have become steadily heavier; and, although these pensions were often transferred by the lay proprietors to monasteries, no advantage accrued to the village church. Even more harmful to the economic position of the village priest was the grant of whole churches to monasteries. Some of the churches were colonized by monks and became cells of the mother house; some were put out to speculators 'at farm' and were served by chaplains for a small stipend; but the later and ultimately standard practice, which was called the impropriation or incorporation of a church, was for the monastery to keep the bulk of the church's endowment for itself, including the tithe of corn, and to endow a priest with a small portion, usually the gifts at the altar and the minor tithes. In this way the 'parsonage' was appropriated to the monastery, and the priest in charge became a vicar. The ubiquity of vicarages today among the old parish churches shows how general became the practice after the Norman conquest of granting churches to monasteries and other corporations. The custom made the monasteries rich and kept the parish priests poor. But so long as the impropriators administered the tithe faithfully—using it for charitable, educational, or building purposes—the arrangement was just and proper. No one minister had any special right to tithe. It was a general church fund, which could better, perhaps, be handled by the monasteries than by the village priests.

Many of the innovations in ecclesiastical affairs which followed the Norman conquest of England worked to sharpen the distinctness of the church as a separate order: the drive to produce a celibate clergy, the acquisition of special courts, the wide application of, and new interest in, canon law, and, above all, the fierce domestic struggles over all the privileges which were now enjoyed. The church had gained a life of its own, and through internal conflict developed its individual constitution. But the more the church was divorced from folk-law and from traditional customs the more at first it felt the control of the king. English kings had often taken ecclesiastical advice when appointing bishops; Norman kings seem to have been more arbitrary; and what is more they invested prelates with their office through livery of the ring and staff—an innovation in England. Ecclesiastical legislation was still under royal supervision, and, although the church was allowed its own law and its own courts, the king was the judge of the competence of that jurisdiction. William, for instance, would not allow his barons or servants to be excommunicated or brought before an ecclesiastical court on a serious charge without his consent; and he required the church to excommunicate his enemies. Church lands were treated as baronies and the bishops as vassals, bound to do homage and swear fealty, and obey the king as they loved their baronies; and William II exploited the feudal theory to the full. William I was a sincere reformer; but he would allow no one and no class to dispute his power. When his half-brother, Odo of Bayeux, in 1082, proposed to draw off his knights and intervene in the papal wars the king arrested him—as earl of Kent, when the bishop protested his order—and kept him in prison despite the anger of the pope. Such a king was not reforming the church in order that it should diminish his authority.

William's masterful purpose is shown equally well in his relations with the papacy and in his restricting the already limited connexion between the English church and Rome. The Old-English church had been free to make what use it could of the pope; and if the intercourse was slight, it was not so because of the will of the king. The way in which William had secured papal support for his English adventure, his ambiguous promises, his equivocal behaviour in 1066, and his use of papal legates in 1070 to depose the native bishops, all seemingly led to a closer connexion between England and Rome. The Roman *curia*, indeed, hoped that William would hold his new kingdom as a papal fief, and William's allowing the papal legates to crown him afresh in 1070 was the last of a series of opportunist moves. For after 1070 William no longer required the services and support of the pope and proceeded quietly but ruthlessly to cut all the ties that had been formed. Gregory VII succeeded Alexander II in 1073, and the newcomer had not only far more radical ambitions but had special reason to expect William to further them. The king, however, resisted every political claim of the pope. He ignored his attempt to deprive the laity of its traditional rights in the church. He would not allow papal letters to reach his bishops except through himself. And, with an eye to the prevalence of schism, he insisted that no pope should be recognized within his dominions without his approval. He supported episcopal opposition to the pope's claim to be the universal ordinary, to have an unlimited primacy within the church. Archbishop Liemar of Bremen wrote to Bishop Hezilo of Hildesheim of Gregory VII, 'This dangerous man wants to order the bishops about as if they were servants on his estates; and if they do not do all that he commands they have to go to Rome or else they are suspended without legal process.' William allowed no papal legate to enter England between 1073 and 1080, and excluded them almost as successfully from Normandy. He permitted no bishop to visit Rome without his consent, and kept Lanfranc at home despite the growing insistence of Gregory. The establishment of the archbishop of Canterbury as primate of all England provided the kingdom with a single supreme ecclesiastical court; and William forbade appeals to go farther than this tribunal without his permission.

These customs, when collected, became known as the 'ancestral customs' of the kingdom. William established in England the practices to which he was accustomed and which had been general in Europe. Once they are expressed they appear to be defensive; but we may well be reading backwards if we regard them as the introduction into England of a consciously reactionary and protective system. William, confident in his righteousness, could treat the revolutionary ideas of the reformed papacy as creating a temporary political problem. Not even a man so shrewd as William could foresee that the papal pressure was going to be sustained and that the world of his father was passing away. Even Lanfranc, who had studied the pseudo-Isidorian decretals, could not have been fully aware that old customs could be made to look like old abuses in the light of even older church law.

As Gregory VII felt the English resistance to his policies he stiffened in turn. At the beginning of 1079 he peremptorily ordered Lanfranc to visit Rome, and a month later he subordinated the province of Rouen together with Sens and Tours to the primacy of Lyons. The archbishop of Rouen with the support of the duke resisted. On 8 May 1080 a legate, Hubert, arrived in England charged with an important mission. The letters he presented to the royal family and Lanfranc developed themes which had already appeared in Gregory's correspondence with William—the debt of gratitude which the king owed him for his favours as cardinal and pope and the papacy's urgent need for help—and also advanced the thesis, expressed in feudal terms and adorned by the famous simile of sun and moon, that all secular rulers were inferior to the pope who had to answer for them before the judgment seat of God. The moral was clear; and the secret mission of the legate was to persuade William to become a papal vassal. Other arguments may have been used in private: the papal claim to islands based on the 'donation of Constantine', the Roman conversion of England, the payment of tribute (Peter's pence), or William's promises in 1066. But William had not acquired a kingdom in order to bow before another lord. He refused the request in few words. He denied that he had ever promised fealty: he had merely undertaken to pay alms each year, and Romescot he would continue to pay.

Gregory's anger at William's intransigence was aggravated when the king imprisoned the bishop of Bayeux, and William was driven to send William of Saint-Calais, bishop of Durham, and, probably, Lanfranc to explain his conduct to the pope. Relations, indeed, between England and the papal *curia* steadily deteriorated under Gregory VII. Lanfranc, no doubt, resented his partiality for Berengar of Tours; William had no use for his novel claims. But William and Gregory respected each other. The pope never raised the question of lay investiture with William, although he fought the emperor to the death for its abolition; and the king never wantonly provoked the man who had done so much for him in the past. Yet it is possible that an open breach was only averted by the increasing misfortunes of the pope; and, after the Emperor Henry IV had occupied Rome on 21 March 1084, William allowed his recognition of Gregory to lapse. Overtures from the anti-pope Clement III, the nominee of the emperor, led to negotiations; and there is some reason to believe that England and Normandy may even have recognized Clement for a time.

Total independence of Rome or faint allegiance to the anti-Gregorian party lasted from 1084 until 1095. It was the logical end to William's policy. And yet, perhaps, more remarkable than the political adroitness that William displayed was the total acquiescence of the English and Norman churches in this state of affairs. Even the ribald tyranny of William II was not enough to create an active

Gregorian party in his dominions or to produce one responsible supporter for Anselm's new ideas; and it was in the reign of Henry I that the Conqueror's policy was defended and given a theoretical justification in the polemical writings of the 'Norman Anonymous', sometimes called 'of York'. The stability proves that William I's need to make use of the papacy at the beginning of his reign had in no way disturbed the traditional position or prejudiced his purpose. He bears no direct responsibility for the revolution which eventually destroyed the old order.

The foreign clerks and monks whom William appointed to English bishoprics and monasteries were dissatisfied with the size and appearance of their sacred buildings. Only Edward's church at Westminster surpassed the churches of Normandy; and before the end of the eleventh century most of the larger English churches had been pulled down and were being rebuilt in the Norman variety of romanesque style. Two main types of plan came into vogue: that with three apses at the east end, and that with an ambulatory passage within eastern chapels (probably the scheme used already at Westminster) which was adopted at Battle Abbey (begun 1070–71) and at many other cathedral and abbey churches. A few insular habits lasted or reappeared: the use of the cushion capital and the twelfth-century preference for the square east end; and some insular modes developed, such as the lofty cylindrical pillars seen at Gloucester, Tewkesbury, and Pershore; but the break in the architectural tradition was fairly sharp. Several of the monuments of this age still stand and still impress. The general substitution of half-circles for the more angular Old-English motifs produced a composition that was more harmonious but no more tender than the old. The small round-headed windows, the massive piers, the heavy vaulting, the simple, geometrical, and often barbarous decoration give an air of gloomy purpose, of power, of a castle built to defend God's people against hostile forces. The tower defied its enemies, its bells shouted defiance, the churchyard guarded both the living and the dead. The crypt of relics reinforced the pavement, and the surrounding altars with their flickering candles kept the faithful secure. Like the Old-English churches the Norman were fortresses in a heathen world.

The wealth of England and the extent of the rebuilding programme led naturally, however, to improvement in technique and in grace; and the Anglo-Norman school of romanesque became the best of its day. At first the naves of the largest churches were roofed with wood, for the method of ribbed vaulting, which was being evolved in Normandy, was still too experimental for its employment on a vast scale. But Durham cathedral, begun in 1093, was the first large church outside Lombardy to be designed to take a complete cover of stone vaulting; and in that magnificent church appear all the structural devices on which the gothic style of architecture was based. The nave vault was completed at Durham about 1130; and pointed arches are already to be found. But this line of development was not pursued in England, probably because the main phase of the rebuilding programme was almost over; and it was in the Île de France that Norman innovations were taken so far that a completely new style of architecture was produced.

In the practice of the fine arts the Normans had no tradition and little skill; and the native crafts deteriorated until new streams of foreign influence caused a general revival. Nor was the effect of the Norman conquest on language and literature any happier in the beginning. The spoken language of the foreign settlers was 'French', a debased Latin dialect. The chansons de geste, notably the song of Roland, were already taking form; but no literature or even laws had yet been written in French, for the learned class, the clergy, also spoke and wrote Latin, and saw no reason to compose in a barbarous medium. Hence spoken English found a rival in French and written English in Latin. Written English suffered the worse: 'official' English disappeared, and literary English gave way. Once English earls, bishops, sheriffs, and thegns had ceased to dominate the shire courts the king's writs were composed in Latin; and it is possible that they gained in authority thereby. But a strange divorce then arose between action and the record of that action. Illiterate kings issued, and illiterate barons received, writs and charters which were incomprehensible even when read to them. And in the translation of business done in oral French or English into written Latin is to be found a falsification which hinders our understanding of the men and their behaviour.

Literary English, the language of the chronicles, the homilies, and the poems, died with the classes which had used and enjoyed it. Before the middle of the twelfth century the Worcester monks asked William of Malmesbury to translate the life of Bishop Wulfstan composed in English by Coleman perhaps as late as 1113. The Peterborough version of the Old-English chronicle was abandoned in 1154. And once the learned class ceased to read and write Anglo-Saxon the rich libraries of vernacular literature began to fall into decay. Had not one manuscript—the Exeter book—survived the general neglect our knowledge of Old-English poetry would have been very small indeed. Anglo-Norman historians wrote in Latin. Written English never completely disappeared. The thread from Alfred to Layamon and Langland is unbroken. But English was declassed for a time, and, without the guidance of scholars and stylists, it relapsed into dialect. It was not until the fourteenth century that one of its branches re-emerged, far simpler in syntax and enriched by many words borrowed from French, to become a new and vital medium for literary expression.

A temporary eclipse of literary English was natural; its long disuse by scholars writing for scholars was inevitable; but its failure to re-establish itself as the vehicle for popular history, adventure stories, and poetry was due to the tenacity with which the lay aristocracy held to its native tongue. The new landowners had no special contempt for the insular vernacular. William I tried to learn English in order to do justice without the help of an interpreter, and most settlers must have picked up a smattering in the way of estate business. It must also be supposed that the children born in England were bilingual, for, except in the greatest households, English nurses, grooms, and servants must have been employed. Had Normandy been far away, and had not most barons held lands on both sides of the Channel, French might easily have died out in England. By the twelfth century English was the cradle tongue and French the second language of the gentry; but in a country so divided by dialects that a Yorkshireman was incomprehensible to a man of Kent, French was indeed a *lingua franca;* and the romance tongue had a history in England similar to that which English is having in India. Native Englishmen in the early Middle Ages found it useful, often indispensable, to speak some French; and the bilingual, or trilingual, tradition took firm root. In the thirteenth century, when the cry of 'hated foreigner' was first raised, French even became the language of English law; and this last, and paradoxical, success was probably the only one which did any harm.

VI

A review of the law and its administration in the Anglo-Norman kingdom serves well as conclusion to this chapter, for the jurisdictional pattern emphasizes many of the features of the new society. The laws of the natives were not abrogated. West-Saxon, Mercian, and Dane law, and all the particular variations, remained intact for those subject to them. *Wer* and *bot* and *wite*, compurgation and ordeal, all the technicalities of Anglo-Danish law still held good in the shire and hundred courts and the many private courts. Indeed, the *Leges Edwardi Confessoris*, *Leges Willelmi Primi*, and *Leges Henrici Primi*, law books made after 1066, are among our best evidences for the old customs. The Norman king took the wonted place in the administration of this traditional law, and, even if the 'reserved pleas' of the Old-English kings became 'pleas of the crown'— *placita coronae*—in the new vocabulary, no new development in this field is perceptible at first. William I made a few changes. A later compiler asserts that blinding and mutilation were substituted by his mercy for capital penalties; and a security measure—the punishment of the locality for failure to produce the slayer of a Norman—was perpetuated in the increasingly profitable *murdrum* fine; but generally speaking natives who lived through the conquest died under the same laws into which they had been born.

The foreign settlers, too, came for most purposes under the old laws of the kingdom. But a large body of unwritten foreign custom was imported, and then modified and developed, to govern the personal and tenurial relationships of the new aristocracy. Feudal law in the beginning affected only those who held fiefs. Its exponents were the *curia regis* and the honorial and lesser feudal courts. At first it hardly touched the native; but in time it influenced all land holding until in the end it provided England with a new land law. Out of the procedure of these feudal courts arose the doctrine of 'judgment by peers', which has had a chequered influence on English jurisdictional procedure; and from the habits of the military aristocracy came the introduction of a new method of irrational proof—the *duellum*, the judicial combat. This new ordeal was from the first allowed to Englishmen; and it outlived ordeal by water, hot iron, and other rustic customs. The two other great legal changes brought in by the Conqueror, the introduction of forest and church courts, affected native and alien alike.

The effect of the Norman conquest was, then, to add to the complexity of an already intricate legal organization. After 1066 there were even more different codes of law for different sorts of men, and there were new types of case for all conditions of men.

The Norman conquest is sometimes regarded as having had a simplifying function. This, it must be recognized, is a very long view. The immediate result of the conquest in almost every sphere of human activity was to increase the diversity, to add new customs to the old. It has already been suggested that in Edward's day the interference of the king in legal affairs, expressed in his writs to his bishop, earl, and thegns in the shire court, might have worked towards a consolidation of custom; and this procedure was not abandoned by the Norman kings. These, like their predecessors, held themselves responsible for seeing that justice was done, and they would intervene on behalf of petitioners; but only after contumacious default of justice did the case come before the king or his officers. Hence the use of a royal writ to start a case, or to obtain justice from a man who denied it, in no way dictated the procedure or the law under which the case was subsequently decided. The development of a new royal law, emanating from the king's court, administered by his servants, and employing its special procedures, notably the inquest and the jury, had hardly begun before the end of the Norman dynasty.

The Anglo-Norman state had barely started to achieve coherence when its existence was threatened by the weak reign of Stephen; and it was rebuilt by Henry II inevitably in a new form. It is, therefore, difficult to generalize on the effect of the Norman conquest. Vast tracts of human affairs were virtually unaffected; in other spheres there was cataclysm enough; everywhere there was some mingling of concurrent custom. Perhaps it is not entirely foolish to dwell finally on two opposing features: the inert persistence of much of the old way of life, especially among the common people; and the extraordinary vitality of the foreign culture introduced by the new aristocracy. It is not surprising that the two races were almost merged by the reign of Henry II; but it is remarkable that the aristocracy still spoke French three centuries after the conquest.

5

ENGLAND AND NORMANDY, 1066-1100

I

ALTHOUGH the kingdom of England was a more valuable and dignified possession than the duchy of Normandy or the county of Maine, William I and his sons were always more interested in their continental lands than in their island acquisition. The pride of race tied them to their ancestral demesnes, and political dangers kept them involved rather with the Vexin and Maine than with the Welsh and Scottish marches. The new aristocracy of England showed in general the same bias. Some, like Eustace of Boulogne, remained foreign princes with English lands; some, like Roger of Montgomery or William fitzOsbern, were sorely divided in interest. A few men of the first generation, including the king, thought to find a solution in dividing their separated inheritance between their sons; but the experiment was premature. Hence the political history of England in the Norman period is dominated by continental themes. The duchy was impoverished by the loss of its best men who could make more splendid fortunes within the kingdom; but English interests followed in the wake of the interests of Normandy.

The late eleventh and early twelfth centuries were not a period of great achievement in Europe. The brilliant success of the Norman conquest of England, the indomitable triumph of the first Crusade, obscure, perhaps, the general mediocrity of result. In military affairs defence had the advantage over attack. A castellated country is defended to the utmost depth; and military engineering had not so developed as to make the reduction of even a simple castle easy. In the sphere of government ambition far outstripped the available means, both financial and administrative. The pope might announce revolutionary reforms; but the impetus ran down quickly in space and time. An active king might require much money for his schemes; but he seemed to extort capriciously rather than to tax. Even the awakening of a new spirit of intellectual inquiry was hindered because scholars possessed an imperfect means of expression. Latin is a gross and imprecise language, unsuited to logic and philosophy; so that the greatest scholastic achievements fell short of what might have been done had the medium been better. Almost every human activity was on a small scale. Feudal society, in its fragmentation of authority and loyalty, in its defensiveness, its conservatism, and its tiny groupings, wasted its energies in trivial aims and lacked sufficient capital for great adventure. The slothful and luxurious Philip, king of the Franks, is, perhaps, a typical ruler of the time. The English kings were harder, wiser, more purposeful; but even they could do little more under these hampering conditions.

Gaul had for long been divided into many parts. But the process of disintegration had been halted in the eleventh century, and some of the dukes and counts had begun to enforce their rule over fairly coherent political entities, of which Normandy was certainly the most centralized. The re-establishment of order within the duchies at first reduced rather than increased the power of the French monarchy, for a strong duke had little need for the help of his over-lord. Hence a characteristic feature of the time was the jostling together of a congeries of duchies and counties as they disputed border fiefs one with another. Normandy had two main points of friction. It rubbed against the northern demesne of the Capetians—the Île de France—in the Vexin; and the county of Maine divided it from Anjou. Maine, with its capital of le Mans, was the more important in the eleventh century; but the problem disappeared when in the third decade of the twelfth, the counts of Anjou became dukes of Normandy. The Vexin, which guarded the valley of the Seine, remained the strategic key to Normandy until the duchy was lost by King John. Among the marcher lordships that of Bellême deserves special mention, for the family possessed fiefs strung along the borders of Normandy from Brittany to the Vexin held variously of the king of the Franks, the count of Maine, and the Norman duke himself. The dynasty, possibly of Breton origin, can be traced back to an officer in charge of the royal siege-train in the latter half of the tenth century; and the family castles at Bellême, Alençon, Domfront, and Séez, gave proof of an hereditary engineering skill. The

Norman bishopric of Séez was under the family's control; and when an heiress—the infamous Mabel, daughter of William Talvas—married a great Norman baron, Roger of Montgomery, who in 1071 received the marcher earldom of Shrewsbury, the family's power became immense. The sons of that marriage—especially the eldest, Robert of Bellême, who reunited for a time the divided inheritance—were for long a power in the Anglo-Norman state, and a power mainly for evil.

In 1066 Duke William was the dominant ruler in north-west Gaul; but in the years in which he became master of a new kingdom his powers waned at home. Philip, king of the Franks, grew to manhood and coveted the Vexin. Anjou became strong once more and cast eyes on Maine. Brittany was restive and Flanders hostile. William's heir, Robert, had no effective outlet for his energies and in troubling his father with his premature ambitions offered himself as a tool to his father's enemies. Hence William is seen again as a count among his peers, on the defensive, fighting hard to keep his territorial position intact.

The rivalry between Normandy and Anjou was already strong, and was to create a national antipathy. The county of Anjou was even more recent in formation than the county or duchy of Normandy. Its ruling family had held the office of *vicomte* under the Robertian counts, later known as the Capetians, and had risen with their overlords, becoming counts when the counts of Angers became dukes of the Franks, and immediate vassals of the crown when Hugh Capet became king. The Angevin counts were warriors; but their energy had been expended more against Blois than to the north. Maine, the county which separated Normandy and Anjou (covered roughly by the modern departments of Mayenne and Sarthe) had its own ruling family, which normally recognized the overlordship of Anjou, and its diocese of le Mans, which lay within the ecclesiastical province of Tours. Maine, therefore, looked south rather than north, and Norman attempts to absorb the county were constantly resisted by the people and opposed by the counts of Anjou.

William, however, was able to get a hold on Maine in the decade before he invaded England. Geoffrey Martel, count of Anjou, had annexed the county after the death of Count Hugh III on 26 March 1051 (?); but William had then given asylum to the widow Bertha and her children, Herbert II and Margaret; and by taking the homage of Herbert and by betrothing Margaret to his eldest son,

Robert Curthose, had prepared the way for a counter-stroke. Herbert died childless on 9 March 1062; and in the next year William conquered the county for Margaret and Robert. But the counts of Anjou could not be reconciled to its loss. Geoffrey the Bearded was induced to take the homage of Margaret and Robert, but only because he was threatened by his brother, Fulk 'le Réchin', who overthrew him in 1068; and Fulk was less complaisant. A series of revolts in Maine, aided by Fulk, disturbed the Norman government; and, although in 1081 William and Robert extorted from Fulk the Treaty of Blanchelande, by which the county was assured to Robert but the overlordship to Fulk, Norman rule was still precarious in 1087.

Duke William had even less success on his other frontiers. On 16 July 1070 died the friendly Baldwin VI, William's brother-in-law, ruler of Flanders, the French county or marquisate lying between the Escaut and the Canche. The rule of the young heir, Arnulf, became so unpopular because of the influence of his widowed mother, Richildis, that a rising in favour of the late count's younger brother, Robert, who was ruling a fragment of Holland, or West Frisia, in the right of his wife, drove Arnulf into Hainault, an imperial fief, the inheritance of his younger brother, Baldwin, and sent Richildis to the court of King Philip I of the Franks to buy help. Early in 1071 King Philip invaded with a feudal army, which included the minimum Norman contingent of ten knights under William fitzOsbern, earl of Hereford, and on 20 February at Bavinchove, near Cassel, the royal army was routed by the usurper, Arnulf being killed and Richildis captured. William fitzOsbern also lost his life. Robert 'le Frison' and Philip then made peace, confirmed by the marriage of the French king to Robert's step-daughter, Bertha of Holland. Robert's accession thus changed completely the direction of Flemish policy. He was already deeply committed to a struggle with his north-eastern neighbours, imperial vassals, and he naturally adhered to his overlord, the French king, and hence opposed the Anglo-Norman family. He gave his eldest daughter, Adela, to Cnut II of Denmark, who had designs on England, and he harboured his nephew, Robert Curthose, when the young man was in revolt against his father, William the Bastard. In return, William stopped payment of the money fief of 300 marks which he had paid to the Flemish counts since Baldwin V.

More actively hostile to Normandy, however, was Philip I, king of the Franks. The Seine on its course from Paris to Rouen receives three tributaries from the north: the Oise, the Epte, and the Andelle. Between the Andelle and the Oise lay the pre-feudal district of the Vexin; and this had been cut in half by the early settlements of the Normans, which had reached as far as the Epte. The eastern half of the Vexin had come into the hands of a family which held it as counts directly of the kings of the Franks; but King Henry I, after he had secured his throne in 1031 largely by the efforts of Duke Robert I of Normandy, to whose court he had fled for help, rewarded his saviour by transferring to him his lordship over Drogo, count of the Vexin. This was an action of which the royal house was certain to repent. Paris and Rouen were too close for easiness of mind, and the Epte was the most satisfactory boundary. Robert had given the sister of Edward the Confessor, Godgifu, to Drogo as wife; and the two counts had been friends; but Drogo's successors had fallen away; French influence had increased during William the Bastard's minority; and when the last of the line, Simon, retired to a monastery in 1077, King Philip I was able to occupy the county while William was busy with Maine.

Philip used every means in his limited power to weaken the position of the Norman duke. In 1074 he offered to establish Edgar Aetheling in the castle of Montreuil-sur-Mer so that he could harass eastern Normandy. In the autumn of 1076 he relieved Dol and routed William's army when the duke was attempting to punish the Bretons for the aid they had given Earl Ralf of East Anglia in his revolt of the previous year. The quarrels between William and his heir offered Philip even more promising opportunities. Robert, nicknamed Curthose, was born about 1052, and had received the homage of the Norman barons in 1066 and again at a later date, and had been enfeoffed with Maine. His father, however, allowed him no power and little money; so that it is not surprising that Robert, after a quarrel with his brothers at the end of 1077, became involved in a series of stupid adventures, which gravely threatened his father's position. In 1078 he tried to seize the castle at Rouen; then raised a border war south of the Seine; and, when driven by the king from the castle of Rémalard, which lay not far from the main stronghold of the rebel, Robert of Bellême, wandered among his father's enemies. Towards the end of the year King Philip tried again the scheme he had proposed to Edgar, and gave Robert the border castle of Gerberoy in the Beauvaisis. At the beginning of 1079 Duke

William marched once more against his rebellious son, and managed to attach the French king to his side; but in a battle with the garrison William was attacked and wounded by Robert, and William's third son, William Rufus, also was hurt. If the father was deeply humiliated, the son was no less repentant; and friends effected a reconciliation. William again recognized Robert as his heir to Normandy; and father and son were often together until 1083, when Robert, possibly on the death of his mother, Matilda, went into exile once more.

From 1084 until 1086 William was in England preparing to meet the threat of a Danish invasion; but the Vexin thrust itself on his attention. In 1087 the garrison of Mantes on the Seine, the capital of the French Vexin, raided west across the River Eure. William retorted by requiring from the French king the surrender of the three principal fortresses of the province: Chaumont-en-Vexin in the north, Mantes in the south, and Pontoise, which bridged the Oise. When the demand was refused, William invaded in July, burst into Mantes while the garrison was abroad, and received accidentally a fatal internal injury while he sacked and burned the town. The dying king was carried back to Rouen, and then moved to the neighbouring priory of Saint-Gervais for the sake of a peaceful end. In the last weeks William disposed of his possessions. Robert was still with his father's enemy, King Philip, and William found it hard to forgive him. The second son, Richard, had been killed in the New Forest. The third son, the faithful William Rufus, was at his father's bedside, and William thought at first to make him his sole heir, as was the custom. He gave him his crown, sword, and sceptre, and sent him to Archbishop Lanfranc in England to be made king. But the archbishop of Rouen and others pleaded for Robert, and in the end William reluctantly recognized his right to Normandy and Maine. Robert stayed in France until after the funeral. To his younger son, Henry, the king allotted part of his treasure, 5,000 lbs. of silver, with which to buy a fief. William ordered his prisoners to be freed, his money to be distributed to churches, and died on 9 September 1087. His end was as squalid as his beginning. His dishonoured corpse, robbed by his servants, was carried to the church of St. Stephen at Caen for burial; his chosen grave was disputed; and his rotting cadaver burst from the integuments as it was forced into a sarcophagus too small for his corpulent body.

It is impossible not to admire the achievements of William the

Bastard; but he has no place among the truly great. From his perilous youth until his unlucky end he was the sole architect of his fortune, and his counsellors, even Lanfranc, were ever his lieutenants. Yet grandeur is lacking in the career of this crafty, determined, and ruthless man because he always planned within the limits of his resources and seldom achieved results greater than his purpose. The bizarre, the capricious, or the astounding gesture was alien to his relentless ambition. He was feared and respected rather than loved. His virtues were forbidding, and he had few personal friends. Marital fidelity and religious piety did him credit as a man; sternness with occasional ferocity and a respect for law became him as duke and king. Avarice was his weakness, and he excoriated England in order to build up a royal hoard. Yet William should be honoured for his justice. He had the power to be a tyrant; but it is seldom that he can be convicted of wanton disregard of the law. He was steeped in the feudal tradition of mutual rights and duties; and when he became king of the English he moved within a maze of strange obligations with surprising patience. William never gives the impression of having been born out of his proper time. He was no barbarian leader. Neither was he a statesman. He had learned the art of government in the hardest school, so that a conquered country groaned under his rule but could not withhold a grudging admiration.

II

The strict hereditary principle had, perhaps, less influence on the transmission of the English crown in the eleventh and twelfth centuries than at any other time. The dying wishes of the late king were usually respected; but a coup d'état by the most advantageously situated competitor was frequently successful. William Rufus, now just over thirty, was fortunate both in having his father's bequest of the kingdom and in being able to seize the throne before another could act. He crossed to England with one of his father's chaplains, Robert Bloet, who could authenticate the testament, and with the prisoners Morkere and Wulfnoth Godwinesson; presented his father's letter to Archbishop Lanfranc; and, after promising to regard Lanfranc as his chief adviser and taking the traditional coronation oath, was consecrated king by the primate at Westminster on 26 September 1087. The kingdom had passed by a will approved and administered by the church; and not even the barons had had much say. Rufus was able to take a general 'oath of allegiance' from his subjects. But considerable sympathy was felt for the eldest son who had been deprived of his full inheritance; much inconvenience was created by a settlement which placed the barons under different lords for their English and continental lands; and many hopes of a milder successor to the stern Conqueror were frustrated when Robert was dispossessed. It was inevitable that Rufus would have to fight hard to keep his crown, but equally certain that if Rufus could ride the storm Robert would in turn be insecure in his duchy. The time for separation had not yet come. The dividing of England from Normandy was as inconvenient to the barons as to the rival rulers.

For some months the barons accepted the unexpected revolution. Rufus, a dutiful son, distributed his father's treasure to the churches and monasteries according to his father's will—an action which left him poor—and he restored his uncle, Bishop Odo of Bayeux, whom the Conqueror's death had released from prison, to his earldom of Kent—an action which threatened his security. By the beginning of the next year, 1088, William II's leading vassals, probably under the inspiration of Odo, were already falling away and preparing to transfer their fealty to Robert should he come to claim the throne. Some, however, including Hugh d'Avranches, earl of Chester, William of Warenne, and Robert fitzHamon, remained loyal; the lesser barons, especially those of the midlands, kept still; and William's vigour steadied the waverers. The English church, with the doubtful exception of the bishop of Durham, William of Saint-Calais, stood by the king. The support of the English laity was secured by the king's promise to give relief from geld and from the forest law and to restore the laws of Edward. In an atmosphere of suspicion, when Rufus did not know which private castle would be closed against him, he proved his merits as a general by striking against the most vital area, Kent and Sussex, a bridgehead for the duke of Normandy, and the seat of his most dangerous enemies, his half-uncles, Odo, earl of Kent, with his castles of Rochester and Tonbridge, and Robert, count of Mortain, with Pevensey. These rebels, strengthened from abroad, had with them Count Eustace of Boulogne, probably the son of the man who had fought at Hastings, and three of the sons of Roger of Montgomery, earl of Shrewsbury —Robert of Bellême, Hugh of Montgomery, and Roger of Poitou. Earl Roger, however, waited on events in his castle of Arundel. He was separated from Pevensey by the loyal William of Warenne, based on Lewes.

Rufus called out the loyal forces, and, although weakened by the defection of the bishop of Durham, attacked and took Tonbridge, and pressed on towards Rochester. But Odo and some of his friends slipped away to Pevensey, where the expected help of Duke Robert of Normandy could be awaited the better. Yet Robert never came in person, and the forces he sent by sea were repulsed. Pevensey was blockaded into surrender on terms: Odo was to suffer disinheritance and banishment, and was to secure the surrender of Rochester. But while Odo was before Rochester he was rescued by the garrison; and the king, wounded in his honour, became implacable. He called up fresh forces for the siege of Rochester under the Scandinavian penalty of dishonour—to be held *nithing*— and gathered round him many of those barons who had by now become more interested in the fate of the besieged than in the defeat of the king. Men were slowly recognizing their master, and Rufus had no intention of relaxing his grasp. Again the king allowed the garrison their lives; but he caused the jeering trumpets to sound as the crestfallen rebels came out on their way to banishment; and his English troops called for the hangman's rope as the traitors passed.

With the conquest of the south-east and the failure of Robert to invade, the western centres of revolt collapsed. From Bristol the Mowbrays—Geoffrey, bishop of Coutances, and his nephew, Robert, earl of Northumberland—and William of Eu had been ravaging the country; and from Hereford, Roger de Lacy had attacked Worcester. Wulfstan, the aged Saxon bishop of Worcester, had inspired the defence of his city; and by the summer conditions were returning to normal. By the autumn only one important conspirator had not made terms with the king—the bishop of Durham.

William of Saint-Calais was one of the best bishops of his time. He had introduced Benedictine monks into his cathedral church, which later he started to rebuild, and at Durham he enjoyed a great reputation. In the first months of Rufus's reign he was the intimate of the king, and his alleged desertion was hateful to his master. Rufus had ordered the confiscation of his temporalities as early as March; but the bishop remained secure in Durham castle, and never appeared before the king without a safe-conduct. The trial of William of Saint-Calais, of which we have a contemporary report, probably drawn up for use in the papal *curia*, to which the bishop appealed, is noteworthy for the complete repudiation by the English church of the more extreme claims to an autonomous jurisdiction which could be based on canon law. Bishop William steadfastly denied that the king's court was competent to try him. He was at all times willing to purge himself as a bishop—presumably by his unsupported oath—in any tribunal of crime and perjury; but he would not submit to the judgment of laymen in a case involving his bishopric; and he claimed that if there were to be a trial it should be in his own province, by his fellow bishops, and according to ecclesiastical law. Archbishop Lanfranc, however, supported by the archbishop of York and all the bishops, though possibly with minor reservations, and with the acclamation of the lay baronage, maintained as determinedly that William's lay fiefs alone were at stake, and that therefore he should plead and submit to judgment in the king's court as a baron. The weighty precedent adduced by Lanfranc was the case of Odo of Bayeux in 1082. When at Salisbury in November 1088 no heed was given to William's initial plea— that, as he had been despoiled of his bishopric without judgment, he should be reinvested before being called upon to plead—he appealed from an irregular tribunal giving judgment against the rules of canon law to the pope for a canonical trial. The king's court, composed in the traditional way of bishops, barons, and royal servants, proceeded nevertheless to the final judgment—forfeiture of fiefs—and the bishop, after he had under pressure surrendered his castle, was allowed to leave the country.

In the spring of 1089 William of Saint-Calais obtained a bull from Pope Urban II directing the king to restore him to his bishopric and to send his accusers to Rome for the lawful settlement of the case. The king took no notice, and the bishop remained with Duke Robert, who had put him in charge of the administration of Normandy. Three years later William of Saint-Calais made his peace with the king and supported him against Archbishop Anselm. Nevertheless, his attitude in 1088 reveals the inherent precariousness of William I's ecclesiastical settlement. The bishop's case was purely theoretical. The customs of both England and Normandy were against him, and on the point at issue English practice was never to change. When William I ordered the separation of ecclesiastical from secular pleas he had no purpose to weaken his hold over the church or to allow rebellious prelates to claim immunity from his jurisdiction. Yet William of Saint-Calais's case was based upon the book, and he had a copy of the decretals with him at the trial. Each time that a radical churchman appeared it became increasingly harder for the bishops to support the customs of England against the universal law of the church. The attitude of Bishop William was portentous; yet so steeped in custom were his contemporaries that it caused no real concern.

The suppression of the rebellion of 1088 set Rufus firmly on the throne He had to put down another revolt seven years later; but his authority in England became even greater than his father's had been. Robert had been accepted without difficulty in Normandy and Maine. Henry has used his legacy to buy from Robert the Cotentin and the Avranchin together with Mont Saint-Michel and the lordship over Earl Hugh of Chester's Norman lands. The characters of the three brothers deserve attention.

It is hard to do justice to William Rufus and his policies because all the writers of the time were bitterly prejudiced against him—for reasons which, in part, appeal also to the modern historian—and there are lacking other memorials of his reign, such as laws or financial records, by which the balance can easily be redressed. Rufus, although he swore by the Holy Face of Lucca, was not a Christian. The conventional churchmen of his day present him as a blaspheming rebel. Some modern interpreters have held that he was a pagan, adhering to the pre-Christian nature religion which was still unconquered by official orthodoxy; yet the strain of scepticism which he often betrays makes it unlikely that he was the devoted follower of a rival cult. The courts of even pacific princes in the early Middle Ages savoured much of the military camp; and Rufus was a brave and famous knight. So we find in his entourage many of the typical qualities of a martial society: a code of honour confined to the elect, together with a ruffianly disregard and contempt for other standards, and a hard and ascetic pursuit of military virtue alternating with luxurious and vicious recreation. William Rufus never married and he begot no children. His private life was an ugly parody of the puritan strain in contemporary morality. He was, therefore, hated by the monks; and monks wrote the histories of his time. Yet the bias of the monastic writers lay deeper than their abhorrence of a perverse and irreligious warrior. Monks were always convinced that any policy of the lay power which ran contrary to the interests of their order, however necessary, was demented tyranny, that any attack on the rights of their monastery, however lawful the procedure, was sacrilege, and that the agents of the prince, however regular their office and action, were invariably irresponsible extortioners. Such views underlie the sweet and reasonable biography written by Eadmer of a sweet and not unreasonable saint— Anselm—with whom Rufus had to deal; and it takes a conscious and sustained effort of will to discount this inherent bias and to supply the want of an *advocatus diaboli.* For William II had meritorious qualities both as a man and as a king; and it was in the thirteen years of his reign that the provisional contrivances of his father were held fast and made firm.

Rufus had little personal dignity and no readiness of tongue. On formal occasions a simulated bluster and a threatening countenance had to do service for the natural sternness and gravity which his father had displayed. Yet he acquired a prestige and a renown even greater than his father's because he had a clear conception of the majesty of his office and neglected none of its duties. He dreamed of boundless military conquest, yet confined himself to the practical ends of a soundly-conceived policy. He was greedy of money, like his father, but spent it to good purpose. He was a formidable defender of his rights, kept firm internal peace, and crushed his enemies, yet with far less chicanery than his father had used and certainly with less savagery. His irreligion and high sense of importance made him a harsh and unpopular master of the English church, and in ecclesiastical affairs he did many things of which his father would have disapproved. But, even so, the Norman church was to welcome his strong rule and to think his mocking jests a small price to pay for peace and order. Although Rufus was not a doting brother, he never behaved unnaturally toward his kin; and, besides being a dutiful son while his father lived, he cherished always the memory of his parents. Many monsters of cruelty and faithlessness lived in the eleventh century; but William II cannot be counted among them.   Had he been less flamboyant he would have been esteemed by posterity at least as good a king as his brother Henry and probably the better man. The younger William's prestige, however, was only partly dependent on his talents as a ruler. His idiosyncrasies of character gave him the same sort of notoriety that the Emperor Frederick II enjoyed a century-and-a-half later. His generosity and chivalry, his innate good nature, his fearless conduct, were readily acclaimed by the knightly class. And even deeper was the call of his scoffing irreligion. Red was the witch colour, the magical hue of blood and fire, the colour fit for the sacrificial king of the nature cults which lay beneath orthodox Christianity. And it seems that Rufus, the red king, who had a servant, Ranulf, bearing the fiery name of Flambard or Passiflamme, played a role in a drama of which he may not have been aware. Like Edward the Confessor William aroused strange expectations; and the myth of sacrifice was fulfilled when he was slain mysteriously in the depths of the forest.

The character of William's elder brother, Robert Curthose, is a variation on the same basic theme; but it received more objective appraisal from contemporary writers for reasons which will become clear. Robert was a weaker, more sympathetic, less violent version of his brother. His incompetence as a ruler cannot be questioned. He was as great a soldier as William, but even more unstable in purpose; equally avaricious, yet a thoughtless spender; more faithless, because more open to influence; no less immoral, but more conventional in his vices; as careless in religion, but without open defiance and ready for high adventure in the church's service. Robert is seen at his best on the first Crusade, a brave knight, a true leader of men, fighting for what Christendom held to be a noble cause. He is seen at his worst in his pitiful misgovernment of his paternal duchy. Henry, the youngest brother, born in England in 1068, was as yet unformed. He had been the darling of his mother, yet seems in time more like his father than either of his brothers, perhaps because he had a similar anxious and arduous youth. Until Rufus died, his sole aim was to win a patrimony from his brothers, and in the tortuous politics of those years he built a character more relentless and more methodical than Rufus's, more conventional and colder than Robert's. Like his brothers he was avaricious and immoral; but he was pious in his father's way.

III

By the end of the year 1088 William Rufus was firmly in the saddle; and he was a wilful man. But rarely did he follow a route that had not been mapped by his father. Despite his glamour, Rufus was a conservative with practical aims. Once he had secured England he aspired to rule Normandy also. When the duchy had been obtained he concerned himself with the Vexin and with Maine. In his kingdom, his attitude towards Wales and Scotland was traditional. If, like Agricola, he toyed with the idea of conquering Ireland, he, too, resisted the temptation; and his grandiose plan of taking the duchy of Aquitaine, or Guienne, in pledge was frustrated by his death. The call of the first Crusade went unheard. Rufus was busy in the west. In matters of government and administration, too, the younger William hardly transgressed the lines drawn by his father. If anything he was more of a king and less of a duke than the Conqueror, tightening his hold over the affairs of the kingdom, sharpening relations with the barons in the royal interest, insisting on every profitable right, exacting every profitable duty. Rufus consolidated the monarchical powers at a time of reaction, at a time when the alliance of king, barons, and church, which a common danger had forged, was weakening; and so successful was he that his brother Henry could maintain the policy despite his irregular seizure of the throne.

Rufus was most martial; and even his petty wars were expensive. He recruited famous knights for his household, and he poured out money in subsidies and bribes. Gelds were imposed. Stern justice was done on malefactors, for the chattels of the hanged, the lands of the disinherited, and the fines of those who found the king's mercy formed no trivial part of the royal revenue. Royal justice, indeed, became hateful to the people. Private war and disturbance were not allowed, for the barons should not waste their military strength or dissipate the country's wealth. The financial obligations of a vassal were rigorously enforced. Rufus emphasized the original precariousness and revocability of the fief. He confiscated and regranted fiefs whenever there was sufficient reason. On the death of a baron he selected the successor—not always the eldest son—and made him buy back the land. He insisted on his right to the fief and the wardship of the children when a vassal died without leaving a mature heir, and he disposed of the marriages of the widow and of the children to his profit. He restricted the right of the laity to leave money by will, and confiscated the chattels of dead prelates, who, of course, had no heir at law. There is some truth in the saying of the St. Albans writer that William was the true friend to none but the dead, and in the statement in the Anglo-Saxon chronicle that he desired to be the heir of everyone, churchman or layman. Yet the king's behaviour should not be regarded simply as tyranny. He opposed himself to a rising tide which, if allowed to reach its flood, could have swamped the monarchy. Fiefs were being transformed by the hereditary principle; and offices were fast becoming fiefs. A strong king had to try to arrest this process. Rufus essayed to push the movement farther back than contemporary habit allowed, and the hereditary fief had in the main to be accepted by his successors. But William's policy was timely and salutary. It produced revenue, and it kept the king in full control of the lands of the kingdom.

Ecclesiastical estates inevitably suffered the worst. The Norman dukes had treated the lands of their monasteries almost as ducal demesne. Rufus showed the same attitude in England. His abbots did not always enjoy the free control of the monastic estates, and vacancies were prolonged so that a part of the revenue could be diverted to the royal treasury. More scandal was caused by William's treatment of the bishoprics. His father had filled vacancies up quickly and had not, it seems, resumed the temporalities during the intermission. Rufus, however, treated the bishoprics as though they were fiefs, and in this connexion he could indulge his views to the full, because there was no heir to demand the succession. He, therefore, made no haste to appoint a new bishop, put out the temporalities at farm during the vacancy as though they had fully escheated, and demanded a relief from the incoming prelate, as at Thetford in 1091, or took a relief from the honorial barons during the avoidance, as at Worcester in 1095. This thorough application of feudal law to ecclesiastical estates was something new in England, although not uncommon abroad, and it was regarded as an abuse by strict churchmen. Its enforcement, however, led to few overt disputes, although it must be recognized as the deep canker in the relationship between Rufus and Archbishop Anselm.

William II's domestic policy should not be condemned out of hand; but clearly it pressed heaviest on those least able to defend themselves. The barons could generally pass on the burden of military service, fines, and reliefs to their under-tenants, and so could worldly prelates. But the pious abbot and bishop, who tried to take the weight, and the mass of the people, from whom the royal treasure was in the last resort extorted, paid heavily for the royal ambition.

Archbishop Lanfranc died on 24 May 1089. Not long since, Wibert, one of the papal claimants, had remembered him as the great pioneer teacher and theologian, the brilliant star that God had given to lighten Europe's darkness; and it is well not to allow the prelacy of his old age to obscure his wider fame. Yet Lanfranc was also a great archbishop. Like his master, William the Bastard, he was a man of his time and one of the best. He had served his king and the church as well as he could, and it can hardly be claimed that either had suffered from the need to compromise. Indeed, it was Lanfranc's strength that he was almost unaware that he played a double role. King William had been also a pious reformer; Lanfranc had been no less a statesman. They pursued the same ends in harmony. Nor should it be assumed that Lanfranc died a disappointed man. Although he must have known the weaknesses of Rufus, he was able to control him, for the prince had been educated in his household and had received knighthood from his hands. But with Lanfranc's death no restraint was left on the king. His uncles had been defeated, the barons had been cowed, and Rufus made no move to appoint another primate. It is significant that in these next years the working of a powerful bureaucratic element in the court can be dimly perceived. The king was surrounded by his military commanders; but the routine business of the royal administration was gradually gathered together in the hands of a trusted royal chaplain.

Ranulf Flambard, a Norman, had been keeper of the great seal when Maurice, later bishop of London, had been William I's chancellor (*c.* 1078), and possibly held the office until the end of the reign. Already an important man in 1087, Ranulf became the key official under William II. His position at first cannot be exactly defined, but it foreshadowed the office of chief justiciar, which is found with certainty in the next reign; and there is no reason to doubt that Ranulf was eventually a precursor of Roger of Salisbury. Ranulf did not normally travel with the king, and he always had an important part in the government while the king was abroad. His essential function was to control the king's legal and financial business while the king hunted or made war. It was Ranulf who drove the local courts hard in the royal interest, who visited the shires on eyre with other royal 'barons', investigating the rights and revenues of the king, who administered the vacant fiefs and ecclesiastical estates, who collected geld, and supervised the treasury and the sheriffs. As the *exactor regis* Ranulf was hated; and the chroniclers vilified him together with his master. Certainly while enriching the king, Ranulf took care of himself and his family; but this was the custom. Rufus's final reward to his faithful servant was the bishopric of Durham; and Ranulf became a respectable figure in Henry I's reign after his initial disgrace and despite some scandalous ecclesiastical adventures in Normandy. He made a good bishop of Durham. He repressed his ambitious monastic chapter, divided his diocese into archdeaconries, enriched his city with new buildings, and infused into his diocese and lordship that business efficiency which he had earlier displayed in the kingdom at large. It is easier, however, to sketch Ranulf Flambard's history than to describe the detailed organization of the royal government. The crisp writs which issued from the chancery and the unfailing supply of money in the treasury prove its efficiency. The notoriety of Ranulf can only mean that its financial and judicial business was expanding. It is known that the abacus, which lay behind the medieval English exchequer system, was familiar to some members of William II's court; but it is uncertain whether the increased volume of business had as yet been matched by an improved technique. What cannot be doubted, however, is that the royal government was rapidly outgrowing its simple domestic organization under the steady pressure of William II's financial needs.

The king never relented except when he was hard pressed. We have seen that in his first year he called the English to him and promised them reforms. Less than six years later, in 1093, when he lay sick and near to death, he issued a written charter of repentance. Prisoners were to be released, royal debts to be forgiven, old offences to be pardoned, good laws to be restored and enforced, and the church to be spared. These acts of William II, like the testament of William I, recognized that the king had done wrong; but the fault was thought to lie as much in the office as in the person. The wrongs were in a sense the almost inevitable burden of sin that any active king had to incur, and which he discharged by repentance and absolution before he died. But if the king by necessity or mistake atoned too soon then he must regard his expiatory measures as promises he could not keep, unless he were to abandon most of his royal purposes. And Rufus had formed one costly ambition, from which only trouble with Anselm and the threats of Wales and Scotland could distract him—the acquisition of Normandy.

IV

When William I died the greater Norman barons expelled the ducal garrisons from their castles, and henceforth, except when William II was in control, did what they pleased. The anarchy which prevailed in Normandy should not, however, be regarded as exceptional. It was William the Bastard's tight rein that had been extraordinary; and Normandy under Duke Robert was no worse than Anjou under Fulk 'le Réchin' (1068–1109) or the French demesne under King Philip I (1060–1108). The frontier fiefs, such as that of Robert of Bellême, inevitably fell away under Robert's indolent government. Maine, which had submitted to Robert on his accession, brought in a rival count in 1090—Hugh of Este, the son of Azzo II, marquis of Este in Venetia, and the grandson of Hubert Wake-dog, sometime count of Maine. And when in the same year Hugh sold his claim to Helias of la Flèche, the great-grandson of Herbert Wake-dog through another daughter, the Manceux obtained a leader who was steadfastly to withstand Norman attacks and to obtain in the end acknowledgment of his position as count. The French Vexin naturally could not be recovered. Robert was at Vernon, south of the Seine and west of the Epte on 24 April 1089, engaged in some hostilities against the French; but in general he and Philip I had a common interest. Robert needed his overlord's help against his brother Rufus; and Philip wished to prevent the reunion of England and Normandy.

The distracted state of Normandy made it easy for William to intervene, and the harassed church and people soon came to regard him as a saviour; but neither prince could readily marshal his adherents; and the campaigns are more notable for hidden diplomacy than for battles or even for important sieges. Only occasionally could the endemic baronial wars be twisted into operations between the rival dukes. Mercenary soldiers were used by both sides. And between the courts of the principal contestants flitted their brother, Henry, determined to hook some advantage out of these troubled waters.

In 1089 Rufus consulted his English vassals and decided to claim Normandy. The pattern of events which had taken place in England in the previous year was then repeated in the duchy. Some of Robert's vassals transferred their allegiance and waited for William's advent. Rufus bought the homage of the lord of Saint-Valery on the Somme, which provided him with an entry to the mainland, and of many barons in eastern Normandy. His only weakness north of the Seine lay in the faithfulness of Helias of Saint-Saëns to his father-in-law, Duke Robert, for Helias's castles of Arques, Bures, and Saint-Saëns almost cut the rebellious territory in half. In November 1090 William inspired a revolt in Rouen; but it was prevented by Robert with the support of his brother, Henry, and of Robert of Bellême; and the leading burgess of the English party, Conan, was thrown by Henry himself from the tower of the city to his death. This success of Robert's showed William that he must intervene in person. He crossed to Normandy in February 1091, and received many submissions at his headquarters at Eu. The brothers came to terms. William was to keep the fealty of those barons who had already become his men. In return the king was to give the duke money and aid him to restore order in his share of the duchy. Finally, if either died before the other without leaving a legitimate heir, the survivor was to succeed him in his territory. Twelve of the leading barons on each side swore to the observance of the treaty. It had the form of permanence, although its terms were more in the nature of a truce. The hostility of both brothers to the cadet, Henry, is most noticeable. Clearly he had, by intriguing with each, lost the favour of both. Although Henry was the heir presumptive to England and Normandy, and although Rufus had no urge to marry and Robert little inclination, Henry was expressly disinherited, and by the allocation of Cherbourg and Mont Saint-Michel to William he was even deprived of territory. When the formalities had been completed Robert and William marched together to dispossess their youngest brother. But when he had been forced to surrender his last fortress, Mont Saint-Michel, and vengeance had been satisfied, a reconciliation took place, and all three brothers joined in more constructive acts. On 18 July 1091, duke and king assembled their barons and bishops at Caen and held an inquest into the rights and customs which had belonged to Duke William the Bastard. The investigation was intended to precede the re-establishment of the ducal government. The plan was then to march against the more recalcitrant barons; but ominous news came from England of Welsh and Scottish trouble; and in August the three brothers crossed the Channel in order to remedy the affairs of the kingdom.

It is possible that William went immediately to the help of the Welsh marcher barons; but the great business of the year was the punishment of Malcolm, king of Scots. Malcolm had done homage to Robert as William I's heir; but he had entered into no engagements so far with Rufus. In May 1091 Malcolm had invaded Northumbria for the fourth time, and had reached Chester-le-Street before he had been driven back. The three brothers organized a powerful show of force. The fleet that was sent up the east coast was wrecked before Michaelmas; but in the middle of November the land army reached Durham, where the king restored William of Saint-Calais to his bishopric. The rival forces met on the Firth of Forth. As neither side stood to gain much by fighting, Edgar Aetheling from the side of Malcolm and Robert Curthose from William's side were able to arrange a settlement. Malcolm did homage to the English king, and was confirmed in possession of his English lands; he gave again, or left in William's train, his son Duncan as a hostage; and William may have promised Malcolm a pension. The three brothers then returned south, and on the way the king showed his renewed confidence in the bishop of Durham by granting him another fief in Yorkshire.

Robert stayed with William until Christmas; but the king's selfishness ruptured their agreement. It was now William's turn to go and help his brother in Normandy; but he found that he had too much to do at home, and he allowed Robert to leave dissatisfied and angry. In 1092 Rufus attended to the Scottish march again. He expelled Dolfin, son of Gospatric and great-grandson of Uhtred, the ancestor of the Bernician house, who was ruling in Cumbria, presumably as a vassal of the king of Scots, restored Carlisle, built a castle there, and colonized the place with English cultivators from the south. The English frontier had begun to move north once more.

Of greater interest to William's English subjects, however, was the state of the English church. Not only had there been no primate since Lanfranc died in May 1089, but no pope had been recognized since Gregory VII lost Rome in 1084. A leaderless church was agreeable to the king; but the avoidance of Canterbury and its exploitation by the treasury were unpopular. The king was already under pressure to fill the archbishopric when in the spring of 1093 he fell seriously ill. In preparation for his death Rufus promised political reform, and he agreed to give Canterbury to Anselm, abbot of le Bec. Anselm, a pupil of Lanfranc and the leading theologian of his day, was already known to England and to the king. He had visited Lanfranc at Canterbury in 1078, and in 1092 he had come to England partly on account of his monastery's estates and partly, no doubt, as the unwitting tool of a widespread pious conspiracy which aimed at securing his appointment as archbishop. The king cannot have been unaware of the plot; he seems indeed, to have toyed with the idea of indulging the schemers; yet nothing might have been done had not his illness brought matters to a head. But when William became eager, it was found that Anselm did not want the primacy: he was a monk and scholar, and knew himself unfitted to hold so great a political office, especially when his master would be Rufus. It was in vain that the defrauded bishops begged, the dying king entreated. In the end the pastoral staff was thrust by force into Anselm's clenched hand and the ring pushed on his finger. This wild scene by the king's bedside was recognized by Anselm as a valid investiture; but so many important questions had been brushed aside that it was to be the start of a momentous series of disputes. Little trouble was found in getting Duke Robert's and the archbishop of Rouen's consent to the promotion; Anselm's abbey agreed with reluctance; the king was quite willing to restore all the Canterbury estates and to agree to take Anselm's advice in spiritual affairs; but the matter of recognizing a pope was not so easily accommodated, for Anselm, on his becoming abbot of le Bec, had made his profession of obedience to Urban II, and it was the Norman custom in England that no pope should be recognized without the king's consent. Anselm was consecrated archbishop of Canterbury on 4 December 1093, with this problem still outstanding; and it could, indeed, be put aside until it was necessary for him to approach the pope for his pallium.

Anselm's appointment to the primacy, for which neither he nor the king can be held fully responsible, had the most unfortunate consequences. Anselm's premonitions were justified in the event, and a series of disputes distracted the English church to its grave hurt for fourteen years. Anselm himself can hardly be blamed for these quarrels, although his insufficiency certainly contributed to them. He was never unreasonably difficult; and the one fanatical party was the king, for the mere suspicion of an insult to his dignity made Rufus rage, whereas Anselm, unless pushed to the very rock of conscience or authority, was always ready to compromise and to suffer. Rufus certainly pressed his advantage too far, and in wilfully provoking a dispute with the church weakened his successor's control over ecclesiastical affairs. The settlement of William I depended on internal harmony, for any domestic quarrel was apt to publish to the world the archaic and peculiar rules which governed the island church.

While William Rufus was acquiring a new archbishop he was also engaged in important negotiations with Scotland. King Malcolm complained that William had broken their treaty—possibly by the annexation of Carlisle—and although Malcolm visited William's court under safe-conduct in August 1093, the two kings did not meet because Malcolm would not accept the jurisdiction of William's court. The king of Scots claimed that by ancient custom disputes between the kings should be settled on the frontier by a court composed of the barons of the two countries. It is clear that Malcolm had no stomach to put himself on the level of any other vassal of the English king; but it is improbable that there was much precedent for the course he proposed, save negotiations such as had taken place when the English kings had invaded. Malcolm returned north only to raise forces for a punitive raid. On 13 November 1093 he was ambushed near Alnwick by Robert of Mowbray, earl of Northumberland, and killed together with his son and heir, Edward. His saintly wife, Margaret, who was already ill, died soon afterwards.

These royal deaths had important consequences in the north. During the reign of Malcolm, who had been as a youth a hostage at the court of King Edward the Confessor and who had been placed on the throne by English power, English influence had transformed the Scottish monarchy. Malcolm's strength had rested more on his English possessions, chiefly Lothian, the alienated portion of Northumbria, than on the Gaelic highlands. He had been, indeed, an independent and often hostile prince, but, for all that, he remained in a way an English marcher lord. On his death a Gaelic reaction took place, and his brother Donald Ban, supported by the Norwegians of the Isles, seized the throne. Duncan, Malcolm's son by his first marriage, was already in England; Malcolm's sons by Margaret found it wise to take shelter there; and it became the policy of King William to help these princes. Duncan (II) tried his fortune in 1094 with the aid of a band of Anglo-Norman adventurers; but he could get no firm grip on the crown before he was slain in the same year. It was then the turn of Edgar; and in September 1097 his uncle, Edgar Aetheling, led a successful expedition and set his nephew on the throne. The dynasty of Malcolm had been re-established, and three of his sons—Edgar, Alexander, and David—were now to rule in succession; and it was in their reigns that the kingdom of Scotland, based on a feudalized Anglo-Norman Lothian, was organized entirely on the English model, and that the church was reformed on the Latin pattern.

It cannot be doubted that it was this very anglicization which made Scottish independence possible. A disunited Gaelic north harbouring an archaic church might have been annexed piecemeal as English administrative competence increased; but a feudal kingdom gained its own polarity. In 1072, as part of the settlement between Canterbury and York, Scotland had been put within the province of the northern metropolitan. But the reformed Scottish church resented the subordination of St. Andrews to any authority other than distant Canterbury; and York was rarely able to exercise its legal powers, despite the support of the papacy. In a similar way the Scottish kings saw no harm in acknowledging their subjection to English kings who were usually on the continental frontiers of their dominions and apprehended no real danger of sinking into the ordinary ranks of the baronage. York was the proper centre for a united Britain; but when England was annexed to a French duchy the Wessex tradition became inescapable. The contrast between Scotland and Wales is noteworthy. In Wales the Norman barons, frightened of Celtic resurgence, looked to the English king for support. In Scotland, except for the episode after Malcolm's death, there was little Gaelic menace; and so the Anglo-Norman baronage strove for independence under the Anglo-Scottish kings. The remoteness of Scotland made autonomy inevitable; and Scotland preserved an ambiguous status until the fourteenth century when it began to draw away from England and develop as a completely separate kingdom.

Before the Scottish position had been clarified, however, Rufus was once more embroiled with Normandy. Towards the end of 1093 Duke Robert, tired of waiting for his brother's assistance, denounced their treaty. The king had already been able to restore friendly relations with the Flemish court owing to Count Robert I's anger at the repudiation of his step-daughter by the king of the Franks; and later he resumed payment to Count Robert II of the traditional fief of 300 marks as a reward for his neutrality, or help, during the Norman campaigns. Thus secured, Rufus raised money by means of an aid from his barons and summoned the feudal host to Hastings in February 1094. But before the west wind blew there was time for Anselm to consecrate the Conqueror's church of Battle on the site of that ever-memorable field and opportunity for the king and the archbishop to dispute over the insufficiency of Anselm's aid, the scandal of the vacant abbeys, and vice at court. Rufus finally got away with his troops on 19 March. At a conference with Robert the twenty-four guarantors of the treaty declared that Rufus was the guilty party; and a desultory war ensued, in which Robert, supported by his overlord, had the advantage. Rufus then called for twenty thousand English foot. But when the fyrd assembled at Hastings, Ranulf Flambard took from the men the ten shillings with which each was provided by his district for his maintenance, and sent the proceeds to the king so that he could hire mercenaries. In the autumn Rufus attracted his brother Henry, now lord of Domfront, to his side, and in October, Henry and the earl of Chester crossed to England. Rufus joined them at the end of December. He had important business to do at home, and Henry was to fight for him in Normandy at his expense.

Rufus was called back to England by rumours of conspiracy, by ecclesiastical troubles, and by news of the desperate position in Wales and of the last Scottish invasion. Anselm met the king with a request to go abroad and get the metropolitan pallium from Pope Urban II. The simplicity of this demand made Rufus mad with anger. In the previous year he had despoiled Herbert bishop of Thetford of his temporalities because he had visited Urban to receive absolution for having 'bought' the bishopric from Rufus in 1091; and he regarded Anselm's calm assumption that Urban was the pope to be recognized as an attack on the royal dignity. But even Rufus could see that there was a real problem to solve. If Anselm was to get the pallium then one of the popes must be recognized, and, as Anselm had already recognized Urban, there was a conflict of loyalty which required consideration. A court was, therefore, summoned to Rockingham (Northants) in March 1095. The easiest way out of the difficulty was to get Anselm to renounce Urban, so that the king could with his advisers make a free choice of pope; and great pressure was exerted on the unhappy archbishop to this end. A more hazardous solution, suggested by William of Saint-Calais, bishop of Durham, was to depose Anselm, and thereby cause the problem to disappear. Rufus, however, was not fully supported by his court. The bishops were willing to withdraw obedience from the primate, but would take no active measures against him; the barons were unwilling to do as much. The technical problem of law was too difficult, and was pushed aside. Incompatible loyalties were in conflict. The king's anger at the impasse made him decide to get rid of Anselm even at the cost of recognizing Urban. During an adjournment of the court, William's ambassadors treated secretly with Urban. The price of recognition clearly was to be the deposition of Anselm; but the king was outplayed. The ambassadors returned in May with a papal legate, Walter, cardinal-bishop of Albano. William then publicly recognized Urban; but the legate, although in other matters complaisant enough to the king, refused to depose Anselm. Rufus in the end took his discomfiture philosophically. He accepted Anselm as archbishop and restored Herbert of Thetford to his bishopric. As Anselm was friendless and also distrusted the papal legate, no reforms were made in the English church.

While these ecclesiastical negotiations were in progress a baronial revolt in England was coming to a head. The deep-seated causes were doubtless William's severe government; the immediate pretext was the king's treatment of Robert of Mowbray, earl of Northumberland. The earl and his men had plundered four Norwegian trading vessels which had taken refuge in a northern port, and Robert disregarded alike the king's order of restitution and the consequent summonses to attend the Easter and Whitsun courts of 1095 in order to stand his trial. It is clear that Robert resented royal interference with the government of his fief, and he drew into a plot those Welsh and Scottish marcher lords who sympathized with his attitude. The earl of Hereford had revolted in 1075 because King William I had sent sheriffs to hold pleas on his lands; and the marches, where independence of the king was so nearly achieved and royal control so irritant, ever flashed quickly into rebellion. In 1095 the earl of Shrewsbury and his brother Philip of Montgomery, Roger de Lacy, a Herefordshire baron, and William of Eu, a kinsman of Rufus, were the leading conspirators with Earl Robert; and their wild plan was to kill the king and replace him by his cousin, Stephen of Aumale, the son of Adelaide, William I's sister, by her third husband, Odo, the disinherited count of Champagne and lord of Holderness in England. After the Whitsun court Rufus left Anselm in command in Kent to prevent an incursion from France, and marched north. He took Newcastle, then, after a two months' siege, Tynemouth, and finally invested the great stronghold of Bamburgh. The king had time to campaign in Wales, in an attempt to relieve the desperate situation, before Earl Robert of Mowbray was captured by a stratagem and his wife compelled to surrender the castle in order to save her husband's eyes. Investigation discovered the conspiracy. Mowbray himself disappeared into prison; and so secure did the king now feel in the north that no successor as earl was appointed. Some of the greater conspirators bought their peace, and it cost the earl of Shrewsbury, so it was said, three thousand pounds. The king's court at Christmas 1095, attended by a great concourse of barons, dealt with the rest of Mowbray's friends. William of Eu failed in the ordeal of battle and was mutilated. His steward was hanged. Others suffered mutilation or disinheritance. In 1088 King William had found it necessary to restrain his anger. In 1096 he could show his strength.

V

Although the royal intervention in Wales in the autumn of 1095 was but a small incident in the marcher world, important events had been taking place in Wales which merit attention. The advance of the Normans into Wales was repeating in the main the pattern of their settlement in England, except that it was accomplished more slowly, largely by force, and often without the express grant of the king. The geographical conditions also gave the conquest a character of its own. The Normans had no desire to settle or to exploit directly the mountainous areas, and were content merely to draw tribute from these. The Welsh political scene had been kaleidoscopic since Harold Godwinesson had broken the power of Gruffydd ap Llywelyn in 1063. Many princes from several lines of descent contended for the kingdoms of Gwynedd—the coastal area of north Wales (western Merioneth, Caernarvon, northern Denbigh, and Flint), Powys —the eastern part of north Wales (Montgomery, eastern Merioneth, and southern Denbigh), and Deheubarth—South Wales; and it was only rarely that native leaders arose who could command the undisputed allegiance even in the lesser principalities. The Welsh princes, just as much as the Norman marcher lords, were vassals of the king of the English; but the instability of their rule, the feuds and intrigues, allowed not only the Normans to encroach but Irish-Scandinavian adventurers, and even the king of Norway, to interfere. The Normans preserved in this period an exemplary solidarity; and their advance could not be entirely checked either by the sporadic general fury of the Welsh or by the forfeitures which followed the occasional baronial rebellion against the king.

William I had created three marcher earldoms, each facing one of the main Welsh kingdoms—Chester against Gwynedd, Shrewsbury against Powys, and Hereford against Deheubarth—and each had a separate history of conquest. But during the reign of the first Norman the barons, except in the north, had been more engaged in consolidating their position in the marches than in making new advances into Wales. In 1070 the earl of Hereford, William fitz-Osbern, lord of Breteuil, left the march for his death in Flanders; in 1075 his unworthy second son, Roger, who had succeeded him in Hereford, was broken and imprisoned by the king for rebellion; and no successor as earl was appointed. In 1078 Rhys ap Tewdwr became king of Deheubarth, was recognized by King William, and paid £40 a year as rent for his kingdom. These events had a depressing effect on the Normans, and in 1087 the outpost castles were still Wigmore, Clifford, Ewias Harold, Monmouth, Chepstow, and Caerleon, which put the frontier on the river Usk in Gwent, far to the east of the modern Anglo-Welsh boundary. Nearly all the southern marcher barons were in active revolt against William Rufus in 1088; and the conquest of Deheubarth did not begin until some years later. Nor had the earl of Shrewsbury, Roger of Montgomery, advanced far into Powys. In 1087 his castle of Montgomery still marked the limit of penetration in the valley of the upper Severn. But in the north Hugh d'Avranches (the Fat), earl of Chester, and his able cousin and vassal, Robert of Rhuddlan, had made good progress, especially along the coastal plain, where the River Clwyd had been the frontier. By 1073 Robert had a castle at Rhuddlan, and from there he pushed on to Degannwy. In 1081 the Welsh-Scandinavian Gruffydd ap Cynan, king of Gwynedd and Powys, was captured and imprisoned; and the whole of Gwynedd seems to have been granted by King William to Robert for an annual rent of £40. Robert had extended his conquests to Conway when he was killed in 1088 at Degannwy by the Welsh. His death, however, was only a temporary set-back in the north. His fief and claims escheated to the earl, who had remained faithful to Rufus in 1088; and by 1092 Hugh d'Avranches had reached the Menai Straits, and was building castles at Bangor, Caernarvon, and Aber Lleiniog in Anglesey. By 1094 the conquest of Gwynedd seemed complete.

The south recovered more slowly from the events of 1088; but the offensive which was mounted in 1092 was to have spectacular results. An advance by Bernard of Neufmarché into Brycheiniog (Brecknock) proved to be momentous, for in 1093 Rhys ap Tewdwr, king of Deheubarth, was killed by the Normans, and was followed by no prince who could command much native allegiance. The Welsh lack of a leader was brilliantly exploited by Earl Roger of Montgomery, who burst through the centre to the sea, and then enveloped the south. In July 1093 he occupied Ceredigion (Cardiganshire) and founded Cardigan at the mouth of the River Teifi. He then pushed into Dyfed, which the king gave as a fief to Arnulf, one of the earl's younger sons. Arnulf of Montgomery built a castle at Pembroke, which he entrusted to Gerald of Windsor, the ancestor of the fitzGeralds, who were later to distinguish themselves in the conquest of Ireland. Meanwhile, Robert fitzHamon had secured Glamorgan and based himself at Cardiff, and Philip of Briouze had advanced into Builth (Radnor), where another famous castle was erected. All these castles were of the simple motte and bailey type, and normally served their purpose well. By 1094 independent Wales consisted merely of a few pockets of land, most of which were in the highland zone.

These catastrophes aroused the Welsh to a heroic struggle under Cadwgan ap Bleddyn, of the royal house of Powys, aided by Gruffydd ap Cynan, of the line of Gwynedd, who had escaped from his prison at Chester. The moment was favourable. Roger of Montgomery died on 27 July 1094 and was succeeded in England by his second son, Hugh. The king was abroad and Hugh earl of Chester with him. In the north, the tide of Welsh insurrection swept over Anglesey and all Norman posts west of Conway, and in the south over all the new castles in Ceredigion and Dyfed except Pembroke and Rhydygors. Only Glamorgan and Brecknock of the new conquests remained in the hands of the Normans. Hugh of Chester had crossed to England in October 1094; but the king, although he returned before the year was out, was prevented from intervening first by ecclesiastical business and then by the Mowbray rebellion. When, however, Montgomery castle fell, Rufus was stirred to action. He invaded North Wales in October 1095, and, dividing his army into detachments, fixed a rendezvous near Snowdon. Woodcutters cleared a way for the slow-moving columns; and the campaign did little more than show the flag to the Welsh. Two years later Rufus invaded again, this time probably in South Wales; and the revolt gradually subsided in the extreme south, where Pembroke castle, held by Gerald of Windsor with such fortitude and so many artful ruses, had never surrendered. The Welsh, however, remained in possession of Ceredigion and Ystrad Tywi (Carmarthen). In the north hostilities had been interrupted when Hugh of Montgomery, earl of Shrewsbury, campaigning with the earl of Chester in 1098, had been killed on the Menai Straits by an arrow shot from the fleet of Magnus Barefoot, king of Norway, which was cruising in these waters after visiting the Scandinavian empire in the western isles; but the earl of Chester recovered Anglesey in the next year. The new earl of Shrewsbury, Robert of Bellême, Hugh's elder brother, could not, however, do much in Powys. As a compromise he invested Cadwgan ap Bleddyn with Ceredigion and with the parts of Powys to which the Welshman had a family claim. Thus by 1099, most of South Wales had been occupied by the Normans; but Powys and Gwynedd remained substantially intact.

VI

In 1095 it seemed as though the painful and unrewarding struggle between King William Rufus and Duke Robert for the duchy of Normandy would be without end. But a wind blowing from an unexpected quarter entirely changed the position. On 27 November Pope Urban II preached the famous sermon at Clermont which called men to a Crusade; and when Robert decided to leave the cares of his duchy and undertake a new adventure a definite settlement with William had to be reached. The pope interested himself in the negotiations; his emissary, Abbot Geronto of Saint-Bénigne at Dijon, was with Rufus in England towards the end of 1095; and during the next summer a satisfactory agreement was made between the two brothers. William was to lend Robert 10,000 marks, and Robert was to give him the duchy in pledge for repayment. William raised the money from England by means of an aid in the form of a danegeld at 4*s.* the hide. Ecclesiastical demesne was not exempted from the tax, and the church, although most prelates were allowed to compound, complained bitterly. In September 1096 William crossed to Normandy with the money, and shortly afterwards Robert led his contingent on the long road to Jerusalem.

The brilliant success of Pope Urban's scheme was due to its irresistible appeal to the chivalrous. The hope of adventure, plunder, and fighting—and in the noblest of causes—stirred the bored and restless population almost to ecstasy. The attraction was weakest where purposeful adventure was to be had at home; and it is significant that few of the greater Norman barons and none of the English took the Cross. But for the frustrated and the failures the Crusade was a heaven-sent chance. With Robert went several distinguished neighbouring rulers, his cousin, Count Robert of Flanders, his brother-in-law, Count Stephen of Blois and Chartres, Count Hugh of Saint-Pol, and Duke Alan Fergant of Brittany, who took with him Ralf de Gael, sometime earl of East Anglia. Robert's uncle, Odo of Bayeux, was also of the party. The count of Maine, Helias of la Flèche, took the Cross; but he stayed at home when he learned that William Rufus would not respect his position. For Robert the Crusade was the beginning of a new life. The purely military character of the enterprise and the clear objective inspired his best qualities. His forces wintered in Apulia (and at Palermo the bishop of Bayeux closed his stormy life), reached Constantinople in May 1097, took part in the siege of Nicaea, the battle of Dorylaeum, and the siege of Antioch, and on 14 January 1099, moved with Raymond of Toulouse and Tancred of Sicily on Jerusalem. On 15 July Robert was in the assault that broke into the Holy City, and in August he was in the centre at the battle of Ascalon against the relieving army under the emir Malik el-Afdhal. Soon after this battle, in which Robert had crowned his exploits by riding down the standard-bearer of the emir, the duke began his return journey. It is unlikely that he had been offered, and refused, the throne of Jerusalem, as one writer maintained; but he had always been among the leaders of the expedition and had gained much renown.

No English and few Anglo-Norman knights took part in the first Crusade; but English sailors struck a blow on their own. A fleet of some thirty English trading vessels penetrated the Mediterranean from Gibraltar, and in 1097, in alliance with the Emperor Alexius, captured the Syrian ports of St. Simeon and Laodicia. From these bases they kept the seas open and provisioned the land forces during the siege of Antioch. Finally, when the fleet had been much reduced in number, the sailors abandoned their ships and joined the army in its advance on Jerusalem. This exploit reveals the great maritime strength of England at the close of the eleventh century and the courage of the ships' masters. We get a similar picture from the life of St. Godric, a hermit who had travelled far in his youth. Godric, a man of the humblest origins, became first a petty chapman and then, as he prospered, a merchant adventurer, taking partnership in trading voyages from East Anglia to Scotland, Brittany, Flanders, and Denmark. The king's financial demands may have fallen heavily on the agricultural community; but it seems that the commerce of England was recovering again.

William II remained in Normandy from the time he took over the duchy as pledge in the autumn of 1096 until Easter of the next year. In that short period the king, who had his chancellor, William Giffard, with him, took vigorous steps to restore the ducal government and the ducal demesne; but he had neither the time nor, probably, the money to deal with the Vexin or with Maine before Welsh trouble called him back to England. In the spring of 1097 Rufus invaded Wales and returned in a bad temper. He informed Archbishop Anselm that the Canterbury knights were of such poor quality and so badly trained that he must answer for it in the royal court. There is no reason to disbelieve the charge, for it is unlikely that Anselm bothered much about the training of his knights or the quality of the mercenaries he could send in their place. The episode served as a final discouragement to Anselm. He had been unable to control his suffragans, or even his monastic chapter, and he could not cope with the king. At Whitsun, and again later, he asked William for permission to visit the pope and take his advice. To Rufus these requests seemed a tiresome attempt to avoid responsibility, and he pointed out that it was forbidden for prelates to leave England without the royal consent. There was far less sympathy for Anselm in the royal court this time than there had been at Rockingham in 1095; and it was decided at Winchester in October that Anselm could leave the country provided he carried away nothing with him. Anselm offered the king his blessing; William accepted; and the two never met again. Rufus took the temporalities of the see into his hands; and, although Pope Urban II threatened the king with spiritual penalties for his audacity in punishing an archbishop for wishing to visit the pope, William's nerve and diplomacy were such that the blow never fell. Urban II died in July 1099 and the king did not recognize his successor.

When the Welsh revolt began to die down the king could devote his attention to Normandy again. In November 1097 he crossed the Channel with the purpose of securing the Norman marches. The task was severe. The indolent and luxurious Philip I of France, now excommunicate for having enticed Bertrada of Montfort away from her husband Fulk 'le Réchin', had in 1092–3 enfeoffed his eldest son, Louis, later King Louis VI, with the Vexin; and Louis, an active and determined boy, won his spurs in the defence of his appanage.

In Maine Helias of la Flèche was in firm possession; and as his ancestral estates lay in the south-east of the county he was well placed to
defend and to call on the help of the count of Anjou, to whose son,
Fulk the Young, Helias at this time betrothed his only daughter.

Rufus raised a large army in Normandy. His plan of campaign was
that he should attack the Vexin castles of Chaumont-en-Vexin,
Mantes, and Pontoise, while Robert of Bellême should prosecute
the war in Maine. The king, however, could take none of the
principal castles, and in January 1098 he went to the help of Robert.
On 28 April Robert captured Helias in an ambush and surrendered
him to Rufus. Fulk of Anjou, Helias's suzerain, then took up his
cause; but he was defeated so decisively by a sortie of the garrison
of Ballon, north of le Mans, that he made peace in August. Rufus
was to have le Mans and all the castles which his father had held,
and was recognized as count. In return he was to surrender all
prisoners, including Helias of la Flèche. Having achieved the half
of his purpose, Rufus turned again to the Vexin. In September he
failed in another attempt to capture Chaumont; and then, together
with William IX, duke of Aquitaine, who had come to discuss an
important proposal, he launched an attack south of the Seine, but
without decisive result. After Christmas the king made a truce with
the valiant Louis and returned to England in April 1099. Rufus was
certainly no military genius; and the advantage which the defence,
secure in its castles, had over an attacking army makes his campaigns
of 1097–9 appear confused and his success fortuitous. But it
should not be overlooked that he won. At the end of July Hugh,
archbishop of Lyons, writing to him about Anselm's exile, addressed
him as 'the victorious king of the English' and remarked on his
repeated triumphs over foreign nations. By 1099 Rufus had completely restored the territorial position which his father had left.
That was no trivial achievement.

William II stayed only a few months in England before he was
called back to Normandy by bad news. That short sojourn in his
kingdom, however, was memorable for a great occasion. For about
two years Ranulf Flambard had been engaged in constructing some
important buildings in London—a wall round the tower (the 'inner
ward'), the first stone London bridge, and Westminster Hall. The
labouring had been done by the men of those shires which owed
work in London; and it is another sign of the traditional flavour of
Rufus's government that the Old-English duties of 'bridge-work',

'wall-work', and 'fortress-work' should still be exploited. The king grumbled that the new palace was far too small; but when Whitsuntide 1099 came round the imposing ceremonies of the coronation feasts that his father had introduced were enacted at Westminster. At last Rufus was duke of Normandy and count of Maine as well as king of the English. South Wales was coming to heel; and the king of the Scots, Edgar, was present at court to bear the sword of state before his overlord. It was at a moment like this, when the ancient rites, rich in association and ambiguous in purpose, had been completed, when the crown had been placed anew on the king's head and the sceptre in his right hand, and when the king sat in state, dressed in tunic, dalmatic, and mantle, with spurred buskins on his feet and jewelled gloves on his hands, surrounded by his household officers, and his bishops, abbots, barons, and mercenaries, that sycophants could compare him with Caesar. And William was still bountiful. He repaid his enormous debt to his loyal servant, Ranulf Flambard, by giving him the rich bishopric of Durham that had lain vacant for three years; and at Durham Ranulf built another stone bridge, constructed another wall round a castle, levelled the open space, known as Palace Green, between the castle and the cathedral, and pushed up the cathedral church from its foundations to the nave vaulting.

The king was not allowed to remain long in peace. In June 1099, when hunting at Clarendon, he heard that Helias of la Flèche had once more entered le Mans and was investing the castle. Rufus rode immediately to the coast, embarked in a storm on a small boat without horse or companions—jesting that never had he heard of a king being drowned—jumped on a priest's mare at Touques, and entered the castle at Bonneville. He then relieved le Mans, harried the countryside as punishment, and returned to England at Michaelmas to resume his hunting.

William had many cares on his mind. By September 1099 Duke Robert was already on his return journey from Jerusalem. It is unlikely that William had decided whether he would restore the duchy if the debt were paid; but his negotiations with Duke William IX of Aquitaine show at least that he was considering another adventure of the same kind. It is reported that William IX, sceptic and voluptuary, and one of the earliest of the troubadours, anxious to go on a Crusade, and as impecunious as Robert had been, was willing to make a similar bargain with the English king. These weighty problems were solved unexpectedly for Rufus. On 2 August 1100, while out hunting in the New Forest, he was killed by an arrow thought to have been shot by Walter Tyrel, one of his own men. An open verdict was returned by the chroniclers, and no later attempt at investigation has conclusively upset that judgment. The pious looked to God's doom on a family that had loved hunting too well. The superstitious saw in the mysterious death of the red king a ritual sacrifice to the old deities. If it was murder— and no contemporary brings the charge—then William's brother, Henry, was certainly implicated. Henry's fortunes were desperate. Robert was approaching Normandy with the beautiful wife he had married in Sicily, and a son born to them would, by the provisions of the treaty of 1091, be heir to all the Norman dominions. Henry's term as heir presumptive to both his brothers was almost at an end. Henry was in Rufus's party, but at a different stand, on the fateful day, and took advantage of his almost exclusive knowledge of the death to seize the throne. Walter Tyrel was related to the Clares, a family most intimate with Henry and handsomely rewarded by him as soon as he succeeded. If Rufus did not die through a common hunting accident we may think Henry guilty. But circumstantial evidence presented so long after the event is insufficient to fasten upon him responsibility for so monstrous a crime.

William Rufus is a controversial figure; but the events of his reign speak for themselves. He confirmed the royal power in England and he restored the ducal rights in Normandy, yet never made a sad labour of his humdrum task. He was a buffoon with a purpose, a jester who accepted his father's mantle but spread it in extravagant caprice.

6

THE ZENITH AND THE NADIR OF
NORMAN RULE, 1100–1154

I

WITH the reign of Henry I, the youngest son of William the Bastard, Norman kingship reached its splendid apogee in England. With the reign of Stephen, a grandson of King William, it fell to its lowest level. The first William had been famed as a conqueror; the second William shone as a magnificent and eccentric knight; but Henry I impressed contemporaries by his learning. The impression developed into a myth, so that by the fourteenth century Henry was called 'Beauclerk'. But, although we know that Henry was illiterate and had little if any Latin; although to us, looking back, he seems as tyrannical as his brother and much crueller; and although, like his father and his brother, he spent his life in warfare and hunting, his reputation is proof that there was a new spirit in the court. If Henry could not write he had many clerks who could; and the experiments towards an orderly bureaucratic administration, which under Rufus had been detested, under Henry for the first time aroused admiration; and it may well be that Henry's true greatness lies in causing this revolution in attitude. Of his successor, his nephew Stephen, Walter Map wrote, 'A fine knight, but in other respects almost a fool', and under Stephen the imposing façade of a coherent kingdom disconcertingly crumbled. The failure and the success were not entirely disconnected. The sons of the Conqueror had pushed the royal powers too hard and had strained the capacities and loyalties of their servants far too severely. The succession of a weak man—an accident that no dynasty can avoid for ever—not only caused the pressure to slacken but allowed the inevitable reaction to destroy much that had been achieved. Nevertheless, if proof were required of the basic soundness of the polity which the Normans had developed in England, the quick recovery of the kingdom under Henry fitzEmpress after the nineteen long winters of Stephen's reign is surely evidence enough.

The speed with which Henry acted after the death of his brother on 2 August 1100 shows that he was prepared for such an emergency. He rode immediately to the royal treasury in the castle at Winchester and forced the unwilling custodian, William of Breteuil, the son of William fitzOsbern, to surrender it. He secured the adherence of most of the late king's household, including the chancellor, William Giffard. He was accepted as king by some of the leading baronial families, notably the Clares and the Beaumonts; and on 5 August he was crowned at Westminster, before the arrival of Archbishop Thomas of York and in the unavoidable absence of Archbishop Anselm, by Maurice bishop of London. An anointed head was as safe as ever a medieval head could be; but the irregularity and the suddenness of the *coup* meant that supporters had to be recruited and that a price had to be paid. Henry immediately granted the bishopric of Winchester to the chancellor and the abbey of Ely to Richard of Clare. Later, one of the Beaumont brothers, Robert count of Meulan, was made earl of Leicester. The unpopular Ranulf Flambard was imprisoned in the Tower of London. The exiled Anselm was begged to return and to excuse the hasty coronation. And to the kingdom at large Henry issued a promise of good government.

The coronation charter of Henry I, attested by three bishops, three earls, and five barons, is especially famous because it was confirmed by the next two kings on their accession and because it had a direct influence on the even greater charter of King John. But in essentials it differed in no way from that which his predecessor had issued in similar circumstances. It was a bid for the support of all those law-abiding men who could be expected to rally to the crowned king once they saw that he was prepared to rule in the traditional way. Henry promised that the church should be 'free' and that it should not be despoiled by the king during vacancies. He renounced the 'unjust oppressions' of his brother, and undertook to maintain firm peace and to re-establish the good old laws— the laws of King Edward as amended by the Conqueror. Various abuses of feudal custom and the remedies offered were listed in detail. Reliefs were to be 'just and proper', and Henry remitted arrears owed to Rufus; permission to marry a daughter or other female relative was to be given without payment; widows could remain single; not the king but the relatives were to have the wardship of a minor; chattels could be left by will or distributed by the family of the dead man; and forfeitures were to be governed by the custom of the Conqueror's predecessors. These concessions Henry made to his own earls, barons, and tenants; and he ordered that they should do the same to their barons and men. To the knights, in the hope that thereby they would be more able to perform their military service, was extended a privilege hitherto allowed only to the barons: freedom of their demesne from geld and the Old-English 'works'. To the country at large was granted a pardon for certain classes of debt and plea owed to Rufus, including the 'murdrum' fine, and an indemnity for unlawful acts committed during the interregnum, provided that restitution was made. In the charter was something for all free classes; and something also for the king, for even at this moment of crisis Henry reserved to himself his forests, but only those which his father had held.

Henry I, no more than his brother William or his nephew Stephen, entirely kept his promises. Yet each undertaking to recall the good laws recognized that there was a body of custom to which all were bound; and each promise of remedy for specific abuses acknowledged that in defining the law the just interest of all parties should be taken into account. These principles, inherent in feudalism, sprang from the very roots of Germanic society; and in the long run, perhaps, their constant assertion was of more importance than the repeated failure of the kings to honour them completely.

Archbishop Anselm returned to England on 23 September, and Henry received him cordially. It must have been to the great distress of Anselm as well as to the disappointment of the king that a conflict immediately and unexpectedly arose.

After half a century of propaganda and acrimonious dispute the question of lay investiture had become a real political issue. The new attitude of the church had been expressed with startling novelty and clarity in the third book of Cardinal Humbert's *Libri adversus simoniacos*, published in 1057, and had immediately been adopted by the papal *curia*. The first decree forbidding clerks to receive their churches from the hands of laymen had been issued at Rome at Easter 1059; and Pope Gregory VII had enacted a succession of laws to the same effect. This revolutionary demand was considered of fundamental importance by the reformers because it almost

epitomized their attitude. Lay investiture, by recognizing the political superiority of the laity and through its association with the
theocratic nature of kingship, conflicted with their conception of
the true order of the universe; it was closely connected with the sin
and heresy of simony (the buying of church appointments); and it
hindered the reformers' attempt to eradicate nicolaism (the marriage
and unchastity of priests). The reckless challenge thus offered to
the traditional order had caused a storm throughout Europe, but
had had no immediate effect on practice.

In 1095, however, Pope Urban II returned to the attack, and at the
councils of Clermont, Bari (1098), and Rome (1099) lay investiture
was condemned more rigorously than before, and, so as to leave no
doubt what the prohibition meant, the doing of homage by a clerk
to a layman was also proscribed. Anselm had been at the councils
of Bari and Rome and had lived at Lyons, a centre of Gregorian
reform; so, when Henry required him in the traditional way to do
homage before receiving his fiefs, the archbishop could do no other
than refuse; and he declined also to consecrate these prelates whom
Henry had already invested by ring and staff. After the initial unpleasant surprise, both parties accepted the fact that lay custom and
canon law were in opposition, and it was agreed that the pope should
be consulted and that Anselm could enjoy the temporalities until a
decision was given.

With this problem successfully postponed, Henry engaged
Anselm in the business of his marriage. He had decided to propitiate
his English subjects by marrying Eadgyth, the orphan daughter of
Malcolm Canmore king of Scots and Margaret, the sister of Edgar
Aetheling, and so through her mother in direct descent from Alfred
and Cerdic. There was, however, a difficulty. It was rumoured that
Eadgyth had taken the veil during her education in an English
monastery. But when Anselm investigated he found that the girl
had never really become a nun and that there was no valid impediment. Henry's successor, Stephen, was to impugn this judgment in
order to bastardize the issue of the marriage; and certainly the
children—Matilda, 'empress of the Romans' and, for a short time,
'lady' of the English, and William the Aetheling, drowned in 1120
–had evil fortunes. Yet, although some of the Norman barons
mocked at this rustic marriage of 'Godric and Godgifu', which was
celebrated on 11 November 1100, it, like the charter, served its
immediate purpose well. Later, Henry went back to his mistresses,

while Matilda, as Eadgyth was called after her marriage, devoted herself again to religion.

Before the year was out Henry took an oath of allegiance from all his subjects, and at Christmas 1100, Louis, the heir to the French crown, paid Henry a visit at Westminster. The king's position was acknowledged. But the claims of his elder brother were still outstanding. Duke Robert had arrived back in Normandy at the end of August or the beginning of September, a few weeks after Henry's coronation. On account of his splendid Crusade and his fine marriage to Sybil of Conversano, whose father, Geoffrey, was a grandson of Tancred of Hauteville and so the nephew of Robert Guiscard and Roger count of Sicily, he was received with enthusiasm; and he took possession of the whole duchy except for the castles held by Henry's men. There was, indeed, sweetness as well as gall in the death of Rufus, for, if England had eluded Robert again, he had at least recovered Normandy without trouble and without the need to repay the loan. There remained, moreover, the hope of dethroning his brother. He built up a party in England, which included the three sons of Roger of Montgomery—Robert of Bellême, Arnulf, and Roger—Walter Giffard, earl of Buckingham, the son of the Conqueror's companion, and William of Warenne, earl of Surrey. In February 1101, he was joined by Ranulf Flambard who had escaped easily from the Tower he knew so well. And by July Robert had assembled a fleet at Tréport at the mouth of the Bresle. In the course of these anxious months Henry took all the precautions he could. At Dover on 10 March (and the year is proved by the presence of the chancellor, William Giffard) he renewed the traditional money fief to count Robert II of Flanders; and for the first time we learn the exact duties of the vassal. The count was to aid Henry against all men, saving his fealty to his liege lord, King Philip, and provide him with mercenary troops on specified occasions: 1,000 knights in England, if Philip or some other enemy invaded the island or should a serious revolt break out, and in each year the same number of knights in Normandy or half as many in Maine if required by Henry. Furthermore, Robert, if obliged to attend his liege lord on an expedition against Henry, was to take with him only the minimum contingent owed by his fief—10 knights—and leave the other troops with their paymaster. This treaty, renewed in 1103 and 1110, contained provisions of great value to a rich king; but they seem seldom to have been invoked. Certainly there is no evidence that Henry brought over a Flemish contingent in 1101. Instead, he renewed his coronation promises in a charter reissued to his English vassals, and ordered all men to swear fealty to him and promise to defend his cause against Robert until Christmas. The naval forces he sent to intercept went over to the invader and Robert was able to outflank the royal army assembled at Pevensey and land on 20 July at Portsmouth. But so strong had the king become that when the rival armies met at Alton in Hampshire a battle was avoided and a settlement advantageous to the younger brother was made. It was agreed that Henry should keep England and pay his brother a pension of £2,000 a year, that Robert should have all Normandy except Henry's castle at Domfront, that each brother should be the heir presumptive of the other, and that both would forgive their rebel vassals.

The Treaty of Alton was another of those promises that Henry could not keep. The only man he forgave was Ranulf Flambard. The bishop of Durham received back his lands without delay and was reconciled to Anselm. Even if he had not always been in secret alliance with Henry—and his honourable entertainment in the Tower and his ability to stupefy the guards with wine and escape with his aged mother and a boatload of treasure, point that way—he certainly bought the king's mercy by playing a double game in the next five years. He lived in Normandy, ostensibly as an exile, and controlled the bishopric of Lisieux. But there can be no doubt that he was there as Henry's agent. The English barons who had supported Robert were punished one by one as legal pretext arose. By Easter 1102 the turn had come of the greatest of them all, Robert of Bellême. The king summoned him to answer in the royal court to forty-five charges of offences against him and his brother, the duke. Robert did not comply. Henry urged Robert Curthose to strike against the continental possessions of the family while he himself advanced against the English castles. Arundel was then blockaded into surrender, and Bishop Robert Bloet sent against Tickhill in Yorkshire. In the autumn Henry attacked the rebel in his stronghold, the Welsh march. He took Bridgnorth, and advanced on Shrewsbury, the earl's headquarters. Robert of Bellême surrendered without a fight. He and his brothers were deprived of their English honours; and so terribly did the king hate this family that he even confiscated the lands of the Norman monastery of Almenèches, because the abbess was Robert's sister.

Duke Robert fared no better than his English supporters. Even if Henry had been sincere in 1101 the renewed evidence of Robert's incapacity and the growing anarchy in Normandy encouraged the king to despise his brother, to interfere, and finally to compass his destruction. Duke Robert had already lost Maine to Helias of la Flèche. In 1103 he made war on Robert of Bellême, who was now ravaging Normandy; but with no success. He fell foul of the church because of his simony and bad government, and by 1105 was engaged in an investiture struggle with Pope Paschal II. The Crusade had taught him no wisdom; and he played into the hands of his crafty brother. Towards the end of 1103 Robert crossed to England to complain that William of Warenne had been deprived of his earldom of Surrey contrary to the spirit of the Treaty of Alton. Henry restored the earl; but he made counter-charges against Robert, and forced him to surrender his pension as price of his liberty. The conquest of Normandy was planned by Henry with the greatest care. He had his supporters and agents in the duchy; he harboured useful exiles from Normandy, such as Serlo bishop of Séez and Ralf abbot of Saint-Martin at Séez, who had fled from the tyranny of Robert of Bellême; and he spun a web of alliances round the duke. In March 1103 he met Count Robert II of Flanders again at Dover; and he is believed to have made arrangements similar to the two-year old Anglo-Flemish treaty with the rulers of Maine, Anjou, and Brittany. To neutralize Robert of Bellême, who was certain to join the duke in an emergency, Henry gave a natural daughter, Matilda, in marriage to Rotrou II of Mortagne, count of Perche, an enemy of the house of Talvas. There can be no doubt that Henry was a brilliant diplomatist. The rulers of Flanders, Maine, Anjou, and Brittany and, above all, the king of the Franks and his son stood to gain by the weakness of Normandy and its separation from England. Yet they all were brought to favour Henry's schemes.

In 1103 Henry sent the trusted Robert of Meulan to suppress disorder in Normandy and, doubtless, to make useful contacts. In the autumn of 1104, Henry himself visited Domfront and Normandy, and so frightened his brother that he ceded him the homage and the county of William of Évreux. In April 1105 Henry invaded in force. He landed at Barfleur in the Cotentin, his old lordship, and was welcomed by Serlo, bishop of Séez. He called on his allies and vassals for their promised help, took Bayeux and Caen, and marched on

Falaise. In May the two brothers met but could not come to terms; and, although Henry had to return to England in August, he gave no heed to the pleas of his brother and Robert of Bellême, who both visited him during the winter, and in the following June (1106), much later than he had intended, invaded again. The duke's most powerful supporters were Robert of Bellême and William of Mortain, both disinherited in England. The king was joined by Helias of la Flèche, count of Maine, and Alan Fergant, count of Brittany. In September Henry began the siege of William of Mortain's castle at Tinchebray, twelve miles north of Domfront. The duke advanced to its relief; negotiations were fruitless; and on 28 or 29 September 1106 one of the rare pitched battles of the time was fought. Each army was composed of cavalry and foot, and each was drawn up in column to face the other. Henry, however, had a fourth squadron on his left flank, composed of the troops from Brittany and Maine. The battle opened with a charge of the Norman van, led by William of Mortain. The English vanguard dismounted to take the shock; and during the mêlée the Bretons and Manceaux charged in from the flank. Robert of Bellême, who commanded the rear squadron, fled the field. The battle became a rout. The duke was captured by Waldric, the king's chancellor, William of Mortain by the Bretons, and among the many captives—400 knights and 10,000 foot, according to the king's boasting dispatch to Anselm—was the unlucky Edgar Aetheling, whom Henry immediately pardoned and released.

The battle of Tinchebray ended all resistance to Henry in Normandy. Robert Curthose was kept in honourable captivity until his death in 1134, barely two years before that of his supplanter. The only son of his marriage, William Clito, was given by Henry in ward to Helias of Saint-Saëns, the duke's son-in-law—a generous act that Henry was to repent. William, count of Mortain, was imprisoned for life. Robert of Bellême submitted, and was shorn of all the ducal demesne he had occupied and of some of his Norman estates. Councils were held by Henry at Lisieux in October 1106, at Falaise in January 1107, and at Lisieux again in March for the reformation and settlement of the duchy. The king's peace was proclaimed; ducal demesne was resumed from its detainers; the title to all lands justly held at the time of the death of the Conqueror was guaranteed; and the destruction was ordered of all adulterine castles—those built without ducal licence. The English king had become once more duke of the Normans; and once again defence of his continental possessions was to cause the king constant disquiet.

During this period of conquest Henry had also found time to reach a settlement with the church. Anselm remained at Henry's side during the invasion of Robert in 1101; but by 1103, despite protracted negotiations, the pope had definitely refused to tolerate English custom, and in April Anselm left again for Rome, this time to wait until his two masters should come to terms. None of the parties desired an open rupture. The king, supported by the English bishops and magnates, stood on his traditional rights, but could not afford to be excommunicated while planning the conquest of Normandy. The pope was unwilling to make the first example of Henry I, whose piety had aroused strong hopes in reforming circles, but found it hard to go back on his avowed policy. Anselm regarded the problem as a simple matter of obedience.

Hitherto none except the weak king of the Franks had abandoned the custom of investing prelates with ring and staff; and the investiture dispute had largely been confined to polemical writings. The extreme decrees of Urban II and Paschal II (Lateran, 1102) had provoked an equally extreme reply, the *Tractatus de consecratione pontificum et regum*, from the 'Norman Anonymous', sometimes called 'of York', a publicist, or possibly a group of writers, whose identity, despite the efforts of several historians, has not yet been convincingly proved. In this tract the Anonymous answered theocracy by Caesaro-papism. He advanced the view that while both king and priest were ordained by God for the rule of the church, so that the king was also a priest and the priest a king, the dignity and power of the king were the greater, for he represented Christ as God, whereas the priest only represented Christ as man. At his coronation and unction the king was married to his bride, the Church-kingdom, and became a priest, Christ, and God. And in virtue of his superiority, of his being head of the national church, standing above the archbishops at the apex of the hierarchy, he invested bishops with their authority to govern, that is to say, with their inferior royal powers.

With one side proclaiming the pope-emperor and the other the king-priest the ordinary working compromise was refused. In practice the prelate was generally regarded as a man with two lords, owing fealty and homage and secular duties to the king for his temporal estates and loyalty and obedience to his ecclesiastical superiors and the church in virtue of his spiritual office. This conception had dominated the attitude of such men as Archbishop Lanfranc. The need was for a formula which, while accepting political reality, would do the least injury to the theoretical claims of the rival powers. Several writers groped towards a compromise. The celebrated canonist Bishop Ivo of Chartres advanced the old view, which had been rejected by Cardinal Humbert, that lay investiture by ring and staff, although offensive, was of little matter as it conveyed only the temporalities and not the office. Shortly after 1102 Ivo's friend and disciple, Hugh of St. Mary, monk of Fleury, wrote his *Tractatus de regia potestate et sacerdotali dignitate,* dedicated to Henry, in which, although he did not deny theocratic kingship, he advised the king to give up investiture with the spiritual symbols and use some other token to convey the estates.

   The polemical warfare might have continued indefinitely had not Henry's need for money forced him to disregard his coronation charter and to restore those practices which had made his brother so odious in ecclesiastical circles. In 1105 Paschal II and Anselm began to threaten to suspend no longer the excommunication which should rightly have fallen on the king's head. Henry, in the midst of his Norman campaign, was vulnerable, and a settlement became imperative. A practical solution was always to hand if each side would yield some dignity. Henry met Anselm at Laigle on the Risle on 22 July 1105 and offered to waive investiture by ring and staff if he could retain the right to take homage from the bishop- or abbot-elect. This proposal was sent to the pope. Paschal was anxious that Henry should support Bohemund's crusade against Byzantium, and on 23 March 1106 gave a grudging consent to Henry's offer. Without positively disavowing his previous attitude, the pope allowed Anselm, until God should soften the king's heart, to consecrate bishops properly elected even though they should have become the vassals of the king. On 1 August 1107, in a council at London, king and archbishop ratified the compromise they had reached at le Bec on 15 August 1106: lay investiture was forbidden, but no prelate was to be refused consecration because he had done the king homage for his fiefs. And on 11 August the many vacancies in the English church—the result of the twelve years breach with Rome—were filled at last when Anselm consecrated the candidates. The compromise of London (or of Bec, as it is often called) had wide repercussions. Although it satisfied neither side—Henry was the first king formally to renounce investiture by ring and staff, and Paschal had made the first relaxation of the papal decrees—and was regarded merely as a temporary expedient, it was to abide in England and was to influence the settlement in other countries. Each party had made painful concessions. The pope had abandoned an extreme theocratic policy which no secular ruler would accept and had recognized lay investiture under less offensive forms. The king had surrendered important spiritual functions and had acknowledged that his power was only temporal. There had been victory to neither side.

II

With the conquest of Normandy and the agreement with the church a new phase of Henry's long reign begins. The baronial revolt of 1102 was the last of the reign and the last in the kingdom for thirty-six years. Wales was exceptionally quiet. In 1114 Henry had to chastise Gruffydd ap Cynan, king of Gwynedd, and in 1121 Maredudd ap Bleddyn, king of Powys; but the Welsh princes turned their fury on each other while the conquest and colonization of Deheubarth was completed. About 1108 the king cleared south Dyfed and settled Flemings in place of the natives; and soon after he established a new baronial family in South Wales—the Clares. In 1110 he gave Ceredigion to Gilbert fitzRichard (of Clare) and before 1119 the lands forfeited by Earl Roger of Hereford in Netherwent, including Chepstow (Striguil), to Gilbert's brother, Walter fitzRichard. English control was so firm that the king was able to influence the appointment to bishoprics and secure the subordination of the Welsh church to the Canterbury metropolitan. The absorption of Wales into the English kingdom seemed to have been achieved. The duchy of Normandy, however, gave Henry trouble enough, and his active foreign policy had considerable influence on English affairs. The bureaucratic government which Rufus had bequeathed, geared to providing the king with money, was brilliantly developed and steadfastly enforced.

It has sometimes been said that Henry followed an anti-baronial policy. This judgment is misleading. His closest friends in the first half of his reign were the brothers Robert and Henry of Beaumont. The elder, Robert, had succeeded his mother's brother as count of Meulan in France and his father as lord of Pontaudemer and Beaumont in Normandy. He had his grandfather's English fiefs in Dorsetshire and Gloucestershire, and obtained the earldom of Leicester. He married Isabel, the grand-daughter of Henry I, king of the Franks. The younger brother, Henry, had been made first earl of Warwick by William Rufus. When Robert died in 1118 his lands were divided according to his wishes between his twin elder sons, Waleran and Robert, and the king continued his favour to the family, educating the boys in his household and taking their sister, Elizabeth, as his mistress. The Beaumonts were nobles of the Bellême type. Their castles of Meulan and Vatteville on the Seine, and Pontaudemer, Brionne, and Beaumont, strung along the valley of the Risle, put them in a commanding position in eastern Normandy; yet Henry felt no alarm.

It is, of course, true that by 1103 many of the great families of the Conquest period had been broken as a result of their rebellions—fitzOsbern, Eu, Mowbray, Montgomery, Bellême, Mortain, and others. But Rufus and Henry, far from adding these escheats to the royal demesne, alienated even more lands to new barons and to the church. That vast demesne which William the Conqueror had reserved to himself was already shrinking fast. Rufus had favoured men from Maine. Henry advanced many from his old lordship, the Cotentin, and from neighbouring Brittany. In the view of one *laudator temporis acti*, Ordericus Vitalis, Henry raised men from the dust and exalted men of ignoble birth. But the aristocracy of England has always been composed of the parvenus of yesterday. And since the new men were often given the heiresses of the old, they stepped easily into their shoes.

King Henry was naturally most generous to his kinsmen. To his eldest bastard, Robert of Caen, he gave manors from the royal demesne and from the lands of the bishop of Coutances together with the services of some minor tenants-in-chief, and also Mabel, the only child of Robert fitzHamon, lord of Glamorgan, and Sybil of Montgomery; and in 1122 Henry promoted Robert's honour of Gloucester into an earldom. To the queen's brother, David, later David I of Scots, he gave the eldest daughter of Earl Waltheof, the widow of Simon of St. Liz I, who carried the earldoms of Huntingdon and Northampton to her husbands. To Brian fitzCount, the illegitimate son of Count Alan Fergant of Brittany, he gave the lordships of Abergavenny and 'Overwent', and marriages which brought him the office of royal constable and the honour of Wallingford.

He so enriched his nephew, Stephen, the son of his sister Adela and Stephen count of Blois, that this favourite was able to snatch the crown on his death. An accumulation of escheated honours and fiefs—Eye and Lancaster in England, and in Normandy the county of Mortain (about 1115) and some of the Bellême lordships (1118)—prepared the way for Stephen's brilliant marriage to Matilda, daughter of Count Eustace III of Boulogne, who took the cowl in 1125. Matilda brought to her husband not only her father's Flemish county and his important English honour but also the advantage of her distinguished lineage, for her mother Mary had been a daughter of Malcolm III of Scots and St. Margaret and a sister of the English queen.

There came, also, into the English baronage William d'Aubigny *pincerna* (the butler), Humphrey de Bohun, one of the king's stewards, who received in marriage Margaret, eldest daughter and eventually co-heiress of Miles of Gloucester, by then earl of Hereford, Alan fitzFlaald of Dol, the ancestor of the English fitzAlans and of the Scottish Stuarts, and Richard, lord of Reviers, Vernon, and Néhou in Normandy, the ancestor of the earls of Devon. Some substantial men in England were made more powerful. In 1121, Henry gave Sybil, the heiress of Bernard of Neufmarché, lord of Brecknock, in marriage to Miles, one of the king's constables and hereditary sheriff of Gloucester. So new men replaced the old, and became indistinguishable from those they succeeded. In the last years of Henry's reign there were six English earls—Chester, Buckingham, Surrey, Warwick, Leicester, and Gloucester—and three of these were closely related. Leicester was the twin brother of the count of Meulan, Surrey was their step-brother, and Warwick their first cousin. In addition, the king of Scots, Henry's brother-in-law, held Northampton and Huntingdon. Yet if the power of the nobility was greater in 1135 than in 1066, so was the strength of the king; and it seems that Henry, confident after 1102 of his authority, felt no need to thwart systematically the territorial ambitions of the baronage.

Nevertheless, the dissipation of the royal demesne affected the king's fiscal policy. Both Rufus and Henry preferred the services of vassals to demesne revenue; and therefore they had to outdo even their father in the exploitation of their rights as feudal over-lord. Despite Henry's charter, reliefs remained arbitrary, amerce-ments were heavy, heiresses were sold, and the wardship of minors stayed with the king; and the English barons were mulcted and controlled as nowhere else in Europe. At the same time the first signs of decay in the very heart of feudalism can be seen. Frankish feudalism had been introduced late into England and was then denied its proper atmosphere—insecurity and war. Hence the military relationship between lord and vassal, the close tie of men who hazard their lives together, began to wither except on the marches. The military obligations of tenants were already becoming unsatisfactory. William I had needed an abundance of knights in England to defend his conquest; but William II and Henry I required knights to fight in their continental campaigns, often of long duration; and both kings, despite new enfeoffments from demesne, had often to reinforce the feudal host with mercenary troops.

Then the comparative peacefulness of England created special problems. In 1097 William Rufus had found that the Canterbury knights were badly trained and equipped; and it is not surprising that Henry should on occasion have commuted the knight service owed by ecclesiastical baronies for money—scutage. There is no evidence that Henry absolved lay vassals from personal service with their military quotas; but the barons themselves were levying scutage on their knights, for some whom they had enfeoffed could no longer fight—they were old, or sick, or had died leaving children—and where a baron had enfeoffed more than the quota owed to the king he sometimes obtained from scutage an additional contribution towards the cost of his service. Castle-guard, too, had become less urgent. Henry I released the bishop of Ely from guard service due at Norwich castle, and commutation in time of peace was, perhaps, already allowed. These early signs of the obsolescence of some of the feudal duties point to the break-up of the Conquest settlement. In 1087 king and barons were still engaged in a common enterprise and relations were still personal and intimate. But by 1135 much of the warmth had gone out of the relationship. Wardship, marriage, relief, and even military service were becoming financial rights of a one-sided kind, which all lords, and the king as the greatest lord of all, were perverting. The barons fretted under the yoke, and only the strongest of kings could control them.

Henry's attitude towards the church was equally severe. The compromise with Pope Paschal over investiture did not weaken the king's power to nominate to bishoprics and abbacies. The election took place on the king's initiative in the royal court. A delegation

of the chapter or cloister was usually summoned to attend; but the
will of the king and the concurrence of the lay and ecclesiastical
magnates were of most importance. After the king had given his
formal consent the elect did homage for his temporalities and then
received two writs, one putting him into possession and the other
ordering his consecration. Consequently, Henry's bishops were all
men promoted out of his chapel, kinsmen, or friends. Nor did
Henry relinquish easily any of the other ecclesiastical rights that his
father and brother had enjoyed. He maintained his royal control
over church councils and jurisdiction; he restricted the entry of
papal legates into the island; and he limited and supervised relations
with Rome. Archbishop Anselm died on 21 April 1109, and until
1114 there was a virtual breach with the papacy. The archbishopric
was not filled, no appeals went to the pope, and the payment of
Peter's Pence fell into arrears. In 1114 the king on his own authority
translated Ralf d'Escures from Rochester to Canterbury, and,
although Paschal scolded Henry for his unfilial behaviour, he sent
the desired pallium.

It was in the first years of Henry's reign that the 'Norman Anonymous' wrote many of his pamphlets against Gregorian reform, one
of which—that justifying lay investiture—has already been discussed. The writer in effect vindicates actual Anglo-Norman conditions in the last half of the eleventh century. He was a royalist,
opposed to the papal monarchy and to the pretensions of primates.
He justified the territorial church, blurred the distinction between
the clergy and the laity, defended clerical marriage, and championed
episcopal control over monasteries. But his generation was passing
away. The views of the Gregorian reformers—however little they
were observed in practice—were obtaining a legal and a moral
ascendency in Europe. They were felt to be right, and they were
justified by the new editions of canon law. They were taught in the
schools, especially in those of France, and by the twelfth century
had been disseminated into every corner of western Christendom.
Henry accelerated the movement by promoting only Norman
clerks, for these, since the decline of le Bec, went usually to Laon or
Paris for instruction. Hence all the rising clerics were imbued with
Gregorian ideals, and the tone of the English church gradually
changed. In 1119 at Gisors the king persuaded Pope Calixtus II to
confirm the customs of the Conqueror; but he could not keep the
English church independent and aloof. In 1115 had begun again a

quarrel between Canterbury and York over the primacy, which was not halted until Pope Honorius II at the end of 1125 made the archbishop of Canterbury, William of Corbeil, papal vicar and legate for life, and hence automatically the superior of York. The traffic of those years permanently affected the position of the English church. Appeals to Rome had been numerous, and papal legates had entered the kingdom to hear the case. The 'ancestral customs' had become, according to the ecclesiastical view, special privileges depending solely on the goodwill of the pope and liable to forfeiture if abused. In practice the royal powers over the church in England were considerable; but few clerks, even those in whom Henry placed his trust, would have cared to defend them in theory.

Henry's piety contributed to his failure. He encouraged the reformers at home. For the first time for centuries new dioceses were erected. In 1109 Hervey was translated from inhospitable Bangor to a new see in the monastery of Ely, and in 1133 Athelulf, an Austin canon, was made bishop of Carlisle, Rufus's conquest. The reign of Henry I, coming between the hard-hearted frivolity of the reign of Rufus and the anxious turmoil of the reign of Stephen, was the golden age of Anglo-Norman monasticism. For the Benedictines it was a period of rebuilding rather than of new foundation, and a time when religious zeal, undimmed, yet softened in the new prosperity, turned to the arts. The monastic historians—Eadmer, William of Malmesbury, Simeon of Durham—were the greatest since Bede. Manuscripts were again as fine as ever, for the native style of illumination, which had been reinforced by similar styles brought in from Normandy—themselves, perhaps, of English origin—had begun to be enriched by romanesque ornaments. Henry's reign, moreover, saw the first settlement of new orders in the island. The king, the queen, and the court favoured the Austin canons; and more than forty abbeys and priories, including Carlisle, the seat of the new bishopric, were founded during this reign. The king's nephew, Stephen, brought in 1124 the first Saviniac monks to Tulketh near Preston (later at Furness); and in the following decade six other houses were founded. Even more momentous was the establishment in the waste lands of five Cistercian monasteries— Waverley (1128), its offshoot Garendon (1133), Tintern (1131), Rievaulx (1132), and Fountains (1132)—and three Cistercian nunneries. The orders of Fontevrault and Grammont and independent Augustinian orders also made a lodgement. Many of the new communities settled north of the Humber and some on the Welsh march, which helped to redress the old disparity between north and south. The fresh influx of monachism was, indeed, fateful. All the new orders owed their origin, and were committed, to ecclesiastical reform. All were under the special patronage of the pope and most propagated ultramontane ideals. The orders of Savigny and Cîteaux, moreover, were organized on a 'feudal' pattern—mother houses having authority over their offspring—which cut across the national groupings. They did much to break down the insularity of the English church.

Henry also supported the reformers in their drive for clerical celibacy. At the Westminster council of 1102 Anselm tightened the laws that had lapsed under Rufus, and even extended to sub-deacons the ban on marriage. When the archbishop returned from exile he resumed the attack at the London council of 1108. The king, through a mixture of zeal and greed, imposed royal fines on married clergymen; and so effective was this double assault that it was generally recognized thereafter that no priest could make a valid marriage. But neither the church nor the king could keep the clergy chaste.

It is abundantly clear that the unprecedented freedom enjoyed by the church in Stephen's reign was but the flowering of a plant that had for years been extending its roots. Willingly in some directions, unwillingly in others, Henry had allowed its development; and when the firm pruning hand of the king was removed the growth was all the more luxuriant.

In the firm peace of the reigns of William II and Henry I the towns recovered their prosperity and trade increased. Three of the great medieval fairs were founded by royal grant in this period: St. Giles at Winchester by Rufus, and St. Ives in Huntingdonshire and St. Bartholomew at Smithfield by Henry. Henry tried hard to maintain the quality of the English coinage; and the silver penny of 240 to the pound, known as the *esterlin*, was worth two pennies of le Mans and four of Rouen, Angers, and Tours, the commonest currency in Normandy. With the new trading and industrial wealth towns bought privileges from the king. York, Wilton and, perhaps, Salisbury and Lincoln acquired the right to have a merchant gild. In 1130 weavers' gilds existed at London, Winchester, Oxford, Lincoln, and Huntingdon, a fullers' gild at Winchester, and a cordwainers' gild at Oxford. Wool was being exported to Flanders through Dover; but cloth was already becoming an important manufacture. Administrative privileges, too, were bought by the towns. By 1130 Lincoln was farming the borough directly from the crown. In 1129 London leased the shrievalty of London and Middlesex for one year, and about 1132 obtained the same right in fee at the traditional, but often disregarded, farm of £300 a year. London also received some judicial privileges, including the right to appoint its own royal justiciar, who was to hold all the pleas of the crown without interference. For these charters the towns paid handsomely. Henry was accumulating the hoard which was to maintain his heir, and he was hoping for the support of the towns for his schemes. But exaction was more evident than concession. Quick to exploit the new prosperity, Henry reformed urban taxation and began to take 'aids' from the more important boroughs in place of the fixed danegeld. In 1130 London gave £120; and Henry is believed to have imposed geld, or a substitute, annually on the kingdom. Henry was seldom at London. He preferred Winchester, where he could hunt and keep an eye on the treasure and easily cross to Normandy if necessary, Woodstock, where he founded a menagerie, and Windsor, where the hawking was good. But London was forging ahead, and had become an important commercial centre.

Henry, like Rufus, had his military companions and friends; but the tone of his court was different. Although Henry's mistresses were many and his illegitimate children numerous, he chased away the ribalds and fops who had surrounded his brother; and even short hair and shaven cheeks came back occasionally into fashion. The organization of the household in the last years of his reign— and it seems that Henry had made reforms—is known from a document, the *Constitutio domus regis* (the establishment of the royal household), drawn up early in Stephen's reign for the use of the new king, in which all the servants are listed and their 'liveries'—their pay and allowances—described. The pattern still conformed to the physical division of the medieval house into hall, chamber, chapel, and yard. The priests and clerks of the chapel, who maintained divine service and acted as the royal secretariat, were ruled by the chancellor. The hall—the main living and dining room—was under two servants, a steward or sewer (*dapifer*), who controlled the dispensers of bread (pantry) and meat (larder), and the butler, who was in charge of the cellar. The chamber—the private and sleeping quarters of the king, and also the finance office of the travelling court—was governed by the chamberlain. In the courtyard were the constables, who, with the aid of the marshal, maintained the stables, the kennels, and the mews, and also protected and policed the whole court.

The first entry in the *Constitutio* will convey the simple and domestic atmosphere of the court:

'The chancellor shall have 5*s*. a day, and one lord's simnel (a loaf of best quality) and two salt simnels, and one sextary (? 4 gallons) of dessert wine, and one sextary of ordinary wine, and one large wax candle and 40 candle ends.' (In addition, of course, to the two main meals he took in the common hall.)

Yet it is easy to be misled by this simplicity. Service in the king's court was ever the way to wealth and influence. Already some of the chief servants had become too grand to perform their duties in person except at coronation feasts and on other solemn occasions. Most of the royal clerks accumulated lands and churches. The more important received bishoprics as a matter of course and advanced their relatives. Even so obscure a man as Bernard, Henry's scribe, built up a modest estate and had esquires in attendance.

The king travelled with his court in attendance and did business wherever he might be, in Normandy or England, in hunting lodge, castle, or palace, at mass or in the saddle. But no king had an unlimited appetite for business; and Henry I both divested himself of routine administration and solved the problem of ruling a divided empire by creating a resident government for each part under an episcopal chief justiciar. About 1109 he appointed to the Norman office John bishop of Lisieux and to the English Roger le Poer bishop of Salisbury. After this reform the royal servants in the shires and bailiwicks, the sheriffs, castellans, local justices, reeves, bailiffs, foresters, and others, were responsible to the chief justiciar as well as to the king. There were in effect three main tiers of royal government. Henry remained the undisputed master. He roamed round his dominions, engaged in large schemes and private pleasure, keeping an eye on what he could see, intervening everywhere at will by means of writs dispatched by his chancellor, and settling all matters which were referred to him for a decision. Money was always on his mind, and the head financial office was in his bed-chamber. To this he directed for his own spending money from the English and Norman treasuries, from individual debtors, and, if need be, from moneylenders. His concern with justice was considerable, for it had to be politically directed in order to help his friends and destroy his enemies. But no king had the time or patience to hear many cases in person, and a hearing *coram rege* was usually a fiction.

Justice was, of course, one of the main responsibilities of the chief justiciars; but their court—the Exchequer—owed its name to their financial duties. Administration and finance were almost inseparable from justice; and since the chief justiciar was the king's *alter ego*, presiding over a royal court, he was no less omnicompetent. He carried on the day to day administration of the kingdom, whether or not the king was in England. He relieved the king of most legal business. The extent of royal jurisdiction, even before its spectacular growth under the Angevins, was considerable. Feudal (honorial) courts had only a limited competence, and there was no system of appeals running up the feudal ladder. Land cases were grave matters and could raise difficult points of law. Feudal courts often shirked them, and if the parties held of different lords the case was heard in the shire court. Moreover, the king was issuing writs of right, which often led to a hearing before a royal judge; and the king may already have decreed that no man need answer for his freehold unless compelled by such a writ. These factors transferred cases from the honorial courts into the king's hands. The chief justiciar's court was convenient and soon became popular with litigants. He sat at the exchequer with a number of 'justices of the whole of England', a group of about six bishops and barons, who, although not professional lawyers, were through practice acquiring the authority of a regular bench of judges. They heard every type of case which could come into the king's court, and especially those disputes over land in which the king was not directly involved—'common pleas'. The chief justiciar also sent periodically from his court parties of two or three of his colleagues to perambulate the shires. These itinerant justices on their 'general eyres' carried out many duties in the shire courts: they investigated all pleas of the crown; they enquired into all royal rights; they heard common pleas; sometimes they tallaged the royal demesne; and they fined all and sundry for derelictions of duty. They developed devices, such as juries of presentment and trial juries, which were to become characteristic features of royal justice and the common law. And they brought back to the exchequer a list of the penalties they had imposed, so that the sheriffs, who had the duty of collection, could be held to account.

The financial duties of the chief justiciar and his court were considerable. He had to supervise the collection of the king's revenues and audit the accounts of the collectors. By 1116, it seems, the system described later in the century by Richard fitzNeal in his *Dialogus de Scaccario* (Dialogue about the Exchequer) was already in existence. Twice a year, at Easter and Michaelmas, the court sat at the exchequer board, the table marked out as an *abacus* and which resembled a chess-board, to audit the accounts of the sheriffs and of some others who accounted directly, and to settle disputes which arose out of them. The final reckoning was at Michaelmas, and a summary of each account—mostly for the individual shires—was recorded on a 'pipe'—two sheepskins sewn end to end; and the pipes were then filed at the head and rolled up to form the Great Roll of the Exchequer—the pipe roll. The earliest rolls have not survived; but that for the thirty-first year of King Henry I is extant, and the series runs practically unbroken from the second year of King Henry II. The use of the *abacus* certainly came from abroad, possibly from Laon or Lorraine, and seems to have been introduced into the king's court in Henry's reign; but whether the reform was tried first in England or in Normandy has not yet been determined. Arithmetical calculations according to the Arabic system were becoming familiar at about the same time, and an adoption of the new method would have simplified the treasury accounts. But the sheriffs were laymen, and deemed illiterate, and the virtue of the *abacus* system was that it made visible and indisputable the processes of addition and subtraction.

The court of the chief justiciar was inventing routines of government and keeping records. Henry I and his deputies, Roger of Salisbury and John of Lisieux, were creative administrators. Roger le Poer, a Norman from Caen, who had held an important position in Henry's household before he became king and was appointed royal chancellor in 1101, was probably the master mind. Both these 'curial' bishops founded important dynasties; and their nephews and great-nephews were bishops and royal officials under Stephen and Henry II. Two of John's nephews were John, bishop of Séez, an exchequer clerk, and Arnulf, bishop of Lisieux, for a time justiciar of Normandy; and among his great-nephews was Hugh of Nonant, bishop of Lichfield. Roger of Salisbury's son, Roger the Poor, became Stephen's chancellor; his nephew Nigel (bishop of Ely), Nigel's son, Richard fitzNeal (bishop of London), and Richard's kinsman, William of Ely, became royal treasurers in turn; and another nephew,

Alexander, obtained the bishopric of Lincoln. The office of chief justiciar reached its fullest dignity and importance under the early Angevins when the business of the royal court increased rapidly and the great area of the royal demesnes caused the king always to be on the move; but it was already a responsible position under Henry I.

Such an active royal government could not fail to affect the local officials, especially the sheriffs; and many expedients are found in Henry's reign designed to augment the yield from the counties. Some of the old shrieval families kept their places; but many were displaced by new men and under new conditions. Henry either sold the shires for sums above the traditional farm of the royal manors or appointed custodians who paid the actual profits and not the stereotyped farm into the Exchequer. Henry also granted groups of counties to members of his court. In 1129–30, for instance, Aubrey de Vere, who was appointed Master Chamberlain of England in 1133, and Richard Basset, one of the king's justiciars, jointly held eleven shires as custodians. This direct and centralized exploitation of the royal demesne could not, however, be entirely maintained; and it seems that several of the new men were acquiring the position of the old and were fast making the office of sheriff hereditary in their own families. But this severe disturbance was decisive in the history of the office. Henry II was to repeat it; and other kings after him. And so it was that the office remained a royal appointment at the king's pleasure, strictly accountable and carefully controlled, and never developed into a fief. The sheriff was, indeed, losing ground. Rufus had appointed local justiciars to hear the royal pleas, and the use of itinerant justices further restricted the omnicompetence of the sheriff in the shire. Nevertheless, the sheriff remained an invaluable royal servant and a great man in local affairs.

III

The reforms in the government, the precocious centralization, the harsh exploitation of financial rights, and the ferocious justice were all stimulated by the cost of Henry's continental schemes. The conquest of Normandy had been expensive, and the duchy remained chargeable, for the increasing jealousy of Henry's neighbours was matched by the aggressive ambition of the king. The general acquiescence in Henry's policy on the Continent barely outlasted his campaigns against Robert Curthose; and Henry was involved in wars from 1109 until his death in 1135. King Louis VI of the Franks was always among or behind his opponents; but the organization of society prevented the rivalry from assuming an acute or really dangerous form. Warfare was a social habit. Fighting was the business, the sport, the very life of the feudal knight. Yet, since the knight shirked regular campaigns as too boring and avoided pitched battles as too dangerous, warfare, even when manipulated by a strong and clever man, such as Henry I, seldom led by itself to a decisive result. Loyalty was too dispersed, individual interest too immediate, and effort much too sporadic. Far more cogent was the feudal diplomacy—the attraction of vassals, the buying of allies, the acquisition of strategic castles, the dynastic marriages—which underlay the bellicose groupings, for the man deprived of friends collapsed in the ordinary rough and tumble, while the man in the ascendant steadily increased his gravitational pull. Henry obtained many vassals outside his duchy, often by enfeoffing them with pensions, a practice which his brother and, perhaps, his father had followed. This method, although feudal in form, approached the system of paying subsidies to allies, and suffered from the disadvantages inherent in both, for the mercenary vassals were still obliged to follow their liege lord, even against Henry, and their performance never equalled their greed.

Yet if Henry's field of action and diplomacy seems more extensive than William II's it should not be inferred that his policy broke sharply away from the conservative tradition formed by his father and brother. Although interest in Maine may appear to be absorbed in the wider issue of relations with Anjou, and diplomatic exchanges with the Low Countries and Germany may seem to transcend military preoccupation with the Vexin, Henry, like every other feudal lord, was basically concerned with the retention of his inheritance, the acquisition of new fiefs, and the safe delivery of his lordship to his heir. Henry was a conventional man. He built up coalitions designed to squeeze the king of the Franks; but there is no evidence that he thought Louis VI's destruction either possible or desirable. Normandy was encircled by enemies; Henry took counter-measures; and the result usually was equilibrium.

Philip I, king of the Franks, although since 1104 no longer under the ban of the church for his adulterous union with Bertrada of Montfort, remained lethargic until his death in July 1108. His successor, long his associate, Louis VI, the Fat, a simple and decent warrior with little political sense and a weakness for money, devoted himself to the limited task of crushing his vassals on the royal demesne. He had, perhaps, been discouraged by the Vexin war of 1097–8 against Rufus; he was perpetually embroiled with Theobald IV of Blois; and he contented himself with harming Henry whenever he could at small cost. Flanders chose to expand eastwards at the expense of the Empire and was one of the most loyal French fiefs, so that Norman schemes never achieved much more than its neutrality. On 17 May 1110 Henry succeeded in renewing the treaty of 1101 by confirming to the count his fief of 400 marks in return for half the previously stipulated military aid; but Robert II died in 1111 fighting against Henry's ally, Blois, and his successor, his son Baldwin VII, was resolutely hostile to Normandy. Anjou was greatly feared by Henry. The old Fulk 'le Réchin', a scholarly man but a mediocre ruler, died on 14 April 1109, and was succeeded by his son by Bertrada of Montfort, Fulk V, the Young. Fulk was a stronger man than his father; and when he also acquired Maine in 1110 on the death of his father-in-law, Count Helias of la Flèche, Anjou passed to the offensive, often in alliance with France and with the support of Robert of Bellême, malignant in his frontier castles. Henry's danger from these enemies was all the greater since there was a pretender to Normandy in the person of his nephew, William Clito, the son of Robert Curthose and Sybil of Conversano. When Henry tried to lay hands on the boy, his guardian, Helias of Saint-Saëns, took him out of danger; and it was Baldwin VII of Flanders who knighted William in his fourteenth year. William Clito grew into a man of great charm, and he always commanded some Norman support until his death in 1128. For Henry's external enemies he was a useful tool.

The English king was not, however, without firm friends. The subordination of Brittany was almost complete. In 1106 Alan Fergant IV did homage to Henry, and his son and successor, Conan III, married one of the king's bastards. The fief of Blois-Champagne was divided among members of its ruling house. Hugh I, count of Champagne, was loyal to the French crown; but his nephew, Theobald IV of Blois and Chartres, who inherited Champagne as well in 1125, was rancorous. His office of count-palatine and his geographical position allowed him to disturb the French royal demesne, and he was well placed to threaten Maine and Anjou.

After 1109 Theobald fought almost continuously for twenty-four years against King Louis; and naturally he was always in the party of his uncle, Henry I, the brother of his mother Adela. Theobald's younger brother, Stephen, a good soldier, was, as we have seen, a close friend and dependant of his English uncle. When Henry placed him in Boulogne he gained a useful agent against the over-lord, the count of Flanders. More reputation but less profit came from Henry's imperial alliance. In 1109 the Emperor Henry V asked for the hand of Henry's daughter, Matilda; and she went to Germany in the next year and was married in 1114. The Emperor, preoccupied with his own troubles, did little for his son-in-law apart from the abortive expedition of 1124; but the connexion was a warning to France. The popes, although depending on Louis VI for protection against the emperor and his anti-popes, could not afford to alienate the difficult English king; and Calixtus II proved more indulgent to the erring son than to his devoted supporter.

Louis recognized Henry's conquest of Normandy in the autumn of 1107; but within a year of his succession to the throne the two were at war. In the spring of 1109 Louis demanded that Henry should abandon the Vexin frontier castle of Gisors on the Epte, which he had taken, and that he should do homage for his fiefs. In the two years' war which followed Henry's refusal Robert of Beaumont, count of Meulan in the French Vexin, was in the centre of the hostilities and was Henry's most active lieutenant. In 1110 Louis captured Meulan, and in March 1111 Robert, in revenge, raided Paris. The men of Flanders, Ponthieu, and the Vexin ravaged the Norman frontiers; and the confused and indecisive struggle lasted until it became part of a more general war. Henry naturally took offence when Fulk V inherited Maine in 1110 and refused to do homage for it. In the autumn of 1111 he attacked Anjou; his ally Theobald of Blois pushed into Brie; and Robert of Flanders came to Louis's support, only to die through an accident. By the next year each side had stirred up rebellion in the territory of the other. In Normandy Amauri, the brother of Bertrada of Montfort, lord of Montfort-Amauri in France and in 1118 count of Évreux in Normandy, William Crispin lord of Dangu, and Robert of Bellême were the leaders; but on 4 November 1112, Henry had Robert arrested when he came on an embassy from the French king, and never released him from prison. In February 1113, Fulk of Anjou sued for peace. He did homage to Henry for Maine and betrothed his daughter Matilda to Henry's son, William the Aetheling. In March Louis followed his example, and at Gisors surrendered to Henry the suzerainty of Bellême, Maine, and Brittany.

Henry had triumphed in his first war with France. He had enlarged his territory, and he had removed a dangerous threat to the internal security of his duchy by the final destruction of Robert of Bellême. Henry's second war was due to the behaviour of Theobald of Blois. In 1115 Theobald ambushed and imprisoned William II, count of Nevers, a friend of King Louis; and by April 1116 the parties were once more in arms. King Henry supported his nephews, Theobald and Stephen of Blois; Fulk of Anjou and Baldwin VII of Flanders rallied to Louis; and the French party and some Norman barons recognized William Clito as duke of Normandy. The Vexin was again the main theatre of war, but campaigns were fought also in Picardy, Brie, and in the neighbourhood of Alençon and Chartres. In September 1118 Baldwin of Flanders was fatally wounded in the northern marches of Normandy. Henry then managed to detach his southern adversary. Fulk of Anjou wanted to go on a Crusade and he needed peace and money. In June 1119 he visited Henry's court and married his daughter to William the Aetheling. He settled Maine on the girl and, should he die on the Crusade, Anjou as well. Louis answered this diplomatic success by crossing the River Epte into Normandy and fixing his headquarters at les Andelys on the Seine. On 20 August Henry met him at Brémule, routed his army, put him to headlong flight, and captured his archives, his standard, and his war-horse, all of which he generously returned. But even this humiliation did not discourage Louis completely. In September he invaded Normandy again and then attacked Chartres; and he complained in person to Pope Calixtus II about Henry and Theobald at the Council of Rheims, which opened on 20 October 1119. Henry replied to the charges at a personal interview with the pope at Gisors a month later. Calixtus, although a Frenchman and the French queen's uncle, was also a third cousin of Henry, and he negotiated a peace rather favourable to the English king. Henry promised to quieten his nephew, Theobald of Blois, and to compensate William Clito with English lands. Louis again recognized Henry's possessions, and in 1120 took homage not from Henry himself but from his son William. The new count of Flanders, Charles the Good, a grandson of Robert 'le Frison', entered into friendly relations with Normandy. Henry was at the height of his power. His influence stretched from Flanders to Anjou; Boulogne, Normandy, Brittany, Bellême, and Maine were under his control; his nephew ruled Blois and Chartres; his son-in-law was emperor; and his son, William, was recognized as his heir in England and on the Continent and stood to succeed to Anjou should Fulk die on his Crusade.

In less than a year the great enterprise was destroyed. On 25 November 1120 William Aetheling was drowned when the White Ship was wrecked off Barfleur on its passage from Normandy to England. The catastrophe was almost irremediable. Henry had no other legitimate son. His daughter, the Empress Matilda, had become his heir presumptive; and a crowd of rival pretenders could easily be perceived. It was an almost annihilating blow; and that Henry recovered, planned anew, indomitably pursued his new aims, and appeared to regain control, reveals the true qualities of the man. His first wife, Eadgyth-Matilda, had died in 1118. On 1 February 1121, two months after William's death, Henry married again. True to his policy he chose Adelaide, daughter of Godfrey VII, count of Louvain, duke of Lower-Lorraine, and marquis of Antwerp. The marriage might give Henry an heir; it strengthened his position on the northern marches of France; and it brought him closer to his daughter and his son-in-law, the Emperor Henry V.

The fatality encouraged Henry's rivals. In 1121 Fulk of Anjou returned from the Holy Land; and when he required the surrender of Maine as well as the return of his widowed daughter, war broke out in 1123. In Normandy, Amauri of Montfort again rebelled in the interest of William Clito and drew into the conspiracy even Henry's protégé, Waleran, count of Meulan, a son of the late Robert of Beaumont. Fulk then supported the rebels by giving his second daughter, Sybil, to William and enfeoffing him with Maine. Henry was hard pressed, for he could get no help from Charles of Flanders. But in October 1123 he took some of Waleran's castles, and in March 1124, when the campaigning season reopened, his chief Norman opponents were routed and captured at Bourgthéroulde. He also scored diplomatic successes. He persuaded the papal legate to annul the marriage between William Clito and Sybil of Anjou on the grounds of consanguinity, and he incited the emperor to invade France. In August 1124 Henry V marched on Rheims; but the threat aroused so much popular support for Louis that the emperor, badly supported by his vassals and distracted by an uprising at Worms, turned back at Metz. The great schemes of both sides had failed.

Henry I's second marriage was barren. But in 1125 the emperor died childless and fresh diplomatic moves became possible. The widowed Matilda could now be made Henry's heiress and could be married again in order to assure the dynasty. Matilda came sadly back on her father's summons, and at the Christmas court 1126 was presented by Henry to the English barons. Henry asserted her rightful claim to succeed him, for she was descended on both sides from lines of kings; and on 1 January 1127 at London the barons swore that in case Henry died without male heir they would immediately recognize Matilda as ruler (*domina*) of England. The primate swore first, then the rest of the bishops. David king of Scots led the laity, and was followed by the queen. When Robert of Gloucester, the king's bastard, was called, Stephen count of Mortain and Boulogne, the king's nephew, disputed his precedence, and won his point. He may have regretted this ostentation when he seized the throne to the exclusion of his cousin on Henry's death. The remainder of the barons then took the oath without demur.

Henry's success provoked the French king to counter-measures. At his Christmas court he appealed to his barons for support for William Clito's claim to Normandy; and then, when he heard of the oath of the English barons, he married William to Johanna of Montferrat, the half-sister of Queen Adela, and enfeoffed him with the Vexin and its castles. William soon appeared at Gisors on the frontier with an army; but, before much had been done, the childless count of Flanders, Charles the Good, was murdered while praying in a church at Bruges (2 March 1127), and the rival powers were able to dispute about the succession. All the numerous pretenders were descended from Count Baldwin V who died in 1067. Baldwin IV of Hainault represented the senior branch; Thierry of Alsace and William of Ypres, a bastard, were grandsons of Robert I 'le Frison'; and the Norman family claimed through Matilda, daughter of Baldwin V and wife of William the Conqueror. Among the Normans themselves William Clito was of the senior line, Henry I stood closest of all the claimants to the common ancestor, and Stephen of Mortain and Boulogne held a Flemish county. The feudal overlord, Louis VI, entered Flanders with an army, and in March and April persuaded many of the barons and most of the towns to recognize William Clito as count. Henry, in alliance with his father-in-law, the duke of Lower-Lorraine, realistically supported other candidates. Louis left Flanders in May after capturing William of Ypres and searching in vain for the late count's treasure; and William Clito, a bad ruler and hostile to the aspirations of the important,merchant class, began to lose ground. He had to fight against Henry's lieutenant, Stephen of Boulogne, and other rivals; Louis's personal intervention in May 1128 only provoked Henry's invasion of France a month later; and when William Clito died towards the end of July of a wound received at the siege of Alost, Thierry of Alsace was the claimant in possession. The situation was accepted by all parties. For Henry it was a substantial victory. He now had a friend in Flanders and could plan a close alliance between Flanders, Normandy, and Anjou.

Henry has always feared Anjou, and he distrusted it all the more since his heir was a woman. A political solution was to marry Matilda to the Angevin heir; and during the Flemish war Henry negotiated the marriage of Matilda and Fulk's son, Geoffrey Plantagenet. Henry agreed that in default of a male heir Geoffrey should be king and duke; and on these terms the betrothal was celebrated in 1127 and the marriage on 17 June 1128 at le Mans. This brilliant dynastic coup was, however, threatened by many practical difficulties. Matilda disliked the marriage. She had been an important woman, and at the age of twenty-six resented marrying a youth ten years her junior. The English barons had not been consulted, and suspected the arrangements. The Norman barons, equally disregarded, detested the idea of submitting to an Angevin count. The French king feared the alliance, and was the more alarmed when Flanders was included through the marriage of Thierry to Sybil of Anjou, the divorced wife of Willliam Clito. Indeed, the Norman-Angevin marriage disappointed all immediate hopes. But it was fateful enough. When Henry knighted Geoffrey a week before the marriage he hung round his neck a blue shield painted with golden lions. The device of Geoffrey's son, King Henry II of England, is not known; but his grandson, King Richard I, like William fitzEmpress, bore a single lion on his shield at the beginning of his reign and later three of the beasts walking. This coat of arms, gules three leopards, was worn unchanged by his successors until 1340, when Edward III quartered the Plantagenet lions with the fleurs-de-lis of France.

Although Henry I's policy triumphed in the end and his grandson was to acquire one of the greatest principalities in Europe, it was to send him to his grave a disappointed man. Geoffrey repudiated his

haughty wife soon after the marriage, and Henry took her with him
to England in 1131. On 8 September at a solemn court at Northampton the oaths of the English baronage to Matilda were renewed,
so as to bind all those who had murmured that the arbitrary re-
marriage had absolved them from their former undertakings, and
it was decided to give Matilda back to Geoffrey since he had asked
for her again. In August 1133 Henry left England for the last time.
His only purpose now was to safeguard the succession. Fulk V of
Anjou had in 1128 been offered Mélissende, the heiress of Baldwin
II king of Jerusalem, and in 1129 had left his county to Geoffrey
and departed for the East. On 5 March 1133 Matilda had given
birth to a son, Henry, later king of England, and on 3 June 1134 to
another son, Geoffrey. The king could feel that the dynastic problem was settled. But his satisfaction was quickly soured. The ambitious Geoffrey demanded to be put into possession of his wife's
dowry and to receive the homage of the Norman barons. Matilda
supported her husband because she saw that unless Geoffrey had a
firm base in Normandy before Henry's death her father's plans
would go awry. But Henry had no love for his presumptuous son-
in-law, and had begun to doubt his usefulness once he had provided
Matilda with sons. So, when the king refused, Geoffrey raised war
in Normandy in the summer of 1135; and it was in these melancholy
circumstances that Henry died on 1 December in the forest of
Lyons, not far from the battle field of Brémule, having feasted too
well on lampreys after a hard day's hunting.

In the prophecy of Merlin, which forms the seventh book of
Geoffrey of Monmouth's *Historia regum Britanniæ,* written between
1130 and 1138, it was predicted—after the event—that there would
succeed a lion of justice, at whose roar the castles of Gaul and the
dragon-[standards] of the island would tremble; that in his days
gold would be extorted from the lily and the nettle and silver would
flow from the hooves of oxen; that those who used curling tongs
[on the hair] would affect various fleeces so that the outward appearance would betray the inner man; that the feet of dogs would be
mutilated, the venison have peace, and men lament their punishment; and that the coins of commerce would be divided and the
half [penny] would be round. In these cryptic words we have one
of the earliest judgments on Henry's reign. He was a lion, terrible
to his enemies, terrible to the malefactor, terrible above all to the
poachers of his game. He tampered with the coinage and wrung

money from every source. His courtiers were sheep. There is much truth in these remarks. Basically, Henry's reign was very like his brother's. The main phases are strangely repeated. But Geoffrey misses an important side. Thirteen years of shifts and expedients at an impressionable age had smoothed and hardened Henry's character. Henry was more methodical, more diplomatic, more eloquent, more sinister than Rufus. He made government an art. He wept when his only son was drowned, and then schemed afresh, undaunted and merciless, for the sake of the empire he had built, and for its descent to a babe in arms by way of a hard woman and her brash, unpopular husband.

IV

On the news of Henry's illness those barons who could, gathered to hear the king's last will. His bastard, Earl Robert of Gloucester, his son-in-law, Count Rotrou of Perche, the Beaumont twins, Earl Robert of Leicester and Count Waleran of Meulan, and their step-brother, William of Warenne earl of Surrey, were present; but Geoffrey of Anjou and even Matilda stayed away. The dying king left all his possessions to his daughter, as he had planned; but he seems to have ignored her rebel husband.

Although the rules of succession to fiefs and kingdoms were still incompletely formed, and although a French fief and the English kingdom did not necessarily follow the same custom, Geoffrey's right to be recognized as duke of Normandy and king of England seems fairly strong. Hereditary succession to the French fiefs was becoming the rule; Stephen of Blois held the county of Boulogne in the right of his wife, and in 1137 the duchy of Aquitaine passed without trouble to a girl and was carried by Eleanor to her successive husbands. The English position cannot be stated so simply, for the precedents are confusing. But the kingdom of Jerusalem went to Fulk of Anjou on the death of his father-in-law in 1131, and there seems no good legal reason why England should not have fallen to Geoffrey in 1135. The one impossibility was for a woman to succeed as sole ruler in her own right and expect to remain in that position. If the dying king had decided to exclude Geoffrey then he must have imagined that Matilda could rule as the guardian for her infant son. Had either Geoffrey or Matilda been acceptable to the baronage there would have been no crisis. But Geoffrey, who was hated for his character and his race, was rejected as king and duke; and Matilda, whose early charm had been spoiled by the shame of her second marriage, was refused as guardian for her child. It is clear that Henry's mistake had been to put territorial ambition before the happiness of his daughter and the contentment of his vassals.

On Henry's death the barons who were in Normandy came together at le Neubourg (Eure) to discuss the position. On 20 December they decided to recognize as duke Theobald IV of Blois and Champagne, the eldest grandson of William the Conqueror and the nephew and ally of the late king. But in the meantime Theobald's younger brother, Stephen of Mortain and Boulogne, the greatest landowner in England, had crossed the Channel with a few determined knights, brushed aside Robert of Gloucester's garrisons at Dover and Canterbury, and accepted the fortune destined for the audacious. London, where the Norman trading influence was strong and where the anarchy was already being felt, had welcomed him and proclaimed him king. Henry of Blois, bishop of Winchester, had then used his influence to secure for his brother the castle and treasure at Winchester and to persuade the primate, William of Corbeil, to perform a hasty coronation. And when news of Stephen's crowning at Westminster on 22 December surprised the Norman barons, who were still in company with their new duke, Theobald gave his approval, and then was mortified when the barons, wishing to have only one lord, transferred their undivided allegiance to his younger brother. The count of Blois went sadly home, made his peace with Louis VI, and thereafter supported Stephen in a quiet but useful way.

From the point of view of Geoffrey and Matilda, Stephen was a perjured usurper; and their attitude was reasonable, for the strength of their case has already been shown. Stephen, in fact, could adduce no single claim of superior merit. But he could present many persuasive arguments. According to the celebrated canonist of the time, Ivo of Chartres, a man could be lawfully crowned if the kingdom belonged to him by hereditary right and he had been chosen by the common consent of the prelates and magnates. Stephen made little show of his hereditary title; but he had conservative tradition behind him, since hitherto in both England and Normandy an adult male of the ruling house had been preferred always to a woman or a son-in-law and usually to a child; and if this argument would seem to favour Theobald, Stephen could have replied that England

since the Conquest had been the portion of the younger sons. He
had obtained only a restricted consent to his action, but as much as
Rufus and Henry in similar circumstances, and he hardly needed the
exaggerated claim the Londoners produced, that it was their special
privilege to elect a king when the succession was in doubt.

Stephen's tacit acceptance by the communities, his legitimate
coronation by the church, and his unopposed exercise of the royal
office made him the lawful possessor; and feudal law, baffled by the
problems which pleas of better right presented, was always favourable to lawful possession. And, indeed, if there had been a court
competent to entertain pleas of better right, then David of Scots
and Stephen's wife could have put in their claims. The law of succession was still far too vague for the strictly legal issues to be argued
with profit; and controversy was confined to subordinate issues.
Stephen's greatest weakness was his perjury, and to this charge,
which was argued in the ecclesiastical courts, he replied to the pope
that the oath he had taken in 1127 to recognize Matilda as Henry's
heir was void for two principal reasons: first, because it had been
extorted by force, and secondly, because a bastard could not be a
legal heir, and Matilda was the issue of an uncanonical marriage
between Henry I and a nun. The church had no special interest in
hereditary right. It esteemed suitability and effectiveness. Stephen's
pleas were accepted by a very respectable pope, Innocent II, and
seem to have satisfied the public conscience.

Stephen owed his happy accession to many factors. He was an
important European figure, yet educated in England and Normandy
and married to a woman of the line of Cerdic. He was popular with
all classes for his affability, generosity, and good manners, so that
even hostile chroniclers were willing to attribute his faults to bad
counsel. He was acceptable to the church because he had favoured
the new monastic orders on his fiefs and because among his relatives
were cardinals and bishops. He was familiar to the trading classes
and wool merchants through his holding the county of Boulogne
and his connexion with the fairs of Champagne. And among the
barons he was recognized as a fine leader, a brave and honourable
knight, and a man of mild temper.

Stephen was luckier at first than his two immediate predecessors,
for a single *coup d'état* had secured him the double inheritance and he
was without important enemies in England. His initial confidence
is revealed by the brevity of his coronation charter, in which he

merely confirmed the concessions of Henry and reaffirmed the good old laws of King Edward. Yet his lucky start was due principally to the general reaction against the harsh government of his uncle; and the very forces which swept him into power were dangerous. Instead of having to face an immediate military crisis, like Rufus and Henry, Stephen had to meet his friends. And, since Henry's tyranny had been great, the sufferers required an assurance from Stephen more ample than that embodied in the coronation oath and implied in the mutual oaths of fealty. The bargaining had become traditional; and both Rufus and Henry had proved that early weakness could be overcome and the power of the crown re-established. But Stephen was unable to turn an immediate and temporary danger to his lasting advantage. It was only when he began to reassert the royal authority that the first crisis in his reign occurred, and by then he had a rival in the field. Hence, although the typical phases of the last two reigns reappear, the forces were more balanced and the resulting pattern was less sharp. Stephen's reign breaks into three main periods. Until 1139 he tried with some success to restore and maintain the rights of the crown. In the next decade he was nearly overwhelmed by the Angevins, losing Normandy, and in England almost succumbing to the disorder which the dynastic war unleashed. But he fought through to a relatively peaceful end (1149–54).

Stephen paid a heavy but not a reckless price for his irregular succession. In December 1135 the Londoners promised him their loyal services provided that he established peace in the kingdom. Although Stephen could never carry out this engagement in full, and although in December 1141 he had to take away from the city some of the privileges it had bought from Henry towards the end of his reign, the memory of fiscal oppression was so strong that London never deserted the king it had chosen. Kent and London were always the bastions of Stephen's power; and in the following century Stephen was a popular baptismal name in the South-east.

The church had made Stephen's accession possible. His brother, Henry of Winchester, had warmly supported him; Roger of Salisbury, the justiciar, had brought over the administration and surrendered the treasure; the primate had crowned him; and the pope had withstood the charges of his rivals. Stephen paid its price by making concessions which had generally been allowed elsewhere in Europe. Already, before his coronation, he had given the primate an assurance that he would restore freedom to the church; and at the Oxford council in April 1136 Stephen redeemed the promise for which his brother had stood bail. In appearance the king gave little more than Henry I had conceded in similar circumstances. Both kings granted that the church should be free; but the policy of the church had gained in clarity since 1100, and Stephen was required to elaborate in even greater detail the freedom which was to be allowed. He promised to protect church property and to respect ecclesiastical customs. He renounced most of the royal rights over the persons and property of clerks—'simony', jurisdiction, the escheat of church temporalities during vacancies, and the seizure of the chattels of dead clerics. The one ambiguity was due probably as much to clerical as to royal hesitation. Free elections were not explicitly granted, for, although royal nomination was disliked by reformers, free election by chapters could be equally inconvenient to the church authorities. In the sphere of external relations Stephen made no concessions, presumably because they were not required. Again the prelates were not anxious to escape from royal control merely in order to submit themselves unreservedly to another. Their dominant aim was to establish the church as a separate and independent order in the kingdom; and in 1136 Stephen accepted the programme with the one reservation that all concessions were made saving his royal and just dignity. Clearly the concordat could not last without the moderation and loyalty of the bishops as well as the good faith of the king; and the conditional fealty which the prelates swore in return for the charter, a fealty which was to last as long as Stephen preserved the liberty of the church, was no good omen for the future.

At the Oxford council Stephen was able to announce that Pope Innocent II had recognized him as king and duke. This recognition was crucial, and the important influence of the church on political events during the reign cannot be doubted, although the clerical authors of the chroniclers and the clerical drafters of royal charters have exaggerated it unduly. A real change had, indeed, occurred in noble society. The evil reputation which had surrounded William Rufus and his military friends was disappearing in the newer age of chivalry. Unlike Rufus and his circle Stephen and some of his companions—as, for example, the Beaumonts—were conventionally pious and great patrons of monks. Their religion was, however, largely the private cult of martial families and hardly affected their behaviour towards the ecclesiastical hierarchy. Hence Stephen's church policy was much like Henry I's and William I's: from conviction he allowed what he believed to be the just aspirations of the church and from policy he then strove to control and direct them in his own interest. And like all his Norman predecessors he had to face that tricky problem of how to deal with those barons who were protected by a special law—the bishops. Henry's administrative reforms had enhanced the status and the power of the episcopate. The dynasty of Roger of Salisbury disposed of important offices and possessed vast estates and many castles; and a new star was rising in Henry of Blois, bishop of Winchester and abbot of Glastonbury. Stephen and his brother were in some ways very alike: Stephen a knight who wanted to be a king; Henry, a monk who made his annual retreat at Cluny, yet aspired also to be a prince of the church. Both were ambitious, adventurous, even reckless. Their paths soon diverged. Stephen was determined to keep the crown at any cost, and in his well-meaning way blundered from expedient to expedient. Henry, a great builder, an importer of heathen statues from Rome, and a magnificent patron, identified his personal ambition so closely with the cause of ecclesiastical privilege that a blow at either aroused a double resentment; and when Stephen refused to be Henry's tool the church became as uncertain in its support as the lay aristocracy.

Unlike the church the baronage had no political programme. It resented King Henry's new afforestations, and Stephen renounced them in his Oxford charter. But Stephen, unlike Henry I, was not required to make detailed reforms in feudal law. Each baron had private ambitions and hoped that they would be satisfied. Stephen naturally rewarded his friends and bought the waverers; but he gave as little as he could. He had the great advantage of his adversaries' unpopularity. Only relatives and a few close vassals ever warmly espoused the Angevin cause; and at first the attitude of even these was doubtful. Robert earl of Gloucester seems to have done nothing for his half-sister, the empress, before 1138. King David I of Scots was the uncle of the queen as well as of the empress, and the honour of Huntingdon was a hostage in Stephen's hands. When, however, the civil war began there emerged a number of self-seeking men, some already great like the earl of Chester, some on the rise, like Geoffrey de Mandeville, hereditary castellan of the tower of London, who exploited the situation simply in their private interests. Yet few barons changed sides.

The under-tenants and the mass of the people were loyal by instinct. The policy of the first three Norman kings had been to attach that loyalty to the crown and to weaken mesne allegiance. Stephen, however, was baronial in sympathy; and in the insecurity of his reign the more immediate loyalties regained their strength and English feudalism began to draw closer again to that parent stock from which it had been diverging. In his Oxford charter Stephen promised to control the sheriffs and to reform some abuses in the administration of the law. These tasks were beyond his capacity; but the magic of a crowned and anointed head was never completely destroyed.

With these general promises and some timely grants Stephen bought the crown. Few but his close friends had seen his coronation. But when he wore his crown at Westminster at Easter 1136 he gathered all his vassals round him in a brilliant assembly which was a sign to all that the harsh and miserly days of the late reign were gone for ever. All three archbishops—Canterbury, York, and Rouen —were present; and among the laity were the future leaders of the Angevin party, Miles of Gloucester and Brian fitzCount. Henry of Scots, the son of King David, was there. Even Robert earl of Gloucester was on his way to submit and take up his fiefs. Early in April the court moved to Oxford to meet him, and the earl swore fealty for as long as the king completely respected his dignity and preserved their agreement. At Oxford Stephen granted the charter of liberties which has already been discussed, and so ratified the compacts he had made with his vassals and with the church. The future seemed bright. He had at his side a loyal and courageous wife; and in William of Ypres he had found an able captain to command the Flemish and Breton mercenaries whom he recruited. William, one of the disappointed candidates in the Flemish war of succession in 1127–8, was rewarded by Stephen with lands in Kent. He never failed his master. Yet this rich, popular, and martial king was not to be a success. He was, perhaps, always conscious of his father's cowardice in 1098 at Antioch, when the count of Blois and Chartres, commander-in-chief of the First Crusade, had abandoned his army and returned home. Ostentatious bravery, even rashness, and also an unshakable persistence, which sometimes in his more desperate moments brought him close to trickery, seem to have been Stephen's answer to the dishonour which was still attached to his name. His initial mistakes as king were over-confidence and failure to appreciate the full magnitude of his task. When the old king died it was as though a dam had burst. Too many ambitions had been pent up too long, and the new king found it hard to keep his feet, for the weakness of his title and the existence of a rival sapped his strength at critical moments. It became easy for decent men in despair to decide that more hope of security lay in acknowledging the Angevins than in buttressing a crumbling power. Yet Stephen never lost heart and never gave in. Louis VI of France, a man much like Stephen and another who spent his reign in petty wars against his vassals, is considered the real founder of the Capetian power, largely because his predecessor was even weaker. By the standard set by the Norman and Angevin kings Stephen was unworthy. But his successor, Henry II, owed more to Stephen's persistent assertion of royal rights than is commonly allowed.

Stephen was in the beginning as successful in foreign as in domestic affairs. After his coronation and after the burial of the late king in the greatest of his monastic foundations—the Benedictine convent at Reading—Stephen marched north to encounter David of Scots. The two kings met at Durham on 5 February 1136. David refused to forswear the oath he had taken to Matilda as Henry's heir; but Stephen allowed David's son, Henry, to receive his father's English fiefs, the honour of Huntingdon, part of the inheritance of Waltheof, and do homage for them; and he added Carlisle and Doncaster. The arrangement was to the advantage of David, for it left his hands free; but Henry of Scots attached himself for a short time to Stephen's court as an English earl and became some security for his father's behaviour. Stephen, in fact, had done as well as he could. Normandy also urgently needed attention. The duchy was becoming chaotic. Geoffrey of Anjou had invaded immediately after the death of King Henry, but he had been glad to negotiate a truce with Theobald of Blois, acting for Stephen, until Whitsun 1136 because he had a serious revolt on his own hands in his county. On 21 September 1136 Geoffrey again crossed the Sarthe only to retire when wounded at the siege of le Sap on 1 October. Geoffrey's expeditions were without strategic purpose and caused great hardship. Towns were ransomed, sacked, or burned and the countryside pillaged. But Geoffrey was, perhaps, no worse than most of his contemporaries; and it was because of the patriotism of the Normans that his warfare has been so harshly described. Waleran count of Meulan and William of Ypres, Stephen's military commanders in Normandy, were no more gentle; and when Lisieux was burned on 29 September 1136 the Breton defenders were responsible.

In 1136 minor disturbances detained the king in England; but hatred of the Angevins kept the duchy loyal. And when Stephen crossed in March 1137 he was received with enthusiasm, and in his nine-months' stay firmly secured his title. Most of the barons, including Robert earl of Gloucester, acknowledged him. He paid compensation to his brother Theobald, and in May obtained a complete recognition from Louis VI of France. The French king had decided that the attachment of Normandy to Anjou was to be feared even more than the familiar peril from the union of Normandy and England, and he allowed Stephen's eldest son, Eustace of Boulogne, to do homage for Normandy and the other French fiefs—an arrangement which Henry I had contrived and which was similar to Stephen's settlement with Scotland. Finally, after an abortive raid from Anjou, Stephen made a two years' truce with Geoffrey at the cost of 2,000 marks of silver a year. The Angevin cause was in complete eclipse, and Stephen may well have thought that Geoffrey would be no more troublesome to him than Fulk V and William Clito had been to Henry I. The king was busily engaged in restoring peace to the distracted duchy when disquieting news from England sent him back there in December.

V

By 1138 the initial enthusiasm for Stephen was cooling. He was not carrying out all his promises; and some of his undertakings had led to discord. His concessions to the church had included a review of all encroachments on church property since the death of the Conqueror; and Henry of Winchester's claims for his abbey of Glastonbury caused baronial unrest in Devon. Then Stephen had disturbed the church by seizing the personal treasure of the archbishop of Canterbury after his death on 21 November 1136. And he was undeceiving the barons by withstanding their demands for favours and resisting trespasses on royal rights. In 1136 he had quarrelled with Hugh Bigod, one of his earliest supporters, over his usurpation of Norwich castle when it was rumoured that the king was dead, and he had forfeited and expelled Baldwin of Reviers for occupying the royal castle at Exeter. Moreover, at Brampton near Huntingdon he had impleaded several barons for forest offences.

At the end of 1137 King David of Scots was disturbing the border in the hope of extorting from Stephen the last of the earldoms which Waltheof had held—Northumberland—and when the king naturally refused to put even more provinces in the hands of David's son he had to prepare for war. In February 1138 Stephen invaded Scotland; and when David retaliated at Easter the English had to rely mainly on local defence, for the king had reached the first crisis in his reign.

In June 1138 Geoffrey invaded Normandy, Robert earl of Gloucester, who was on his lands in the Bessin, renounced his fealty to Stephen, and rebellions broke out on both sides of the Channel. The eldest bastard and the favourite nephew of King Henry I may well have been rivals in the past—certainly they disputed precedence in 1127—and it is likely that Robert, a man eminently suited to rule, resented that hardening of opinion against the legal rights of natural children which deprived him of a claim to the throne. His upright character was recognized by all, and his talents as a statesman were proved abundantly in the struggle with Stephen. The new king had tried to attach him to his side, and seemed to have succeeded. But when Robert saw a chance for his half-sister he changed allegiance and remained stubbornly loyal to her cause in the face of every temptation. Robert became the real leader of the Angevin party in England and the centre of Geoffrey's hopes in Normandy. He and Stephen were well matched; and it seems that in the end neither bore the other much personal ill will.

In England the area of revolt was largely confined to the Welsh march and the South-west. Robert's castle at Bristol was the key position, Salisbury the outpost, and Wareham in Dorset the essential port. Of the scattered centres of rebellion Dover, held by Robert's castellan, Walchelin Maminot, was the most inconvenient to the king. Queen Matilda, who could call in her men of Boulogne, was sent against Dover, and Stephen attacked the West. He took Hereford before Whitsun, and from the base he made at Bath reconnoitred Bristol and found it too strong. Stephen's rapid changes of direction and incompleted designs give his campaigns an aimless and haphazard appearance. This, however, is characteristic of the time rather than of the man. Defence still kept its advantage over attack. The two basic forms of the Norman castle—the motte and bailey, with its conical mound surmounted by a wooden stockade, and the residential castle, with its flatter mound supporting a wooden hall, both protected by dry ditches—had not changed much by Stephen's reign; and the simplest earth castles were thrown up in the course of the civil war. But since the beginning of the century many wooden halls had been rebuilt in stone, either with common hall and chamber side by side over a storage basement, a type called the hall-keep, or with the rooms stacked to form a lofty tower of three or four stories—storage basement, entrance chamber (but only in the more elaborate), common hall, and, at the top, the lord's private chamber—a structure known as a tower-keep, and familiar through its prototype, the Tower of London. And in the same period the motte and bailey castles were being strengthened by the replacement of the wooden palisading at the top of the motte by a circular stone wall—the shell-keep. Castles, therefore, were of various strengths; but any stone building could be held until starved out or smashed by assault engines and mining operations, unless it fell to surprise or was yielded to inducements or threats. Hence Stephen darted against the enemy posts, and, whenever one held, had to decide whether it was possible, and worth while, to mount an expensive blockade which would weaken his strength in the field. On occasion, when the operation was crucial, Stephen himself sat for months before a place. Sometimes he left a beleaguering force under a lieutenant. Often he ravaged the surrounding country and husbanded his men. Nor was the defence any more capable of decisive action. Each rebel castle became a robber stronghold from which raids were mounted against the friends of the king and royal property. The insurgents never put a substantial army into the field, and their one material success—the capture of the king—was the unexpected result of a siege and relief.

While the queen reduced Dover and the king campaigned in the West, the northern barons, inspired by two old men, Archbishop Thurstin and Walter Espec, lord of Helmsley and Wark or Carham, prepared to protect Yorkshire from the ravages of a motley host drawn from all parts of Scotland and always out of the control of the 'sore saint', its commander. The Anglo-Norman forces advanced to Thirsk; an offer of Northumberland no longer satisfied the Scottish king's ambition; and when David crossed the Tees the English moved up to Northallerton. The archbishop's troops flew the banners of St. Peter of York, St. John of Beverley, and St. Wilfrid of Ripon from a standard surmounted by a silver pyx and erected on a cart; and on 22 August 1138 in the hard-fought battle 'of the standard' David was defeated and fled the field. He did not abandon his attack on Northumberland; but Yorkshire at least had been spared. Nor was Geoffrey of Anjou any more successful in Normandy. It was not until November that Waleran of Meulan and William of Ypres could force the invader to retire; but Geoffrey's fourth incursion was the last until Stephen was a prisoner in Matilda's hands. Normandy was without a proper government; it was suffering severely from the anarchy; but it would clearly not accept Geoffrey as duke. And the count of Anjou had much to do at home. He was engaged in reducing his own barons to order after the revolt against his father's severe repression. He was young and could afford to wait.

By the end of 1138 Stephen had weathered his first storm. The western and extreme northern districts of England had passed out of his control; and Wales had almost been lost. On the death of King Henry I the Welsh had risen simultaneously and, although thwarted by most of the castles, had wellnigh overwhelmed the foreign settlers, for the natives had learned the art of cavalry war from their masters, intermarriage had aggravated intrigue, and a great leader was emerging in Owain Gwynedd, the son of Gruffydd ap Cynan. The Welsh church, in sympathetic revolt, tried to break free from Canterbury, and the bishop of St. David's advanced a claim to metropolitan authority over a national province. Stephen had soon been screened from the conflict by the rebellion of the marcher lords; but Canterbury was not so hampered by schism, and the bishop of St. David's was to find that the ecclesiastical chains had been better forged than the political and that the papacy stood immovably behind Canterbury's historic rights. The western marcher barons could get independence only at the cost of great suffering. But the king of Scots could legalize his position cheaply. In 1138 a papal legate, Alberic, cardinal-bishop of Ostia, was in England for the affairs of Canterbury, and interested himself in negotiations with Scotland. The queen, David's niece, also played her part, and on 9 April 1139 a treaty was made at Durham. David swore fealty to Stephen for the term of his life and gave five hostages. Stephen enfeoffed Henry of Scots with the earldom of Northumberland less Newcastle and Bamburgh on condition that the laws of Henry I should not be changed. The Scottish heir was brought into the Beaumont circle by his marriage to Adeline, the sister of the earl of Surrey, and Henry rejoined Stephen as one of his barons.

The treaty of Durham was most unwelcome to the earl of Chester. Ranulf de Gernons, the fourth earl, had inherited vast estates and even vaster claims. His father had held the honour of Carlisle, and the son was inclined to dispute with the Scottish royal family control of the land between the Mersey and the Forth. As the lesser evil, Stephen favoured the Scots, for Ranulf's eastern ambitions threatened the interior security of the kingdom. Among the many appendages to the palatine county of Cheshire was a string of estates and castles running along the line of the Trent into Lincolnshire. When Ranulf's father, Ranulf 'le Meschin', had married Lucy, already twice widowed, he stood to gain other fiefs and claims in Lincolnshire. But King Henry I had pollarded this spreading tree. The honour of Carlisle had been taken away; the honour of Lancaster had been placed in the safe hands of Stephen of Blois; and most of the Lincolnshire fiefs had eventually passed to Lucy's son by her second marriage, William de Roumare. But Ranulf de Gernons and his half-brother were close friends, and their aim was to control a triangle in the heart of the kingdom with Chester and Lincoln as the base-line and Coventry its southern point. The establishment of a semi-autonomous honour on the natural cleavage line of the country was even more dangerous to the integrity of the kingdom than the thrust of the earl of Gloucester and his satellites from South Wales into the Thames valley. Ranulf had, indeed, married a daughter of the earl of Gloucester; but his faithlessness to Stephen was matched by his indifference to the Angevin cause. Self-interest alone guided his steps; and Stephen strove to isolate and contain him. The king's most spectacular scheme was the reinforcement of the power of the Beaumonts in the gap between Chester and Gloucester. By 1140 the three Beaumont brothers, Waleran count of Meulan, Robert earl of Leicester, and Hugh the Poor, held the counties of Hereford, Worcester, and Leicester and the Beauchamp inheritance in Bedfordshire, their cousin, Roger, was earl of Warwick, and their brother-in-law, Gilbert de Clare, had been made earl of Pembroke. When Henry of Scots received Carlisle and Northumberland and married Adeline of Warenne, the half-sister of the Beaumont brothers, the net was closed. Nevertheless, Chester's dominant position astride the kingdom was always an embarrassment to the king and occasionally had a decisive effect on the fate of the realm.

Between 1138 and 1142 Stephen granted new earldoms to others than the Beaumonts. William of Aumale was given York and Robert of Ferrers Derby for the part they played in the battle of the Standard. William d'Aubigny, the husband of Henry I's widow, was made earl of Lincoln, and William of Roumare, who coveted that position, was half-compensated by the grant of Cambridge. Gilbert de Clare's nephew and namesake was created earl of Hertford; and to Geoffrey de Mandeville and Hugh Bigod went the counties of Essex and Norfolk respectively. All the new earls were substantial men; and the reason for each creation is clear. In the north and midlands Stephen was strengthening and encouraging his own friends against the Scots and Chester. Elsewhere he was buying the support of key men. He created no new earldom after 1142. His policy was traditional and, in the main, justified by results.

The king's success in the temporal sphere in 1138 explains his momentary firmness in ecclesiastical matters. His brother, Henry of Winchester, aspired to succeed William of Corbeil at Canterbury; but Stephen felt that he had done enough for Henry, and at the end of 1138 in an election held in the royal court but controlled by the papal legate, Alberic, Theobald abbot of le Bec was preferred. As consolation Henry was appointed papal legate and vicar by Innocent II on 1 March 1139, and a situation without precedent was created in the English church. The policy of William I and Lanfranc and of their successors had been to insist on the historical primacy of Canterbury over all Britain and to foster a unified church under the protection of the crown. The northern metropolitans had struggled against their subjection, and the papacy, hostile to independent primacies and jealous of its exclusion, had since the pontificate of Calixtus II favoured York and undermined the primatial privileges of Canterbury. At the end of 1125, so as to quieten for a moment the internal rivalry, Honorius II had made Archbishop William of Corbeil his permanent legate in England. Henceforth the unity of the *ecclesia Anglorum* depended on papal grant and not on historical precedent. Here again, Henry I had given way in principle and, owing to his strength, had thought he conceded nothing. And once more Stephen was to pay the cost. Archbishop Theobald, a fine canonist and a man of outstanding merit, was for some years condemned to a secondary role unfitting his historical position; and Henry of Blois, now rancorous towards his brother and ready to use the church for political ends, had supreme power but was unsupported by tradition. The English church was divided; and when, after Innocent II's death in 1143, no permanent legate was appointed for England, the church was for a few years deprived of a local leader. The advantage was to the pope and not to the king. Litigation flourished in the new freedom, and the papal court so extended its jurisdiction through unrestricted appeals that never again in the Middle Ages could it be reduced to its former position.

In 1139, however, Stephen may have thought that he could divide and rule. Encouraged by his barons, and especially by the Beaumonts, he decided to destroy the over-mighty family of Roger bishop of Salisbury. Roger was still chief justiciar, his son, Roger the Poor, was chancellor, his nephew, Nigel bishop of Ely, was treasurer, and another nephew, Alexander, was bishop of Lincoln. Stephen feared that this family would change sides if the rumoured Angevin invasion occurred, and open its strategically important castles to the enemy; he coveted its enormous wealth which he thought had been embezzled; and he quite rightly believed that such a concentration of power threatened his security. He summoned the bishops to his court at Oxford at midsummer 1139, demanded the surrender of their castles as satisfaction for a breach of the peace that their men committed, and, when Nigel escaped to Devizes castle, arrested Bishops Roger and Alexander. This resolute action was successful; and the bishops were released only when Salisbury, Sherborne, Malmesbury, Newark, Devizes, and Sleaford had been restored to the king. But the stroke alarmed Henry of Winchester, who had built some six castles and feared he might be the next to be despoiled. So he flew the banner of clerical freedom and summoned the clergy to a legatine council at Winchester on 29 August. The church, however, was divided in opinion. There were the precedents of Bishops Odo of Bayeux and William of Durham; and, despite the canons, it seemed reasonable to all moderate churchmen that traitorous bishops could be deprived of their fiefs by judgment of the royal court. There was also the royal and ducal custom that any private castle could be garrisoned by the prince when security required. So, when the legate called upon the king either to justify his action or to submit to judgment on this violation of clerical immunity, Stephen's attorney, Aubrey de Vere, defended his master and forbade the clergy on pain of outlawry to appeal to the pope. The archbishop of Rouen, another Cluniac, championed the king, and the council broke up on 1 September without having taken action.

Stephen had both destroyed his enemies and stifled the church's resentment. Bishop Roger of Salisbury, Roger the Poor, and Nigel lost their offices, and the former chief justiciar died, mourned by few, in December 1139, four months after his disgrace. Only Nigel came back into favour. Under Stephen he again obtained a post at the Exchequer and from Henry II he bought the treasurership for his son Richard, the famous author of the *Dialogus de Scaccario*. Nevertheless, Stephen's victory was to prove expensive. His brother, the legate, became even more dissatisfied and the English church withdrew its unanimous support. But if the king's suspicions of Roger of Salisbury were justified, he did well to scotch the danger while he was still strong rather than postpone action until a time of invasion and revolt. Moreover, the disgrace of the bishops and the death of Roger brought him treasure and military stores when most needed. Some of the booty went to re-equip his troops and some went to the French king to confirm their alliance. The betrothal of Eustace, Stephen's son and heir, to Constance, the sister of King Louis, was one of the happy consequences of the fall of a powerful family.

VI

The Angevin attack on England, which took place soon after the council of Winchester, was mistimed and should have been destroyed. David king of Scots had already been defeated at the battle of the Standard when Baldwin of Reviers disembarked at Wareham at the beginning of September 1139 and took refuge in Corfe; and when, a month later, Matilda and Robert of Gloucester landed at Arundel, a castle of their step-mother, Adelaide, King Henry's widow, Stephen was on his guard. Robert managed to slip through to the West; but Matilda was trapped. In the end, acting on the advice of the legate, Stephen let his rival go and gave her safe-conduct to her half-brother. Stephen was blamed by contemporaries for the frivolity or simplicity of his chivalrous behaviour; and later historians have condemned his lack of political sense. Even if Stephen's moral code disarmed him against a woman and prevented him from dealing with a rival in the way of a Henry I or a John, he could have taken Matilda prisoner and sent her back to Anjou. In England, despite her unattractive character, Matilda could rally Stephen's opponents and legitimize rebellion. Robert of Gloucester was always the real leader of the rival party; but without his sister he could have done little. Once Robert and Matilda were safe in Bristol her secret supporters unmasked. Miles, sheriff and castellan of Gloucester, joined her party and gave her devoted service; and the war of siege and relief was mostly restricted to the arc which confines Gloucester and Bristol, a strip running south from Worcester into Wiltshire, Somerset, and Dorset. The one important outpost in regular communication with the main Angevin base was Wallingford in the Thames valley, where Brian fitzCount, the constant companion of Henry I in his last years, renounced his fealty to Stephen, renewed his childhood friendship for Matilda, and, as that deepened into love, remained true despite the ruin of his isolated fief. At Christmas 1139 Nigel bishop of Ely revolted in the Fenland, and then William fitzRichard with Reginald, an illegitimate son of Henry I, rebelled in Cornwall. The peripheries of the kingdom had fallen away; but Stephen had the interior lines, safe communications with the Continent, and always complete freedom of manœuvre except to the north. He took Ely directly and then recovered Cornwall. In the summer of 1140 the church tried to mediate between the parties. At the end of September Henry of Winchester crossed to the Continent and conferred with Louis VII of France and Theobald IV of Blois; but a military stalemate had as yet discouraged neither side and satisfactory terms could not be discovered.

The deadlock was broken unexpectedly. Just before Christmas 1140 the earl of Chester and his half-brother, William of Roumare, dissatisfied with the king's treatment of Chester's claims in the north and enraged by the Scottish alliance with the Beaumonts, occupied the castle at Lincoln. Stephen, always careful of the royal boroughs and castles, acted with haste. Compelled at first to tolerate, even reward, the invaders of Lincoln, he returned without warning—and, some held, dishonourably—to the city, almost captured Ranulf de Gernons, and set siege to the castle in which the countess of Chester, Robert of Gloucester's daughter, held out. Within a month Ranulf had raised a relieving force in Wales and its borders and, together with his father-in-law, marched back to Lincoln. On 2 February 1141 Stephen gave battle against the odds and against advice. Most of his friends fled when the day went against them; but Stephen fought dismounted, 'like a lion', until he was overwhelmed and taken prisoner to Gloucester and then to Bristol. Proof of his bravery was bought at a price.

This accidental result of a private quarrel between the king and
the earl of Chester filled the Angevin party with fresh hope. But
nothing proves more surely the general unpopularity of the Angevin
cause than the very limited advantage which Matilda and Geoffrey
were able to extract from this most lucky chance. So many had
snatched the crown in the last century that the procedure was well
known: the citizens of Winchester and London must open their
gates and the church must be persuaded to perform the coronation
ceremony. On 2 March Matilda met the legate at Wherwell, near
Winchester. She promised him that she would take his advice on all
the major matters of the kingdom, especially on ecclesiastical
appointments (a promise which corresponds to the assurance which
a new king normally made to the primate); and the legate recognized her as his lord (*domina*) and swore allegiance for as long as she
kept her oath. The castellan of Winchester surrendered to Matilda
the castle and treasury, almost empty except for the crown; and
Matilda moved on to Wilton to negotiate with the archbishop of
Canterbury. Theobald, cool in his support for Stephen, yet bound
by the papal recognition and unwilling cynically to abandon his
fallen master, said that he must receive Stephen's permission before
he did Matilda homage. From the captive king came only the advice
that men should bow to necessity. Theobald acted discreetly, and
allowed the legate to burn his fingers.

In April Matilda ventured as far east as Oxford, where the
castellan, Robert d'Oilli, recognized her; and on 7 April Henry of
Blois held a legatine council at Winchester. After a secret session
the legate addressed the open assembly. God had passed judgment
on his brother, he said. And as the kingdom could not be left
leaderless, and since it was the prerogative of the church to elect
and consecrate kings, they chose Matilda, King Henry's daughter,
as ruler (*domina*) of England and Normandy. The response of the
audience was lukewarm; and the legate hastened to add that he had
invited the Londoners to attend and that he expected them shortly.
But when the representatives of the metropolis arrived they merely
asked that the king should be released. The council of Winchester
had not been a great success.

The legate's claim that it was the right of the church to elect a
king was as opportunist as the claim of the Londoners in 1135.
The series of *coups d'état* since 1066 had prevented a sound procedure
from developing, and the necessity that the postulant should be

anointed and crowned exaggerated the role of the church. In 1141 the Angevin party was merely a junta, devoid of popular support, and ready to exploit any path which might lead to the throne. Only five bishops were in regular attendance on Matilda—Winchester, Lincoln, Ely, St. David's, and Hereford—and the magnates were confined to relatives—her uncle, David of Scots, her half-brothers, Robert of Gloucester, Reginald of Cornwall, and Robert fitzEdith, and her distant cousin, Brian fitzCount—and west-country magnates, of whom Miles of Gloucester was the most important, together with such other barons as were willing to follow the highest bidder, like Hugh Bigod and Geoffrey de Mandeville. Indeed, the capture of the king hardly increased the real strength of the Angevins in England. Even on the morrow of defeat three kinsmen, Waleran count of Meulan, his half-brother William of Warenne earl of Surrey, and Simon of St. Liz earl of Northampton, Robert of Beaumont's son-in-law, swore that they would support the captive king and his heirs; London did no more than waver; and public sympathy went out to the prisoner.

The only man who could put pressure on London was Geoffrey de Mandeville, hereditary constable of the Tower. In 1140 Stephen had made him earl of Essex, and in 1141 Matilda was prepared to pay his price. By midsummer the Londoners had been cowed and the empress was able to enter the city in the hope of being crowned. But already her conduct was disgusting the waverers and her new supporters. Arrogance sharpened by humiliation and intransigence heightened by failure were fatal to her cause. The legate was offended when she would not confirm his nephew, Eustace, in at least Mortain and Boulogne during Stephen's captivity; the queen's plea for her husband's release commanded much public support; and when Matilda tried to tallage London she was asked to follow not the laws of her father but those of St. Edward. The queen and Earl Simon of St. Liz advanced on Southwark with forces they had raised in Boulogne and Kent; and on midsummer day the citizens drove the Angevins out. Matilda fled to Oxford and then to Gloucester. Her supporters dispersed. The legate met the queen at Guildford and changed sides. The captive king was still the only asset of the opposition.

Even this advantage was soon lost. The legate returned to Winchester and tried to regain the royal castle. He was then attacked by the empress from Oxford, and, while he fought off the Angevins from his own stronghold in the town, a relieving army under the queen, reinforced by the Londoners and many adventurous young men, and strong enough to reject with contempt the services of the earl of Chester, invested the city. In this concentric operation every advantage lay with the outer army which sat across the Angevins' communications with the West and which could afford to wait indefinitely now that it had all the enemy leaders in the net. According to the tradition in the Marshal family Robert of Gloucester decided on 14 September to dispatch the empress with a small select escort to John fitzGilbert the Marshal's castle at Ludgershall before the main body broke out. The empress got through to Devizes with Brian fitzCount and was carried exhausted in a litter to Gloucester; but John the Marshal, who covered her passage of the Test against the pursuit of William of Ypres, had to take refuge with his men in the abbey church at Wherwell, and lost an eye when the Flemish captain set fire to the buildings and molten lead from the roof dripped on to the defenders. The main sortie from Winchester disintegrated into a rout; Miles of Gloucester broke clear; Archbishop Theobald was despoiled and roughly handled; King David was taken, bribed his captors, and hastened back to Scotland; and Earl Robert of Gloucester was captured at Stockbridge on the Test. Matilda's miraculous luck still held, but her party had fallen in pieces, and the only memorials of her brief rule in England were the honours she bestowed on her supporters. Western earldoms were given to her half-brother Reginald (Cornwall), and to Baldwin of Reviers (Devon), William de Mohun (Somerset), and Miles of Gloucester (Hereford). Even Matilda was not so stupid as to give counties held by Stephen's earls; and, like her rival, she did not continue the practice. Aubrey de Vere was created earl of Oxford in 1142; and then, some seven years later, Patrick, constable of Salisbury, obtained the earldom of Wiltshire. The pensioner earls of Stephen's reign are a myth.

With Stephen held at Bristol and Earl Robert at Rochester the opportunity for an honourable and lasting settlement had arrived. The confidence of Stephen's party, however, is shown by its failure to offer any terms which the other side could honourably accept, such as, for example, a reversion of the crown on Stephen's death to Matilda's heir. Negotiations were limited to finding the conditions on which Robert of Gloucester would recognize Stephen; and, when Robert turned down even the offer of a regency, the intermediaries followed the counsel of despair and agreed to a simple exchange of the leaders and acceptance by both sides of the territorial position. On 1 November 1141, Stephen was freed and then Robert was released in turn. Robert's obstinacy had saved the Angevin cause; and the price was eight more years of civil war.

On 7 December the legate assembled a church council at Westminster. With shameless plausibility he brought the church back to its original position. He had been forced to recognize Matilda, he said; she had not fulfilled her pledges, and God had withdrawn his aid. Now he asked the clergy to support the king again. At Christmas Stephen and Queen Matilda were recrowned at Canterbury by Archbishop Theobald. The king had still to meet and overcome the full strength of his adversaries in England, and he could not prevent the loss of Normandy; but he had awakened as one out of sleep.

Stephen's capture had lost him Normandy. There the anarchy had been worse, and by 1141 the feeling was gaining ground among all classes that even the rule of Geoffrey of Anjou would be the lesser evil. Even so, it is significant that when Geoffrey on hearing of his wife's success in England ordered the leading barons to surrender their castles they gathered at Mortagne in March 1141 and made a desperate appeal to Theobald of Blois to take over the duchy. On his refusal the barons reluctantly prepared to submit to Geoffrey. In 1141 central Normandy surrendered, and, in the general despair, Waleran, count of Meulan, made his terms with the Angevin. Waleran, who had been betrothed to an infant daughter of Stephen, now married a sister of the count of Évreux and left his English interests under the care of his brother, Leicester. The problem of loyalty had become too great even for a baron whose main holding was in the French Vexin. During 1142 and 1143 Geoffrey secured all Normandy west and south of the Seine; and on 14 January 1144 he crossed the Seine and entered Rouen. The conquest was almost over. Geoffrey's systematic campaigns of 1141–5 are in marked contrast to his raids of 1135–8; but it may well be that the change in the political situation rather than an improved strategic plan was responsible. In the first phase every hand was against the hated invader; in the second, the population was resigned to submit.

In England there was peace until Whitsun 1142. Both parties

were reorganizing. Territorially, the Angevins were stronger than
before. They held Somerset, Gloucestershire, the modern Mon-
mouthshire, Herefordshire, and most of Worcestershire, and were
now firmly entrenched in the Thames valley. King David was consolidating his hold on the extreme North. David's new ambition was
to add the patrimony of St. Cuthbert to Northumberland and
Carlisle, and in furtherance of this scheme he was intruding his
chancellor, William Cumin, a nephew of the late bishop, into the
see of Durham. The Empress Matilda had been about to invest
William when she had been expelled from London, and all hope
of lawful aggrandizement disappeared when the legate rejoined his
brother's party. The monks of the Durham chapter, supported by
Ralf, archdeacon of Northumberland, a nephew of Ranulf Flambard,
remained loyal, and managed to elect William of Ste.-Barbe, dean
of York. The loyalists were in dire straits; but the Scottish king had
not yet securely pushed his frontier to the Tees.

Stephen's first action after his coronation was to visit the north.
In the spring of 1142 he conciliated the earl of Chester and William
of Roumare and passed through their territory to York, where he
rallied his friends and raised troops for an attack on Oxford. But
he fell ill at the end of April, and nothing could be done. On the
Angevin side a desperate appeal had been sent to Geoffrey to come
and aid his wife; and at the end of June the earl of Gloucester sailed
reluctantly and secretly from Wareham to convince his brother-in-
law of the need of his presence. Geoffrey, however, was faced with
a revolt in Anjou and committed to the conquest of Normandy and
would not further disperse his effort. He kept Robert with him; and
only in October or November allowed him to return with Henry
fitzEmpress, his son and heir, a boy nine-and-a-half years old.
Geoffrey's policy was shrewd; but it was aided by good fortune.
When Stephen recovered and learned that the earl was away he
pushed through the gap between Gloucester and Oxford and took
many places including Wareham, the Angevin port. Then, in
September, having isolated Oxford, he turned against that great
water fortress where Matilda tarried in false security. This time
Stephen was determined to take his rival; and his brilliant tactical
campaign, distinguished by personal bravery, was frustrated only
when, just before Christmas, Matilda was lowered at night on a rope
from the castle and escaped in the snow over the frozen waters to
Wallingford. Oxford castle surrendered; but Robert of Gloucester

had recaptured Wareham and landed with his nephew and their troops. The king's counter-attack failed ignominiously at Wilton on 1 July 1143. Once more the Angevin cause had been saved.

The third crisis of Stephen's reign, like the others, was precipitated by his determined effort to restore the royal authority. In the autumn of 1143, while the royal court was at St. Albans, he arrested Geoffrey de Mandeville and released him only when he had surrendered his castles. The king had a personal grievance, long dissembled, against the earl of Essex and he feared the concentration of power that that man had built round London through blackmailing each side in turn. His possession of the earldom of Essex, the shrievalties and justiciarships of London and Middlesex, Essex, and Hertfordshire, and the constabulary of the Tower of London threatened the king's lines of communication. Geoffrey, despoiled, broke into furious revolt. He seized Ely in the absence of the bishop, and with the connivance of Hugh Bigod, earl of East Anglia, established a reign of terror in the Fenlands. Stephen could do no more than contain him, for Ranulf of Chester likewise took the opportunity to rebel, and attacked the king's Yorkshire friends. In 1144 the anarchy reached its peak. The sons and vassals of the earl of Gloucester were ravaging from the eastern borders of Gloucestershire and Wiltshire; and Durham was in the hands of William Cumin. Early in 1144 Stephen failed to take Lincoln, and about this time his honour of Lancaster is found divided between the earl of Chester and the king of Scots. But Stephen held on grimly. In May 1144 William Cumin had to abandon Durham. In August Geoffrey de Mandeville was fatally wounded when attacking a royal post, and before the end of the year his son, Ernulf, had been captured and banished. On Christmas eve Miles of Gloucester, earl of Hereford, was killed while hunting in the Forest of Dean. In the summer of 1145 the king took Faringdon in Berkshire, which Robert of Gloucester had fortified as a base against Oxford, and at the end of the year one of Robert's sons, Philip Gai, made his peace with Stephen and turned his arms against his father. Ranulf earl of Chester followed his example, only to be arrested in the summer of 1146 by the king and deprived of the royal castles he had obtained, including Lincoln and Coventry. Ranulf, like Geoffrey de Mandeville three years before, revolted when released. But he could not recapture Lincoln and Coventry, and his midland scheme had been foiled. Even so, his position was safe. The Beaumont party had broken up. Hugh the Poor had relapsed into obscurity; Waleran of Meulan had become an Angevin supporter; and Robert of Leicester fell back into neutrality. Younger men were now taking the field; and the seniors concentrated on safeguarding their fiefs and honours.

The king always forgave rebellion more easily than the church absolved men from sacrilege; and after 1146, when the second Crusade was preached, men stained with crime in the civil war could wash away their sins by fighting for Christ on alien soil. An Anglo-Norman contingent, which included Arnulf bishop of Lisieux and Waleran count of Meulan, went in 1147 with Louis VII of France to Jerusalem, and a trickle of repentant soldiers followed after. The hardest blow, however, was struck for other motives and by another class of adventurer. On 23 May 1147, perhaps inspired by the naval expedition of 1097, a mixed force of English, Normans, Flemings, and Germans sailed from Dartmouth in 164 ships and on 25 October captured Lisbon from the infidel. An Englishman, Gilbert of Hastings, was then elected the first bishop of Lisbon since 688. He was back in England in 1150 preaching the Crusade against the Moslems of Seville. English interest in the Iberian peninsula was never thereafter to fail.

By 1147 the Angevin leaders in England were becoming old and disillusioned; and their spirits lifted for no more than an instant when the Empress's son, Henry, a boy of almost fourteen, who had left England in 1144, returned in the first months of the year with resources inadequate even for a desperate venture; and in the end it was the king himself who generously and, perhaps, not unwisely sent the boy money so that he could pay off his knights and return home with honour unstained. Five months later (31 October) Robert earl of Gloucester died. He had fought unceasingly, if vainly, for his half-sister, and with him was extinguished her cause. The Empress left England in 1148 never to return, even when her son was king. In April 1149, Henry fitzEmpress landed again in England to make a desperate effort to rally his friends while the earl of Chester still nursed his grievance. All depended on harmonizing Chester with his old rival, King David of Scots. On 22 May David knighted Henry at Carlisle, and Henry promised him a boundary on the Tyne should ever he become king. Ranulf de Gernons joined them, was ceded the whole honour of Lancaster in return for his renunciation of Carlisle, and agreed to marry his son to a daughter of Henry of Scots. Lancaster was chosen as the spring-board for an offensive against Stephen, who established his head-quarters at York. But the rebels, dismayed by Stephen's strength, refused battle and were chased away. Henry slipped past Eustace, who had crossed from London, and left Bristol for the Continent at the end of the year. His father gave him the duchy of Normandy.

The civil war was over. Normandy had been lost; only a part of the kingdom was ever under Stephen's control—even Wallingford on the Thames held out until the end of the reign; but since 1143 the barons had begun to give up their temporary castles; and once the initiative had clearly passed to the king his rule was relatively peaceful. It is hard to assess usefully the extent of the disorder and devastation which the country had suffered. Acts of violence and petty disturbances were common even under strong kings. Baronial revolts had occurred in all reigns since the Conquest. And the peaceful progresses of a king like William Rufus were not unlike the military expeditions of others. Moreover, some of the main theatres of war in Stephen's reign were in the traditional areas of lawlessness. Even so, it cannot be doubted that there had been an aggravation of the congenital malady of medieval society. The campaigns waged by both sides with mercenary soldiers, the private feuds, the banditry, the burnings of towns, the fortifications which all contestants had made and which neither ruler managed entirely to control, and the serious and often prolonged fighting in such usually peaceful districts as Wiltshire, Berkshire, the Thames Valley, and East Anglia had greatly disturbed the life of the country, temporarily reduced its wealth, loosened its political bonds, and caused local famines and pestilence.

Yet to picture a scene of unrelieved misery and anarchy would be false. Some parts of the country, such as Kent and Sussex, were hardly ever disturbed. The king of Scots and the earl of Gloucester ruled well in the territories under their control, although Welsh resurgence hampered the western marcher powers and ruined many English settlers. In the loyal areas the king's government continued in form as before: the coinage was good; the exchequer system never collapsed; writs went out from the chancery; sheriffs were more or less obedient to the king's commands; justices were appointed to hear cases. The skeleton of an organized kingdom endured. And society took its own measures for its protection. The feudal bond became of real value again. Men looked to the local magnate for security, and groupings and loyalties shrank to the fief. Barons made treaties one with another. Shortly after 1141 John the Marshal came to terms with his local enemy Patrick constable of Salisbury. John divorced his wife and married Patrick's sister. Patrick transferred his allegiance to the Empress—an act which brought him an earldom. And the two men became good neighbours. Between 1148 and 1153 the old rivals Ranulf de Gernons earl of Chester and Robert de Beaumont earl of Leicester made peace in an elaborate compact which ignored the king by name; and about 1150 Robert married his daughter Hawise to William fitzRobert earl of Gloucester, the son of his old enemy.

The texture of the kingdom was becoming looser. Even the territorial boundary between the English and Scottish kingdoms was being blurred again. But so securely had the Normans stamped the pattern of royal administration on the country that there is a provisional air about many of the expedients of Stephen's reign. Old men remembered the old times, which began to seem the good old times. Warfare has its pleasures; but they are extravagances that even a wealthy kingdom cannot indefinitely afford. By 1148 the barons had dissipated their resources; and, even if many were little disposed to answer obediently to the king, all were anxious to restock their ravaged demesnes and restore their devastated estates. After 1154, when they accepted a new master, the recovery of the kingdom was quick.

VII

Stephen's control of the church was as lax as his control of the baronage. His sporadic blows, such as the disgracing of Roger of Salisbury, no more cowed the episcopate than did his periodic arrests of leading barons curb the aristocracy. They were counted with the general insecurity of the country, the disregard of the coronation promises, the invasions of church lands, and the pillaging and fortification of churches as the sins of a frivolous tyrant. The Norman church had been as loyal as the baronage until the disaster of 1141. The English followed the papal lead and answered as best it could to the divided government of Henry of Winchester and Theobald of Canterbury. From 1142 until 1150 it was passive and without much influence on events.

The papacy never formally renounced its early recognition of Stephen as king. The complaint of the Angevins that Stephen was a perjured usurper was argued juridically before the Lateran Council of 1139; but, after hearing the pleadings, Innocent II adjourned the case *sine die* and continued to give Stephen and Henry of Winchester his steady support. Henry's plan to make Winchester a third ecclesiastical province and his see the metropolitan of the West came, however, to nothing, and by 1151, when negotiations were reopened, it had become an idle dream. Indeed, Innocent II's successors, especially Celestine II (1143–4) and Eugenius III (1145–53), favoured Count Geoffrey against Stephen and Archbishop Theobald against Henry, and Innocent's caution in avoiding a definitive sentence on the rival claims to the throne in 1139 allowed his successors to thwart the crowning of Stephen's son and to recognize without embarrassment Geoffrey Plantagenet as duke of Normandy and Henry fitzEmpress as the rightful king of England. Henry of Winchester's legateship lapsed with the death of Innocent II and was never restored to him. Eugenius III appointed Theobald his legate before 1150, and Henry finally lost his political importance. Stephen was never subservient to hostile popes and he always tried to maintain the rights of the crown; but his political weakness made real success impossible.

The king's impotence in ecclesiastical matters is shown by his failure to appoint to bishoprics after 1139. First his brother, the legate, obtained control, and then, after 1143, when the legation lapsed, an anarchic period, corresponding to the secular disorder, ensued until Archbishop Theobald reaffirmed the influence of Canterbury. Freedom from royal control brought new dangers to the church. While the king had virtually appointed bishops in the royal court there had been few difficulties. Once the traditional form had been destroyed there were disputes over procedure and participants (as at Coventry in 1149), double elections (as at York in 1147), and internal conflicts (as when the metropolitan refused to confirm the Durham election of 1153). Uncertainty and strife caused many appeals to go to the pope, and for the first time the *curia* interfered often and successfully in English diocesan affairs. The York schism was typical of the new ecclesiastical anarchy. Archbishop Thurstin died on 5 February 1140. The king and legate nominated their nephew, Henry of Sully, abbot of Fécamp; but he was rejected by the pope because he would not surrender his abbey. Stephen then gave the arch-see to another nephew, William fitz-Herbert, treasurer of York, only to face a host of objectors, including the Cistercian abbots, now powerful in Yorkshire and anxious to get a sympathetic archbishop; and, although the legate consecrated William on 26 September 1143 after the elect had purged himself of the charges, a Cistercian pope, Eugenius III, acting under pressure from St. Bernard, deposed him in 1147. A divided election then occurred, which the pope resolved by consecrating St. Bernard's favourite, Henry Murdac, abbot of Fountains, on 7 December 1147 and consoling the loser, Hilary, a papal clerk, with the see of Chichester. When Archbishop Henry died in 1153 William fitzHerbert was elected again, and Pope Anastasius IV reinstated him. In the next year he died, poisoned it was said; and in 1226 he was canonized. But the mischief had been done: the feud had split the northern province; the one English suffragan see, Durham, had almost escaped from subjection; and the authority of the York metropolitan had been permanently maimed. The church had wrestled free from royal control; but its own discipline was insufficiently developed as yet to replace it satisfactorily.

The decisive influence of the Cistercian order on the York appointment reveals the position that the new monasticism was acquiring in England during this period of ecclesiastical freedom. In Stephen's reign Cistercian foundations proliferated and the number of Augustinian canonries increased apace. New orders were introduced. In 1143 the first house of Premonstratensian canons was established at Newhouse (Lincs.); the Knights Templars gained a footing; and the rule of Gilbert of Sempringham, the one purely English order, began to spread from Lincolnshire into Yorkshire. Benedictine expansion, however, had ceased except in one significant direction. A popular interest in nunneries had arisen, and some fifteen Benedictine and a few Cluniac and Cistercian houses for women were founded in Stephen's reign. St. Gilbert's order, too, was devoted to the religious life of women. And at no other time in the Middle Ages, it seems, had women better educational facilities or more opportunity to embrace a corporate devotional life. Nuns, however, were not as a rule politically conscious and abbots rarely had much political weight in the Middle Ages. With a new order still militant, and fortunate in counting among its members a powerful spiritual leader and a pope, conditions at this time were exceptional.

King Stephen did not accept the intervention of hostile popes. At Easter 1147 Eugenius III and Geoffrey of Anjou conferred at

Paris. In December Stephen refused to allow Henry Murdac to return to England and be installed at York; and during the winter he prevented John Paparo, the papal legate to Ireland, from travelling through England because he would not swear that he intended no harm to the king. In 1148 Stephen forbade Archbishop Theobald to go to the council which the pope had summoned to Rheims, and when the primate defied him he banished him too. That Stephen dared exile his two archbishops and warn off a papal legate was due to his confidence after the death of Robert of Gloucester. By English custom he had ample justification for all three acts, and the pope, insecure in Italy, was, as the king's advisers foresaw, unable to take drastic measures. But once again Stephen's dynastic weakness hampered his policy. He was getting old. He needed the support of the church for the succession of his heir. So he had to allow the archbishops to return and then to patch up his quarrel with the pope.

The suddenness of the revolution in the English church led inevitably to uncertainty in form and procedure. But the incoherence was a passing phase, a sign of rapid growth and attempted readjustment. A new interest in canon law started with Theobald of Bec's appointment to Canterbury. He built up a household of lawyers and scholars, and among them, to name only the most famous, were Roger of Pont-l'Évêque, his archdeacon, archbishop of York in 1154; Thomas of London (Becket), Roger's successor as archdeacon, archbishop of Canterbury in 1162 and martyred in 1170; John of Belmeis, bishop of Poitiers in 1163 and archbishop of Lyons in 1182; John of Salisbury, his chancellor, bishop of Chartres in 1176, a humanist and philosopher; and Master Vacarius, Roman lawyer and theologian. Thomas Becket studied law at Bologna, and Gratian's *Decretum*, which became the standard textbook of the old canon law, was to be found in England soon after its publication about 1140. The new autonomy brought increased business to the ecclesiastical courts, and they developed quickly. Archidiaconal courts were established, and the hierarchy of appeals to the papal audience with frequent remittance of the case to local delegate judges became familiar. Law was becoming a key to the door of preferment. Archdeacons, skilled in the law, were beginning to get bishoprics. And with the study of canon law went also interest in Roman law, that pattern of a civilized jurisprudence which fascinated those bred to custom and unreason. The Lombard Vacarius,

whom Theobald brought from Italy between 1139 and 1154 and
who became the juridical oracle in his court and later went with
Roger of Pont-l'Évêque to York, wrote about 1149 his *Liber
pauperum*, an abridgement of the Digest in nine books, known in
time as the *Pauperistae* from its use as a textbook of Roman law by
poor scholars at Oxford. King Stephen forbade Vacarius to teach
law in the schools. The system which contains the phrase 'Quod
principi placuit legis habet vigorem' never harmed a prince; and
Stephen in his ignorance shot down the wrong bird. But he was
right to be uneasy.

The intellectual life of Europe was fast gathering momentum.
The migration of scholars was standardizing European culture.
The University of Oxford was not born until the next reign; but
already Robert Pullen, Geoffrey of Monmouth, and, perhaps,
Vacarius had taught in that place where so many roads converged.
Paris was replacing Laon as the fashionable intellectual centre; and
just as there were foreign teachers in England so were there English
at Paris: the theologians Robert of Melun and Robert Pullen and
the grammarian Adam of the Little Bridge. Englishmen were also
finding places at the papal court. Robert Pullen was called to Rome
by Lucius II in 1144 and became papal chancellor until his death or
retirement in September 1146. John of Salisbury was a papal clerk
between 1147 and 1154, and Boso, the famous biographer of popes,
who died about 1178, became in turn clerk, chamberlain, and cardinal. Henry of Winchester's clerk, Hilary dean of Christ Church
in Hampshire, gained an important legal practice at the papal
court before his return to England in 1145 and his election to
Chichester through papal influence in 1147. Baldwin was appointed
by Eugenius III at Ferentino in 1150–1 instructor to Gratian, a
nephew of the late Pope Innocent II, and rose to be archbishop of
Canterbury. But the most spectacular career went to one who was
not famed as a scholar. Nicholas Breakspear, born at Abbot's
Langley in Hertfordshire, the son of a clerk in the king's chamber,
was educated at the Austin priory of Merton (Surrey), migrated to
the Austin abbey of St. Ruf near Avignon, where he was abbot by
1147, and about 1149 was made cardinal-bishop of Albano by Pope
Eugenius III. At Christmas 1154, as Adrian IV, he became the first
and last Englishman to wear the triple tiara. Almost simultaneously
the writing of the Anglo-Saxon chronicle was discontinued at Peterborough. English insularity had wellnigh disappeared.

VIII

King Stephen had been born not later than 1100, and when he entered the sixth decade of his life he became anxious to secure the succession to the throne of Eustace of Boulogne, his elder son. His natural disquietude nurtured an unprecedented plan: he would, like the Capetians, have his son crowned in his lifetime, and so both avoid an interregnum and remove the need for his heir to bargain with nobles and bishops, and he would obtain, if possible, papal sanction for the act, and so prolong that invaluable protection. But Stephen's negotiations with Pope Eugenius in 1151 for permission to have Eustace crowned led only to a papal prohibition to Theobald; and when, after the barons had accepted Eustace as Stephen's heir at the Easter court at London in 1152 and done him homage on 6 April, the king required Theobald to perform the ceremony the primate escaped to France in order to avoid the threats of his disappointed lord. Eustace and the implacable pope both died in the next year, and it was not by Stephen but by Henry fitzEmpress that the unlucky scheme was revived, and this time importunately driven to a disastrous end. Later kings left it alone.

While Stephen's fortune stagnated the Angevin power increased. Geoffrey Plantagenet assumed the title of duke of Normandy in the early summer of 1144, and in September 1149, when Louis VII was back from the Crusade, obtained his overlord's recognition of the conquest in return for the surrender of most of the Norman Vexin. Until 1149 Geoffrey divided his time between the duchy and the county. In Normandy he showed his political wisdom by restoring the traditions of the dukes. The sworn inquest was used extensively to recover ducal revenue and demesne; and the privilege of using this ducal machinery was sold to others who had suffered in the anarchy—a dissemination of the greatest importance, especially when Geoffrey's son introduced the practice into England. The exchequer and the chancery were restored to full working order, and the superior methods of the Norman chancery were imitated in Anjou. The duchy had little to learn from the county, and the only obvious Angevin influence is seen in the suppression of the office of chief justiciar and the transformation of the seneschal into the principal judicial officer. Geoffrey's apt improvisations prove him to have been an administrator of the highest class. Yet he failed to restore the church to its accustomed position; and his lack of success puts Stephen's difficulties into perspective. The church had taken advantage of the anarchy to strike off all the ducal fetters, and although Geoffrey acted violently against bishops and abbots elected without his consent (as at Lisieux in 1141, Séez in 1144, and Mont St.-Michel in 1149) the tide of clerical freedom bore him down. In Normandy the stakes were high, for owing to the attraction of French schools, the growth of papal centralization, the frequent presence of the popes in France, and the extinction of such local organs as the provincial council the isolation of the Norman church had almost completely disappeared. And when the Norman church considered itself as part of the French church the political autonomy of the duchy was deeply compromised.

At the end of 1149 Geoffrey resigned the duchy to his eldest son, Henry fitzEmpress. Henry was always an active man and between 1149 and 1153 his energy was amazing. In 1149 he had made his completely unsuccessful attempt to acquire the other part of his maternal inheritance. Until 1151 he was involved in a sporadic and tiresome war with his overlord, Louis VII, who returned from the Crusade with grievances against the Angevins and naturally allied with his brother-in-law, Eustace of Boulogne. In August 1151, however, Henry made his peace with Louis by doing homage for Normandy and surrendering the whole area between the Seine, the Epte, and the Andelle; and he began feverishly to prepare an attack on England. But first his father died. On 7 September 1151 Geoffrey's intemperate life closed in his thirty-ninth year. He was never a pleasant man; but the epitaph on the lovely enamel portrait which hung over his tomb at le Mans does him less than justice: 'By your sword, seigneur, the troop of brigands has been put to flight and, through the restoration of peace, repose given to the church.' He left all his fiefs to his eldest son, Henry, and counselled him to keep the various customs distinct. But, as Henry was forced to swear to observe the will, it is possible that there was a provision that he should surrender the paternal inheritance—Anjou and Maine —to his younger brother, Geoffrey, besides the three castles of his immediate bequest, if ever he obtained England. Then in March 1152 King Louis VII divorced his wife, Eleanor, duchess of Aquitaine, and in May Henry, still greedy at nineteen, married the heiress eleven years his senior, and so outwitted his brother, Geoffrey, and Theobald of Blois and Chartres who each had tried to seize her. Almost without pause Henry once again assembled an army against England. But even Louis VII was dismayed at this sequel to his foolish action, and while the lord of all the western fiefs of France stood at Barfleur at the end of June a coalition of his rivals—Louis VII, Theobald of Blois, Geoffrey Plantagenet, and Eustace of Boulogne—attacked him. By the end of August, Henry had smashed his enemies; and in January 1153 he at last invaded England.

When Henry landed and attacked Malmesbury, Stephen was besieging Wallingford. The king was eager for a decisive action; but all through that year accidents of weather and the reluctance of the barons frustrated his purpose and prevented an ordeal by battle. Most men felt that it was too late to begin all over again; and the desultory war of raids and sieges diverted contestants deep in negotiations and manœuvring for diplomatic advantage. Henry bought Ranulf de Gernons with promises so extravagant that they must surely have been made in bad faith: Stafford and most of Staffordshire, the castle and town of Nottingham, the Avranchin in Normandy, and a string of fiefs in England including that of William Peverel of the Peak—a fatal gift, for it was to poison administered by William that rumour attributed Ranulf's death on 16 December 1153 when at the height of his power. But it was not through defections, serious as they were, that the king was brought to terms. On 3 May 1152 had died Matilda, the wife to whom he owed so much; and on 10 August 1153 his son and heir Eustace, a fine young soldier, followed her to the grave. Broken at last by these calamities Stephen's sole interests became to keep the crown until his death and to assure for his last surviving son, William, the inheritance of all the family estates. On these terms peace could be made, and the church, ably led by Theobald, busied itself with the details. On 6 November a treaty was negotiated at Winchester and later proclaimed in London. Stephen was to be king for life; but he adopted Henry as his son and heir and confirmed to him the reversion of the kingdom in fee. The claim to the throne of Stephen's son, William, was barred; but he was to succeed to all the fiefs which his father had had before he became king and keep his own endowment and the great Warenne inheritance which he had obtained by marrying Isabel, heiress of William, third earl of Surrey. As a security measure, Stephen's son was henceforth to hold those fiefs directly from Henry. The king was to associate his adopted son with the government and act on his advice; and, to safeguard the treaty, the vassals of each party were to do homage to the rival leader, saving their fealty to Stephen. The church added its threats of anathema. This dynastic settlement was wise. There seems also to have been a no less sensible understanding that all castles built since the death of Henry I were to be overthrown, foreign soldiers, especially the Flemings, were to be expelled, and the old privileges of the kingdom and the rights of the crown were to be restored and recovered.

On 13 January 1154 at Oxford, on the boundary of the two zones, the homages were done. In Lent father and adopted son received Count Thierry of Flanders and Sybil his wife, Henry's aunt, at Dover, doubtless to confirm the settlement in so far as it concerned Boulogne. And at Easter Henry returned to the Continent. Stephen made a rapid circuit of his recovered kingdom, and appeared once more to have gained control. But his reign was almost at an end. On 25 October he died in Kent and was buried near his son Eustace and his wife Matilda in the Cluniac monastery they had founded at Faversham six years before. On 8 December Henry fitzEmpress landed on the Hampshire coast and inherited the kingdom without difficulty.

7

SOCIAL CHANGES IN ENGLAND

I

A NEW era seems to begin with the reign of Henry II. The recuperation and rapid growth of the royal institutions, the development of the kingdom as a coherent unit within a mighty assembly of fiefs and honours, the renaissance of historical writing and the beginning of systematic records, and the greater sophistication of society, which appear under the Angevins, all dazzle after the 'nineteen long winters' of Stephen's rule. But this turbulent reign should not be denied its share of the glory. The civil disorder had in part been due to, and certainly had greatly encouraged, a vigorous sectional and local growth, which, when here pruned and there forced, transformed the texture of medieval life.

The reigns of Henry I and Stephen are often seen merely as in contrast. But it is also possible to regard them as forming a whole—as a bridge between the old world and the new. Few leading characters overlap, and fewer have the same influence on either side. Moreover, most of the notables have the contradictory attributes of men conscious of change: Anselm, the monkish theologian disturbed by new attitudes of mind: the Cluniac Henry of Winchester, a prince-bishop of the old school, but a passionate defender of clerical freedom: Theobald, the last archbishop taken from le Bec, yet collecting round him students of the modern philosophy and jurisprudence: Robert of Gloucester, a conservative feudal magnate but also a patron of the arts. For the church it was an age of intellectual and emotional disturbance, an age of strain. For the baronage it was the hey-day of chivalry. For the merchants it was a period of expansion, of new hopes, new ambitions. For the English people as a whole it was a time when the tensions of the Conquest period were abating and when, out of the confusion caused by the revolution in land tenure, new social classes were forming.

The intellectual and religious revival of the early twelfth century transformed European civilization. Movements which had remained local and spasmodic in the eleventh century suddenly gained momentum and were gathered into a general and turbulent advance. A rush of exciting new ideas shook all scholars, and spilled over from the professionally learned class—the priests, monks, and clerks—to affect all men eventually. This upsurge of intellectual and emotional life forced and broke many barriers which had constrained the church. The influence of individual kings on the history of the church in this period has, therefore, been exaggerated. Both Henry I and Stephen favoured it, and each in moments of weakness admitted some of its legal claims. But the new culture was as a tide that individuals could only momentarily help or thwart. Henry and Stephen granted 'freedom' by charter, and then saved what royal powers they could. Anselm lived at Lyons and brought back the decrees of papal councils. Count Stephen introduced Saviniac monks, Walter Espec monks from Cîteaux. Archbishop Theobald sent Thomas Becket to Bologna and enticed Vacarius away from there. These men each played a part. But the world was changing, and with it England.

A striking feature of the old world is that many different, and even hostile, views of the universe had been in circulation, yet remained, as it were, inert, because the political conditions only gave practical outlet to one: the belief in the theocratic authority of kings. It was the king, with the aid of his bishops, who had ruled the church, who had led the people to salvation, and who had reformed ecclesiastical institutions. The Emperor Henry III (1039–56), completely pious and entirely autocratic, is the classic example of the eleventh-century theocratic king; and William I and Henry I of England were of the same type. But by the twelfth century the political situation had changed, and other conceptions of the hierarchical construction of the world could acquire practical significance.

The most astonishing revolution was that which had occurred in the secular church, and which had led to the investiture disputes. The papal *curia* suddenly adopted, and then ruthlessly applied, ideas which, although based on fundamental catholic belief, had been obscured by other modes of thought. The sacramental or priestly conception of world order stressed the importance of clerical office and assessed value according to dignity of function. In such a view the laity had a passive and lowly status, monks, as monks, a place of little importance, and the king a doubtful role depending on how much significance was given to the coronation ceremonies. This view of the universe, when taken up by the papacy, which Henry III had reformed, and translated into a policy, threatened to smash the old order and the familiar way of life. It stimulated thought and controversy, and set the canon lawyers on new searches through the disorderly mass of law which they had inherited in order to produce collections both more coherent and more 'correctly' aligned. The sacramental conception could hardly be reconciled in theory with the theocratic, for it was difficult to find a suitable place for a king in a hierarchy arranged according to the dignity of the clerical office. And by the twelfth century the pope was advancing towards monarchical powers in the church, kings were being stripped of their priestly character, the laity were being forced out of active participation in ecclesiastical affairs, and the clerical hierarchy had undertaken a mission to reform the world, a mission which was to lead to the excommunication and even the deposition of kings, to the pope's feudal lordship over secular kingdoms, and to the political authority which made of Pope Innocent III the real emperor of Christendom.

Some of the kings, however, did not stand quietly by. A movement to canonize King Edward was begun after Henry I had married Edward's great-grand-niece, and was brought to fulfilment when her grandson, Henry II, became king. To have saints in the royal family helped to reinforce the religious veneration for kingship which the attitude of the Gregorian reformers was reducing. Moreover, Edward the Confessor was credited with thaumaturgical powers. The Capetian dynasty in France had, since Robert II, acquired the virtue of being able to cure scrofula (tubercular infection of the lymphatic glands—the 'King's Evil'); and it seems that, in imitation, a similar ability was attributed to Henry I of England. This new manifestation of the sacred character of English kingship was contemporary with the tracts published by the 'Norman Anonymous'. It was part of a counter-offensive by the conservatives against the Gregorian programme. Despite the novelty of the claim, it obtained acceptance. Peter of Blois, defending his service

under Henry II, wrote, 'I think it is a holy thing [for a clerk] to
serve the lord king, for he is a saint and the Christ of the Lord: it is
not in vain that he has received the sacrament of royal unction, for
the efficacy of that rite, should anyone not know it or bring it in
doubt, is amply proved by the disappearance of the plague which
attacks the groin and the cure of scrofulas.' Although the church
hastened to deny that the unction of a king was a sacrament, and in
the thirteenth century gave it no place among the seven sacraments
which were then officially recognized, the disavowal had little effect
on popular belief. People continued to think that in virtue of the
coronation ceremonies the king became something more than a
layman, even though his exact position in the clerical order was hard
to define. This feeling preserved the awe in which kingship had
been held, and, as the effective power of kings increased, allowed
new myths to form round it. The attack of the reformers on the
contemporary idea of kingship was sharp, and not without effect;
but it failed as a whole because it lacked popular support. The failure can be compared instructively with the victory in the battle
against clerical marriage. In this matter the reformers were aided by
superstition, for the people believed in the magical virtues of
virginity and continence, and were inclined to the heretical idea
that the conduct of the minister could affect the sacraments. At a time
when education was designed to promote a single cause, the gulf
between the thesis developed by the intelligent servants of the church
and the conservative beliefs of the illiterate people became dangerously wide.

Nevertheless, in theory at least, the sacramental view of the world
triumphed over the theocratic; and it also dominated a rival and
equally venerable conception which found its true home in the
monasteries. According to the ascetic view of the world value was
assessed according to individual merit, according to holiness and
closeness to God. It was not necessarily in opposition to the theocratic, for kings could be good, and a church preoccupied with
individual holiness needed a king to govern and protect it. It could
also, in practice, subsist beneath the sacramental theory, for it was
pietistic and led to non-resistance. Acceptance of this ancient
attitude had kept reformed monasteries, such as Cluny, almost
neutral during the investiture dispute. Indeed, only when a great
prophet arose, whose call to righteousness trumpeted beyond the
cloisters, could the ascetics shake the clerical hierarchy and the

temporal powers. Such a man was St. Bernard, a product of Cîteaux; and for a time the world was edified to see a simple abbot of Clairvaux ruling princes and popes and denouncing the worldliness of the papal *curia*. But the situation was unusual and the effect of small duration.

All the same the influence of monasticism on the individual man and woman was immense. In the reigns of Henry I and Stephen the enthusiasm for monasticism, chiefly for the reformed Benedictine orders, was in its flood. In the eleventh century monasteries had been founded by the nobility as necessary aids to the salvation of their families. The deed in itself was meritorious, and the prayers for the living and the dead, the just and the unjust, made the endowment of lasting value. The old Benedictine houses were, therefore, in a sense private institutions; and a monastery, like a castle, was a sign and an adornment of baronial rank. The first generation of Normans, however, had never been really at home in England, and so had rather enriched their ancestral monasteries than built new ones on their acquired estates. But by the twelfth century the foreign barons were settling down; and when they felt the need to found monasteries on their insular fiefs the new orders were available to satisfy their desires.

The preambles to the foundation charters still expressed the traditional hopes. In 1127 Stephen granted land to Savigny in the extravagant, almost untranslatable, literary style of an older age:

> In the name of the Father and of the Son and of the Holy Ghost, and in honour of St. Mary the mother of our Lord Jesus Christ. Amen. I, Stephen, count of Boulogne and Mortain, seeking in God to provide for the salvation of my soul and for that of my wife, the countess Matilda, and for the soul of my lord and uncle, Henry king of the English and duke of the Normans, and for the souls of all the faithful, both the living and those who have paid the debt of death, in the year from the birth of our Lord 1127, the 5th indiction the 17th epact, seeing each day that the periods of time are rushing to their destruction, that all the pomps of this collapsing age and the flowers and roses of blooming kings and the garlands and palms of emperors, dukes, and all rich men are withering away, and that all separate things are suddenly reduced to one and all things hasten with swift flight to death . . .

In 1142 at Devizes the empress issued a charter written in chancery style to the Cistercian abbey of Bordesley in Worcestershire:

> Matilda, empress, daughter of King Henry and lord (*domina*) of the English, to the archbishops, bishops, abbots, earls, barons, justiciars,

sheriffs, and all the faithful of England, both present and future, greeting. Know that I, for the love of God and for the soul of King Henry my father and of Queen Matilda my mother and of my parents and ancestors, and for the salvation of Geoffrey count of Anjou my lord, and of me, and of Henry my heir, and of my other children, and for the peace and stability of the kingdom of England . . .

The style alters; the sentiment shows some change; but the basic purpose remains.

Each order—Augustinian, Premonstratensian, Gilbertine, Saviniac, Cistercian, and those of Fontevrault, Grammont, and the Temple—made a contribution to English religious and social life. But the entry of the Cistercians had the widest repercussions. Cistercian monasticism is difficult to describe, for it is characteristic of a transitional period, and contained within itself many contradictions. The old monasticism had reached its highest point in Cluny. The intimate ties of the Cluniac houses with the feudal world of the day were revealed by their princely abbots of noble stock, their elaborate liturgy which allowed the maximum effort of intercession, their splendour of building and decoration in the most sumptuous style of the age, and their production of manuscripts and histories to suit the cultivated aristocracy, whether ecclesiastical or lay. King Henry I had paid for the rebuilding of Cluny's church, and in England had founded the Benedictine abbey of Reading; and all the greater English Benedictine communities were of that world, cultured and good mannered. In origin the Cistercian order was in reaction against this feudal monasticism—against the dullness of those who lived either richly under lay protection or ignorantly in squalor.

From the beginning Cîteaux fought on two fronts. The Englishman, Stephen Harding, who composed the rule and was in some ways the real founder of the order, insisted on simplicity, sobriety, and poverty, but also took fine manuscripts to his monastery. And when Bernard, abbot of Clairvaux, became the leading Cistercian and the most influential moral leader in Europe, the number of targets increased. Bernard, who once described himself as the chimera of the century, had within himself many of the contradictions of this revolutionary period. He attacked violently the attitude of Cluny; yet, a Burgundian noble by birth, he became a new type of prince of the church. He condemned the old civilization in a literary style which was the very flower of that culture; and his literary work itself and his preaching do not fit easily into the Cistercian interpretation of the three marks of monastic life: holy contemplation, sincere prayer, and honest toil. His religion, his whole attitude, was emotional; and he denounced those purely intellectual streams in contemporary life—the 'rationalism' of Abailard, with its consequence the revolutionary schemes of Arnold of Brescia, and the scholarship of the canon lawyers, with its consequence the new sort of worldliness in ecclesiastical courts. Against Cluny he stood as a revolutionary, a spiritual humanist with a new conception of God and of the mystical union of the soul with a loving deity. Against Abailard he stood as a conservative, a defender of the old faith against a false prophet.

The righteousness of the Cistercians disturbed all but the most complacent. The white monks, clothed in undyed wool, spun and woven from the pure fleece of the sheep—'dressed as the angels might be', according to the English monk, Walter Daniel—were so humble that they knew they were superior to other men. 'Welded together by such firm bonds of charity that their society is as "terrible as an army with banners" ', they professed the purest monastic rule and regarded all other monks as condemned to imperfect orders. The great landed families of northern England competed in making Cistercian foundations and in contributing converts to this harshest of rules. Benedictine monks and Austin canons migrated from their comfortable houses; and many sensitive men were tormented by the challenge. Maurice left Durham and became the second abbot of Rievaulx. Waltheof, or Waldef, the second son of Earl Simon of St. Liz I and Matilda (the daughter of Earl Waltheof and Judith the Conqueror's niece), a man who had been brought up at the court of his step-father, David king of Scots, left the Austin priory of Kirkham which he ruled to become a Cistercian monk and, in 1148, abbot of Melrose, a daughter of Rievaulx. For there was among the Cistercians a sweet and mystical faith which was both more gentle and more spiritual than the crude legalistic beliefs of the older churches. Their rule was the *Carta caritatis*, the rule of love. Mary, the mother of Jesus, was their patron, to whom all their churches were dedicated; and the Christ Himself appeared softened in the new vision. The too frequent self-righteousness and the occasional stridency were the only shadows on the brilliant illumination that irradiated the more receptive converts.

And some seem to have escaped those faults entirely. We have a biography of Aethelred, or Ailred, abbot of Rievaulx from 1147 until his death twenty years later, written by his friend and disciple Walter Daniel. Ailred, the son of the last of the line of hereditary priests of Hexham, became steward of King David's court and a friend of Waldef. About the year 1134, on a business trip to York, he turned aside to visit Rievaulx, and found it impossible to depart. Ailred came through the harsh discipline with his personality intact but purified as though by fire. In humility he found the way to a more perfect self-expression; and even at the end, when through sickness and old age some weaknesses in his character had begun to show again, he still seems a much better man than he could ever have been had he stayed in the world.

Yet for some, the discipline was more than the spirit could bear. One monk complained to Ailred,

> Lord, my inconstancy is not equal to the burden of the Order. Everything here and in my nature are opposed to each other. I cannot endure the daily tasks. The sight of it all revolts me. I am tormented and crushed down by the length of the vigils, I often succumb to the manual labour. The food cleaves to my mouth, more bitter than worm-wood. The rough clothing cuts through my skin and flesh down to my very bones. More than this, my will is always hankering after other things, it longs for the delights of the world and sighs unceasingly for its loves and affections and pleasures. [Sir Maurice Powicke's translation.]

Ailred managed to keep that man until his premature death; but the struggle was severe. Another of Ailred's monks went mad and threw his abbot on to the fire. The true spirit of Cîteaux was only for the elect; and it is obvious that admission to the order was given sometimes too lightly.

St. Bernard and his followers dissolved the old materialistic view of the relationship of God and men in the solvent of love. Yet the founder and the prophet of this new order had not seen sufficiently clearly whither they were leading; and unexpected tendencies soon appeared. The original Cistercians tried to avoid all the temptations which had pressed on the old monasticism. They were to inhabit the wilderness and work with their hands; they must own land free from secular obligations; their churches should be simple, their ritual plain, their life austere. It was, indeed, cheap to endow these monks, for they accepted with gratitude the most worthless and inconvenient sites. Walter Espec settled William and his companions in the wooded valley of the Rie, not far from his castle at Helmsley, and a daughter house at Wardon in Bedfordshire, known as Sartis (*de assartis*—the clearing). The first monks did, indeed, labour, felling the trees, making a garden, building a rude church; and the pride of noble converts was broken by the menial work. But no endowment was refused. When Ailred was abbot of Revesby in Lincolnshire (1143–7), he accepted grants of land from knights in free-alms,

> since he had realized that in this unsettled time such gifts profited knights and monks alike, for in those days it was hard for any to lead the good life unless they were monks or members of some religious order, so disturbed and chaotic was the land, reduced almost to a desert by the malice, slaughters, and harryings of evil men. And so he desired that that land, for which almost all men were fighting to the death, should pass into the hands of the monks for their good; and he knew that to give to God what they owned helped the possessors of goods to their salvation, and that, if they did not give, they might well lose both life and goods without any payment in return.

Thus Ailred made Revesby 'rich and fruitful'. And such estates, through the industry, prudence, and thrift of the monks, became great capitalistic ventures—often sheep runs—which perverted the original character of the monks. Laymen had been barred from the properties; and hundreds of lay brethren (*conversi*—men who shared in some of the privileges of the monks) and ordinary servants had to be recruited. At Rievaulx in 1143 there were 300 persons subject to the abbot, and in 1167 more than twice as many. Of these little more than one-fifth were monks. In 1167 there were 140 monks, and the remainder were divided, probably, into 240 *conversi* and 260 servants. The abbeys became wealthy, and, since they were withdrawn from the world, they could not put their riches to practical works of charity.

The failure of the most radical of the twelfth-century attempts to reform Benedictine monasticism on traditional lines helps to explain why later expressions of the monastic ideal were usually so different in purpose. In the long view the Cistercians, despite the revolutionary ideas of Bernard, belong to the old order; and Bernard himself, like most revolutionaries, was more representative of the society he tried to reform than would appear at first sight. Although he humanized the spirit of religion his methods were reactionary. Vital monasticism was part of the dying world. It flourished when a gross and brutal society was rocked by periodic crises of revulsion and despair. Already, in Henry II's reign, wits at court found the ascetic ideal uncouth. Jests could be made about St. Bernard's miracles. The justiciar, Ranulf Glanville, when considering which order to favour, is said to have remarked that the Cluniacs were gluttonous and the Cistercians avaricious and fraudulent. And monastic influence, except on the chosen soul, was gradually to decline. The heaviest of Bernard's thunderbolts were cast at the hypocrite, the deceiver Abailard. And it was Abailard's spirit, incarnate in the schools, which was indeed the real enemy and which conquered in the end. Bernard had proclaimed the *schola Christi*. But to the ebullient classrooms of the secular schools the culture of the old-fashioned monasteries seemed musty, while the passionate mysticism of Bernard appeared morbid and hysterical.

The leaven of the secular schools worked powerfully in the new age. Abailard shared Bernard's spirituality and his hatred of the feudalized church and of the materialistic ethics of the day; but he combined with his refined attitude a rationalizing tendency, which appealed especially to the bourgeoisie—to the merchants and lawyers of the Italian cities and the restless urban clerks of northern France. Abailard's theological collection *Sic et non* (yes and no) and his influential *Introductio ad theologiam*, and Gratian's *Decretum*, a compilation of canon law in a similar form, were landmarks in the development of scholastic method. Abailard's work marked the successful application of reason to theology and philosophy, Gratian's to jurisprudence. In the second half of the twelfth century clerks who went to Paris, Northampton, or Oxford—to mention three schools popular with Anglo-Normans—could not fail to imbibe some ideas for which these rationalistic co-ordinators were responsible.

The whole movement under discussion, the surge of ideas and emotions, is sometimes called the twelfth-century renaissance. But the tag is unfortunate in its implications. There was no proper rebirth of classical culture; and such influence as it exerted was superficial. The art of Latin composition was improved; but hardly any of the twelfth-century writers have a true classical feeling. Roman authors were more carefully studied, Greek ideas were perceived through translations; but the ancient texts were used mostly as a quarry for an elegant quotation, an apt point, or an argument which could be used under contemporary conditions. In architecture, indeed, the trend was away from classical models.

And the 'Gothic' style, like Bernard's humanistic mysticism, Abailard's rationalism, and the logic of the lawyers, were fruits of a native European movement which can be traced in almost every particular to pioneers in the previous century. Two main lines of development went side by side. There was the regeneration of the ascetic ideal and its dissemination through the new monastic orders; and there was the novel drive in the church's ministry to the world, supported by the intellectual activities in the schools.

The diversity in aim and approach among twelfth-century intellectuals is very noticeable. And even the one jewel which all seem to prize—the freedom of the church—is found on careful examination to be a stone with many facets. For *libertas* meant no more than proper position, rightful status, appropriate privileges; and as thinking men were much concerned with the proper place which each individual, each rank, each class, should have in the scheme of the universe they created, there was much talk of liberty. But the freedom of a monastery as conceived by its abbot was different from that allowed to it by the bishop. A religious writer could grant a serf complete freedom in his relations with God. Royalist writers envisaged the liberty of the church in different terms from those current in papal or monastic circles. Freedom was a word which meant all things to all men, and which has always to be defined in its individual context. In a similar way the phrase 'free and canonical election', which appears in every reformer's programme, had no one constant meaning. There never was a united reform movement with a standard vocabulary and an agreed interpretation.

Even so, a small general advance was made on a wide front. Some of the ideas created or rediscovered during the intellectual and moral upheaval passed into common currency. Clerks and monks came to believe that the *sacerdotium* was at least superior in dignity to the *regnum*, and that the church had not yet acquired its proper place (*libertas*) in the world. And lay society could not remain ignorant of their feelings or avoid being influenced by them. Above all, clerks became more aware of their uniqueness. They knew that they should be chaste, wear distinctive signs, live under a special law, and hold their possessions free from all earthly service. But uniqueness is always a strain and is resented unless it is the certain badge of superiority. Ideals have little practical effect until they are not far removed from actual conditions. And so the revolution was never so rapid or thorough as the more ardent spirits desired.

England received these continental influences diluted. There was no Bernard or Abailard in England. But the circulation of men and ideas was considerable. Bernard sent his secretary, William, to be the first abbot of Rievaulx; and Rievaulx became one of his favourite daughters. Nor were the Cistercian monasteries intellectually withdrawn from the kingdom. Rievaulx soon acquired a firm place in the religious life of the north. Ailred revered St. Cuthbert and established close ties with the Benedictine chapter at Durham; and his friend Waldef was prior of the Augustinian house of Kirkham. Ailred preached to the people; and it is significant that on his deathbed he fell back into the English tongue, calling on death to hasten 'for Crist luve'. His biographer excuses this lapse by explaining that 'Crist', a word of one syllable in English, was easier to utter and— he could not help adding—in some ways sweeter to hear. The books Ailred wrote show his double character as Cistercian and Englishman. The titles, The mirror of love (*Speculum caritatis*)—which he wrote at the command of Bernard—On spiritual friendship (*De spirituali amicitia*), and On the soul (*De anima*) are typical of the new order. But his Genealogy of the kings of England, Life of St. Ninian, Tract on the Battle of the Standard, and Life of Edward the Confessor reveal the true native of this island.

The English Cistercians also played some part in the religious controversies of the day. The observance of the feast of the Conception of the Virgin Mary had been an Anglo-Saxon peculiarity which came into fashion again in the early twelfth century. By 1150 the festival was observed in some of the greatest English Benedictine monasteries and was becoming popular in Normandy. This was a sign of the times. The Cistercians, of course, were devoted to the Blessed Mary and helped to spread the cult. But St. Bernard opposed the dogma of her immaculate conception, and consequently came into conflict with several Benedictine theologians. In England Nicholas, a monk of St. Albans, wrote a treatise against Bernard's views, and Walter Daniel replied with a treatise against Nicholas.

The influence of the Cistercians on English religious life is unquestionable. But in some ways the traditional English culture proved highly resistant to change, and was usually powerful enough to modify the alien influence, as can well be seen in the life of Ailred. The great old Benedictine monasteries, like St. Albans, never surrendered to the more sensational movements. They kept their tone and their social pre-eminence.

The heads of daughter houses in the Cistercian Order had to visit the mother church once a year. Secular clerks were sometimes peripatetic. Laon, under Master Anselm, was the popular resort of Anglo-Norman clerks in Henry I's reign. Later, Paris took its place. And there were many other schools of repute for the restless student to visit. John of Salisbury, the pupil of Abailard and the protégé of Bernard, was a clerk of the new type. Born at Old Salisbury between 1115 and 1120, he studied dialectic, theology, and rhetoric at Paris, grammar at Chartres, and learned administration, and possibly law, in the papal *curia*. His circle of friends included all the intellectual and spiritual leaders of the day, and friendship was an art he cultivated through his letters. He was a true European, and his real love was Chartres, where he died as its bishop. But he spent some years in England as secretary to Archbishops Theobald and Thomas Becket, and played a part in its politics. John was not only an accomplished writer, a good dialectician, an interesting political philosopher, and a firm believer in the liberty of the church, he had also that humane spiritual outlook which was so characteristic of those who had felt the influence of both Bernard and Abailard and who had come under the spell of Chartres. Men like John worked a great change in England. A larger class of well-educated clerks enabled all in authority to expand the operation of their governments; the study of canon and civil law made possible an English jurisprudence; and the increasing number of university graduates in the church strengthened its ministry.

Not the least important consequence of the rise in the standard of learning among clerks was the spread of literacy among the laity. Medieval grammar schools are not always given their proper importance. The schools which developed into universities are, naturally, the most interesting; but the simpler schools made the universities possible and also influenced a very much larger circle of men. There had been many schools in Anglo-Saxon England. After the Norman conquest English was replaced by French as the language of instruction; and in the twelfth century, with the growth of urban populations, public schools became popular institutions. Some of the best schools were attached to secular minsters—to those churches and cathedrals served by bodies of clerks and having a schoolmaster among the dignitaries—but almost all boroughs and market towns had their schools, and in the villages the priest was often capable of teaching. London had three famous public schools dependent on the churches of St. Paul's, St. Mary-le-Bow, and St. Martin-le-Grand. A school mentioned by the Durham monk Reginald in his collection of miracles of St. Cuthbert—a book which gives us much information about social life in the north of England in the middle of the twelfth century—will serve as an example of the humbler sort of school. At Norham in Northumberland, he writes, where, 'according to a custom now common enough, boys went to school in the church both for the love of learning and, sometimes, for fear of the master's whippings', a boy thought to get a holiday for himself and his fellows by throwing the key of the church into the River Tweed. But he had not taken St. Cuthbert into account; and the priest recovered the key from the jaws of a salmon.

The fundamental subject taught in these public schools was grammar (the study of the Latin language). But the whole of the *trivium*, that is to say, grammar, rhetoric (the art of public speaking in Latin), and dialectic (logic, or the art of argument), was within the competence of most schools; and some of the more ambitious may have completed the arts course with the *quadrivium* : arithmetic, geometry, astronomy, and music. William fitzStephen, in his famous description of the London in which Thomas Becket had been bred, tells us how on feast days the senior schoolboys of London competed publicly in rhetoric and dialectic, while the juniors held contests in grammar and, to the great delight of the audience, lampooned each other in epigrams and verse. Holidays seem to have been gay. There was no lack of sport. On Shrove Tuesday, the day of Carnival, London boys took their game cocks to school, and there were 'mains' all the morning, followed by football in the afternoon. In Lent there were tournaments; at Easter there was a water carnival with tilting at a target from boats; in summer the boys devoted themselves to archery, athletics, and dancing; in winter there was the baiting of boars, bulls, and bears, sliding, skating, and sledging. And the young men could always hawk and hunt in the extensive forest liberty of London.

In the Middle Ages the only men who remained illiterate were those who had no need for letters: the peasant who had nothing to read and the nobleman who could employ a secretary. The true purpose of the grammar school was to provide for the elementary instruction of clerks—of those who intended to serve the church— and they were licensed and controlled by the bishops; but clerkishness had become of value to all engaged in business, whether commercial or landed, and in the larger towns the grammar school seems to have been acquiring secular characteristics. Canon 17 of the legatine council of Westminster (1138) prohibited schools to be let for hire. They were profitable institutions. Literacy had become the basic qualification for many lucrative careers. There was the church itself; and in the twelfth century it might have seemed to any shaveling clerk that he had at least a mitre in the purse at his girdle. And there were all the opportunities to be found in the royal and baronial courts and in the merchant houses. Many famous men of Henry II's time had learned their letters at grammar schools in Stephen's reign; and for every one who gained an important position or fame as a scholar there were scores of others who were just a little more efficient, a little more civilized because they had been to school.

II

The new culture was hostile to feudal ideas and drew some of its strength from bourgeois virtues, even if its exponents in the twelfth century came mostly from noble families. Yet it was not without its effect on the lay aristocracy. Nobles who founded religious houses were in frequent contact with their monks and were interested in the condition of their monasteries, for the more devout the monks the more efficacious their prayers. Great men had relatives among the brethren. Earl Simon of St. Liz II disapproved of the excessive zeal of his younger brother Waldef. But the monkish life was the popular ideal of piety and set the pattern for all. A fresh fervour in monasticism had wide repercussions. Even oaths show the change in the religious climate. King Stephen swore by the Birth of God (*La naissance Dieu*), Roger bishop of Salisbury by his Lady St. Mary, and Robert earl of Gloucester, according to his admirer William of Malmesbury, depended on the patronage of the Holy Ghost and St. Mary.

The bridge between monasticism and the knightly ideal was the Order of the Temple, founded after the establishment of the Latin kingdom of Jerusalem, which spread rapidly in England after its introduction in 1128. With its aim to raise funds for the Crusade and to provide a corps d'élite, the *militia Templi*, in the Christian forces, it appealed both to religious leaders, such as St. Bernard, and to the cultivated aristocracy. King Stephen is often remembered for

bringing Saviniac monks to England and for founding the Bene-
dictine-Cluniac abbey at Faversham; but his patronage of the more
active orders, especially the Templars, was probably much closer to
his heart. Both the king and the queen were intimately connected
with the crusading movement. The king's father, Stephen count of
Blois and Chartres, had been one of the leaders of the first Crusade;
the queen's family of Boulogne had provided the kingdom of
Jerusalem with two rulers; and the two founders of the Order of
the Temple originated one from Champagne and the other from
Boulogne. It is significant, perhaps, that the bulk of the endowments given to the Temple in England were situated in the eastern
half of the kingdom (apart from a puzzling absence from Norfolk
and Suffolk), in the sheep-rearing counties and those connected with
Flanders and the fairs of Champagne. The word 'pilgrimage' comes
from the Latin *peregrinatio*, meaning a living abroad and, by extension, a travelling abroad; and pilgrimage and trade were closely
connected in the Middle Ages. Queen Matilda, backed by her
husband, was particularly generous to the Templars out of her
English honour of Boulogne. But there was no political division.
The house of Anjou was no less involved with the Crusading
cause; and opponents as well as friends of Stephen advanced the
Templars.

English knights enrolled in the *militia Templi*. But there was unaccustomed opportunity for warfare at home. And the rebellions
and civil war of Stephen's reign provide us with a good occasion for
studying the behaviour of the nobility. A code of conduct for the
knightly class had gradually been forming. King William II, according to Ordericus Vitalis, had declared that no honest knight would
break his parole, for if he did he would be for ever an object of
contempt as a man outside the law (i.e. he would be an 'outsider', a
cad). By the twelfth century these rules of conduct were well-estab-
lished. What is more, men seem more civilized, less prone to those
orgies of senseless destruction which had disgraced earlier times.
But if there had been an improvement in behaviour, it was not due
directly to the ecclesiastical view of the knight as the secular counterpart to the clerk, a Christian soldier fighting for Christian standards
—which John of Salisbury expresses in the sixth book of his
Politicraticus—for every clerical writer of the period charges all
soldiers indiscriminately with contempt for the church. Even
Stephen is dismissed by Henry of Huntingdon (whose *Historia*

Anglorum was dedicated to Bishop Alexander of Lincoln) as one who had never loved clerks. Nor can the slightest evidence be produced for the influence of 'courtly' love. Women, as women, have still no part in military society. In the contemporary *Historia regum Britanniae*, the pseudo-history in which Geoffrey of Monmouth created the story of Arthur and provided the basic material out of which a great cycle of courtly romances was spun in the following centuries, the feminine—and the ecclesiastical—interest is small, and two kings, the evil Mempricius and the good and great Malgo, are described as homosexual. Geoffrey, however, was aware of the new ideas. Ladies watch a tournament organized by Arthur, and it was their custom, we are told, to refuse their love to anyone who had not thrice distinguished himself in arms. But this is merely a harbinger of a new literary fashion. The chivalrous code of the time seems purely masculine and entirely worldly, and influenced by the rising culture only in the most general way.

No knight of the time is famous for his chivalry towards women. And it is significant that the two most distinguished women in England were Amazons. The Empress was served by Robert of Gloucester, Miles of Hereford, and Brian fitzCount, and the Queen by William of Ypres and the loyal earls, not so much as hapless 'widows', but as substitutes for their lords, forced by circumstances to exercise rights which normally were latent and vested in their husbands. A woman's proper place was in her chamber; and such civilizing influence as she could exert was private and personal. In this limited way her influence could be considerable, for the twelfth-century gentlewoman was well-educated. Adelaide of Louvain, Henry I's queen and later countess of Sussex, was a patron of literature. She commissioned an otherwise unknown poet, David, to write a life of her first husband—and Dame Custance bought a copy of this lost work for a mark of silver—and accepted the dedication of Philippe de Thaun's *Bestiaire* and of a forgotten monk's life of St. Brendan. Feminine influence, therefore, like ecclesiastical, was more a channel through which a variety of new ideas could reach the knights than a force with a cultural direction of its own.

William of Malmesbury, the author of some of the best histories of the Norman period and the chronicler of the first years of the civil war as seen from the no-man's land between the contending parties, judged the soldiers by a standard which he describes as *mos militum* (the custom of knights) or *mos majorum* (the custom of the barons). He regarded Robert earl of Gloucester, to whom he dedicated his works, as the best example of this code, and Stephen, to whom he was opposed, as almost equal.

His picture of Robert exemplifies the fashionable virtues. Robert had the basic qualities of nobility of blood, military skill, learning, and justice; and these were enhanced by the queen of virtues—munificence. Robert, he tells us, had been given a good education by his father, and loved both to hear books read and to read them himself. Robert's position as a patron of learning is well attested. Geoffrey of Monmouth, too, dedicated his History to him; and when Gaimar was looking for material for his *Lestorie des Engles* (history of the English), a copy of Geoffrey's work was procured for him by Dame Custance, his patron, by way of her husband, Ralf fitzGilbert lord of Scampton, and Walter Espec, who borrowed it from Robert himself. Characteristically, we know the name of the tutor Robert provided for his nephew, Henry fitzEmpress, while he was with him at Bristol; and it was possibly at this time that Adelard of Bath dedicated to the boy his *Libellus de opere astrolapsus* (treatise on the astrolabe). Adelard was the great popularizer in Europe of Moslem science, which was beginning to pour out of Sicily and Spain, mainly from Toledo. The astrolabe is almost symbolical of the new science, for by permitting the astrologers to make more accurate observations, it was the link between science and the occult. It is, indeed, quite evident that Robert's court at Bristol was not only a rival political centre; it was also the focus of a provincial culture. London and Bristol faced different ways.

Robert's military reputation, however, seems less secure. William of Malmesbury tells of his success in repressing Norman rebellions for his father. But in the speech to the royalist troops before the battle of Lincoln which Henry of Huntingdon puts in the mouth of Baldwin fitzGilbert (of Clare), Robert is scorned with the words, 'It is his custom to threaten much and do little. He has a lion's mouth and the heart of a hare.' And the malicious Walter Map describes Robert as 'a man of great cleverness and much learning, though, as often happens, lascivious', and relates an anecdote in which Robert, in order to excuse his muddled actions before a battle, remarks to his knights, 'I serve Venus as a volunteer, but fight for Mars only when I must'. This was a side to his character which the librarian of Malmesbury may have chosen to ignore.

King Stephen's character can be regarded as complementary, for we know nothing of his learning and much of his military skill. He was *bellator robustissimus*. His rescue of Prince Henry of Scots at the siege of Ludlow in 1139, his intrepid attack on Ely in the winter, his gallant fight with battle-axe and sword before Lincoln, and his assault on Oxford in 1142 are famous examples of a reckless courage which most kings of the period were too prudent to display. Only Louis VI of France and, much later, Richard I of England, were of similar metal. Yet Stephen's family, that of Blois-Champagne, was one of the most cultured of the time. Through the fairs of Champagne flowed some of the most important commercial traffic of Europe; and the county was a great centre for the exchange of ideas, witness the fame of Chartres. Hugh of Fleury dedicated his *Historia ecclesiastica* to Adela of Blois, Stephen's mother; but Stephen himself seems to have collected few dedications. He was pre-eminently a knight. His good manners and chivalrous virtues are fully acknowledged even by William of Malmesbury. French chroniclers called him *debonaires*.

The art of war seems to have made no radical advance in Stephen's reign, although, no doubt, there were tactical and engineering improvements of which we are unaware. Geoffrey of Anjou read the fourth-century Vegetius's *De re militari* during a siege in 1150. But there was no contemporary handbook for generals. Organized armies were composed of cavalry and infantry, in the proportion of at least five foot-soldiers to one knight. The main types of soldier available were knights, serjeants, *routiers*, and crossbowmen.

All knights and their attendant squires (apprentice knights) were of gentle birth, but were divided into the social and economic ranks of counts or earls, barons, vavassors (rear-vassals with a fief), and bachelors (household retainers). On the evidence of the *History of William the Marshal*, the effective elements in the feudal cavalry army were a small number of great men (counts and barons) and famous captains together with their forces of bachelors. The vavassors were regarded by the bachelors as an unmilitary class: they were either rustic sluggards or bachelors who had foresaken the game and retired to live on their rewards. Among the captains of Stephen's reign we may notice John fitzGilbert, a royal marshal, who, according to his son, 'although neither count nor rich baron' kept 300 knights in his household, supplying them with 'robes, money, horseshoes and nails, liveries, and rich gifts'. The cavalry contingents were organized in squadrons, some 10-40 strong, under a knight-banneret, who flew his banner of command. Bachelors normally wore the device of their lord on their shields.

Serjeants (*servientes*) were of much lower rank. They were usually foot-soldiers, and their pay was 1*d.* a day against the knight's 8*d.* In Stephen's reign both leaders recruited infantry abroad, especially from Flanders; and the rebel marcher barons used Welsh auxiliaries. But both seem to have stopped short of employing the deadly cross-bowman and the pitiless *routier*, professional soldiers under their own captains, drawn mainly from Brabant, Navarre, and the Basque country.

A knight's equipment had not changed much in the two genera-tions since the Norman conquest. In the stirring speech which Henry of Huntingdon ascribes to the bishop of the Orkneys before the battle of the Standard, the bishop encourages the small York-shire army with the words,

> Raise up your hearts, sweet sirs, and, relying on your native strength and even more on the presence of God, rise against this most wicked enemy. . . . For they do not know how to bear themselves in battle; you drill in peace time so that in war you will not experience the accidents of war. Our heads are covered with helmets, our breasts with coats of mail, our thighs with greaves, and the whole of our bodies with shields. Wherever the enemy strikes he will not find one unpro-tected by iron.

The knight was, indeed, well guarded. His hauberk seems to have been impervious to the lance or pike—splintered lances always littered the field and troubled the horses—and his weakest point, the helmet, was a small target. The helmet was attached by laces at the last moment before action; and if struck severely it could be crushed, reversed, or even forced off. After one tournament William the Marshal was found by a delegation bringing him a prize with his head on the anvil in a blacksmith's shop in the process of having his distorted helmet removed. The arms of the knight were the lance, the sword, and, sometimes, the mace. Foot-soldiers were more lightly protected, and fought with bows of yew, pikes, halberds, and hooks for pulling knights off their horses.

Horses were the knight's chief interest and concern. Eudo viscount of Porhöet, it is said, advised knights, in case of a surprise attack, first to mount and then, if possible, to arm. An unarmed knight on horseback could at least save his person and his horse.

If the knight fought often he needed two destriers (warhorses), a palfrey for riding, and rounceys for carrying his harness and baggage. And he had to mount his squire, valet, and boy. Fine warhorses, which were never ridden except in battle or tournament, were greatly prized. Spanish, Lombard, and Sicilian destriers of proved merit could be valued by their proud owners at from £30 to £100 Angevin. But the poor bachelor only dreamed of these: normally he was equipped and mounted by his lord.

Yet in the twelfth century, except in tournaments, knights seem to have fought horsed only in individual combat or as a squadron with special duties. At the battle of the Standard the Yorkshire knights fought dismounted in a phalanx like the thegns and housecarles at Hastings; and the only cavalry engaged were the Anglo-Norman-Scottish household troops of Prince Henry of Scots. At Lincoln, Stephen put the earls and their cavalry contingents in front, while he commanded a large body of dismounted horse and foot soldiers. But his cavalry screen, which expected, so the *Gesta Stephani* asserts, to fight 'justs', in which art the royal knights were skilful, was disconcerted and routed when the enemy attacked with swords for close combat instead of with the couched lance; and the phalanx of infantry did not have the same fortune as on the field of Northallerton. At Winchester there was no pitched battle. But during the period of siege and counter-siege individual contests of knightly skill took place daily outside the city. The same impression is gained from a reading of Geoffrey of Monmouth's fictitious *Historia*. Feats of bravery are performed by mounted knights, but battles are fought on foot.

In the twelfth century the difference between a battle and a tournament was not very great, as can be seen from the youthful adventures of William the Marshal as related in his biography. Every type of military stratagem, even the employment of infantry, could be used in the general conflict of the tournament—the *mêlée*; and only the provision of lists, where knights could rest, and the total absence of lethal intention, distinguished the sport from the real thing. The whole civil war was, in fact, little other than a series of sieges and tournaments. And the war itself encouraged its imitation. Young soldiers had to be trained. Sieges could be boring (and not every knight would care to read Vegetius), and the interludes between the fighting could become tedious to those who had lost the arts of peace. The reference to jousts at Lincoln, and the jousts which were

fought at Winchester, show that the rules of the tournament were
familiar to English knights, for jousts were often held before the
mêlée. In 1139 a force of knights whom Stephen had left to beleaguer
Ludlow castle, 'so arrogantly active that they could not keep off
fighting for a moment', arranged a tournament which attracted a
small army of knights. The continuator of 'Florence of Worcester'
remarks how distressing it was to see knights brandishing their
spears at each other and preparing to run men through with their
lances without giving a thought to the judgment which would fall
on the souls of those killed. The king, however, who was on his
way to London, hurried back and put an end to it. After Easter 1142
Stephen, intent on raising an army to fight against the Empress,
stopped a tournament (*militares nundinas*) which had been arranged
at York between the two Yorkshire earls, William of Aumale and
Count Alan of Richmond, in which, presumably, their feudal armies
would have fought. And it should be noticed that there are many
examples of chivalrous contests in Geoffrey's History, such as
Arthur's 'joust' with Frollo, as well as a description of a three-days'
tournament at Arthur's court, at which the knights 'contrive cavalry
games in mimicry of war'. The speech attributed to the bishop of
the Orkneys at the battle of the Standard stresses the *disciplina
militaris* of the English knights and their thorough training. This
military skill was developed on the mimic as well as on the deadly
field of war.

The code of conduct which governed the behaviour of the
military aristocracy in tournament and war was strictly observed by
the barons and knights; and neither side could charge the other with
serious infractions. Rebellion seems always to have been preceded
by the *diffidatio*, the renunciation of fealty; and William of Malmesbury actually blames Stephen for attacking Lincoln castle at Christmas 1140 without first renouncing fealty 'as was the custom of the
barons'. Peace was usually kept in Lent and at Christmas. Truces
were observed. When Philip, the renegade son of Robert of Gloucester, captured Reginald earl of Cornwall during peace negotiations, Stephen made him release him. But Philip was a thoroughly
unsatisfactory knight. He once laid an ambush for Philip Musard
outside his castle, and then, by twisting a rope round his neck,
persuaded him to surrender the place. The threat to hang castellans
and garrisons was used frequently by the rival leaders, and was
normally successful when the castellan was in their hands. In 1138

Stephen actually hanged some of the garrison at Shrewsbury. But then his title was undisputed. Later, castles reduced to extremities were usually given the customary period in which to ask their lord to relieve them, and, if abandoned, allowed to make an honourable surrender. Robert of Gloucester even permitted this privilege to Wareham in 1142, although he was racked by impatience to rescue the Empress at Oxford. When Walter Espec's castle at Wark surrendered with honour to David king of Scots in 1138, the victor dismissed the garrison with their arms and replaced the warhorses they had been forced to eat. He then destroyed the castle.

Hostages were regularly taken both to secure waverers in their loyalty and to bind contracts. Even Robert of Gloucester and Miles of Hereford named sureties when they made a formal treaty in June 1142; and when Robert left shortly afterwards for Normandy he took with him hostages from those to whom he was entrusting his half-sister's cause. But there were unscrupulous men who took advantage of the decent knight's disinclination to hang another for no fault of his own. When the earl of Chester was released in 1146 he gave the king as hostage for his good behaviour his nephew Gilbert of Clare, earl of Hertford, yet immediately rebelled and 'exposed his hostage to danger'. In 1152 Stephen attacked Newbury, a castle which belonged to his rebel marshal, John fitzGilbert. He threatened to hang the defenders. The garrison asked for a truce in which to consult the marshal. Stephen agreed. The marshal requested that the truce should be extended so that he could consult the Empress. Stephen demanded a hostage, and accepted the marshal's fourth son, William, a boy of five or six. The marshal then reinforced Newbury and cheerfully abandoned his son to his fate. Stephen was enraged, and went to hang the boy. But when he saw the innocent lad his natural mercy prevailed; and he withstood later suggestions that he should catapult the boy into the castle. William was spared to become one of the greatest men in the kingdom. And in his old age he told how he had picked out plantains—ribwort—from the flowers and herbs which strewed Stephen's tent before Newbury and played at 'knights'—conkers we call it today—with the gentle king.

Death was an accident of battle. It was not a very serious risk for the knight. Ordericus Vitalis thought that nine hundred knights were engaged in the battle of Brémule (1119) and could learn of only three fatal casualties.

'For,' he writes, 'they were clad entirely in iron, and they spared each other for the love of God and for the sake of their fellowship. Nor did they seek to kill the fugitives but rather to take prisoners. Christian soldiers do not thirst to spill their brothers' blood, but, God willing, rejoice in lawful victory for the good of the holy church and the peace of the faithful.'

The monk of St. Évroult paints an idealized picture. But wars were fought by social equals with a strong sense of comradeship; the permutations of feudal politics often forced a knight to fight with his personal enemies against his friends; and the purpose of the war seldom aroused strong feelings. So captives were willingly taken and then ransomed. After the battle of Lincoln Robert of Gloucester showed respect to Stephen as cousin and king; but when the Empress's cause collapsed Stephen was chained. Robert, however, was well treated by the queen at Rochester. He was even allowed to receive rents from his Kentish estates and with the money buy fine horses which were most useful to him later. It was, indeed, the custom of ransom which helped to keep the fighting civilized and made it similar to the tournaments of the period. When it was proposed in 1141 that Robert should be exchanged for Stephen, the crafty baron argued that an earl was not equal in value to a king and that the royalists should release all their prisoners with him. As the queen's captains had several valuable prisoners, this suggestion was, of course, successfully opposed.

There are few recorded violations of the code of knightly behaviour. The Empress claimed in December 1141 that Bishop Henry of Winchester had broken his promise to serve Stephen with no more than twenty knights; but Henry was a 'new sort of monster —half-monk half-knight'. Nor were there committed many atrocities, in the contemporary sense. The one inevitable charge from the ecclesiastical writers was that of sacrilege—disrespect for the clergy, the interference with church lands and goods, and the use of churches as castles when convenient; and, since they were built of stone, they were most convenient. The evil was denounced in synod. Canon 10 of the legatine council of Westminster (13 December 1138), held by Alberic, cardinal-bishop of Ostia, who had had first-hand experience of the effects of Scottish raids and had done much to mitigate the suffering, proclaimed the excommunication of those who did injury to clerks or usurped their goods or lands, and reserved to the pope the absolution of those guilty of violence. The

legatine council held at London in March 1143 elaborated this
enactment. Anathema was pronounced on those who assaulted,
imprisoned, chained, or held to ransom ecclesiastical persons, and
an interdict was to be placed on their fiefs. Nor was the interdict to
be avoided by having services held privately by chaplains in fortresses and castles. The countryside 'was to mourn with the mourner'.
Some of these provisions were certainly enforced. Alfred of Beverley
tells us in his *Annales* that after the council of London his church
ceased to function and that he was only saved from madness in his
tedium by taking up Geoffrey of Monmouth's History to read.

Barons and knights may well have been influenced by ecclesiastical censures; but the less punctilious mercenaries can hardly have
been deterred. And the church did not show quite the same zeal in
protecting other classes from savagery. It probably did its best. The
London council condemned all exactions and unlawful demands for
work on castle building, and, according to Matthew Paris, decreed
that the peasants and their ploughs were to have the same peace in
the fields as they would have enjoyed in a churchyard—the normal
place of refuge in troubled times. But the morality of the age was
more shocked by sacrilege than by atrocities on civilians. William
of Malmesbury, when describing the battle of Lincoln, contrasts
complacently the mercy shown to knightly prisoners and the
slaughter of the burgesses. The chivalrous code was limited in its
application. Devastation of the countryside, burning of crops,
driving off of cattle were normal ways of subduing a castle or
hurting an enemy. Many captains, and even some knights and barons,
seem also to have lived by simple banditry. One of Robert of
Gloucester's captains, Robert fitzHildebrand, a good fighter of low
birth, whose 'greed, drunkenness, and lust dishonoured and
destroyed the glorious flower of chivalry', deserted his master and
seized a castle for himself. This freebooter died by God's judgment,
according to the *Gesta Stephani*. But another mercenary, a Fleming,
Robert fitzHubert, who took Devizes castle for his own use, was
hanged by the earl. The Anglo-Saxon chronicler, writing at Peterborough, tells a doleful tale of the misery of the meaner folk. Yet
sometimes the bandit did not go unscathed. In 1141 Count Hervey
of Brittany was besieged in Devizes by a mob of peasants. Walter of
Pinkeny took the castle of Christchurch and behaved very cruelly to
the inhabitants. One day a band made up of citizens, countrymen,
and even some of his own knights, ambushed him between the castle

and the church, and, when he refused to promise amends, killed him with a battle-axe. Occasionally the people were able to restrain the knights. Robert of Gloucester on his return from Normandy in 1142 proposed to attack Southampton. But his sailors, who had kinsmen there, would not let him.

The warfare helped to harden the knightly caste. William of Newburgh, delighting in the ignominious end of tyrants, tells how Geoffrey de Mandeville was killed by an arrow shot by the commonest of footsoldiers, and how Robert Marmion, helpless in a trench into which he had fallen, was decapitated by an ignoble ranker. After the rout of Winchester, according to the scornful *Gesta*, 'knights and even great barons threw away their military equipment, and, on foot and in dishonour, hid their desertion and their real names'. The ignominy here was that *equites* did not shrink from becoming *pedites* and posing as inferiors. Stratagem was allowed. While Stephen was besieging Exeter in 1136, a relieving force mingled undetected with the attackers and managed to get into the fortress. Similar deceits are common in Geoffrey of Monmouth's History. The ability to deceive implies the general use of distinguishing marks by knights. Few of these early devices are known. According to Nicholas Upton, the fifteenth-century author of *De officio militari*, Stephen's arms were gules three sagittarii, adopted, he tells us, either because he gained the crown when the sun was in the sign of sagittarius or because he won a battle with the aid of his archers. But Edward the Confessor, and even Arthur (azure three crowns), were given imaginary coats by romancing antiquarians. Some of the knights portrayed on the Bayeux tapestry fly heraldic banners; but these seem to have been flags of command. In Stephen's reign, however, a revolution took place. The individual signs of recognition, painted on the shield of the knight and sometimes on his helm, became hereditary; and coats of arms were adopted which disclosed kinship or feudal relationship to the skilled observer. Mandeville carried a shield quarterly gold and gules; the kindred families of Say, Beauchamp of Bedford, Clavering, and Vere wore his coat with differences. These armorial bearings were passed down. English heraldry had been born.

The rebirth of the military spirit among the aristocracy in Stephen's reign is the change easiest to see; and the developments in law and organization, which the turmoil must have inspired, are far more difficult to illustrate. Yet it is significant that at least two baronial treaties should have survived from this period; and it cannot be doubted that in proportion as royal influence declined, the importance of the honorial courts increased. A baron would want to keep his men more tightly tied in their allegiance, and he would often need their advice. Independent earls, like Gloucester and Chester, were forced by circumstances to organize their honours as principalities. Moreover, the more fluid political situation must have provoked many legal disputes concerning feudal duties.

The treaty made between the earls of Chester and Leicester (1148–53) settled some difficult points of law raised by the conflict. Both parties reserved their fealty to their liege lord (King Stephen), but severely circumscribed his rights. He was not to be allowed to attack either of the allies from the territory of the other. If he summoned one to fight with him against the other, the one was to take no more than twenty knights to the royal army and was afterwards to restore to his ally any booty he had seized. Neither was to attack the other until a fortnight had elapsed after the renunciation of fealty (*diffidatio*). The limitation of the *servitium debitum* in this case to twenty knights is of some interest, for, when Henry bishop of Winchester submitted to the Empress in 1141 he, too, agreed, apparently, to serve his brother with no more than that number of knights. The knight service owed to the king from the bishopric of Winchester and the abbey of Glastonbury and from the earldoms of Chester and Leicester was, of course, much larger than this unit. Clearly the question of knight service was of the greatest importance to all during a period of rival claimants to it and of protracted campaigns. It is said that at Lincoln in 1141 Stephen's barons appeared with only their minimum contingents and sent the rest of their knights to fight with the enemy. If, indeed, a revision of the amount of service due and of the conditions governing it was forced on the king by barons placed in an unusual situation, then Henry II's difficulties in this matter are understandable. It is likely, too, that the numerous sieges of castles in Stephen's reign must have led to an elaboration of the law about the responsibilities of castellans and garrisons. But of this legal side we know almost nothing, for feudal law was seldom written down.

Nor can the changing organization of an honour be traced, for baronial documents have not survived in quantity. We can get some idea, however, of the state of honorial administration from the witness-lists to charters. A charter in favour of Bordesley abbey,

Worcestershire, which Roger earl of Warwick addressed to all his
barons and vassals (*fideles*), French and English, will serve as an
example. It is witnessed by his brother Henry, his steward Henry,
his chaplain Walter, and his chamberlain Geoffrey, and by two
other men. Roger had, therefore, at least the three basic curial
officers: a steward to look after his table and, more widely, his
estates, a chaplain to watch over his soul and act as a secretary, and
a chamberlain to supervise his bedchamber and his money. The
greater barons imitated the king closely. Towards the end of Henry
I's reign Roger's cousin, Robert earl of Leicester, confirmed to the
monastery of St. Léger at Préaux his father's grant of rent-charges
on Stratford and Harbury in Warwickshire together with an annual
pension at his exchequer. As Robert's father had died in 1118 this
baronial exchequer seems as early as the king's.

The greatest alteration in the life of the honours came probably
from the need to put them on a war-footing again. Labour had to be
organized for castle building, knights had to be recruited, trained,
and equipped, and money had to be raised for these purposes and,
occasionally, for the payment of ransom. But some of these changes
were ephemeral. Later, there was a general opinion that actions
caused by the state of hostilities were extraordinary and should not
create precedent. Indeed, efforts were made to undo them. In Henry
II's reign the pope tried to rid the English bishops of their superfluous and costly new vassals; and all barons stoutly maintained in
the face of the king that no enfeoffment made since Henry I's
death should be counted against them when scutage was imposed.
Again, the elaboration of feudal law was in the event of little
importance, because from Henry II's reign the royal court became
dominant and honorial courts began to decay. Yet Stephen's reign
cannot be regarded simply as an aberration or as a retrogression in
the history of the English kingdom. There was much lasting good
in the ethics of the knights. Stephen's generosity to his rival, the
Empress, at Arundel, when he gave her safe-conduct to Bristol,
which, says William of Malmesbury, 'it was not the custom of
praise-worthy knights to deny to anyone, even their worst enemy',
and his kindness to his young rival, her son, when he sent the youth
money so as to spare him embarrassment, were virtues which could
transcend their military setting and operate for good in every rank
of society. And even the growing solidarity of the military caste,
short-lived as it was to be, was not without useful effects. The

Angevin tyranny was great; but it would have been greater and far more pernicious had there not been this reaction against the Norman tyranny and a space in which healthy counter-forces could develop.

III

In April 1112 King Henry I's sometime chancellor, Waldric, bishop of Laon since 1107, was murdered in the cellars of his cathedral while the rebel citizens proclaimed a commune and put fire to the town. In June a party of canons set out with their most holy relics—principally the shrine of Our Lady—on a begging mission through 'France' for the restoration fund of the church. In three months they toured Issoudun, Tours, Angers, Caen, and Chartres. The money was used up in the autumn and winter; and next year nine canons, including Robert, an Englishman, visited England. Their report on the mission is of the greatest interest.

The canons were frankly collectors, making use of a miraculous shrine in a way which was common at the time. But they seem also to have practised ordinary medicine. Abbot Guibert of Nogent-sous-Coucy suggests as much in the short account of the tours which appears in his *Vita ;* and the 'miracle' at Bath, when a boy, half-drowned in the hot bath, was suspended head down between two fires with a stick between his teeth, is evidence of orthodox medical skill. The normal procedure for 'miracles', however, was that the patient should confess his sins to the priest who was of the party and make amends if this was necessary for absolution, and then drink water in which the shrine had been washed. By this means a number—but not an extravagant number—of sick (crippled, feeble, blind, and mute) were cured. And the report is so free from the more spectacular type of miracle that we can give it credence. The shrine was set up in the local church whenever possible; and there were, of course, the inevitable disputes with unsympathetic clerks who grudged seeing the pennies of the faithful going to an alien church. On the whole, however, the collectors were treated with charity.

The school of Laon was well-known in England. Its master was Anselm, who himself had studied at le Bec under Anselm of Aosta, later archbishop of Canterbury. Anselm of Laon was the last famous exponent of an outmoded theological method. Abailard, who visited Laon in order to study theology, ridiculed Anselm's pains-taking exegesis of the text of the Bible, and the unruly pupil's *Sic et non* was, perhaps, his challenge to the uncritical and pedantic dogmatism of the old school. But Laon seems to have satisfied English clerks in the first half of the twelfth century; and the canons were sure to find friends in the island.

The party set off from Laon on 24 March 1113, and, travelling by way of the textile towns of Arras and St. Omer, reached the Channel port of Wissant a month later. There they were joined by a party of Flemish merchants, going to England with 300 marks of silver to buy English wool, who wanted to cross with them under the protection of their relics. They chartered a pooped sailing vessel, with a master named Coldistan; and their worst fears were realized when they were chased by a pirate vessel manned by mailed sailors carrying lances and shields. But by a miracle the pirate was dismasted; and the collectors' ship drew away to reach Dover in safety. The wool merchants, in their fear, had offered all their money on the shrine, but took every penny back, leaving only their thanks, once the danger was spent. For this impiety they were truly punished. After travelling nearly all round England buying wool, they stored their serpels (*acervi*) in a warehouse on Dover strand, and there it was all destroyed by fire before they could ship it home.

From Dover the collectors rode to Canterbury, where William of Corbeil, later its archbishop, who had studied at Laon under Anselm, put them up at St. Augustine's abbey. They then, apparently, followed the prehistoric Harroway—the so-called Pilgrims' Way—which runs along the foot of the North Downs, for they are next found at Winchester in the middle of May. At the seat of the royal treasury they cured two typical residents: a retired royal butler, named Ralf Buarius, who had gone blind and whose office had passed to his sons, and a usurer named Walter Kiburo. The usurer was a very wealthy man. When he gave three gold rings and three silver dishes as well as money and ornaments to the canons after his cure, the citizens said it was not enough, for he had £3,000 in his treasury. But this, he pleaded successfully, was money he had to restore to his debtors under the conditions imposed by the collectors.

From Winchester the canons rode through the New Forest to Christchurch on the coast. They arrived not only in a torrential downpour but also to find all accommodation booked, for it was Saturday 30 May, the eve of the fair on the octave of the Ascension. What is more the dean and canons of the minster resented competition for the offertory. However, a pious lady persuaded her husband to put his new house (or two empty houses, according to

Abbot Guibert), already let to merchants for 2 marks, at the disposal of the collectors. The fair lasted only until dinner time, when the merchants packed up; and we are told nothing of the merchandise except for three bells which come incidentally into the story. As the canons departed another storm came up from the sea, and a thunderbolt set fire to the church—Ranulf Flambard's building—and the houses of others who had not helped them. The canons then continued westwards through Dorset until they came to Exeter, where the archdeacon Robert (possibly Bishop William Warelwast's nephew, who succeeded to the bishopric in 1155) was another who had studied at Laon. But after ten prosperous days they had to leave for Salisbury in order to complete the cure of a native of that place. At Salisbury all ended well, and they were welcomed by Bishop Roger, whose nephews, Alexander and Nigel, had been pupils of Anselm of Laon. The canons then returned by way of Wilton and Exeter (which this time they skirted), and pushed on across the moors. They were shown King Arthur's oven (? King's Oven on Dartmoor) and his seat (? Arthur's Hall on Bodmin moor). At Bodmin in Cornwall they met a clerk Algar, later bishop of Coutances, another of Anselm's pupils; but they also got involved in a dispute and brawl over King Arthur, one of their number taking exception to the claim of a local inhabitant that Arthur was still alive.

Bodmin seems to have been the most westerly point of their itinerary. The return journey took them up the northern coast to Barnstaple in Devon, where they had better luck, for there they found the west-country baron of Breton descent, Juhel of Totnes, whose wife, a sister of Germand de Pinkeny (Péquigny), a woman from Amiens, hailed them as compatriots. Juhel gave them a silver dish, a precious cup, tapestries and other ornaments, a horse, and a good sum of money, and invited them to visit his castle at Totnes, sending them with an escort of his men across Devon. At Totnes, however, they had a vexatious adventure. Three young men, wanting the price of a drink, accused them of being magicians, and one of them took a mouthful of the offertory while pretending to kiss the shrine. But after drinking alone at a tavern he went and hanged himself (or, more likely, like Absalom, was caught in the branches as he rode through a wood), and the money was restored.

Crossing the peninsula once again, the collectors came to the river-girt fortress of Bristol. As an Irish merchant fleet had just put in the travellers thought to buy new clothes. They went on board the ships—to the horror of their host, who explained that Irish merchants were fond of getting strangers aboard and then sailing off and selling them to barbarians. Undaunted, however, by this disclosure of Bristol's traditional trade, the canons paid a second visit. But a third trip was prudently cancelled. From Bristol the travellers moved up the Avon to Bath, where they duly inspected the thermal springs and performed the cure which has already been described. At this point, unfortunately, the account of the journey is cut short. The canons got home on 6 September with 120 marks as well as tapestries and various ecclesiastical ornaments. The alms of France and England allowed the church of Laon to be restored. It was re-dedicated exactly a year after the collectors' return.

The strange itinerary through southern England cannot be explained by the following of any major trade route; for the wool merchants, presumably, travelled through the eastern shires of England. The interests of the English canon Robert may have had something to do with the choice of places; or it is possible that their celebrated teacher, Anselm, had given them a list of addresses of his old students. Adelard of Bath had studied at Laon, as he tells us in the introduction to his *Quaestiones naturales;* and certainly they seem to have met with *alumni* of Laon at several places they visited. The murdered bishop, too, had several times returned to England—in search of money, if we can believe the hostile Guibert of Nogent. However that may be, England had been chosen, we are told, because of its wealth; and it seems that the canons' expectations were not disappointed. There is no hint in the narrative of barbarism. The canons rode easily and securely through a civilized kingdom.

London was avoided by these collectors, perhaps because of its very size and importance. In the previous year they had circled round Paris. There can be no doubt that by the twelfth century London was becoming almost the capital city of England. It is the place most frequently mentioned in Geoffrey of Monmouth's fictitious history; and Geoffrey gives it a dignified origin. Trinovantum, he says, means *Troia nova,* the new Troy, the name given to it by the Trojan Brutus, its founder. To the author of the *Gesta Stephani* it was 'the metropolis and queen of the whole country'.

Urban wealth in this period was based on trade rather than industry, for manufacture was on a small scale. Crafts were practised by masters and their households in their own workshops. The craftsmen were organized in gilds; and the regulations of these monopolistic bodies were designed to divide equitably between the members a volume of business which was relatively inelastic. The responsibilities of monopoly, however, were not shirked. The gilds insisted that prices should be just and that the maker should answer for the quality of his products. Both the dominant morality and the condition of the market worked to restrain private enterprise and the reckless pursuit of profits.

Trade, however, offered more opportunity to the ambitious. The Pipe Roll of 1130 mentions various articles which were procured for the royal court in London: cloth, cendal (taffeta) and samite (satin), towels, and linen; herrings, onions, oil, nuts, wine, pepper, cummin, and ginger; and basins and silver cups—mostly articles of a luxury trade, and proof that London's merchants had rich warehouses. Citizens grown wealthy through trade could use their capital profitably in the mortgage business—a form of money lending which was immune from the usury laws. The charter of King Henry I to London (*c.* 1132) confirmed to the citizens their lands, property mortgaged to them (*vadimonia*), and debts. In 1141 Queen Matilda, desperately raising money for her captive husband's redemption, mortgaged a Cambridgeshire manor of her honour of Boulogne to a leading London citizen, Gervase of Cornhill; and between 1146 and 1148 Hugh Tirel, son of the reputed slayer of King William Rufus, sold his manor of Langham in Essex for 100 marks to Gervase, in order to raise money to go on the Crusade. Warfare, with its risk of capture and ransom, must have stimulated the mortgage market; and many a London merchant may have gained property by foreclosing as well as by purchase.

The enormous wealth accumulated in Stephen's reign by the Anglo-Flemish wool financier, William Cade, was, perhaps, unusual; but several great merchant families rose to prominence in London during this period. Osbert 'Eightpence' (Huitdeniers), 'great not only among his fellow citizens but among men at the royal court', held one knight's fee in Kent of the earl of Gloucester, and employed as his clerk and accountant a kinsman named Thomas —Thomas of London—a young man who rose to be archbishop of Canterbury and a martyr. Gervase of Cornhill, justiciar of London in Stephen's reign and one of its sheriffs in Henry II's, was the founder of a family which supplied the Angevin kings with many loyal and expert servants. Gervase fitzRoger, a Norman, married before 1136 Agnes, daughter of Edward of Cornhill (a member of the cnihtengild), and adopted his father-in-law's English name. One of the sons of Gervase and Agnes, Henry, married Alice de Courci, the heiress of a baron; and a daughter of this pair, Joan, married the chief forester of England, Hugh of Neville. It is no wonder that Henry bishop of Winchester at his important council in 1141 described the Londoners as 'sort of barons in England (*quasi optimates in Anglia*) on account of the size of the city', or that the citizens themselves should have advanced a claim to elect the king.

The towns had both their ambitions and their fears. The chief ambition was to obtain a measure of self-government. After Henry I's death, the citizens of London, encouraged perhaps by the limited privileges sold to them by that king, seem to have joined together in an association sworn to extort liberties, and to have secured Stephen's adherence to their 'commune' in return for their championship of his cause. But they were hampered by the military strength of Geoffrey de Mandeville, the hereditary constable of the Tower. In May 1141 Aubrey de Vere, Geoffrey's father-in-law, who had been an important financial servant of Henry I, was killed in a riot in the city; and when Geoffrey extorted a charter from the Empress in July it was agreed that neither she nor her husband nor her son would make peace with the burgesses of London without Geoffrey's consent, 'because they are his mortal enemies'. The great fear, then, of the citizens was anarchy and seignorial oppression; and because of this fear the towns always supported Stephen, impotent though he often was. The citizens of Exeter and Lincoln appealed to him when a local baron seized the royal castle; and in 1149 the citizens of York, according to John of Hexham, promised the king much money if he would come to their city, placed in danger by the meeting of the king of Scots, the earl of Chester, and Henry fitzEmpress at Carlisle. Stephen repaid their loyalty by allowing them to destroy a little castle which had been terrorizing them and by fining the rival town of Beverley.

Of the commerce which produced the wealth of the towns the wool trade must have been the most important; and it is noticeable that much capital was reinvested in the eastern and northern parts of England. Nigel bishop of Ely was active in draining the fens; the Templars created and colonized the village of Temple Bruer between 1150 and 1189 on a high heathy ridge twelve miles from

Lincoln; and we have evidence that east-country barons were interested in the reclamation of land from forest. Geoffrey de Mandeville, earl of Essex, in a charter he obtained from the Empress in 1141, secured pardon for all forest offences, wastes, and assarts committed on his land, and permission to cultivate and plough the clearings freely. Aubrey de Vere, earl of Oxford, who had large fiefs in Cambridgeshire and Essex, obtained a similar pardon in 1142. And it is significant that by Henry II's reign the barons of the exchequer had obtained the collective privilege of freedom from all pleas of assarts made before the death of King Henry I. Control over the royal forest was relaxed in Stephen's day (the author of the *Gesta* was horrified to see the indiscriminate slaughter of royal beasts at the beginning of the reign); and farmers took the opportunity to encroach and improve. There was important building work done, too. Lincoln's port was improved by the reopening in 1121 of the Roman Fossdyke, a canal which ran from Brayford Pool to the Trent at Torksey. And the new monasteries, some of them built and equipped with Jewish money, represented a heavy capital investment. Kent and East Anglia had always been the richest parts of England; and it is possible that with the expansion of the wool trade the lead of the eastern coastal area increased.

But there is evidence of greater wealth for many parts of the country. The abbot of Evesham from 1122 to 1149 was Reginald, formerly a monk of Gloucester and nephew of Miles, constable of that city and later earl of Hereford. It is recorded of Reginald that he moved the houses of some of the abbey's knights away from the monastery so as to improve the amenities, that he built a wall round the abbey and cemetery and proposed running a moat round the vill (a project which Miles discouraged on the grounds that the vill would then become the sort of fortified place that the king might occupy), that he built a large part of the wall of the nave, the refectory, the parlour and chapel, a guest hall and chamber, and a large kitchen, that he restored the shrine of St. Egwin, and that he enriched the monastery by acquiring a pair of thuribles and a pair of candlesticks, all parcel gilt, a large bell named 'Benedict' with its companion and a small bell named 'Gloucester' with its companion, besides tapestry-hangings, vestments, books, and ornaments. He was also able to indulge in the luxury of a lawsuit against the bishop of Worcester and pay for a papal privilege.

The trade of the country passed through fairs and markets, the fairs usually annual events and attracting sometimes foreign merchants, the markets usually weekly for local exchange. In 1185 almost every tenant on the estates of the Templars was paying a money rent, and so must have been growing a cash crop. And such produce was sold in the local market, which, for the convenience of the farmers, was commonly on Sundays. The fairs were often on saints' days and in origin associated with religious festivals. At Durham, we are told, the people used to crowd into the city on the feast of the Translation of St. Cuthbert (4 September); but all had not the same devout intention. 'Some there were who came chiefly, or even solely, to seek the protection of such a father; but there were others who were more concerned with the marketing which was done at that time than with the benefits which the saint could give.' The right to create new fairs and markets was reserved to the king. And the ambitious barons of Stephen's reign extorted mercantile among other privileges from the king and his rival. In 1141, for example, Geoffrey de Mandeville obtained from Matilda the manor of Newport with permission to transfer its market and all its franchise, with a guaranteed right of way, to his nearby castle of Saffron Walden. The market at Walden was to be on Sundays and Thursdays, and there was to be a fair beginning on the vigil of Pentecost and lasting for the whole week. Geoffrey also secured the right to a Thursday market and an annual fair of three days starting on the eve of St. James at Bushey in Hertfordshire.

Trade was thus still canalized. But merchants could not be compelled to attend a specific market or fair; and the arrangement was to their advantage. Nor could the owner of the franchise afford to be tyrannical or extortionate; and the special peace which protected these licensed trading occasions, and the regular concourse of people, suited the itinerant merchants as well as the local craftsmen and traders. A special royal peace lay also on the great arterial roads. Occasionally there was heavy traffic. Siege-engines, owing to their bulk, were usually made locally. But about the year 1100 the monks of Durham had a great bell cast at London, and transported it the length of the kingdom on a waggon pulled at times by twenty-two oxen.

The chroniclers give us occasional glimpses of the towns and the merchants; but the only occasions on which they notice the rustics are when they tell of some disastrous raid by the Scots or of some brigandage more terrible than usual. And then the story is always the same. Old men and children are slaughtered, women and girls dishonoured, while the survivors stream into the towns, the churches, and the graveyards for protection. They return to blackened fields and looted homesteads; and there is famine in the land. Yet the recovery from devastation seems to have been rapid enough. David king of Scots could ravage Northumbria time after time and still always find more to plunder. And when he died the same Hexham chronicler who had often bewailed the inhuman behaviour of the Scots broke into a great eulogy of this David, this pious king, who had founded many monasteries and washed the feet of the poor, and who had always done his best to restrain the natural ferocity of his subjects. It is likely, indeed, that the havoc caused by small feudal armies, although terrible enough on the line of march, was always exaggerated, and that even in the swathe of destruction domestic animals could be rounded up again once the troops had passed on. Despite the disorder in Stephen's reign there is no evidence that the country as a whole was other than prosperous. The king seems never to have been seriously short of money. And this must mean that the royal demesne, enlarged by the enormous private estates of Stephen and his wife, was still producing a big profit.

The agricultural organization of the country had not changed very much since Edward the Confessor's day. Some of the provincial differences in culture can be seen plainly in a survey which the Templars made of their widely scattered lands in 1185—a survey of particular interest since almost all the estates had come from lay fees and in no case had they been in the brethren's hands for more than two generations.

Cowley, near Oxford, will serve as an example of a midland nucleated village-manor. This manor of four hides, which was given to the Templars in 1139 by Queen Matilda out of her honour of Boulogne, has the regular pattern of manorial husbandry, in which the labour service of the tenants is organized to work a substantial seignorial demesne. In 1185 half of the manor lay in demesne and half was held by the tenants—sixteen half-virgaters, headed by the reeve, the tenants' representative. Each tenant paid 3s. a year rent and also had much work to do for his lord. The agricultural year was divided into two seasons; and the 'works' were assessed on the land. In the summer (9 June–14 September) each virgate (hence these half-virgaters would only do half the labour specified) had to work on every weekday (with Saturday work if it was necessary to carry corn to market), and do three boon works in autumn with four men, the Templars providing food on the last day. In the other months each virgate had to work only two days a week. In addition, at the winter and Lent sowings, each virgate had to plough, sow with the Templars' corn, and harrow one acre of demesne. There were also twenty cottagers on the manor, each holding a house and a garden (messuage and curtilage), who paid rents varying from 9*d.* to 3*s.*, and who had less to do on the demesne. They had to work two days a week between 1 August and 29 September and one day a week for the rest of the year. They had to perform the three boon works in the autumn like the half-virgaters, and on 11 November, if married, give four hens, otherwise two.

In the West Riding of Yorkshire, at Temple Newsam, an estate of 16 carucates, most of which had been bought by the brethren early in the reign of Henry II, we find conditions much altered in appearance. Six carucates and three bovates (apparently 255 acres) were in demesne; and in the subordinate hamlet of Newbiggin were 13 bovates (some 65 acres) of tenant land. Nine men, or partners, held a bovate (five acres) each, and two men two bovates each. Rent was assessed throughout the estate at 6*d.* an acre. In addition, each bovater had to give two hens and 20 eggs a year, and do two ploughing and two harrowing services, one reaping and one hay-making service, repair the pond when necessary and carry mill stones, wash the sheep on one day and shear them on another, and do four boon services in autumn with one man. Three cottagers held two acres apiece, and paid 1*s.* rent, and gave one hen and ten eggs. They owed four boon services each, but lighter labour than the bovaters. In this estate, with its large demesne, small arable, and small labour force performing no week work, we can, perhaps, recognize a manor concerned mainly with the raising of sheep.

In Lincolnshire the pattern is once more different. On the estate lying in the vills of Cawkwell and Goulceby in Lindsey, the gift of Robert Basset, the distinction between the farmers and the cottagers is again the basic economic division between the tenants; but there is no mention of seignorial demesne, and the labour services due from the men are negligible. Thirteen tenants had each, for the most part, one bovate (probably 20 acres) and one toft (an enclosure for sheep folds) and fourteen tenants had only tofts. The farmers paid 6*s.* a year rent for toft and bovate and were free of all labour services. The toftholders paid 1s. a year rent and had to do four days' work a year and give four hens as a 'present'. This estate, apparently typical for Lincolnshire, consisted in effect of a rent-roll.

An estate in Kent will complete this picture of diversity. Temple Ewell, a holding of some 250 acres of arable with woodland rights (a denn) on the Weald, was given to the Templars by William fitz-Empress and William Peverel of Dover before 1164. The tenants divide into three groups; but the dominant feature is the fragmentation of holdings, due to the custom of gavelkind, and the absence of pattern. The first group was made up of 40 tenants holding houses, garden plots (? vegetable gardens), or parcels of arable land at competitive rents (6d. to 1s. for houses, 6d. to 9d. for gardens, and 3d. to 2s. 2d. an acre for arable). The second group, twelve tenants who held 49 acres in parcels of from one-and-a-half to ten acres, paid rent at a uniform rate of 3d. an acre and were also responsible as a body for a large number of miscellaneous services round and about the manor house, the dairy farm, the sheep farm, and the arable demesne, for most of which they were paid in food or produce. Finally, seven cottagers or small-holders performed services but paid no rent. Four were swine herds and summoners to the halimote of the Weald (presumably the forest Swainemote), and also had fencing duties. The other three were responsible for sheep folds only. At Ewell, it appears, we have no economic community, but an individualistic and intensive type of farming, suburban in character.

The Templars' inquest of 1185 gives us only the landlord's side of the picture. The village communities and the individual households, the rotation of the fields or the changing of the pastures, the farmer's long day and his seasons always too short, his struggle to make a livelihood from under-nourished or barren land and from half-starved beasts of poor breeding, find no place in such a record. Nor is there concern with the tenant's personal status. Merchet (the fine paid by servile tenants for permission to marry) and heriot (the relief or succession duty, usually the best animal) are occasionally mentioned, the manor courts even less frequently. There is, perhaps, a lesson here. The interest of the medieval landlord was not primarily social but economic. He had no mission to perpetuate or impose a special way of life. Some servile customs, such as merchet and heriot, were profitable; some, such as the inability to leave the manor, could be valuable under certain conditions. The obligations

by which the peasant was bound—even his personal status—could
be altered through the pressure of the lord or by agreement. There
was little the villein could do for himself. Sometimes the saints
would help. Reginald of Durham relates how St. Cuthbert restored
to a man the cow which the reeve of the earl of Northumberland
had unjustly seized as merchet, and how a tenant of the lord of
Middleton in those parts, driven to desperation by the exactions of
his lord—more was being required than the annual rent—piled his
goods on his cart and fled by night with his family and his stock,
oxen, sheep, and lambs, to Lindisfarne, which he reached in safety
after St. Cuthbert had confused the manorial servants in pursuit.
Men were more concerned with duties than with status; and the
question 'free or unfree?' can seldom have arisen at this time. It
was a customary society, yet capable of change; and, although
economic trends governed all, the immediate master was the lord
of the manor.

The emphasis on tenure, which is characteristic of feudal society,
probably at this time worked to the advantage of the rural communities, for it allowed them to make some use of economic movements in their favour. Reginald of Durham tells us that the lord of
Middleton had difficulty in getting his estate cultivated, so few were
the men who could bear his tyranny. Lothian, as well as the sanctuary of St. Cuthbert, offered a refuge for northern peasants pushed
too hard. At the beginning of the twelfth century money, although
more plentiful than it had been, was still scarcer than labour and
dearer than goods. Hence most recipients of labour services and
farm produce were willing to commute these into rents. We find,
for example, about the year 1125 a man being enfeoffed with Wol-
verton in Warwickshire to be held as one-third of a knight's fee, but
at a money rent of 20s. a year. And the principle applied particularly
to agricultural services, for manorial demesne was shrinking. The
abbots of Glastonbury seem to have reduced their demesne slowly
and, apparently, steadily between 1086 and 1201, established many
rent-paying tenancies, and commuted agricultural services. These
policies were inter-connected, for as the demesne diminished,
absolutely owing to alienations or relatively through the widening
of the tenants' land, so the labour force became excessive. One great
landowner of this period, the Temple, was interested only in money;
and the Templars seem to have preferred whenever possible to
collect fixed rents (rents of assize) from individual tenants.

It appears, therefore, that the movement which had led to the economic servitude of the small landholder had not only been halted but was here and there in reverse. A large number of rent-paying (socage) tenures in the eastern part of England had survived the Norman conquest; and these were being reinforced both by commutation of services and by the creation of new free holdings. Indeed, the impression gained from a study of twelfth-century agricultural conditions is of an archipelago of manors in central England surrounded by a sea of freer communities. And even in the Midlands around the islands of customary holdings were being formed new plots and fields—assarts—held, since new labour was not required, mostly at rent.

It was not until the close of the twelfth century, when there were rapid alterations in the economic situation, that owners of estates began to make and use records in abundance. Surveys, accounts, and custumals imply change, and their absence stability. Estate management could not become flexible until there was plenty of money in circulation; and in the twelfth century estate management was still on the traditional pattern. Whole manors, or parts of them, could be leased at a fixed money rent (put at farm), or the individual rents and services could be collected by agents. For example, between 1155 and 1160 the abbey of Tavistock leased three Cornish churches to Andrew dean of Petherwin for the term of his life at an annual rent of 30*s*. payable in three instalments. This type of bargain meant an assured and stable revenue for the lessors, but was disadvantageous at a time of rising profits. There was also the danger of dilapidation by the tenant. Tavistock's lessee, Andrew, was forced to take an oath before the bishop that he would be a faithful administrator. But damage was usual. At Michaelmas 1130 a former sheriff or farmer of Oxfordshire, Restold, was brought to account at the royal exchequer. Not only was he £120 in arrears with the farm and guilty of embezzlement, but he was also held responsible for dilapidations assessed at £270. He had wasted woods, lost stock, produce, and men, reduced the wealth of the tenants, and allowed the buildings to fall into ruin. There were, therefore, disadvantages in the method of putting to farm. But direct administration involved the recruitment and training of stewards, bailiffs, and auditors; and if the estates were small and scattered it was hardly worth while. The Templars, although their lands were of this type, managed to dispense with 'farmers', but only because they could establish administrative cells—preceptories—and had the free service of the brethren.

No great change in farming technique occurred in the century-and-a-half after 1042. But the area under the plough had been steadily expanding and the animal population had been increasing even faster. The staple field crop was still corn, with peas and beans as subsidiaries. Here and there commercial crops were grown, such as flax for making linen, and woad and saffron for dyes. But these were not very important. Much food was produced in the cottage gardens and the suburban market gardens. Alexander Neckam, in his *De naturis rerum* written late in the twelfth century, tells us—a little fancifully, perhaps—what should be grown in the gardens of the nobility. It is a catalogue of herbs, vegetables, and fruits; and the few flowers mentioned—the rose, lily, viola, heliotrope, peony, daffodil, poppy, purple iris, and yellow gladiolus—all had their uses. Among the herbs are found the familiar lettuce, parsley, mint, and sage; and beet is listed under pottage vegetables. He advises setting beds of onions, leeks, garlic, pumpkins, and shallots, and recommends the cucumber or gourd. In the orchard should be medlars, quinces, warden-trees (a pear), peaches, pears of St. Riole, pomegranates, almonds, and figs—and, for the really ambitious—lemons, oranges, and dates. Neckam, apparently, did not consider either the apple or the pear a noble fruit. He believed pears to be harmful unless taken with wine, because they were hard, difficult to digest, and of a cold complexion; and he advised that all soft fruit, such as cherries, mulberries, grapes, and even apples, should be eaten on an empty stomach and never after dinner. Pears and figs, he thought, were laxative when eaten after a meal, binding when taken before.

The vineyard was separate from the garden in Neckam's scheme. In the Pipe Roll of 1130 royal vineyards are mentioned at Huntingdon, Rockingham, and Maldon (the two here, apparently, a new venture); and it is known that on ecclesiastical estates vines were grown as far north as Derbyshire and as far west as Gloucestershire. But English viticulture languished after 1154 owing to the competition of superior Gascon wines.

The two most important machines on the farm were the plough and the cart. Neckam describes the plough, complete with tail, handle, beam, two mould boards, coulter, and ploughshare, and the cart, a two-wheeled affair with a wicker carriage on the shafts. In his treatise *De utensilibus* he gives us more information about the farmer's implements and stock. The prudent villein, he writes, will have his house stored with all sorts of wicker baskets and panniers, besides the moulds in which cheese is formed after the whey has been given to the children to drink. He will keep chaff and bran for his poultry, and he will need a sieve and a bolter cloth for sifting meal and straining beer. He will have spades and mattocks, a threshing sledge, a seed-bag for sowing, a wheelbarrow, a trap for mice, and a gin-snare for wolves. He will need stakes hardened in the fire, an axe for rooting up thorns, thistles, brambles, suckers, and butcher's broom so that he can make and repair the protective hedges round his yard, a small knife for cutting grafts and budding trees, and a hoe and a hook for weeding. He will be furnished with nets and snares for catching hares and deer, keep hunting dogs, and have a gaff for fishing.

According to Neckam, the villein will have a stable and cowshed and employ an oxherd and a shepherd. If he prospers he may keep a groom, a muleteer, and a stallion to stand at stud. The shepherd will sit in a hut at night with his dog on account of the wolves. The sheep will be folded to enrich the soil with their dung, and the fold will be moved often so that the whole of the field will get the benefit. Neckham declines to describe the scarecrow (*larva*) and the masked image of Priapus—the tutelary gods of the fields—but he lists some of the farmer's tasks. Manuring and liming the fields and cleaning them up 'under the Dogstar or Procyon or the setting Kids', harrowing stubble fields that have been burned, rolling the ground, hedging the fields with thorn, harrowing to cover the seed-grain, reaping, harvesting, and thrashing, cleaning up with a rake, winnowing and then grinding the corn. Clearly Neckam had the vision of a prosperous countryside.

Just as the area under the plough had been expanding, so had the animal population of the farms. The domestic animals listed by Neckam are the horse, mule, ass, and ox (draught beasts), the sheep and goats (milch animals), the pig which was valued for its flesh, and the bee which produced wax and honey, the only sweetener at a time when cane sugar was almost unknown in England. In the poultry yard he places capons, cocks and hens, geese and ganders, ducks, swans, herons, cranes, coots, divers, pigeons, woodcock, pheasants, and peacocks. He has much to say of the dog, the trusty friend of man, but little of the cat.

On the mixed farm sheep were indispensable. From their milk was made cheese, from their skins parchment, and their wool was the raw material of cloth. Moreover, sheep were the most efficient means of turning corn stubble (which, owing to the use of the sickle for reaping, was long) and rough pasturage into manure; and most cornlands needed flocks of sheep for the sake of the fertility of the fields. Almost every farmer must have kept some sheep; and we know that the eleventh-century sheep population of England was large. For example, in 1086 the abbey of Ely had 13,400 sheep on its manors in six shires. And in the areas described in the unabridged Domesday documents—Cornwall, Devon, Somerset, and Dorset (the Exeter Domesday) and Norfolk, Suffolk, Essex, and Cambridgeshire (the Little Domesday)—there were some 300,000 sheep on seignorial demesne. Large figures can also be provided for the twelfth century. In Henry I's reign the abbey of Holy Trinity at Caen was keeping 1,700 sheep on Minchinhampton common in the Cotswolds. A typical mixed farm with the emphasis on sheep raising is described in a benefaction made about the end of Stephen's reign to the Premonstratensian abbey of Newhouse in Lincolnshire: a farm house, four acres for a sheep fold, five bovates of arable, and pasture for 700 sheep in the fields of Cabourne.

There were two main breeds of sheep—the small short-wool and the large long-wool. The former, the mountain sheep, which was distributed throughout England, grew wool with a high felting quality which could be carded into soft woollen yarn. The best clip came from the Welsh border, the worst from Cornwall. The long-haired breeds did best on the good grazing of the Cotswolds and on the lush pastures of the Fenlands and Lincolnshire, but were also to be found in the Midlands, especially in Leicestershire. Their long wool could be combed into a smooth lustrous yarn suitable for the weaving of fine worsteds. Lindsey produced the top-grade clip and the Midlands the lowest.

Besides the flocks and herds kept on the mixed farms there were also more specialized stock and dairy farms, often on land unsuitable for cultivation. We can learn something about the herds of cattle which drifted over the uplands of the north and west, the stud farms which bred horses, and the dairy farms which produced butter and, especially, cheese from the Pipe Roll of 1130. The king was receiving £85 8s. 8d. a year from the tax on animals at Carlisle, and payment was also made (the amount has been lost) from Westmorland. Moreover, the keeper of the vacant diocese of Durham rendered £100 5s. 5d. for the 'cornage' of the animals in the bishopric. Geoffrey of Monmouth says that in Henry's reign silver flowed from the hooves of oxen; and we can see that it was coming from the north. The king had a stud farm at Gillingham (Dorset), for the sheriff had paid Svein, the king's groom, 30s. 4d. when he was there with a stallion for serving the king's mares. Those royal dairy farms which are mentioned were run by the family of Croc, royal huntsmen. Walter Croc was managing two farms in Staffordshire, and Ruald Croc seven in the New Forest. The woodland farms consisted of twenty cows and one bull, and each rendered annually to the king ten cheeses of Wilton weight.

More important, however, for the economy of the country was the growth in the flocks of sheep. Much of the wool was made up into cloth in England, for homespun was produced in most villages, and weavers' gilds were active in the towns in the twelfth century. But the greatest impetus to sheep farming in England was given by the industrial development of Flanders. The Flemish towns, favourably placed for trade, had turned also to manufacture. In the twelfth century fifteen towns, led by Bruges, formed the 'Hanse of London', and handled much of the wool trade; and the leading textile centres were Arras, St. Omer, and Douai. The rising demand for English wool was met not only by the expansion of the flocks on the mixed farms but also by the creation of great ranches wherever there was suitable land. Some of the new monastic orders, especially the Cistercians, the Premonstratensians, and the Gilbertines, which obtained estates mainly in the north and east of England, were able to join in the movement. But it was by no means confined to church lands. Indeed, those older foundations which had been curtailing their demesne had also been reducing their livestock. On the Glastonbury estates far fewer oxen, cows, and sheep were being kept by the monks at the end of the twelfth century than at the beginning. Wool had probably always been the main English cash crop, and small men as well as great estate-owners profited from the increase in demand.

The terms of trade assured the prosperity of the English farmer. The quality of the best English wool made it prized even so far off as Florence, the other great cloth-manufacturing centre of Europe, and above African and Spanish merino. Hence the balance of advantage lay with the producer of the raw materials and not with industrial Flanders.

The English mining industry must have been sharing in the general boom, for it is found in a most flourishing condition under the Angevins. A growing population used more iron tools and pewter dishes, and the new buildings needed lead in abundance for their roofs. The Forest of Dean in Gloucestershire was the most important English iron field at this time. Tin was still being produced in Devon and Cornwall. And lead came mainly from three areas—Alston moor in the neighbourhood of Carlisle, Derbyshire, and the Mendips. Silver was found in many lead mines. At Durham, in the middle of the century, the bishop's mine was leased by the moneyer or mint-master named Christian, who persecuted a free-miner by accusing him of concealing treasure-trove. In 1130 the king was getting £40 a year from the lease of his silver mine at Carlisle; and after Stephen had granted the honour to the king of Scots, Archbishop Henry Murdac of York complained that the royal miners were wasting his forest. Mineral coal, however, was still neglected.

Of the other natural resources of England fish deserves special mention, for, with meat in short supply and fasts obligatory on all classes, fish was an essential food. All the ports were engaged in off-shore fishing and in the curing of their catches. But perhaps the biggest harvest was taken from the rivers and the fens. Salmon and eels were trapped in large quantities—the eel rents of some Fenland estates were prodigious—and trout and coarse fish were taken from the streams. Alexander Neckam, in his *De utensilibus*, although relying too much on other vocabularies, extends this list considerably. Mullet, sole, conger-eel, lampreys, whale, sprats, gudgeon, sea bream, chub, cod, tunny, ray, pike, turbot, mackerel, herring, 'lobster fried in half an egg', oysters, and bêche-de-mer are among the more likely fish he mentions. The hippopotamus seems improbable. Most manor houses and monasteries had their fish ponds in which the creatures were kept fresh until required for the table.

From a contemporary standpoint England had a flourishing economy. It produced sufficient food for its population, and it had an exportable surplus of two basic raw materials: metals and wool. The carrying trade, however, was only partly in English hands. Flemish and German merchants were influential in the south-east ports, and there were even Italians in London. Liquid capital—coin —was still the key to mercantile power, and this was more abundant in industrial Flanders and at the great continental fairs than in

England. But the amount of small-scale trading done in English ships was considerable. The west-coast trade was shared with the Scandinavian Ostmen of the Irish ports. Gloucester as well as Bristol took part in it. The north-east coast traffic—especially that to Scandinavia—was even more a purely English concern. Lindisfarne, the Holy Island off the Northumbrian coast, where Durham priory had a cell, was a favourite port of call. The stone guest chamber often harboured sailors taking refuge from a storm, waiting for a favourable wind, or seeking food and water; and on the near-by island of Wedume were buried those who had reached journey's end. Reginald of Durham tells us of the merchants who also spread their nets for fish when the sea was calm, of the great piles of fish landed on the island, of the sailors from Lothian, Berwick, Durham, and Bamburgh, of Englishmen trading to Norway, and of an English ship almost driven into the snares of the 'pagan' Frisians. He mentions the sons of a tenant of Earl Gospatric in Lothian who subscribed with others to buy a ship at Newcastle, and names as steersman and master of one ship William fitzMalger of Berwick, the brother of Thor, archdeacon of Lothian. And he relates how in Stephen's reign Eystein (II) king of Norway ravaged the coast, and from Lindisfarne stole sheep for roasting and broiling and wood for repairing his ships.

Norway required English corn and wool. And among the return-cargoes were the precious falcons from the snowlands which the English aristocracy bought in the East Anglian fairs, especially at the fairs of Boston, Lynn, and Yarmouth, and at the port of Grimsby. As we can see from the Pipe Roll of 1130 a man named Outi of Lincoln had the office of providing the king annually with 100 Norwegian falcons, of which four had to be white, and as many gerfalcons, of which six had to be white. Adelard of Bath wrote in Henry's reign a treatise on falconry, and in it refers occasionally to English methods of training. But Reginald of Durham had a poor opinion of this trade. It was only novelty, he thought, which gave to the goods exchanged so high a value, and, although the business was profitable to the undertakers, it was of little benefit to the deluded purchasers of their vain and useless things.

England was by nature a fortunate country. Washed by the warm Gulf Stream and covered by moist air blowing in from the western ocean, it was fruitful beyond compare. The rainfall was sufficient to nourish great forests and rich pasture, yet not so heavy as to prevent the ripening of grain. And the equable temperature favoured the raising of stock on open pasture. If the standard of living was low it was because the available capital and the traditional techniques were insufficient to exploit the natural resources to the full. The farming routines were inefficient, and there was still no means of producing enough fodder to carry large herds of animals through the winter months. The annual slaughter of beasts at the coming of winter, so that they could be salted, was typical of this primitive husbandry. The same generalities are true of the mineral wealth of the country. Few of the resources had been discovered and the exploitation of these was crude. Nor had manufacture made much advance. Goods were produced mostly for a local market. But there had been progress. Trade was quickening throughout Europe; and the livelier exchange of goods stimulated production everywhere. Ideas were changing, too. Men were becoming more alert, more inquisitive, better educated. Granted peace, England could reap a finer harvest. When Henry fitzEmpress became king, the movements which were beginning could gather pace and carry England on to that most expansive of its medieval periods, the thirteenth century.

8

THE RE-ESTABLISHMENT OF THE
MONARCHY UNDER HENRY II

I

ALL contemporaries agree that Henry fitzEmpress was a restless man. And he had need to be. When at the age of twenty-one he added the kingdom of England to his French fiefs only a fine physique and an unquiet and persistent curiosity could have enabled him to govern his far-flung estates by the only satisfactory means at his disposal—constant perambulation. A bow-legged horseman, he led his retinue along all the tracks of western Europe; and if he tarried for a while it was to hunt. Yet this aggressive physical energy seldom clouded his intelligence. Schooled in warfare, he did not make soldiering his career. Even if his appetite for territorial acquisition was not completely sated when England was won, the task of maintenance became so heavy that he learned to renounce the more grandiose opportunities which came his way and to content himself with recovering his legal or pretended rights and exploiting them profitably through improvements in technique. In the turbulent years of his boyhood he had threaded the labyrinth of feudal diplomacy and had learned all the lessons of the world except patience; and that he was never to master. At quiet times he had had his tutors—Master Matthew when he lived with his Uncle Gloucester at Bristol and William of Conches, the most famous Norman grammarian of the time, while he was with his father—and, although not much of a scholar, he always had the air of a cultured prince. A professional to the core, Henry set a new standard for kings. He collected useful men; he could always find the right man for the job; and, since he was a clever lawyer and was never at a loss for a legal or administrative expedient, his control was both firm and creative. His father had been a capable ruler as well as a fighter; his mother had poured the maxims of a disappointed Roman empress into his ears; and he took as model his grandfather, Henry I. Never imperial, no doctrinaire, Henry II ruled a patch-work inheritance by opportunist methods. With all his faults he became a great man. His early and habitual betrayal of his wife, his crises of unreasoned anger, his impatience, his legal chicanery, his cynical use of men as tools, in which he often, and sometimes tragically, miscalculated, were held by contemporaries, and have seemed to posterity, but flaws in his brilliance. He was a great king in his day; and through his deft contrivances in law and administrative method he established a pattern of royal government that was capable of unlimited development within its basic form.

Henry succeeded to a peaceful kingdom. The generation that had fought the civil war and mauled the countryside was passing away. In the last seven years of Stephen's reign had died the two Gilberts of Clare (Pembroke in 1148 and Hertford a few years later), Henry of Scots (12 June 1152), his father, David I of Scots (24 May 1153), and their rival for the midland earldoms, Simon of St. Liz II (August 1153), Roger of Warwick (12 June 1153), and Ranulf of Chester (16 December 1153). The heir to the Scottish throne, the son of Henry of Scots, Malcolm IV (the Maiden), was a boy of twelve at his accession and the heir to the Chester earldom, Hugh of Cyveiliog, was born only in 1147. In 1155 the earldoms of Hereford and Somerset lapsed when Roger became a monk and William of Mohun died, and in October 1159 King Stephen's son and heir, William count of Boulogne and Mortain and earl of Surrey, died without issue. Only eleven of the earls of the last reign survived into the 'sixties and none of these had been an active supporter of Stephen in his later years.

It was fortunate for Henry that death was striking so shrewdly, for he was a stranger in the kingdom and unable, even had he desired, to be vindictive or to use drastic methods. In his coronation charter he promised merely to uphold the liberties and customs which his grandfather had approved and to avoid those bad customs which the first Henry had condemned. He made no mention of his predecessor, but the new earldoms of Stephen and Matilda were not suppressed, the grants of the usurper were not automatically invalidated, and, even if the rank and file of the mercenaries, now unserviceable and under royal displeasure, departed, the leader of the condottieri himself and the greatest recipient of crown lands, William of Ypres, Stephen's friend and captain, was spared in his blindness and old age and allowed to keep his estates, including the city of Canterbury, until Easter 1157, when he retired to the monastery of St. Peter at Loo in West Flanders, to which he had transferred his patrimony. .

The king's main concern was to recover his legitimate rights and destroy unlawful privileges as the first step towards re-establishing orderly government and the smooth collection of his revenues. He probably held an inquest into purprestures (illegal encroachments on the royal demesne); he pressed on remorselessly with the destruction of adulterine castles; and in the first decade of his reign received a formal surrender of most of the royal strongholds in baronial hands. There was opposition at the start. William of Aumale, Stephen's earl of York, refused to surrender Scarborough castle; Roger earl of Hereford closed Hereford and Gloucester; and Hugh Mortimer, the greatest of the Welsh marcher lords, fortified Wigmore, Cleobury, and Bridgnorth. But in January and February 1155 Henry moved through the eastern shires to York, where the earl submitted; in March Roger of Hereford, wisely counselled, opened his castles to the king; and in the summer Henry took Hugh's castles by main force. No penalties were exacted—Henry was at first as wary as Stephen had been—but the marches had been cowed and a principle triumphantly asserted. In 1155 Henry of Blois, bishop of Winchester, lost his castles, and in 1157 William earl of Surrey and Hugh Bigod, earl of Norfolk, surrendered theirs. The beginner was not squandering his advantage.

No king since the Conquest had possessed a more legitimate title or a wider appeal. Henry was the first who could trace back his lineage to Alfred and Cerdic and the first to succeed without a dynastic rival. Ailred abbot of Rievaulx, in his *Life and miracles of Edward the Confessor*, greeted the young man as the cornerstone which bound together the two walls of the English and Norman races. In 1161 the pope at last agreed to canonize Edward; and when the Confessor's body was translated to a new shrine in Westminster abbey two years later the shame of Hastings was finally allayed. The security of Henry's position allowed him to apply himself intrepidly to the many tasks which awaited him. On all frontiers there were lands to be recovered and dormant rights to enforce. The counties of Berry, Auvergne, and Toulouse had fallen away from Aquitaine; Blois was nibbling at Anjou; the Vexin had been ceded to the French king; the Welsh princes had encroached; and the king of Scots had acquired an ambiguous and threatening position. There was also the question of the inheritance of Henry's brothers. Geoffrey had a claim to the patrimonial fiefs, and the castles he held in Touraine cut Henry's continental dominions in two. William, the youngest brother, lacked an endowment. Henry attempted to solve all these problems in his first years, and with some measure of success.

These multifarious activities of the king could not have been possible had not Henry I's scheme of government—especially the resident chief justiciars and their courts in each territorial unit—been fully restored. The king had arrived in England with a Norman suite; but as soon as the English barons and royal servants had rallied to him he gave them his trust. He appointed as chief justiciars Robert of Beaumont, earl of Leicester, one of his stewards, a man who had been loyal to Stephen as well as to Henry I, and Richard of Lucy, a diligent servant of the late king. As chancellor he took on the advice of the bishops a new man, a Norman by blood, Thomas, son of Gilbert Becket of London, Archbishop Theobald's clerk and archdeacon; and the routine of the royal secretariat was immediately improved. Thomas, a lawyer and a man of business, a clerk with a taste for secular and military glory, was a lieutenant after the king's heart and shared all the royal amusements except one. Thomas was chaste.

Henry naturally turned first to family problems. On 19 December 1154 he was crowned; on 10 April 1155 the English barons recognized his eldest son, William or, failing him, his second son, Henry, as his heir to the kingdom; and on 29 September, as soon as the civil disturbance was over, the king held a council at Winchester to discuss the conquest of Ireland for his youngest and favourite brother, William Longsword. The barons agreed, and in October an embassy was sent to the English pope, Adrian IV, to obtain his sanction. The mission, aided by John of Salisbury, an English clerk at the *curia*, was successful. But when the ambassadors returned with a gold ring set with an emerald—a symbol of investiture, for an emerald signified *fides:* faith, or fealty—and with the letter 'Laudabiliter' commending Henry's intention of going to Ireland and reforming the scandals to be found there, they found the scheme abandoned. The empress had recalled her son to more immediate

tasks. In January 1156 Henry crossed to the Continent. On 5
February he did homage to Louis VII for his French fiefs, and then
turned against his second brother, Geoffrey, who had already shown
himself an awkward rival and who now, it is thought, demanded the
inheritance of his father's fiefs, Anjou and Maine. Henry stopped at
no half-measures. By July he had stripped Geoffrey of his three
castles and returned him no more than the castle of Loudun and
compensatory pensions on the exchequers; and although Geoffrey
was able to acquire the county of Nantes, while rivals disputed
Brittany, it was only to enrich his ruthless brother, for Geoffrey
died on 27 July 1158, and Henry inherited the county. Possession of
Nantes gave the count of Anjou control over the mouth of the
Loire. It had long been desired. Nor was William Longsword ever
properly endowed. He got the *vicomté* of Dieppe and some English
fiefs; but he was still in the king's household when he died on 30
January 1164, aged 28.

In April 1157 Henry returned to England. Scotland and Wales
required his attention. In July, while he was at Chester preparing
to invade Wales, the young Malcolm IV of Scots was brought to
him and did homage. Since Scotland was distracted by feud and the
boy king was in uncertain health Henry was able to sell his friendship dear. Malcolm and his brother William surrendered all their
northern fiefs, including the honour of Carlisle and the earldom of
Northumberland, and in return Malcolm was confirmed in the
earldoms of Huntingdon and Northampton and William was
enfeoffed with Tynedale. In the West the position was quite different. There the prince of North Wales, Owain Gwynedd, was at the
height of his power and it was the earl of Chester who was a boy.
A show of force was required. Henry and his troops advanced
along the coast road from Chester while a fleet sailed from Pembroke
to meet them, and, although some ignominious reverses were
suffered, when the king reached Rhuddlan on the Clwyd, Owain
was ready to submit. He did homage, gave hostages, and surrendered the territory over which Henry had passed. In January 1158
Henry visited his northern acquisitions, Bamburgh, Newcastle, and
Carlisle, and in the summer invaded South Wales, where Rhys, the
surviving son of Gruffydd ap Rhys, held much of Deheubarth and
Ceredigion. South Wales could not be defended against a strong
attack, and Rhys was content to surrender all the former Norman
lands in return for peace. Thus by the end of the year 1158 Henry

had restored the kingdom to its fullest territorial extent. He could return to his continental fiefs.

Of the thirty-four-and-a-half years Henry II reigned as king, he spent about twenty-one on the Continent. Necessity conspired with personal taste, for the strategic centre of Henry's dominions was his father's county of Anjou. The Angevin empire—and there can be no objection to using the word 'empire' in a descriptive sense—was, like most of the principalities of the day, weakly articulated, for it was held together only by common allegiance to the same feudal overlord. And, since it was a new grouping, and lacked a tradition and a myth, it had less stamina than some of the historic kingdoms which seemed to be breaking up. Geoffrey Plantagenet had counselled his son to respect the customs of the various units; and Henry had little choice in the matter. But through his judicial and administrative reforms he gradually built up a fairly coherent superstructure which might have helped to weld the parts together—especially England, Normandy, and Anjou—had the empire lasted beyond the second generation. Geographically, the territories were compactly grouped, and the lines of communication were adequate, for Tours was a great road centre and the sea lanes could not be blocked. The legal position was well understood. Henry held a kingdom in his own right and various counties and duchies as fiefs of the French king: Aquitaine in the right of his wife, and Anjou and Normandy by inheritance. In a similar way the king of Scots, the count of Boulogne, and the count of Brittany held fiefs in England of the English king. The only singularities about the Angevin 'empire' were its size and its compactness; and just as Henry disliked the Scottish holdings in northern England, so Louis VII felt uneasy at Henry's possession of the western counties of France. Louis, indeed, was envious of Henry's wealth, and irritated that his rival was begetting sons from the woman whose person and duchy he himself had so fruitlessly enjoyed.

In 1158 Louis VII was the father of three children, all daughters, two by Eleanor of Aquitaine and one, Margaret, by Constance, daughter of Alfonso VIII, king of Castile, whom he had married in 1154. In the autumn of 1158 Henry and Louis renewed their friendship by betrothing Henry, the English king's eldest surviving son, to Margaret. This scandalous engagement between a boy of three years-and-a-half and a girl of six months, whose fathers had both been married to the same woman, was a political stroke of some importance. The dowry consisted of the Vexin castles which Geoffrey Plantagenet had surrendered; and the Vexin had always been and was to remain a bone of contention between the two parties. Moreover, the projected marriage put the young Henry close in succession to the French throne. The good understanding between the two kings was, however, quickly destroyed. The dukes of Aquitaine had a long-standing claim to the county of Toulouse. Louis VII had claimed the county *jure uxoris* in 1141, and in 1158 Henry II renewed the claim. But the king's summer campaign of 1159 was frustrated when Louis threw himself into the city of Toulouse and Henry realized that he had ventured with his mercenary infantry too far from his base at Cahors. Louis had no wish to see Henry pushing farther east, and, besides, he had given his sister Constance, Eustace of Boulogne's widow, to the count of Toulouse. In October the two kings skirmished in the Beauvaisis and in November they made a truce, which became a peace in May 1160. The projected marriage was worth more to Henry at this time than the county of Toulouse, and it is clear that he was acting with caution and restraint.

The prize fell to the schemer, however, even earlier than he could have expected. In September 1159 Pope Adrian IV died, and a double election was made to the papacy. In February 1160 the council of Pavia, assembled by the Emperor Frederick I, recognized the Cardinal Octavian as Pope Victor IV. By July the English, Norman, and French churches had decided in favour of the other candidate, Cardinal Roland Bandinelli, the chancellor, who had taken the title of Alexander III. Papal diplomacy began again; and among the rewards that Henry obtained from Alexander's grateful legatees was permission for the children to be married. On 2 November 1160 the ceremony was performed and Henry took over the dowry from the trustees. Louis had been completely tricked, and, although in May 1161 he attacked the Vexin, Henry had re-established his frontier on the Epte. At the end of 1160 Louis married for the third time. But it was not until 21 August 1165 that Adela, daughter of Theobald count of Champagne, gave him the ardently wished-for son.

Henry's considerable success in recovering territorial rights lost since the reign of his grandfather was due as much to diplomacy as to war; and the marriage of his heir to Louis VII's daughter kept what might have been a dangerous rivalry within the bounds of family squabbles. The king could, therefore, always find time for administrative matters; and the attention that he and his subordinates gave to improvements in the technique of government was usually fruitful.

II

By 1162 Henry had become interested in the jurisdiction claimed by the church within his dominions. His father had been a doughty, if unsuccessful, champion of the lay authority in his fiefs; and Henry, although a pious prince, was most jealous of his rights. During Stephen's reign the lack of governance had compelled a willing church to encroach on the half-paralysed secular administration; yet, although the church's power had increased almost as haphazardly as the baronial, its acquisitions lay mainly within a sphere already staked out by its lawyers and militant members and could be regarded more as a tardy and partial satisfaction of outstanding claims than as a usurpation. Even so, the English church moved warily when Henry succeeded to the throne; and under the guidance of the old and prudent Theobald flattered the young man in order to conserve its new position. Henry was no less cautious. Faced with an ageing body of bishops, most of whom had been elected under abnormal conditions, and requiring the moral support of the clergy while he established his rule, he avoided cause for offence and bided his time. But no one expected the peace to last long. Most of the clergy were aware that some regrettable compromises would have to be accepted, some odious wrongs endured; and it was largely with pained resignation that the bishops accepted the promotion of the royal chancellor to the primacy on 27 May 1162, a year after the death of Archbishop Theobald.

The church was still engaged in defining the legitimate interest it allowed the lay government in the appointment to bishoprics. On 5 February 1156 Pope Adrian IV had tightened the regulations by making general Eugenius III's judgment in the William fitz-Herbert case that secular pressure on an electoral body invalidated the election; but, although a twelfth-century prince had to walk with circumspection, Henry could not doubt that once he became strong, chapters would elect his candidates in canonical form. The election of Thomas Becket to Canterbury was Henry's first success. Thomas had served the king well as chancellor, and the king required an archbishop who would serve him just as faithfully. But both Theobald, who had recommended Thomas as his successor, and Henry, who with some hesitation accepted the choice, had miscalculated. Theobald had chosen a man who, he believed, would defend the liberties of the church adroitly while remaining a friend of the king. Henry had selected a man who, he imagined, would help him restore the church to its traditional position. The hopes of both were defrauded. The adroitness with which the humble clerk had risen to such eminence had been an almost intolerable strain on his inclinations and natural character, and he discarded it with relief as soon as he could with safety. As archbishop of Canterbury he needed no longer be all things to all men. He had become a great man in his own right. On 10 August 1162 the archbishop, bare-footed in his cathedral, received the pallium sent by the pope, the livery of his new splendid servitude. Before the year was out he had imitated his predecessors and returned the chancellor's seals to the king.

Henry suffered this deception at the very moment when he had started to put his plans into action. With Archbishop Theobald dead and the papacy distracted by schism he foresaw no great hindrance to his policy of depriving the national churches of their novel independence, especially as he could appeal to ancient custom and the undoubted privileges of the pious princes, his ancestors. Henry's main attack was directed against the gains of the ecclesiastical courts, for they touched one of the principal functions of kingship and one of its most profitable rights. Ecclesiastical jurisdiction was generally superior in method to its secular rivals. Canon law was being developed by professional lawyers under the influence of Roman jurisprudence and the discipline of scholastic logic, and it displayed a coherence and a rationality which gave it strong powers of attraction. It was, moreover, easy to bring all manner of cases before the *forum ecclesiasticum*, if the litigants so wished, for most disputes involved broken faith and most crimes were sins. As the king was determined to improve the procedure in the lay courts he could hope to recover much 'civil' jurisdiction from the church without provoking more than professional rivalry. But it was quite otherwise when he expressed dissatisfaction with the way in which the church punished its own offending members, for to trespass on the immunity of the clerical caste, to threaten to lay sacrilegious hands on God's anointed, aroused the passionate fears of an institution which was never confident that it was winning its war against the world, the flesh, and the devil.

In February 1162 at Rouen Henry renewed the canons of the Council of Lillebonne (1080), which had defined the competence of ecclesiastical jurisdiction in Normandy in the Conqueror's day; and in 1163 he ordered his officials in Poitou to stop the abuses of the church courts in connexion with cases of land. Becket, sensitive to the royal attitude, began to increase the severity of his penalties. A clerk convicted of theft was branded, another exiled; and a canon of Lincoln, Philip of Brois, who had insulted a royal justice, was sentenced to a heavy fine and a public flogging. But this policy made matters worse, for Henry considered that the church courts were now usurping royal penalties, and in the case of banishment the charge was true. On 1 October 1163 at Westminster Henry complained to the unsympathetic bishops of the unsatisfactory justice done on criminous clerks in ecclesiastical courts. He was convinced that there had been a change since his grandfather's time, and, after a lively debate, he asked the bishops if they were prepared to observe the customs of the kingdom. No bishop, especially the canonists, could with good conscience agree to be bound by lay custom without reservation, all the more since they were aware that by such an action they would be abandoning hard-won privileges which they believed to be theirs by right. But the king had put his case on a reasonable foundation, for he could pose as the conservative reformer who asked for nothing more than the just rights he should have inherited from his ancestors.

The issue had been joined; and Henry concentrated all his effort on bending the bishops to his will. His affection for Archbishop Thomas had already cooled. He had watched with impatience the archbishop, fresh from recovering royal rights for the king, devote all his talents to the recovery of rights lost by Canterbury; at Woodstock in July 1163, when Henry had proposed to transfer to the exchequer a customary payment from land known as the sheriff's aid, Thomas, who had himself been a sheriff's clerk, had shown his new independence and change of allegiance by the stiffest opposition; and after the council of Westminster Henry abruptly disgraced the archbishop and detached the bishops from his side. In January 1164 at Clarendon, near Salisbury, the king brought matters to a head. Once more he required the bishops to assent to the customs of the kingdom as they had stood in his grandfather's day; and, after some bitter sessions, Archbishop Thomas, aware that the pope counselled moderation, and overwhelmed by threats, took an unconditional oath to conform. The rest of the bishops then with reluctance followed his example. But the customs of England had never been written down. So Henry used his favourite device of the inquest and ordered his court to declare the customs. A record of 16 articles was then produced which, when engrossed as a chirograph, the bishops were required to confirm with their seals. The prelates were dismayed. It was one thing to swear to observe customs which were uncertain and open to varied inter-pretation and another to confirm in full knowledge practices which no good churchman could honourably approve. The primate recovered his courage and refused; the other bishops, however, bewildered and disillusioned, gave way.

For a time the king put his trust in an insecure pope. But repeated missions to the *curia* failed to obtain papal sanction for the constitutions or the grant in satisfactory form of a papal legation to the archbishop of York. And in the end, Henry deliberately con-trived the ruin of the primate by trying him for secular offences in the royal court. At Northampton on 8 October Becket was condem-ned for failing to perform suit in September when he had been summoned to answer the charge of one of his vassals, John fitz-Gilbert the marshal, that justice had been denied him in the arch-bishop's honorial court; and for this offence all his movable goods were adjudged to lie at the king's mercy. On 9 October the king began to demand account of various sums of money which had passed through Becket's hands while he had been chancellor. And on 13 October, when Becket appealed to the pope against the bishops, who, he feared, would next pass judgment on him on a criminal charge, the king was presented with the very opportunity he sought, for by appealing to the pope the archbishop contravened the customs of the kingdom as recently recorded by the Clarendon inquest. But the bishops evaded pronouncing judgment on this charge of treason; the lay barons faltered in the task; and the primate pushed his way out of court, and by the morning had fled, secretly and in disguise, to the coast.

Henry's callous and intemperate behaviour had defeated its purpose. The agony of conflicting loyalties, the terror of concealed threats, the strain of following an unreliable and irresponsible leader had racked the English bishops almost beyond endurance and had destroyed the cohesion of what must surely have been the finest episcopal bench in Europe. The archbishop himself had gone defiantly, broken-heartedly, into exile. And the Constitutions of Clarendon remained a royal programme devoid of clerical support and discredited through the measures which the king had used to extort assent.

The Constitutions of Clarendon purport to record the royal rights in ecclesiastical affairs as they existed before the recent lawlessness. And the truth of the record was never disputed: the question at issue was whether such archaic practices could still be tolerated by the church. Naturally, the more venerable the custom the more likely it was to be obnoxious to the reformers. The church could accept the Norman custom that clerks who held baronies of the king should owe him all the usual feudal services except those irreconcilable with their order (cap. 11); but it could hardly approve those rules of the Conqueror which hindered free appeal and recourse to the pope (caps. 4, 8) and which restricted the use of ecclesiastical penalties (caps. 5–7, 10). And, although the agreement between Pope Paschal, Archbishop Anselm, and King Henry I underlay the procedure described for episcopal elections (cap. 12), even that method was beginning to look outmoded and undesirable to the canonists. The clauses which concerned the competence of the rival courts were more debateable, for in the past church and crown had been more concerned with engaging the help of the other to buttress their threatened authority than with disputing each other's jurisdiction. In the Constitutions the king claimed cases of debt (cap. 15) and of disputed advowson (cap. 1), and, of course, maintained that he should supervise the punishment of criminous clerks.

The position of a clerk accused of felony or of a breach of the king's peace (crimes reserved to the king) is described—far too concisely—in article 3 of the Constitutions. Such a clerk is to appear in the royal court when summoned and plead to the charge. If he pleads his clergy the court will consider where he is to stand his trial. If it is decided to hand him over to the bishop so that he may be tried according to canon law a royal officer will go with him to watch the proceedings for the king. Finally, if the accused is found, or pleads, guilty in the ecclesiastical court he is no longer to be protected by the church. It is clear that two separate threats to clerical immunity can be detected in this procedure. In the first place it is recognized that the clerk, when identified as such, may have to face a trial in the royal court itself. The charges to which clerical immunity could not be pleaded are not listed; but it is known that in the Anglo-Norman period, forest offences and treason fell within this category. The second threat is more oblique but more consequential, and it is that which aroused the most opposition. The cryptic conclusion to the clause—that the church was not to protect clerks found guilty of the crimes in question—was generally interpreted as meaning, and was probably intended to secure, that the condemned clerks should be degraded from their sacred orders, re-arrested as laymen by the royal officer who had been present at their trial, and taken back to the royal court to receive without further trial the ordinary secular penalty for the crime—usually mutilation or death.

This article 3 of the Constitutions was most offensive to the primate, presumably because it pronounced on the controversy which had provoked the king to hold the inquiry. But Becket could find little in the current text books of canon law on which to base his case. It was certainly illegal to try a clerk on a criminal charge by secular law in a lay court; but Henry infringed this principle only by making exceptions to the rule, and these exceptions were allowed in the final settlement. Moreover, such guidance as the canonists gave on the practice of punishing a degraded clerk by secular penalties favoured the king. In the year 539 the Emperor Justinian had enacted in his 83rd Novel just such a procedure as was declared to be English custom; and, although the canonist Gratian ignored this regulation, he was perfectly familiar with the procedure whereby clerks guilty of heinous clerical offences, such as rebellion against their bishop, were degraded and handed over to the lay power for punishment. Indeed, it would seem that during the preceding centuries the church had taken little interest in the fate of those members it had expelled. Nevertheless, it may be thought that Henry's insistence on the initiative to be taken by the secular power and his intention to use the church courts in this matter simply as instruments for the condemnation and degradation of criminous clerks were out of harmony with the general spirit of the reformed ecclesiastical jurisprudence, and that his plans to establish a royal police system under which clerical criminals should be effectively caught and then suffer almost automatically as laymen was contrary to the policy of the church. What is more, his project did injury to sentiments which, although poorly presented by the canons, were strongly felt. The early church had been prodigal with threats of degradation—and these can be read in the *Decretum*—but the medieval church, under normal conditions and when left to itself, was less severe. To add capital punishment to degradation did violence to its idea of justice, and, since the belief was spreading that Holy Orders were a sacrament and that they left an indelible mark, the too sudden change of character offended its sense of decorum. Archbishop Thomas argued that degradation was a sufficient penalty in itself and that degraded clerks should be punished by the lay power only if they offended again, and used, not unreasonably, Jerome's commentary on Nahum, as employed by the Apostolic Canons and as quoted by Gratian (*Decretum* I, 81, 12)— 'Non judicat deus bis in idipsum' (For God does not judge twice for the same offence)—to justify his view. But this argument had its weaknesses and dangers, for Henry was not advocating a double trial or judgment for a single offence, and the canonists themselves required the prince to add a second penalty in certain cases.

It cannot be doubted that, while the inquisition of January 1164 declared with substantial truth the customs of England, some of those customs were directly opposed to the law of the church and others had become most unpopular. The opponents of the Constitutions did not question their authenticity. Their appeal lay from custom to the law, from history to justice; and Archbishop Thomas in exile based his case upon the book, on the latest codification of canon law, Gratian's *Decretum*, although, as we have seen, that work was not without ambiguity on the subject of criminous clerks. Yet, even if the English customs were at variance with the law of the church as interpreted at the time they could still be tolerated as special custom provided that they were not wrong in themselves. There were always radicals ready to invoke fundamental principle whenever the sphere of ecclesiastical clashed with secular government, and it was not difficult to condemn some of the Anglo-Norman regulations as inherently bad; but in general the Constitutions dealt with matters which were usually treated as political and as subject to diplomatic agreement between the pope and the lay powers. Indeed, the whole juridical controversy was in its nature no more intractable than other disputes, such as that over the investiture of clerks, which had run their courses and been settled by compromise.

In 1164 the situation was envenomed by bitterness and distorted by adventitious elements. Henry pursued the 'traitor' archbishop with passionate animosity and refrained from no action, however mean and cruel, which could hurt. Thomas, less powerful and, perhaps, more affected by their old friendship, directed his occasional rash acts of severity against the 'traitor' bishops and archdeacons. None of the principal parties, however, wanted the quarrel to get completely out of hand, and the violent expressions of a violent age (so voluminously preserved) to some extent obscure the patient negotiation between king, pope, and archbishop, which continued almost without interruption. Although no English bishop was uncritically loyal to the king—and men so deeply influenced by canon law and the new spirit in the church could not be expected blindly to follow a lay prince in such a cause—none was prepared to enlist under the doubtful banner of the archbishop. Thomas's promotion had disappointed the ambition of some and outraged the sense of propriety of others. His intimacy with the king in the past made his motives suspect and his tactlessness unforgivable, while his ostentation both as courtier and as archbishop stamped him as a parvenu; so that his championship of the common cause made the cause itself appear less honest. And these taints, which no extreme of asceticism, no discipline in the new life could wash away, deprived him of that integrity, that natural holiness, and that moral authority which illuminate a saint in his lifetime and which Anselm had so conspicuously displayed. It was an act of murder which made Thomas a saint, and even his passion was smirched by a foul word.

No one hated Thomas more than another who might have become a saint and an archbishop, Gilbert Foliot, sometime prior of Cluny, prior of Abbeville, abbot of Gloucester, bishop of Hereford (1148), and, since 1163, bishop of London, a man of noble birth, an able governor, and a famous ascetic, and one who could not forgive Thomas because he was the wrong man championing the cause of right. For the archbishop of York, Roger of Pont-l'Évêque, Canterbury's disgrace was York's opportunity. There had been enmity between the two men in Archbishop Theobald's household—Roger, who became archdeacon of Canterbury in 1148, resenting Thomas's climb to importance through the old archbishop's doting favour—and, when Thomas fell, Roger aspired to keep and to extend the privileges he had acquired for his metropolitan see while the southern province had lacked a pastor. This personal struggle, clothed now in constitutional garb, was, perhaps, the bitterest ingredient in the whole conflict. Chichester and Salisbury, too, were opposed to Becket. Others vacillated or shut their eyes. Worcester went abroad to study. Only the aged Henry of Winchester, secure in his rank and his fame, dared, quietly but consistently, to take the exile's side.

The judge to whom all the disputants looked, Pope Alexander III, a Sienese, was the finest canonist and theologian of them all. His *Summa*, known as the *Stroma*, one of the earliest commentaries on Gratian, and his *Sententiae*, a theological exercise influenced by Abailard, had adorned his teaching career at Bologna; and his work as papal chancellor had given him a clear understanding of the working of the papal government. Indebted to Henry for his recognition and threatened by a rival under the patronage of the Emperor Frederick I, Alexander showed himself to be a statesman with the true Italian touch. Although Becket's stand was inopportune and his behaviour often an embarrassment, the pope never let the archbishop down, and his diplomatic finesse was such that neither was Thomas completely disheartened nor was Henry entirely unhopeful during the seven years the quarrel lasted. Alexander, in exile at Sens, did not hesitate to confirm immediately the archbishop's condemnation of certain of the Constitutions. Obnoxious chapters were those which restricted the right of appeal and of exit from England (8 and 4) and the freedom to punish and coerce the king's tenants-in-chief and servants by sentences of excommunication and interdict (7), that which restored to the royal court disputes over the advowson of churches (1), and, of course, the clause concerning criminous clerks (3). Other chapters were anathematized as the quarrel developed, until about half of these English customs came under the ban. But the pope, prudent and conciliatory both by nature and training, was not prepared to take offensive action; and Becket retired with a few devoted companions to the Cistercian abbey of Pontigny, near Auxerre in Burgundy, where he devoted himself to the study of the *Decretum* and the prosecution of his case, while striving through austerity to prepare himself morally for the lonely path he had chosen.

A fallen upstart has few friends. One, however, Thomas kept, and one worth a thousand: John of Salisbury, the famous author of the *Policraticus* and *Metalogicon*, both of which works he had dedicated to Becket, a man familiar with the papal court and skilled in diplomacy and the composition of persuasive letters. But in general the beneficed members of the church, while professionally sympathetic, were unwilling to risk much for the exile's cause. Nevertheless, a fire was lit which has never since been put out. The poor and oppressed, those who groaned under the weight of the world and suffered under Angevin rule, took the archbishop to their hearts. For them he became a symbol of revolt, until legend made him an Englishman resisting the foreign yoke; and this feeling ensured his sanctity when at last he had been struck down by the servants of the tyrant, and made possible the many miracles at his tomb.

In the beginning, with Henry defiant, Becket stubborn, and the pope shackled by political necessity, the incessant negotiation and the flood of polemical writing did little more than sharpen the forensic skill of the disputants. The international situation governed all. In 1165 Henry opened negotiations with the emperor, and at the council which began on 22 May at Würzburg, Richard of Ilchester, archdeacon of Poitiers, and John of Oxford, soon to be dean of Salisbury, swore allegiance in Henry's name to the new anti-pope, Paschal; but it was a manœuvre, and the king disavowed his envoys once the threat had sunk in. The pope, in return, appointed Thomas his legate on 24 April 1166; and on 12 June at Vézelay the archbishop published the papal condemnation of some of the Constitutions of Clarendon and excommunicated several of the royal ministers. The king himself was reprieved only, it was said, because he was ill. Henry retaliated by approaching the anti-pope again and by so threatening the Cistercian General Chapter that Thomas, in order to spare his hosts, moved from Pontigny to the papal residence at Sens and settled down in the suburban abbey of Ste.-Colombe, a Benedictine foundation. The strategy of the royalist bishops was to anticipate Becket's strokes by preventive appeals to the pope, and in this way render him harmless while the tedious technicalities of law were argued. Henry's policy was to cajole, weary, or threaten, according to the circumstances, the many special commissions appointed by the pope to mediate a settlement. At first time was on the king's side. He could manage without a primate and Thomas might die. With a new man at Canterbury, more wisely chosen, everything could be arranged.

By 1169, however, the king was becoming impatient. Bishoprics were falling vacant and could not be filled while Becket was in exile; and, moreover, Henry wished to have his eldest son crowned.

On 18 November 1169 at Montmartre Henry and Thomas almost reached an agreement. The king offered grace and security to the archbishop and the complete restoration of his possessions; but he would not seal the compact by giving the kiss of peace, and the archbishop, no doubt rightly, doubted his good faith. By this time negotiations were no longer concerned primarily with the Constitutions of Clarendon. Since the papal position had been made clear a personal reconciliation was now considered sufficient, to be followed, it was hoped, by a compromise negotiated in an atmosphere of good will. But this side-tracking of the juridical issues made agreement all the more difficult, because there was a complete absence of trust between the two parties. And when the Montmartre conference failed each side stiffened in the hope of forcing the other to concede that last inch. Henry tightened up his security measures in the kingdom in preparation for a complete rupture and Alexander announced that he would place an interdict on England if peace were not made before 2 February 1170. Negotiations were still dragging on when, on 3 March, Henry abruptly left the Continent with his eldest son and put a complete embargo on cross-Channel shipping.

Henry's patience had snapped at last. On 15 August 1169 the Emperor Frederick had had his son Henry crowned at Aachen, and the English king was determined to follow his example. He was aware that if he persuaded York to perform the ceremony Canterbury's pride would be wounded and the personal issue exacerbated beyond measure; and it may be that such was his intention. By Anglo-Norman custom the right to crown the king belonged indisputably to the archbishop of Canterbury. Since the reign of Henry I, however, the primacy of Canterbury had not only been undermined in authority but also had been deprived of much significance. It had been papal policy to sap metropolitan and primatial jurisdictions in order to centralize the bishops under the pope; and since 1164 Henry had encouraged the anarchy in the southern province and supported York's independence. In the years 1161–2, just before Thomas's promotion, Alexander III had gravely weakened Canterbury's primacy by granting some notable privileges to Roger of Pont-l'Évêque as a reward for his devotion to the papal cause during the schism. The northern metropolitan was exempted from the jurisdiction of the archbishop of Canterbury whether as primate or as papal legate; and on 17 June 1161 he was given permission to crown the king's son should Canterbury be unable to perform the ceremony. Once the quarrel had started, however, Alexander supported Canterbury as strongly as he dared. Pressed by Henry to give a legation to York for the whole of England, the pope issued on 27 February 1164 such an unsatisfactory commission that the royal agents returned the bull to the chancery and Roger had to be content with a legation for Scotland. Then on 24 April 1166 Alexander appointed Thomas his English legate, but excepted the diocese of York and the person of Roger, since one legate ought not to be subject to another. By these compromises effective authority was divided between the two; but the pope also reaffirmed Canterbury's superior dignity by confirming its primacy in November 1164 and April 1166. From the papal standpoint the primacy was merely an honour; yet there was one privilege attached to it in England that had become of some importance—that of crowning the king. On 5 April 1166 Alexander expressly forbade the archbishop of York to crown the king's son, and in February 1170, at Becket's urgent instigation, he issued new bulls forbidding York or any other bishop to perform the ceremony. But there is no evidence that these latest prohibitions got through Henry's blockade. On 14 June 1170 the archbishop of York, assisted by six or seven English and Norman bishops, crowned the young Henry in Westminster abbey.

The act of defiance done, Henry returned to the Continent to face the papal legates, the archbishop of Rouen and the bishop of Nevers, and to take his punishment. But his diversion had succeeded. He arranged a meeting with the exiled archbishop at Fréteval, a castle in Touraine, greeted him with simulated warmth, and Thomas, hopeful of a change of heart and eager to return, easily accepted on 22 July the terms he had rejected at Montmartre, dispensed with the kiss of peace, and asked only for permission to vindicate Canterbury's primatial authority in the kingdom. Henry made no demur, and said that Thomas should recrown the young Henry together with his wife. He had turned the archbishop on to a new quarry, he was to get him once more in England within his power, and he had made no explicit concessions to the church. But then Becket tarried. The returning avenger wanted many papal bulls and required them in satisfactory form. Alexander renewed his grant of the primacy and conceded him a legation throughout England, excepting this time only the royal family from his authority; he suspended York and all bishops who had sworn to observe the Constitutions and confirmed that London and Salisbury had relapsed into excommunication; and he protected the agreement of Fréteval by providing for an interdict to fall on the continental fiefs of the king in case of its infraction. Becket, however, thought the punitive bulls too offensive to the king in their reference to the Constitutions, and wished rather for the suspension of those bishops who had taken part in the coronation. But, before the substitute documents arrived from Italy, the archbishop heard that elections to the vacant bishoprics had been arranged in England and that the prelates and electors were crossing from England to complete the ceremonies in the king's court. This flagrant adherence to the Constitutions, this insulting reward to his enemies, who were now to be made his colleagues, this total disregard of his position, touched off the explosion which had been hanging fire. On the last day of November Becket published the offensive papal sentences, and on 1 December crossed to England with John of Oxford, whom, with typical bad taste, Henry had appointed as his conductor.

The populace greeted the returning exile with joy; the regency and the bishops met him with anger. He had, indeed, brought not peace but a sword into the kingdom; and when York, London, and Salisbury, backed by the royal officials, asked for their absolution, which the pope had reserved to himself, Thomas could offer no more than conditional absolution to the two bishops provided that they would give security for standing to judgment. This they would not do, for the procedure was contrary to the Constitutions, they did not want to desert York, and, besides, they thought the sentences unjust. The archbishop had never dealt a more provocative or a clumsier blow. The bishops resumed their journey to Normandy and complained venomously to the king. Henry became mad with rage. In his anger he railed at the cowardice of his men who could not rid him of a humble clerk. Four knights of his household, Reginald fitzUrse, William de Tracy, Hugh de Morville, and Richard le Bret, took him at his word and crossed swiftly to England. At Canterbury, on 29 December, they forced an interview on the archbishop and demanded that he should absolve the bishops. He answered as before. And when the knights had armed they struck him down in the north transept of his cathedral church as he stood by a pillar between the altars of the Blessed Virgin Mary and St. Benedict in the lamplight at the end of a winter's afternoon.

'For the name of Jesus', the wounded man had whispered, 'and for the protection of the church I am prepared to embrace death.' Friends and enemies alike proclaimed the martyr and hailed the saint. A murmur of indignation ran through Christendom. On 25 January 1171 the archbishop of Sens, despite the protest of his colleague of Rouen, let fall the sentence of interdict on Henry's continental fiefs. Henry himself, bowed with grief and in despair at the wanton destruction of all his hopes in the very hour of victory, kept his chamber for three days. His nuncios, however, sought out the pope at Tusculum, and Alexander was merciful and wise. He excommunicated the murderers and their accessories; but, although he confirmed the interdict laid by the archbishop of Sens and for-bade the king to enter a church, he refrained from excommunicating Henry by name.

Henry did not wait for the papal legates who were to investigate the crime, but retired to Ireland. It is possible, indeed, that the Irish 'Crusade' was the price he paid for the pope's forbearance. And when he at last returned to meet the legates in Normandy, sixteen months had passed in which passions could subside. By May 1172 all the bishops, except Salisbury whose infirmity had hindered the business, had been absolved and restored; and on 21 May at the episcopal city of Avranches it was the king's turn. After much hesitation Henry swore to the legates Albert and Theodwin that, although he had been an unwitting cause, he had neither intended nor desired the murder and that he would accept correction for his fault. The pope's terms were severe. In addition to private penance the king was to maintain 200 knights for one year in the defence of the Holy Land and was himself to crusade for three years unless the pope should later dispense with this condition. But Alexander was not vindictive. He required that freedom of appeal from the English church to the papal court should be allowed (with permission for the king to take security from appellants that they would not harm him or his kingdom), that all customs hostile to the church introduced by Henry should be abolished, that the possessions of the church of Canterbury should be restored in their entirety, and that all exiles and sufferers for the cause should be pardoned and reinstated. Henry straightway added the phrase *dei gratia* to his official title; on 2 September the pope confirmed the sentence of his legates; on 27 September the ratifications were exchanged; and on 21 February 1173, owing to the insistence of the French clergy and people, Thomas was canonized by papal bull. The incident was closed.

Sincere regret at the murder of a saint and a general feeling of relief at the extinction of a disturbing force cleansed the juridical dispute of almost all its bitterness. The pope had not abused his advantage in 1172, and by contenting himself with the expression of general principles had prepared the way for a detailed agreement. In the next two years Henry attempted to recover lost ground on the plea that he had introduced no innovation hostile to the church; but he found the pope so reasonable and so helpful to him in the troubles which began with the rebellion of his wife and elder sons in 1173 that he ceased to prevaricate. Alexander's complaisance was proved abundantly in the course of the elections to the vacant bishoprics, which had been postponed again when Becket died and which were completed to the entire satisfaction of the king in 1174, despite the opposition of the young Henry who tried to gain the church's support for his rebellion. A blameless mediocrity, Richard prior of Dover, was elected to Canterbury with the agreement of all the interested parties; but most of the bishoprics went to the king's nominees, to men who had stood by him loyally during the conflict and who had been detested by the martyr. Richard of Ilchester, archdeacon of Poitiers, was promoted to Winchester, Geoffrey Ridel, archdeacon of Canterbury, to Ely, and Reginald fitzJoscelin, archdeacon of Salisbury, to Bath. Even more scandalous was the king's nomination of his eldest bastard, Geoffrey, to Lincoln; yet the pope dispensed with his uncanonical age and irregular birth. The friends of Becket were left in the cold. John of Salisbury wrote to the pope on behalf of Richard of Ilchester; but there was no English bishopric for John. The pope humoured the king and at the same time strengthened his own legal hold. The young Henry's appeal against the elections had gone to the papal court, and it was thanks to a papal decision that the king's candidates got their sees. Alexander III was a great rather than a heroic pope.

When the revolt of his sons was over Henry began to negotiate again with the church over the Constitutions of Clarendon, and between 1176 and 1180 all the controversial problems were settled by agreement. In 1175 Henry asked Alexander to send a legate to England to hear his case against his wife, Eleanor of Aquitaine, who had encouraged her sons in the late rebellion. The divorce proceedings came to nothing; but Henry negotiated a concordat with the legate *a latere*, Hugh of Pierleone, cardinal-deacon of St. Angelo, before he left the country in June 1176. The cardinal allowed the king to keep jurisdiction over clerks who offended against the forest law, for hunting was prohibited to clergymen by the canons, and the king agreed that for no other crime would he try or punish clerks in his court. Yet Henry's abrogation of chapter 3 of the Constitutions was the only important concession he made after 1172. He promised Cardinal Hugh that he would not force clerks to undergo the ordeal by battle and that he would not keep archbishoprics, bishoprics, or abbeys vacant for more than a year unless there should be special cause. But the cardinal agreed that cases involving the lay fiefs and the lay services of clerks should be heard in the appropriate feudal court and he confirmed the agreement which Henry had recently made with the English bishops that despite the 15th canon of the Second Lateran Council of 1139 (*Si quis, suadente diabolo*), the king should punish the murderers of clerks. This concordat cleared up most of the difficulties. The few which remained were quickly settled. On 1 October 1179 the pope abandoned to the king the examination of all cases concerning the possession of land, even if it should be held in free alms, and so legalized the assize *Utrum;* and in 1179–80, to avoid the regulation of the Third Lateran Council of 1179 that the presentation to a benefice lapsed to the bishop if delayed more than three months, the king devised a new possessory assize (*de ultima presentatione*) which refined chapter 1 of the Constitutions and enabled him to keep cases of advowson in the royal court without doing violence to the canons.

Henry had failed to establish the whole of his claims as expressed in the Constitutions of Clarendon. The political customs of the Norman age had fared the worst. But freedom of intercourse between the English province and Rome was a basic right for which the reformed church had never ceased to strive; in the later years of Henry I and during the weakness of Stephen there had been little royal obstruction to appeals to Rome in purely spiritual cases, and it would seem that only brute force, consistently applied, could have stopped a practice which for a generation had been accepted as normal. The papal *curia* had become in fact as well as in theory, owing to the pressure of the litigants themselves, the international court for Europe; and it is significant that Henry and his servants should have appealed frequently to the pope during the very time that the king was denying the right to English clergymen at large. Even so, Henry retained some control over ecclesiastical business. He had not given up the established procedure for episcopal elections; he had kept the right to supervise the going of prelates and the coming of papal legates; and he had not remitted the protection he gave to his barons and servants from ecclesiastical sentences. In the jurisdictional sphere Henry had done much better. True, he had been forced to surrender his scheme for the punishment of criminous clerks. But again, it may be thought that the king had been asking for too much. In proportion as the clerical caste developed its singularity by insisting on a special mode of life enforced by its own discipline so it became ever more difficult to constrain it by the processes of secular law. This immunity of the clerical offender made a gap in the king's police system and became in time a scandal; but it did his plans of reform no serious harm in a period when franchises were common and unremarkable. And except on this one point the king was almost completely successful. Nearly all cases involving land had been brought back into the secular court and a method by which cases of disputed advowson could be properly entertained had been invented. Moreover, it had been clearly recognized by the pope—indeed, had hardly been in dispute—that those clerks who held secular fiefs were bound by feudal law; and the king had retained the right to enjoy the revenues of bishoprics and royal abbeys during their avoidance just as though they were escheated fiefs, a right which Stephen had renounced in his second charter but had never surrendered in practice. This papal release of the bishop and his temporal possessions to feudal law balanced Henry's concession of freedom of appeal. In general to control the fief was to control the 'free and canonical' election and then to control the man. After the 1173-4 rebellion Henry forced Bishop Arnulf of Lisieux to resign by forfeiting his temporalities; and one example was enough.

Henry's reactionary policy had failed on two issues, both of crucial importance to the reformed church. But, like his grandfather, he had retained much of the substance of his claims while sacrificing objectionable forms; and this was the type of compromise which best suited the two parties. Perhaps the most remarkable feature of the struggle was its peaceful subsidence. Once tempers had cooled everyone could see that the original dispute, although important, had been small, and that even the fury of the king and the archbishop had not widened it dangerously. Henry had in the beginning meant no harm to the church. He had been interested only in his rights. And the pope had done little more than insist that any change in ecclesiastical affairs must be scrutinized and approved by the church. Hence, after the polemic and violence were stilled, little was changed. Adjustments were made and some doubtful matters defined, but within the framework laid down by the Chartrian school at the beginning of the century. It was recognized that the clerk was a vassal with two lords; and Henry and Alexander defined his duties to God and to Caesar with good sense. Both respected the concordat. Indeed, Henry, chastened by Becket's death and harassed by domestic troubles, treated the church most generously in his later years. Once he had obtained bishops of his choice he entrusted them with his business, and the pope seems to have dispensed with the 12th canon of the Third Lateran Council which forbade clerks to accept secular judicial appointments. What is more, the king, through the influence of a new friend, Hugh of Avalon, prior of the Charterhouse at Witham, one of the king's penitential foundations, and bishop of Lincoln in 1186, zealously furthered the cause of ecclesiastical reform. A professional rivalry continued to exist between the royal and ecclesiastical courts for civil cases, and the royal court invented writs of prohibition designed to bar the hearing of a particular action by its competitor. But these writs were obtained by clergymen when advantageous, and the royal chancellor who issued them was usually a clerk. There could be no simple conflict of Church and State so long as clerks held secular possessions and appointments; and the radical claims of both powers—pope and king—always failed because the subjects for whom they were competing—laity as well as clergy—were deeply aware of their double allegiance and bitterly torn whenever they were required to choose a single lord. At the height of the quarrel between Henry and Thomas, Bishop Arnulf of Lisieux had written, 'the ecclesiastical authority promotes rather than detracts from royal authority, just as royal authority usually preserves rather than abrogates ecclesiastical liberty', and had argued that the two powers were mutually beholden 'since kings cannot obtain salvation without the church nor can the church without royal protection get peace'. These sensible views prevailed in the end.

But under Becket's influence the church renounced for a time one measure of royal protection. About the year 1177 Alexander III, by then a convert to the martyr's views, had issued a decretal to Sicily (known as *Licet praeter* or, from the first words of the relevant sub-section, *At si clerici*), in which he condemned the procedure of accusing a clerk by a lay jury as invalid and the imposition of a second penalty on a degraded clerk as illegal. Such independence of the secular courts was, however, inconvenient to the church, especially in the thirteenth century, when it made determined efforts to stamp out heresy. A series of decretals after *At si clerici*, culminating in Innocent III's *Novimus* of 1209, weakened the prohibition. Becket's revolutionary position could not stand unimpaired. After 1209 the ecclesiastical courts were permitted to deliver men condemned by canon law to the lay power and require the prince to impose a secular penalty. But the initiative was to lie with the church. Thus Henry's attempt to manipulate ecclesiastical procedure and Becket's determined opposition had caused the church to define the law; and it had defined it largely in its own interest.

III

Normally Henry got on excellently with the English church and the pope. They had a common interest in peace and good order. Henry's main achievement in England was to restore the monarchy of Henry I—the three-tier system and the general eyres of justices—and to render it indestructible. He made no revolutionary changes in the government of England: indeed, he and his servants seem to have been less inventive than Henry I and Roger le Poer, and many measures for which Henry II has been praised can be traced back at least as far as his grandfather's reign. But the reconstruction itself was no light task, and, while rebuilding, Henry enriched the Anglo-Norman tradition from other French sources and improved the system by making many pragmatic adjustments. So soundly did he build that the administration continued to develop through Richard I's absences and under John's somewhat capricious direction, so that by the end of our period (1216) the question is no longer whether the kingdom can again disintegrate but rather who can and who should control this machinery which runs remorselessly and even dangerously almost under its own momentum. Clerks served Henry in many governmental departments. They staffed the chancery and the writing-office at the exchequer, and the guardians of the bureaucratic ritual were clerical families in which the secrets of royal administration were handed down from uncle to nephew and, sometimes, from father to son. Clerks influenced the development of law. Illiterate laymen might have a great knowledge of feudal custom, even, perhaps, some fragmentary acquaintance with the *laga Edwardi*, the old laws of the English; but few except clerks disposed of a set of rational principles, for these could be derived only from a study of civil and canonical jurisprudence.

The eagerness of educated clerks to serve the king, and their willingness to accept judicial appointments under papal dispensation revolutionized English law; and it was in Henry's reign that there began to issue from the royal court a coherent and common body of law which was in time to cover and to destroy the mass of disorderly custom. Henry II, like his forebears, was no legislator. The new law developed out of new procedures, sometimes solemnly, sometimes informally introduced; yet all his measures were contrived in the spirit of the new jurisprudence emanating from the schools of Italy and based on the study of Roman and canon law. And it was exactly in the field of procedure that the influence of canon law could be most easily exerted, for the ways of the church were in advance of the traditional practices of the secular courts. The church was creating its own system of sworn inquisitions, and had probably anticipated the lay powers in using possessory actions. What is more, canon lawyers were building up a rational method of pleading. Bishops and archdeacons serving as royal justiciars, and clerks acting as advocates and attorneys, had the power to remodel the form of royal justice. The systematic development of the English common law owed much in its beginning to the church. Henry's error in 1164 was to over-strain the loyalty of his clerical advisers; but such was the basic harmony that the quarrel over the punishment of criminous clerks was never much more than a vexatious complication.

Henry II was naturally much preoccupied with his revenue. Although he re-endowed the monarchy first by contributing the revenues of Normandy, Anjou, and Aquitaine, and then by adding most of Stephen's lordships after the death of Stephen's son, William, in 1159, his territories were in disorder and his government was expensive. Most of his reforms, including the judicial, had a financial purpose. He improved the exchequer's work as a finance office by making a number of small changes, and he made sure that it was under his control. The king's chamber (*camera regis* or *camera curiae*) had always been used as the king's personal treasury on his travels. It received money for the household expenses from the Westminster and Winchester treasuries and directly from royal revenue-collectors and debtors, and paid it out to purveyors and other creditors. But under Henry's direction it not only accounted for its own monies but also began to supplement and reinforce the main exchequer. In the early part of the reign sheriffs were slack and often in arrears with their 'farms', and important men, like Thomas Becket, were sometimes careless about their accounts. The king appointed men from his chamber to the exchequer, and also transferred the accounts of unsatisfactory sheriffs from the main exchequer to the chamber, so that he could put drastic pressure on the defaulters.

There was, moreover, the problem of the novel independence of the sheriffs. At his accession Henry was content to appoint the strongest among his supporters to the office, and four earls and even a bishop and an abbot served for a time. He made a few changes in 1155 and 1162; and then in 1170, after he had been abroad for four years, he jolted the financial administration even more severely. In reply to the many complaints of fiscal oppression which greeted his return Henry sent out itinerant justices to investigate in each shire the behaviour during the last four years of all royal officers— sheriffs, bailiffs, and foresters—and also baronial officials, including the spiritual agents of the bishops, the archdeacons and deans. He required to know what exactions had been made on hundreds, vills, and individual men whether by judicial process or without, what had happened to the chattels of all those who had suffered under the assize of Clarendon and whether the assize had een properly enforced, what had become of the money collected in 1168 as an aid when his daughter was married, whether the royal manors were properly maintained and stocked, and, generally, what financial peculation had occurred. It is obvious that Henry suspected that the rapacity of the administration was not devoted entirely to the royal interest; and since most of the sheriffs and bailiffs were removed after the inquest it is clear that his suspicions were well-founded. The new sheriffs were mostly men connected with the royal court and, more especially, with the exchequer; so that the office was restored to the status which it had had under Henry I.

But the sheriffs had more to do under the second Henry. Their basic duty, the collection of the royal revenue and services in the shire, and all the administration which directly or indirectly con-

cerned it, became more onerous; and the extension of royal jurisdiction, although reducing the purely judicial character of the
sheriff, put many new burdens on him, for it was he who had to
handle the writs, summon the various juries, guard prisoners, and
generally prepare for the visits of the itinerant justices. And the
perambulation of the royal justices brought the sheriff under closer
supervision. Henry II may have been a tyrant; but he was not prepared to let the people suffer under a host of petty tyrants.

Danegeld had become obsolescent in Henry I's reign, and seems
to have been replaced by *dona* (gifts) taken from the shires and
auxilia (aids) required from the towns. In the earlier part of Henry
II's reign Thomas Brown, the king's financial expert from Sicily,
began to revise Domesday Book. But the revision was not carried
beyond Herefordshire. Henry imposed geld only in his second and
eighth years. General taxation had always been considered tyrannical,
and it was a measure which Henry could not reimpose. Instead, he
and his sons concentrated on the exploitation of the royal demesne
and the extortion of casual profits. Henry tallaged 'his own': his
demesnes the towns, sheriffs, the moneyers, and the Jews, under
the guise of taking *auxilium*, *assisa*, or *donum*; he extracted the
maximum gain from his feudal rights; he made royal justice more
profitable; and he accepted greedily all those 'fines', offerings, and
bribes, without which he would grant no favour. Among feudal
rights wardship (especially of the vacant bishoprics) remained the
most lucrative and marriage the most politically valuable. Baronial
reliefs were commonly at £100 or 100 marks, but they were still at
the will of the king, and Henry used his discretion so as to punish
his enemies and reward his friends.

But while the English kings were abandoning the most venerable
tax on the kingdom, the church, familiar with tithe, was developing
a new and better method of taxation. In 1166, 1184, and 1188 Henry,
in agreement with his cousin of France, sanctioned for England and
his continental fiefs the pope's plan of taking an aid for the relief of
the Holy Land in the form of a fraction of a man's movable property
and revenue; and the Saladin Tithe of 1188—a compulsory tenth—
remained a precedent which all later kings sought to turn to their
own use. In the Norman period the kings seem to have imposed a
more than usually heavy danegeld when entitled to an aid; Henry II
levied the aid of 1168 for his daughter's marriage on knights' fees.
Both carucates and knights' fees remained units of assessment in

the thirteenth century; but the taxation of movables, which in conception owed much to the church and in machinery everything to tallage, was to supersede the land taxes.

No less perplexing to the king than the financial problems was the state of the feudal army. The royal 'empire' had suddenly expanded; but a knight's tour of duty in the field had been reduced to the training period of forty days. Yet the difficulties of the situation were avoided for a time, and an ambiguous position bequeathed to succeeding kings, because there were always some barons and knights who wished to share the prestige and adventure of royal expeditions in whatsoever theatre they might be, and because the king was usually willing to commute the service of the more pacific for money. Henry I had allowed some ecclesiastical barons to pay scutage. Henry II in the first eleven years of his reign took five scutages (the first from the church baronies only) at 1 mark, £1, or 2 marks the knight's fee, the lowest rate representing 40 days at 4*d.* a day. Initiative lay with the king. He could require a baron to furnish knights, or commute at a standard rate, or pay an arbitrary fine to be quit. In 1166 Henry tried to put fresh life into knight service by requiring each baron to make a detailed return of the knights enfeoffed on his honour. But if the original purpose of the inquiry was to take fealty from those rear-vassals who had not done their liege homage to the king—and so strengthen the allegiance of the kingdom at a critical period (Matthew of Boulogne planned an invasion of England in 1167 to recover his sequestrated English honour)—the use made of the returns was financial. For the aid of 1168, taken in the form of scutage, Henry attempted to revise the obligation of his barons by making them responsible for either the *servitium debitum* (the contract figure as settled after the Conquest) or the actual number of knights enfeoffed on the barony, whichever was the greater. But the opposition of the barons to a revision in their rating was fierce and sustained, and successful. Henry's sons created some new knights' fees; but the feudal host was going the way of all venerable customs.

More malleable, however, than the financial and military customs were the judicial customs of the kingdom; and Henry both tightened up the police system and also fostered the growth of the 'civil' jurisdiction of his court. The old Germanic system of *wer* or *bot* and *wite* was moribund. The more serious crimes (felonies and treasons) were unamendable, and placed the culprit's life and limbs at the king's mercy and forfeited his land either to his lord (with felony) or to the king (with treason). For the less serious crimes arbitrary money penalties were being introduced by all courts. The guilty man was usually held to be 'in mercy' (*in misericordia*), and his amercement was then assessed. Even when imprisonment was imposed the sentence could usually be compounded by a 'fine' (*finis:* an ending, a composition), for prisons were costly. With the introduction of discretionary penalties instead of the antiquated fixed tariffs modern criminal law began to take shape. But the prosecution of crime was still largely a private affair. It was the individual who had been wronged, or his kin, who 'appealed' the malefactor. And when most crime was punished through private action and all cases in the royal court, even those concerning the title to land, involved punishment, the distinction between criminal and civil jurisdiction, which was recognized by the *Tractatus de legibus et consuetudinibus regni Angliae*, written in Henry's reign, will be seen to be in advance of practice.

Since money was the chief interest of those who owned jurisdiction few vagrant criminals were ever caught and hanged. Henry tried to remedy this weakness. The quarrel over felonious clerks was a prelude to the king's attempt to repress crime; and in 1166 (assize of Clarendon) and 1176 (assize of Northampton) Henry decreed extraordinary hunts for criminals. He used the ancient duty of local communities to denounce malefactors to the king's servants, and provided for the summary punishment by his itinerant justices of the defamed. According to the assize of Clarendon all those denounced by juries of twelve men representing each hundred and four men representing each vill as notorious robbers, murderers, thieves, or their harbourers, were to be deprived of the right of purgation. The most manifest criminals were to be allowed no defence at all, the others were to go to the ordeal of water and, even if they succeeded, were to abjure the realm. It is possible that in organizing these savage swoops, which disregarded the traditional law, respected no franchise, and were entirely to the profit of the crown, the Angevin was merely imitating his grandfather, reviving, indeed, a most ancient practice; but the procedure has a continuous history from 1166. The machinery for catching and punishing all those who had broken through the ordinary meshes of the law was crude, and it is significant that mutilation was the severest penalty under this rough justice. But the punishments were, no doubt, salutary. Even so, it is doubtful whether Angevin police measures were very successful. Many of those appealed came clean from the ordeal or swore the charge away; the eyres collected much money and hanged few men; rarely was a man kept in prison. Indeed, it seems that few desperate malefactors were ever haled before a court, and that outlawry—a violent confession of failure—was the most usual sequel to the commission of a serious crime.

More ingenuity was expended on the development of the civil jurisdiction of the king's court. As an honorial court it heard disputes between tenants-in-chief and cases concerning their feudal duties. Complaints of denial of justice and of arbitrary wrong had always reached the king; and his normal response was either to order the appropriate feudal lord to do justice—otherwise a named official, usually the sheriff, would do right (writ of right)—or to make a simple order of restitution (writ *praecipe*) which often led to a case in his court. Hearings before royal judges, sitting either at the exchequer or on eyre, were becoming so popular with litigants in land cases because of the expertise of the bench and the superior procedures employed that Henry and his justiciars, interested in land titles and peaceful possession, eased and cheapened the approach to them. The most useful procedures they offered were those which employed a jury. The right to empanel a representative body of local inhabitants and make them swear to answer truthfully a question which was to be put to them was a royal prerogative, acquired by the Norman dukes from the Frankish kings and normally used for ascertaining and recovering royal demesne and customs. But Geoffrey Plantagenet had sold the right to hold an inquest quite freely to his bishops during the pacification of Normandy; and it was his son's achievement to standardize some approaches to the royal court which hitherto had been occasional and extraordinary and to promote some new ones. The king had always favoured lawful possession and discountenanced arbitrary eviction of a man from his free tenement without the judgement of a competent court; and in 1166 Henry, in his assize of Novel disseisin (*de nova disseisina*), offered a general remedy for unlawful disseisin. Henceforth the victim could purchase a writ from the royal chancery directing the sheriff to empanel a jury to answer the simple question whether or no the plaintiff had in fact been disseised since a certain statutory time. If the jury 'recognized' that the plaintiff had suffered this wrong he was restored to possession and his oppressor was amerced. In 1176 a second 'possessory' assize, that of Mort d'ancestor (*de morte antecessoris*), was devised by the king, by which an heir was to be given seisin of his father's lands if a jury recognized that his father had died in possession and that the plaintiff was his father's heir. These two assizes, together with the assize *utrum* incorporated in the Constitutions of Clarendon, 1164, but presumably older (lay fee or free alms) and the assize of Darrein presentment of 1179–80 (permitting the patron who last presented to a church to present again in case of dispute), both of which have already been mentioned, became known as the Possessory Assizes, and they had in common their summary procedure and their simple interest in possession. Possession and ownership were contrasting concepts familiar to the civil and canon lawyers, and, owing to the form of Henry II's legal changes, became concepts of great importance in English common law. Nevertheless, English lawyers, affected by feudal conditions, gave possession much of the character of ownership and were unwilling to treat of ownership as a radical property valid against all comers.

Under real feudal conditions it was difficult to speak of the absolute ownership of land, for any particular parcel of land, unless it were royal demesne, had an ascending series of owners under the king. English lawyers, by conceding that the man who held land in demesne (that is to say, in direct exploitation) and in fee (by hereditary right) or for life was the owner of that land and by reducing the concurrent rights of the superior lords in it to an entitlement to services and customs, managed to avoid this negation; but there was, nevertheless, a general inclination to pose the question who was the more lawful possessor rather than who was the more rightful owner, for the issue was far simpler and the answer could readily be given by a jury. Indeed, he who wished to prove better right (and this was the only way of removing a lawful possessor with an inferior title) had a long and hazardous road to travel. Procedure under writs of right or *praecipe* (the usual methods of initiating proprietary actions) was solemn and dilatory, as befitted so serious a matter, with the decision depending on God's judgment, usually expressed through the ordeal by battle. Every advantage lay with the man in lawful possession (the tenant), and Henry II even increased his advantage by allowing him to avoid the duel by purchasing the privilege to have the issue of better right decided by a jury of twelve local knights (the Grand Assize, introduced before 1182, possibly in 1179). Thus Henry II's legal reforms made it extremely difficult to remove a lawful possessor—however doubtful his title—and gave rise to the proverb that possession is nine-tenths of the law. They also made available a new type of title to land. Litigants in the royal court often came to a private agreement and offered money to the king for leave to withdraw. The agreement they made—the *finalis concordia*, the 'fine'—was drawn up as a chirograph (in duplicate) under the supervision of the justices; and from 1195 a third copy, the 'foot of the fine', was kept by the court. The fine served as a title deed; and it became so useful that by John's reign fictitious suits were being brought before the king's court merely in order to obtain this type of authoritative title.

These new actions—the Grand and Possessory Assizes—were royal benefits which could be bought from the king. They met an obvious need and were popular from the start; and the increase in business began to strain the organization of the royal court. What made the reforms possible was the emergence under the chief justiciar of a corps of almost professional judges, clerks and laymen. Their headquarters were the exchequer at Westminster where they formed what can now be called the Common Bench. When the king was in England they mostly sat (notionally) with him, *coram rege*, although it is doubtful whether this made much difference. From 1188, when Henry left England for the last time, until 1199, when John succeeded, the bench at Westminster was rarely disturbed. This continuity was momentous. By 1168 Henry had got the general eyres working again and had almost abolished the local justiciars of the Norman period. Parties of judges were dispatched from Westminster through the shires to hear cases and control and exploit the judicial, feudal, and domanial rights of the crown. The instructions given to the judges—the articles of the eyre (*capitula itineris*)—grew wider as the years went by and after 1168 usually included the hearing of some or all of the assizes. Litigants were being spared expensive, and sometimes interminable, journeys in order to get justice. To suit the convenience of the judges, however, cases could be transferred from the eyre to be terminated at Westminster. And occasionally, of course, the judges halted proceedings to allow them to speak with the king.

The law administered in the royal courts, whether before the king, the common bench at Westminster, or the itinerant justices, was a special royal law, distinct from all local and feudal customs and monopolizing certain forms of action. Proceedings were usually originated by means of a writ. This document, except in the 'assize' procedures, did not determine the form of the action—that was oral and traditional, and far older than the writ system—but the language of the writ and the plaintiff's story (his plaint or count) gradually came together as the method developed, until by the late thirteenth century an action based on any one writ followed a unique and stereotyped course. From this feature arose both the strength and the weaknesses of the English common law before it was reformed in the nineteenth century. Once the plaintiff had chosen a writ the trial proceeded remorselessly according to the appropriate rules. If the plaintiff had chosen wrongly he could not amend his plea nor could the judge use his discretion. All parties to the trial were shackled by the rules, and the one redeeming feature of this archaic formalistic rigidity was that it kept the judge in his place. He soon became, as he had been before, but the umpire of a complicated game. This lack of plasticity was not, of course, inevitable. So long as the king and his judicial officers could vary the writs to suit the circumstances paralysis could be avoided. But by 1272 the king's power to invent new writs and to interfere with the working of his courts had been severely curtailed; and this restriction led not only to atrophy but also to the exclusion of the common law from all new spheres of legal activity, such as commercial jurisprudence.

Another factor which influenced the development of the common law in England was Henry's practice of making changes by means of assizes. The *assisa*, a 'sitting', hence a judicial bench, and hence the decision of such a body, was not properly a legislative act, and it inaugurated a change in procedure rather than made an alteration in the substantive law. The customs of England were often appealed to, but there was no written code, and they had to be discovered and declared. The law was, therefore, made by judicial decisions: it became 'case-law', increasingly bound by precedent. It was on the bench at Westminster that the common law was created. Already before the end of Henry's reign justices had begun to keep rolls of their judgements (plea rolls have survived from 1194), and before long the young lawyer had a mass of 'unwritten' (that is to say, unenacted) law to study. Also during this formative stage in the history of the common bench was written by one of the clerks or judges that important treatise on the rules of the king's court known as 'Glanvill', after Henry's chief justiciar. But although here again the cumulative effect of precedent was to stereotype, the immediate results of establishing an irresponsible royal court of law, staffed by bold men with wide vision and a natural leaning towards simplification, were revolutionary. Two fundamental peculiarities of the English land law were, for example, created by the royal court towards the end of the twelfth century. The court insisted on the impartibility of tenements, except among heiresses, and their descent to the eldest son: hence the English rule of primogeniture and the disherison of the younger sons (better, indeed, to be a bastard than a younger son); and a little later the court began to favour the free alienation of land. Both these rules have been of major importance in English history. The rule of primogeniture prevented the creation of a caste nobility and threw many younger sons of gentle birth into the professions and into commerce and industry; and the refusal to shackle the land market helped to keep English society mobile.

Most of the judicial assizes of Henry's reign extended the use of the jury; and thereby another characteristic feature of English common law was created. The Angevin jury was not much like its modern descendant. It was an instrument of royal prerogative, a purchasable royal favour, not a popular right; it was a body sworn to tell the truth about something it knew or had investigated, not a body called to give a verdict solely on the evidence presented to it; and it was a body which represented some community, a vill, a hundred, or a county—in a wider sense, the *patria*, the country—in a far more meaningful way than any modern jury can be said to do; but it had one essential feature in common with the modern jury which proves the lineage and dissociates the two from the witnesses and oath-helpers familiar to the old law: it was summoned by an indifferent authority, a royal official, to declare the truth about a specific matter in the sole interest of justice. In France, under the influence of canonical procedure, the jury disintegrated into witnesses whom the judge interrogated individually and sometimes in secret in order to discover the truth. But English juries, owing to their early and regular use, had developed a tradition quite different from this more rational—and authoritarian—inquisitorial approach, and were strong enough to withstand it. In Henry's day judges were unaccustomed, and reluctant, to do more than declare the law. Final judgment lay with God, or could be extorted from a jury. Hence judges showed a preference for unanimous and anonymous verdicts, and ceased to inquire too carefully into the special knowledge of the jury. This prudence on the part of the judges gave the

English jury its characteristic form.

The new procedures were open to all freemen who could afford them. It was taken for granted that justice should be profitable; but Henry's willingness to take gifts in order to hasten the process of justice caused misgivings even in the faithful heart of Richard fitz-Neal, his treasurer. Yet far more pernicious in its ultimate effect than the venality of royal justice was the denial of its benefits to all but the free. This English peculiarity was due to the precocious development of the king's jurisdiction at a time when the power of the territorial nobility was still great. Henry had neither the strength nor, perhaps, the desire to interfere between a lord and his peasants, to meddle in the affairs of the manor court; and the effect of this rule was to depress even further the status of the villein. The very dilemma, free or unfree, produced a novel sharpness in the classification of society, for if a man were unfree he must, according to those who were familiar with Roman law, be a slave. Moreover, masses of Englishmen had for long been in an ambiguous position —free ceorls in origin and still free under the old law, but economically dependent and socially despised—and this cruel dilemma was posed when they were beginning to suffer under new pressures, when demesne farming was coming into fashion and labour services were being increased, and when a greater national wealth made more obvious the stratification of classes. It was in the second half of the twelfth century that writers under the influence of the civilians, such as Richard fitzNeal in his *Dialogus de Scaccario*, treat the villein as a thing without rights, as a mere chattel of his lord; and that hardening of sentiment sealed his fate. A great class of serfs—despite the Roman lawyers the villein was never treated quite as a slave—had been recognized and perpetuated by the law. Only the villeins on the royal demesne escaped the full condemnation. In their case there was no landlord to hinder the king's action, and naturally the king was interested in the well-being of those peasants whose labour produced much of his wealth. Hence the king's itinerant justices, often employed to investigate the condition of the royal manors, began to entertain complaints from royal villeins, and in course of time these were allowed to purchase not the ordinary but nevertheless useful writs. Moreover, they were permitted to keep their privileged status even when the king alienated the manor; and between 1154 and 1272 'ancient demesne' became the one area protected from some of the forces which were steadily driving the villeins into greater servitude.

But if Henry's legal reforms sharpened the cleavage between the free and the unfree they helped to preserve the essential equality of the free. Tenure was already beginning to be an uncertain guide to a man's wealth and importance. Already there were baronial families which had alienated so much land that their standing had deteriorated and men who held so many under-fiefs of other barons that they counted among the more powerful in the kingdom. Moreover, feudal England was ceasing to be a society organized for war. Henry II would not allow tournaments in England; and without those miniature battles there could be no real chivalrous life and no proper military training. The English barons were no longer as a class the king's captains in the field and the country knights had long ceased to be professional soldiers. After Stephen's reign England relapsed into its traditional rusticity; and it was in the tournaments of France, Flanders, Burgundy, and Champagne that adventurous men like William the Marshal acquired their professional skill and made their livings. In England, fiefs, which in origin had been impartible and inalienable, had been allowed to split among heiresses, and sub-infeudation, imperfectly controlled, had scattered and complicated the burdens for which the fief was responsible. For the chivalrous under-tenant scutage was becoming a rent, and many who held but a fraction of a knight's fee were almost indistinguishable from rent-paying socagers. Serjeanties were becoming unreal and obsolete. Into this confused and dissolving feudal world royal justice pushed its way and offered equal remedies for all free men. No earl or baron was 'dearer born' than a knight or socager. Society was still as aristocratic as ever; but it had been too fluid since the Conquest to precipitate a new caste nobility.

With knights losing their martial skill, changes in the military system had become imperative. Henry II had no great enemy to fight and no ambition which a large cavalry army could serve. He needed a force sufficient to check the rivalry of neighbouring princes, to overawe the 'colonial' dependencies, and to crush the sporadic baronial risings. For these purposes the Flemish and Welsh mercenary infantry he maintained was usually adequate; and he was content, therefore, to allow the military organization of the kingdom as established by the Conqueror to decay and to take money instead of knight-service from most of his vassals. But the rebellion of 1173–4 severely shook his authority. His subjects could become too pacific and his dominions lie too easily at the mercy of rival professional armies. In 1176 (assize of Northampton, cap. 11) he held an inquiry into castle guard in England; and four years later he reformed the ancient duty of all free men to bear arms and to bear them solely in the king's service. In the Ordinance of le Mans (Christmas 1180), for the continental fiefs, and the Assize of Arms (1181), for England, the king decreed the scale of armament to be maintained by each man according to his wealth, and prohibited the export of military stores and ships from the kingdom. In England, all freemen and burgesses were to have at least a gambeson (a quilted tunic), an iron cap, and a lance. Those worth 10 marks in chattels and rents were to be better accoutred, and those worth 16 marks were to equip themselves as knights. All knights were to fit themselves out correctly, and those responsible for a quota of knights were to keep harness for the men they had not enfeoffed. Local juries of knights and other freemen, under the supervision of itinerant justices, were to enforce the plan; and all whom the order concerned were to take an oath of fealty to the king and be prepared to serve his cause. The effect of the assize is unknown. Equipment had become expensive: a knight's charger (*dextrarius*), for instance, costing some £10. But the very restatement of military duty in a financial idiom was important. The count of Flanders and the king of France imitated Henry immediately; and Henry III of England was to revise his grandfather's enactment. Once more it had been recognized that every freeman, irrespective of his tenure, had the duty to fight for the king.

This general military obligation was founded on the direct allegiance which all Englishmen owed their king. Henry II restored the practice of William I and his sons of taking oaths of allegiance from as many men as he could outside the circle of the tenants-in-chief. One of the purposes of the inquiry into knight-service in 1166 was to make sure that all the knights enfeoffed on the honours had done homage to the king. By the Assize of Clarendon of the same year all men were to swear to keep the peace; and by the Assize of Northampton (1176) not only peace-oaths but also oaths of allegiance to the king were to be taken by all men, even rustics, in the shire courts. Henry II's sons continued the policy. And the law of England became that every subject of the king must swear allegiance to him and swear to keep his peace. Thus to replace the feudal loyalties, which had become perplexingly involved, the king was offering a simple loyalty to his person. The new relationship was in the same form as the old. Men swore fealty, not obedience, to the king; and fealty was always a contract obliging both lord and vassal. In this way the English kingdom, while growing out of its feudal phase, preserved one of the greatest virtues of feudalism: the insistence on a code of mutual rights and duties which could be disregarded by either party only at its peril.

In his quest for the recovery of his rights Henry II was forced to refashion many of the obligations he reimposed. His rights over the church, his rights over the barons, his judicial and military rights, all suffered change, either because Henry willed it or because he was forced to compromise with rival powers. Hence Henry's reforming activity both secured the basic continuity of English institutions and gave them a new beginning and often a different direction of advance. It also gave rise to a more exact record. As an imposer of *ius scriptum* Henry II can compare with William I. None of his records can by itself rival Domesday Book; but the Constitutions of Clarendon of 1164, the collection of returns to the inquiry into knight-service of 1166, and the Assize of Woodstock of 1184, in which the customs of the royal forest were for the first time committed to writing, form an impressive whole; and, if taken with the historical and technical works of the reign, reveal the new dominance of the written word. It was in Henry's busy court, especially under the justiciar at the exchequer, that clerks learned to appreciate routine and precedent; and the new records of the royal government which seem to begin in his reign and which took more regular shape under his sons are a memorial to this training.

IV

Because of Henry's intelligent direction his reign marks more the start of a new epoch than the culmination of the past. But the more important changes in the economic life of the kingdom, those which were to produce the familiar thirteenth-century manor and self-governing borough, were only inchoate. The general trend from the eleventh to the fourteenth century was for the population of Europe to increase and through pressing ever heavier on the land under cultivation to cause rents to rise, and also, of course, to stimulate the reclamation of waste, fen, and forest. But for a century at least after the Norman conquest, while the aristocracy was pre-occupied with war, estates were still organized on the traditional subsistence pattern with customary services and payments producing stable 'farms'. In the firm peace of the Angevins, however, with the security of the empire entrusted increasingly to professional soldiers, the English landed class began to turn its attention to rational estate management. Prices were rising—in the 1180's plough beasts rose from 3s. to 4s. or 5s. and sheep from 4d. to 6d.—farming was profitable; and there began a century and a half in which the large landowners through a professional staff (seneschal, travelling auditors and bailiffs, and their clerks) pursued that high farming which made the thirteenth century the most buoyant epoch of the Middle Ages. With the new drive and efficiency and through reorganization the rising profits from tillage and grazing were appropriated by the lords; and the tenants, rack-rented and intelligently directed by centralized bodies which loved uniformity, constrained to new terms and sometimes to renewed labour, gained little as a class from the novel agricultural prosperity.

Another factor, too, worked to encourage domanial exploitation. It was towards the end of the twelfth century that the water-driven cloth-fulling mill was introduced into England, perhaps by the Templars; and in hilly districts the fulling mill began to take its place with the lord's corn mill and oven as a profitable seignorial monopoly. Hence it seems that the clothing industry began to escape from the towns on the plains, where hitherto it had flourished, as at York, Beverley, Lincoln, Louth, Stamford, and Northampton, and take root in the West Riding of Yorkshire, the Lake District, Cornwall, Devon, Somerset, the Cotswolds, Wiltshire, and the Kennet valley. Nor was this an isolated feature. In 1204 the sheriff could buy 4,000 plates and 500 cups in Staffordshire for the king's Christmas feast at Tewkesbury. Some landlords, therefore, were on the way to becoming petty industrialists as well as corn and wool growers for the market.

But if the towns began to lose some of their industrial pre-eminence there was ample compensation in the growth of trade. Henry's acquisition of Guienne stimulated the west-country ports. The industrial centres of Flanders depended on English wool and welcomed grain from the fertile East Anglian and Kentish fields. Barren Norway took corn. There was a European demand for English metals. England had a most favourable balance of trade; and silver flowed in with the wine and other luxuries. The English towns, as local commodity and money markets and, especially, as the site of fairs, profited from the commercial boom. Typical of this phase of their development is the merchant gild, an association of burgesses sworn to protect and share the trading privileges of the borough.

Towns were attracting settlers from the free peasantry of the hinterland; and it was not unusual for the more fortunate of these to retire to new and better estates in the country. Jews, on the other hand, could have no place in feudal society. But as they could practise usury, which was forbidden to Christians, they had a useful urban occupation. In England the Jews were a royal monopoly. The king protected and exploited them, and controlled their movements. Segregated in the ghettos, pursuing a leisurely business, and intensely religious, Jews lived a more intellectual life than most of their contemporaries. In every Jewry was a master, a Rabbi, usually a rich businessman, for a professional rabbinate had not yet emerged, who taught the Talmudical students; and several eminent Jewish scholars are known to have visited England in Henry II's reign. In 1158 the greatest, most versatile, most encyclopædic Jew of the time, the Spaniard, Abraham ibn Ezra, visited London, where the Rabbi was Joseph, son of Joseph of Moreilles in the Vendée, and wrote a book there. In 1189 Rabbi Jacob of Orleans, one of the most erudite Talmudists of the day, was caught in the London massacre, and in the next year Rabbi Yom-Tob of Joigny, a versifier and biblical commentator, fell in the carnage at York. It is also possible that Berechiah ben Natronai haNakdan, author of the famous Fox Fables (Mishle Shualim), translator into Hebrew of Adelard of Bath's *Quaestiones naturales*, and composer of a lapidary, lived for a time at Oxford. But, even more than the monks, the Jews lived apart, and their world, a private world touching all the European centres of trade, made little real impact on Gentile society.

Jews were more isolated in backward England than in most European countries; and it is only from the middle of the twelfth century that a slight weakening of the barriers can be discerned. The predominant interest among Christian biblical students in the Old Testament led some scholars to consult Jewish masters. Andrew of St. Victor, in Stephen's reign abbot of the Victorine cell at Wigmore (Herefords.) and possibly an Englishman, led the way; and an indubitable Englishman, Herbert of Bosham, secretary and biographer of Archbishop Thomas Becket, imitated him. Herbert was a competent Hebraist and wrote a commentary on the Psalter. Moreover, in the later twelfth century some Jews were employed at the exchequer and a few were used by bishops and abbots as stew-

ards. But this amelioration in their standing was probably a misfortune for the Jews in the end, for the reaction was drastic. New
Crusading ideals, a greater attempt at Christian practice, and the too
ruthless milking of Jewish wealth had transformed them by the
end of the thirteenth century into undesirable aliens.

In the period of toleration the Jews amassed the liquid wealth
which not only allowed kings and nobles and prelates to realize
their landed assets but also made possible many capital developments,
such as building. It was Jewish money which enabled several of the
English Cistercian houses to turn forest and moor into sheep runs.
The part they played in the financing of English trade is, however,
obscure. Yet vast fortunes could be made from trade at this time, as
can be seen from the career of a Christian usurer, William Cade, who
died in England about 1166.

Cade, a Fleming, possibly of St. Omer, was owed some £5,000
when his assets escheated to the crown on his death. His principal
debtors were in the centres of the wool trade: in England, in Essex,
London, Lincolnshire, Yorkshire, Northamptonshire, Cambridgeshire, and Norfolk; and in Flanders mainly in Ghent. It is clear that
Cade was financing this Anglo-Flemish trade—possibly in the main
by advancing money to the growers—and using his profits to lend
to the king and other leading men. In the first ten years of Henry's
reign he lent the king on the average over £600 a year in anticipation of the exchequer renders; and after Cade's death Henry had to
turn to the Jews. Cade cannot have been an isolated phenomenon.
Trade was bringing wealth to the towns. But the increased prosperity did not immediately allow the boroughs to buy greater privileges. Henry II offered no more than his predecessors in the way of
autonomy; and it was his sons, more needy and, perhaps, under
greater pressure, who began to grant by charter those rights of self-
government which transformed the boroughs into little republics.

V

The ramifications of Jewry and the rise of a great Anglo-Flemish
financier are signs of a more settled age. Never since the Roman
Empire and never again, perhaps, until the eighteenth century was
western Europe more open than in the second half of the twelfth
century. Many of the greater barons still held lands on both sides of
the Channel, and in chivalry had arisen a culture common to all
French-speaking knights. Clerks studied a standard curriculum.

Although the schools at Oxford and Northampton were acquiring a local importance—and, indeed, the Oxford schools seem to have been recognized in Henry's reign as a *studium generale*, a university—it was to Paris, Tours, and Bologna that the ambitious English and Norman clerk went for preference. Latin-speaking clerks were at home everywhere in a church which was losing its provincial peculiarities, and several Englishmen obtained bishoprics abroad. The closest ties were between the French-speaking countries—England, France, Sicily, and Jerusalem; and Henry II, as head of the house of Anjou the expected patron of the Crusading movement, had an exalted position in this Latin world. The Teutonic people were apart, distinct in language and habits and often schismatic in religion. Yet England was already the link between the northern and Mediterranean cultures. Henry's political connexions with the Empire were always intimate, and when he married his daughter Matilda to Henry the Lion, duke of Saxony and Bavaria, an alliance of some moment was created. The Scandinavian powers, Norway and even Sweden, kept in touch with the English king. Indeed, Henry's court was the centre of an intense diplomatic activity. His couriers were on all the European routes, and his confidential agents, men like Richard of Ilchester and John of Oxford, were familiar in every important court. Europe had suddenly become much smaller.

The king himself, no Englishman, yet no Norman or Angevin, was a typical cosmopolitan of a cosmopolitan age. His tutor, William of Conches, in dedicating his *Dragmaticon* to Geoffrey of Anjou, had praised that prince's care for the education of his sons; and in his treatise *De honesto et utili* William had made a collection of ethical maxims for his pupil. Henry grew into a cultured if worldly man. He seems to have been able to understand most of the languages used in his dominions and to have spoken Latin as well as French. His wife, Eleanor of Aquitaine, came from a province with the strongest tradition of secular education, and she has a controversial position in the history of European culture, for some of her reputed judgments in the, perhaps mythical, courts of love are reported in that systematic treatise on *courtoisie*, Andrew the Chaplain's *Tractatus de amore et de amoris remedio*, written between 1174 and 1182. But there is no evidence that Eleanor influenced the tone of her husband's court: the king was busy, and after 1164 was estranged from his wife. Yet Eleanor never lost her hold over her sons. From 1170 until her imprisonment after the 1173 rebellion she held court at Poitiers for her son Richard, who had been recognized in 1169 as count of Poitou and duke of Aquitaine, and there in the company of her female relations and dependants she may well have formed a sophisticated coterie, and so, directly or indirectly, influenced her sons.

By this time the phrase *rex illiteratus asinus coronatus*—an unlettered king is a crowned ass—had become proverbial, and most of Henry's sons spent some time at school. The young Henry was placed in Becket's household until the primate's disgrace; but there, it is thought, he learned more of jousting than of books. Among the younger sons Richard and John were well educated. Both could read and write. Richard is credited with composing *sirventes* in the Poitevin manner and with making jokes in Latin; and John built up a royal library. But the most elaborate education was bestowed on the one least ready to receive it, Henry's eldest bastard, Geoffrey fitzRoy, who was destined for the church, and, indeed, became in the end, and much against his will, archbishop of York. Geoffrey went to school at Northampton and Tours; and he might easily have become a great patron had he not been so difficult and so unfortunate.

The results of a general higher standard in education are plain to see. What is usually called the twelfth-century renaissance was in its flood. It was a very literary age. Literate men began to take a naïve pleasure in self-expression. All centres of intellectual activity were stimulated. In England William, a canon of the Austin priory of Newburgh (Yorks.), wrote his *Historia rerum Anglicarum*, a typical product of more critical times; and history and homiletic literature were written in most monasteries. But more remarkable was the literary work of busy administrators, of the men who were transforming the governments of western Europe. The bishops had become great letter-writers, and their correspondents were widely spread. Arnulf bishop of Lisieux, the nephew and brother of exchequer clerks and himself for a time chief justiciar in Normandy and then an influential courtier, published two editions of his letters. Collections of the correspondence of Thomas Becket and of many of his contemporaries, of John of Salisbury and of Gilbert Foliot bishop of London, to name only the more famous, were made by other hands. Some of these men wrote solely in the way of business, some of them composed with an eye on posterity; but all had risen far above the standard of the grammar school.

Most of Henry's bishops after 1173 had been royal clerks; and it was natural that such a powerful and generous prince should attract brilliant men to his service. Peter of Blois, a voluminous letter-writer and pamphleteer, and Master Thomas Brown, an Englishman, a financial expert employed by Henry as his Remembrancer at the Exchequer, had experience of the Sicilian as well as of the English court. That prolific writer, Gerald of Barri (Giraldus Cambrensis), the historian of the Norman-Welsh in Ireland and author of a most readable book on the sacraments and the duties of priests—the *Gemma ecclesiastica*—was no stranger to Henry, and Walter Map, who left a collection of amusing literary pieces, *De nugis curialium* ('Concerning the Trifles of the Court'), was a royal clerk and itinerant justice. Even more praiseworthy, however, and characteristic of the new age, were the technical productions of royal clerks. Henry's treasurer, Richard fitzNeal, wrote his *Dialogus de Scaccario* to explain the working of the royal exchequer, and in his lost *Tricolumnis* kept a register of important documents. Under the inspiration of the chief justiciar, Ranulf Glanville, the law of the royal courts was recorded and discussed for the first time in the *Tractatus de legibus et consuetudinibus regni Angliae*. And Roger, parson of Howden, a king's clerk who served as a justice of the forest and who later accompanied Richard I on his Crusade, produced—if the anonymous *Gesta regis Henrici secundi Benedicti abbatis*, as well as the better authenticated *Chronica*, can be attributed to him—an authoritative and documented presentation of European history as seen from the Angevin court which did credit to the government in which he had his small place. The king's court had become one of the best schools in the land.

The new vulnerability of England to foreign influence led, of course, to rapid changes in fashion. English ecclesiastical architecture provides a good example. Anglo-Norman romanesque, which in the eleventh century had been simple and plain, burst into flower in the twelfth. Arcading of intersected blind arches decorated walls; doorways, surmounted by elaborate tympana, were packed with carvings, usually disposed in medallions, or were picked out in rich patterns: chevron and lozenge, disk and rosette, chain and cable, and the more savage beak-head. The 'English' cubical cushion capital was scalloped, fluted, or gadrooned, or elaborately carved. Floors were tiled in mosaic pattern and the walls were painted in a

fine style derived from the art of manuscript illumination. Into this
florid magnificence had been introduced here and there some new
alien features. The Cistercians had popularized the pointed arch and
the ribbed vault. But the Anglo-Norman style was still developing
when it fell suddenly from fashion. In the first half of the twelfth
century in the Île de France a new 'Gothic' style had been evolved,
with pointed arches, ribbed vaulting, and, most characteristic, the
buttress used to transmit thrust. The flying buttress was an engineering invention of major importance, for it allowed pillars and
walls to be reduced in weight and bulk, and permitted, when fully
developed, those caskets glowing with stained glass to be suspended
within an intricate framework of stone. By 1171 Bishop Arnulf had
begun to rebuild his cathedral at Lisieux in the new style with help
from Noyon. In 1174 Canterbury cathedral was burned down, and
the French architect, William of Sens, took his inspiration from his
native church. By the end of the century the great English romanesque tradition was destroyed and a style of the purest French extraction had taken its place.

The only outlandish thread which managed to get woven into
this polite French civilization was the Celtic. Between 1130 and 1138
Geoffrey of Monmouth had invented a British history from which
the French romancers were to take the story of Arthur. Under the
Angevins Gerald of Barri ruined his career, and sacrified a royal
pension, for the sake of a Welsh archbishopric and wrote of the
mysteries of Wales and Ireland, while Walter Map, another from the
Celtic fringe, told stories from Welsh folklore. And there ran
through the Angevin empire the strange excitement of Merlin's
prophecy, that 'The mountain-ox will collect the herds of the
Albani and of Cambria, which will drink dry the River Thames',
that 'Wales will call Brittany and join with Scotland; there will be
bloody slaughter of the foreigners; the hills of Armorica will burst
out; the crown of Brutus will be restored; Wales will be glad and
Cornwall flourish; . . . the Bretons will be felt even in France.'

English culture was still disparaged. The Old-English chronicle
was no longer written. Even the old phrases of the law were losing
their magic. In Henry's reign Denis Pyramus, a monk of Bury St.
Edmund's, wrote a life of the convent's patron saint in French
verse, translating from the English and Latin sources so that all,
both great and small, could understand. Normans and English had
by this time so intermarried that only in the highest and the basest

society were pure strains still to be found. And this hybrid society imitated its betters. The French tongue was the real solvent of provincialisms.

Yet underneath the surface the vernacular tradition was moving again. Before the end of Henry's reign Glastonbury abbey had 'discovered' the bodies of Arthur and Guinevere, neatly labelled in their graves, and claimed to be Avalon. In John's reign Layamon, a Worcestershire priest, rewrote Wace's *Brut*, a French poem based on Geoffrey of Monmouth's *Historia*, in English verse. Henry, perhaps the most foreign king of England since William I, refashioned the country's plastic institutions so skilfully that in restoring he built anew; and by reopening the land to new and powerful streams of continental influence he made possible its transformation. But his restoration of the kingdom, and with it the spirit and genius of its people, was to prove no less momentous. Within the ephemeral Angevin empire the *regnum Angliae* was beginning to live again.

9

THE ANGEVIN EMPIRE

I

THE Angevin empire did not outlast Henry II and his sons. A personal accumulation of fiefs could be no stronger than the family which united the parts; and the domestic feuds which rent Henry's house undid its strength. In the beginning the family power seemed without measure. 'The wealth of the king of the Indians is in precious stones, lions, pards, and elephants. The emperor of Constantinople and the king of Sicily glory in gold and silk, only their men are empty boasters. The emperor of the Germans has many soldiers but no riches or splendour, for Charlemagne gave it all to the church. But your king', said Louis VII of France to Walter Map, 'the lord of England, who wants for nothing, has men and horses, gold and silk and jewels, and fruits, game, and everything else, while we in France have nothing but bread and wine and gaiety.'

Yet, according to contemporaries, there was a canker in the Angevin tree. Gerald of Barri in a savage ⌐⌐pter of his *De principis instructione* (On the education of princes) laid bare the worm. Henry fitzEmpress, he observed, was of rotten stock bred from a witch. He had married a bigamist who had been his father's mistress. He had debauched his son's betrothed. Like his father he had oppressed the church. Small wonder that his son, Richard I, jested that from the devil they came and to the devil they would return. So wrote the moralist reflecting on the misery and misfortune of the proud. And even the great king himself, as though oppressed by the doom, uttered wild blasphemies while his cruel son hunted him to his death. But the problem of keeping adult sons in a long and contented pupillage—familiar to all hereditary societies—was especially acute at a time when men were still undisciplined and passionate; and of Henry's Norman predecessors only the insecure and lovable Stephen had held the affection of his wife and children. Family discord was a commonplace of the age.

The size of the Angevin empire taxed even Henry II's strength. Administrative machinery was still too primitive and the experiments towards a centralized bureaucracy too untried for the king to regard his empire as a unity to be transmitted undivided to a single heir. That Richard inherited the whole was due to the death of his elder brother, the young Henry, and that John took all on Richard's death was even more fortuitous. Henry II's original intention was that his heir, Henry, should succeed to the paternal lands—England, Normandy, and Anjou—and that his second son, Richard, should have his mother's duchy, Aquitaine. For the others, Geoffrey and then John, heiresses had to be found.

Henry made provision for his sons as early as he could. He intended to do better than his grandfather and Stephen. Richard was invested with Aquitaine in 1167. On 7 January 1169, when the young Henry was almost 14 and Richard 12, the boys did homage for their fiefs to Louis of France. In 1170 the young Henry was crowned king of England and in 1172 Richard was installed as duke at Poitiers, in a specially devised 'coronation' ceremony. An heiress was found for Geoffrey in 1166. It was agreed with the youthful Conan IV of Brittany and earl of Richmond, whose county, disrupted by faction, was being eroded at both ends by Henry, that the seven-year-old Geoffrey should marry his only daughter, Constance, if the church would dispense with their kinship. John was born in October 1165, the last child of the marriage and the dearest to his father and second only to Richard in his mother's affection. In 1171 the king, bewildered after Becket's murder, found refuge in Ireland—a country which might serve eventually as an appanage for John, and whose subjugation and reform might be an agreeable offering to the pope. Already, in 1155, Henry had planned the conquest of Ireland under the papal banner. By 1171 Norman adventurers from Wales were repeating in the western isle the story of Apulia. An independent feudal power in Ireland could be dangerous. Henry decided to intervene and reap the harvest.

Ireland was a poor country. The Romans had left it alone. The Germanic hordes had not troubled it. Only the Scandinavians had found it tempting and had colonized the coastal areas and built trading towns at Dublin, Waterford, Wexford, Cork, and Limerick. But the Norse, as was their wont, had intermarried with the natives, accepted much of the local culture, and shown little political ambition. Nevertheless, since they were traders and seamen, they had brought some disturbing influences into this backwater of Europe. Ireland, with a damp and mild climate, was a pastoral country. Wealth was counted in terms of men, cows, and precious objects; and even in the twelfth century no coins were struck except in the Ostmen towns of Dublin and Waterford. A sheltered position and a passion for history and law had worked to preserve an archaic way of life. The social organization was tribal, the spirit of the lords heroic. Amid the general anarchy seven kings ruled uneasily over many under-kings according to elaborate rules, and disputed for the almost empty honour of being High King of Erin. The tribal leaders, rich in cows and men, fought unceasingly among themselves; and, isolated from the feudal battlefields of Europe, they fought unarmoured and with primitive weapons. In the twelfth century the dominant kings aped the style of the English court; but Anglo-Norman influence had no more than touched the surface. Yet there was one institution in Ireland inherently susceptible to outside influence. Its church had been as archaic as its aristocracy. But the Irish-Norse of the towns had since 1066 looked to Canterbury for bishops and spiritual guidance; and it was not long before there were native clerks ashamed of Irish peculiarities and disgusted with the loose morals of their compatriots. The pope was approached, Bernard of Clairvaux showed interest, and by 1152, when a reforming synod met at Kells to greet the papal legate, John Paparo, the old Celtic church, tribal and monastic, with all power concentrated in the hands of the abbots, was under heavy attack. At Kells a territorial government for the Irish church on the usual western pattern was decreed. Thirty-six dioceses were subordinated to four provinces—Armagh, Cashel, Tuam, and Dublin—and Armagh was to have the primacy. And this plan of reform was fatal to the political independence of Ireland. The reformers were insecure; the new Cistercian foundations were in an alien and hostile world. They needed the comforting support of a reliable High King. In 1171 Henry II came to Ireland as though in answer to their prayers.

Norman intervention in Ireland was not to be expected while England, Scotland, and Wales offered fields for adventure; and it was not until the peacefulness and stability of Henry II's reign that restless men were ready to push further into the West. The political state of Ireland at this time was in no way unusual. On the death in 1156 of Turloch O'Connor, king of Connaught and High King, Murchertach MacLochlainn, king of Tyrone, had fought his way to titular supremacy with the aid of Dermot MacMurrough, king of Leinster. Both had raised the normal host of enemies in their ruthless climb to power, and in 1166 Rory O'Connor, the son of Turloch, with the help of Tighernan O'Ruairc, king of Tefni, whose wife Dermot had abducted in 1152, won the high kingship from Murchertach. O'Ruairc then marched against Dermot to settle old scores, and Dermot, instead of accepting his fate, sailed on 1 August 1166 to Bristol with his daughter Aoife intending to interest King Henry II in his cause.

The persistence which Dermot showed in tracking Henry to Aquitaine is proof enough that he was aware of the king's interest in Ireland and of the old papal authorization. But Henry was still occupied with continental problems, and all he could offer Dermot was permission to recruit soldiers within his dominions. Dermot, therefore, returned to South Wales and enlisted allies and captains. Richard fitzGilbert (of Clare), earl of Pembroke, known as 'Strongbow', was offered Dermot's daughter and the succession to Leinster, and, while the earl sought the king's licence to accept, subordinate leaders were engaged from among the Cambro-Normans and Flemings. In August 1167 Dermot returned to Leinster with a Flemish vanguard under Richard fitzGodebert. In 1169 Robert fitzStephen and Maurice fitzGerald—sons of Nesta, daughter of Rhys ap Tewdwr, last king of South Wales, by different Norman husbands—Stephen constable of Cardigan and Gerald of Windsor castellan of Pembroke—together with other knights from Wales and their troops, joined him. And on 23 August 1170 Earl Richard himself landed at Waterford with 200 knights and 1,000 men-at-arms.

The force that Dermot had assembled, although tiny, was capable of winning a kingdom against a disorganized and ill-equipped opposition; and the reckless adventurers wasted no time. From Waterford, where Earl Richard married Aoife, Dublin was attacked and captured (21 September 1170), despite the intervention of the High King Rory and his friend Tighernan; and to Dublin the Normans held grimly throughout 1171 although troubled by Henry II's embargo on shipping and his order that all his vassals should return before Easter, weakened by the death of Dermot on 1 May, and tested almost beyond endurance by a massive counter-attack launched by the Irish and their Viking auxiliaries in the summer. By the autumn the army of the High King had been destroyed. The adventurers had established a firm base and had discredited the native rulers.

But their overlord had been no less alarmed. The scope of the enterprise had exceeded his expectations. Already Henry was distraining on the English lands and chattels of those who had disregarded his order, and on 17 October he landed near Waterford with a substantial army, not as a reinforcement to his disobedient men but as a king requiring the submission of all powers in Ireland, whether native, Norse, or Norman. So had his predecessors behaved in England and then in Wales; and, indeed, no other course was to be expected of Henry. His only interest was in prestige and in appearing as a crusader and a pacifier; and it would have been dangerous beyond measure for him to allow the Welsh barons to establish a remote and independent base. Henry, therefore, balanced the Irish against the Normans and one baron against another. Most of the Irish kings submitted and did homage, for they required Henry's protection against the ruthless invaders. Earl Richard, precarious in Ireland and with his English earldom in peril, could do no other than accept Henry's terms. He took the land of Leinster as a barony to be held of the English king for the service of 100 knights and allowed the king to reserve for himself an ample demesne and the more important towns—Dublin, Waterford, and Wexford. Henry garrisoned the towns and granted Dublin to the burgesses of Bristol with the same privileges as they had at home. A visitor with the king, Hugh of Lacy, lord of Ludlow, was made warden of Dublin and chief justiciar of Ireland, and then given Meath to be held as an earldom for the service of 50 knights. On 17 April 1172 Henry left Ireland in haste, having heard that papal legates had arrived in Normandy to give him absolution for his part in the murder of Becket.

Henry had, perhaps, done as well as he could in his fleeting holiday from continental cares. The trip had served its purpose, and the king had arranged matters to suit his convenience. The real profit lay in the flattering acceptance he had received from the Irish church. Under his auspices a synod had been held at Cashel in the winter of 1171–2 at which reforming canons had been decreed, including the provision that mass was to be celebrated according to the English usage. And so it was as a pious reformer, as a man who had won another church for Rome, that Henry could meet the papal legates. PopeAlexander III appreciated Henry's work. In September 1172 he confirmed Henry's lordship over Ireland. The scheme that Adrian IV had blessed had been compassed in a strange and unexpected way.

II

From 1154 until 1173 the Angevin empire was relatively peaceful. In 1159 Henry had tried to secure Toulouse, from 1166 to 1171 he skirmished against his overlord, King Louis VII, while he reaffirmed his borders, and always he had to be on the alert against rebellious barons; but the preponderant military power in his hands and his generally defensive purpose limited the scale of warfare. Henry's strength lay in the barrels of silver pennies which his efficient government provided. With these he hired mercenary armies, against which no feudal troop could stand, and organized a siege train capable of reducing quickly the ordinary castle. His soldiers were drawn from all quarters. A cosmopolitan group of engineers and artillerymen built and worked the mangonels or siege-engines, the catapults, the ballista, and the new trebuchet, with which fortresses were battered into surrender. Crossbowmen, valuable as garrison troops and useful for covering an assault, were recruited mainly from south and east Europe. The rank and file of the infantry pikemen were drawn from the Low Countries, from Spain, and, after 1166, from Wales and its borders. And as a monstrous fringe to the more reputable forces were the *routiers*, that nomadic, denationalized scum, called at the time Brabançons or Cotteraux, who flocked to the standard of any martial prince and thereafter terrified his foes and his friends alike. Feudal cavalry, although no longer required in bulk, still had its place in such an army. The leaders needed mounted escorts, the columns of foot protection on the march; while horsemen were indispensable for skirmishes, raids, and scouting. Moreover, it was from the knights that the king chose his subaltern officers to command the foot. The knight had risen in military as well as in social status.

The Anglo-Danish kings had kept mercenary soldiers; William I had recruited them for his invasion of England; William's sons had employed them in their continental wars; Stephen had brought them into England; but their habitual and specialized use by Henry II

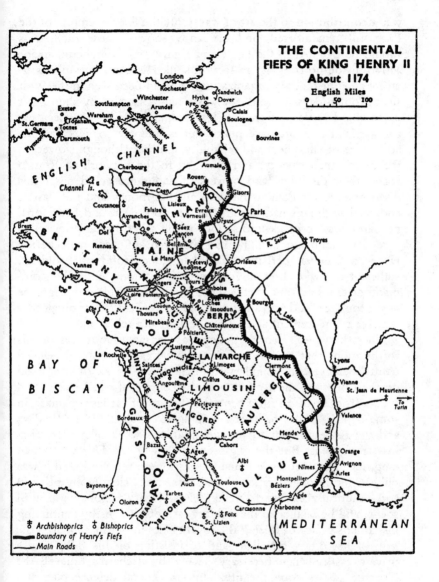

THE CONTINENTAL
FIEFS OF KING HENRY II
About 1174

English Miles
0   50   100

ENGLISH CHANNEL

London
Rochester
Sandwich
Dover
Hythe
Rye
Hastings
Winchelsea
Calais
Boulogne

Winchester
Southampton
Arundel

Exeter
Topsham
Wareham

St.Germans
Totnes
Dartmouth
Plymouth

Bouvines

Cherbourg
Eu
Aumale
Channel Is.
Rouen
Gisors
Bayeux
Caen
Coutances
Lisieux
Falaise
Evreux
Paris
Avranches
Verneuil
Dol
Séez
Alençon
Dreux
Chartres
Troyes
R. Seine
Brest
Bellême
NORMANDY
Rennes
MAINE
Le Mans
BRITTANY
Orléans
Vannes
Loir
Fréteval
Vendôme
Angers
Blois
Tours
Amboise
Nantes
Loire
Fontevrault
Chinon
Loches
Bourges
Loudun
Issoudun
Thouars
Châteauroux
R. Loire
Mirebeau
BERRY
Poitiers
POITOU
Lusignan
Lyons
LA MARCHE
Vienne
La Rochelle
Limoges
Clermont
St. Jean de Maurienne
Saintes
ANGOUMOIS
Châlus
To Turin
AQUITAINE
SAINTONGE
Angoulême
LIMOUSIN
AUVERGNE
Valence
BAY OF
Périgueux
BISCAY
PERIGORD
Bordeaux
R. Lot
Mende
GASCONY
Bazas
Cahors
R. Rhône
Orange
AGENOIS
Agen
Avignon
R. Garonne
Albi
Nîmes
Arles
Bayonne
Auch
Toulouse
TOULOUSE
Montpellier
Béziers
Oloron
Tarbes
Agde
BEARN
Foix
Carcassonne
Narbonne
BIGORRE
St. Lizien
MEDITERRANEAN
SEA

☥ Archbishoprics   ☥ Bishoprics
━━ Boundary of Henry's Fiefs
── Main Roads

was a contribution to the art of war. Only the Roman empire of the East still remembered, and brilliantly showed, how such arms should be handled in the field; and Henry, who fought no major action, made no progress in tactical skill. His contribution was to create a better military organization than had been seen in the West since Roman days. He did not waste feudal cavalry by shutting it up to guard castles. He showed his sons, and also his enemies, that for garrison and ordinary police duties infantry soldiers had the advantage of cheapness and reliability and that although slower on the march than cavalry, and confined to the network of Roman roads, their discipline and powers of endurance could offset this disadvantage. He demonstrated to all that money and not vassals endowed with fiefs had become the key to power; and henceforth no baron was to break into serious revolt and no rival prince plan a regular campaign until he had recruited sufficient mercenaries. Henry had never, perhaps, more than 6,000 professional soldiers, sufficient to make three or four tactical divisions, under his command at any one time; yet, except in his last bitter campaign, he never fought at a disadvantage. Royal power had at last obtained a decisive reinforcement against disaffection and rebellion.

Since, however, Henry's policy was conservative it was on his fortifications that he lavished the greatest care. Normandy lacked natural defences. Its boundary from Eu on the Bresle to Pontorson on the Couesnon mostly followed the courses of small rivers; and such a frontier called for a protective screen of castles organized in some depth. Castles had been built in stone since Henry I's day; and the Angevin resumed his grandfather's work of modernizing his strongholds. But the engineering skill of the Eastern Roman empire had not yet made much impression on the West, and it was only in the next generation that castles were scientifically planned and beautifully executed. Nevertheless, Henry's money was well spent; and he facilitated the military task of his sons by continuing his father's policy of freeing the royal castles in Normandy from the grip of hereditary castellans and of insisting on his right to use private castles when necessary. Hence by Richard's time all the Norman castles could be fitted into a general defence plan and castellans could be changed as easily as sheriffs and bailiffs. Henry II, without being in any way a military genius, was able to bequeath to his sons a healthy position. He had organized an administration to produce the necessary money; he had introduced a soundly organized field army; he had kept his fortifications in order and assembled valuable garrison troops; and by his assizes of arms he had widened the areas from which foot soldiers could be recruited.

At the beginning of 1173 Henry was at the height of his power. The errant border fiefs, the Norman Vexin, Berry, and Auvergne, had been recovered; and when Raymond V of Toulouse met him in the marches of Gascony and did homage for his county to the king, his heir, and Richard duke of Aquitaine, Henry's territorial claims had at last been satisfied. The Angevin empire had reached its greatest extent. The rule of such a vast territory gave Henry a commensurate influence outside. The Angevin followed the traditional Anglo-Norman policy of making friends to the north. Money fiefs had been granted in 1163 to Thierry of Alsace, count of Flanders, who had appointed Henry in 1157 guardian of his fief and his heir Philip while he visited Jerusalem (500 marks), and to many of his barons and castellans, and in 1172 to Baldwin, count of Hainault (100 marks) and six of his barons. All had the service of providing Henry with stipendiary knights, especially against the king of France. In 1168, again in imitation of his grandfather, Henry had married his eldest daughter, Matilda, to Henry the Lion, duke of Saxony and Bavaria. But his possession of Aquitaine gave him a preponderant and largely novel interest in the south. Englishmen were in positions of trust in Portugal. Marriages had been arranged between Henry's daughters Eleanor and Joan and the kings of Castile and Sicily. Since 1169 Henry had been subventing the communes of the Lombard League in revolt against the Emperor Frederick Barbarossa. And early in 1173 Count Humbert III of Maurienne and Savoy agreed to marry his heiress, Alice, to Henry's youngest son, John, and to give a dowry in the Alps and Rousillon.

This net of alliances looks menacing. If it had been purposely spun it would seem to prepare for an intervention in Italy, presumably in concert with a Welf attack on the Hohenstaufen emperor in Germany. But Henry, who had so cautiously abandoned his attack on Toulouse in 1159, was no military adventurer; and once his feudal claims in France had been satisfied he never made a hostile attack on his overlord. The alliances cannot, therefore, be considered a preparation for war. They enhanced Henry's importance, strengthened his hold on Toulouse, gave promise of casual territorial gain, and served a diplomatic purpose in threatening the king of France and the Roman emperor and in easing the position of Pope Alexander III. And Henry found even these modest aims difficult to maintain. By the spring of 1173 he seemed to be fighting for very existence.

III

The great rebellion of 1173–4 arose out of the marriage treaty with the count of Maurienne. Humbert asked that his future son-in-law should be fittingly endowed. Henry decided to give John the three castles in Anjou which had been his brother Geoffrey's appanage: Chinon, Mirebeau, and Loudun. But the young Henry, titular king of England, duke of Normandy, and count of Anjou, who possessed not a single castle, objected to the scheme, demanded the effective government of his inheritance, and, when denied, escaped in March 1173 to France. His mother, Eleanor of Aquitaine, sent his brothers, Richard and Geoffrey, to join him; but she herself was captured and put in prison. Louis VII took his son-in-law under his protection and rallied his vassals to the boy's cause. The young Henry made extravagant promises of money and lands to French barons, especially to Philip count of Flanders and Theobald count of Blois; and to the pope and the church he addressed a manifesto in which he both denounced his father's tyranny and promised reform. The signal had been given for a general insurrection. Twenty years of strong government had created an unbearable tension. Outwitted rivals, repressed vassals, and all those with concealed grievances threw off the yoke. Severe uprisings occurred in Gascony, Anjou, and Normandy; Brittany revolted under Ralf lord of Fougères, who had troubled Henry before; English earls who rebelled were Hugh of Cyveiliog earl of Chester, Hugh Bigod earl of Norfolk, and Robert ès Blanchemains earl of Leicester; and William the Lion king of Scots and his brother David disturbed the north of England. In June the counts of Flanders and Boulogne and the king of France invaded Normandy.

As his empire dissolved Henry kept his head. At the beginning he hunted assiduously. In the autumn his soldiers took Dol and captured Ralf de Fougères and the earl of Chester, and the king himself chased the invaders out of Normandy. Before Christmas Henry smashed the Angevin revolt and could then use the valley of the Loire as his base. Meanwhile the chief justiciar of England, Richard of Lucy, was smothering the English rebellion. On 29 September, while Lucy had been harrying Lothian, the earl of

Leicester had invaded Suffolk with Flemish mercenaries and linked up with the earl of Norfolk. On 17 October the constable, Humphrey de Bohun, with the earls of Cornwall, Gloucester, and Arundel defeated them at Fornham, near Bury St. Edmunds, and took the Leicesters prisoner. The church resisted temptation and did not desert the king. In the spring of 1174 Alexander III at last confirmed the election of Richard of Dover to Canterbury and granted him the pallium and a legation in his own province. In July Henry crossed to England and did penance at Becket's tomb. He had much to be thankful for, but could hardly have hoped that the martyr would work a miracle for his old master. Yet on 13 July, the morrow of the scourging, Robert of Estouteville, the sheriff of Yorkshire, and others of the king's friends captured the king of Scots while he besieged Alnwick. By August all the English rebels had submitted and Henry could return to the Continent. The invasion of England from Gravelines, which the count of Flanders and the young Henry were planning, could not take place.

On 22 July 1174 King Louis and the young Henry, with the help of Philip of Flanders, Hugh of Burgundy, Theobald of Blois, and Henry of Champagne, set siege to Rouen. Henry's very appearance with his army of Brabançons drove them off; and on 8 September Louis at last agreed to a truce. His timid hostility had brought him nothing but shame; and he was glad to withdraw from the conflict and leave Richard to his fate. The duke of Aquitaine was rallying his Poitevin barons; but even this young warrior could not hold out against his resurgent father, and in the third week of September he too laid down his arms. With all his enemies captives or chastened, Henry dictated terms. A family peace was made at Montlouis, between Tours and Amboise, on 30 September 1174. The king of France and the count of Flanders gave up their conquests in Normandy; and in 1175 the count was granted a larger English fief (1,000 marks). Henry forgave most of the rebels and tried to make a fair provision for his sons. The young Henry was given two Norman castles and a pension of £15,000, Richard two Poitevin castles and half the revenues of that county, and Geoffrey half the rents from the dowry of his betrothed, Constance of Brittany—and to have all after the marriage; and the youths did liege homage to their father and swore that they would be content with the settlement. Yet the king saw to it that they were punished through John. The Maurienne heiress had died, and Henry gave John in compensation the castle and shire of Nottingham and the castle of Marl-borough, two castles in Normandy, and three in Anjou, besides substantial pensions on the English and Norman exchequers. But it was more of a threat than a penalty. John was only eight years old.

The humiliating failure of this great rebellion increased Henry's outward strength. Secret enemies had stood revealed and had been struck down. Louis VII had been completely discouraged; the queen was a prisoner; the presumptuous sons had been whipped. The king was not vindictive. He had fined the rebel barons and had made some minor confiscations; he demolished their castles; he forced one Norman bishop to resign; but in general he observed his promise to forgive his enemies. He could afford to be generous, because, when the dust had cleared, it could be seen that he had never been in real peril. Nowhere had there been a popular rising; his viceroys and officials had remained loyal; and the bishops had, with a few exceptions, stood firm. His mercenaries had proved their use-fulness; and not every member of his family had deserted. His eldest and favourite bastard, Geoffrey, had been most helpful in England, and his youngest and dearest son, John, was still too young to reveal his treacherous nature. The rebellion had been a sort of blood-letting which had purged Henry's empire of some of its bad humours.

In one direction Henry had even increased his power. The captive William the Lion, king of Scots, was forced to accept stringent terms (Treaty of Falaise, December 1174). He took Scotland back as a fief; his five most important castles were to be surrendered to Henry as security for his good behaviour; and Henry reserved the right to take oaths of fealty from the Scottish clergy and homage from the Scottish laity without a reservation in favour of their king. On 10 August 1175 the ceremonies were performed at York. The king of Scots had been reduced to the position of an English earl.

IV

In the years after 1174 Henry made some changes in the adminis-tration of the empire. It had become his policy to construct a similar independent government in each major division which he could control by directives and by visits. Yet in perfecting this system, which in form owed something to Anjou, in machinery almost everything to Normandy, and in spirit much to England, little disturbance was offered to native customs. The ducal or comital **government existed above and outside ordinary provincial life. The** replacement of the duke or count by a deputy made little difference to the vassals, and the reorganization of the ducal or comital demesne was of private concern. The power of the Angevin over-lord decreased as he travelled from north to south. As king in England he was all but despotic; as duke in Normandy he was invested with a traditional and almost autonomous authority. In Anjou, however, he had inherited merely what power his bellicose father had wrested from the turbulent barons; and in Aquitaine—outside the county of Poitou, where most of the ducal demesne was concentrated—he came into nothing more substantial than a tenuous lordship over powerful mesne counties and fiefs. As ruler of the whole, Henry was stronger in each part than his predecessors had been; and so he was able to complete the work of his father in Anjou and Normandy and begin the task of consolidation in Aquitaine.

Normandy's long and intimate connexion with England had given the two a general similarity in organization, and, although the ten years' break in the union, the accession of a new dynasty, and the gradual separation of the English and Norman honours had cut some of the more vital ties, Henry's government reinforced the official uniformity. At the beginning of his rule, to please the bishops, Henry had restored the office of chief justiciar in Normandy. But the office of seneschal, exalted by his father, soon recovered ground; and Henry, by appointing some of his best servants to this post and by entrusting ever greater powers to them, trans-formed the seneschal into a viceroy similar to the chief justiciar in England. The seneschal presided over a court which transacted both judicial and financial business, and, as the king's political and military deputy, he governed the duchy subject to royal control. Norman administration can be considered in no way inferior to English. Richard of Ilchester, after his appointment as seneschal in 1176, reorganized the financial system which had suffered during the rebellion of 1173–4; and William fitzRalf, the son of a small Derbyshire landowner, seneschal from 1178 until his death in 1200, was a most able governor. Henry also reformed the local govern-ment. By 1172 the ducal demesne, which had been administered by vicomtes and prévôts, relics of the old Frankish division of the kingdom into counties, had been regrouped into bailiwicks, each dependent on a castle. Since there existed in Normandy no public territorial subdivision as vital as the English shire, Norman local government was never as simple or logical as the English. But in the old vicomte or the new bailiff can be seen the equivalent of the sheriff.

In Normandy's dependancy, the county or, as it was more frequently styled by its rulers, the duchy of Brittany, Henry revolutionized the government. Influence was exerted on the bishops; the restless and almost independent barons were brought to heel; and in 1185, when Geoffrey issued an assize introducing primogenital succession to the more important fiefs, the first comital law in the history of Brittany was promulgated. The seneschal, hitherto a purely domestic official, was remodelled on the standard Angevin pattern, and the county was divided into eight bailiwicks, each under an inferior seneschal. Angevin rule over Celtic Brittany was short in time; but its effects endured.

Henry had little trouble from the Angevin baronage and church; and he was able to organize a more regular comital government than his ancestors had possessed. He transformed the seneschal into his single lieutenant for Anjou, Touraine, and Maine, and gave him powers similar to those enjoyed by his counterpart in Normandy. The deputies of the count and seneschal, the prévôts, like the Norman bailiffs—and the prévôts seem sometimes to have been called bailiffs—administered the comital demesne from nuclear castles. Normandy and Anjou had been influencing each other; and in the second half of the twelfth century Anjou, with an integrated administration invigorated by the enhanced power of the count, could for the first time take its place alongside Normandy as a centralized fief. It is significant that during the political disturbance which followed Richard's death Anjou did not break up again, but as a whole transferred its allegiance first to Arthur and then to Philip Augustus, king of France.

In Aquitaine Henry could only attempt a more elementary task, that of reducing his vassals to obedience and of establishing the physical authority of the duke; and in this his son Richard was his tool. Aquitaine, once a kingdom, divided racially between Gascony and Poitou, loose in texture and anarchic in temperament, presented problems which, perhaps, a duke could no longer solve. The great barons, in order to preserve their independence, were quite ready to appeal from the duke to his overlord, the king of France; and once Philip Augustus was firmly established it had become impossible for the duke to act without interference. Richard used rough methods against the Aquitainian barons between 1176–8—he even penetrated the Pyrenees to seize the count of Bigorre—but the recurrent complaints that he was violating local custom revealed the political danger he was incurring. Henry introduced into Aquitaine the Norman-Angevin organization. He had his seneschal —sometimes his sons appointed more than one—to act as his lieutenant, and the seneschal had his deputies for the local administration of the ducal demesne. But since the ducal government was restricted in scope, the ducal servants were far more seignorial in character than their counterparts in the older portions of the Angevin empire.

A separate administration for each historic unit in the empire was inevitable at the time. The most obvious connecting link was the ambulatory king with his permanent officials and secretariat pursuing a general policy divorced from local patriotism and enforcing it by means of the standard writ. The king legislated for the parts or for the whole; the exchequer system was used throughout; his own itinerant court and the courts of his seneschals had a fairly uniform policy of legal interpretation; and in time a common law of limited scope might have been established by the action of the king and his agents. The interchange of royal and church officials could also help to create a sense of unity. England and Normandy were already closely tied in this way. Anjou was affected much less. In 1162 Henry had a Norman elected bishop of Angers and in 1196 Richard appointed an Englishman, Robert of Thornham, his seneschal. And Aquitaine, which was to replace Normandy as the origin of foreign careerists in England, until the loss of Normandy remained very much apart. In 1163 Henry made John of Belmeis (or of Canterbury) bishop of Poitiers and in 1196 Richard appointed his favourite nephew, the Anglo-German Otto of Brunswick, count of Poitou—solitary and disconnected examples of an imperfect centralization. Such a government as Henry II devised for his empire depended for its success on the quality of the persons with responsibility. The main burden lay on the king. Ubiquity, industry, prescience, firmness, and generosity were required of the man in whose hands all strands were gathered. And much depended on the calibre of his servants, for the seneschal needed to be loyal, steadfast, and impartial to a degree far above the standard current in those days. Henry II lacked generosity and, perhaps, foresight. Richard pursued wayward aims. John was without moral authority.

The man was still more important than the office. The task of consolidation and of creating a national spirit was immense. The very spread of royal justice stimulated rival forces, because inquests and recognitions encouraged the recording of local custom and the fixing of provincial idiosyncrasy. And the denationalized character of the overlord weakened traditional loyalties. As a rule, medieval government succeeded only when it was personal. Henry II was becoming too remote from his subjects. Compensation could be found in the formation of a myth. Henry II and Richard I enjoyed great prestige; and both gave their reputations material support by building—Henry palaces and hospitals, Richard castles. Henry's greatest works were in Anjou—the embankment along the Loire and the causeway south-west from Chinon—Richard's in the marches of Normandy. The feeling of security did not outlast the creator of the empire.

V

During the last lingering years of Louis VII, an old man with only a boy to succeed him, the Angevins pursued their ambitions without hindrance. Henry consolidated his position by making an agreement with the church, improving his administration, and picking up an occasional strategic fief or castle, as when the count of la Marche sold him his county for £15,000 in 1177; Geoffrey was occasionally sent to visit Brittany, and ruled it personally after his marriage to Constance in 1181; Richard fought against his ducal barons; and only the heir, Henry, had no useful job to do and chafed impatiently and jealously while he waited for the king to die. By 1177 the church was already planning a new Crusade for the defence of tottering Jerusalem, and when trouble between Louis VII and Henry II threatened to impede the plan the papal legate, Peter of Pavia, forced Henry under threat of interdict to make peace. On 21 September 1177 at Nonancourt, between Ivry and Verneuil, in the presence of the legate and the barons of both kings, Henry and Louis protested their amity and swore they would crusade together. Their disputes over Auvergne and Berry were to be settled by arbitrators. On 1 November 1179 Louis had his only son Philip crowned king at Rheims; and on 18 September 1180 the senior king died after a long illness.

Henry did not take advantage of the succession of a boy. In-fluence over Philip was disputed between the queen-mother's relatives of the house of Blois and Philip count of Flanders, whom both kings preferred. On 28 June 1180 Henry met King Philip near Gisors and promised him his full support; and thereafter he kept him under his protection until he grew out of it. Henry fitzEmpress was getting old; and it may be that he had become sentimental. But by his chivalrous behaviour in the last decade of his life he atoned for some of the rougher actions of his youth. Henry suffered his first great personal loss when his heir died in 1183. It is doubtful whether the young Henry would have made a good king. Destined for England, Normandy, and Anjou, he had most of the qualities of his Aquitanian ancestors: a fatal charm and a gay spirit, which attracted fools—and some wiser men despite themselves—an ungrateful and jealous nature, and a treacherous streak. In January 1183, after some recent waywardness, the young Henry renewed his fealty to his father. The king then desired Richard and Geoffrey to do homage to their elder brother. Richard refused; as duke of Aquitaine he claimed an independent position; and in the end the two other brothers, envious of Richard's position, revolted and tried to maintain themselves in Poitou. But the young Henry fell ill of dysentery at Martel, and on 11 June he died, forgiven by his father, but unapproachable.

The new heir was Richard duke of Aquitaine. His active experience of government in his duchy had given him a useful basic apprenticeship for the greater task; and had he been willing to give up Aquitaine and continue his political education with his father he might have become a great king. Henry in fact proposed to Richard that he should surrender Aquitaine to John and take the young Henry's place at his side. Richard refused. The inactivity of an heir was uncongenial, and his work in Aquitaine was only begun. Richard, a blond warrior of great physical strength, was a true Norman despite his gloss of Provençal culture. He fought the Poitevins and Gascons with their own wiles but also with a steady determination which was born of the north. He was not to be wooed from his purpose; and he brushed aside his brothers, Geoffrey and John, whom the king sent to despoil him. Richard kept Aquitaine. It was a misfortune for the empire. Engrossed in a struggle with a hydra-headed disaffection Richard became completely ignorant of the rest of his father's possessions, quite unversed in the secrets of their government, entirely indifferent to the wider strategy and diplomacy. He devoted his considerable talents to imaginative projects of his own choosing—projects, indeed, of importance by contemporary standards—and shirked the more prosaic life with which his father had been content.

John still lacked a proper inheritance. In May 1177 at Oxford, in consequence of a papal privilege to give the kingdom of Ireland to one of his sons, Henry had had John proclaimed king; and in April 1185, again taking up this plan, Henry knighted the youth and sent him to visit his dominion. Norman rule was prospering in Ireland despite the premature deaths of most of the original leaders and the king's suspicion of the planters. Earl Richard, lord of Leinster, had died in 1176 leaving young children; and Eva (Aoife), 'countess of Ireland', went to live on her English dower lands. But a new star had then risen in John of Courcy, who in 1177 set out on his intrepid conquest of Ulster. A steady flow of knights from Wales and England made possible the sub-infeudation of the honours; and the many motte and bailey castles ensured the security of the new aristocracy, while their new monasteries spread their culture. Yet the history of the Normans in England and Wales was already being repeated. The Normans were marrying into the native families. In 1180 John of Courcy married Affrica, daughter of Godred king of Man, and so allied himself with the Norse-Gaelic world; and in the same year Hugh of Lacy, earl of Meath and royal justiciar, married Rose, the daughter of Rory O'Connor, who still ruled with maimed power over the native parts of Ireland. And the Norman-Irish were soon to be *Hibernis ipsis Hiberniores*—more Irish than the Irishry. Norman adaptability had its dangers. John's visit of eight months, despite the presence of the great justiciar of England, Ranulf Glanville, his tutor, merely upset an already uneasy situation; and it lost all purpose when his elder brother, Geoffrey, died in August 1186, for John then became second in succession to the English throne. Henry dropped once more his plan of settling John in Ireland; and the golden crown set with peacock feathers, which he received in 1186 from Pope Urban III with a privilege authorizing him to have a son anointed king, seems never to have been used.

Geoffrey's death was involved with the emergence of King Philip of France as a formidable power. By 1186 the stripling had tamed the lesser barons of northern France and felt ready to challenge even the Angevin king. Henry II was failing in health and had lost his old zest. He wanted only to die in peace. But he soon learned that peace could not be bought by modest concession. Philip was intent on his ruin and cared nothing for the humiliation of his old benefactor. He had determined to destroy the Angevin empire; and his faithless, fraudulent, and mean diplomacy achieved its purpose, while robbing the achievement itself of all splendour. The tortuous and discreditable methods which Philip used were due in part to his character and his reaction from his father's well-meaning ineptitude, in part to the political situation. The church, alarmed by the peril of Jerusalem, wanted peace in the West and war in the East; the French barons had begun to fear the ambition of their young master; and Philip's financial resources were limited. He was, indeed, compelled to use underhand tricks in order to weaken this dangerous vassal; and it is only the absence of the occasional scruple, the occasional abandon, the occasional generosity which makes his behaviour so unpleasant.

The strategic key to the Angevin empire was Touraine, which Anjou had wrested from Blois by 1044. Tours on the River Loire was the great junction of western France, and the roads from le Mans through Angers and Tours to Poitiers were the vital arteries between north and south. The valley of the Loire was thickly defended by castles. Tours, Loches, Chinon, Loudun, and Angers were the great fortresses which guarded the heart of the territory; Fréteval and Vendôme on the Loir protected the left flank; and on the right were Graçay, Issoudun, Déols, and Châteauroux, all in Aquitanian Berry, screening the land between the River Cher and Poitiers. If Philip could push down the valley of the Loire he would cut the Angevin empire in two. All his warfare and diplomacy was directed to weakening the defences of Tours; and he tried to extort concessions from Henry in the Vendômois and Berry by encouraging the thwarted ambitions of Henry's sons.

Henry, however, with Richard firmly established in Aquitaine, had been giving much of his attention to German affairs, for in the autumn of 1182 his son-in-law, Henry the Lion, duke of Saxony and Bavaria, had joined him in Touraine after his banishment by the Emperor Frederick Barbarossa and the German princes. For three years Henry maintained the duke, the Duchess Matilda, their children, except the second son, Lothair, and their many dependants and used all his diplomatic skill to further their return. He fostered English relations with Flanders, arranging a second marriage between Count Philip and a daughter of the king of Portugal, and negotiated with the archbishop of Cologne and with the pope. At the end of 1184 the emperor agreed to pardon his dangerous vassal; and in the autumn of 1185 the duke and duchess went back to Germany, leaving their younger children in Henry's care. Little profit accrued to Henry from the Welf connexion. When Henry the Lion, once more an exile, returned in 1189 to his father-in-law's court, the old man was dead; and it was Richard who found a useful marriage for his niece, Eleanor, by giving her soon afterwards to Geoffrey, son and heir of Rotrou III count of Perche.

In these circumstances Philip of France allied with the Emperor Frederick and stirred up trouble within the Angevin family. In 1186 he intrigued with Henry's son, Geoffrey; but the rumoured threats were stilled when the count of Brittany died on 19 August from a tournament accident in France. Geoffrey left an only daughter, Eleanor; and the posthumous Arthur was born on 29 March of the next year. Philip then looked to Richard duke of Aquitaine. His demands on Henry were usually framed so as to tempt Richard's cupidity, yet were designed so that they could also be used against the duke when convenient. Philip had a number of basic grievances against the English king; and a selection of them could always be advanced in order to justify aggression. He resented Henry's acquisitions in eastern Berry and in Auvergne, the marches of Poitou, for these pushed into the middle of France, and his retention of the Norman Vexin, his half-sister's dowry, after the death of the young Henry. He was suspicious of Henry's long guardianship of his other half-sister, Alice, and his failure to marry her to Richard. He claimed the wardship of Eleanor of Brittany. And he complained of Richard's behaviour in the Languedoc. Perhaps the most embarrassing problem was Alice's marriage. If she had been seduced by Henry, as Richard seemed to believe and Philip to suspect, Philip's constant demand that Richard should marry her immediately and be put into possession of even more fiefs was cunningly contrived. Until 1187 Philip complained, but was not strong enough to fight. At the beginning of May 1187 he invaded over the River Cher, obtained Issoudun and Fréteval by treachery, and laid siege to Châteauroux. Henry made proposals—possibly that John should marry Alice and inherit all the French fiefs except Normandy, which should go with England to Richard; and, when Philip cynically disclosed them to Richard, Henry was glad to make the truce of Châteauroux with the invader at the expense of ceding his two flanking outposts, Issoudun on the right and Fréteval on the left.

Henry had bought an unsubstantial truce by making his first unrequited territorial surrender since he became king. It was not to be the last. Richard had ceased to trust his father, and feared what he might do for John. Moreover, Richard wanted to crusade; yet he could depend on no one to protect his interests in his absence. While the western princes plotted and bickered the True Cross was lost at Hittin (July 1187) and Jerusalem fell (October). But not even the horror which these events inspired nor the active efforts of the church for peace could smother Philip's conviction that the vital chance had come to break his old rival. True, the two kings met near Gisors in the third week of January 1188, exchanged kisses of peace, took the cross, and taxed their lands for expenses; but while they took formal action, a revolt in Aquitaine provoked a muted but deadly struggle. Richard suspected that the rebellion, in which the count of Toulouse was involved, had been instigated by his father in order to keep him at home. He hit savagely at his rebellious barons and invaded Toulouse. The count appealed to his overlord. Philip first ordered Richard to stop and then required Henry to control his son. But Henry, who was in England, was powerless; and Philip, despite all Henry's pleas and remonstrances, invaded Berry in June. By autumn, when the mounting wrath of the church at this squandering of Crusading funds in an impious cause, the reluctance of the French barons, and the exhaustion of Philip's resources, brought the French king to a temporary halt, he had conquered Berry, Auvergne, and most of Touraine, and had gained Vendôme by treachery. But he was still not ready to offer reasonable terms. When the two kings and Richard met on 18 November 1188 on the frontier of Normandy and Perche at Bonmoulins, Philip, with the secret approval of Richard, demanded that Richard should be put into possession of Touraine, Maine, and Anjou. Henry refused. Philip then offered a truce on equally unacceptable conditions: that Richard should straightway marry Alice and be recognized as his father's heir to the whole of the empire and receive the homage of all the barons. Henry prevaricated; and Richard joined Philip. The duke did homage to the French king for all the continental fiefs, being promised the return of Châteauroux and Issoudun and all Philip's conquests in Berry, and then helped his overlord in the war. In January 1189 Brittany revolted and the fiefs on the Loire fell away. By June the invaders were halted again. But a last attempt of the church to mediate failed. When the two

kings met on the border of Maine and Perche at la Ferté-Bernard
Philip's demands were as stringent as before, and he required also
that John should go on the Crusade with Richard. But Henry could
not agree to risk both his sons; so Philip and Richard invaded
Maine and uncovered le Mans, Henry's birthplace, where the old
man and Geoffrey, his bastard, sheltered. A defensive fire on 12 June
turned against the defenders and drove them out; and William the
Marshal had to unhorse Richard to save the king from the shame of
being captured by his son. That night the fugitives reached Fresnay,
almost within the protection of the Norman castles. Geoffrey wished
to hold it in order to cover his father's retreat; but Henry, with the
perversity of an old man driven too far, decided not to flee, but
instead to break south to Anjou, his real home. With a few companions he slipped through the net of his enemies and waited for
Geoffrey to rejoin him. Geoffrey led the main army towards Normandy, and then, at Alençon, he too abandoned safety, and with a
hundred chosen knights eluded Richard and Philip and made his
way back to his father at Savigny, from where they rode to Chinon.
It was a gesture. Henry would not fight.

By 30 June Philip and Richard were ready to assault Tours. Henry
asked for terms and was offered unconditional surrender. Tours fell
on 3 July; and on the next day Henry went to Colombières, between
Azay-le-Rideau and Tours, to make his submission. He was to be in
mercy and renew his homage to Philip. He was to recognize Richard
as his sole heir and cause all the barons to do homage to him. He was
to put Alice in ward to Richard's nominees until their wedding,
which was to be celebrated after the Crusade. He was to crusade
with Philip. He was to lose Auvergne and the baronies of Issoudun
and Graçay in Berry. He was to pay 20,000 marks towards Philip's
expenses. And he was to cede le Mans, Tours, Trou, and Château-
du-Loir (unless he would exchange them for the Norman border
castles) until all the articles were fulfilled. Henry was sick and
feverish. He asked only for a list of those of his men who had conspired with Philip. When the schedule was read to the king, John's
name came first. Henry had no wish but to die. He had been carried
back to Chinon by Geoffrey, and he lay there sometimes cursing
and blaspheming, sometimes talking gently with the few friends who
remained with him. The summer heat was oppressive. Geoffrey
supported the king's head and shoulders in his lap and brushed the
flies from his face. The agony was not long. On 6 July Henry died

before the altar of the church, where he had been placed. John had broken his father's heart, and Richard was the sole heir.

VI

Philip Augustus had, indeed, pushed Henry too far. A fortnight after the king's death Richard was invested as duke of Normandy at Rouen (20 July); and two days later the new duke met Philip at the Norman frontier and recovered from his confederate all their conquests except Auvergne and the baronies of Issoudun and Graçay. He had to agree to pay Philip 4,000 marks besides the 20,000 promised by his father; but the feudal relief was disguised, it seems, as an indemnity for Philip's expenses in the campaign. On 3 September Richard was crowned king of England at Westminster. The Angevin empire had passed almost intact into strong hands.

Richard Coeur-de-Lion was a great man, perhaps too great a man. Let loose as a boy in Aquitaine, where exalted ideas of individual grandeur were held, since 1183 he had gone his own arrogant and selfish way. Preferring men to women, dedicated to a chivalrous way of life, but no simple knight-errant or careless troubadour, Richard was at his finest superhuman, at his worst unpleasant and inhumane. Although pre-eminent as a soldier and engineer, he was shrewd in politics and also capable of diplomacy on the grand scale. More generous than his father, nobler, more imaginative, less careful, he bid for more glittering prizes and took far graver risks. Not as clever as Philip, more wayward, he tried by tremendous efforts to win back those advantages which in his rasher moments he gave his rival. During his short life his reputation was fabulous; and time has not greatly disturbed it.

Richard's brief stay in Western Europe was devoted entirely to preparation for his Crusade; and among the basic problems was the establishment of a government for England. The kingdom was accustomed to the absence of its king; and all that was necessary was to confirm a suitable and loyal administration. But Richard was incapable of making a simple and obvious settlement. He had been in revolt against his father and could not help breaking some of Henry's most faithful men, such as the chief justiciar of England, Ranulf Glanville; he had his own men to reward, yet dared not act too suddenly; he was so greedy for money that he could not resist selling any office to the highest bidder, often in bad faith; his ignorance of English life made his touch clumsy; and he had the awkward problem of settling two dangerous brothers while he hazarded his life far from home. If there was a principle underlying his initial arrangements it must have been the fragmentation of authority and the balancing of powers, a natural policy for one who had been educated in Aquitaine. Yet in the end the familiar pattern of government was re-established; and, although a secret thread of design may be hidden in Richard's tortuous actions, it is more likely that the habits of the English government as confirmed by Henry II were too strong to be entirely broken even by the incoherent instructions of the new king.

Four members of the royal family needed special attention: Richard's younger brother John, his elder illegitimate brother Geoffrey, his infant nephew Arthur of Brittany, and his distant cousin William the Lion king of Scots. John was at last properly endowed. Between July and December 1189 he was given the Norman county of Mortain, and in England, besides the earldom of Gloucester, which came to him when he married, without papal dispensation, the youngest of the co-heiresses, Isabella, on 29 August, the four south-western counties, Somerset, Dorset, Devon, and Cornwall, and a group of counties and honours centred on the Midlands: Nottinghamshire and Derbyshire with the honour of Peverel and the castles and honours of the Peak and Bolsover; the castle and honour of Lancaster and the Yorkshire honour of Tick-hill; the honour of Eye in Suffolk; the honour of Wallingford in Berkshire; and in Wiltshire the castles and honours of Marlborough and Ludgershall. The castles of Nottingham, Peverel, Tickhill, Gloucester, Wallingford, Eye, Exeter, Launceston, and some others were, however, retained by the king. The intention was to give John wealth and independence but restricted military and political power. Moreover, he was banished from England for three years. With the bastard brother, Geoffrey, who had been faithful to their father, Richard played cat and mouse. He allowed him to be elected archbishop of York and to buy some offices, forced him to take priest's orders so as to remove the dynastic threat, and then hindered him in every way from getting the archbishopric. Geoffrey, too, was exiled from the kingdom for three years. The king of Scots was permitted to buy for 10,000 marks release from the conditions imposed on him by the treaty of Falaise after his capture at Alnwick in 1174. Arthur was in ward with his Breton relations; and he could be used as a threat to John. Richard was still unmarried and might easily die on the Crusade. Indeed, it was widely believed that he would never return. But he had not yet named his heir.

The policy of giving at a price—and often at a crippling price—honours which were not always quite what they seemed, which dictated the family settlement, was applied to the distribution of offices. All the sheriffdoms were sold; some unwisely: Gerard of Camville, who bought the sheriffdom of Lincoln, was already castellan in the right of his wife. A loyal and trusted servant of Richard, William Longchamp, whose family had risen from humble origins through service to Henry II, was made chancellor; and the office of chief justiciar was split between two representatives of the old order, Richard's kinsman, Hugh of le Puiset, bishop of Durham, who also bought the earldom and sheriffdom of Northumberland, and Henry II's old servant, William of Mandeville, earl of Essex and count of Aumale. The intention was to balance the north against the south, with Count John holding the ring, and also to check the king of Scots with Bishop Hugh's palatinate. But on 14 November 1189 Mandeville died; and in December Longchamp was sent back to England apparently to take his place. The king's man was moving up; and it may have been Richard's intention to advance him unobtrusively. The chancellor had ability and confidence; but as a pure Norman he was insensitive to English customs and as a haughty and strident parvenu he aroused prejudice. In March, Longchamp was made superior to Bishop Hugh; and after he had arrested his colleague for exceeding his authority, Richard made him sole justiciar (6 June 1190). Richard's man had come out on top. On 31 December he had been consecrated bishop of Ely; on 5 June 1190 he was made papal legate in order to take the place of the archbishop of Canterbury who was going with Richard; and this 'monster with many heads', as Gerald of Barri called him, had concentrated more than royal powers. But he could never be more than a servant of the king; and Richard was well aware that he would find it difficult enough to keep his feet in the whirlpool of jealousy and frustration he had left behind.

VII

Richard was a sincere Crusader. But he had business to do on the way. Embarking at Marseilles on 7 August, he broke his journey at Naples and spent some weeks at Salerno before sailing into Messina. His business with the Norman kingdom of Sicily concerned the affairs of the late king, his brother-in-law, William II. The old family connexions between Sicily, Normandy, and England had been given formal recognition in 1177 when Henry II at the pope's prompting had married his daughter Joan to William; and when Henry and Philip had planned their Crusade they attached much importance to William's aid, for he had already adventured in the East, having taken Thessalonica and threatened Constantinople in 1185. But William had died childless on 18 November 1189, and in 1190 Richard was in quest of his widowed sister, her dowry, and a legacy, which, it was believed, William had left his father-in-law, ignorant that he was already dead. But the political situation was tricky. In 1186 the Emperor Frederick Barbarossa had married his son Henry (VI) to William II's aunt, Constance. But when William died unexpectedly and childless and the middle-aged Constance inherited the kingdom, Pope Clement III, more sensitive to encircle-ment than Lucius III, who had furthered the alliance, took alarm, and a Sicilian party hostile to German domination, led by Richard Palmer, an Englishman, archbishop of Messina, and the vice-chancellor, Matthew of Ajello, secured the coronation of Tancred of Lecce, an illegitimate grandson of King Roger. Any action which Richard took was bound, therefore, to have wide repercussions, and to touch especially the Welf-Hohenstaufen feud, in which he was already involved through his eldest sister's marriage to Henry the Lion.

Richard began by seizing the fortress of Bagnara and the Greek monastery of St. Saviour's *de Lingua Phari* in order to secure the straits of Messina, and then occupied Messina itself. Tancred was obliged to buy him off. On 6 October 1190 the two princes made a treaty of alliance. Richard would take his sister back with 20,000 oz. of gold in place of her dowry; he would accept an equal sum in clearance of his other claims and for the marriage of his nephew, Arthur of Brittany, whom he recognized as his heir presumptive, to a daughter of Tancred, and this money he would settle on the girl; and he would defend Tancred against all men while he remained in the kingdom. On 6 March 1191, Richard gave Tancred the sword of King Arthur, Excalibur, a graceful reminder of an agreement fateful for both princes.

Richard also made an important treaty with King Philip of France while they waited at Messina. The joint enterprise was already breaking up. Philip's sense of inferiority in wealth and prestige, exacerbated by Richard's arrogance, burst into active resentment when the old Eleanor of Aquitaine left France with a new bride for Richard, Berengaria, daughter of Sancho VI of Navarre. Philip naturally raised the question of his long-suffering sister, Alice, and her dowry, the Norman Vexin; and in March 1191 an agreement was patched up. For 10,000 silver marks of Troy, Richard was released from his engagement to Alice and was to hand her back to Philip. Gisors, however, was to return to Philip only if Richard left no son to succeed him. If Richard had two sons the younger was to hold one of the three main 'baronies'—Normandy, Anjou, or Aquitaine—directly of the French king, while the elder was to be responsible for all the services to the overlord. In the second half of the treaty the area and juridical position of Richard's fiefs were defined. Richard was to hold all the fiefs he had inherited, less those parts his father had surrendered—Auvergne and the baronies of Issoudun and Graçay—and he was to perform all the services and judicial customs due from each fief. Especially was it agreed that all Richard's claims as duke of Aquitaine on the count of Toulouse were to be heard in the French royal court.

The treaty of Messina, although in appearance generous to Richard, was in fact a severe punishment for the impiety of the Angevin family. The empire which Henry II had ruled for so many years without interference had been broken up again into its component parts, each fief held separately of the French king by its appropriate services; and the overlord had emphasized his position by regulating the rules of succession and by insisting that quarrels between his feudal vassals were not to be decided by private war but by judicial process in his court. The subjection of Richard's fiefs to strict feudal law, and the application of a parage tenure to the succession, promised future advantage to Philip, provided that his power did not weaken. But he was not satisfied with his juridical success. When he reappeared in France after his brief Crusade he made use of a draft or forged version of the treaty in which Richard surrendered the Norman Vexin and the counties of Aumale and Eu as well as Alice.

On 10 April 1191 Richard sailed from Sicily. A storm broke up his fleet; and, after a narrow escape from disaster in the Gulf of Adaliya, he hastened back from Rhodes to Cyprus, where he found two of his ships wrecked and a third, bearing the precious cargo of his sister Joan and his betrothed Berengaria, in danger of capture by the local tyrant, Isaac Ducas Comnenus, a member of the imperial house, who had enjoyed an independent lordship since his revolt from the Eastern Roman Emperor, Andronicus I, in 1185, and who was hostile to the Latin cause. Richard avenged the ill treatment of the survivors from the wrecks and the insult to his ladies by forcing a landing at Lemesos (Limassol) and driving Isaac into the northern hills; and once more his sojourn on an island involved him in matters of great political importance. While he prepared for his marriage with Berengaria, which took place in the chapel of St. George at Lemesos on 12 May, Guy of Lusignan with his suite arrived, wishing both to hasten Richard's arrival at the siege of Acre and to interest him in his private cause. Guy, titular king of Jerusalem in the right of his dead wife, Sybil, the daughter of King Almaric I and sister of Baldwin IV, had lost all prestige in the East since his defeat and capture at Hittin in 1187, which had led to the fall of Jerusalem and the reduction of the Frankish territory in Syria to Tripoli, Antioch, and Tyre; and, despite his hazardous and tenacious attempt to recover Acre, most of the settlers wished to replace him with Conrad, marquess of Montferrat and lord of Tyre, to whom in November 1190 the barons had married Isabella, the other daughter of Almaric I. Philip Augustus had accepted Conrad as the better claimant; but Richard, as duke of Aquitaine, rallied easily to a Poitevin baron, although the Lusignans were a family which had given his father and him much trouble. Guy helped Richard to round up Isaac Comnenus. At the end of May Isaac surrendered, and was imprisoned, fettered, it was said, in chains of gold and silver, for Richard had promised that he should not be bound with iron. Richard then assumed the rule of Cyprus, promised the inhabitants the laws and liberties they had enjoyed under the Emperor Manuel Comnenus, left two of his trusted men, Richard of Camville and Robert of Thornham, in charge, and, enriched by a subsidy paid by his new subjects, departed on 5 June for Acre.

Richard arrived at Acre on 8 June 1191; and on 12 July the city, invested and counter-invested since August 1189, fell to the Crusaders. Philip of France then decided to go home. His engineering skill had been invaluable at Acre; but he had no real interest in the Crusade; he found the rivalry of Richard embarrassing; and he had claims on the estate of the count of Flanders who had died during the siege. He left Richard 10,000 knights under the duke of Burgundy, swore that he would protect his interests and do him no harm, and departed at the beginning of August amid the jeers of the

Norman-Angevin forces. Richard took over the military command, for he would not accept the marquess of Montferrat and Guy had no following. His plan was to recover the Syrian coastline and then, based securely on the sea, to push inland to Jerusalem. In August he marched south accompanied by a flanking fleet, and, after defeating the Sultan Saladin at Arsūf (7 September), reoccupied and re-fortified Jaffa. At the end of October he wheeled left against Jerusalem and spent Christmas at Latrūn within twelve miles of the Holy City; but he feared a repetition of the siege of Acre under even more disadvantageous conditions, and in the spring returned to the coast and rebuilt Ascalon.

Bad news from England contributed to Richard's decision to limit his commitments. In April 1192 he heard that his trusted servant, William Longchamp, had been expelled from England by a conspiracy in which John was implicated and that John was intriguing for the succession to the throne, even, perhaps, negotiating with Philip of France for an immediate usurpation; and Richard's growing anxiety to return, together with his acclimatization to Syrian politics, led him to accept more and more the colonial attitude. He had soon established diplomatic relations with the Sultan Saladin and his brother, Mulik al-'Adil, and before long began to try through negotiations to restore a viable Latin kingdom which could survive his departure. In such a scheme the Holy Place itself was of no importance, for its maintenance as an outpost would be beyond the capacity of the settlers. Richard also came to accept the local view of Guy of Lusignan. At a great council convoked by Richard to Ascalon in April 1192 Conrad of Montferrat was recognized as king, and then, after Conrad's murder by the agents of Rashîd al-Dîn Sinân, grand-master of the Assassins, on 28 April, Guy was again passed over in favour of Henry II, count of Champagne, a half-nephew of both Richard and Philip of France, but Richard's friend, who was given in marriage to Conrad's widow, Isabella. To complete the political settlement Richard transferred Cyprus from the Temple, to which he had sold it during the siege of Acre, to Guy on the same conditions: a life-fief in return for 100,000 gold dinars, 40,000 down and the balance by instalment; and, on leaving Syria, Richard remitted his rights over the island to Henry of Champagne.

The restoration of political unity forced the leaders to make a last attempt to recapture Jerusalem. In June Richard came within

sight of the city once more; and again, despite the sneers of the
French knights, he refused to attack or invest. He thought that a
coastal expedition to the north against Beirut or to the south against
Egypt would be more profitable.

Meanwhile diplomatic exchanges between Saladin and Richard
continued. In October 1191 Richard had proposed that his widowed
sister Joan should marry Saladin's brother, Mulik al-'Adil, and be
secured in the lordship of most of the old kingdom of Jerusalem;
and in November he proposed his niece, Eleanor of Brittany, instead. Later he had suggested that Henry of Champagne should
hold the kingdom as a vassal of Saladin. The sultan was wise,
amiable, and tolerant, and his military power was unreliable; but
he had time on his side, and could afford to wait for better terms.
On 26 July 1192 he attacked Jaffa; and, although Richard relieved
it from the sea and on 5 August hurled the enemy back, he accepted
the warning. On 2 September Richard agreed to a peace for three
years, three months, three weeks, and three days on the conditions
that the Franks should keep their holdings in Syria, except Ascalon,
Gaza, and Darun (Deir-el-Bela) (which threatened Saladin's communications with Egypt), and should also have free access as pilgrims to Jerusalem. The bishop of Salisbury, Hubert Walter, was
among those who visited the Holy Place; and on 9 October 1192
Richard and his forces re-embarked for home.

Owing to the inopportune death of the Emperor Frederick I and
the rivalry between the surviving Christian leaders the Third
Crusade had not achieved its avowed object, the capture of Jerusalem and the restoration of the kingdom. And there had been no
concerted subsidiary plan, for, except on the unrealizable major
scheme, the Eastern Franks and the transitory Crusaders could not
possibly agree. The colonists desired a defensible kingdom in which
they could live in ordinary peace after the visitors had gone home.
The western Crusaders wished to perform an act of piety regardless
of its political effects. Richard, by coming round to the colonial
point of view, deprived the Crusade of spectacular success; but, by
his conquest of Cyprus—a source of provision and a secure military
base—and his conservation of the coastal strip of Syria from Tyre in
the north to Jaffa in the south, he had re-established the kingdom
on a new and stable footing. It became a trading and tourist outpost
of the Latin world, another of those cosmopolitan entrepôts which
dotted the Mediterranean shores; and it is significant that although

the capture of Jerusalem remained the official object of the Crusading movement, the later Crusades were never aimed militarily at the city itself.

VIII

Once free from Near Eastern politics, Richard hastened home, anxious to escape the winter storms. His first plan was to return as he had come by way of Sicily and Marseilles; but, on hearing that the count of Toulouse, suborned by Philip and John, was laying an ambush, he sailed up the Adriatic, intending, presumably, to pass in disguise to the friendly Rhineland. Wrecked near Venice, Richard tried to flank the wintry Alps; and on 17 December 1192 he reached the suburbs of Vienna with only a knight and a boy left of his companions. Three days later he was arrested by the servants of Leopold IV, duke of Austria, whom he had insulted at Acre and who was related to the Comneni, the family Richard had dispossessed of Cyprus; and thereafter, for more than a year, he became the focus of European diplomacy.

Richard as a returning Crusader was under the special protection of the church and his person should have been sacrosanct even to those Christian princes who were his enemies. But his proud behaviour and insolent diplomacy had made him so feared and disliked that, despite papal efforts, the question became not whether Richard should be imprisoned but who should be his gaoler. The Emperor Henry VI had even more reason than Leopold of Austria for wishing to lay hands on Richard. He was still unable to wrest Sicily from Richard's ally, Tancred of Lecce; and in Germany the Welf nephews of Richard, in alliance with the Netherland princes and Denmark, with whom English relations had always been close, were giving him much trouble. With Richard a captive he could put pressure on all his enemies. Accordingly, on 14 February 1193 he forced his vassal, the duke of Austria, to transfer the prisoner. In the person of Richard, Henry acquired a golden key that would open every door. For equally anxious to acquire the captive was Philip of France, another related to the Comneni; and, since Richard and his friends were terrified at the thought of such a transfer, they were prepared to pay the emperor's price. Moreover, Henry disliked the French alliance his father had made in 1187 to counterbalance the Welf-Angevin connexion. His inordinate and, perhaps, chimerical ambition included the subjection of France to his rule; and in this task Richard would be an invaluable ally. With these aims in view the 'philosopher emperor' handled his captive well. He used French importunity to extort the maximum concessions from Richard and his friends; yet was able to make an alliance, based on common interest, with the man he was wronging.

The basic terms on which Richard was to be freed were settled on 29 June 1193 at Worms. He was to pay a ransom of 150,000 marks of silver to the emperor and the duke, of which a third would be remitted if he could reconcile Henry of Saxony to the emperor; and he was to marry his niece, Eleanor of Brittany, to the son of the duke. By the spring of 1194 the Welfs were coming to heel and security had been given for the payment of the ransom, which seems to have mounted to the full 150,000 marks again, possibly owing to the intrusion of the Sicilian business. In fact Henry used English money to conquer Sicily in 1194; and it was in the very castle of Trifels, where Richard had spent a few uncomfortable days, that Tancred's widow, heir, and daughters were imprisoned. On 4 February 1194 Richard was released at Mainz. With Philip of France meddling in Denmark in order to detach it from the Welf-Angevin alliance and to obtain a fleet for the invasion of England, the emperor had decided that the time had come for Philip to be restrained. Henry had proposed enfeoffing Richard with the kingdom of Arles—in effect, Cisjurane Burgundy—over which he had little control, and which, with Toulouse and Aquitaine, would give Richard a great concentration of power in the south, and the coronation had been fixed for 24 January 1194; but, although that plan fell through, Richard surrendered the kingdom of England in order to receive it back as an imperial fief and was encouraged to enlist imperial vassals to fight against Philip Augustus. Richard granted money fiefs to the magnates of the Rhineland—Conrad of Wittelsbach archbishop of Mainz, Adolf of Altena archbishop of Cologne, Henry III duke of Limburg and his son Simon bishop-elect of Liége, Henry I duke of Brabant (Louvain), and Dietrich VII count of Holland; and with this influence he was able to detach Baldwin count of Hainault and Flanders and Reginald of Dammartin count of Boulogne from Philip of France, to whom they had turned. Indeed, Baldwin's son, the future ninth Baldwin of Flanders and emperor of Constantinople, became another of Richard's vassals and pensioners.

These alliances restored Richard's prestige and held out hope that he would be able to reconstruct his damaged empire. Even when in eclipse his renown had served him well. Philip's desertion of the Crusade had allowed him to secure his inheritance in Flanders and to plan the destruction of the Angevin power in France in concert with Richard's ambitious brother, John count of Mortain; but the two conspirators, one prudent and one callow, had not dared come into the open until they learned that Richard was a prisoner. In January 1193 John crossed the Channel and made a treaty with Philip. The king invaded Normandy, assembled a fleet at Wissant in order to reinforce with Flemish soldiers John's revolt in England, and negotiated with Denmark for a princess with an archaic claim to the English throne and for ships and men as her dowry. By the summer he had taken Aumale and Eu in Caux, and Ivry and Pacy in the valley of the Eure and had obtained Gisors by treachery; but he had been beaten back from Rouen by that gallant crusader, the earl of Leicester. John had been even less successful. His castles of Wallingford, Windsor, and the Peak had been besieged by the archbishop of Rouen and the justiciars while his half-brother, Geoffrey of York, and the bishop of Durham had attacked his northern strongholds; and after Hubert Walter had returned to England on 20 April with authentic news of the king's fate the rebel had been glad to make a truce from May to November, and in July rejoined Philip in France. On 9 July Philip in turn made a truce with the envoys of the captive king at Mantes. Richard was to pay 20,000 marks of silver (double the amount paid at Messina) and give the key forts of Arques and Drincourt (Neufchâtel-en-Bray) in Normandy and Loches and Châtillon-sur-Indre in Touraine as pledge. The terms were severe; but the invasion fleet had never sailed, and the loyalty of the kingdom and fiefs had frustrated the attempted revolution.

Nor was the diplomacy of the confederates making much headway. In August 1193 Philip accepted 10,000 marks of silver with his Danish bride, Ingeborg, the sister of King Cnut VI, and on the day after the marriage repudiated her. This mysterious action, whether due to cynical policy or to physical revulsion, cost Philip twenty years of conflict with the church which hindered his later attacks on the Angevins. By December the plan to bribe the emperor to keep Richard in prison had also failed; and the allies became desperate. In January 1194 John completely lost his head. He agreed to cede to Philip all Normandy north of the Seine, except Rouen,

and most of the duchy's frontier castles south of the Seine together
with Tours and its covering fortresses. Such a surrender would have
put the whole Angevin empire north of the Loire at Philip's mercy.
In February Philip invaded up the River Eure; but Rouen withstood him again. On 13 March Richard landed at Sandwich. He
quickly reduced John's last castles of Nottingham and Tickhill; he
held a council at Nottingham at which he changed most of the
sheriffs and disseised John and his supporters of their lands; and
finally he had himself recrowned. On 12 May he disembarked at
Barfleur. His second and last visit to England was over.

IX

Richard was given a great welcome in Normandy. Men felt that
the knightly hero had returned to rescue his vassals from the strain
of the squalid politics of the last four years. And, indeed, this was
the king's intention. He had come back with a burning anger at
Philip's treachery and with the single aim of recovering his losses.
His attitude had been affected by his captivity. He had always had
a chivalrous disdain of the church. He had avoided Rome when
cruising to Messina in 1190; and in Sicily, after hearing Joachim of
Flora expound the Apocalypse, he had actually suggested that
Antichrist was no other than Pope Clement III. This aversion had
been turned into hostile scorn by the failure of the church to protect a crusader. He had also come to recognize and estimate correctly his temporal enemies. But his character had not been warped.
He received the recreant and tearful John with good-humoured
contempt, and promised merely to punish those who had led him
astray. Richard's strategic position was hardly desperate. Although
he had lost the defensive outposts from Flanders to Auvergne he
was nowhere hemmed in or disrupted; and the remedy was obvious:
to recover the more vital castles piecemeal and so to wear Philip
down that he would restore the rest by treaty. To accomplish this
end Richard organized an army and rounded off his great system of
encircling alliances.

Richard balanced his power in northern Europe with an influence in the south which was formidable even without the kingdom of Arles. He had the Navarese alliance through his wife and
the Castilian through his sister; and in 1196 he settled the long
feud with Toulouse. He ceded some disputed territory to the young
Count Raymond VI and gave him his widowed sister Joan to

wife. In return, Raymond was to send him 500 knights for a month should there be war in Gascony. In September 1196 Richard made his nephew, Otto of Brunswick, Henry the Lion's son, count of Poitou; and even more dazzling prospects opened when the Emperor Henry VI died a year later. Henry, when in his last illness and aware that his young son Frederick, later Frederick II, would not easily be accepted as his successor, had tried to conciliate his enemies and victims in his will. To Richard he gave release from his position as a vassal of the empire and promise of compensation for the unjust ransom. But the testament was suppressed until its capture in 1200; and Richard pressed on with a private scheme. The late emperor's brother, Philip of Swabia, was elected as his successor by the Hohenstaufen party in March 1197; and in June Richard contrived the counter-election of his nephew, Otto of Brunswick, by those Rhenish princes who favoured the Welf. Richard's schemes had become as grandiose as the late emperor's. In January 1198 a new and vigorous young pope, Innocent III, was elected, committed to oppose the Hohenstaufen plan of uniting Sicily with the empire, determined to organize yet another Crusade, and inclined to act as an effective moral authority in Europe. Hence the Emperor Otto IV gained a powerful champion, the delinquent King Philip a stern corrector, and Richard, as a proved Crusader, a warm friend.

Richard's overwhelming diplomatic advantage over his rival, although valuable enough, was costly and could only work slowly against the immense advantages enjoyed by the possessor and defendant in any feudal action, whether legal or military. Nor was Richard able to assemble sufficient military strength to force a decision. He had more money and more fame than Philip and was a better field commander; but Philip was at least as good an engineer and organizer; and with the improved technique of castle building the defence was increasing its advantage. Richard devoted all his resources to war. In Normandy the frontier castles were supplied from arsenals at Falaise, Domfront, Caen, and Montfort; and behind these were the base ports, of which Barfleur was the most important. In 1197 he built his greatest castle, Château Gaillard, the saucy castle, at les Andelys on the Seine, to replace Gisors as a cover to Rouen. Inspired by the Syrian castles, which in turn had used Byzantine models, this fortress was a gem of military engineering. Richard bought the ground tenant out, built a new

town and organized a new bailiwick; and on the great limestone
rock, protected by outworks and fortified by two massive wards,
he constructed an elliptical wall beaded with turrets to curtain a
cylindrical keep. The simple unity of design and the geometrical
precision, which provided for an elaborate system of fire over
ground meticulously traversed, made the castle a thing of austere
beauty. It had been built for a single purpose and answered that
purpose to perfection. Richard also attracted the best mercenary
captains. Mercadier, a Brabançon, had been with him on the Crusade
and remained loyal even to Richard's successor, John. Louvart and
Algais served him well. The Crusade had made men more professional, more pitiless. Richard employed, it was said, Muslim
troops and used the murderous Greek fire. But the reduction of
castles was a painful and costly undertaking. Indeed, the unparalleled
intensity of the war defeated its object.

The war of 1194-6, in which Richard ignominiously routed his
rival near Fréteval (early July 1194), secured the return of Aquitainian Berry, some important castles south of the Seine, and all eastern
Normandy except most of the Vexin; but left the Norman castles of
Gisors, Neuf-marché, Vernon, Gaillon, Pacy, Ivry, and Nonancourt and the county of Auvergne in Philip's hands (Peace of Louviers, 13 January 1196). The war of 1196-9, in which Philip was
again defeated in the field (Courcelles, near Gisors, 28 September
1198), forced from Philip the surrender of all the disputed Norman
territory except the castle buildings which he held—Gisors, Pacy,
Ivry, Nonancourt, and some others—and these were to be retained
only as pledges for the observance of the five years' truce. All
through 1198 the papal *curia* had been busy with peace negotiations;
and on 13 January 1199 Richard met Innocent III's legate, Peter of
Capua, cardinal-deacon of St. Mary in Via Lata, at a place between
Vernon and le Goulet. The English king, suspicious of the church
and convinced that Philip had seduced it, exploded with justifiable
wrath when the legate asked for the release of the bishop of Beauvais, Philip of Dreux, a kinsman of Philip, whom Mercadier had
captured in battle on 19 May 1197. The bishop had been among
the French king's ambassadors to bribe the emperor to keep Richard
longer in prison; and it had given Richard no little satisfaction to
capture him *flagrante delicto* and then to load him with chains. He
was still in fetters when Richard died. Nevertheless the five years'
truce was agreed, and suggestions were made for a permanent peace.

Richard should marry his niece, Blanche of Castile, to Philip's heir, Louis, and should give Gisors and 20,000 marks to Philip. The French king should restore all the other Norman castles and surrender the lordship he claimed over the archbishop of Tours. Then, if Philip would abandon the alliance he had made with the Hohenstaufen emperor, Philip of Swabia, in June 1198, Richard and Philip and the true emperor, Otto IV, could plan a new Crusade.

While the terms were being discussed Richard heard that a great treasure had been found on the fief of Adémar V, viscount of Limoges; and he went to Aquitaine to vindicate his right to treasure-trove, all the more essential if a new indemnity had to be paid. But on 26 March 1199, while besieging with Mercadier Adémar's castle of Châlus in Limousin, Richard was wounded in the left shoulder by an arrow from a crossbow. The wound turned septic, and ten days later (6 April) Richard died.

Even if the legate's peace proposals were fanciful, it may be that Richard was robbed of the fruits of his ambitious diplomacy and determined warfare by his untimely death in his forty-second year. Certainly he was the only man with the ability and the reputation to push the French king back. But his disappearance before a final decision had been reached was fatal to his enterprise. In the piecemeal recovery of castles he had been fairly successful; but in the wider purpose of grinding Philip down he had failed. In fact once Richard was dead it was apparent that he had merely exhausted his own empire. The Crusade, the French subsidies, the ransom, the payments to allies, the imperial scheme for his nephew, and then the incessant and savage war had been an intolerable strain on the richest of lands. In Richard's reign the worst features of war finance were displayed: the severe exploitation of every possible source of revenue and the reckless dissipation of money so painstakingly acquired. The ordinary revenue of the crown was drastically increased by the rack-renting of all public offices. Tallages, carucages, and aids foreshadowed a system of regular and direct taxation. And loans raised from individual persons, towns, Jews, and merchants supplemented those other sums which accrued from an avid hunt for casual profits. The centralized system of Angevin finance, in which money was a commodity stored in barrels which could be moved on the simple instruction of a royal writ, insured that the burden was not localized. Indeed, it is possible that Normandy itself contributed less in money than England; for it is a general rule that money, which is stringently gathered in the safe provinces, spills over the advanced bases. Yet the theatres of the war had suffered. The armies had pushed deeply into Normandy and Anjou. Mercenary captains had pillaged friend and foe indifferently. Privileges granted to towns hardly compensated for their loss of trade. And, above all, the church had been alienated. However pious Richard might be in the conventional knightly way, however great his reputation as a Crusader and as a champion of the Welf, he had not restrained his anti-clerical bias and he had not respected or protected church property. Hence the Norman church, in despair at the futile ruin, and professionally committed to peace, began to act as a neutral party between the rival kings. It no longer had an interest in the autonomy of the ecclesiastical province; it had nothing to gain under an independent duke; and its cultural and sentimental ties were all with *la douce France*. It was the church which had forced the exhausted combatants to make truces and treaties; and it was the church which first came to the despairing conclusion that if the Angevins could not reach an understanding with their overlord then it were better that they should be vanquished.

Richard, by recovering some border castles and building some substitutes for his losses, had made the empire militarily defensible, but at the cost of its life. And he had also been losing a more intangible war. The Angevin possessions had become juridically and almost in fact ordinary fiefs held of the French crown. The sustained pressure of the French kings, the disputes among the Norman and then the Angevin ruling family, the rising tide of feudal jurisprudence, and, perhaps, the contamination of Anjou and Aquitaine, had all worked to change the relationships. A few special privileges still remained. No Norman duke had as yet paid a feudal relief on succession. But from the standpoint of Philip and his court the English king who held Normandy, Anjou, and Aquitaine was for those honours only another of his vassals, subject to all the burdens and restraints incumbent on a baron. And even if this view was still discordant with the facts, and could not be applied logically owing to the strength of the vassal, it helped to influence the course of history. The juridical climate had changed; and Richard as well as Philip had played his part in the development. Ever since he had become duke of Aquitaine he had stood on his rights as duke; and this proudest of English kings had also been one of the most feudal.

He had, indeed, been the unconscious victim of a subtle change in atmosphere which his own behaviour had encouraged.

X

Richard had indulged his whims and had never worried much about the future. He left no undisputed successor and no claimant with sufficient prestige to cope with the difficulties. The choice lay between John—the last surviving son of Henry II—and Arthur of Brittany—the son of John's elder brother Geoffrey. Feudal law, although working towards primogeniture and the principle of representation, still hesitated over this nicely-balanced problem. Norman custom favoured the brother and Angevin custom the nephew. English precedents led nowhere, but indicated in general a preference for the adult man against the boy. Aquitaine did not have to decide, for the ducal right was vested in the queen-mother, Eleanor, that remarkable old lady who was still ready to bring up troops and then travel into Spain in the interests of her family. Richard had been hesitant or indifferent. In 1190 he had recognized Arthur as his heir; but since his return from captivity Arthur had been in the ward of Philip of France, and an even more favoured nephew, Otto of Brunswick, had been elected emperor, so that a gradual understanding that John would succeed led naturally to his being named by the dying king. The situation was all the more difficult because neither claimant was popular. Arthur had been associated with Breton nationalism and had spent his twelve years either among his own people or at the court of Philip of France. He was counted a foreigner by the Anglo-Norman baronage and was believed to reciprocate the attitude. John was generally despised; but he had lived his thirty years in England and Normandy, and familiarity with his faults had bred a kind of tolerance. Hence it is clear that, although there could be no enthusiasm for either claimant, John was the more likely to secure a grudging recognition.

In the event things turned out well for John. William the Marshal quoted Norman custom to the archbishop of Canterbury; and the Anglo-Norman barons and officials prepared to accept him. Eleanor of Aquitaine was for her son. And in Anjou, which unhesitatingly declared for Arthur, the English seneschal, Robert of Thornham, held some of the key castles for his dead master's brother. The rudimentary centralization was standing up well to its first severe test. On 25 April John was girded with the ducal sword of Normandy and on 27 May was crowned king of England. The crucial problem was whether the Angevin lands could be crushed between Aquitaine and Normandy before Philip of France could consolidate the breach. On 16 August John, back from England, met Philip near le Goulet. Philip, who had already conquered Évreux, reproached him with his irregular and arbitrary succession to Normandy and demanded the surrender of all the Norman Vexin as price of his recognition and the transfer of Anjou, Touraine, and Maine to Arthur. John naturally refused; on 18 August he renewed the traditional alliances with the counts of Flanders and Boulogne; and in the war which followed the Angevin barons began to feel the pull of their old allegiance. On 22 May 1200 John was able to make the treaty of le Goulet with Philip.

The treaty of le Goulet, like the treaty of Messina of 1191, although superficially favourable to the vassal, marked in fact another stage in the growth of the French royal power. John was recognized as Richard's lawful heir for all his fiefs, including Anjou and Brittany, and was to pay a relief of 20,000 marks sterling. In defining the extent of the fiefs the treaty of Louviers (January 1196) was taken as a basis; and the only major loss John had to accept was the county of Évreux. The baronies of Issoudun and Graçay in Berry and some other disputed lands were to be settled on John's niece, Blanche of Castile, who was to marry Philip's heir, Louis. In return, John was to abandon his hostile alliances with Flanders and Boulogne and with his nephew, the Emperor Otto IV, and was to do justice in his court to Arthur of Brittany. On the day after the treaty Arthur did homage to John and was then placed in ward to Philip, and Louis married Blanche of Castile.

The next treaty between the kings of England and France was the Peace of Paris in 1259, in which John's son, Henry III, renounced his claims to Normandy, Maine, Anjou, Touraine, and northern Poitou. All the seeds of that disaster can be discerned in the treaty of le Goulet: the subjection of the fiefs to strict feudal law as interpreted by the court of the French king and the claim to the English throne that Louis VIII was able to advance in the right of his wife. Nevertheless, John had done extraordinarily well. He had had the advantage of effective possession; he had capitalized the value of Richard's coalition; and he had been able to exploit the belated penalty Philip was paying for his premature attack on the Crusader, for on 15 January 1200 the church had laid an interdict on his kingdom in order to force him to take back his rejected wife, Ingeborg of Denmark. Yet in the great lawsuit between the Angevins and the Capetians Philip was making progress. His court had awarded disputed fiefs to John. If the balance of power continued to shift in his direction there might come a moment when he could enforce a sentence of forfeiture.

In the unaccustomed peace which followed the treaty of le Goulet, John seemed to be firmly establishing his authority. In 1200 he increased his power in Aquitaine by having his uncanonical marriage to Isabella of Gloucester annulled (he was related to her in the third degree), and marrying on 24 August Isabella, daughter and heiress of Audemar Taillefer, count of Angoulême and claimant to the county of la Marche. By this marriage John drew to his side a family which had been troublesome to Richard—and through its control of the road from Poitou to Gascony it could be very awkward—and stood to gain through his wife two strategic counties. But the marriage of John's Castilian niece to Louis of France had drawn the closely inter-related Castile, Aragon, and Toulouse (Joan had died in 1199) into the French orbit; and when on 14 October 1201 and 4 February 1202 John allied with his third brother-in-law, Sancho VII of Navarre, the two were almost isolated in the South. Yet it was the Angoulême marriage which was to be the immediate cause of John's collapse. Isabella had been betrothed to Hugh le Brun (IX), the elder, count of Lusignan and rival claimant to the county of la Marche. The Lusignans revolted. John put the rebellion down and offered them crooked justice; and in October 1200 the family appealed to the French king against John's unlawful behaviour. Richard had withstood many such appeals; and Philip was still not ready to act. Although the interdict had been raised from his kingdom on 8 September 1200 on his promise to submit to judgment, the affair of his marriage was in its most critical stage. In the summer of 1201 he entertained John sumptuously at Paris; and it was not until the following spring that he made use of the Lusignan appeal. He summoned John as duke of Aquitaine to answer the charge of injustice in the French royal court, and required him to surrender Château Gaillard, Arques, and Falaise as security for his performing suit. John dared not comply; and his contumacy allowed Philip's court on 28 April 1202 to condemn the absentee to forfeit not only Aquitaine but all the fiefs he held of the French crown.

John's treatment of the Lusignans was merely the pretext Philip used in order to justify his reversal of attitude and to legalize a war against Normandy that was already planned. Any excuse would have served. But it was also typical of the way in which John had been undermining his moral authority. To marry another man's betrothed was ordinary enough; but to treat the wronged family with contempt and to punish it in disregard for the law weakened respect and bred fear. John was always without nobility and honesty; and Philip had done well to wait two years, for a feudal lord despised and feared by his vassals had no real power at all.

After the sentence of forfeiture John revived those alliances of his brother which he had abandoned by the treaty of le Goulet, and Philip armed his tool, Arthur of Brittany. In April 1202 Philip promised to give Arthur his daughter Mary and in July he knighted him and took his homage for Brittany, Maine, Anjou, and Aquitaine. Normandy and Touraine were, apparently, to fall to the royal demesne. Philip's plan was that he himself should push up the Seine and conquer Normandy while Arthur attacked up the Loire into Anjou. But the clever scheme failed. Philip overran north-east Normandy and Arthur with 200 French knights burst into Touraine. But when the boy attacked Eleanor of Aquitaine in Mirebeau John swept down from le Mans and on 1 August captured Arthur and many of the greatest Poitevin barons, including the Lusignans, as they prepared to storm the keep.

Had John been a 'philosopher king' the possession of his nephew Arthur and of some of his chief enemies might have been his golden key. Philip raised the siege of Arques on news of the disaster and shifted his efforts to Touraine. But John spoiled his advantage. His cruel treatment of the prisoners alienated his supporters and enraged his enemies. By December it was already rumoured—prematurely— that Arthur was dead. In an atmosphere of suspicion and fear the Angevin empire dissolved. John had William the Marshal, the most respected of the Anglo-Norman baronage, at his side as adviser and some good mercenary captains in the field. He seems to have understood the military problem and to have been feverishly active. But he dared not risk a battle; and the immediate reasons for the astonishing collapse were the absence of several of his allies, especially the count of Flanders, on Crusade, Philip's superior force and wealth, and the reluctance of the baronage to fight hard for John's losing cause. By the spring of 1203 Maine and Anjou were beyond

John's control; and it was possibly on 3 April that Arthur suffered the fate of a traitor at Rouen. In the summer Vaudreuil, which covered Rouen on the south-east, was surrendered by its English garrison. In the autumn Philip laid siege to Château Gaillard. Pope Innocent III tried to halt the wave of French successes; but Philip would not listen. On 22 August he replied that matters of feudal law were no concern of the church. In December 1203 John abandoned the scene of his humiliation and crossed to England. On 6 March 1204 Roger of Lacy was forced to yield Château Gaillard after an heroic defence of five months. On 24 June Rouen surrendered. On 10 August Philip entered Poitiers, the capital of Poitou. After Easter 1205 he captured John's last castles in Anjou— Chinon and Loches. In 1206 he secured Brittany. It was a stupendous victory.

The recovery of the lost fiefs became one of John's principal aims; and his son and successor, Henry III, inherited the policy. But long before 1259, when Henry renounced his claim to Normandy, Maine, Anjou, Touraine, and most of Poitou, all hope of military success north of the Loire had disappeared. The old ancestral fiefs of the English crown had been irrevocably lost, and only the latest acquisition, Aquitaine or Guienne, remained in part. Aquitaine— and especially its most southerly province, Gascony—had few ties with the French king. Its duchess, Eleanor, had lived until 1204, and John had been her only surviving son. Moreover, Gascony had developed a flourishing wine trade with England, and to its commercial interests Bordeaux remained for ever true. Hence the English kings were to retain a substantial holding on the mainland of Europe.

Of the forfeited baronies only Normandy had been intimately bound to England; and even this bond had been weakening through the gradual division of honours between different branches of the families. In 1204 there were few barons whose holdings were not predominantly on one or the other side of the Channel and who could be in any serious doubt over which they were to abandon. William the Marshal, to John's annoyance, did liege homage to Philip in 1205 for his French fiefs and contrived to be a vassal of both kings; and Leicester, too, made an arrangement. But, in general, Normandy lost most of its major barons and could easily be absorbed into the French royal demesne. Indeed, the shock of amputation was probably greater for Normandy than for England. Norman clerks and Norman knights had constantly made their fortune in England; whereas the number of Englishmen who had made their way on the Continent had never been many. To place the rebirth of English nationality in 1204 is both too late and too soon. Too late because already the mass of the Anglo-Norman landowners had sunk their roots firmly into the country their forbears had conquered. Too early because for at least another century the English kings and the highest baronage remained completely European in culture. It is possible to view the loss of Normandy as a symptom rather than a cause of English nationality. Had there still been so close a tie between the kingdom and the duchy as there had been in the century following the Conquest, then the separation could never have been achieved so easily and so conclusively. In retrospect it appears that Henry II's cosmopolitan outlook had weakened the traditional connexion, while his development of efficient local administrations had strengthened provincial unity. Already in Richard's reign a pure Norman, like William Longchamp, could cause offence in the kingdom because of his reputed contempt for the English; under John the captains from Normandy and Touraine were most unpopular; and in Henry III's reign the Lusignans, the king's half-brothers and -sisters, were regarded as aliens. But since the aristocracy was still French in culture the thirteenth century is for England an age of paradox. Henry III was at once the most English and the most foreign of kings. The rebellious barons first invited Louis of France to rule over them, then denounced Henry's ministers as foreigners, and finally chose Simon of Montfort, an alien of the aliens, as their leader. Boroughs swore communes and introduced the foreign title of mayor. The bishops were mostly Englishmen; but almost all the intellectuals had been at the schools of Paris and were œcumenical in outlook. England was always too small and provincial for the restless man. But the loss of Normandy had made the development of English nationality easier. No other French fief could replace the duchy as a home from home.

10

THE ANGEVIN DESPOTISM

I

KING HENRY II gave alms on all the great church festivals: on Christmas day he disbursed two marks of gold and on Easter day and Whitsunday one mark of gold, with lesser sums on the three following days of solemnity; and on the feasts of the Circumcision, Epiphany, the Purification of the Blessed Virgin Mary, Ash Wednesday, the Annunciation of the B.V.M., Palm Sunday, the Ascension, the Birth of St. John the Baptist, Saints Peter and Paul, the Assumption of the B.V.M., the Nativity of the B.V.M., St. Michael, and All Saints, he gave one ounce of gold. His almoner, Thomas Brown, took a note of the system. A highly ritualistic society was beginning to record its behaviour.

Of all the political groupings only the church had an ideal pattern, fervently displayed, and strenuously applied to a recalcitrant world. The lay princes might employ civil lawyers who saw in the Roman empire a model for a secular kingdom; but the imperial idea was so foreign to feudal politics that it contributed far more to the church than to the state. In polemical warfare with the church the lay authorities were always the losers, for their advocates were either apologetic or clumsily strident. But in workaday politics the secular state held its own. It had an obvious function; it wielded the sharper if inferior sword; and it was supported by inveterate custom. The church justified its aims and ideals by appealing to the past: to the Scriptures, the Fathers, and the decisions of earlier popes and councils. The secular state also looked to the past, but only to justify present practice or a reform masquerading as a restoration. The church's danger, intensified by the intellectual revival, lay in excessive attention to the ideal, in creating a logical system too remote from the actual conditions of a sinful world. The danger to the secular state, enhanced by its development of the record, lay in routine, in putting too much value on precedent. In the kingdom of England, with its long tradition and peaceful evolution, the danger was very real. The witness of history dominated the kings and the baronage; the secrets of administrative method were held by close and privy societies of clerks; and the long absences of the kings from England left control in the hands of men who dared not innovate. Typically, the English coinage was unchanged in design between 1180 and 1247, neither Richard nor John troubling to put their names on the 'short cross' pennies. The peril of stagnation, however, was rudely dispelled. It was John's enforced sojourn in his kingdom, marked by energetic improvisation and brutal decisiveness, which inspired a new ferment in secular society and warded off for a time the danger that the only men capable of freedom might become prisoners in a web of etiquette and routine which they and their ancestors had spun.

Richard I's ignorance of English affairs provided a severe test for the system of government which his father had bequeathed. The dispersal of power which characterized his preparations for the Crusade and the complete trust he placed in his servant William Longchamp, who was unacceptable to the English magnates, led to unrest once the king had passed out of regular communication. Longchamp, bishop of Ely, royal justiciar and chancellor, and papal legate, held every office necessary for supreme power. But the man, despite his ability, self-confidence, and loyalty, was not quite big enough for the position; and as Richard disappeared into the East, men turned to the brother he had left in the West, and who had returned to England despite his oath, John count of Mortain. John's enormous English honour, which reached from his southwestern shires across the midlands, severely circumscribed the chancellor's power; he had friends in England, especially Hugh of Nonant, one of Arnulf of Lisieux's nephews, bishop of Coventry and sheriff of Warwickshire, Leicestershire, and Staffordshire; and he courted all those whom Longchamp offended. John cannot have been without hope of succeeding his brother; and Richard's recognition at Messina of Arthur as his heir almost forced John to return to England in the winter of 1190–1, in order to prepare for the future. Queen Eleanor's absence from the kingdom on Richard's matrimonial business was an unsettling factor; and after Clement III's death in March or April 1191 Longchamp's legation was for a time in doubt. John's first aim was to gain effective power in the Midlands; and, in alliance with Bishop Hugh of Coventry and Gerard of Camville, sheriff and castellan of Lincoln, he disputed with the legate custody of Tickhill and Nottingham castles. In the summer Longchamp punished the disaffected Roger Mortimer by taking his castle at Wigmore, and then marched on Lincoln to dispossess Camville, whom he had removed from his shrievalty. John reoccupied Tickhill and Nottingham and ordered Longchamp to desist.

Complaints against Longchamp had been chasing Richard across Europe; and on 2 April 1191, possibly after hearing of John's return to England, the king had sent Walter of Coutances, archbishop of Rouen, back from Messina. Walter, who returned by way of Rome, arrived in England on 27 June at the time of the disturbances. In his portfolio of royal commissions was one dated 23 February, addressed to Longchamp and the justiciars, ordering them to act on his advice; and he immediately began to negotiate a settlement between the rival parties. The agreement of 28 July between Longchamp and John left the former in control; but with John rallying the forces of opposition, Longchamp's grip became insecure. The king's brother rather than his menial servant appeared as more representative of the crown.

In the autumn Longchamp gave the conspirators a perfect opportunity. Richard's other brother, the bastard Geoffrey, archbishop-elect of York, had like John been banished from the kingdom, and had needed the absence in order to get papal permission for his consecration and papal support against his ambitious suffragan, Hugh of le Puiset, bishop of Durham. The accession of Celestine III in the spring of 1191 reversed the hostile attitude of his predecessor; and on 18 August, more than two years after his election, Geoffrey was consecrated archbishop at Tours and received the pallium on the same day. He had also obtained a privilege freeing him from all jurisdiction inferior to that of a legate *a latere*, and an order to the bishop of Durham to make his profession of obedience to York. With or without royal permission (and it appears that Richard, possibly in bad faith, had remitted the exile) Geoffrey was determined to return to England in order to take revenge on his enemies. He would force Longchamp, who had once been in his

household, to account for the unlawful detention of the temporalities of his archbishopric; he would compel the bishop of Durham to
make submission; and he would punish the unruly and unfriendly
canons of his cathedral church. John encouraged him to come. He
could use another discontented man.

Longchamp had not dared withstand John; but he thought he
could deal with Geoffrey. He gave orders that the archbishop should
be prevented from landing and arrested if he persisted. On 14
September Geoffrey crossed to Dover and, having shaken off the
guard, took refuge in St. Martin's priory, a cell of Christ Church,
Canterbury. On the next day the castellan of Dover, the husband of
Longchamp's sister, required the archbishop either to return to
Normandy or to take an oath of fealty to the king and the chancellor.
Geoffrey would do neither; and on 18 September a force sent by
Longchamp dragged the archbishop from the altar of the priory
church and imprisoned him in the castle. Geoffrey's biographer and
many contemporaries naturally thought of the scene at Canterbury
in December 1170. The monks spurred the bishops to action against
this violation of sanctuary; John collected troops; and on 26
September Geoffrey was replaced in the priory. But Longchamp's
concession was too late. At last a focus had been provided for the
many discontents against his rule; and he was driven from the
kingdom by force.

The engineer of the plot against Longchamp was the bishop of
Coventry, Hugh of Nonant; and, since the church's irritation at
being ruled by a diocesan bishop flamed into anger when the legate
imprisoned an archbishop, private ambitions and personal resentments could easily be concealed. Longchamp never moved from his
plea that he was merely serving the king his master and doing his
simple duty; but as his unpopularity grew his associate justiciars
began to desert him, and he dared not attend the trial on 5 October
at Loddon Bridge, on the Thames between Reading and Windsor,
to which he was summoned by John. The archbishops of Rouen
and York, the bishops of London, Winchester, Bath, Lincoln, and
Coventry, John, and the earls of Arundel, Norfolk, Surrey, and
Pembroke, together with their followings, listened to Geoffrey's
complaints against the justiciar, and the trial turned into a revolutionary meeting. The archbishop of Rouen had a second royal letter
in his portfolio, dated 20 (or 9) February, addressed to William the
Marshal, one of the justiciars, and other barons. They were to give

heed to the archbishop because he knew the secrets of the king's
heart and were to disregard Longchamp if he refused to act faithfully in accordance with the counsel of the archbishop and of the
other justiciars. It was, therefore, decided to depose Longchamp as
useless to the king and the kingdom. On the morrow Longchamp
was excommunicated by the bishops and his arrest was entrusted to
the barons. Longchamp tried to rally London, where he held the
Tower; but the citizens, too, were fishing in the troubled waters,
and opened their gates to his enemies. On 8 October at a meeting in
the city it was ordained 'by the common deliberation of the king's
vassals' that John should be regent and Rouen chief justiciar. An
oath of fealty was taken to the absent king; but John was recognized
as his heir should Richard die without children—and London's
support could be decisive. Longchamp, who had taken refuge in the
Tower, was forced to submit; and on 29 October he crossed to
Wissant after some embarrassing adventures suffered in his disguise
as a woman.

The revolution of 1191 is not of direct constitutional importance.
A chief justiciar, who believed he was faithfully serving his absent
master, and who, indeed, never forfeited the confidence of the
king and of the pope, was forced to make way for another servant
of the king on the authority of the king's own missive. Yet there
are undertones which will become louder in the next century.
Among the terms of the Winchester agreement (28 July) was a
clause that no man was to be disseised without lawful judgment, a
clause which was to be elaborated in chapter 39 of Magna Carta.
John made his appeal against Longchamp in October to the *communitas Angliae*, to a body which, although in practice narrow and
in action partisan, could yet be imagined as representing the
whole community of the realm. The wider charge against Longchamp was undoubtedly his autocratic behaviour, his neglect of
the advice of his fellow justiciars and of his new colleague; and a
principle which could seldom be enforced against a king was successfully asserted against a lonely viceroy. Clearly Longchamp's
removal had been possible only because the ambitions of the king's
brothers, John and Archbishop Geoffrey, happened to agree on this
one point, and because they and Hugh of Nonant were able to
exploit the accumulated resentment in church and state against the
agent of a harsh government devoid of immediate royal support.
But the opposition carefully observed legal forms and all its proceed-

ings were characterized by moderation and good sense. This was possible—and here can be noticed the essential difference from the revolutionary actions of 1215—because most of Longchamp's enemies were loyal to the royal Crusader. Even Geoffrey of York, whose behaviour had caused the crisis, was to prove himself un-hesitatingly on the side of the brother who had not treated him too well. Nevertheless, the opposition effected for a time a real change in the type of government. Longchamp had been Richard *in parvo*. John's ambition soon took him on to a lonely path; and the government stayed in the hands of a body representing the faithful. Walter of Coutances, an Englishman, and trained as a royal clerk under Henry II, worked closely with his fellow justiciars; and until Richard returned, it was the actions of the council rather than those of the justiciar which were noticed by the chroniclers. Feudal society never required, or wanted, active government at the head. It could subsist satisfactorily provided that the *communitas regni* had a sense of duty and put a proper restraint on the many private ambitions.

The steadfastness of the kingdom at large was proved by the course of events between the return of King Philip of France from the Crusade at the end of 1191 and Richard's release from prison in February 1194. John's intrigues with Philip came to nothing because the Norman barons shunned him and because in England the queen mother, Eleanor of Aquitaine, and Archbishop Geoffrey of York were able to squeeze John's midland palatinate between them. When John revolted in the spring of 1193 on hearing that Richard was a prisoner, he was unable, despite his possession of the castles at Lancaster, the Peak, Nottingham, Tickhill, Windsor, and Wallingford, his raising of Welsh mercenaries, and his call to the French king to invade from Flanders, to do much harm. The coast was protected against a landing; towns and castles were fortified; the justiciars invested Wallingford, Windsor, and the Peak; Arch-bishop Geoffrey and Bishop Hugh of Durham attacked Tickhill; and had there not been a general disinclination to go to extremes against a man who might yet be their king, John would have lost all his castles and honours. On 20 April 1193 Hubert Walter, bishop of Salisbury, brought certain news to England of Richard's fate; and with the return of the Crusaders and the resumption of regular communication with the imprisoned king English condi-tions returned almost to normal.

II

In the past when the royal power had been weak the advantage had been reaped mainly by the baronage and the church. By Richard's reign both those communities had achieved their main ambitions; and it was, perhaps, the mercantile class which gained most profit from this slackening of royal control. The traders were becoming increasingly wealthy. Richard was able to summon a large English fleet to Marseilles to transport his army to the Holy Land. But mercantile society was still short of privileges and was constantly exploited by the crown. Its dissatisfaction and its impatience of competition from the Jews led to the pogroms which swept through the towns on Richard's accession, a change from the baronial revolts which had marked royal deaths before. On coronation day the Jewish quarter was sacked in London; and on 6 February Norwich, on 7 March Stamford, on 17 March York, and on 18 March Bury St. Edmunds murdered their Jews. Only Winchester among the greater towns was spared a massacre. Little pity and less shame was felt by contemporaries at this cruel treatment of defenceless communities whose religion barred sympathy and whose profession bred hatred; but the king and then William Longchamp punished the rioters, for the Jews were the king's own and their destruction was wastage of his property.

Henry II had repressed all the municipal ambitions which had been conceived in Stephen's reign, and had granted few privileges. The boroughs still had no self-government, few beyond trading privileges, and no common organ except in the merchant gild which many of them possessed. To the crown they were merely especially wealthy parts of the demesne. Royal revenue was drawn from the tolls imposed in the markets, the profits of justice, and the burgage rents; and one of the wishes of the boroughs was to exclude the sheriff and his officers and pay directly to the crown. Henry II allowed a few boroughs to farm their revenues at his pleasure; but from London, to which his grandfather had granted the right in perpetuity at the low farm of £300, but which had consistently opposed his mother, he extorted more than £500 a year, except between June 1174 and midsummer 1176 when he was buying support during the later stages of the great rebellion. Even more onerous to the boroughs than the heavy farm, whether collected by the sheriff or by themselves, were the aids or gifts which the king took as tallage; and as they had no government of their own they could not bargain satisfactorily with the crown. Henry II had created an explosive situation in the towns; and the few concessions which Richard sold in order to raise money for the Crusade did not dampen it.

In the main commercial centres of Europe—Lombardy, France, and the Low Countries—a movement to check seignorial exploitation had been spreading. Citizens joined together in a town to form a 'commune', an association sworn to resist oppression and to obtain liberties. London had made its first abortive attempt at liberty in Stephen's reign. Movements at Gloucester and York had been quickly stifled by Henry II. At Michaelmas 1189 London was entrusted to keepers who were merely to account for the royal revenues, and a year later the farm was restored to the citizens at £300. But London was not satisfied; and its great opportunity had arisen. In October 1191, while William Longchamp and John were struggling for power, London rejected the former, who was identified with Angevin tyranny, and gave its allegiance to the latter, who was prepared to pay its price. On 8 October John took an oath to the commune of London, and the citizens set up a municipal government under an official with the foreign title of mayor. Richard on his return to England was unable to repress the new forces; and his successor, John, sought to direct them to his profit. Within a quarter of a century of London's revolution the communal movement, although attenuated and restricted in England, had wrought a great change in the condition of the larger royal boroughs. By 1216 some 23 towns had received the grant of their farm in fee, there were more than a dozen towns ruled by mayors often assisted by a sworn council, and municipal common seals were coming into use. The greater royal boroughs had at last by purchase from the king achieved a degree of corporateness and a measure of self-government under their elected rulers. Yet it is doubtful whether the mass of the burgesses gained. In mercantile society wealth automatically gives power; but it may be that the more the king and his agents were excluded from the borough the less were the oligarchical tendencies controlled. There was no place for democracy in urban self-government.

The English church had already won its battles against the crown; and its desire to order its own affairs under the guidance of the pope had been granted in Henry II's reign. But Richard had no sympathy for the freedom of the church. In the first months of his reign he broke with the benevolent tradition of his father's last years and distributed the vacant bishoprics to men of his choice without allowing much semblance of free election to the chapters. However, his departure together with the primate, Baldwin archbishop of Canterbury, prevented a period of reaction and had some far-reaching effects. The ecclesiastical anarchy born during Becket's exile had never been completely destroyed owing to Henry's relaxed control after his concordats with the papacy; and with the local rulers away the English church suffered a period of institutional disorder not unlike that which had appeared under King Stephen. Once Henry had withdrawn his opposition to appeals to the pope, the old order was put at the bar to be tested by the law. The flow of papal decretals was creating a new common law for the church; and rights and customs at variance with this norm became ever more difficult to maintain. At the same time the political atmosphere which dominated the new creation favoured the universal ordinary, the pope, against the local ordinary, the bishop, and was hostile to all petty popes such as primates and archbishops. Under these conditions the traditional ecclesiastical organization in England could not remain unchanged.

Canterbury's primacy, already undermined, was reduced to a title of honour. The papacy, once the need to support Thomas Becket against Roger of Pont-l'Évêque had passed, resumed its policy of balancing Canterbury and York. Usually each metropolitan was given a papal legation within his own province; and the primacy which Canterbury secured conferred dignity and a few privileges rather than power. Indeed, so concerned were the archbishops with maintaining their metropolitan and ordinary authority in their own provinces and dioceses that the old rivalry began to subside. York was in collapse. Between 1175 and 1186 Glasgow and in 1188 or, more likely, 1192 the whole Scottish church had escaped from its metropolitan authority. The anomalous arrangement during Richard's absence, whereby the bishop of Ely as papal legate within England, Wales, and that part of Ireland subject to John ruled the English church, and the unusual situation in Scotland, where, owing to the rivalry of St. Andrews and Glasgow, there was a church depending directly on the pope without the intermediacy of a provincial archbishop, were characteristic of this disordered period.

The insecurity of the bishops arose from the reduction of their

jurisdiction through unrestricted appeals to Rome and the growing
independence of the archdeacons, and from the spirit of freedom
working in the monasteries and cathedral chapters. After the short
interruption in Henry II's reign the hierarchical organization of
church courts had been consolidated, so that few important law-
suits were determined by the ordinaries in England, but were heard
mostly by special judges in England to whom the pope remitted the
case (judges delegate) or, more rarely, at Rome itself or by judges
whom the pope dispatched from his court (legates *a latere*). All
local ordinaries were affected. But the worst sufferer was the archbishop of Canterbury, whose primatial court lost its traditional
position as the highest court of appeal for all but the most exceptional English cases. At the same time the bishops were abandoning
a great field of petty jurisdiction to the archdeacons and various
privileged persons and bodies. The archdeacons had wielded
episcopal powers as agents of the bishop; the owners of a franchise
had secured their privileges by grant or usurpation. Towards the
end of the twelfth century the bishops gave up the struggle for
recovery, and by developing a superior court and superior rights of
visitation both recognized and debased the alienated functions. The
archdeaconries and peculiar jurisdictions became subordinate
territorial divisions within the diocese. And when the archdeacons
went out of the episcopal court the bishop appointed a new personal
helper, the 'official'.

Equally disturbing was the ambition of the monasteries to escape
from episcopal control and the struggle of the cathedral chapters
for independence under their prior or dean. At Durham, the monastic
chapter was usurping rights from the bishop under cover of forged
charters. At York, Geoffrey was almost impotent in the face of his
rebellious canons. And at Canterbury the archbishops lost finally
their long war against the exemption of St. Augustine's and became
involved in a vexatious quarrel with their chapter, the monks of
Christ Church.

The quarrel at Canterbury reveals most of the contemporary
frictional points, because the archbishops' scheme to establish a
college of canons in honour of St. Stephen and St. Thomas succeeded
in arousing every separate fear of the monks and in appearing to
threaten each of their most cherished privileges and ambitions. The
days of Lanfranc's Customs, with their ideal of a cathedral monastery in
which the bishop should be the abbot and father of the monks and the

monks his family and council, were far behind. No twelfth-century bishop could satisfactorily harmonize his monastic and diocesan duties; the permanent corporation of monks could hardly avoid encroaching on the internal rights of the transitory bishops; and when a secular clerk was appointed to such a see a difficult situation was created. The history of all cathedral monasteries was marked, therefore, by a growing cleavage between the bishop, with his secular archdeacons and clerks, and the monks striving for autonomy under their prior. A few twelfth-century bishops, such as Hugh of Nonant—like his uncle Arnulf of Lisieux an admirer of regular canons and a doughty fighter against decadent and insubordinate monasteries—tried to reform their chapters by substituting canons for monks; but tradition was too strong for such a change. The desire of all monastic chapters was to elect one of their own monks as bishop who could be expected to condone its usurpations and consolidate its rights; and since this ambition was usually frustrated by the king the disappointed convent cold-shouldered and thwarted the unwelcome intruder. In 1173 and 1184 the electors at Canterbury had also been embittered by the claim of the bishops of the province to share in the election on the ground that they had an interest in the choice of their superior. In 1184 the candidate of the bishops, Baldwin bishop of Worcester, sometime abbot of Ford, a learned and austere Cistercian, had been forced on the monks after a desperate procedural struggle; and it was in Baldwin's episcopate that the fiercest quarrel between the archbishops and their chapter had begun.

Both as a Cistercian and as a scholar Baldwin was dismayed at the worldly condition of the monks, at their wealth swollen by the offerings which showered on the tomb of the martyr, St. Thomas, and at their insubordination. He therefore took up the unrealized project of his predecessors of founding a college of canons in honour of St. Stephen, and proposed to add the name of St. Thomas to the dedication. In this way Baldwin hoped to endow learned and useful clerks and to divert some of the convent's usurped and superfluous wealth to a worthy cause. The scheme aroused the hysterical opposition of the monks. Baldwin's attempt to recover archiepiscopal revenue, which some of his predecessors had wrongfully alienated to the convent, at a time when the cathedral church was still being rebuilt after the fire of 1174, and his efforts to re-establish his power to deprive and appoint the monastery's prior and other obedientiaries were hateful enough; but the suspected implications of the scheme were horrifying. The monks feared—and Baldwin's proposal that each of his suffragan bishops should have a stall in the college sharpened the fear—that it was intended that the college should supersede them as the electoral body; and, since the foundation was to be dedicated also to the latest martyr—possibly in origin a placatory gesture—the monks suspected that Baldwin planned to translate the body of St. Thomas to the new church. Such was the desperation of the monks that, although their archbishops were supported by the crown, most of the English bishops, and the Cistercian order, they fought through to a successful issue by means of constant appeals to the pope and by using every artifice of deceit and obstruction against the archbishops and the kings. Baldwin's successor, Hubert Walter, more supple than the Cistercian and less confident of King John's support, abandoned in 1201 the college which had already been moved from Canterbury itself (Hackington) to Lambeth. The case had never been judged on its merits. The reforming zeal of the Cistercian and the worldly progressive attitude of the royal clerk had alike gone down before the tenacity of a corporation and the prejudiced view of the papacy. Monks were acquiring a taste for litigation and had the leisure for its timeless prosecution. And if the bishop tried to restrain them by limiting their funds he provided them with yet another charge to make at the papal court.

The thirteenth-century bishop, with his official, his chaplains, and his clerks, was still the greatest power in his diocese. But he was no longer master in his own cathedral church; he had no control over many monastic foundations; he could not prevent appeals from his court; and he could not trespass on the archdeaconries and franchises. A great process of redefinition was taking place. Traditional rights and claims were being tested by the law through the facility of appeal to the pope; and by the time that another century had passed the organization of the medieval church in England had settled down quietly into its new and lasting pattern.

Many abuses were uprooted during this period of critical review. The concordat of Avranches was followed by a reforming council held by the Legates Albert and Theodwin (Avranches, 28 September 1172); the decrees of papal councils were published without hindrance in England; and the bishops became accustomed to enforcing the law. Hubert Walter, archbishop of Canterbury 1193–

1205, although in origin and in sympathy a royal clerk, held provincial and legatine councils. The maintenance of discipline according to the law had become a matter of administrative routine. The weakest institutions suffered the most change. Parish churches were prised from the grip of families of hereditary parsons, but were then rarely left intact under a rector. Monasteries and other ecclesiastical owners seized avidly on the property which had at last fallen in, transferred the parsonage to themselves (impropriation), and appointed a priest to serve the church at a small wage. Bishops were unable to withstand the policy; and they succeeded only in securing that the priest in charge should have a firm tenure with the title of vicar and a competent, but usually slender, revenue.

Although the spiritual ferment in Europe was susbiding England still received impulses from abroad. Perhaps the strangest incursion were the visits of Eustace, abbot of the Benedictine house of St. Germer de Flay, near Gournay in the diocese of Beauvais, a disciple of the revivalist preacher Fulk of Neuilly. Eustace preached the holy war, denounced the sins of the age, in particular usury, and had as his special theme the profanation of Sundays and other holy days by labour and trade. In 1172 a stranger had accosted Henry II at Cardiff and ordered him in the name of Christ and the saints to abolish Sunday markets. In 1200 Eustace of Flay visited the southern counties of England. He then secured a copy of that curious document, a letter of Christ condemning the desecration of holy days, said to have fallen on to the altar of St. Simeon on Golgotha. And, supported by this authority, Eustace had in 1201 a more successful tour of the eastern shires up to York. Meanwhile St. Dominic had been born in 1170 at Caleruega in Old Castile and St. Francis in 1181 or 1182 at Assisi.

All these momentous changes in the English church can easily be studied owing to the wealth of narrative and documentary evidence which has survived. The history of secular society is far more obscure, and generalizations even about the condition of the baronage must be considered tentative. The royal government still offered no impersonal threat to baronial liberties. The effect of Henry II's legal reforms was to define franchises rather than to subvert them; and if uneasiness persisted after the last revolt, that of 1173, there was no overt common expression of it. The private resentments caused by a personal type of government were many; and in 1191 there was enough aggravation to provoke a fairly concerted attack on the king's minister. But it is significant that in 1191 the party of opposition put forward no special plan of reform. The panacea was the replacement of a bad justiciar by a good one. If there was one widespread grievance it was, perhaps, the tight hold which the crown kept over castles. Many adulterine fortresses had been over-thrown in the early years of Henry II's reign; more private castles had been razed during and after the 1173 rebellion; and in 1191 there were still some important barons, such as William of Mowbray, who possessed not a single castle. But John was the only malcontent who in the years 1191–4 dared to try to acquire his detained castles by force.

The baronage did not form a homogeneous class. The advance-ment and ruin of individuals lay in the king's hand. With the king's favour went the admission of legal or pretended claims, the grant of escheated honours and valuable heiresses, the gift of lucrative custodies and offices, and support against rivals. With the king's displeasure justice was denied and enemies closed in. Even the greatest English magnate after John, Ranulf earl of Chester, thought that he was more likely to establish some of his insatiable claims through the king's good will than through violent action. Fortunes were easily made and lost. In the *Histoire de Guillaume le Maréchal* can be read how William the Marshal, who began with little else than his hereditary marshalcy and a few grants from the royal demesne, became an earl and one of the greatest barons in the land; and in the romance *Fouke fitzWarin* is told the story of Fulk, a simple knight who was educated with Henry II's sons at court, became the leader of an outlaw band in Shropshire, and in the end made his peace with John and received a castle and a valuable widow for wife. In the same period the great family of Beaumont, which had risen under Henry I and overshadowed England under Stephen, crashed during the loss of Normandy. In this turbulent and emulous society men fought to stand in the warmth of the royal glance. As yet no cleavage had developed between the barons and the royal government. The Angevin bureaucracy could not have existed without its clerks; but the court was always thronged by knights and barons eager to serve the king. Henry II attracted men largely through his power; Richard added the martial qualities of a hero. The father was dilatory and secretive, the son so open that the importunity of his suitors made his actions often contradictory and incoherent. No man despaired of Richard's favour, and baronial ambitions remained individual and competitive.

III

No English baron of any standing conspired with John during Richard's absence; and there was a general relief from anxiety when the king was at last discovered in a German prison. The anarchical tendencies began to subside; and the enormous ransom, the cost of the king's homecoming, was raised without political difficulty. In England in the years 1193-4 the justiciars took every type of tax that they knew of: a scutage at 20*s.* the knight's fee; a talliage on the royal demesne; a quarter of a man's movable goods and revenues (or fines instead); a geld at 2*s.* on the more comprehensive 1084 assessment; from the Cistercians and Gilbertines the year's crop of wool; and from the churches their treasure. It was an obligatory duty on vassals to redeem their captive lord; and the contributions seem to have been fairly apportioned. William Longchamp had rejoined his master at the first opportunity and had been kindly welcomed. But England could not stomach him; and Richard acquiesced. Longchamp remained the royal chancellor until his death at Poitiers on 31 January 1197. But Hubert Walter was the man Richard advanced in England.

Hubert, a man of outstanding ability, was a nephew by marriage of Henry II's chief justiciar and sheriff of Yorkshire, the great Ranulf Glanville; and Hubert repaid his uncle for the education he gave him in his household by founding in 1188 the Premonstratensian abbey of West Dereham for his soul and also, perhaps, by writing the *Tractatus de legibus et consuetudinibus regni Anglie* which goes under his benefactor's name. Such a family had much influence over ecclesiastical patronage. In 1186 Hubert was allowed to accept the deanery of York; but the archbishopric to which he was then elected was considered too great an honour for a chancery clerk, and he received in consolation from King Richard the bishopric of Salisbury on 16 September 1189. He went on the Crusade; and his distinguished conduct in Syria and his loyal attendance on Richard when captive induced the king to give him the primatial see (30 March 1193), which the death of Baldwin at Acre on 19 November 1190 had left vacant. Early in 1194 Richard made Hubert chief justiciar of England; and on 18 March 1195 Celestine III sent him a legation for the whole of the kingdom. The punishment of the conspirators against Longchamp gave Hubert a quiet country to rule. John, lord of Ireland, recovered only the county of Mortain, the earldom of Gloucester, and the honour of

Eye, without their castles, and a money fief of £8,000 Angevin in compensation (May 1195), and was kept at the king's side abroad. And with Geoffrey of York's entanglement in provincial and diocesan troubles and Hugh of Durham's death in 1195 the church offered no great difficulties.

For the first time all the threads of power which a royal servant could hold had been brought together in a single hand; and an office without precedent and without regular succession had been created. Leicester, Lucy, and Glanville had had no standing in the church; Longchamp, the real prototype, had not managed to add Canterbury to his titles. Hubert Walter did well. His was the slow, characteristic rise of a favoured royal clerk, such as the baronage and church were prepared to accept. His lack of scholastic learning and sacerdotal polish, which would have passed unnoticed at Ely, was almost a scandal at Canterbury; his absence of fervour had a deadening effect on a church seldom remarkable for its zeal, and his inherited quarrel with the monks of Christ Church was unfortunate; but he was a great patron of the Premonstratensian canons; he performed his ecclesiastical duties conscientiously and efficiently; his recovery of a papal legation for the whole of the kingdom restored a broken tradition; and in a large measure he gave stability again to a church which had been losing coherence. So too in secular affairs Hubert took up where Henry II and his uncle had left off. No man knew more of the laws and customs of the kingdom; and his steady elaboration of the bureaucratic system to which he had been bred and the important chancery reforms he introduced when King John suceeded insured that Henry's work was the beginning of a new age and not the culmination of the past. Had William Longchamp, a clerk with only foreign experience, been restored to power the history of England might have taken quite another turn under Kings Richard and John. Hubert was the conservator of English tradition; and so firmly was he placed in the quiet centre of his different characters that he felt hardly at all the clash of loyalties that would have racked a more idealistic man.

Hubert Walter was chief justiciar of England from January 1194 until 31 July 1198 and chancellor from the day after King John's coronation until 13 July 1205, when he died. His main duties under Richard were to restore and maintain the peace and to raise the money necessary for the king's continental wars. In the year of his appointment he set on foot a great judicial, financial, and administrative investigation, and thus not only revived the Norman and Angevin general eyre but also extended its scope. The itinerant justices were given 25 articles of instruction. Besides holding the pleas of the crown and recognitions they were to discover royal escheats, advowsons, wardships of boys, marriages of girls and widows, and various other sources of revenue; they were to survey the lands and possessions of John, so that those parts which had been forfeited could be resumed by the king; they were to investigate the collection of the aid for the king's ransom and all complaints of wrongful exaction by royal bailiffs—justices, sheriffs, constables, foresters, and the rest; they were to survey and restock all royal custodies and escheats; they were to tallage all cities, boroughs, and demesne manors of the king; and they were to initiate two important reforms: all Jewish business was to be put under control, and custody of the pleas of the crown was to be entrusted to three knights and one clerk elected in each shire. At the same time no sheriff was to be a justice in his sheriffdom or in any shire he had held since Richard's accession. The crown was investigating its financial rights and also providing for their better administration. The suspicion that sheriffs accepted bribes to conceal offences against the king had led to another curtailment of their judicial capacity and to the general appointment of a local commission to keep the pleas of the crown in which can be seen the germ of the coroner's office.

In the next year, 1195, the justiciar issued a proclamation for the keeping of the peace—the *Edictum regium*—which was based on the Assizes of Clarendon (1166) and Northampton (1176) but which introduced yet another procedural novelty. All men over the age of fifteen were to take an oath before local knights assigned for the purpose that they would keep the peace and denounce and capture breakers of it; and these knights responsible for the maintenance of peace in the shire are believed to be the forerunners of those keepers of the peace who became justices of the peace at the end of the fourteenth century. On 20 November 1196 Hubert ordered that standard weights and measures should be used throughout England, an ordinance which, as Magna Carta proves, was popular in London.

Although some of Hubert Walter's administrative expedients were to have a long lineage, his government was of necessity oppressive. In 1196 he had to put down an insurrection in London raised by William fitzOsbern in protest against the unequal distribution of the heavy taxation and the suspected peculation by the city oligarchy; and in December 1197 he was defied in a Great Council at Oxford by the bishops of Lincoln and Salisbury, who temporarily defeated the king's request that the English barons should provide him with a fraction of their knight service for a whole year by protesting that their bishoprics owed no military service abroad. Hubert's last measure was to plan a geld at 5s. on the arable carucate. The necessary survey of lands was extremely unpopular; and in July 1198, perhaps even before its completion, Hubert had taken advantage of increasing papal pressure to resign his royal office.

Hubert Walter's administration is noteworthy for his intelligent development of the principles underlying Henry II's reforms. On the one hand can be seen the fresh impulse given to the bureaucratic machine and, on the other, the extension of the practice of employing local knights on the king's business. With the growth of royal government the established local officers of the crown, the sheriffs, bailiffs, reeves, and constables, had become over-worked; and the king had either to increase the cost of his administration by creating new officials or to impose more duties on the only class capable of doing them—the knights of the shire.

The gulf between those knights with fiefs and those kept in the household (knights bachelor) was still fundamental; and a new distinction was arising between knightly tenure and knightly status, because many who held knight's fees or fractions of them were no longer soldiers and hence avoided being dubbed knights. Since the number of landed knights in a shire was relatively small and their prestige among the rear vassals considerable, the royal court found them much to do. It required them to form the Grand Assize and to sit on other juries; the itinerant justices used knights to verify excuses of absence (essoins), to view boundaries, to assign dower, and perform all those tasks for which local knowledge and a good social standing were necessary; and knights bore the record when a case was transferred from court to court. In the thirteenth century the king imposed duty after duty on them, some lucrative, some not, using them as itinerant justices, coroners, keepers of the peace, forest officials, tallagers, assessors for taxation and for arms, constables of castles, custodians of escheats. And for those who accepted the load and did not try to pose as socagers there were rewards in social prestige and a busy interest in local affairs, besides the customary and illicit profits and the occasional bounty of a grateful king. By Henry III's reign knights were complaining of the burden. But there were always some who regarded the commands of the prince as honourable and coveted duties.

The knights were especially trusted by the king. But all freemen were becoming increasingly involved in the operations of the king's government. 'Good and discreet' men, 'legal and discreet' men were summoned for inquiry after inquiry, jury upon jury. And legal procedure needed many men. The litigants required an imposing 'suit', and had often to find pledges and then better pledges. The defendant must be summoned by 'good and lawful' summoners. Hindered parties had to send essoigners. Issues of fact were decided by juries. Amercements were fixed by affeerors. There was no pay and some risk for the participants, for the king's justices enforced the salutary rule that false claims, false opinions, and errors in procedure should incur an amercement. Thus all free men, and on the royal demesne all men, were required to help the king govern his realm.

Hubert Walter's resignation was due to the growing impossibility of satisfactorily combining the spiritual office of primate with the temporal duties of justiciar. His quarrels with the monks of Christ Church and his act of sacrilege in 1196, when he had William fitzOsbern smoked from sanctuary in Bow Church, London, and dragged to the gibbet, made it impossible for the new pope, Innocent III, to dispense with the 12th canon of the Third Lateran Council, which forbade clerks, from subdeacons upwards, to accept administrative or judicial offices from laymen. Hubert's successor as chief justiciar was Geoffrey fitzPeter, sheriff of Yorkshire and Staffordshire, who held the office until his death in 1213. Geoffrey, too, had been a clerk of Ranulf Glanville, and was a product of the same tradition. After serving as a sheriff and forest judge he had been named an assistant justiciar in 1189 and became one of that inner circle of professional administrators on which the king could draw for a variety of purposes. But, unlike Hubert, Geoffrey's ambitions were entirely secular. While Richard was absent he had obtained the English inheritance of William de Mandeville, earl of Essex, to whom his wife, Beatrice de Say, was distantly related; and just as Hubert had achieved high honour in the church so Geoffrey obtained a good place among the English baronage. But Geoffrey had been lucky. True, Richard of Lucy, chief justiciar under Henry

II, had died holding some 13 knight's fees in chief, 19 fees held of the earldom of Cornwall, and the castle and barony of Ongar in Essex held of the honour of Boulogne; but the general policy of the crown was to reward its servants mainly with casual profits— wardships and marriages and the custody of escheats. An hereditary estate with a good title (and that was the weakness of Geoffrey's position) was granted with reluctance. Geoffrey was as faithful and as efficient as Hubert; but less rapacious and, perhaps, less creative. His task was quite as heavy. Richard never revisited England after his brief stay in 1194, and John was absent for most of the first four-and-a-half years of his reign.

IV

Richard's death caused more disturbance in the kingdom but less change in the administration than had Henry's ten years before. In his weakness John could do no other than quieten baronial unrest by promising redress of grievances and accept without demur the officials his brother had bequeathed. Geoffrey fitzPeter remained chief justiciar and, content with his recognition as earl of Essex, served John faithfully. Hubert Walter was brought out of retirement and given the chancellorship. A descendant of the exchequer family which sprang from Henry I's Roger of Salisbury, William of Ely, continued to be treasurer. Richard's chief forester, Hugh of Neville, a nephew of Henry II's chief forester, Alan, became one of John's most intimate friends. So, too, Richard's justiciars and sheriffs, men who had served their apprenticeship under Henry II, such as Hugh Bardolf and William Brewer, remained in employment. The great William the Marshal, a repository of Angevin history, was the king's constant companion until Normandy was lost. These were the men who, steeped in the tradition of Henry II, had without much hesitation preferred his last surviving son to his Breton grandson; and their staying in office determined the basic continuity of the royal administration. Yet John soon made his influence felt. He was not one to be governed by servants. And in the course of his reign there were few institutions which were not shaken up by his personal action.

John's true character has been perplexingly obscured by the evil legend, full of contradictory attributes, which was quickly created in order to explain his failure; for, although it is not difficult to reduce each separate charge to its proper proportion, it is less easy to be confident that in consequence the whole case fails. John, like his great-grandfather Henry I, was a youngest son, pampered, and then twisted and hardened by the failure of too many premature ambitions; and although his vices seem ordinary enough—the conventional weaknesses of the age—and only moderately pursued, it is possible that his coarse sense of humour could aggravate his offence and that his intelligent, even scholarly, outlook could make his misbehaviour revolting. It may be that in John, as in William Rufus, there was the occasional flash of conscious defiant evil which could horrify the ordinary sinner. There must also have been a flaw in his majesty, for, despite his magnificence, his restoration of the splendour of the crown-wearing at the great festivities, his love of finery and jewels, and his generosity—he was indulgent to the queen and his divorced wife, open-handed to his men, liberal to churches, and prodigal to the poor—he earned contemptuous epithets. He was 'lackland' or 'softsword'; and his consistent failure would seem to justify the taunts. King Stephen had failed because he possessed in too great a measure the ideal qualities of his age, John, perhaps, because he was under-endowed with popular virtues.

But failure is one of the shallower judgments. John's problems were immense and his near-successes brilliant. The loss of the continental possessions was almost inevitable; and such a beginning was fateful. Richard had left him an empty treasury, a people wakening to disenchantment, and a difficult and costly foreign policy. Monetary inflation added to the task. Professionalized warfare had become ruinous to the crown. A mediocrity in John's position would have retrenched, and, by seeking less, have salvaged more. John would rarely bargain; and he accepted uncompromising defeat as a springboard to total victory. It may be that John was too clever, too opportunist, too mercurial. Aware of mistrust and dislike, he was suspicious and elaborately careful; but he aroused only greater fear. Although an intelligent diplomatist and general, and always meditating conquest, his diplomacy usually outran his means, and his campaigns were too often unlucky. He had his father's gift of finding useful men, and handled them even better, possibly because he chose rougher tools. William of Wrotham and Reginald of Cornhill, the most able administrators of the time, were his servants. Peter des Roches and Hubert de Burgh, great names in English history, were from his household. Gerard d'Athies, Fawkes de Bréauté, Engelard de Cigogné, and Philip Mark, infamous names, but borne by staunch and efficient servants, were his men. He kept the loyalty of his own creatures, and they remained faithful to his family in the years of its greatest danger. But their employment imperilled the throne. John, the pupil of Ranulf Glanville, had too his father's technical grasp of law and administration which enabled him to comprehend and solve his problems and judge and govern in person; yet his impatience and versatility give an air of improvization to his whole reign. The man who first sanctioned the recording of his chancery's business finished like a condottiere living from hand to mouth on the country. In short, John lacked stability of character; and his undeniable talents only made his failure seem all the more grotesque, ignoble, and complete:

V

The abbot of Coggeshall's verdict on John was that he reigned indefatigably (*satis laboriose*). The appointment of Hubert Walter to the chancellorship and the king's love of experiment led to the opening of a new chapter in the history of the royal government. A great change in the business habits of men was affecting in turn all the chanceries of Europe. In feudal society before the twelfth century written documents were rare. Intention was conveyed by a symbolical act and witness secured by the publicity of the ceremony. The conveyance of land was as real as man could make it; and if a charter was drawn up to provide a physical memorial of the transaction it merely recorded a completed and perfect act. The spread of literacy and greater familiarity with business affairs had, however, gradually accustomed men to the use of written documents; and the growing flocks of sheep provided abundant parchment for the purpose. By the reign of Henry II every little knight had a seal, as the justiciar, Richard of Lucy, noted with disapproval; and they had acquired seals because of the number of documents they had to sign. In the second half of the twelfth century the art of writing was for the first time in the Middle Ages put to general use. The monasteries compiled and fabricated their collections of charters, their cartularies. The hated starrs of the Jewish moneylenders obliged their debtors. Landlords, now entrusting their estates to professional stewards, found accounts and manorial extents essential. Records began to accumulate in all archives.

The documentary habit was, of course, found in its most advanced phase in the papal and royal governments from which it had spread.

The papal court had always led the way in devising specialized routines and forms, and its chancery had made spectacular growth under Alexander III (1159–81), a former papal chancellor. The Anglo-Norman royal chancery had followed its own unique tradition based on the Old-English scriptorium. But in Richard's reign the influence of papal practices can be seen. William Longchamp and Hubert Walter, both papal legates, the former the author of *Practica legum,* the latter most skilled in English practice, both drew on their knowledge of the papal *curia* when governing in England. To William is possibly due the innovation of giving royal charters a dating clause similar to that in papal privileges and of dating other royal documents by the day and the month on the analogy of papal letters; and Hubert may well be responsible for the more systematic keeping of chancery records.

Until the end of the twelfth century governments rarely took copies or extracts of the documents they issued. Clerks made notes; but the business was so small that much of it could be kept in the head. Financial records were the first to be kept. Debt collectors need long memories. The English exchequer, by 1199 a department stationed at Westminster, had been systematically recording its business for at least half a century. Even the king's household had been keeping duplicates of the financial writs it sent to the exchequer (the origin of the close and *liberate* rolls). Next to adopt the habit were the royal law courts, partly, no doubt, because the exchequer had to collect the fines and amercements which were 'estreated' from their rolls. But the keeping of records was outgrowing the purely financial stage. Land titles were of the utmost importance. Rolls of the Grand Assize seem to have been kept from the beginning. And in 1195, at the conclusion of a final concord made in the royal court, it was decided (in imitation of the procedure introduced the previous year for the recording of Jewish contracts) to make the chirograph, or indenture, in triplicate, so that the court could keep the third copy, the 'foot of the fine'. In this way began a new class of records of the court of Common Pleas. Hubert Walter was justiciar in 1194–5. Papal registers have been preserved in unbroken series from the accession of Innocent III in 1198. At John's coronation Hubert became chancellor. On 7 June 1199 the king issued a constitution reducing the fees charged in the royal chancery; and thereafter charter rolls (with their offshoot the patent rolls) began to be kept. Within a few years separate rolls were being made for registering all the different classes of chancery documents, except legal writs, which were never recorded. In 1216 Hugh of Wells, bishop of Lincoln, a former royal chancery clerk, began to keep the first English episcopal register. The record habit had taken firm root in England; and its inspiration seems to have been ecclesiastical. Nevertheless, English practice remained peculiar. Most writing offices chose to enter their records on gatherings of parchment which later were bound into a book, a register. The English court used the roll—the chancery rolls consisting of twenty or more membranes sewn end to end, the exchequer and law rolls made up of a number of sheets secured at the head, all written on both sides—a primitive and inconvenient method which it preferred not to change.

The need to record departmental business was one sign of the growing importance and complexity of the once single *curia regis;* and the inauguration of chancery enrolments hardened the divisions. Developments in the formerly standard chancery handwriting, the 'court hand', point the same way, for by John's reign distinct chancery, exchequer, and legal versions of it can be distinguished. But, although by 1199 most royal justice was done by benches of judges operating away from the king and controlled by the chief justiciar, John's long residence in England closed the gap between his itinerant court and the exchequer and allowed him to intervene more easily, while his interest in business made the whole organization for a time more fluid. To convey his will the king had merely to give a personal order to the chancellor or one of his chief clerks, and the appropriate document then went out to set in motion the exchequer, the sheriff, or other royal official. And John would not abide independence. Like his father he could draft a charter himself; and at the end of 1200 he broke Hubert Walter for a week and acted as his own chancellor because Hubert was appearing to rival the king in the magnificence of his state. The chancery was the mainspring of the Angevin government; and from the first year of King John until chancery in its turn went out of court and was controlled by writs sent from the household under the small, or secret, seal, chancery enrolments provide a day-to-day record of the king's movements and actions. Hence 1199 is a real turning point in English history. The materials available to the historian suddenly become more numerous and more exact. Institutions can be studied from their own archives.

John also influenced the development of English law. His training and interest in jurisprudence, his policy of selling his justice cheap, and his inexhaustible pleasure in hearing cases in person gave a fresh impetus to his father's reforms. He popularized the writ *praecipe*, which could be used to transfer a case from a feudal to the royal court, and from it there developed a class of writs of entry, useful in land actions. Men both small and great would pay to have their cases heard by John; and if the centralization of justice led to some new inconveniences, which Magna Carta sought to remedy, it can hardly be viewed as the policy of a megalomaniac. The king was resident in England, anxious to do justice; and other royal courts inevitably lost some of their standing.

VI

John did well to start by putting his own house in order, for he had to face a financial blizzard. The increased activity of the European markets, the greater abundance of silver, the medium of exchange, and the vast war expenditure which released capital reserves, together with the relatively slow expansion of the area of land under cultivation and the even slower improvement in farming techniques, were causing the price of agricultural produce to rise and driving up the cost of labour. Gainers were all those men who lived by the direct exploitation of land and those who had the right to free services; losers were the recipients of fixed rents and the employers of hired labour. The English landowners countered the effects of monetary inflation by recovering immediate control over their estates and by high farming. Kings Henry II and Richard had moved in the same direction. The Inquest of Sheriffs (1170), the Assize of Northampton (1176), and the Eyre of 1194 had been steps towards the routine supervision of the royal demesne and its welding into a centrally controlled unit. But the intensive exploitation of the demesne manors, characterized by regular restocking and rack-renting, had been nullified by the necessity of all kings to alienate demesne to those with a claim on their gratitude. The Norman kings, as we have seen, granted much away. The rivalry of Stephen and Matilda was expensive. And even Henry II, in so many fields the restorer, was generous with his estates. By 1200, it seems, but a third of the demesne that William I had had in 1086 was still in the hands of the crown.

John introduced no novelties into the administration of the shrunken demesne, the escheats, and the custodies; but he probably increased the pressure. He both withdrew items, such as manors, boroughs, and the customs of seaports, from the sheriff's farm, in order to let them to the highest bidder, and also tried to enhance the sheriff's offer for the remainder. Like his predecessors he also experimented with making some sheriffs and bailiffs custodians rather than farmers, that is to say accountable for the net profits; but the expedient was unpopular and seldom profitable to the crown. Indeed, tallages, which until 1206 John took almost annually, remained the easiest way of tapping the hidden wealth of the boroughs and royal manors.

More radical was John's attempt to restore the coinage, the silver pennies, to full standard and weight. By the ordinances of 9 November 1204 and 26 January 1205 he initiated the gradual withdrawal of all faulty money and its exchange for new coins, superior, but of the same general pattern (the short cross). The trusted William of Wrotham and Reginald of Cornhill were in charge of the operations; the mint would issue penny-weights for the checking of the old coinage; and the sheriffs were to appoint four lawful men in every market to carry out the plan.

The king suffered also as a great employer of labour. A manorial lord could force his villeins to plough and reap his demesne again; but the king was unable to exact profitable services from his tenants-in-chief. The feudal host could not provide him with an expeditionary force; the serjeants and their deputies were indifferent servants; his vassals could not supply the sort of counsel and administration he needed. John created a few more serjeanties and knights' fees; but more characteristic of this transitional period between the feudal benefice and the pure salary were the money fiefs which he gave so prodigally. In 1200, for example, he granted a fief of 400 marks to Robert count of Dreux in return for the service of the count and three knights who were to be at Verneuil within fifteen days of their summons to serve forty days in any part of France. He also granted money fiefs to recruiting agents, principally to captains and nobles of the Low Countries. Much money was involved. Besides the annual charge there was the collateral security which important feoffees required to be deposited in the treasuries of the Templars; and the soldiers were paid when used and also compensated for loss. Against this account John could only put the sums raised from the English baronage in lieu of military service, the scutages and fines; and these were insufficient. John imposed eleven scutages in his first sixteen years, a great increase on Richard's three in his ten years and Henry II's eight in his thirty-four years; and he forced the rate up to £2 the knight's fee on occasion. But it was not enough. Warfare was costlier in men and equipment; John's principal enemy, Philip of France, was wealthier and more powerful than his predecessors. The balance had to be found elsewhere.

The demesne produced much. But John was able to increase the yield from the traditional sources of revenue only by straining them. Radical reform was impossible both because it was opposed by vested interest and because no government as yet could force all its servants to keep accounts. John, therefore, like all the Angevins, sold favours, hunted voraciously for all the incidents of government, and reviewed the various methods of taking an aid. In 1200, to pay his relief to the king of France, he took a carucage at 3s. on the carucate (or, possibly, on the plough team). In 1203 he collected a seventh and in 1207 a thirteenth of movables and revenues for the cost of the war. Even more notable were the customs duties he imposed as a war measure between July 1202 (or 1203) and October 1206 in the form of a fifteenth of all merchandise passing between England and France and Flanders. But gracious aids required consent. After 1207 no consent was forthcoming. So John reaped the harvest of his quarrel with the papacy and took four scutages for which no consent was necessary; and the experiments in taxation ceased until his son's reign. But John's measures were of the greatest importance in creating precedent. John failed, like all his successors until modern times, to solve the basic administrative problem of how to assess accurately the liability of unwilling taxpayers. His half-brother, Geoffrey archbishop of York, struggled against the carucage of 1200 and was forced into permanent exile over his opposition to the thirteenth of 1207; and John usually allowed the prelates and sometimes whole counties to 'fine'—pay a lump sum in commutation of the tax. But he had kept new expedients alive and had done something to transform them into customs. At the centre a special committee of the royal household under a group of John's financial experts, such as William of Wrotham and Reginald of Cornhill, supervised the levy of each tax; each shire was given its local commission of knights and clerks; for the customs duties, on the precedent of the Assize of Arms of 1181 and the carucage of 1198, juries were used to assess the individual liability—a most unpopular device; and collection was made usually by the barons of the shire who paid to the sheriff for delivery to the exchequer. The subsidies of Tenths and Fifteenths of the sixteenth century trace back to John's seventh; and the new customs system of Edward I had its forerunner in John's temporary and novel expedient.

John's financial policy was experimental and opportunist. He needed money; he tried every method. He was not a fiscal reformer; and when one method ceased to be profitable or aroused too much opposition he tried another. All taxation was detested unless its purpose was obvious and popular. And John's purposes were seldom popular in England. The English baronage as a whole quickly lost interest in the recovery of the king's continental demesne and grudged the cost. It also feared lest John should become too strong. This attitude forced John to exploit windfalls to the full; and his greatest opportunity occurred when he quarrelled with the pope.

VII

John returned to England from his disastrous campaigns in defence of his French fiefs at the end of 1203; and he was never again to leave the kingdom for long. At first his bad luck persisted. Just as he had lost his fiefs through a quarrel not of his own choosing and because of factors largely outside his control, so his great struggle with the pope was not in origin of his own making or connected directly with his special vices. From his accession until May 1200 and after April 1202 his warfare with Philip Augustus and his alliance with his nephew, Otto IV, the Welf claimant to the Empire, had aligned him exactly with the papal policy; and Innocent III knew him as a useful if undependable ally. In domestic affairs John had done nothing to disturb the entente. In 1204 the pope actually helped him to secure the bishopric of Winchester for his financial adviser, Peter des Roches, by quashing a divided election and allowing the delegation of monks at Rome to re-elect Peter. On 13 July 1205 Hubert Walter, primate of all England and royal chancellor, died; and the rival interests which had clashed in 1173, 1184, and 1193 collided again with even greater violence and with far more unfortunate results.

The three parties were as before: the monks of Christ Church, the cathedral chapter, who claimed the sole right to elect, and who were determined after the repression of Archbishops Baldwin and Hubert to elect one of their own brethren; the bishops of the province, who desired to share in the election, and who were likely to support the king's nomination of one of themselves; and the king, who wished to reward a trusted servant, in this case John Grey, bishop of Norwich, formerly a senior clerk in the chancery. On hearing of Hubert's death John hastened to Canterbury, and, when he found the monks and the bishops already in dispute, he either imposed a truce until December or authorized the contestants to settle their quarrel by law before proceeding to an election. However that may be, both sides approached the papal court; and the monks, hardened to deceit, secretly and irregularly elected in advance the head of their mission, the sub-prior Reginald. In December, when John revisited Canterbury, the sorry story came out; and the king in order to safeguard his purpose forced a compromise: the monks and the bishops were to drop their suit; and an archbishop was to be elected by the chapter alone subject to the assent of the bishops. Accordingly, on 11 December 1205 Grey was elected archbishop. But when Innocent III was confronted with two delegations of monks, each with a candidate, he quashed Grey's election (May 1206) and ordered a thorough investigation. In December 1206 he gave definitive sentence in the two cases. He pronounced that the right to elect belonged exclusively to the cathedral chapter, and he invalidated in turn Reginald's election, partly because the king regarded him as unsuitable. Then, as in the Winchester case, he authorized the monks to re-elect; and the division between the supporters of Reginald and of Grey was resolved when he suggested a third candidate, Stephen Langton, cardinal-priest of St. Chrysogonus, a distinguished Englishman at the papal court. The royal proctors at Rome, however, refused their assent. Their business had been to secure Grey's election, not to accept a papal candidate. Innocent finally disregarded the objection, and on 17 June 1207 he consecrated Stephen archbishop and gave him the pallium. He had made war inevitable.

Stephen Langton, the son of a freeholder of Langton-by-Wragby in Lincolnshire, was then just turned fifty years of age. He had gone to the Paris schools about the year 1170, and had stayed to teach in arts and afterwards in theology. During a quarter of a century he had lectured on the *Histories* or *Historia scholastica* of Peter Comestor, on the whole of the Bible, and on Peter Lombard's gloss on the

Pauline epistles, while discussing the outstanding theological problems in complementary courses—a comprehensive study which led to his revision of the order of the books of the Bible and of their arrangement into chapters. Langton was pre-eminently a Biblical scholar; but the purpose of his teaching was to train men for office in the church: to give them a course in practical morality based on the Scriptures. He was a poet, too, and an eloquent preacher both in Latin and in the vulgar tongues. His fame had brought him canonries in the cathedral churches of York and Paris; and when Innocent III called him to Rome in 1206 to teach theology in a cardinal's hat he took a doctor whose glosses or postils (commentaries on the Scriptures) and *questiones* (theological disputations) had contributed to the advancement of the science and had deeply influenced the younger masters, his pupils. The pope's candidate for Canterbury was, then, exemplary. But Innocent was naively imperious in imagining that John would accept him without a struggle.

The pope's action showed a contemptuous disregard for the residual rights of patronage which were commonly allowed to the laity. Ecclesiastical lawyers had completely undermined the old conception of the private ownership of churches; but lay patrons were still allowed to present to benefices where no ecclesiastical procedure of election was possible, as Innocent had expressly allowed in a privilege to England dated 3 August 1200, and kings were still permitted to exercise some control over the election of bishops, for it was against the church's interest to force unwelcome candidates on the king. The bishops, as Alexander III had recognized, were the king's vassals for their fiefs; and the archbishop of Canterbury was traditionally the first counsellor of the king. Never before had the king failed to obtain an archbishop of his choice. John, therefore, had two valid lines of protest: that Langton was personally unacceptable (a stranger who had been living under the protection of his enemy, the king of France) and that his right of patronage had been set aside. Innocent regarded the first objection as perverse and foolish. He knew better than the king what was good for him. And he regarded the second as irrelevant. Langton had been canonically elected and consecrated, and John's regrettable attitude could have no legal force. The quarrel was, then, mainly political in character. John did not deny that archbishops should be elected; he only insisted that the man elected should be agreeable to him. And Innocent in his way concurred. Nevertheless, the pope's action threatened another assault on the rights of the laity; and the English barons, as jealous as the king of their ecclesiastical patronage, supported John in his stand. The bishops, too, were quite aware that the ancient rights of the king had been flouted by a troublesome chapter and an interfering pope; and they had no interest in Langton. But they were the servants of two masters.

John answered Langton's consecration by expelling in July the monks of Christ Church. On 27 August 1207 Innocent gave instructions to the bishops of London, Ely, and Worcester to lay an interdict on England and Wales if the king would not submit. John then stated his terms: the new archbishop was to give satisfactory security for his loyalty and the pope was to confirm the royal right, dignity, and liberties. In effect, John would make a grudging exception if the pope would explicitly recognize it as an exception. Negotiations failed, however, to convince either side that the other was sincere. On 18 March 1208 the king announced the appointment of commissioners to confiscate the property of all clerks who observed an interdict; and on 23 March the three bishops published the papal sentence and retired to the Continent.

Although the interdict had become a common political weapon of the papacy no common law governing it had yet evolved; and it seems that the sentence was interpreted with slight differences in the various English bishoprics. The basic feature was the suspension of all church services, except baptism of infants and penance for the dying, so that there could be no confirmation, no Christian marriage, and no Christian burial, no mass, no absolution of sins, and no consecration. Church bells were silent. The loss to the people was severe. The pious were left without comfort and ordinary men and women without the familiar ceremonies. Yet there is no evidence of popular unrest in England. Men become accustomed to absences; and to withhold Christian ministration too long was to endanger the faith. Early in 1209 Innocent gave permission for conventual churches to celebrate mass behind closed doors; and late in 1212 he allowed the last communion, the *viaticum*, to be administered to the dying. The interdict lasted for more than six years. It was remembered as a hardship, but, it seems, as nothing more.

On the publication of the sentence John immediately imposed his simple reprisal. Distraint and forfeiture of land for failure to perform service were familiar feudal processes; and the sequestration of church property caused no trouble. More unusual, however, and certain to amuse, was the order to arrest all the clergy's house-keepers and concubines, the *sacerdotissae*. Wits averred, and moralists feared, that the priests felt the loss of their women more than the loss of their land; and for once John's humour was of political value. But John was fighting against Innocent III, not against the English church; and, after he had shown his power, he allowed the clergy to pay fines for their lands and mistresses. A few beneficed clerks fled the country and left their estates in the king's hands; more and more bishoprics and abbeys fell vacant and were exploited by royal custodians; and naturally John continued his practice of asking the church for *dona*, gifts. The interdict solved John's financial problem for a time. But for the clergy who kept quiet there was no special penalty after 1208. Benefit of clergy was observed. Church courts functioned, although, certainly after 1210, no appeals could go to Rome. Ecclesiastical business went on as usual, with the bishop's official and the archdeacons administering the spiritual-ities of the vacant dioceses. Episcopal elections were held, although the bishops-elect, all friends of the king, could not be consecrated. Church building was not abandoned. The king protested his ortho-doxy by maintaining his customary alms and even, perhaps, by having a heretic burned at London in 1210. He was certainly less violent than his father had been during his quarrel with a pope.

As on the previous occasion negotiations between the parties were never broken off. In the spring of 1205 John had ordered Reginald of Cornhill, sheriff of Kent, to send him two tuns of wine to Windsor and a history of England in French. He was preparing a brief to persuade the barons, whom he had summoned to North-ampton, to support his projected continental campaign. After his break with the pope he turned to his books again. He collected a theological library and seems to have closely investigated the rights of his predecessors in church elections; but there was no flood of polemical literature. Langton had sent a manifesto to England in 1207, at the beginning of the breach, and proved that feudal analogy could serve both sides by arguing that vassals were not bound to follow a ruler who rebelled against his superior lord, the King of kings. In November 1209 a sentence of excommunication was published against John in the churches of northern France; but Langton does not seem to have appealed again to the English baronage. To spurn the divine law was the greatest treason; but the archbishop was no extreme papalist, and the political effect of spiritual censures was still a dark question. Nor did the sentence make much difference. The king himself was undismayed; the usual barons were to be found at court; and, although the clerical contingent inevitably declined, two bishops, two Cistercian abbots, some Templars and Hospitallers, and the considerable body of secular clerks stayed in regular attendance. Yet the king could not fail to be concerned with the possible effect of the sentence on his vassals. Langton's views were a warning; and the king began to pay special attention to internal security.

VIII

After Henry II's strife with the church there had been a great baronial revolt. Events followed a similar course in John's reign; but this second rebellion, although less cataclysmic in its beginning, has attracted disproportionate attention because among its incidents was the royal grant of the Great Charter and because John died while engaged in suppressing it, an accident almost as harmful to the monarchy as Henry I's death in similar circumstances. John's relations with individual barons and with groups of magnates have been studied intensively as the prologue to Magna Carta. But in the early Middle Ages private motives are inexplicable and characters enigmatic; and the isolation of family groups, supposedly united in aim through kinship and marriage alliance, is arbitrary and delusive, since most of the baronage was inter-related and because kinsmen are not always friends. The common frictional points between the crown and the baronage are obvious from the history of the preceding reigns, and are confirmed by the demands of the insurgents in 1215. A king such as John, avid for money to finance an unpopular policy, had only to drive the inherited system of government hard to create a general feeling of oppression and to provoke many individual hatreds. John was no more of a tyrant than his predecessors; but his enforced stay in the kingdom after the loss of his French fiefs increased the latent tensions and brought on him all that odium which his brother and father had shared with their chief justiciars; his conflict with the church weakened one bond in society; his surrender to Innocent and the disastrous close to his continental schemes gave an opportunity to the malcontents; and his comparative weakness in 1215 allowed the revolt to get out of hand.

Yet until 1214 John seemed to be overcoming his difficulties. If his personal government provoked private quarrels it also allowed him to impose exemplary punishment; and while he built up a war chest and an army to bring him victory against Philip Augustus he kept in training by crushing the traditional anarchy on the English marches. John had a special interest in the frontier areas. He had been king designate of Ireland since his boyhood; his marriage to Isabella of Gloucester in 1189 had brought him the lordship of Glamorgan; and Richard's grant of the honour of Lancaster had introduced him to northern politics. John's military skill did not impress contemporaries; and clearly he lacked Richard's power of leadership and probably also his personal courage. Yet John was quite as martial as his brother; and the ten years of campaigning which ended in 1203 had given him some of the worst features of the professional soldier: the profane humour, the ruthless exploitation of subordinates, and the irresponsibility. Nor had John returned to England in order to settle down. He prowled round his kingdom, circling incessantly through the southern shires to the Welsh march and then back along the Trent, lashing occasionally at Wales and Scotland and the difficult baron, while he built up power for the counter-stroke on the Continent. He was, therefore, committed to war, and his whole reign bears the marks of military expediency.

John was most generous to soldiers. He collected engineers and could always take a castle. He kept a force of crossbowmen distributed between his English strongholds. He rewarded barons who would fight for him, such as his half-brother, William Longsword earl of Salisbury, William the Marshal earl of Pembroke, and Roger of Lacy constable of Chester. William of Briouze was extravagantly prized. This descendant of a Conquest family, holding the rape of Bramber in Sussex with its two castles, half the barony of Barnstaple in Devon, and the marcher lordships of Radnor, Abergavenny, and Brecon, had been with Richard when he died and had pressed hard for John's succession. In 1201 John granted him most of Limerick and in 1202 the wardship of Glamorgan, Gwynllwg, Gower, and the Beauchamp land in Worcestershire. It was he who captured Arthur at Mirebeau; and through rewards which come ever closer in appearance to the fruits of blackmail he became with William the Marshal one of the greatest barons in South Wales and in Ireland. His eldest son married the daughter of Richard of Clare, earl of Hertford, and another son, Giles, became bishop of Hereford. William of Ferrers, earl of Derby, was his nephew; Hugh Mortimer, heir to Wigmore, and Walter of Lacy, lord of Meath, were his sons-in-law. William's ambition had overtopped prudence. John also advanced men from his household who could be entrusted with a castle. Hubert de Burgh, originally Richard's servant and then John's chamberlain when count of Mortain, was employed as sheriff after 1201, and in 1202 was given the key command of warden of Dover castle and of the Cinque Ports. Thereafter he always held a post of danger in time of war. And after Normandy and Anjou had been lost John welcomed soldiers from his old fiefs and gave them English employment: Fawkes de Bréauté from Normandy and Gerard d'Athies and his kinsmen from Touraine.

The loss of Normandy and Brittany and the defection of Flanders and Boulogne created new strategic problems for John. For the first time since 1066 control of the sea became a military requirement. And the Channel Islands, the only portion of the duchy remaining to the king, became an essential link between England and Aquitaine. John reacted with typical quickness. The traditional forces at his disposal were the royal yacht, the duty fleets of the Cinque Ports (and it was in the years just before 1207 that the burgesses of Hastings, Romney, Hythe, Sandwich, Rye, Winchelsea, and Pevensey as well as those of Dover were recognized by the king as barons), and such merchant shipping as he could requisition. By 1205 John had assembled at least 51 galleys, the long warships of Mediterranean origin, and had created a chain of naval command. Reginald of Cornhill, of the great London merchant family, was one of his chief agents in the project; but his senior admiralty official, with the title of 'keeper of the ports and ships', was the indefatigable archdeacon of Taunton, William of Wrotham. The main base for the royal fleet was Portsmouth, which Richard I had built in the years after 1194, a safe harbour, equipped with warehouses and a dock, and conveniently placed near Southampton, the largest sea-faring town after London. There was also the problem of the military defence of the kingdom. In 1205, in anticipation of a French landing, John reorganized the fyrd. Chief constables were to be appointed in the shires to command the forces of the local 'communes'—the hundreds, cities, boroughs, and groups of townships —each under inferior constables; and all men over twelve were to take an oath to obey their officers and be loyal to the king. The scheme does every honour to John's ingenuity. It drew on the basic Assize of Arms (1181) and on John's experience of Norman communes;

and, by redefining fyrd service in the current idiom, it was a notable
step in the evolution of the military and peace system of the kingdom.

John was not the first king to lavish money on soldiers and
financiers, on military stores and equipment; but he was the first
since the Conquest to live permanently on his English estates and
conduct war at home. As a result the traditional financial administration soon broke down. At his accession the main English treasury
was at Westminster, with Winchester used as a subordinate store-
house: a convenient arrangement for an absentee king, for from
both hoards money could be sent easily to the French fiefs. But as
John perambulated ceaselessly through the southern half of his
kingdom he imposed an impossible strain on the treasury couriers.
The obvious remedy was to follow the precedent set by Henry II
when resident in England: to authorize the household to collect
money direct from debtors. The king's chamber, of which Richard
Marsh, the future bishop of Durham, became clerk in 1207,
gathered in all the royal revenue available as the king's retinue
travelled across the country and loaded it on to the wardrobe carts.
Since more money was collected than was required for current
expenditure, the scheme was carried a stage further by the establishment of local treasuries in which the surpluses could be placed.
During the war years in France John had deposited his money,
silver pennies barrelled or packed in units of £100, as military stores
in the castles; and by the summer of 1207 he had developed a similar
system in England. Rochester (Reginald of Cornhill), Marlborough
(Hugh of Neville, the chief forester), Devizes (Thomas of Sandford),
Corfe (Ralf Parmenter), Exeter (William Brewer), Bristol, for the
Irish receipts (after March 1208 Gerard d'Athies, sometime
seneschal of Tours), and Gloucester (Engelard de Cigogné) were the
main treasuries on the western circuit; and Nottingham (Robert of
Vipont or Vieuxpont; and after October 1208 Philip Mark) and
Northampton (Robert Braybrook) were the main northern deposits.
The exchequer still kept its accounts in the traditional manner; but
it handled less money. The king was in residence, and he had his
own little ways.

John knew what he wanted to do and reorganized his English
administration to that end. He searched hard for money and he
stored it conveniently in the hands of trusted castellans. It could be
poured into Flanders or Poitou if need be; it could be used in Wales
or Ireland; and with a little adjustment it was ready for a Scottish

campaign. John found much to do at home. Richard had completely sacrificed his English to his French claims. On Henry II's death Rhys ap Gruffydd, prince of Deheubarth, had begun to attack and capture castles in South Wales, and, although John had been sent to chastise him, no real stand had been made. Symptomatic of Welsh resurgence was the renewed and again unsuccessful attempt by St. David's, this time under Gerald of Barri, who had been elected bishop in 1199, to claim metropolitical status independent of Canterbury. Then Richard had sold freedom from vassalage to William the Lion, king of Scots, and returned the castles of Roxburgh and Berwick; and on John's accession William had demanded the shires of Cumberland and Northumberland. Under these conditions the marcher barons had become intractable, and the royal power in Ireland had dwindled. John was naturally most interested in Wales and Ireland; and had not his authority suddenly collapsed in 1214 he might have anticipated the achievement of his grandson, Edward I.

While Rhys ap Gruffydd, prince of Deheubarth, grew old, two young men rose to power in north Wales, Gwenwynwyn in southern Powys and then Llywelyn ab Iorwerth, known to history as Llywelyn the Great, in Gwynedd. Hubert Walter had humbled Gwenwynwyn in September 1196, and in August 1198 Geoffrey fitzPeter had decisively defeated him. John at first pursued the traditional royal policy of encouraging rivalries and of balancing the Welsh princes against the marchers. In the north he cold-shouldered the earl of Chester; and in order to check Gwenwynwyn betrothed a bastard daughter, Joan, to Llywelyn in 1204. In the south, where Rhys had died in 1197, he built up William of Briouze to balance William the Marshal. In the spring of 1205 the Marshal did liege homage to Philip Augustus for his French fiefs and thereafter refused to serve John in France against Philip. John was furious, and encouraged his justiciar in Ireland to attack William's lands. But this quarrel was ephemeral. John had decided to break William of Briouze. The king seems to have become jealous and mistrustful of his old confederate in 1206. Early in 1207 he replaced him as bailiff of Glamorgan and Gwynllwg by Fawkes de Bréauté, and a year later put in Gerard d'Athies as sheriff of Gloucestershire and Hereford. About the time of the interdict John asked William for his eldest son as hostage. The boy's mother, Matilda, referred indiscreetly to the fate of Arthur of Brittany; and John became without mercy. He used the summary procedure for recovering exchequer debts to deprive the heavily indebted William of his lands, and when William's family took refuge in Ireland at the end of 1209 (or 1208) they found there as chief justiciar John Grey, bishop of Norwich, a strong man whom John had just appointed to watch Briouze, the related Lacys, and the Marshal. The fall of Briouze in 1208 disturbed the balance throughout Wales. Gwenwynwyn ravaged the central area, but obeyed in October the order to meet John at Shrewsbury, and suffered the loss of his estates. Llywelyn then marched into Powys; and he in his turn had to be restrained.

In 1209 John turned to Scotland. On hearing of a conspiracy among some northern barons, in which Philip of France was meddling, John decided to settle matters with William the Lion. In July, with Llywelyn of Gwynedd in his army, John marched to the Scottish border and at Norham charged William with harbouring his enemies and interfering with the fortifications the bishop of Durham had built at Tweedmouth to compensate for Richard's surrender of Berwick. The Scottish king was old and his heir, Alexander (II), a boy. He did liege homage, promised an indemnity of 15,000 marks, and surrendered his two daughters as hostages. In return John agreed to leave Tweedmouth open. Both frontiers were safe; and John met the threat of papal excommunication by summoning all his vassals to attend him at his favourite castle of Marlborough in September and swear fealty to him and his infant son, Henry, and by receiving the homage of the Welsh princes and some of their men at Woodstock in October.

The next year, 1210, it was the turn of Ireland. After punishing a group of eastern barons—Henry of Bohun earl of Hereford, Robert fitzWalter lord of Dunmow, the traitor of Vaudreuil, and Geoffrey and William of Mandeville, the two sons of the chief justiciar Geoffrey fitzPeter—John assembled the feudal host, a bodyguard of Flemish knights, and several companies of mercenary serjeants and crossbowmen, and marched through South Wales. He brushed aside William of Briouze's offer of 40,000 marks for pardon, and in two months (20 June–24 August) without having to besiege a single castle, he broke and expelled the Lacy brothers, Walter lord of Meath and Hugh lord of Ulster, for the crime of harbouring Walter's father-in-law, William of Briouze, took hostages from William the Marshal, lord of Leinster, and received the submission of most of the Irish kings. The destruction of all but one of the great principalities which had been created during the Norman conquest enabled John to bring Ireland under the ordinary pattern of royal government; and the two justiciars he appointed, John Grey, bishop of Norwich (1208/9–1213) and Henry of London, archbishop of Dublin (1213–5), both confidential royal servants trained in the English legal and financial tradition, carried out the work of reconstruction. They extended the area and the authority of the royal government by attempting to assimilate independent Irish kings into the baronage, by building castles, and by improving communications; and they brought the law of the settlers into conformity with current English practice. Norman Ireland became peaceful, prosperous, and loyal. But by taming the great Norman barons in Ireland John possibly prevented the occupation of the whole of Erin. Only two-thirds of the country was under direct Anglo-Norman rule. Control over the south was weak; and the north and the west were almost completely independent.

Ireland, Wales, and Scotland each kept its Celtic hinterland; and this could be to the advantage of the English crown. The king of Scots was pliable whenever a rival arose in the north; the Welsh marcher barons were submissive when powerful Welsh princes emerged; and after 1210 Ireland became one of the main buttresses of John's power. Nor were John's punishments easily forgotten. Hugh of Lacy and Matilda of Briouze and her sons fled from Ulster to Scotland. Matilda and her eldest son, William, were captured by Duncan of Carrick and surrendered to John. There was still talk of the 40,000 marks, which her husband did not possess. But when William of Briouze, the elder, fled from Wales to France, his wife and son were starved to death in a royal castle. The Lacys were pardoned in 1213 and Walter recovered Meath. But Hugh would not pay the fine for Ulster.

The desperate return of William of Briouze to his Welsh estates while John was in Ireland led in some way to hostilities between the king and Llywelyn. In the summer of 1210 the earl of Chester, the chief justiciar, and the bishop of Winchester invaded Gwynned; and at the end of November John restored to Gwenwynwyn his estates in south Powys. In May 1211 the king himself pushed into Gwynedd from Chester and in July had more success in an expedition based on Oswestry. Llywelyn accepted heavy terms. He surrendered the Four Cantrefs in the Middle Country, between Snowdonia and Chester, together with thirty hostages, and promised

an enormous tribute in cattle. Fawkes de Bréauté had meanwhile
built a new castle at Aberystwyth to complete his conquest of
northern Ceredigion. The native areas were being squeezed hard.
Llywelyn and his wife Joan spent Easter 1212 with John at Cambridge. On 16 May Reginald king of the Isles, or of Man, became
John's liege vassal, and so confirmed a relationship which had been
close since 1205. In the summer John went north to the help of the
king of Scots, troubled by a Celtic pretender from Ireland, and was
granted the marriage of the Scottish heir, Alexander, his 'liege man'.
But in his absence Llywelyn rebelled.

John had been intending to invade France that autumn. In May
he had summoned his foreign vassals to join him. In June, to prepare
for maximum military and financial demands on his barons, he had
ordered an investigation into the state of the baronies. His recruiting
agents in Flanders and Scotland had orders to raise every man they
could; and John Grey and William the Marshal were instructed to
bring 200 knights and as many serjeants as advisable from Ireland.
John, however, decided to turn his army against Wales and deal the
crushing blow. Labourers were impressed. Money was assembled
at Nottingham. The feudal host was summoned to Chester for 19
August. On 14 August John hanged some of the Welsh hostages
surrendered the year before. And on 16 August he countermanded
all the preparations. Rumours of a conspiracy against his life turned
him on to another quarry.

Llywelyn had recovered the Four Cantrefs except the castles of
Rhuddlan and Degannwy, and these he captured early in 1213. He
had survived a critical moment; and the baronial revolt in England
followed by an unquiet minority was to give him the opportunity to
undo all John's labour and to create a Welsh principality greater
than had ever been seen before. And yet there was something of
permanence in John's work. By fettering Ireland, Wales, and Scotland again he had reinforced the tradition of subjection and had
given a new impulse to a neglected English policy. Edward I, in
character the antithesis of his grandfather, but in purpose strangely
alike and in fortune not dissimilar, was his true successor.

IX

The conspiracy of 1212 which saved Llywelyn was so quickly
smothered by John that its ramifications and purpose are obscure.
When John demanded hostages from those he suspected Robert

fitzWalter, lord of Dunmow, fled to France and Eustace of Vesci, lord of Alnwick, took refuge with his father-in-law, William the Lion, king of Scots. Both these barons had been in trouble before; and either they were the ringleaders in 1212 or they were too deeply implicated and too hostile to risk submission. Certainly they re-emerged three years later as men committed to destroy the king. It is likely that Robert fitzWalter, a baron of the first rank, was the tool of France. Both kings were engaged in suborning each other's vassals; and Robert was the man who in 1203 had surrendered Vaudreuil under mysterious and suspicious circumstances.

The war between John and Philip was still going in the French king's favour. The stupendous expedition planned in 1205 had not sailed owing to the opposition of the primate and the earl marshal. John's successes in his campaign up to the Loire in 1206 had not long survived the two years' truce made on 24 October, for in the course of those years Philip had reconquered most of Poitou. John was still seriously hampered by the state of Flanders. In 1202 Count Baldwin IX had gone on the Fourth Crusade, and, after becoming emperor of Constantinople, had died in 1206, a prisoner of the Bulgars. His heiress had passed under Philip's wardship; and although John made a treaty in 1211 with the most important towns it was a poor substitute for the traditional lordship over the count. In January 1212 Philip married his ward to Ferdinand, son of Sancho I of Portugal, intending to use the new count as a pliable servant; but from the beginning he overplayed his hand. On 3 May Reginald of Dammartin, count of Boulogne, who had changed sides so often before, at the emperor's bidding accepted a money fief from John and did liege homage, and thereafter acted as John's agent in organizing a northern coalition. Nor had the career of John's nephew, Otto of Brunswick, been of much comfort to England. From 1204 to 1208 his rival, the Hohenstaufen Philip of Swabia, had been in possession of Germany; and, although he regained the throne after Philip's murder (21 June 1208) and was crowned emperor by Innocent III on 4 October 1209, he was deposed by the pope on 22 December 1210 for daring to lay his hands on the patrimony of St. Peter, and confronted with a new Hohenstaufen rival, the young Frederick of Sicily, the Emperor Henry VI's son. Otto had taken refuge in England in 1207; his brother, Henry of Saxony, since 1195 *jure uxoris* count palatine of the Rhine, had visited England in 1209; and in September 1212 Duke Henry III of Limburg came over to have his fief renewed. The Angevin and the Welf clung together; but neither could do much for the other.

John's diplomatic position in the south was no less precarious. His sometime brother-in-law, Raymond VI of Toulouse and duke of Narbonne, had been excommunicated and deposed by the pope in 1206 for favouring the Albigensian heresy, and, although the count had submitted in June 1209, a Crusade against the heretics launched from the north of France in July, under the command of a papal legate, but soon dominated by Simon de Montfort, claimant to the earldom of Leicester, succeeded in conquering most of his territory. In 1212 Peter II king of Aragon and count of Barcelona intervened to aid Raymond, his brother-in-law; but the French hold on the eastern marches of Aquitaine had become much firmer. In general, the victims of Pope Innocent III's sentences were the natural allies of John against Philip of France. And the pope could not turn without reserve to the French king, for, although Philip's mistress, Agnes of Méran, had died in August 1201, the queen, Ingeborg of Denmark, was still neglected. It is possible that John had the diplomatic advantage in 1212; and he had the money—some 200,000 marks at call in his castle treasuries. All he needed was a free hand. And if Philip was, indeed, behind the abortive English rebellion of 1212 he had gained two years' grace.

The disappointment convinced John that he had undertaken too much. Rumours were circulating that he as well as his brother-in-law and nephew had been deposed by the pope; and the Welsh princes were making use of the story. A crazy prophet, Peter of Wakefield, was forecasting his doom. The easiest way for John to limit his liabilities was to make peace with the church. In November 1212 he sent envoys to accept the terms which the nuncios Pandulf and Durand had offered him at Northampton at the end of August 1211. On 27 February 1213 Innocent repeated the conditions and ordered John to confirm his acceptance and provide pledges before 1 June, otherwise he would take stronger measures. The terms embodied the pope's original and consistent attitude: John was to submit to ecclesiastical discipline for the offences which had caused his excommunication; he was to receive the archbishop and take back all the clergy and laity who had been exiled during the controversy and guarantee them full restoration and safety; and he was to return everything he had stolen from the church. He could take oaths of fealty from the returning archbishop and bishops; but should he violate his guarantee he would lose his remaining rights over ecclesiastical property. John decided to offer the pope even more. He summoned the nuncio Pandulf to him, and on 15 May 1213 at the Temple near Dover issued a charter surrendering his kingdom to God and the apostles Peter and Paul for the service of 1,000 marks, 700 for England and 300 for Ireland. The tribute was light, the advantage considerable. By making England a papal fief he secured a powerful overlord and changed in a twinkling his stern opponent into a benevolent protector. He faced the returning archbishop as a vassal of the pope his master. The charter was attested by the archbishop of Dublin, the bishop of Norwich, seven earls, the count of Boulogne, and three barons. There was no contemporary opposition. Indeed, a few years later the rebellious barons claimed that it was on their advice that John had taken the step. Richard had surrendered the kingdom to the Emperor Henry VI and received it back as an imperial fief for the service of £5,000 sterling a year. John made a more profitable arrangement.

A month after John's agreement with Pandulf, Archbishop Stephen Langton landed in England, and on 20 July 1213 at Winchester, after requiring the king to swear an elaborate coronation oath, absolved him from excommunication. Both the king and the pope were anxious for a quick settlement. John wished to be free to attack Philip of France. Innocent was planning the Fourth Lateran Council which was to be the prelude to a new Crusade. The raising of the interdict, however, depended on the fulfilment of the terms John had accepted. The exiles returned, among them three personal enemies of the king—Giles of Briouze bishop of Hereford and the two leaders of the 1212 conspiracy, Eustace of Vesci and Robert fitzWalter—all of whom had posed as martyrs for the church; and only the complicated business of restoring John's exactions from the church caused difficulty. The investigation itself took time; and the problem of distinguishing the illicit from the lawful profits and the forced from the willing gifts spun out negotiations. At the end of September Nicholas, cardinal-bishop of Tusculum, arrived from Rome to wind up the business; and on 23 January 1214 Innocent accepted John's offer of 100,000 marks in full settlement and later his request to pay by instalment. The interdict was lifted on 2 July 1214. Political events had made the exaction of substantial damages impossible.

When two great powers quarrel and then come to a mutually

advantageous alliance the subject of the quarrel often loses all importance, frequently becomes, indeed, an embarrassment to the erstwhile champion. Becket had spared the pope further vexation by his splendid martyrdom; but Langton lived to displease his master. Trained as a theologian and casuist, inexperienced in administration and politics, Langton could not easily accommodate himself to the world of expediency in which he now found himself. It is believed that he disapproved of John's surrender of the kingdom to the pope; and as primate of all England, with a position of honour and duty in the state, he could not see eye to eye with papal legates who were concerned merely with the superficialities of the current situation. He had returned to England to vindicate in his person the right of freedom of election, to punish the transgressors, to insure that those who had suffered for the cause were indemnified, and, more widely, to enforce the rule of law. He saw the wicked pardoned easily, the sufferers defrauded, and his own cause betrayed. And he knew that the trivial restorations with which the pope was satisfied were no guarantee of sound and just government. The method by which the vacant bishoprics were filled was bound to cause him the liveliest distress. Innocent had ordered the legate Nicholas to co-operate with John and see that men useful to the kingdom and agreeable to the king were promoted. Hence Pandulf got the revenues of Norwich, Exeter was given to Simon of Apulia, dean of York, as a gracious gesture to the pope, Rochester was confirmed under Canterbury's patronage, but Worcester, Lichfield, and York went to royal nominees and Durham escaped only through the pertinacity of the monks and a series of accidents. The alliance of pope and king to defraud the electors of their legal powers was the strangest sequel to a quarrel which had arisen out of John's assertion of his right of patronage. But there was no real illogicality. Innocent had never denied that bishops should be acceptable to the king; and in 1213 John was a papal vassal facing internal difficulties. Langton was obstructive. The provincial subordinate could not appreciate the full import of the wider curial policy as interpreted by legates *a latere*. In January 1214 Pandulf returned to Rome and complained. Langton was concerned with justice as he saw it in England, and for him there was no turning aside. His suspension by the pope in 1215 was the inevitable result.

John's foreign policy must have caused Langton equal distress. John was making peace with the church in order to fight in alliance

with the pope's enemies against the pope's friends. In 1213 John
and Philip stood poised, each ready to attack the other if the opportunity arose. On 19 November 1212 Philip had allied with Frederick
of Sicily and secured his election to the German crown. In February
1213 John ordered an 'inquest of sheriffs' as a final administrative
review. On 29 March William count of Holland, in the presence of
Henry count palatine of the Rhine and Reginald count of Boulogne,
did homage to John at London for a money fief of 400 marks. On
8 April Philip at the council of Soissons ordered the French army to
assemble at Rouen a fortnight later, and at last he took Ingeborg
back as queen. John collected his fleet at Portsmouth, mustered his
army at Dover, and invited his Rhenish vassals to join him. Early in
May he reviewed a great host, which included a large Irish contingent, at Barham Down near Canterbury. Money began to flow eastwards in tens of thousands of marks. In June 100,000 were transferred from Bristol to Corfe and Devizes and in July Bristol provided
a further 20,000 for the king at Canterbury. Philip decided that he
must first punish Ferdinand of Flanders, who, although not yet an
ally of John, was moving in that direction. On 22 May Philip invaded
up the coast and within a week had taken most of the towns. But
on 28 May the English fleet sailed under the earl of Salisbury and
the count of Boulogne, destroyed the French fleet and transports on
the beach at Damme, the port of Bruges, and forced Philip to desist;
and during the autumn and winter Philip lost all his acquisitions
except Douai and Cassel.

Control of the sea had given the initiative to John. In July he
completed his pacification of the Welsh march by pardoning the
Lacys, and summoned the feudal host to reassemble at Portsmouth
to cross with him to Poitou. On 25 July he sent an embassy to
Germany. The great counter-stroke was about to be launched. The
Emperor Otto IV with John's Rhenish and Flemish allies and some
English reinforcements would invade France from the north while
John and his southern friends would strike up from Poitou. But
again domestic trouble frustrated John. The discontent which had
been repressed in the previous year had found an outlet in the
negotiations concerned with the lifting of the interdict and a sympathetic auditor in Stephen Langton. Some northern barons refused
the second summons to serve and alleged that their military service
was not owed outside the kingdom; and when John, after getting
no farther than the Channel Isles, marched in his fury against the

laggards the archbishop held him back by reminding him that at the
time of his absolution he had sworn that he would not use force
against his barons except after the lawful judgment of his court. In
August John postponed the invasion again. And on 12 September
Peter II of Aragon was defeated and killed at the battle of Muret by
Simon de Montfort, while attempting to defend the Languedoc
against the French 'Crusade', and Raymond of Toulouse was forced
to take refuge in England.

If the return of the king's personal enemies reanimated baronial
discontent, it was Langton's arrival which gave it purpose. He
regarded the remedy of wrongs and the establishment of just government as a single problem. At a council held at St. Albans on 4 August
1213 under the archbishop and John's representatives, Geoffrey
fitzPeter and Peter des Roches, to investigate the injuries to church
property, a proclamation of peace was made. Royal officials were to
behave themselves and the laws of King Henry I were to be observed. At the next council, held on 25 August at St. Paul's, London,
the coronation charter of Henry I was produced and discussed.
Langton was exploring both public opinion and history in order to
find a true basis for peace. Henry I was the last king to promise
remedy of specific abuses; and by 1213 the *leges Henrici primi* were
becoming as respectable and as unintelligible as the *laga Edwardi*.
Negotiations may have been opened with the king on this basis,
for some historians believe that the document in the French royal
archives (the 'Unknown charter'), consisting of the charter of Henry I
with a draft or notes of additional clauses, comes from this time
or the spring of 1214 when John was raising his army for France.
Others would date it later. It is clear that the idea that the king
should be persuaded or compelled to grant a charter of liberties on
the style of Henry I's was making ground.

But the Angevin leopard was still too strong to be caged. And his
enemies did nothing while he made his last preparations for a continental victory which would make them helpless. In October 1213
the old justiciar, Geoffrey fitzPeter, died; and in February, after
negotiations with the barons, John appointed the more cosmopolitan Peter des Roches, bishop of Winchester, his Poitevin financial adviser, in his place. Money was again moved to the southern
ports. The treasuries at Bristol and Nottingham were emptied.
Peter de Maulay, who was to be John's paymaster with the expeditionary force with his headquarters at la Rochelle, took 40,000 marks

from Devizes with him when he sailed from Portsmouth. In January 1214 John met Ferdinand of Flanders at Canterbury in order to receive his homage and perfect their plans; and on 9 February the king embarked for Poitou with his troops, including a number of barons who were later to revolt. The great coalition was at last putting its armies into the field.

At first all went according to plan. The Aquitanian barons rallied to their old lord, and John recovered Poitou. In June he crossed the Loire, occupied Angers, and laid siege to the new and neighbouring castle of Roche-au-Moine, his last hindrance to an advance towards Paris. But on 2 July Louis, Philip's son whom he had left to contain John, raised the siege with an inferior force. The Poitevin barons would not fight against the French king or his heir. John realized that his projected offensive was impossible; and he devoted himself to re-establishing his power in Aquitaine while his northern allies tried their luck. Towards the end of July Otto arrived at Valenciennes to reinforce the troops of Flanders, Boulogne, and other Netherland fiefs. Philip, from Péronne, attempted a flanking movement to the north-west; but at Tournai decided to fall back on Lille. As he retreated on Sunday 27 July the allies followed, and when he crossed the river Marcq near Bouvines they fell upon his rearguard. A regular battle was given on the higher ground to the east. Each army faced the other with three divisions in line. The allied left under the count of Flanders was overwhelmed and the commander taken. In the centre both Philip and Otto were unhorsed; and so roughly was the emperor handled that he left the field. The right under the count of Boulogne and the earl of Salisbury fought desperately until the earl was struck down by Philip bishop of Beauvais, Richard's old enemy whom John had released, and the count was encircled and captured. A bloody and a fateful battle had been fought to a decisive end. The counts of Boulogne and Flanders were kept in prison. Philip again dominated the Low Countries. In Germany the discredited Otto of Brunswick went down before his young rival, Frederick of Sicily. John made peace on 18 September. At Chinon he bought a five years' truce for £60,000. Philip Augustus had become the most powerful king in Europe.

X

On 13 October 1214 John returned to England. He himself had not done badly; but all his greater hopes had been destroyed and his money was exhausted. When he imposed a scutage of 3 marks the knight's fee on those who had not campaigned collection proved difficult; and so poor had he become that in January and February 1215 he put his new chancellor, Richard Marsh, formerly clerk of the chamber, over the exchequer to see if anything more could be squeezed out of the disturbed kingdom. Conspiratorial meetings were again taking place. The baronial malcontents were threatening to make war on the king unless he would grant them their just rights. John looked desperately for friends. In the winter he strengthened his alliance with the church by abandoning the customary procedure in episcopal and abbatial elections, as stated in chapter 12 of the Constitutions of Clarendon, and reducing his rights to the grant of a *congé d'élire* (charter of 21 November, reissued 15 January 1215); and on 6 January at London, when confronted with a baronial demand for the abolition of all innovations made by himself, his brother, and his father, he replied that he would answer at Easter. He summoned mercenaries from Poitou; and then on 13 March dismissed them, for on 4 March he had taken the Cross and so reinforced his position as a papal vassal with all the privileges allowed a Crusader. But the barons still wanted an answer; and when the truce expired they carried out their threat, assembled in arms at Stamford, and moved towards London. John sent the cardinal archbishop and the earl marshal to ask what they wanted; but he rejected in fury the schedule of their demands. Whereupon the rebels renounced their fealty, elected Robert fitzWalter their leader with the title of Marshal of the Host of God and Holy Church, and marched from Brackley against Northampton castle. On 9 May John issued an indulgent charter to keep London loyal, and on the next day Langton and the moderate courtiers at Reading again attempted to mediate. John offered to submit to the arbitration of a body of eight, chosen from both sides, under the guidance of the pope. He also promised the rebels that he would take no action against them except according to the law of his kingdom or the judgment of their peers in his court—a promise which with small alteration was repeated as chapter 39 of Magna Carta. The 'unknown charter', already mentioned, may represent these proposals. The offer, however, had no result. Northampton had held; but Bedford fell. It came ever closer to war. Mercenaries were arriving from Flanders. Hubert de Burgh landed from Poitou. On 12 May John ordered the sheriffs to confiscate the land of the rebels and sell their chattels. On 17 May the barons occupied all London except the Tower. On 27 May John asked Langton to arrange a truce. He had been defeated, perhaps, as much by his friends as by his open enemies.

John's indecisive behaviour between his return from Poitou and the autumn of 1215, when the civil war broke out undisguised, is reminiscent of his conduct at the beginning of his reign while Normandy was being lost; and at both times William the Marshal was at his side. It may be that the earl, the flower of chivalry, believed he could negotiate a fair settlement, and restrained his lord's bellicose instincts. Certainly William had arranged his own affairs satisfactorily in 1205; and in 1215 his son and heir joined the rebels. Moreover, in 1214–5 Stephen Langton was at court, desperately anxious that his conception of a just peace should not be hazarded by the violence of either side; and John could not openly disregard his advice, for as a papal vassal he was bound to the church and relied on it for protection. Hence the negotiations. But since John would not make substantial concessions he invalidated his public policy, and by inaction he frustrated his real purpose. But whether John given a free hand could have crushed the rebellion of 1214–5 as easily as that of 1212 is doubtful. On the former occasion he had had the appearance of strength, a full treasury, and an army at command. In 1214 he was discredited and bankrupt. What is more, the opposition party had grown in numbers and in coherence owing to the opportunities for free expression it had enjoyed. Although the core of the rebels still consisted of a collection of embittered enemies of the king, such as Robert fitzWalter, Eustace of Vesci, Roger Bigod earl of Norfolk, Geoffrey de Mandeville who styled himself earl of Gloucester and Essex, and Henry de Bohun, earl, and Giles of Briouze, bishop of Hereford, together with their kinsmen and vassals, by appealing to the good old days and the excellent customs of the past the leaders recruited some men of good will and enjoyed for a time the sympathy of a wide circle which saw much to criticize in the Angevin system of government. The immediate use of force against the eastern rebels might have caused the conspiracy to collapse; the timely concession of reforms under an acceptable guarantee might have isolated the implacable. But John was prevented from striking hard and he had no intention of making a radical surrender of his rights. In May 1215 he was engulfed and had to sue for terms. The exact course taken by the negotiations, which lasted from 10 to 23 June and were conducted

on the Thames in 'the meadow called Runnymede between Windsor
and Staines', is not entirely clear. But out of them came first the
'Articles of the Barons', which may have been accepted as heads of
agreement on 15 June, and then the Great Charter itself. On 19 June
the rebels renewed their homage, probably after both sides had
sworn to observe the charter, and by 24 June copies of the royal
grant (dated 15 June) were being issued for publication. 'Firm
peace' had been made.

The charter of 1215 was the product of at least two years' thought;
and many interests had moulded it. The rebels had studied the
coronation charters of at least the two Henries, and they adopted
Henry I's as a model. So John's charter can be regarded as a modern-
ization and expansion of that grant. But the original aim to recover
Anglo-Norman customs and abolish all Angevin innovations had not
been pressed in an antiquarian way. The impossible idea of returning
to a mythical past had been replaced by an insistence on practical
reform once the terms began to be negotiated. Many of the rebels
had served the king; some had been sheriffs and justices; Geoffrey de
Mandeville was the son of the late chief justiciar; Robert fitzWalter
was the grandson of Henry II's justiciar, Richard of Lucy. They had
a fund of experience which no rancour could entirely obliterate. The
intermediaries had also played their part. William the Marshal, earl
of Pembroke, was trusted by both sides; and no man knew more
about royal courts and feudal customs. The archbishop of Canterbury stood by the king but sympathized with the just aspirations
of the rebels. As a professor of moral theology he could turn an
individual grievance into a general principle of law. The king
himself no doubt had his say; and the contribution of his chancery
was of considerable importance. Despite its imperfections in
arrangement, Magna Carta is a splendid chancery production. In
its brevity and precision, its technicality and polish, it is a worthy
memorial to the system of government which was under attack.

Magna Carta is a code of some sixty clauses. It declares the law in
the technical language of the royal court on the points which the
insurgents had raised. It reforms specific abuses, some of general
interest, some of local or sectional importance, some of long
standing, some few introduced by John himself; and although the
characteristic brevity of the enactments can cause difficulty to the
modern reader we may be sure that there was no ambiguity at the
time. The charter is the largest body of enacted law since the code of

Cnut, and was worthily placed near the front of the *Statutes of the Realm*. Yet in substance the charter is curiously disappointing. It displays no real understanding of the problems of government, and in fact exerted no detailed influence on the development of the royal administration; and it ignores some of the most important matters which the king and baronage had to settle, such as military service. It comments mostly on the periphery of the royal sphere of action and condemns mainly those abuses of power by subordinates which were universal at the time and regularly investigated by the Angevin kings through their 'inquests of sheriffs'. It was an inadequate judgment on the past and an impracticable guide for the future.

The first chapter revises the corresponding clause in Henry I's coronation charter. The church is to be free and have all its liberties, especially freedom of election; and all 'free men' are to have the enumerated liberties. A group of feudal clauses follow, similar to those in the prototype. The law of custody, wardship, and marriage is declared in a manner to protect the vassal against the king (caps. 2–8); and the vexed question of the amount a baron is to pay as relief is fixed for the first time at £100 (cap. 2). As in Henry's charter the king's barons are to pass on these gains to their vassals; and this was intended to be no mere form of words, for most of the rebels held substantial mesne fiefs. Chapters 9–11 reform the practice of distraint for debts due to the crown and to the Jews. Chapter 12 attempts a bold solution of the problem of scutage: no scutage or aid—except the compulsory aids, which are defined—is to be placed on the kingdom unless by the common counsel of the realm; and chapter 14 gives the organization of the council that is to be consulted. John's development of scutage into an almost annual tax on those barons who did not serve in the army may have been equitable, both historically and in the circumstances, but it was resented as a burden; and in 1215 the rebels forced the king to agree to obtain the prior consent of a body consisting of all the greater barons summoned individually and all the lesser barons summoned collectively through the sheriff. The vexed problem of military service, however, remained unsolved. It is merely conceded that no one is to be distrained to perform more service from a knight's fee or any other tenement than is due from it (cap. 16).

No opposition can appreciate a government's financial difficulties and policy; and John was forced to abrogate every Angevin expedient to increase the yield of traditional sources of revenue except the exploitation of his own demesne. It can, however, often make a grudging appraisal of its legal reforms. John's barons accepted almost without demur the astonishing growth of royal jurisdiction since the early Norman period and were concerned only with its reform. Feudal courts in general were incompetent to deal with any but the simplest cases. Skilled lawyers were lacking; the power to secure the presence of those concerned in the case, especially third parties and warrantors, was not available; and if the matter at issue was of any complexity or importance it usually suited demandant, tenant, and the lord of the feudal court for the case to go before royal justices. There is no evidence at all that John's court had been wilfully encroaching. And the only defensive move the barons made in 1215 was to secure the abolition of the writ *praecipe quod reddat* (cap. 34) and thus make sure that a feudal lord could retain jurisdiction over his tenants if he so wished. The main complaint of the barons was of the insufficiency, the venality, and the inconvenience of the existing facilities.

The basic principle of the rule of law was expressed in chapter 39: 'No freeman shall be arrested, or kept in prison, or disseised [of his freehold], or outlawed, or banished, or in any way brought to ruin—and we will not act against him or send others against him—unless by the lawful judgment of his peers or by the law of the land.' Legal practice was suspended uneasily between two ages. The traditional, and for the most part irrational, forms of proof were falling into disfavour and oblivion. Both the enlightened laity and the church were becoming dissatisfied with the ordeal; but, although experiments towards more satisfactory procedures were being made, no generally accepted method had as yet emerged, and vigorous rulers were apt to choose the most expedient method of punishing their enemies. Hence it was taught in the schools and generally held that a lawful judgment of a competent court must precede punishment (as both Longchamp and John had confessed in 1191); and it was impossible to be more precise at the time for there were many courts and many customs. Langton, when lecturing on obedience at Paris, had argued that a vassal was bound to ride with the king to attack a castle provided that there had been a formal judgment, even if that sentence was unjust; but that there was no moral necessity if the king attacked both unjustly and arbitrarily. Chapter 39 of Magna Carta was in protest against all lawless acts of the royal government and particularly against John's use of special methods for condemning barons to forfeiture. In October 1201 those Poitevin barons required by John to disprove his charge of treason by fighting a duel with his professional gladiators had refused to accept any judgment except that of their peers. In 1208 John had broken the family of Briouze by distraining for debts under exchequer procedure, and in September 1211 Langton had buried William of Briouze at Corbeil. In 1213, when Langton removed John's excommunication, he is believed to have made the king swear that he would judge his vassals according to the just laws of his court; and he had in mind, no doubt, the returning 'martyrs', Eustace of Vesci and Robert fitzWalter, who had fled or been outlawed in 1212. During the negotiations in May John had repeated this promise; and the first chapter of the Unknown Charter states that John had conceded that he would arrest no man without judgment. Hence chapter 39 embodies a principle of crucial importance at the time. It does not specify the form of trial—there were many lawful procedures—but it does insist that there should be a proper trial before execution of sentence.

Several of the clauses were designed to secure that lawful judgment in the king's court. The next chapter (40) reads, 'To none will we sell, refuse, or delay right or justice'. Writs, the necessary preliminary to a hearing in the king's court, cost too much; and the king accepted gifts to hasten or impede a suit. In chapter 45 the king undertakes to appoint no justice, constable, sheriff, or bailiff who does not know the law of the kingdom and mean to observe it. Chapter 20 promises that amercements shall be reasonable, and that in no case is a penalty to be so heavy as to endanger a man's means of livelihood. Other clauses were intended to make royal justice more convenient. Chapter 18 concedes that possessory assizes are to be taken in the shire courts and that itinerant justices are to visit the shires four times a year. Chapter 17 reversed John's policy of centralizing his courts, and restored the court of common pleas (the bench sitting usually at the exchequer at Westminster) to a fixed place divorced from the ambulatory king, as it had been before 1209. The opposition understood this legal problem to the core. They were litigious men. They knew the courts. They accepted royal justice as a convenience; but they saw a danger in its control by the king in his own interests and in its freedom from traditional rules. So they insisted on a healthy and popular principle, a principle of permanent value for safeguarding individual liberty.

A remarkable feature of the charter of 1215 is the inclusion of some concessions to the mercantile community, proof of the growing power of the merchants and due to the help given to the insurgents by London. The rights and liberties of London and of all other cities, boroughs, towns, and ports were guaranteed by chapter 13. Freedom of movement was promised to merchants in chapters 41–2, with relief from all but the old customs except in time of war. And by chapter 35 it was decreed that there should be one measure of wine, ale, and corn (the London quarter), and a fixed width of cloth, together with standard weights throughout the kingdom. But London did not achieve its full ambition. Its attempt to make both aids and tallages subject to its consent (chapter 32 of the Articles of the Barons) had been too revolutionary; and in chapter 12 of Magna Carta only its aids were equated to baronial scutages and aids.

As a code of enacted law Magna Carta was inadequate and in-effective. Few of its specific decrees could be observed. It is doubtful whether every weir was destroyed on every English river; the plan for the great councils was unrealistic; itinerant justices could not visit the shires four times a year. But if most of the general reformative provisions were lifeless, those clauses which concerned directly the state of hostilities were drastic both in purpose and effect. Chapters 52 and 55 gave a bite to chapter 39. John promised to restore immediately all lands, castles, and liberties taken by him from anyone without the legal judgment of the man's peers and to investigate after his Crusade the claims of those who had been despoiled by Kings Richard and Henry II. And he agreed to pardon all fines and amercements imposed unjustly and contrary to the law of the land. Canonical theory and baronial aspirations met here in an impossible condition. Wrongful gains must be restored before absolution could be given. But to call in question all royal actions since 1154 threatened to tear the kingdom in pieces. Barons had been broken and others had risen. Society was riddled with counter-claims, and only the inert pressure of seisin, of lawful possession, guaranteed by the crown, kept order. But respite was allowed for the entertainment of the remoter claims until after the Crusade—tantamount, perhaps, to an act of oblivion. What is more, although John had been reducing the area of his forests—during the financial stringency of 1204 he had sold part of Essex and all of Devon and Cornwall to the local inhabitants—he was forced to abrogate such afforestations as he had made, to consider after his Crusade those of his brother and father, and to hold immediately an inquiry into bad customs of the forest (caps. 47–8, 53).

Even more objectionable to the king was the final security clause, providing machinery for the enforcement of the charter and, especially, of those clauses which were intended to be implemented at once. The rebel barons were to elect twenty-five of their choice (and could co-opt to fill vacancies) who were to supervise the charter's execution. Any complaint against the king or his servants was to be presented to four of the body, who were to ask the king or, in his absence abroad, the justiciar for redress. Emendation was to be made within 40 days, otherwise the whole twenty-five would constrain the king by force, saving the immunity of his and his family's person. The restoration of unjust disseisins, fines, and amercements was also placed under the control of the twenty-five. All men were to be invited, and, if recusant, compelled, to take an oath to help the twenty-five control the king.

The security clause was similar to the guarantee to a treaty, and is remarkable only in its use between a king and his rebel barons and in its one-sidedness. English kings had granted charters of liberties before and had incontinently forgotten them. This charter was to be executed under threat of war in accordance with the baronial resolutions made while extorting it. The right of resistance to a king behaving unlawfully was one of the deepest constitutional ideas of the Germanic people. It was implicit in every oath of fealty. The obligation of the king to respect every individual right and, more widely, the law, which was seen as containing within itself the totality of those individual rights, was universally held, and was expressed publicly in the coronation oath. In 1215 the rebels set up guardians of the law. The expedient was novel and clumsily designed. The council of twenty-five was to be chosen by the barons and its majority decision was to have full force. In the event the barons appointed John's personal enemies to it, and, by putting the idea to a vindictive purpose, robbed it of any chance of success. But even when the plan was tried again against later kings in more refined forms it never worked. Kings would not act under obvious restraint.

Magna Carta has been much studied, and with reason. It was a partisan judgment on 60 years of Angevin rule and also a precedent for future trials. The king's government had been developed to suit the royal purpose alone, and by 1215 it touched nearly every man in the kingdom. It had been extended haphazardly according to the needs of the moment and was subject to no control except the king's; and he was less interested in the general welfare than in efficiency. At Runnymede the king was forced, through the temporary combination of selfish rebels and a moderate party anxious for peaceful reform, to grant the charter. And although the measure was almost without immediate effect and never had much influence in detail it reinforced some healthy precedents and reaffirmed some salutary principles. One of the themes of the charter is 'to each man his just rights held under the dominant law'; and behind the crude attempt of the barons to insure that the king would respect the law was an idea, which, when differently applied, was to produce the constitutional monarchy. It became of political importance again in the seventeenth century, when antiquaries, using the 1225 edition and misunderstanding the technicalities, read trial by jury and no taxation without representation into its clauses. Yet their interpretation was not completely ludicrous. Magna Carta guaranteed the thirteenth-century equivalents. The spirit lived after the words had lost their original meaning.

In 1215 the charter represented the terms on which John expected to get peace; and after Runnymede the king began to give effect to some of his promises. He released a number of hostages, dismissed most of his mercenaries, displaced some of the sheriffs, changed the justiciar of Ireland, superseded Peter des Roches by Hubert de Burgh as chief justiciar of England, satisfied a number of claims under chapter 52, inaugurated the investigation into onerous forest customs, and directed all men to take an oath of fealty to the twenty-five. But chancery could not cope with the pressure. And when John met the barons at Oxford shortly after 16 July, as agreed at Runnymede, in order to review progress and complete the peace, copies of the charter had still not reached all the shires and the oaths of fealty to the twenty-five were far from complete. In these circumstances the barons would not agree that the conditions had been satisfied. They refused to restore London or to give charters of fealty; and in the end John had to agree to leave the Tower in the hands of Langton and London in the possession of the barons, but as royal custodians.

Even if John had been completely sincere during the first month after his capitulation the course of events was hardening his attitude. He had found the conduct of the barons overbearing and rapacious.

The earl of Chester had taken advantage of the turmoil to demand and be given the lands of his kinsman, Simon de Montfort, earl of Leicester; and the flood of doubtful claims was unreasonable. At Oxford it was decided that the parties should meet again in the middle of August. But John did not appear. There was to be no final peace.

Neither side could trust the other. On 28 May John had taken back from the Templars the 'German' set of regalia and coronation robes; and on 24 June he had recalled all his jewels and silver plate from the monasteries in which he had deposited them. He believed civil war to be inevitable. Moreover, he was using the pope to defeat his enemies. On 19 March 1215 Innocent had written letters to all parties: the king was to do justice to the aggrieved in his court; the archbishop was to repress disorder; the barons were to be quiet. On 18 June Innocent had ordered ecclesiastical sentences to be imposed unless the barons submitted within eight days. On 7 July he had expressed astonishment at the behaviour of Langton and the bishops, and had ordered them to excommunicate the rebels forthwith and place their lands under an interdict, otherwise three papal commissioners, the bishop of Winchester, the abbot of Reading, and Pandulf, would execute the mandate and suspend those refusing to act. The archbishop would take no action and in September was suspended. He set off for the Lateran Council, and on 4 November, a week before its opening, Innocent confirmed the sentence. On 24 August the pope annulled Magna Carta on the grounds that it prejudiced the king's rights and his honour, absolved the king from his promise to observe it, released all men from the oath they had taken to the council of twenty-five, and excommunicated all adherents of the charter. But before the letter of annulment arrived in England war had already broken out again. It took couriers at least a month to reach Rome; and John usually found the papal instructions disappointingly inappropriate by the time they arrived.

The rebel barons unaided could not have withstood the king for long. Advances in the art of engineering had given greater military power to the rich. The introduction at the end of the twelfth century of a new siege machine, the trebuchet, an engine which worked on the tip-cat principle, forced owners of castles to make revolutionary changes in order to withstand its higher trajectory and heavier missile. Hitherto the motte or the hall or tower had been the main defensive structure; henceforth all attention was concentrated on the surrounding walls, which were raised to form a defensive

curtain round the dwelling place and studded with towers—
square, semi-circular, or round—to enfilade the lists and prevent
mining and escalade. These alterations were costly; and in 1215
the rebels possessed hardly any first-class strongholds. Even
in the few areas where the insurgents were territorially preponderant
—Cumberland, Yorkshire, and the land between the Wash and the
Thames—the royal castles, generally in safe hands, threatened their
security. Robert of Vieuxpont and Hugh Balliol controlled the road
south from Carlisle through the valleys of the Eden and the Tees.
John had the honour of Lancaster and the vacant sees of Durham
and York. The valley of the Derwent was watched by the castles of
Scarborough and Pickering; and in the West Riding of Yorkshire
the king's cousin, the earl of Warenne, had Conisborough and
Sandal. Lincolnshire was well held. And in the angle between the
Thames and the Welland the royal castles at Norwich and Orford,
Wisbech, Cambridge, and Berkhamstead formed advanced posts
based on Nottingham, Northampton, Oxford, Wallingford, and
Windsor. John had also the support of the only barons who could
put a feudal army into the field—the Welsh and Irish marchers,
especially Ranulf of Chester and William the Marshal—and had
available that formidable cadre of professional captains on which a
mercenary army could soon be built. The insurgents for the most
part were men of small military experience. Indeed, the rebels had
only one advantage—possession of London—and only one hope—
that their foreign allies would fall for the temptation to destroy the
Angevin king. The young Alexander II of Scots, who had succeeded
to the throne on 6 December 1214, hated John and had claims to the
northern counties. Llywelyn ab Iorwerth naturally remained true
to his eastern allies. And in September or October 1215 an embassy
was sent to Louis, the son of Philip of France, inviting him to invade
and take the crown to which he had a just title. In these circumstances the rebels waited in London on the defensive.

The flexible administration which John had forged was well
designed to take the strain. Corfe under Peter de Maulay and
Nottingham under Philip Mark served as his main financial centres
for the south and midlands; and each of his castellans could live off
the country. John's immediate tasks were to isolate London, prevent a French landing, and keep communications open with the
recruiting ground, Flanders. He therefore fixed his headquarters in
Kent, laid siege to Rochester, which Reginald of Cornhill had given

to the barons, and sent Fawkes de Bréauté on a containing expedition from Oxford to Lincoln. By the end of November, when Rochester was taken by mining, John's army had become substantial, despite the loss in October of Hugh of Boves, one of his Flemish recruiting agents, and his contingent by shipwreck; and the king left his half-brother the earl of Salisbury, Savary de Mauléon, and Fawkes de Bréauté to operate against London while he took an army to subdue the north and drive off Alexander of Scots who had entered Northumberland. John reached Nottingham, by way of Northampton and Rockingham, on Christmas eve; and after a campaign up to Berwick was back at Bedford on 29 February 1216. The expedition had been a great success. Many baronial castles had been taken, many submissions received; Berwick had been burned as a reprisal for the firing of Newcastle; and the field treasury had been replenished with the fines taken from rebels and their supporters. Meanwhile the southern army had ravaged Essex and East Anglia. In March the reunited royal forces operated again to the north of London and captured the earl of Norfolk's castle of Framlingham, a recent structure with great curtain walls, Oxford's castle of Hedingham, and the royal castle at Colchester. By April, with the disheartened barons wavering in isolated London, the rebellion seemed about to collapse.

Pope Innocent III was doing all he could for his vassal. On 16 December 1215 Innocent excommunicated many of the leading rebels by name and authorized his commissaries to add others to the list. In the new year he dispatched Guala Biachieri, cardinal-priest of St. Martin, to help John and, in transit, try to prevent the French from giving aid to the insurgents. The rebel barons were in legal as well as military difficulties. They had organized their own administration, imitated from the king's; but, however just their cause, they could never be more than rebels until they acknowledged some king. Louis's claim to England—as the husband of a younger daughter of the queen of Castile (Henry II's daughter)—could not acquire even a specious respectability unless John could be shown to have forfeited his rights. And so the French court put out a medley of arguments, such as that John by his alleged condemnation for treason in Richard's day was a usurper, that he had lost his title by surrendering his kingdom to the pope without the consent of his barons, that he had been deposed by his barons for his misdeeds, and—to add an impudent lie to misrepresentation—that he had been condemned in the French *curia* for Arthur's murder. The pope found the stories ridiculous. Innocent seemed even to approve of John's summary justice on a traitorous nephew. Yet the tissue of special pleading served to cover Capetian aggression and to legitimize rebellion.

In December and January Louis sent French knights to London by way of the Orwell (Geoffrey de Mandeville was killed by one of them in a tournament in March); and by April he had an expeditionary force ready. John made careful preparations. On 14 April he offered a safe-conduct to any rebel who would make peace within a month after Easter; and on the same day he ordered all his ships to concentrate at the mouth of the Thames. But John was unlucky to the end. The cardinal's interview with Philip Augustus and Louis on 24–5 April at Melun was unsuccessful; and on 18 May a storm wrecked and dispersed the royal fleet. Two days later Louis embarked and landed some 1,200 knights and supporting arms on the English coast. John, a student of history, chose not to bar the invader's way to London. On 2 June Louis entered the beleaguered city amid great rejoicing and received the homage of the rebels.

The intervention of the French prince as a pretender to the throne completely transformed the situation. He was an energetic young man, provided with an excellent army and a great siege-train of trebuchets, and he had command of the sea. His admiral, a pirate from Boulogne, Eustace the Monk, who had once been in John's service based on Winchelsea, suborned the Cinque Ports, and with their aid captured the Channel Islands. The irreconcileable core of the rebels saw for the first time the hope of victory. And, more significant, many waverers and even a few of John's intimates began to desert to his rival.

John fell back on Winchester and then on Corfe. When Louis took Winchester the earls of Arundel, Surrey, and Salisbury, and the inconstant count of Aumale submitted to the invader. The defection of his half-brother, Salisbury, followed by the treason of such friends as Hugh of Neville and Warin fitzGerold was a sign that few barons were prepared to fight vigorously for either side. John remained at Corfe from 23 June to 17 July. When Louis returned to the south-east to secure his communications and besiege Dover (magnificently fortified by Henry II and now gallantly defended by Hubert de Burgh) John perambulated the Welsh March to rally his friends. On 25 August he was back at Corfe; and on the next day he set off to retrieve his position in the eastern midlands. Riding by way of Reading, where he relieved the pressure on Windsor, to Cambridge, where he tried to intercept the king of Scots who had visited Louis at Dover, he then struck north through Stamford to the relief of Lincoln under siege by Gilbert of Ghent. From Lincoln John moved south to Lynn, which he reached on 9 October. On 11 October, sick with dysentery, he set off for the north again, and reached the abbey of Swineshead on the following day, having skirted the Wash by way of Wisbech. But his baggage train, loaded with the spoils of the campaign and with some of his personal treasure, had taken the direct road from Lynn, and in crossing the Wellstream, now the Nene, at that time a broad estuary into which most of the Fenland streams drained, got caught in the quicksands and was overwhelmed by the tide. John was seized by a feverish despair. On the morrow he rode to Sleaford castle and on the next day struggled on to Newark. He could get no farther. In the night of 18–19 October he died among his captains, an unquiet ending to a disordered life.

John's premature death in 1216 just before his 49th birthday, leaving a widow with little interest in England and two young sons to represent his line, was not to prove the calamity it must at first have seemed. He bequeathed a military situation uncompromised by defeat, a cadre of captains faithful to the family, and some advisers of ability and standing. He had provided an overlord devoted to the care of widows and orphans; and with the children no man had a quarrel.

Most medieval reigns end in ruin. The boyish hero becomes in time a broken old man. The unrestrained power which he has acquired in his manhood cracks through the caprice and stubbornness of his ageing brain. Ambitious sons and rivals throw off restraint; the weight of accumulated grievance bears him down. The Norman and Angevin kings died badly; and the formal effigies on their tombs commemorate incongruously the passionate creatures who knew no peace in life. John had left his body to his favourite saint, St. Wulfstan; and it was before the altar at Worcester that he was buried. He dated his regnal year from the day of his consecration—the moveable feast of the Ascension; his alms to the poor had always been generous, his interest in monasteries considerable. He was a cultivated man. He died a papal vassal, a frustrated Crusader. Yet he was remembered as an oppressor of the church, as a tyrant. The standards of the monastic chroniclers were simple and severe.

EPILOGUE

THE administrative units of the Roman world, neatly arranged and clearly defined, had been submerged in the Dark Ages by haphazard groupings of private family estates which respected neither ancient frontiers nor geographical barriers. Real states almost disappeared from western Europe. Boundaries were well nigh impossible to define. The fiefs of the Norman and Angevin kings of England sprawled uncertainly across western Gaul; even the kingdom of England, which developed many features of a coherent unit, was blurred at the edges; and within the Norman and Angevin 'empires' there was a confused jumble of fiefs. Yet in 1216 as in 1042 the kingdom of England was a unit in the contemporary sense; and in 1216 it was larger than it had been at the beginning. The king of Scots had been pushed back again beyond the Liddel and the Tweed; most of Wales had been added; and part of Ireland had been conquered; while all the rulers in the British Isles acknowledged the overlordship of the English king. But even in 1216 it could easily have been imagined that at some moment a king of Scots might have faced a king of France across the Trent. Homogeneity was still lacking. The England known to the kings was only that Wessex and Mercia which John circled so assiduously, the area bound by trade to Flanders, Normandy, and Aquitaine. Beyond were the more loosely attached members, like the earldom of Chester and the honour of Lancaster; and then the marches, disputed by almost autonomous barons with Anglo-Celtic princes. Dover was more closely connected with Boulogne, London with Rouen, Southampton with Bordeaux, and Bristol with Dublin than any one of them with York or Carlisle.

In 1042 there were Norwegian, Danish, Anglo-Norman, and West-Saxon claimants to the English throne. In 1216 an Angevin and a Frenchman were disputing the crown. For two centuries the kingdom of England had been ruled by men of foreign race who had not regarded the island as their real home. Throughout this period most of the lay and ecclesiastical aristocracy had been of foreign extraction and habits. At no time had the kings pursued a policy based on purely insular considerations. The interests of

Denmark, Normandy, Anjou, or Aquitaine had always come first. Yet from the beginning to the end the kingdom was the richest and most important unit in the continental groupings of which it formed part; and by 1216 it is apparent that the weight of purely English interests was beginning to tell again. Moreover, although Frankish feudalism had been imported wholesale in the years after 1066, so that England became the most perfectly feudal kingdom in the West, particular characteristics due to the power of the crown and vernacular idiosyncrasies resulting from the influence of native institutions had always been apparent.

The importance of the eleventh and twelfth centuries in the history of western Europe is immense. In the eleventh century England was part of a strange, sub-antique, barbarized world, into the inner life of which we can but dimly see. According to the dominant beliefs, God, angels, men, beasts, plants, and things, all the visible and the invisible universe, were bound together in a theocratic order. The kingdoms of the earth and the Kingdom of Heaven, the customs of the people and the Law of God, the rulers of the world and the King of kings, each merged into the other. All offices were many-sided, all words were ambiguous. God ruled and the king ruled. God was King, and the king was God.

In the course of the twelfth century a revolution occurred in western Europe. Logic—Aristotelian logic—became the key to all arts and sciences. Theology was *more geometrico demonstrata*. The old cosmos was split into the natural and the supernatural. Two enemies, St. Bernard and Abailard, inspired a new conception of God, in which the just avenger of the Old Testament, the harsh feudal lord of the Dark Ages, was replaced by the God of love, the sweet Christ, and the Holy Ghost the comforter; while Mary became the queen of Heaven, the protector and advocate of the sinner. At the same time open heresy appeared, for orthodoxy implies heterodoxy, and the intellectual ferment inspired wayward and unacceptable speculation both in those areas which had been but superficially Christianized and in those, such as the towns, which resented the traditional ecclesiastical pattern. Men began to discover and to assert their individuality, their spiritual personality. Stable governments, both ecclesiastical and lay, with all the characteristic apparatus of mature political states, took shape. The imperial romanesque style of architecture gave way to French gothic.

The sociological developments caused changes in the meanings of words. Men began to separate and to define. Words acquired more limited meanings. For example, *rex* was emptied of most of its spiritual content, while *beneficium* fell out of feudal use and referred simply to an ecclesiastical benefice. Technical vocabularies were formed. Theological, scholastic, legal, and literary forms of Latin appeared, and all showed a growing divergence from popular speech. There was, consequently, much dispute over words and phrases. But the controversies were not completely childish and the very misunderstandings are proof of change, questioning, and the desire for a more perfect expression.

England was affected by most of these European developments; and between 1042 and 1216 enormous changes occurred in its society. Most obvious, perhaps, is the apparently steady increase in wealth, proof of which lies in the capital expenditure on stone buildings, castles and houses, churches, and bridges. At the same time wealth had become more 'liquid'. Mortgages and loans could be raised and taxes collected. Money flowed in abundance along the trade routes and from treasury to treasury. Yet no government in western Europe had found the need to issue a coin of greater value than the silver penny. Marks and pounds still remained units of account.

The firm establishment of a money economy had had a differential effect on power. A king could hold thousands of pounds at call. Greater projects could be achieved in a shorter time. The influence of capital had become more immediate. It is, however, more difficult to discover whether there had been much change in the distribution of wealth among the classes under the king. Little is known about the life of the peasantry at this time. Rightless slaves, without land or chattels, had disappeared, and many new plots had been cut out of the waste; but there were still too many mouths to feed. The barons seem always to have been short of money. On the evidence of the *Rotuli de dominabus* of 1185 the honours were seriously under-stocked; and men with wide possessions still lived in squalor relieved by moments of splendour. Even King John, as he rode with his knights and squires and clerks, his hunting packs and his 30 baggage carts, gave no impression of luxury. And although in *L'histoire de Guillaume le Maréchal* the simplicity of manners when William was a boy is contrasted with the pride at the time of writing (about 1226)—in 1154 a king's son would go on a journey with no baggage except for his mantle rolled up and carried as a bandoleer, whereas now-a-days even a squire requires his sumpter beast—it is likely that among the laity a greater total of wealth was spread almost as thinly as before owing to the increase in population. The church had certainly increased its estates and drew bigger sums from tithe and offerings. It had also forced out the lay parsons from the parish churches. But it had enfeoffed many vassals and built many costly edifices; and its capital wealth had probably grown more rapidly than its revenue. There certainly had been a redistribution of wealth within the church. Almost all the new endowments had gone to monasteries; and the monks had also secured a large share of tithe.

The growing wealth of the country was due almost entirely to the improved husbandry of a larger acreage and to the greater facilities for the marketing of surplus crops and wool. No radical change in farming method had occurred; but estate management had become a professional business. Forests were being felled and swamps drained. The buoyant commodity market stimulated efficiency; and, wherever the fertility of the land allowed, an unrecorded substitution of a three- for a two-field rotation must have been taking place. Under these conditions merchants prospered; and the mercantile is the one class which had undoubtedly grown in relative wealth and importance since 1042. London with its suburb of Westminster had become the political and the mercantile capital of England; and its mayor was treated as a major baron in 1215. The main artery of trade was between the south-eastern ports and Flanders; the counts of Flanders had usually been vassals of the English kings; one count of Boulogne had worn the English crown; and the English government had already learned that an embargo on the export of wool was a useful political weapon. And in return for the wool and other exports came the silver and all the luxuries which had raised the standard of living in England.

No less remarkable than the increased wealth of the kingdom was the transformation in the power of organized religion. In 1042 England was passively and ignorantly Christian. By 1216 unorthodoxy was unthinkable. The priestly caste, well-organized, well-disciplined, and resolutely led by the pope and his court, had established a dominating position in society. So confident had the hierarchy become that it was waging open war against the last remnants of dissent and paganism in Europe, the 'heretics' of the Languedoc. In 1216 England was a papal fief directed by a papal legate; all clerks were under a special law withdrawn from royal control; and spiritual jurisdiction, centralized in the pope, had become an accepted and potent force. The old Benedictine monasteries had kept their social pre-eminence in the kingdom; but their spiritual leadership was disputed by the numerous and widely-spread houses of the reformed orders, which were exempt from the local diocesan and ultramontane in tone.

Secular society had gone through a revolution. The replacement of an Anglo-Danish aristocracy by Norman barons had brought changes in fashion—the use of the French language and the influence of courtoisie and chivalry—and changes in the law. Yet, in retrospect, it is the impossibility of the feudal ideal which is striking. Feudalism is the law of a people escaping out of anarchy; and under peaceful conditions it loses its spirit. In 1087 the Norman barons and knights were still living precariously in a conquered land. By 1216 the barons had failed in their duties, the serjeants had fallen by the wayside, and the knights had grown as rusty as their old swords. Once the vassal is endowed with a benefice and peace returns to a country he begins to slip away from his lord. His duties become onerous customs, his heirs are remiss. By 1216, as John had found to his cost, English society was no longer organized for war. On the *Curia Regis* rolls can be found writs of peace like this: 'Geoffrey fitzPeter, &c. We order you not to allow B. to be impleaded before you about anything as long as his money is in the service of the king beyond the sea, &c.' Feudalism had become a system of land tenure.

Nevertheless, within the general process of settling down, there had been remarkable instability. The baronage had suffered many casualties since the Conquest. Few families had escaped the hazards of forfeiture, childlessness, division of lands between girls, crippling fines, and extravagance. Always there was a group of royal favourites on the rise and a crowd of younger sons struggling for survival. Society had not been static. Some knights had entered the baronage; some knight's fees had been so broken up that the holders were peasants. Some socagers became knights, others villeins. Even out of the peasantry men were using the ladders of the free boroughs and the church, or were simply climbing from bovate to bovate or from acre to acre.

The most striking feature of the whole period, however, is undoubtedly the unusual power of the crown. Germanic society wrapped in the law, insistent on the sanctity of private rights, and hostile to change, obstructed an active governor at every turn. Legislation was violation of custom. Taxation was robbery. A foreign policy was the whim of a despot. And the unlawful acts of a king were protected by no theory of necessity or of special standards. Hence an ambitious and energetic king was inevitably a tyrant. The kings of England, owing to the power given by conquest and their exceptional abilities, had been strong; and because of their strength England had escaped the worst effects of the prevailing ideas. For feudal society believed in rights, but could not protect them; it held to ancient tradition, but kept an imperfect record; it worshipped the law, but had unsatisfactory courts. And under those conditions a partly enfranchised monarchy was a beneficent force. But an active king could not hope to avoid baronial revolts and conflict with the church; and in 1135 and 1215, owing to the pressure having been applied too hard, there were general explosions. Yet from the unusual strength of the crown had sprung the precocious development in England of royal justice and a common law, of royal taxation, and of a royal administration which had outgrown the seignorial economy of a feudal lord.

The arbitrary power of the king was probably at its greatest under the two sons of the Conqueror. Edward the Confessor had been constrained by local magnates stronger than he; William the Bastard had had to act with circumspection. And Richard and John, despite their authoritarian natures, were limited by a routine which their father had confirmed. The re-endowment of the English monarchy by William I and the wastage of demesne under his successors provide an economic explanation. The extent of the royal forests and the severity of the forest laws is a good guide to the wilful power wielded by each king. By John's reign the area of the royal preserves was shrinking; and in 1217 the worst excesses of the forest law were checked.

In 1205 John borrowed a history of England written in French. He swore 'par les piez De' (*per pedes Dei*); but he bequeathed his body to St. Wulfstan. The dominance of French culture and the persistence of an indigenous tradition, the strength of Germanic and feudal custom, the influence of canonical jurisprudence, and the power of a strong monarchy—all contributed to the rich heritage of the national kingdom that developed in the centuries to come.

NOTE ON BOOKS

As excellent bibliographies for this period are contained in several easily accessible works, the purpose of this note is simply to show the student the way to further study.

1. BIBLIOGRAPHIES

The basic general bibliographies are C. Ulysse J. Chevalier, *Répertoire des sources historiques du moyen-âge* (1883–99) and A. Potthast, *Bibliotheca historica medii aevi* (1862–96), and, for English history, Carl Gross, *The Sources and Literature of English History to about* 1485 (1900) and Sir T. D. Hardy, *Materials relating to the History of Great Britain and Ireland* (Rolls Series, 3 Vols., 1862–71). But of greater use to the ordinary student will be the bibliographies given in the *Cambridge Medieval History*, vols. II, V, and VI and in the *Oxford Histories* (Stenton and Poole); while in *English Historical Documents*, 1042–1189 (ed. D. C. Douglas and G. W. Greenaway, 1953), a valuable source book, are detailed and exhaustive lists arranged under subjects. All these bibliographies can be kept up to date with the help of the *Annual Bulletin of Historical Literature* published by the Historical Association.

2. STANDARD SECONDARY WORKS

W. J. Corbett's contribution to vol. II of the *Cambridge Medieval History* is still of value; but the most authoritative general history of the Anglo-Saxon period is Sir F. M. Stenton's *Anglo-Saxon England* (Oxford History of England, 1943). Stenton's impeccable original scholarship will give his book a long life; yet it should be noticed that there is much dissatisfaction in some historical circles with the underlying assumptions of the Freeman–Stubbs–Stenton school (the 'Germanists'), even when presented as reasonably as by Sir Frank Stenton. Dorothy Whitelock's *The Beginnings of English Society* (Pelican book, 1952) forms an interesting supplement.

For the later period A. L. Poole's *From Domesday Book to Magna Carta* (Oxford History of England, 1951) replaces all earlier histories, although the chapters by Corbett, Doris M. Stenton, and F. M. Powicke in the *Cambridge Medieval History*, vols. II, V, and VI, can still be read with profit. Dr. Poole's book, the work of many years, is especially valuable for its study of social and cultural conditions; and its arrangement according to subject matter makes it most useful for reference. Lady Stenton's unrivalled knowledge of legal and financial records makes her *English Society in the Early Middle Ages* (Pelican book, 2nd ed., 1952) of quite exceptional value.

The standard history of Wales is J. E. Lloyd, *A History of Wales from the Earliest Times to the Edwardian Conquest* (2 vols., 2nd ed., 1939).

Medieval Ireland has two excellent historians in G. H. Orpen, *Ireland under the Normans*, 1196–1333 (4 vols., 1911–20) and E. Curtis, *A History of Medieval Ireland from* 1086–1513 (4th ed., 1942). Scotland, however, has been less fortunate. P. Hume Brown's *History of Scotland to the Present Time* (3 vols., 1911) is comparatively slender on the early period.

It will be seen that the student is well served with general histories. But there is no one constitutional, ecclesiastical, or economic history of this period that is entirely satisfactory. William Stubbs's *Constitutional History* (3 vols., 1875–8, and several later editions) is definitely outmoded, although his deep knowledge of the twelfth century preserves his work from neglect. A. B. White's *The Making of the English Constitution* (2nd ed., 1925), a slighter and more analytical study, has also, perhaps, had its day. J. E. A. Jolliffe's *The Constitutional History of Medieval England* (1937) is a stimulating and often provocative essay; but it has incurred much detailed criticism and must be used with caution. Some aspects of constitutional history are discussed in the light of recent specialist work by G. O. Sayles in his *The Medieval Foundations of England* (1948), and a useful summary of an involved subject is to be found in S. B. Chrimes's *An Introduction to the Administrative History of Medieval England* (Studies in medieval history, ed. G. Barraclough, vol. 7, 1952). The *History of English Law before the time of Edward I*, by Sir Frederick Pollock and F. W. Maitland (2 vols., 2nd ed., 1923) is the best work of its type; and anything written by Maitland keeps a freshness and vitality that more than compensates for the occasional waywardness and the inevitable obsolescence of some of his views.

English economic and, especially, ecclesiastical history have aroused much interest in recent years, so that articles and monographs abound; but the standard interpretation in the light of modern research is still lacking for both. The first volume of E. Lipson's *The Economic History of England* was published in 1915, and, although it has been revised through eight editions (1945) and has not been bettered, it still keeps too much of its original form. Dom David Knowles's *The Monastic Order in England* 943–1216 (1940) is a masterly account of monasticism in England. But the secular church is without its modern historian. The best short study of the culture of this period is R. W. Southern's *The Making of the Middle Ages* (Hutchinson's University Library, 1953).

3. NEW BOOKS

Since this book was written several important studies and monographs have appeared. Peter Hunter Blair's *An Introduction to Anglo-Saxon England* (1959) is outstandingly good and gives proper attention to northern history. Eric John, *Land Tenure in Early England* (1960), makes some interesting suggestions. Tryggvi J. Oleson, *The Witenagemot in the Reign of Edward the Confessor* (1955), demolishes the witenagemot as an institution. I. J. Sanders, *Feudal Military Service in England* (1956) discusses the baronies and their military duties. Jacques Boussard, *Le Gouvernement d'Henri II Plantagenêt* (1956) studies the government of the Angevin empire as a whole and as a feudal entity. J. E. A. Jolliffe's *Angevin Kingship* (1955) is a brilliant if idiosyncratic essay on some aspects of Angevin rule. Important contributions to English ecclesiastical history have been made by Norman F. Cantor, *Church, Kingship, and Lay Investiture in England 1089–1135* (1958), Avrom Saltman, *Theobald archbishop of Canterbury* (1956), C. R. Cheney, *From Becket to Langton* (1956), and G. V. Scammell, *Hugh du Puiset bishop of Durham* (1956). On the economic side, Reginald Lennard, *Rural England 1086–1135* (1959), reinterprets Domesday evidence to good effect. The Bayeux Tapestry has been better reproduced and well edited (Phaidon, 1957), and *Medieval England,* ed. A. L. Poole (1958) is an excellent companion to medieval studies. Nelson's Medieval Texts provide the student with some attractive editions of historical texts with a translation; and K. R. Potter's *Gesta Stephani* (1955) is especially important because a more complete MS. is edited for the first time.

4. POSTSCRIPT 1971

Although there has been a steady stream of books and articles since 1953, it does not seem that the general picture of the period or even much of the detail has been greatly altered. The spate of publications in connexion with the nine-hundredth anniversary of the Norman Conquest largely confirmed the accepted interpretation. Respect for Henry I continues to grow and renewed interest in Stephen has made some new views available. But the Angevins and their ministers, despite the commemoration of 1215, stay much as they were. Perhaps the most interesting and influential work to have appeared, certainly the most provocative, is H. G. Richardson and G. O. Sayles, *The Governance of Mediaeval England from the Conquest to Magna Carta* (1963). A companion volume, *Law and Legislation from Æthelberht to Magna Carta,* was published in 1966. Also in the field of constitutional history are D. M. Stenton, *English justice between the Norman Conquest and the Great Charter* (1965), F. J. West, *The justiciarship in England, 1066-1232* (1966), and J. C. Holt, *Magna Carta* (1965). C. Warren Hollister has produced two important studies of the miiltary organization, *Anglo-Saxon military Institutions on the eve of the Norman Conquest* (1962) and *The Military organization of Norman England* (1965). Among the political studies and biographies should be noticed Frank Barlow, *Edward the Confessor* (1970), David C. Douglas, *William the Conqueror* (1964), Frank Barlow, *William I and the Norman Conquest* (1965), R. H. C. Davis, *King Stephen* (1967), H. A. Cronne, *The Reign of Stephen* (1970), W. L. Warren, *King John* (1961), and J. C. Holt *The Northerners* (1961). On the ecclesiastical side there are Frank Barlow, *The English Church 1000-1066* (1963), A. Morey and C. N. L. Brooke, *Gilbert Foliot and his letters* (1965), David Knowles, *Thomas Becket* (1970), and C. R. Cheney, *Hubert Walter* (1967). In 1966 was published a revised edition of volume I of the *Cambridge Economic History of Europe.* V. H. Galbraith's *The Making of Domesday Book* (1961) is the most original and intelligible work on that enigmatic document. W. C. Dickinson has written *Scotland from the earliest times to 1603* (1961) and A. J. Otway-Ruthven, *A history of medieval Ireland* (1968). A good history of the Irish church in this period is J. A. Watt, *The Church and the two Nations in medieval Ireland* (1970) and of the Welsh, Glanmor Wilhams, *The Welsh church from Conquest to Reformation* (1962).

MAP AND CHARTS

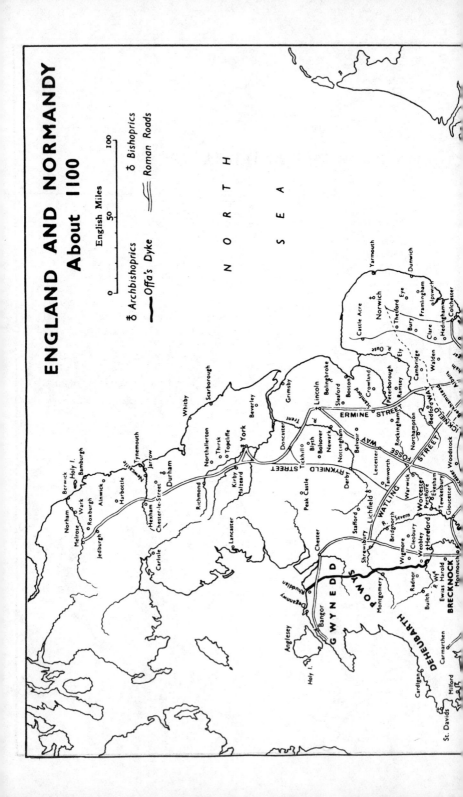

ENGLAND AND NORMANDY
About 1100

English Miles

0   50   100

☩ Archbishoprics   ♉ Bishoprics
—— Offa's Dyke   〰 Roman Roads

NORTH

SEA

Norham
Berwick
Holy I.
Melrose
Wark
Bamburgh
Roxburgh
Alnwick
Jedburgh
Harbottle
Tynemouth
Carlisle
Hexham
Jarrow
Chester-le-Street
Durham

Lancaster
Richmond
Northallerton
Thirsk
Topcliffe
Kirby
Malzeard
York
Whitby
Scarborough
Beverley

Doncaster
Tickhill
Blyth
Bolsover
Newark
Nottingham
Belvoir
Derby
Ashbourne
Leicester
Tamworth
Peak Castle

Trent

Grimsby
Lincoln
Sleaford
Bolingbroke
Boston
Crowland
Stamford
Peterborough
Ramsey
Ouse

Castle Acre
Yarmouth
Norwich
Thetford
Eye
Framlingham
Bury
Clare
Hedingham
Dunwich
Ipswich
Walden
Colchester

Cambridge
Ely

St. Albans

ERMINE STREET
RYKNIELD STREET
WATLING STREET
FOSSE WAY
ICKNIELD STREET

Rockingham
Northampton
Bedford
Warwick
Woodstock
Worcester
Pershore
Evesham
Gloucester
Tewkesbury
Hereford

Stafford
Lichfield
Shrewsbury
Bridgnorth
Cleobury
Weobley
Wigmore
Radnor
Severn

Chester
Rhuddlan

GWYNEDD
POWYS
SAMOD
BRECKNOCK
DEHEUBARTH

Bangor
Anglesey
Holy I.
Montgomery
Builth
R. Wye
Ewias Harold
Monmouth
R. Deganwy

Cardigan
Carmarthen
St. Davids
Milford

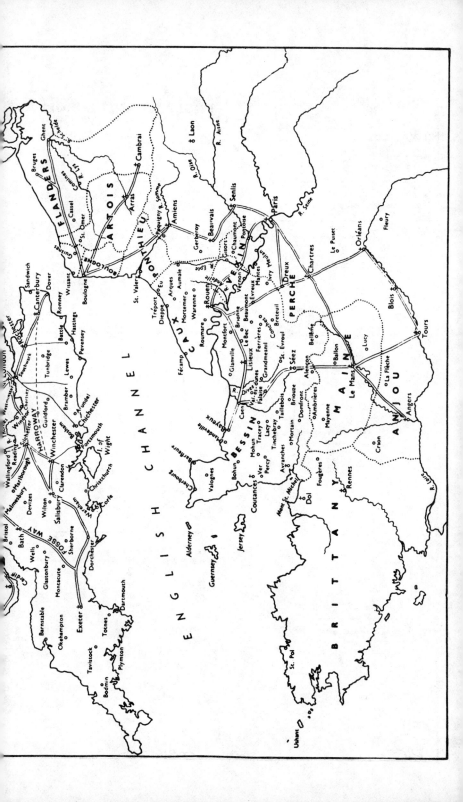

ENGLAND AND EUROPE IN
(English Kings

NORMAN LINE

ENGLISH LINE

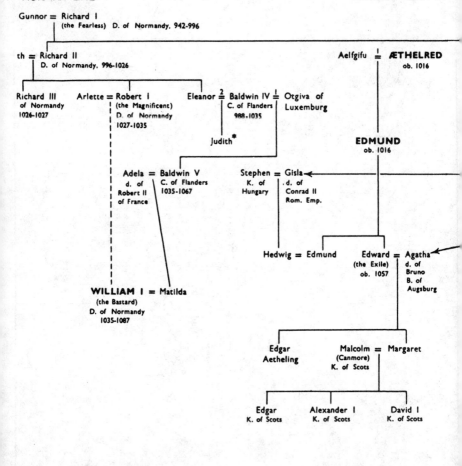

Gunnor = Richard I
(the Fearless) D. of Normandy, 942-996

th = Richard II
D. of Normandy, 996-1026

Aelfgifu = ÆTHELRED
ob. 1016

Richard III
of Normandy
1026-1027

Arlette = Robert I
(the Magnificent)
D. of Normandy
1027-1035

Eleanor = Baldwin IV = Otgiva of
C. of Flanders   Luxemburg
988-1035

Judith*

EDMUND
ob. 1016

Adela = Baldwin V
d. of   C. of Flanders
Robert II   1035-1067
of France

Stephen = Gisla
K. of   d. of
Hungary Conrad II
         Rom. Emp.

WILLIAM I = Matilda
(the Bastard)
D. of Normandy
1035-1087

Hedwig = Edmund

Edward = Agatha
(the Exile)   d. of
ob. 1057   Bruno
           B. of
           Augsburg

Edgar
Aetheling

Malcolm = Margaret
(Canmore)
K. of Scots

Edgar
K. of Scots

Alexander I
K. of Scots

David I
K. of Scots

Judith* indicates the same person

THE ELEVENTH CENTURY
in heavy type)

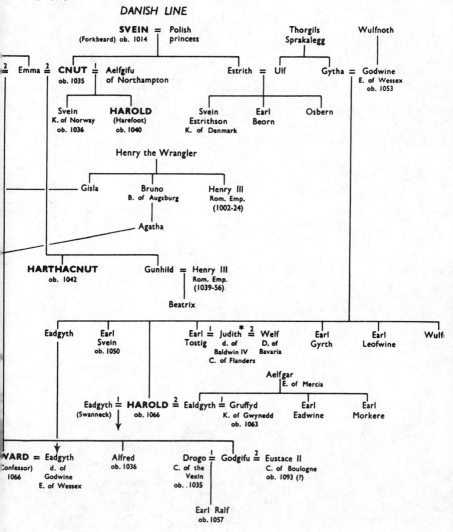

DANISH LINE

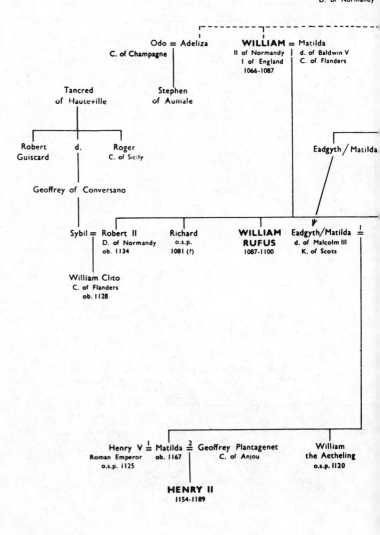

THE NORMAN
(English Kings

Robert I
D. of Normandy

Odo = Adeliza
C. of Champagne

WILLIAM = Matilda
II of Normandy | d. of Baldwin V
I of England | C. of Flanders
1066-1087

Tancred
of Hauteville

Stephen
of Aumale

Robert
Guiscard

d.

Roger
C. of Sicily

Eadgyth / Matilda

Geoffrey of Conversano

Sybil = Robert II
D. of Normandy
ob. 1134

Richard
o.s.p.
1081 (?)

WILLIAM
RUFUS
1087-1100

Eadgyth/Matilda
d. of Malcolm III
K. of Scots

William Clito
C. of Flanders
ob. 1128

Henry V = Matilda = Geoffrey Plantagenet
Roman Emperor ob. 1167 C. of Anjou
o.s.p. 1125

William
the Aetheling
o.s.p. 1120

HENRY II
1154-1189

DYNASTY

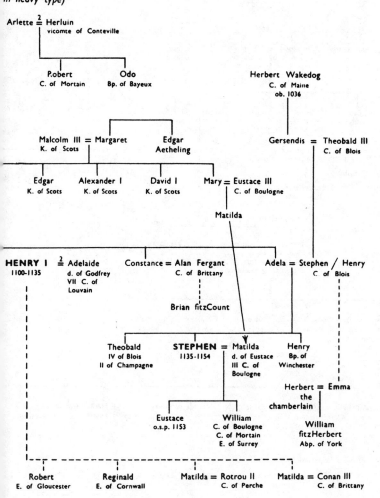

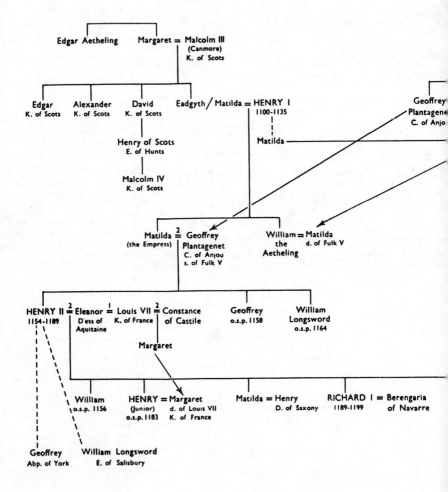

KINGS

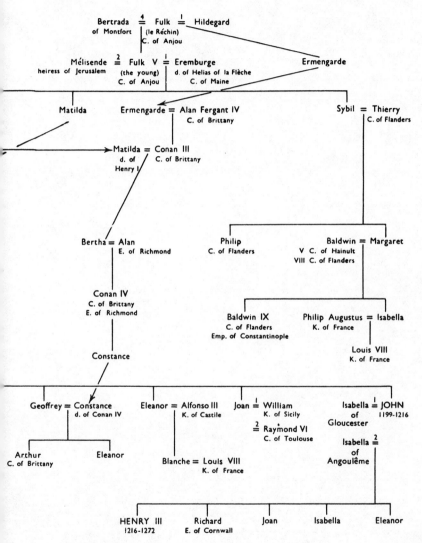

INDEX

(Persons are indexed under their first name)

Calligraphy, 40–1, 309, 398
Cambridge, 414, 432, 435; earl of, *see*
William de Roumare; shire, 325
Canons, 32, 36; *see also* monasteries
Canterbury (Kent), 26, 202, 264, 285,
421; church of, 27–8, 30, 32–3, 38, 62,
123, 127, 159, 181, 186, 212, 214,
300–1, 303, 329, 333, 383–6, 402–7;
abps. of, *see* Augustine, Eadsige,
Robert of Jumièges, Stigand, Lan-
franc, Anselm, Ralf d'Escures, William
of Corbeil, Theobald, Thomas Becket,
Richard of Dover, Baldwin, Hubert
Walter, Stephen Langton; St. Augus-
tine's abbey at, 264, 384
Cardiff (Glam), 164
Cardigan, 164
Carlisle (Cumb), 156, 158, 208, 213, 224,
278, 280, 287, 432, 436; church of,
186; bishop of, *see* Athelulf
Carolingian empire, 7, 23, 29, 34, 37–8
Carucages, 367, 389, 392, 401
Carucates, 17, 25, 50–1, 272, 312
Cashel, church of, 333; synod of, 335–6
Castellans, 109, 256–7, 261, 338, 392,
410, 432
Castile, kingdom of, 364, 371; kings of,
see Alfonso VIII, IX
Castles, 23, 61–2, 68, 83, 89–90, 106,
111–12, 137, 164, 178, 210–11, 215, 225,
234, 258, 285, 338, 343–4, 348, 365–6,
388, 431–2; castle-guard, 111–12, 114,
117, 184, 321
Cawkwell (Lincs), 272
Celestine II, pope, 227
Celestine III, pope, 377, 389
Ceorls, 7, 15, 19–22, 319
Cerdic, 2, 3
Châlus (Haute-Vienne), 367
Chamber, royal, 46, 113, 188–90, 230,
310, 410, 422; ducal, 107
Chamberlains, 44, 46, 106–7, 113, 188,
190–1, 262
Champagne, 250, 320; fairs of, 203, 250,
253; counts of, *see* Hugh I, Theobald II
(IV of Blois), Henry I, II
Chancellors, royal, 45, 113, 188–9, 398, *and
see* Osbern bp. of Exeter, Maurice
bp. of London, Robert Bloet, William
Giffard, Roger bp. of Salisbury,
Waldric, Roger the Poor, Thomas
Becket, Geoffrey Ridel, Geoffrey
fitzRoy, Walter of Coutances, William
Longchamp, Eustace bp. of Ely,
Hubert Walter, Walter de Gray,
Richard Marsh, Hugh of Wells
Chancery, royal, 35, 106, 108–9, 153,
225, 286, 308–9, 396–8, 424, 430; *see
also scriptorium*
Channel Is., 409, 419, 434

Chansons de geste, 133
Chapel, royal, 8, 44–5, 109, 113, 185, 188
Charles the Good, count of Flanders, 196–9
Chartres (Eure-et-Loire), 196, 253, 263;
counts of, *see* Blois; schools of, 247
Château Gaillard (Eure), 365–6, 371, 373
Château-du-Loir (Sarthe), 352
Châteauroux (Indre), 349, 350, 351;
truce of, 350
Châtillon-sur-Indre (Indre), 363
Chaumont-en-Vexin (Oise), 142, 168
Chepstow (Mon), 163
Cherbourg (Manche), 155
Chester, 23, 24, 93, 287, 413–14; church of,
123, *and see* Lichfield; earldom of, 89,
114, 436; earls of, *see* Hugh d'Avran-
ches, Ranulf le Meschin, Ranulf de
Gernons, Hugh of Cyveiliog, Ranulf
de Blundeville
Chichester (Sussex), 65; church of, 123;
bps. of, *see* Stigand, Hilary; earls of,
see Arundel
Chinon (Indre-et-Loire), 232, 286, 287,
340, 349, 352, 373; truce of, 421
Chirographs, 45, 293, 316, 397; *see also*
records
Chivalry, 235, 250–62
Christchurch (Hants), 259, 264
Christian, Durham moneyer, 280
Church in England, 439–40; Anglo-
Saxon, 8–10, 26–41, 43, 48, 54; under
William I, 95–6, 123–32; under Wil-
liam II, 145–8, 151–2, 156–7, 160–1,
165, 167; under Henry I, 172–4, 179–
81, 184–7; under Stephen, 204–6, 209,
212, 214–16, 217–18, 222, 226–30, 236–
49, 258–9; under Henry II, 290–309,
311–41, 375; under Richard I, 382–7;
under John, 402–7, 416–18, 422, 425;
see also bishops, monasteries
Church-scot, 31
Cinque ports, 26, 49, 60, 66, 86, 409, 434
Clare, family of, *see* Baldwin fitzGilbert,
Gilbert de Clare earl of Hertford,
Gilbert de Clare earl of Pembroke,
Gilbert fitzRichard, Richard, Richard
fitzGilbert
Clarendon (Wilts), 169, 292; constitu-
tions of, 292–300, 302, 304–8, 322, 422
Clement III, pope, 356, 364, 377
Clement III, anti-pope, 131, 151
Cleobury (Salop), 285
Clifford (Herefs), 163
Cloth manufacture, 187–8, 278–9, 323
Cluny (Saône-et-Loire), 32, 102, 126, 206,
240, 297
Cnihts, 7, 9, 10, 14, 26, 116
Cnut, king of England, 2–3, 5, 13, 28,
32–5, 43, 45–7, 50, 52–7, 75, 80, 101,
108, 424